The Hidden Game of Football

THE HIDDEN
GAME OF
FOOTBALL

Bob Carroll, Pete Palmer, John Thorn

A FOOTBALL INK BOOK

WARNER BOOKS

A Warner Communications Company

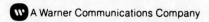 A Warner Communications Company

Printed in the United States of America

First Printing: September 1988

10 9 8 7 6 5 4 3 2 1

Library of Congress Cataloging-in-Publication Data

Carroll, Bob
  The hidden game of football / Bob Carroll, Pete Palmer, and John Thorn.
    p.   cm.
    1. Football. 2. Football—United States—History. 3. National Football League—Statistics.
I. Palmer, Pete. II. Thorn, John, 1947–   . III. Title.
GV951.C48   1988
796.332′2—dc19   88-3533
                  CIP
ISBN 0-446-51414-4

Book design and diagrams by Arlene Goldberg

For Sue—B.C.

For Beth—P.P.

For (my) Sue—J.T.

1

A Flying Wedge into the Future

At first we thought someone was kidding us, but the voice at the other end of the telephone insisted politely that it really belonged to a newspaper reporter calling from Denmark. We recognized an accent of some sort, but with our iron ear for nuances, it could just as easily have been Doughnut as Danish.

"Your name was given to me by someone at the American Embassy as someone who can tell me about American football," the caller explained. Now it made sense. Not that we're used to being recommended by the U.S. government for much other than filing our tax returns on time, but we do have a friend who does something or other for the State Department. The last time we'd talked to him, he was on his way to Europe.

"What do you want to know?" we asked.

"Everything," he said.

He meant it. His editor had assigned him to write an article on American football, and he candidly admitted that about all he knew was the term "Super Bowl." What he really needed was a brief but accurate history of professional football from its origins up to yesterday.

So we started with Walter Camp.

About the time we got to the 1950s in our telephone lecture, we were struck by a sense of irony. For nearly a year, we'd been spending most of our thinking moments at a keyboard trying to explain *The Hidden Game of Football* to what we expected would be rather football-sophisticated readers. Now, we were trying to come up with the words that would interpret a hundred years of football to an obviously bright but completely uninitiated listener.

As we rattled into the 1960s, panic replaced the irony. Had we gauged our readers correctly? Our listener on the telephone could ask for further explanation when we hadn't been clear enough, but what could a reader do, stop in the middle of a chapter and send a telegram?

"Ah, yes, the Super Bowl!" said the Dane. We'd finally rung a familiar bell.

We rushed through the '70s and '80s, anxious now to get back to the keyboard.

"And what about the strike?" he asked.

It had been a disaster for the players, we said. And, although the fans came back to the stadiums and their TVs readily, the failure of the strike would put the players into the courts, which might ultimately be disastrous for the owners. "And," we added, "it's had quite a strong effect on our own work." We didn't explain that part to the Dane, but we'll tell you about it in a moment.

After the Dane thanked us and hung up to write his story, we did a lot of thinking about you, the reader. Here's what we decided:

You already know a great deal about football. You may have played it in high school, college, or professionally. Perhaps you're a coach. Perhaps you're a bettor. Certainly you've been watching games for years. You're an informed fan.

So why are you reading this book? To find out *more*!

We think we can help you. We think that by showing you the statistical side of football, including some stats you've never seen before and some familiar stats used in new ways, we can increase your football fun. Stats can be a lot of fun. They give us a basis for evaluation and comparison of teams, players, and coaches. They may start more arguments than they settle, but that's part of their appeal, too. We can't teach you how to block or tackle, and we won't diagram any plays, but by the time you finish this book, you should have a greater understanding and a deeper appreciation of what goes on between the goalposts.

The ideas we're going to investigate should have some application to high school and college football, but we're going to focus on the pros. That's partly by choice; we're pro fans. And it's partly by necessity; pro football, despite some serious gaps, has a more complete statistical history. We'll be traveling through sixty-seven years of pro football statistics here, but our primary target will be the last ten years. The game changes. New strategies, new concepts, and new rules make the averages and ratios of today very different from those of a couple of decades ago. What's happening now?

To come up with our answers, we've used the statistical footprints of literally thousands of pro football games. We've calculated more than five hundred NFL games on a play-by-play basis. That's more than two seasons' worth. For specific reference, we'll use all of the games played in the 1986 season.

Why not 1987? You've probably figured that out already. The strike. As we told the Dane, it affected our work. The use of replacement players for one-fifth of the season threw everything out of kilter. Some teams completely altered their personalities—and, of course, their statistical tendencies—while the replacements were on the field. And once the regulars returned, it still took some of the teams a couple of weeks to get back into character. The result is that we just don't trust the numbers from 1987.

It may sound contradictory, but we think the 1986 stats are more predictive of 1988 than the closer year. The bright side is that we had more time to delve into the 1986 figures. And that extra time allowed us to go deeper in some areas than we originally planned.

We're going to cover a lot of ground here.

Part One of this book deals with history and general concepts. That sounds a little dry, but we're betting you'll find it exciting.

In the next chapter, "How Football Got That Way," we'll give you *History of Football 101,* an off-tackle smash through the whole history of the game, starting from before it was football and ending with the 1980s. We'll explain why the pro game depends predominantly on passing, how the two-platoon system changed the size of players, explore the effects of some significant rule changes, and generally prepare you for what comes next.

"What's Wrong with Traditional Pro Football Statistics," the third chapter, lets us cheer for the numbers that are available and complain about the ones that aren't. Fortunately, we've been able to come up with some of the missing pieces. We'll also begin our main mission: to make you a better interpreter of what you see.

Our handy-dandy computer has been essential in creating this book, and in "Punch, Zip, Whirr . . . Touchdown," we'll show you how the face of football has been reshaped by bits and bytes. As much as some old-timers long for the good old days when they made decisions by the seat of their pants, those days are as long gone as moleskin leggings.

The fifth chapter, "Looking for a Winning Situation," is a lot of fun. We'll take a play-by-play account of a real game—there's an official record for every NFL game—and show how such accounts could create new and more meaningful statistics for individual players. For example, it's quite possible to have numbers that actually measure a runner's effectiveness in clutch situations.

In "Driving for Glory," we'll look at some real drive charts and show how you can estimate Win Probability (just what it sounds like —the probability of winning the game) by correlating the score, time left, and field position. Obviously, this is at the root of all strategic decisions, but that doesn't mean every coach understands it. We'll even look at a couple of extreme examples, a blowout and a game where the "wrong team" won.

With "You *Can* Get There from Here," the seventh and last chapter in Part One, we introduce the concept of point potential related to field position. We've examined hundreds of drive charts to arrive at some surprising answers. For example, we'll show you why a team may be better off going for that first down than punting—even if it's deep in its own territory. And did you know a successful field goal may actually cost the kicking team points?

In Part Two of the book, we'll take the game apart and see how the various parts can be measured—and how much they contribute to the final score.

For example, in "The Joy of Sacks, and Other Mistakes," we'll calibrate the effects of fumbles, interceptions, and, naturally, sacks. We think they may be a bit less important than those glitzy TV graphics would have you think, but judge for yourself.

In "Special Teams," we measure actual kickoffs (now where else can you find that?), punts, and returns. There are some simple things teams could do with these to improve their Win Probability. We'll tell them about it.

"Kicking Up a Storm" gives us the opportunity to return to one of our favorite subjects: the importance of not kicking that field goal.

Here we can go after it in depth. And did you ever wonder what happened to the quick kick?

The longest chapter in the book is "The Glory, the Blame, and the Ratings," but that's not our fault. You see, before we could show you how passers should be rated, we had to explain how they *are* rated. Joe Montana says he doesn't understand the NFL's Passer Rating System, but by the time you get through this, you will. And you'll know how it can be fixed.

Ever hear of YPSG? It's an easy way of looking at the records of running backs that tells you more than traditional totals. You'll read all about it in "The Running Game."

Of course, no one runs or passes very well without a good, strong— but always anonymous—line in front of him. In "Opus for the Unsung," we'll show you the good, the bad, and the ugly among NFL lines.

Everybody has heard of the two-minute drill. We'll explain why it's really a minute longer, and how teams could better use that time, in "Three Minutes to Fat Lady."

We end Part Two with "Profile of a Winner," where we put all the parts back together and see if it'll fly.

The third part of the book takes on some of the more exciting and controversial side issues. These are the kinds of things fans argue about until the early morning hours, and we'll give them plenty of ammunition.

"The Draft Dodge" tells why the event that's been described as a "new national holiday" is really a rip-off, raising false hopes of positive change while preserving the status quo. Can it be improved? Yes. Will it be? Probably not.

Pro football games are America's most popular wagering events. From friendly backyard bets among buddies to serious bettors, everybody's looking for an edge. In "Wanna Bet?" we'll give you a primer on how it works, tell you what to look for, and suggest some ways you can improve your odds of winning.

Debates over who was the "greatest" never lose their fascination, but unless you know how to interpret the numbers, you won't win many scuffles. Players from ten, twenty, and thirty years ago *can* be compared to today's stars, but not by simply putting one number next to another. Jim Brown, Don Hutson, Sammy Baugh, and others who thrilled the fan of yesterday will always lose in that kind of confrontation.

In "Great Performances," we'll look at some of the best (and a couple of the worst) efforts ever made on a football field. And in "Rumblings in the Pantheon," we'll see how some players who were the very best of their time have been ignored by the Hall of Fame and name a few inductees and candidates who have questionable credentials for enshrinement.

And finally, in "The Tables," we'll give you a season-by-season review, along with the most significant numbers for each year.

As you read *The Hidden Game of Football*, you will find many of your suspicions confirmed and many of your confirmed beliefs challenged. That's what makes football the great game it is. Long after the final gun, we can investigate, analyze, and just plain enjoy our experience. Yogi was wrong; the game is *never* over.

2

How Football Got That Way

There's probably no chance at all that they'd consider changing their name to the National Armball League, but that would be a lot more descriptive of the NFL's version of America's Game than the present *foot*-ball misnomer. The colleges play "foot" ball, using the run as their regular *modus operandi*. The pros live and die by the pass. And while a foot is a necessary item for any passer, neither the left nor right is the featured part of his anatomy. The last NFL quarterback to win a job with his feet was the Bears' Bobby Douglass, and that mistake happened in seasons they'd just as soon forget in Chicago. As far as the pros are concerned, the kick and the run—two efforts showcasing the feet—are definitely secondary to what happens in the defensive secondary.

Cynics think the NFL emphasizes passing only to improve its TV ratings. They insist the pros are afraid to run the ball as God intended because viewers will get bored and switch to "Cagney & Lacey." Throwing—the football version of the cop-show car chase—is more exciting to watch than running and keeps the viewers' hands off the dials. The cynics are wrong, of course. The pros throw because they have to.

Any pro team that can't put the ball in the air with a high percent-

17

age of satisfactory results can count on an early position come next Draft Day. The same can be said for a team that treats defending against the pass as a lost art. Purists sneer that Rozelleland is beginning to look like a basketball league, but don't hold your breath awaiting a change unless you look good in blue. It's going to be "armball" for the NFL until Punky Brewster gets her pension.

Just how pro football changed from a game based on what players did with their feet to today's celebration of the fly pattern is worth looking at.

A SIMPLE GAME

Actually, the object of the game is very simple: move a previously agreed upon item (a football) a previously decided distance (one hundred yards) within a previously set time period (sixty minutes) more often than your opponent. One side tries to move the item; the other tries to stop them. Pro footballers move their oddly shaped item best by throwing it; college teams excel at running with it. If someone demonstrates that the ideal way to get a football from here to there is by mail, all the coaches will buy stamps the next day. Move the item. In its basics, football is no different from basketball, hockey, water polo, or several other games.

A "game" is played within a prescribed space—a basketball court, a hockey rink, a swimming pool, or a football field. The first three come in preferred sizes with some variations; a football field these days is always 100 yards long and 53.33 yards wide. There are always the same number of players on each side, depending on the sport—five in basketball, six in hockey, seven in water polo, and eleven in football—according to what works best. Put twenty-two men on a basketball court and they'd keep bouncing dribbles off other guys' toes; put that many in a swimming pool and somebody would drown.

The differences lie in the rules—handicaps, if you will—placed on the attackers and defenders, which is why football isn't just dry water polo. In basketball, the attackers can throw the ball but may only move with it if they bounce it. In hockey, the attackers have to shove the puck with a stick. All the games have similar restrictions as to what defenders are allowed to do, varying only in degree: no touch in basketball; don't carry a loaded gun in hockey.

The handicaps placed on football players—both attackers and defenders—have evolved along with the game over many years. Usually someone's new rule was meant to solve a problem that had gotten out of hand. A few rules were tossed in apparently because someone thought they might make things more interesting. Rare is the rule change that did only what it was meant to do and nothing more. Many rules have been added just to contain the carnage caused by earlier rule changes.

The sum total of all the rule changes makes it necessary for a pro football team to pass the ball if it entertains any hope of winning. Football wasn't always like that. But they changed it.

YOUNG WALTER'S GAME

In 1876, when Walter Camp went out for "football" at Yale, he really intended to play an American hybrid, part soccer and part rugby. They used a No. 6 rugby ball which looked like a basketball that had been jammed into a too-small tube for months, and the field was about a third bigger than today's gridiron. At Yale, they'd settled on eleven players to a side a few years earlier when a touring soccer team from Eton School in England told them that was the best number.

As in rugby, a player could run with the ball, and when he was about to be tackled, he could either kick it away, throw it away, or keep it and go down in a heap. If he chose to kick, he could either try for a goal or send the ball off to the other team. If he threw the ball away—hopefully to a teammate—the rules said he could not toss it forward, only backward or sideways. If he let himself be tackled—certainly the least preferred option—a "scrum" followed. A scrum was like a face-off in hockey. Everyone gathered around in a tight circle like seventh-graders sharing a dirty story, and the referee skittered the ball in between the two "centers" for each team, who kicked at it until it bounced to a teammate. Whoever got the ball took off like a scalded dog until he too was about to be tackled. At which point, he had the same three options of kick, throw, or be dumped.

Games must have looked like mobile miniriots with players racing hither-and-yon and every once in a while a kick popping into the air like a leather champagne cork.

As in soccer, all the scoring was done by kicking the ball. Even if a player ran the ball over the goal line, all he got was a free try to kick a goal. To count, just as with today's football kicks, the ball had to go over a crossbar set on matched posts placed on the goal line.

Young Walter Camp proved to be a wizard at this hybrid game; the best in the world, his friends said. Admittedly it was a pretty small "world" in those days, what with only Yale and a couple of other northeastern colleges playing the game, but Camp's talents as well as his brains made him a leader every time a group got together to suggest new rules.

By 1880, he was fed up with the free-for-all, catch-as-catch-can jumble he'd been playing; he decided to develop a more regimented affair wherein a team could know it was going to have possession of the ball for a bit and give some thought to its next move. In other words, the brainy Camp wanted a game where his quick mind was as useful as his quick feet. Working with what he already had, he suggested changing the "scrum" to the "scrimmage," in which only one team's center was allowed to kick the ball back to his teammates (it took a couple of years before they figured out they could hike the ball better by hand). For Camp's scrimmage to work at all, he also had to invent the "line of scrimmage," with the teams set up on opposite sides and the ball in the middle.

ORIGINAL T-FORMATION

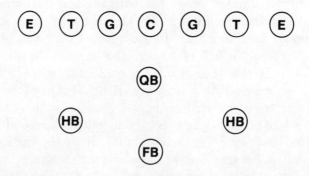

They tried Camp's brainchild in the 1880 season and the result was disastrous. Everybody but Princeton had forgotten that a weaker team could simply sit on the ball, run play after play and never kick, while playing for a tie. The Tigers showed this to Camp's strong Yale team and tied them, 0-0.

In 1881, after a session back at the drawing board, Camp came up with the "downs-and-yards-to-go" idea. The mix sounds a little strange to modern ears—five yards forward *or ten yards back* (!) in three downs to get a first down—but it worked. From here on, the game ceased to be poor-man's rugby and became American football. A couple of years later, they started awarding different numbers of points for different actions: so many for field goals, so many for touchdowns, etc. Like the size of the field and the downs-to-yards ratio, it took them a while to get everything right, but by 1912 they had six points for a touchdown, three points for a field goal, ten yards in four downs for a first down, and a hundred yard field. They also had a legal forward pass.

SAVING THE GAME

The chain of events that eventually allowed the no-no pass to become a yes-yes began in 1887, when the rules makers decided to let defenders tackle ball carriers from the knees down, probably because players were doing it fairly often, by accident anyway. It didn't seem to be any big deal at the time, but, like Pandora and Three-Mile Island, the rulesmakers had unleashed a lot more than they ever intended.

After Camp's yards-and-downs idea in '81, teams had continued playing a wide-open game—more premeditated than before, but still with backs spread out wide to take long pitches from the quarterback. As soon as the low tackle was legal, defenders started charging across the scrimmage line, diving at a halfback's feet, and cutting him down

DOUBLE WING

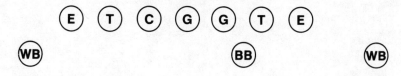

while the quarterback's pitch sailed who-knew-where. To counteract that, attackers moved everyone in tight, surrounded the ball carrier, and everyone churned forward like a human tank. And *that's* why the famous flying wedge and other grind-'em-out plays constituted the dominant style of offense in the 1890s.

They might still run the wedge today except that in the '90s, more and more often a defense would suddenly realize that they only had ten men standing around waiting for the next onslaught. "Hey, what's that sticking out of the mud at the 40-yard line? It looks like Harry's elbow. Harry!"

Finally, fans grew tired of seeing football players treated like grapes at Luigi's Winery. Even President Theodore Roosevelt bullied his way into the act, calling for reforms. The rules makers made up a whole passel of new rules in 1906, all aimed at getting rid of the wedge and opening the game up again. About the least important new rule at the time allowed forward passing, but they put so many restrictions on the maneuver that at first almost no one thought it was worth a darn.

A NEGLECTED STRATEGY

Even when a couple of Notre Damers named Dorais and Rockne used the pass to beat Army in 1913, most coaches okayed it only in desperation—a sort of play of last resort. Twenty years after passing became legal, you'd have to scour the country to find a college team that threw more than half a dozen times during a game. Fans could

V-TRICK
(FORERUNNER OF FLYING WEDGE)

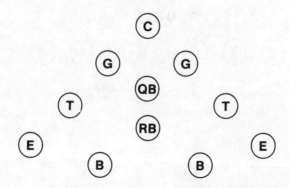

give you details of important forward passes years afterward because they were that rare. Coaches, conservative old duffers that they were, had simply reinvented the flying wedge in the form of the single wing, a formation designed to get an abundance of blockers to a particular

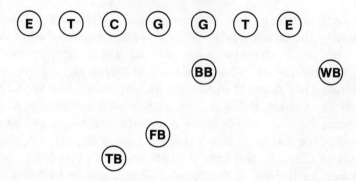

SINGLE WING

spot all at one time. Then, because college teams could practice-prac- tice-practice, they'd run their off-tackle plunges and around-end sweeps over and over until their players could do them in their sleep.

If you quarterbacked the ideal college football team in the '20s, you slugged away on the ground. Most teams knew what to expect and could put eleven decent players against you, so you seldom gained more than a couple of yards a try. Meanwhile, your punter kept your opponent bottled up at the other end of the field. Until you got inside your foe's 30-yard line, you might punt on third down—the most popular third-down alignment was a short punt formation which al- lowed some options—because you were almost as likely to fumble as to break away for a first down. Eventually, something gave—usually in the fourth quarter—and you scored a touchdown to humiliate your rival 6-0.

It was football with the accent on "foot." Teams didn't so much win games as their opponents lost them by making a mistake. Coaches loved running because mistakes were less common, or at least less disastrous, on well-practiced runs than on somewhat ad-libbed passes —"putting the ball up for grabs" it was called. When a team lost with pass goofs, it got buried 20- or 30-0. Scratch a typical college coach in the '20s and you'd find someone who'd rather be certain of losing 6-0 on the ground than take a chance on winning through the air.

THE PROS LEARN TO PASS

By and large, the pros in the '20s copied the colleges. The only difference was that they couldn't practice as much—most pro players held down full-time "real" jobs—so they spent even less time on innovation.

The only pro coach who was an exception to this rule was Curly Lambeau of the Green Bay Packers; his teams would saturate the air with fifteen or twenty passes a game. Curly had two good reasons for taking this tack. First, when he started at Green Bay his roster had considerably less talent than some other pro teams like the Chicago Bears or the Canton Bulldogs, and he needed a gimmick to equalize his chances. Second, he was his own tailback, and either he had absolute confidence that he wouldn't throw a disastrous pass or he realized he'd stay healthier by throwing the ball away than by getting tackled.

Anyway, by the end of the decade, when Curly had lured a whole bunch of all-pros into Packer uniforms, including a new tailback or two, he was used to his aerial circus and had his boys continue tossing

NOTRE DAME BOX

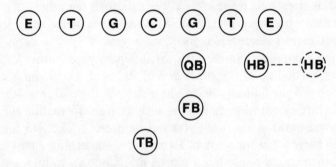

the ball. Because he started winning championships at about the same time, some of the other pro coaches began to think that maybe old Curly wasn't so crazy after all.

Helping to prove the point was a young tailback named Benny Friedman, who'd played college ball at Michigan, one of the few campuses where "pass" wasn't a dirty word. Benny never played for the Packers, but for several seasons after he turned pro in 1927, his passes made his teams runners-up to Green Bay.

Ironically, it was a game in 1932—a year when the Packers didn't win the title and when Friedman was only playing part-time—that really turned the pros toward passing. The title that year came down to a playoff in Chicago between the Bears and a team called the Portsmouth (Ohio) Spartans (if "Portsmouth" doesn't ring a bell, just think of them as the Detroit Lions, which is what they became two years later). Both teams were anxious to get the playoff started, but the weatherman wasn't. Because it snowed so much in Chicago that week, there was no way they could play at Wrigley Field without having every man carry a shovel, so they moved the game indoors to Chicago Stadium.

The problem with Chicago Stadium was that the field was ten yards too narrow and twenty yards too short and the sidelines came right up to the wall. At that time, they "played it where it lay," just as in golf, so if the ball ended up a foot from the sideline, teams just strung out into the middle with the center on the sideline end. Then they wasted a first down running the ball back to the middle of the field. Well, everyone could see right away that that would be a real mess in the truncated stadium, but somebody got the bright idea of putting hash marks ten yards in from the sideline and starting plays there whenever a previous play had concluded within five yards of the sideline. Sure enough, it worked slicker than cow slobber, opening up the game a poke and a half, and the next year the pros adopted it as a regular thing—their first really useful addition to the evolution of football.

The other important innovation to come out of that game was a change in the passing rules. Up to and including the indoor playoff, a passer had to be five yards behind the line of scrimmage before he was allowed to throw. But early in the fourth quarter, with the score at 0-0, Bear fullback Bronko Nagurski started to buck into the line, then stopped, retreated a step or two, and passed to Red Grange for a touchdown. The Portsmouth people swore Bronko wasn't nearly the required five yards back, but the officials somehow held a different opinion.

By the next rules meeting, the Portsmouth reps were still bitching about that pass. Finally, the Spartan coach said, "The hell with it! Let 'em pass from anywhere." And by 1934, pro football had its second innovation.

LEGAL *AND* RESPECTABLE

American football was a little over 50 years old at this point (counting from Camp's yards-to-go invention), but it was still only on the fringe of the modern game. During the '30s, the ball was tapered to make it more passable and, unintentionally, to make drop kicking nigh unto impossible. The colleges followed the pros for a change and adopted hash marks and liberalized pass rules. A few college teams, particularly in the Southwest Conference, made the pass a significant part of their offense.

By 1938 the two brightest stars in pro football were Washington's Sammy Baugh, a passer, and Green Bay's Don Hutson, a receiver. Hutson, a slightly built but speedy Alabaman, practically invented modern pass receiving by creating new patterns, cuts, and moves. He was probably the first man ever to practice catching badly thrown passes. Nevertheless, the highest paid pro that year was Pittsburgh's Byron "Whizzer" White, the present U.S. Supreme Court Justice. White was an awful passer but a terrific runner, and his salary shows where pro football's priorities were at the time.

A-FORMATION

Then in 1940, the T-formation burst on the scene. The T itself wasn't new. In fact, it had originally been drawn up by Walter Camp when he created the scrimmage. But the "old" T was a creaky formation with the quarterback standing a yard or so back from the center (a "quarter of the way back," to be exact). The center hiked the ball the short distance to the quarterback, who then handed off or pitched out while standing there in the open for God, the spectators, and the defense to see. The T lacked power and was about as deceptive as showdown poker. Powerful, wedge-type plays replaced it in the 1890s, and when they were ruled out, the single wing or the related "Notre Dame Box" became the popular attacks. These had a little more deception than the wedge, but essentially their intent was the same—to concentrate as many blockers as possible at the point of attack.

Against all reason, a few coaches kept faith with the T, among them George Halas of the Bears and Clark Shaughnessy, who took over at Stanford University in 1940. They got together with Hunk Anderson, a line coach who knew more about blocking than Freud knew about ids. The result was a brand new T that worked entirely by deception.

The key was to move the quarterback flush up against the center. When he took the snap and turned his back to the defense, they didn't know what he was going to do. And that froze them. Holes and blocking angles had already been created by splitting the offensive line. The defensive backs were spread out of the play by sending a running back in motion or stationing him wide as a wingback. Meanwhile, the remaining offensive backs were in high gear. When the quarterback handed off, the ball carrier was through the line like a shot and running free.

On paper it looked as if it would never work—supposedly, quarterback Sid Luckman cried when Halas showed it to him—but on the

MODERN T-FORMATION
(WITH MAN IN MOTION)

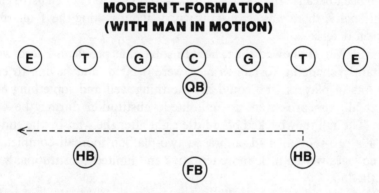

field it was magic. Shaughnessy's Stanford Indians went undefeated and won the Rose Bowl. Halas's Bears crushed Washington 73-0 in the championship game.

Marshalling the creativity football coaches are famous for, head men all over the country scurried to copy the T, X for O. It took about a dozen years, but by the mid-1950s every pro team and nearly every college squad was using some version of the formation.

Although it was designed to break the ball carriers loose, the surprising thing about the "new" T was that it worked even better for the passing attack. All the ideas about freezing the defense and spreading the secondary went together to free up receivers and give the passer more time to throw. For the first time, coaches mumbled about using the run to establish the pass.

By the end of World War II, the average NFL team was throwing about 35 percent of the time, or slightly more than 20 tosses a game.

If the T had a flaw, it was that in the era of two-way players, it demanded speed over bulk, particularly on the part of the receivers.

Hutson was a perfect example, even though his coach, Curly Lambeau, stuck with his old single wing. As a receiver, Hutson was everything a coach could want, but as a 185-pound defensive end he was a liability, just too small to stop a sweep. Under the substitution rules of the time, a player who left the game couldn't return until the next quarter. Lambeau finally solved his problem by putting Hutson at safety on defense and switching his raw-boned blocking quarterback, Larry Craig, to end on defense. Unfortunately, the skills necessary for playing T-quarterback made those people unlikely candidates for the defensive line.

Some of the very best receivers had to sit on the bench or be wasted at halfback because they were too small to do the job at defensive end. Additionally, there was a constant worry about risking the T-quarterback on defense.

World War II showed them how to solve that problem. Faced with constantly changing rosters as men were drafted, and having to employ lots of players who could do one thing well and something else not at all, the pros went to unlimited substitution during the war years. Though they backed off a little right after the war, by the end of the '40s pro football had embraced two-platoon football completely. The colleges were a little more tentative and limited substitutions well into the '50s.

Like every innovation, unlimited substitution had both predictable and unexpected results.

Predictably the new rules brought on the era of the one-dimensional player, or as the pros like to call them, "specialists." Now there was a place for the iron-handed end, the speedster who couldn't tackle, the kicker who couldn't do anything else. Nobody became more specialized than the T-quarterback.

The earliest generations of super T-quarterbacks grew up under limited substitution and could do other things besides pass. Sid Luckman, Sammy Baugh, Otto Graham, Bob Waterfield, Bobby Layne, and Frankie Albert were all versatile athletes who could run, kick, and play defense. Had the T never happened, they still could have become stars. There are still a few like that around today, but most modern quarterbacks would be out of work if they couldn't throw. Where else could such stiff-legged slingers as Dan Marino, Joe Namath, or Sonny Jurgensen play?

An unexpected result of unlimited substitution, one that is not always recognized because it happened slowly, was that linemen got bigger. Until the rule change, there had been perhaps only a dozen pro linemen who played successfully at 240 or more pounds. Very big men simply couldn't last for the extended periods necessary under limited subbing. By the second quarter, they'd turn into sweat-soaked rugs. Up to 1950, most tackles were in the 210- to 220-pound range; guards were often under 200 pounds. "Stocky" was the optimum word, "endurance" the quality.

Once the rules were changed, 280-pound Kongs could rumble onto the field, shove those 215-pounders around for five minutes, and then lumber back to the sideline to gasp oxygen. At first, the behemoths were put on defense. The Lions used to moor 315-pound Les Bingaman right over the offensive center, where he could swat anything that came near the middle. Later, when huge men became as common as nude scenes in movies, there were enough of them to match up along the offensive line. Generally bigger running backs were needed, too, as well as taller quarterbacks to see over all that mass.

It's true that the population itself is getting bigger, but even allowing for steroids, the inflation of football flesh from the lean-means of yesteryear is out of all proportion to the growth of your average accountant. The reason is simply that the mastodons can play today's two-platoon brand of football. Fifty years ago, they were out looking for honest work as Alps.

DEFENDING AGAINST THE BOMB

During the 1950s, the so-called "Golden Age of Pro Football," the passers became easily the most recognizable players on the NFL marquee. Passers sold tickets, but they also won games. The pass was the knockout punch in any team's arsenal. The idea—one that would dominate for a quarter of a century—was to run the ball until the defenses began to tip that way, then zing 'em with a pass. It broke down to 30-35 runs and 20-25 passes every game. Running carried the bulk of the responsibility. If a team couldn't run first, it probably couldn't pass second.

The best friend had most of the lines, but the hero rescued the girl in the last reel.

As the pass grew in importance, defenses reacted by pulling more men back from the line of scrimmage. Up to the '20s, the defensive side had mirrored the offense, with seven men across the line, a full-back-linebacker and three defensive backs. This is called a "7-diamond" or "7-1," after the first two lines of defense. Sometimes, particularly to close down a very strong running attack, a 7-2 was used.

Throughout the '30s and '40s, the six-man defensive line with the center as an extra linebacker (6-2) became popular. In "passing situations," a defense could drop a guard back as a third linebacker (5-3).

Once unlimited substitution was introduced, the linebackers had trouble covering the speedier receivers. Coach Greasy Neale of the Eagles introduced a 6-1 with four quick defensive halfbacks, and it helped win Philadelphia a couple of championships. But Paul Brown's Cleveland team opened the 1950 season by destroying Neale's "Eagle Defense," 35-10. Brown split his offensive line, isolating the linebacker, and sent his receivers into the flat, where they caught passes in front of the defensive backs.

A few games later Coach Steve Owen of the Giants used an "umbrella defense" to stop the Browns' swing passes. He put in a seven-man line but dropped the ends off as linebackers covering the flats, and used four fleet defensive backs as the umbrella in his secondary. This 7-2 into a 5-2-2 was a good defense, but it left a hole in the middle behind the line. The middle guard was still a down lineman, who dropped back only in certain pass situations.

Then Bill George of the Bears showed that he could play back from the middle-guard slot, become a linebacker to disrupt passes over the middle, and still come up to stop the run. Overnight, the versatile middle linebacker, embodied in such as George, Joe Schmidt, and Sam Huff emerged as the golden boy of the defense. The 4-3 became the standard pro defense for twenty years. Interestingly, the fact that some mega-ton brute wasn't playing right over the center allowed pocket-size snappers like Jim Otto and Mick Tingelhoff to excel by their

SLOT-T

(E)   (T)   (G)   (C)   (G)   (T)   (E)

(QB)   (SB)

(RB)   (RB)

ability to cut down linebackers. They would have been too small to put in front of Bingaman-like middle guards.

In the '50s, for the first time, fans began to recognize the guys playing defense. The Giants started introducing their defensive unit before the game—in truth, partly because the offense was dragging; but anyway, the idea caught on.

Offenses reacted to the increased number of defenders in the second-ary by adding another receiver. They couldn't put a twelfth man on the field, of course; and the rules said they had to have seven men on the line of scrimmage, with only the two ends eligible to catch passes. What they could do was split the ends and pull one of the running backs up closer to the line in a slot between an end and a tackle. This helped break loose the "slot back" (or "flanker," if he lined up outside the end), but put more rushing and blocking responsibility on the two remaining backs, another reason why bigger backs became the norm. The "pro-set" was standard for all NFL teams and many colleges by the end of the '50s.

PRO SET

(WR) (T) (G) (C) (G) (T) (TE)

(QB) (WR)

(RB) (RB)

BACK TO BASICS

The two poles of offense in football are power and deception. The T had replaced the single wing because it fooled people. But after twenty years, defenses were seldom astonished by the T anymore. It was time to reinvent the single wing, which is just what Vince Lombardi did.

First he brought one of his ends back in next to the tackle. Instead of using a popular speedster for this position, he put in hulking Ron Kramer, who was built like—and blocked like—a tackle. He pulled both his guards to lead interference and threw in his fullback for good measure. The tight end and tackles blocked the down linemen while the center hooked a linebacker. Split wide, the flanker drew off a

I-FORMATION

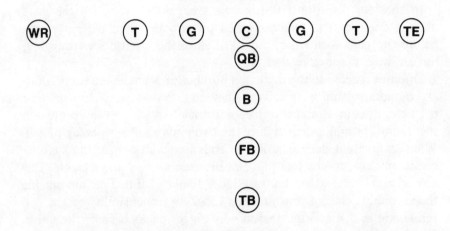

defensive back, and the guards and fullback flattened everyone in between. Then, to make sure it would work, Lombardi practiced his
team over and over just like a '20s single-wing coach. Defenses could
see the Green Bay Sweep coming; they just couldn't stop it.

Lombardi's running attack was so effective it made his passing game
look better than it really was. In truth, the Packers' passing was more
sophisticated than their running, for quarterback Bart Starr's principal
virtue was the strength of his mind, not of his arm. "Setting up the
pass with the run" was a cliché when Lombardi won his first division
title in 1960 (to be followed by five NFL championships), but in the
Packers' case it was absolutely true. The most important job for passer
Starr was that old standby: "Don't make a serious mistake."

Green Bay's conservative "single-wing/T" attack was so successful
that, naturally, most other NFL coaches copied it. In part, that explains why the Dallas Cowboys, one club that didn't clone Lombardi,
became "America's Team." Even while Green Bay was winning as
regularly as the postman rang twice, the Dallas Cowboys were more
fun to watch.

Green Bay won through simplicity and the Cowboys won through
obfuscation. Tom Landry's offense, the most complicated of the '60s,
called for thirty or forty different sets. Many of them were so subtly
different from the norm that the average TV fan couldn't see the
change, but there were enough variations that—coupled with a big-

play philosophy—the Cowboys seemed the embodiment of the ever-popular "razzle-dazzle."

Of course, razzle only dazzles when it wins, and the Packers won earlier and oftener in the '60s than the Cowboys. So when it came time to copy, NFL coaches mostly cribbed from Lombardi. That was a break for the American Football League, which began operation in 1960 amid predictions of disaster.

From its start, the AFL was a so-called passers' league. There were some legitimate, strategic reasons, of course. First of all, with any new team (and the AFL had eight of them in 1960), it's easier to find one thrower and a couple of catchers than to find six or seven blockers and a runner. Second, it's easier to teach a few pass patterns and harder to learn pass defense than to teach running and defend against it. And, remember, in the first few years, AFL rosters were about as stable as a nitro nerf ball. But with all that, there's no doubt the young AFL emphasized passing at the beginning because TV viewers liked to watch them throw. The "war" between the AFL and NFL was fought mainly on TV screens. The new league even started sewing the names of players above their numbers so TV fans could tell who they were without programs.

Sid Gillman's San Diego Chargers threw better passes than anybody else. Gillman, the grand guru of the modern passing game, geared his whole attack to throwing the ball for touchdowns. With Gillman, the run set up the pass, *and* the pass set up the pass. His prize assistant, Al Davis, used much the same philosophy when he took over the Oakland Raiders.

By the decade of the '70s, when the NFL and AFL merged into the monolithic National Football League, most successful pro teams passed about 40 percent of the time and ran 60. Overall league figures were about 45-55, but that included all the losers who threw a ton in the fourth quarter when they were a couple of touchdowns behind. Yet touchdowns were scored 60-40 through the air! Offenses were like fencers, spending most of the time parrying except for a few telling thrusts.

After World War II, colleges mostly looked to the pros for inspiration. What few new offensive wrinkles they had were almost completely aimed toward tuning their running attacks. By the '70s, a successful Big College team was a perfect running machine. Start with a two- or three-deep, monster-size line. A college line bigger than the average pro line still brings gasps from TV commentators, but the phenomenon is common now. As a rule of thumb, huge linemen block better for the run than the pass—run blocking is mostly straight-ahead, where size counts; pass blocking requires balance and clever footwork.

SHOTGUN

(WR)   (T) (G) (C) (G) (T) (TE)

(WR)   (WR) (WR)

(QB)

Behind these mountains come a fleet of quick runners. With rosters of 70 to 100, a Big College team might have a dozen or so.

Then they run, run, run, with only enough passes to keep a modicum of honesty on the defense. Well, why not? A "tough" schedule means only three or four challenges a season. Most of the big colleges can expect at least an 8-3 or 9-2 season going in. Their bulldozer running attacks can average 8 or 9 yards a try, the alumni are happy, and their Designated Heisman candidate tailback will go as a high draft choice. It works for them.

But it wouldn't work for the pros.

First of all, pro teams are too evenly matched. It may not be Rozelle's hallowed "any given Sunday," but there are no soft touches to the extent of, say, two-thirds of Oklahoma's schedule. A Big College team can point toward a couple of games in eleven weeks; a pro team has to be ready every time out of the chute.

Second, pro rosters are limited. A Big College team can send out waves of fresh linemen and backs; with the pros, the well runs dry. Injuries and exhaustion take a greater toll.

And most important, pro defenses are constantly catching up with the offenses. New ideas on offense are adopted slowly; defenses adapt overnight. Pro defenses are nearly as complicated as the offenses, and they close down the run pretty well with 4-3's, 3-4's, 53's, and flexes. About the best a pro offense can hope for with its runners is a 4.0

yards-per-attempt rate. That's not good enough. Any pro team that stays on the ground is going to lose.

About ten years ago, the NFL more or less admitted that the defenses had learned to handle the offenses. They literally gave the offenses a hand by letting the blockers use theirs. At the same time they put clamps on the defensive secondary's custom of hanging all over receivers. In other words, they made it easier to pass, without doing a thing to help the runners.

In 1982 for the first time, NFL teams-in-total passed more often than they ran. It used to be said that teams that threw more than they galloped never won. It also used to be said that the world was flat. Of the four teams in the 1986 AFC and NFC championship games, three had more passes than running plays during the season.

It only took three quarters of a century, but the forward pass has arrived.

3

What's Wrong with

Traditional Pro Football

Statistics?

The year 1971 was a dark one for alumni of West Liberty State College. That was when Bob Campiglio of the Staten Island Stapletons—yes, they were once an NFL franchise—disappeared from the NFL's *Official Record Manual*. From the time we began reading NFL manuals from cover to cover, those of us who'd survived four (or in Bob Carroll's case, five) years at the little, hilltopping West Virginia school could flip open the newest edition and point proudly to West Liberty grad Campiglio at the top of the list of NFL rushing leaders. True, the people we apprised of this wonderful fact seldom gave a damn, but it made West Libbers feel good. We had sat in the same classrooms, listened to the same lectures, sung the same alma mater as the immortal Bob Campiglio. His 504 yards in 1932, the year they finally got around to keeping such records, was enshrined forever, we assumed. The fact that Bob was the *only* West Liberty athlete ever to make any kind of mark in pro football did not lessen his glory or our vicarious pride.

Suddenly in 1971, the Elias Sports Bureau, Inc. (the company that collects, prepares, and issues the league statistics), decided the 1932 rushing leader was really Cliff Battles of Boston with 576 yards.

Our hero was, quite literally, an also-ran. And, vicariously, so were we!

We may never forgive the Elias Sports Bureau, but we have to admire them. No one ever seems to say a harsh word about Elias, and you won't find any here. They do a superhuman job in collecting, preparing, and distributing statistical information on baseball, basketball, and football. Their information is invariably clear, accurate, and reliable. Up to a traditional point (and we'll get to that later), Elias is admirably thorough. Since Elias became the official statisticians for the NFL in 1960, the quality and quantity of available football stats have improved tremendously. And make no mistake, the pre-Elias days left a lot to be desired.

EARLY PROBLEMS

By the time pro football got itself an organized league in 1920, professional baseball leagues had been around for fifty years. Baseball fans were used to studying end-of-season diamond statistics and evaluating the performances of their favorite players. Many newspapers of the period printed complete hitting, pitching, and even fielding statistics at season's end.

Pro football statistics were hit-or-miss throughout the 1920s. When they were kept at all, the keeper was usually a local newspaperman who fleshed out his account of yesterday's home game with a few numbers. His choice of "keeper" records was often very different from those favored by interested newsmen in other towns. For example, a fairly common approach was simply to record all the yardage credited to a player, lumping rushes, passes, and returns, and sometimes making no notation of attempts or opportunities. On the other hand, the *Rock Island Argus*, trumpeter of the Rock Island Independents' games, often divided rushing stats into two columns—"plunges" and "end runs." Few papers concerned themselves with pass receiving stats, at most giving the total number of catches. Passing totals often gave the number of completions but not attempts.

The newspapers that paid the most attention to statistics were in the small NFL towns: Rock Island, Green Bay, Staten Island, Providence, Canton, and, after 1930, Portsmouth. Monday's game account was usually accompanied by a complete play-by-play. The reason was simply that the doings of the local pro teams constituted major stories in these cities; the Chicago Bears or New York Giants were only second or third page in their hometown dailies. An exception was Philadelphia, where the local Frankford Yellow Jackets were well detailed.

A consequence of this erratic "local" coverage is that we can get a reasonably complete picture of the statistical accomplishments of the long-defunct Staten Island Stapletons, Rock Island Independents, and Providence Steam Rollers but only glimpse bits and pieces of the early New York Giants or Chicago Bears.

At the end of the 1931 season, a complete table of individual NFL scoring totals appeared in some newspapers. In four columns after players' names, it listed touchdowns, extra points, field goals, and total points. There was no distinction made for the way touchdowns were scored (by rushing, pass reception, runback, or fumble recovery), no column for safeties, and no indication of missed extra points or field goals. Furthermore, later studies have shown that the totals given were not 100 percent accurate; points were missing or credited to the wrong player. Still this 1931 table is significant because, though uncredited, it must have come from the league itself, including as it does players from all of the NFL's ten teams, and therefore must represent the NFL's first statistical effort. Apparently, it was not considered "official," but it awarded the "first" NFL scoring title to Green Bay halfback Johnny Blood with 72 points.

The next year, the NFL expanded its stat keeping. At the end of the season, it recognized "official" leaders in scoring, rushing, passing, receiving, and field goals. The National League Press Bureau (under the direction of Ned Irish in New York) issued news stories identifying the leaders, and these were picked up by some papers around the country. There is no indication that the league tried to keep complete records of rushing, passing, or receiving for all players. In fact, it seems most unlikely, if only because later studies by Elias have replaced two of the leaders.

In 1933, "top tens" in scoring, rushing, passing, and receiving were issued after the season, and apparently updates were distributed during the season itself because some newspapers showed an awareness that Glenn Presnell of Portsmouth and Ken Strong of New York were engaged in a close battle for the scoring leadership.

Along with the scant individual stats, some maddeningly incomplete team statistics appeared. These showed yards gained, opponents' yards gained, passes thrown, passes completed, points scored, and points against. There was no way to guess how much yardage was made strictly by rushing or by passing, no record of pass interceptions, and no division of the points into touchdowns, extra points, field goals, and safeties.

GM	TEAM	YARDS GAINED	OPPONENT YARDS	FORWARD PASSES	PASSES CAUGHT	POINTS SCORED	POINTS AGAINST
13	Chicago Bears	3029	2326	210	92	133	82
14	New York	2970	2529	180	74	244	101
10	Brooklyn	2207	1754	169	79	93	54
11	Portsmouth	2710	1983	170	65	128	87
12	Boston	2823	2525	106	33	103	97
13	Green Bay	2758	1929	209	88	170	107
9	Philadelphia	1786	2236	149	41	77	158
10	Cincinnati	1206	2319	101	24	38	110
11	Pittsburgh	1887	2761	195	61	67	208
11	Chicago Cards	1508	2308	141	37	52	101

We have no idea why the teams are listed in this apparently haphazard order, but leaving that aside, it's frustrating not to know how many of the Bears' yards came on rushes or how many times they ran the ball. Which team had the better passing attack—Green Bay, New York, or the Bears? We don't have enough information. Should an opponent run or pass against Boston? We don't know. Did Pittsburgh pass more often than it should have?

It's impossible to tell.

The only thing more frustrating than having *no* statistics is having too *few* statistics.

After the 1934 season, the Spalding Company published its first *Official National Football League Guide.* Until then, any statistical information put out by the NFL was at the mercy of heartless sports editors across the country to use or discard as they saw fit.

In his "Introductory," NFL President Joe F. Carr said: "In the face of many obstacles, professional football has now taken its place as one of the seasonal attractions for the sport loving American public, and the initial number of the National Football League Guide is offered as a chronicle of the league's activities and a medium for promulgating the official playing rules of professional football."

Unfortunately the guide concerned itself more with rules and team histories than with numbers. Its summary of the 1934 season contained only the same individual scoring, rushing, passing, and receiving "top tens" and rudimentary team statistics. Not until 1936 were "complete" stats in the major categories listed.

The inadequacy of the 1932 through 1935 NFL statistics was matched only by their fallibility. Those early efforts produced some highly unreliable numbers. Remember Bob Campiglio? Here are some other recounts:

Scoring

The numbers for 1932 leader Earl "Dutch" Clark have moved from 4 touchdowns, 6 extra points, 3 field goals, and 39 points to 6 touchdowns, 10 extra points, 3 field goals, and 55 points.

Jack Manders, the 1934 leader, has lost 3 extra points, dropping him to a season total of 76 points.

Rushing

Battles picked up the '32 leadership when he supplanted Campiglio, but he lost the '33 championship. His 737 yards gained gave way to Jim Musick's 809.

The next year, Beattie Feathers became the first recorded thousand-yard rusher with 1,004 yards on 101 attempts—maybe. The figures released immediately after the season of 1,052 on 107 were revised downward within a few months, but curiously from 1943 through 1947, the manuals printed his attempts at 117.

Passing

Harry Newman, the 1933 leader, has been credited with 4 more pass attempts (to 136) and also added 10 yards (to 973) without gaining a completion (still 53). The 1935 leader, Ed Danowski, is down a yard to 794.

Receiving

Luke Johnsos (24 receptions) has been replaced as 1932 leader by Ray Flaherty with only 21 catches. "Shipwreck" Kelly's 1933-leading totals are up to 22 catches and 246 yards from 21 for 219. The next year's leader, Joe Carter, is up a yard to 238.

And those are only changes for the leaders! We can only wonder about the others in the "Top Ten" lists, some of them members of the Pro Football Hall of Fame.

In addition to early inaccuracy, NFL stats were laughably incomplete throughout the 1930s. Punting records were not kept until 1939, interceptions until 1940, kickoff and punt returns until 1941.

Thanks to Elias, we need no longer question the accuracy of today's stats. Additionally, they've added some interesting columns to existing categories, like field goal range and net yardage on punts.

So what's the complaint?

THE BASEBALL CONNECTION

The problem started way back when. The writer-statisticians looked at baseball stats and used them as a model for football stats. Even the sainted Elias Sports Bureau has continued down this road—after all, they started as baseball statisticians—despite the fact that about the only thing the two games have in common is their second syllable.

Ah, the life of a baseball statistician!

The baseball statistician performs his pleasant duties under a warm July sun or a comfortable August moon. If it should rain, he gets the day off. His subject is easy to observe, its intricacies unobscured. Baseball players perform their rituals in a predictable cadence: pitch, hit, field. The pitcher always begins his performance from exactly the same preordained spot on the field, as does the batter. Should the batter become a baserunner, he is restricted by baseball law to well-worn paths. The fielders have only a little more leeway, posted at historically approved intervals across green grass or kelly carpet. There is never any confusion as to which man did what. Whenever the statistician is perplexed by an event, he has plenty of time to stroll over to someone with a better view—pausing for a hot dog along the way—and ask just wotthehell happened. Baseball is leisurely.

Compare this with the harried football statistician, struggling against a freezing December wind, peering through the swirling snow at drift-covered yard markers, confronted with twenty-two players in constantly shifting alignments, all of them racing against a clock into new configurations. Even on a relatively simple play like a thrust off tackle by Atlanta's Gerald Riggs, the statistician has his hands full. Listen:

"Who was that? Was that Riggs? Okay, where are they putting the ball down? Wait a minute! Was that a fumble? No. Okay, it's on the 32, right? Or is that the 33? No, the 32. Who made the tackle? Did anyone see who made the . . . ? What's that? A penalty? Where's my eraser? No, it's refused. The play stands. Oh, God, they're lining up. Who made that last goddamn tackle!"

There's a lot wrong with traditional football statistics. Some of it stems from the problems encountered in collecting the numbers.

Some comes from how long we've been adding them up. Compared to baseball, football is a very young game.

After a baseball game the statistician adds up his totals of throws, hits, and catches, and from these works out various percentages and averages. He can weigh one number against another, and produce even more numbers to indicate various player abilities. He is guided in this by over a hundred years of record keeping. And incorporating examples from baseball's long history, he can make numerous comparisons among thousands of players who have tried to do the same sorts of things—make runs and put the other side out—in essentially the same ways.

With some small adjustments for the glacial rate of changes in baseball, our statistician can rank a player like Boston's Jim Rice—either by season or career—against every player in the entire history of baseball. Admittedly everyone may not fully agree with the evaluation, but arguments will stem from what weights he attaches to certain figures. Few would argue the need for two or three more columns of numbers.

After a football game the statistician finds himself adding up numbers relating to many different kinds of activities: running with the football, kicking it, throwing it, catching it, and even doing brutal things to others who were trying to run, kick, etc. If the football statistician wants to make a historical comparison, he is confounded by the knowledge that the responsibilities of a given position may have changed drastically during his lifetime and that the game he played as a youth is very different from that of today. He knows many of the numbers he finds significant were not kept until recently, and that some of the most significant actions on a football field are never recorded at all. In that context he tries to make sense out of the flawed and incomplete picture his numbers produce.

THE CULT OF THE INDIVIDUAL

The first thing anyone must understand about football statistics is that they are not baseball statistics. While that may be obvious in detail—no one is likely to mistake an end run for a home run—it is less obvious in interpretation. Hence in scanning stat lines, we should not evaluate Gerald Riggs's contributions to his team with the same cause-and-effect mind set that we use for Jim Rice's contributions to his.

With a baseball player such as Rice, we have all—or nearly all—the numbers we could ever ask for. That's in the nature of baseball. Baseball, is a team game made up of many individual acts, all of which can be counted rather easily. Furthermore, because of the long and stable history of the game, the numbers that were most significant fifty years ago are still, for the majority of fans, most significant today.

Every time Rice saunters up to home plate, the statistician will record an individual act by him—a home run, a strikeout, a base on balls. Conversely, the same actions can be considered individual acts by the pitcher. Should Rice ground out to the shortstop, the statistician records four individual acts: an *at bat* for Rice, a *third of an inning* pitched for the pitcher, an *assist* for the shortstop, and a *putout* for the first baseman. Significantly, on this play the statistician does not have to record any action by the third baseman, the left fielder, or any other player. Indeed, there's nothing to record. And, our statistician can take comfort in the fact that fifty years ago a groundout to the shortstop was statistically just what it is today, no more or less.

Rice's final stat line at the end of the season is, with only a couple of exceptions, a record of actions Rice performed on his own without the aid of his teammates. He did not have to depend on another Red Sox player to knock the opponent leftfielder on his can so that he could register a two-base hit. In theory, a player can achieve excellent marks in almost any statistical category regardless of the ineptitude of his teammates. Ralph Kiner used to lead the National League in home runs with monotonous regularity while playing alongside Pirates who swashbuckled as nimbly as John Candy. A few years ago, Steve Carlton topped the National League in wins while pitching for the phutile Phillies. Ernie Banks went into the Hall of Fame; his Cub teams went into the toilet.

Assuming a dedicated football statistician marks down everything he's expected to on a play, what has he got? Well, certainly not a record of an individual effort by Gerald Riggs.

Is there a record of the transfer from the center to the quarterback or the handoff from the quarterback to Riggs? Is there anything to indicate a good fake into the line by the other running back, a fake that froze a linebacker? Where is it recorded that the Falcon line performed three excellent blocks and missed two?

Football is a team game made up of many interacting efforts.

One lesson from this observation is that whereas baseball glories in individual stats, football's most important numbers are team statistics. Individual football stats are nice to look at, even though they may not always be the most meaningful stats, and I'm not suggesting that we put them all in a bucket and sink them. As a matter of fact, we'll be looking at lots of individual marks a little later. But in football, the team stats take precedence.

Compare Roger Maris's 61 home runs in 1961 with Dan Marino's 48 touchdown passes in 1984, two unprecedented (and, apparently, individual) accomplishments.

No doubt Maris was helped by baseball's expansion that year (he faced more second-rate pitchers) and by Yankee Stadium's friendly right field wall, but those things don't mitigate his individual achievement in taking advantage of his particular situation. How much of his record did he owe to his Yankee teammates? Well, the Yankees hit .263 as a team compared to the league average of .256. Maris probably batted .023 more times by playing for the Yankees than he would have had he played for an average American League team. Credit Maris with 97.7 percent of his record. Given only average teammates, he would have still hit 59 home runs.

Estimating how much of Marino's record belongs to Marino isn't so easy. Factor in a defense to give him the ball, some runners to help move it closer to the goal line, a line that blocked, receivers who caught, and a coach willing to go with an all-out passing attack. Credit him with 40 percent input.

That doesn't mean that any klutz can play quarterback for the Miami Dolphins. It simply puts Marino's 48 touchdowns in a reasonable context. He'd still be an exceptional quarterback in Indianapolis, but his statistics wouldn't be as good.

The contributions of teammates are only one way that football statistics are situational. The play called is dictated by the score, the down, the clock, the field position, the strengths (or weaknesses) of a team and of its opponent, the weather, the philosophy of the head coach, and probably what the play caller had for breakfast. Not even Marino can throw a touchdown pass on a running play.

Marino was able to throw a high number of touchdowns in 1984 because he threw a high number of passes in situations conducive to throwing touchdowns. That Marino has a hell of a strong and accurate arm is only part (albeit a *significant* part) of those situations.

MAKING THE WORST OF A GOOD SITUATION

The situational side of football statistics is like the weather; everybody knows it's there, but nobody does anything about it.

Where football went off the track was way back when they used baseball stats as models. Baseball stats come in two varieties: counting and averages.

Counting stats tell us *how many.* They are obtained simply by adding up like things—so many home runs, so many passes caught, so many strikeouts, so many punts. In baseball, counting stats are somewhat situational; in football they are absolutely so. In baseball, the more situational a statistic, the less meaningful it is; in football, the situation is all.

Averages tell us *how often.* They are obtained by dividing one counting stat by a different counting stat: hits by at bats, yards by rushing attempts, earned runs by innings pitched (multiplying by nine to get an "earned run average" simply makes the final number easier to interpret), pass completions by attempts. In baseball, a batting average has some meaning because it is only slightly situational and it is based on a large sample, a 162-game schedule. In football, averages are based on only a tenth as many games and all of the counting numbers used to create them are situational.

Such averages as yards per attempt or completions per attempt are not quite meaningless, of course. They are simply not as significant in evaluating a player's ability as are such baseball averages as batting average, slugging average, on base percentage, or earned run average. In football, a passer who averages an 8-yard gain per attempt is superior to one who averages 6 yards per attempt, *all other things being equal.* The problem is that all other things are *never* equal. To take a very simplified example: is an 8-yard pass completion on third-and-10 better than a 6-yard pass on third-and-5?

Wait a minute! Isn't a two-out grand slam home run in the ninth inning of a baseball game when a team trails by three runs rather situational? Granted, but a baseball player who bats 600 times in a season may face such a situation 6 times (or maybe not at all). To know what he did in those few crisis situations is only marginally useful (unless you want to show that Bobby Thomson was the greatest hitter of all time). Situational statistics have their place in baseball; they just happen to be more important—indeed, most important—in football.

We don't intend to ignore counting and averaging. They are useful, as far as they go. Certainly we must know *how many* before we can do anything. Knowing *how often* is interesting and sometimes useful. But the most important thing to know about an event on a football field is *under what circumstances.*

A really ironic fact is that baseball, which is situational to a far lesser extent than football, has hundreds of fans across the country making and collecting play-by-play accounts of games (it's called "Project Scoresheet") just so they can create situational stats that are not apparent in traditional box scores. Yet football play-by-plays are routinely kept during a game (by the official statistician) and sent to Elias, along with the final tally sheets. In other words, the apparatus necessary to produce situational football statistics already exists.

All we have to do is figure out how to put it to work.

LOOKING FOR THE LITTLE STAT THAT WASN'T THERE

The football encyclopedia edited by David S. Neft and Richard Cohen, *Pro Football: The Early Years,* has used newspaper accounts to calculate scoring records for individual NFL players and for teams for the years 1920–31. Included are TDs by rushing and passing, field goals, and PATs attempted and made. The 1987 edition also has some yardage records compiled from newspaper play-by-play accounts, but these were only published occasionally. Because they come from unofficial sources, the Neft-Cohen compilations can never be official, although they present tremendous insights into the way football was played in the 1920s.

The NFL started to keep official statistics in 1932, its thirteenth year of existence. By 1935, a reasonably complete set of individual and team rushing, passing, receiving, and scoring stats were kept and published. Defensive statistics were slim-to-*nada* until 1941, while individual return figures came in gradually—interceptions and punt returns in 1942 and fumbles in 1945. Yards lost attempting to pass were counted in with rushing yards through 1946. They were kept separately afterward, although the 1947 and 1948 data were not released to the public. The number of times passers lost yardage (now called "sacks") was not counted until 1961, and no credit was given to the defensive player responsible for the sack until 1982.

Team punting averages started in 1935, with individual stats in 1939. The league made an attempt at team net punting average, subtracting returns from the yardage, in 1943. In 1946 they started subtracting touchbacks. Then, in 1961, they said to hell with it and didn't pick it up again until 1976. This time they also kept individual net punting average and also began including the number of times the punter put the receiving team inside its own 20-yard line.

Among the stats *not* kept are the number and average length of kickoffs. This is sort of odd, if you think about it. The kickoff is as important in establishing field position as the punt (although no one ever blocks a kickoff). But while lots of punting stats are kept, at present there is just no way for the average fan to tell which teams kick off better than others.

Kickoffs occur nearly as often as punts; in 1986, there were 2,311 punts and 2,017 kickoffs (not including 40 on-side kicks and 14 free kicks after safeties). We know from league data that the range in net punting average among NFL teams is plus or minus 4 yards (29.7 to 37.4 yards). Analysis of 1986 play-by-play data shows about the same range for net kickoff average, with the receiving team starting within a range of the 21- to 29-yard lines. Thus the net difference in average and total yards is about the same for kickoffs as for punts.

Another oversight is that no credit is given for the distance gained on intercepted passes. At first glance, this might seem to make sense. After all, should a team receive *credit* for the thin air the ball arched through on its way, via the efforts of an errant quarterback, to the hands of some larcenous pass defender? In a word—yes. Even though it turns the ball over to the other team, an interception still moves the ball downfield. When a fumble occurs, the player and team get credit for the yardage to the point of the fumble. How many times have you seen a running back zip nine yards downfield and get zapped? Although he fumbled, he still can add those nine yards to his total when he negotiates his next contract.

In 1986, there were 581 interceptions (including 2 on fake field goal attempts). The average "gain" on these plays was 19.1 yards. Total it up and it's 11,100 yards, about 10 percent of the gross passing yards of 101,128 and more than the sack total of 9,047. Wars have been fought for less territory than the NFL ignores! In 1986 the one hundred longest net "gains" on interceptions averaged better than 35 yards, including the return—about as good as a punt.

Speaking of fumbles, there is no official breakdown on fumbles by play type. You can get a total, 431 in 1986, but which ones came on runs, passes, returns, or what-have-you is what you don't have—unless you read the rest of this paragraph. Fumbles on rushing plays totaled 176. On passing plays there were 155, 69 by passers and 86 by receivers. An additional 30 occurred on aborted plays where no determination could be made whether a rush or pass was called. There were 65 fumbles on returns (35 on punts, 25 on kickoffs, and 5 on interceptions), and 5 fumbles came on punt and field goal attempts.

The NFL (and just about everyone else) makes a big deal out of turnovers. You get the idea that turnovers are more important in football than in pancakes. Curiously, a loss of possession on downs is not considered a turnover by the NFL. It happened 173 times in 1986.

We can't think of a good reason why loss of possession on downs shouldn't be considered a full-fledged turnover. If fourth down comes up and a team throws an interception, that's an official turnover; if the pass is grounded incomplete, it's not. Does that make a whole lot of sense to you?

Although the loss-of-possession data doesn't appear in the official stat section of the *NFL Record Manual,* it does show up in the individual team figures under fourth-down conversions, where it's been kept since 1984. A failed fourth-down conversion is equal to a turnover on downs. Turnovers on fumbles and interceptions on fourth down are double-counted here by these stats. The 1986 league data shows 195 failed fourth-down conversions, while the play-by-play data shows 173 turnovers on downs and 27 interceptions or fumbles. Apparently the league did not count the 5 times a fumble occurred on botched punt or field goal tries.

And turning to botches, the league has never kept track of blocked punts by the defense. You can find out whose punts were blocked, but you'll look in vain to find who blocked 'em. And yet a blocked punt is one of the most devastating plays in football. We think the number of blocked punts (and blocked field goals, too) should be kept both for the offense and the defense.

In 1986, there were 28 blocked punts, plus an additional 7 partially blocked. Official stats count a punt as blocked only if the ball doesn't reach the line of scrimmage. Of the 28 "true" blocks, 14 were returned for touchdowns. How's that for devastating!

Actually, it was a well-kept secret. It's almost as hard to find the touchdowns scored on blocked punts as it is to find Jimmy Hoffa's toenails. What you have to do is start with all the touchdowns scored, eliminate all the other ways of scoring TDs, and what you have left are the blocked punt TDs. Okay, the official stats break touchdowns into three groups: rushing, passing, and returns. We can skip the first two groups. The return group has six possibilities. In 1986, there were 90 touchdowns on returns: 29 on interceptions, 14 on punts, 7 on kickoffs, 18 on opponent fumbles recovered by the defense, and 6 on fumbles recovered by the offense. That leaves 16 touchdowns on blocked kick returns. Two of those weren't on blocked punts but on the 32 blocked field goals that occurred in 1986. That gets you the team numbers; for individuals you have to do the whole thing all over again —with a lot more counting.

Remember the USFL? Ah, it seems like only yesterday that the $1 League was cavorting through the springtime air! Perhaps the New Jersey Generals and others are a bit unlamented by the NFL, but one idea they had was pretty good. Currently in the NFL, if a team is trying to run out the clock, the quarterback will move backward a step and kneel down for a small loss. This is counted as a rushing play! The USFL had a separate category for clock-consuming plays, which did not count in the overall rushing total either for teams or individuals. Believe it or not, there were 291 plays of this type in the NFL in 1986, for a loss of about 600 yards.

Actually there's quite a hodgepodge of methods used in compiling statistics. For example, the leader in rushing, both team and individual, has always been measured by total yards. Meanwhile, pass receptions and interceptions are measured by total number. Scoring is by total points. And punts, punt returns, and kickoff returns are ranked by average, with a minimum number to qualify for individual leaderships.

Passing—hoo boy!—has been measured ten different ways over the years. The current complicated rating system began in 1973, but is used for individuals only—not for teams. Just why it's not used for teams (both offense and defense) is known only by the NFL and God (and then only if they've let Him in on it). Strangely, touchdown percentage, one of the four items used in the rating system, is not considered a separate category for individual and lifetime records, season or team. You can look up record performances in the other three parts, completion percentage, average gain, and interception percentage.

Another oversight: sacks for individual passers are not shown in the official records, although they *are* given in the team stat section of the *Record Manual.* They first appeared in the league *Media Guide,* starting in 1969. The *Media Guide* and *Record Manual* were combined in 1983, but the sacks were not added to the *Record Manual* side. The data should really be used in the rating system; the reason it is not is apparently that the information on sacks doesn't exist historically as far back as the other items.

We think a better system would be to measure each category except scoring by a simplified method that includes number, yards, touchdowns, and turnovers. This is similar to the passer rating system, and while we find some faults in the way it's set up, we approve of the *idea* behind it. If you set up a Rusher Rating System, Receiver Rating System, and various Return Rating Systems, you could give bonuses for touchdowns and assess penalties for turnovers. Admittedly, this isn't as simple as just adding up numbers, but it's far more accurate. (You want simplicity, just rank everybody alphabetically.) The big stumbling block is fumbles, which—as we said—are currently not broken down as to types of plays.

On the subject of penalties for turnovers, we suggest 50 yards for a fumble and 45 for an interception. Here's the reasoning.

A fumble costs a team about 50 yards in offense, as on the average a team will gain an additional amount in yardage from scrimmage or punting before turning the ball over to its opponent. The fumbler should be charged with the 50-yard penalty for each fumble, with the recoverer getting a bonus for the same amount. Thus if a teammate recovers, the net penalty is zero.

Interceptions should be penalized only 45 yards because the average return of an interception (about 14 yards including touchbacks) is less than the average length of the pass (about 19 yards).

Touchdowns, we figure, should get a bonus of 10 additional yards. This is because the scoring potential from the 1-yard line is still only a bit over 6 points (instead of a full 7). Thus the final inch into the end zone is worth almost a whole point. Since it normally takes about 12 yards of offense to score a point, the actual accomplishing of a touchdown is worth a 10-yard bonus.

We'll get into this in a great deal more detail later. Right now we'd like to summarize what is and isn't available in NFL stats and tell you how long those that exist have been around.

HISTORY OF NFL STATS

CATEGORY	TEAM	OPPONENTS	INDIVIDUAL
Points scored	1920-	1920-	Top 10 1932; all 1935-
Touchdowns	1933-	1941-	1935-
Field Goals Made	1933-	1941-	1935-
Field Goals Attempted .	1938-	1941-	1938-
Field Goals by Distance	1966-	Not Kept	1966-
PAT Made	1933-	1941-	1935-
PAT Attempted	1940-	1961-	1939-
Safeties	1933-	1941-	1942-
Total First Downs	1935-	1941-	N/A
First Downs Rush, Pass,			
Penalty	1941-	1941-	N/A
Third Down Efficiency . .	1981-	1981-	N/A
Third Downs Att./Made .	*1972-	*1972-	N/A
Fourth Downs Att/Made	*1984-	*1984-	N/A
Total Yards Gained . . .	1933-	1933-	N/A
Rushing Attempts	1936-	1941-	Top 10 1932, all 1935-
Yards Gained Rushing .	1935-	1941-	Top 10 1932, all 1935-
Touchdowns Rushing . .	1933-	1941-	All 1941-

(Team rushing totals included touchdowns on all types of returns until 1946)

Passing Attempts, Completions	1933-	1935-	Top 10 1933, all 1935-
Yards Gained Passing .	1933-	1941-	Top 10 1933, all 1935-
†Times Sacked	1961-	1961-	Defense 1982
†Yards Lost Attempting to Pass	1949-	1949-	Defense 1982

(Kept separately and not released 1947-48; included in rushing until 1946)
† Individual data for passers in team section of league media book, 1969-

Touchdowns Passing . .	1933-	1941-	Top 10 1933, all 1935-
Passes Had Intercepted	1936-	1935-	1935-
Passer Rating System	Not Calc.	Not Calc.	1973-
Laterals (att., comp., yards)	1935-1949	1942-1949	1942-1949

(Kept as part of whatever play was originally initiated, 1950)

Kickoffs	1948-1960	1948-1960	Not Kept
Yards on Kickoffs	Not Kept	Not Kept	Not Kept
Punts	1939-	1941-	1939-
Average Distance of Punts	1935-	1941-	1939-

CATEGORY	TEAM	OPPONENTS	INDIVIDUAL
Net Punting Average . . **(Not including touch-backs 1943-45)**	1943-1961 1976-	1943-1961	1976-
Punts Had Blocked . . .	1943-	*1969-	1943-
Punt Returns	1941-	1941-	1941-
Yards on Punt Returns .	1941-	1941-	1941-
Touchdowns on Punt Re-turns	1941-	1941-	1941-
Kickoff Returns	1941-	1941-	1942-
Yards on Kickoff Returns.	1940-	1941-	1942-
Touchdowns on Kickoff Returns	1941-	1941-	1942-
Interception Returns . .	1935-	1936-	1941-
Yards on Interception Returns	1940-	1941-	1941-
Touchdowns on Inter-ception Returns	1941-	1941	1941-
Penalties	1941-	1941-	N/A
Penalty Yards	1935-	1941-	N/A
Fumbles	1935-	1941-	1945-
Fumbles Lost	1941-	1935-	1945-
Yards on Own Fumbles .	1945-	Not Kept	1945-
Touchdowns on Own Fumbles	1945-	1964-	1945-
Yards on Opponent Fum-bles	1945-	1948-1960	1945-
Touchdowns on Oppo-nent Fumbles	1945-	1947-	1945-

(Yards on own fumbles and opponent fumbles combined in 1983)

* Not part of official statistics but contained in the team section of the league media guide, which first came out after the 1969 season and was merged with the record manual in 1983.

4

Punch, Zip, Whirr . . .
Touchdown!

Picture this. The clock is running out on the Cowboys, only a few seconds left and four points down. A desperation Dallas pass from the Giants' 18 fails, leaving them to look at third down with time for only one last play. Instead of moving toward a huddle, the Cowboy players —as they have done all game—begin lining up in a loose T. The Giants rush into an even looser defensive alignment.

Meanwhile high in the stands (in a glass-enclosed booth to minimize crowd noise), a Dallas staff member speaks crisply into a microphone, stating the down, yardage to go, and time left. Below the grandstand, a voice-activated computer absorbs the input. By the time the last syllable has been spoken, every Cowboy player hears the play, formation, and starting count being called in a dry, HAL-like voice through the miniature speaker set in each white-starred helmet.

Similarly the Giant players hear their computer call the defensive set. Several players for both teams turn in place and dash toward the sidelines as appropriate subs sprint on.

But wait! The Dallas man in the booth recognizes the defense and blurts it into his mike. Instantly, the Dallas computer voice changes the play and intones: "Hike!" The Giants' computer calls belated warnings even as the ball is snapped but it's too late for the flesh-and-blood New Yorkers to react.

Touchdown Dallas!

Ecstatically, the victorious Cowboys carry their offensive programmer off the field on their shoulders.

Sounds like Arthur C. Clarke has invaded the NFL? Not really. The technology for this little scenario exists already. The only thing keeping it off the field is that it's against the regulations of the NFL. Ever since Paul Brown's short-lived experiment with a shortwave radio receiver in the helmet of quarterback George Ratterman in 1956, the NFL has lived in fear of the future. The appropriate rule, Section (E) of Article X (Prohibited Conduct), states: "No club, nor any coach, representative or employee thereof, shall use or employ any mechanical or other equipment or device in connection with the staging or playing of any game . . ."

The computer-as-sideline-coach is not yet in sight. But those who think it will remain a Star Wars pipe dream should remember that at one time the rules prohibited coaching in *any* form from the sideline.

For the moment, though they've been ruled out of the game itself, computers affect, enhance, and guide almost every other aspect of NFL life. A team without a healthy, quadruple-threat computer might just as well line up in the Notre Dame Box. The league doesn't crow about its reliance upon microchips, probably because a large segment of the ticket-buying and TV-watching public still regards the computer as a Trojan horse in which the nerds will infiltrate and ultimately take over pro football.

"No computer can tackle or block," the saying goes. Okay, and no linebacker can throw a pass, and no wide-out can kick a 50-yard field goal. Football is the ultimate game of specialists, and, yes, there is even a specialized role for computers to play. After all, coaches and general managers don't tackle or block, but good ones are necessary to a successful football operation—and the good ones can be better with a trusty data-cruncher at their sides.

NO WORSE THAN A REDHEAD

If you're old enough to remember when they were called "electronic brains," you probably still don't know how they work—and we're not going to show you how, because this is a football book, not a hardware manual. For the football fan, *it's what computers do, not how they do it, that matters.* Nobody asks about the innards of his toaster while he spreads jam on the product. Computers basically do three things.

First, they can do mathematical calculations—and darned quick, too. Remember that red-haired girl in fourth grade who learned her six-tables before anyone else? And when you got to high school, she probably did square roots and all those sine and cosine things before you, too. Well, just think of the computer as that red-haired girl to the hundredth power.

The second thing your red-haired computer can do better than you is remember things. Oh, you remember a lot of important things: your Social Security number (most of the time), your anniversary (sometimes), the opening day of trout season (always), but your computer never forgets anything. All right, the red-haired girl knew all the states *and* their capitals while you were still struggling with your Zip Code. So, a computer is the red-haired girl to the *thousandth* power.

Finally, the third basic thing a computer does is sort information to produce lists of things. Sure, you can list five beers that begin with "b," but what if you wanna know all the state capitals that end in "ton"? Or all the sitcoms with a single-parent family? You'll recall, of course, when the red-haired girl started listing your faults. Alphabetically. With sub-heads. A computer is that girl to the *millionth* power.

Yeah, for a long time you really hated that red-haired girl. But then she helped you a couple of times with your homework, and then you started talking to her just for fun, and then—well, we needn't go into details, but you still get a warm feeling when you think of her, right?

Maybe the analogy for even the most user-friendly computer breaks down when you reminisce about all the things the redhead could do that your computer can't. But the point is that a computer doesn't do anything new. It does things you've been doing for years. It just does them faster and more accurately than you and a roomful of redheads.

The computer was essential in putting this book together. If we had had to sit down with a pencil and paper and do all the calculating and figuring on the outcome of every single play in 1986, this book would have been published in the year 2001. And then, in addition to 1986 stats, we went back for just about every stat from 1977 on, and a whole roomful of figures from the 1930s. We wanted to be as accurate as possible because, frankly, a lot of the things we will suggest in *The Hidden Game of Football* may strike you as a little off-the-wall.

Along the way, we got very interested in all the ways the computer has jumped into the game of football. What follows is a brief history.

BUT CAN IT RUN A 4.4?

How can these whizbang calculators be used in football?

Tex Schramm, the longtime Dallas G.M., asked the same thing back in the 1950s when he was working for the Los Angeles Rams before the Cowboys were even little Buckeroos. At that time, the Rams enjoyed a blowout advantage over the other eleven NFL teams on Draft Day. Whereas most teams showed up carrying wrinkled Street and Smith magazines, and puff profiles based on the fertile imaginings of collegiate sports information directors, the Rams had real scouts sending in reports from all over the country.

But every apple has its worm. The Rams had too much information for efficient analysis. Enough scouting reports piled up in the front office to make it look like a recycling center. Just reading them took weeks. Remembering what was read took a miracle.

As if that wasn't bad enough, all the reports weren't created equal. For one thing, different scouts had different preferences and prejudices. Some leaned toward size; some downgraded certain schools; some were better at evaluating players at particular positions. Schramm himself admits he was biased in favor of speed. There were hard and soft graders; one man's "sure all-pro" was another's "adequate." Every scout's idiosyncrasies had to be considered.

On top of all that was the language barrier. The reports were all in English, but you still needed a Rosetta Stone to figure out what they meant. Every scout had his own terminology and the devil take the interpreter. How did "naturally mean" equate with "unusually aggressive"? Is "excellent work habits" the same as "gives 100 percent" (or the sports anomaly "110 percent")?

Sifting through it all "was very time-consuming," Schramm says, sounding like the guy who calls Mt. Rushmore a large statue. And time wasn't all that was lost—so were many prospects. A modern computer could have solved the problem lickety-split, but, of course, this was thirty years ago and they were suspiciously newfangled (and huge) then.

Between his L.A. and Dallas gigs, Schramm worked for CBS, where he participated in the televising of the 1960 Winter Olympics from Squaw Valley. CBS happened to be sharing office space at the games with IBM, which was doing the scoring and statistics. Tex marveled at the technology.

Schramm knew he was going to Dallas the next year, and he

dreaded creating the same paper glut he'd had with the Rams. He wondered if the computer people had any ideas, short of incineration, on dealing with storing and analyzing great gobs of information. They yawned and said, "Oh, sure," as if he'd asked them "Can you read and write?"

The bells that went off at that moment were not in the computers.

So in '61, when Schramm took over the one-year-old expansion team in Dallas, he brought in a computer. The Cowboys kept it quiet for a couple of seasons, for fear everyone would laugh at them, but eventually the secret got out. Sure enough, there were snickers and sneers. But the Cowboys' success by the late '60s—not instantaneous but faster than any other expansion team in any sport—was the proof of the programmers' put-in.

Exhibit A in the look-what-our-computer-has-wrought sweepstakes has always been Calvin Hill, a running back out of Yale(!), whom the Cowboys drafted number one in 1969 to a rousing chorus of "Who?" (If you are still asking that question, look at 6,060 yards in the NFL All-Time Rushing Leaders.) But Hill was only one of several peaks the Dallas computer hit. By the time they started making regular Super Bowl appearances, the Cowboys' roster was dotted with guys nobody ever heard of until they were drafted.

It wasn't as easy as it sounds. Schramm (whose real first name is Texas, by the way) didn't just order his computer C.O.D., plug it in, and watch it spew out Pro-Bowlers. The first year, according to Schramm, was spent mostly devising terminology that would mean the same thing to everyone involved.

The other necessity was to determine what factors go into making a good football player. It took until 1965 before they were sufficiently satisfied to base their draft on the readouts. The final five golden factors have become standard for scouting reports throughout the league:

- Character.
- Quickness and body control (agility and balance).
- Competitiveness and aggressiveness.
- Mental alertness.
- Strength and explosion, which factors quickness into strength.

A sixth factor—speed—wasn't on the list because no evaluation was involved. Nobody has to characterize a 4.4.

Every player needs the golden five and speed, but then the system is further refined by seven or eight characteristics particular to a given position. Finally, the whole system has to be weighted: Some characteristics are more important than others; you can't just add them up and divide by x.

You might be able to handicap a couple of dozen college seniors with a pocket calculator and a ream of paper, but on Draft Day—with twenty-seven other teams depleting the pool—you have to be ready with a list of several hundred prime prospects ranked in order of desirability.

An additional fillip to computerizing all this information is that a team can, in effect, scout its scouts. By collating reports over several years and comparing reports with a player's later accomplishments, a team can spot a particular scout's strong and weak points. Then that can be factored into the total picture.

So the computer moved into the NFL primarily to store, calculate, and sort scouting reports. Today, all league teams except the renegade Los Angeles Raiders and the individualistic San Francisco 49ers participate in one of two computerized scouting combines. Seven teams— Chicago, Dallas, Detroit, Miami, Minnesota, Philadelphia, and Pittsburgh—use Blesto (named for the four founding clubs: the Bears, Lions, Eagles, Steelers Talent Organization). The remaining nineteen use the National Football Scouting Service. The services prepare reports that blend objective and subjective information on just about every draftable player in the western hemisphere and distribute them —along with specially requested reports—to the subscribing clubs. Then the clubs filter the reports through their own computers, adding their own "inside" dope.

The cumulative numerical ratings assigned by the combines (and widely published before Draft Day) are only part of the picture, but they make for fun reading. Blesto ranks upward, from "0.0-0.99: sure starter" to "4.0-4.99: reject." The NFL Scouting Service ranks downward, from "9.0-9.9: superstar" to "1.0: reject." In 1987 they agreed on the top-rated players at nine of the sixteen positions. For example, Blesto had Miami University's Vinny Testaverde at 1.10; National ranked him 9.00. In both cases he was the top-rated college senior.

Each year, computer generated scouting reports become a little more sophisticated, a little more exact. There have been mistakes, of course. In the 1960s, when the American Football League and NFL were dueling to the death, the San Diego Chargers were in a bidding war against an NFL team for the services of an undersized running back. Suddenly the NFL club lost interest and the Chargers signed the kid, who went on to have a terrific rookie year. After the merger, when teams from both sides started talking to each other, the NFL team's head scout told a Charger rep that their computer had given the back almost no chance of making it because of his size. Charger coach Sid Gillman cracked, "When it's third and 3, I can give the ball to that running back, but I can't give it to your computer."

The story has been told and retold as an example of "computer error." In fact, it was a programming error, with too much emphasis on the back's size and not enough on his other qualities. It was for just such examples that they invented the word "GIGO" (Garbage In, Garbage Out).

Subjectivity still plays a part. Larry Wilson, the Cardinals' Director of Pro Personnel, explains: "Every player is rated against every other player by height and weight, speed and strength, and so forth; but the computer can't tell us the size of the heart in each man." Wilson himself was a perfect example of a player who outperformed his apparent abilities. His "heart" won him enshrinement in the Pro Football Hall of Fame.

Sometimes a team has to go against its computer's advice. If it has a glaring need, it may have to choose a player with poorer numbers only because he's the best available at that position. Most teams like to posture about taking "the best available athlete," but if they desperately need a linebacker, they'll take a linebacker.

These days, we might still see a hunch pick on the eleventh or twelfth draft rounds, but with the universal use of computer-generated scouting reports, it's going to be a long time before an early draft choice gets a "who?" If he doesn't have a file in every team's computer, he ranks with Benji as a prospect.

PUSH-BUTTON COACHING

Although scouting reports on college seniors brought computers into the NFL and are still their most visible manifestation to fans, they may not be the most important use. It takes a cocksure coach to prepare a game plan without computer input.

The magic word is "tendencies."

Ever since coaches began sending assistants to scout opponents, they've been trying to spot tendencies, like how often an opponent passes on first down or whether they're likely to run left or right from a particular formation. Obviously every scrap of information helps. If you know your opponent does a certain thing 60 percent of the time when they line up a particular way, you have an edge.

A pioneer in the use of computers to spot tendencies is Dr. Frank Ryan. When he was a journeyman backup quarterback for the Rams, his name seldom got into print, but on those few occasions when it did, a mention of his doctorate in mathematics was *de rigueur.* Later, when he'd won an NFL title as the Browns' signal-caller and thrown a jereboam of TD passes, newswriters had many more footballish things to say about Ryan, and his degree sort of faded from the sports page. When he wasn't developing Brownie touchdowns, Ryan was developing a computer concept called PROBE, in which a user generates reports by posing questions to an existing data base. The system had scads of uses—Ryan's first customer was a Cleveland brokerage firm seeking stock analysis—but the football connection was a natural.

Vince Lombardi was so enamored of Ryan's idea that he worked a trade to bring the aging quarterback to Washington when he took over as Redskin coach in 1969. He even became a vice president in Ryan's company. Perhaps only Lombardi could successfully handle a situation where he gave on-the-field orders to his off-the-field boss.

Although Ryan was quoted in 1973 as saying that he doubted computers could be employed successfully on the sidelines during a game to indicate what should be done in clutch situations—"There are simply too many variables"—he suggested they might be used during games to detect minute changes in an opponent's strategy. Nevertheless, he added, PROBE was designed for pregame, rather than game, guidance.

Of the four major sports, football best lends itself to computer analysis. Basketball and hockey flow up and down the court or rink, one play moving seamlessly into another. They are games that emphasize continuous movement more than strategy. To analyze them would be, in one observer's words, "like trying to measure a flash flood with a shot glass."

Baseball has more than a hundred years of statistics to compare, but strategically the diamond game comes down to a few set pieces: to steal, to bunt, and the ever-popular lefty-righty duel. None of them means very much when a curve ball breaks an extra quarter of an inch.

Football, on the other hand, is the classic battle simulation. The armies align themselves, feint, probe, attack, defend. Strategists can refight Gettysburg or replay the last Super Bowl with equal vigor. Generals study Clausewitz; coaches study Lombardi.

The game film is the traditional coach's textbook. But just as computers have radically changed the printing industry, they've revolutionized the study of game films.

A long time ago, when game film study was in its infancy, coaches pirated films, bought them *sub rosa*, passed them on to buddies, and generally behaved like porno filmmakers in the Bible belt. Obviously that was a mess. Very quickly the exchange of game films was made mandatory. Each NFL team must send films of its last three games to its next opponent.

What computers have done is to speed up the flow of information from the coach's film viewing to the players on the practice field, thus increasing the number and kinds of tendencies that can be noted.

Typically on Sunday night after a game, the offensive coaches go into one room to view reels of their next opponent's defense. The defensive coaches are in another room looking at their upcoming rival's offense. Each play is charted: down, yards to go, offensive and defensive formations, play, results, and any other information deemed significant. Next, all the charts are fed into a preprogrammed computer.

By Monday's practice, a team can have readouts broken down into every conceivable category: short yardage plays, plays inside the opponent's 20, plays run from an I-formation, first down plays, and on and on—all of it itemized, cumulated, collated. At a glance a coach knows how often the opponent tends to run a certain play on, say, first down; which hole the play is likely to hit; its degree of success; and, to a large extent, why that play is selected. Appropriate sheets are handed to the players for study.

Next, the coaches use this information in putting together the game plan, which, for all the mysticism that surrounds it, is nothing more than a list of plays and defenses that are expected to work in certain situations.

In an interview for *Game Day,* Jack Faulkner, administrator of football operations for the Rams, explained, "Everything you need to know about the team you're playing is right there for you. For instance, look at this sheet. It is based on this team's I-left formation.

"See, they ran 15 plays from that formation. Nine were runs, 6 passes. The 9 runs gained 20 yards, or about 2½ a carry. The 6 passes picked up 23 yards, or about 4 per attempt. Now the next thing you want to know is who carried and caught the ball. That's here, too. Turns out, the halfback carried 7 times from this formation and he caught the ball 4 times when they threw it. That tells you something, doesn't it?"

Obviously, it tells you who to key on and how to stack your defense when the opponent comes out in an I-left.

It used to be that coaches would have game films re-edited so that they could watch, for example, all the short yardage plays run consecutively. They might get that near the end of the week. Now, more coaches use videotapes of games. Computers can be tied into the tape, each play coded, and separate tapes of various categories produced immediately.

Studying tendencies probably goes back to Alonzo Stagg, but the computer has tremendously increased the depth and breadth of knowledge while cutting the time element to next to nothing.

In another *Game Day* interview, Tom Landry chuckled over the inevitable Catch-22: "Originally, the computer was supposed to alleviate the workload. They've caused us to work harder, of course, because they've generated so much more information for us to try to absorb and use."

An unlooked for development is the amount of shifting that offenses now do before nearly every play, up 100 percent from the beginning of the decade. Teams are so attuned to opponents' tendencies that as soon as an offense settles into a formation the whole defense can practically bet its lunch money where the next play will go. The only recourse seems to be to wait till the last second and shift, hoping to catch the defense before it adjusts.

In addition to studying opponents, the computer makes it possible for a team to study itself through the season to spot its own tendencies and pinpoint what is and isn't working.

Although no one has done it yet—or, at least, admitted doing it—a coach might have his quarterback play a simulated game against the computer on Wednesday to see how next Sunday's game plan will do. If the computer opponent won 40-0, the coach certainly wouldn't announce it to the press on Thursday—but he'd sure change his game plan.

Still, with everybody's computer whirring away at the same tendencies, the day will come when a coach explains at a postgame interview: "Our computer said we've been doing x too often, so we thought of switching to y, but we don't do that very well, so we were going to do *z,* but we knew their computer would expect that, so we decided to fool them by doing *x*."

And then the coach will excuse himself to go have tea with Alice and the March Hare.

MEANWHILE BACK AT REALITY . . .

Most training rooms have computers now. No, they can't predict injuries—not yet, anyway. But once an injury occurs, they track the player's rehabilitation and use of medication. They also chart workouts, diets, and a player's whole medical history, freeing the trainer of some of the paperwork that often kept him scribbling away in the training room while practice went on without him.

Moreover, computers can sometimes spot a pattern to recurring injuries and help prescribe preventive measures. With the money a club has invested in a player's health, one fewer knee injury might pay for the whole system.

Al Vermeil, younger brother of former NFL coach Dick Vermeil, has developed a computerized device to measure players' speed and reaction times in a series of activities. It can be used to test new players, identify falloffs in performance by veterans, or monitor a player's recovery from injuries. The VTM (for Vermeil's Time Machine) measures time and motion in thousandths of seconds, using sensitized mats, a keyboard, readouts, and light beams.

In a typical test, a back's forward and lateral speed and his ability to make quick changes of direction can be measured exactly as he moves from one mat to another through light beams. "Say you're timing backs for speed and cutting ability," Vermeil explains. "One runs 20 yards in 2.5 seconds and cuts through a slalom in 3.1 seconds. There's another 2.5 guy, but he's timed in 2.6 seconds for the slalom. Which is the [more] effective back?"

The advantage of the VTM is that it can make minute measurements over very short distances. Back-pedal speed, a necessity for defensive backs, is almost impossible to gauge with a stopwatch because it requires a sudden short burst when the back is already moving in another direction. Another VTM test might be to measure exactly a lineman's drive off the snap.

"You can also measure when fatigue sets in," Vermeil says, perhaps trying to win over a few players with the suggestion that his machine could get them a day off from practice.

Vermeil sees unlimited uses for his fifteen-pound VTM (though he's hardly a neutral observer). The Denver Broncos seem to agree. Before the 1987 season they shelled out the $5,000 for a model.

Speaking of money, once a player leaves the locker room, he may sit down with his financial planner and *his* computer to go over his stocks, bonds, and investments. In the meantime his agent—armed with all sorts of performance and comparative readouts—may be talking to the club about next year's contract. Ah, but where do you think the club's G.M. gets his information to prove the kid doesn't deserve a raise?

Punch, zip, whirr.

5

Looking for
a Winning Situation

Don't you hate it when you turn on the game in the middle and you have to wait five minutes before the announcer tells the score? Or have you ever tried to listen to a distant game on your car radio and had it fade in and out so you couldn't be certain of the down or yard line?

Reading current football statistics is kind of like that. You get an intriguing part of the story but not the satisfying whole. You get totals and averages, but not the context.

What do you make of this statement?

John shot Harold.

Unless you're John or Harold, you want to know more. There are all kinds of possibilities.

John shot Harold in cold blood.

John shot Harold because Harold attacked him with an ax.

John shot Harold a dirty look.

John shot Harold a telegram and told him to buy long, and as a result Harold made ten million dollars and now lives a carefree life.

Current pro football statistics are like "John shot Harold." We need the rest of the story. The situations!

If we're going to try to make pro football statistics more situational, we'd better take a look at what kind of can of worms we're opening up. We can assume that it's going to cause us more work, so we'd better decide if it will be worth it.

A CLOSER LOOK

Let's run through the philosophy.

Whether we were able to watch a particular game or not, we want to be able to sit down later and analyze it. For that, we need a play-by-play account. Here's a tiny part of the third quarter of the San Francisco 49er-New England Patriot game of December 14, 1986. New England had just scored to take the lead, 17-16.

Franklin kicks off for NE to Ring at the 15, returns 15 yards to the 30 (Reynolds)

SF1-10	SF30	(8:59) Montana at QB. Cribbs runs left for 7-yard gain (McGrew)
SF2-3	SF37	Cribbs runs up middle for 1-yard loss (T Williams)
SF3-4	SF36	Montana's pass deflected at line by Rembert—incomplete.
SF4-4	SF36	Runager punts for SF to Fryar at NE15, returns 12 yards to the 27 (Ferrari)—49-yard punt

NE1-10	NE27	(7:29) Collins runs draw for 3-yard loss (Turner)
NE2-13	NE24	Eason passes complete to Baty for 5-yard gain (Walter)
NE3-8	NE29	Eason scrambles left, passes right, intended for Fryar—incomplete
NE4-8	NE29	Camarillo punts for NE to Griffin at SF33, returns 6 yards to 39 (Tatupu)—38-yard punt

All right, we don't have everything. No blocking detailed. "Runs left" isn't much of a play description. We can't tell just why a play did or did not work. Who missed that block on Rembert? There are limits to what can be marked down during a game.

Still, within the realm of practicality, we're given an awful lot of information in this tiny, three-minute section—downs, yards to go, yard lines, ball carriers, passers, receivers, intended receivers, where a play was headed, the tackler. In fact, we're given far too much information to hold in our reeling heads at one time. Without looking back, can you remember how many yards Cribbs gained in the series? Now, imagine reading the entire game play-by-play! At best, we might be left with a few impressions, but undoubtedly possessing a much foggier idea of what took place on the field than a fan who watched the game from the end-zone stands with a fat guy jumping up and down in front of him.

Sportswriters—most of them experienced and competent observers —watch the game from a better vantage point and then file their stories, highlighting what they consider the most significant plays, adding a little color and background, and interpreting the ebb and flow for us. They've done it for years. We'd like to get more out of a game than someone else's ideas.

Once we have the play-by-play, we can list all of the similar kinds of things in appropriate columns.

Here's a list of San Francisco passes in the first quarter:

Montana passes to Craig for 11 yards
Kemp passes short right to Rice—incomplete
Montana passes over middle to Rice for 22 yards
Montana passes complete to Craig for 11 yards
Montana passes left intended for Cribbs—incomplete

This kind of list is better in one way; we can get a little feel for how the San Francisco passing game was working. We're not really able to measure how well or how badly it did. We only get an inference. We begin measuring when we turn *raw data* like a list of all San Francisco's passes for the game into *counting stats* by adding all the similar things—attempts, completions, yards gained, touchdowns, and interceptions—and putting the totals in appropriate columns.

ATTEMPTS	COMPLETIONS	YARDS	TOUCHDOWNS	INTERCEPTIONS
26	14	202	0	1

We gain knowledge by gathering a large enough sample to allow us to draw some basic conclusions: San Francisco completed more than half its passes, gained a fair amount of yardage, threw for no touchdowns, and had one pass intercepted. We can now compare 49er passing with that of the Patriots.

ATTEMPTS	COMPLETIONS	YARDS	TOUCHDOWNS	INTERCEPTIONS
37	22	227	2	2

Let's see, New England completed more, gained more, had two touchdowns, but turned the ball over twice. We can improve our ability to measure and compare the two passing attacks by using some *averages*. For example, we can divide attempts into completions to get a *completion percentage*: SF 53.8, NE 59.4. Or we can divide attempts into yards gained and come up with the *average yards gained per pass*: SF 7.77, NE 6.13. We can get a *touchdown percentage* and an *intercep-*

tion percentage the same way. The NFL has an involved *Passer Rating System* for balancing all four of these averages against each other and coming up with an overall rating. We'll have a lot to say about that system later, but for right now let us simply say that it won't tell us the one thing we most want to know—*which passer did the better job?*

We've all seen players who produced wonderful stats while losing. We usually just assume that they are stars on poor teams. Maybe. How do we explain players who have very ordinary stats for winning teams?

Of course, there are many explanations, but many times the apparent anomalies occur because *we didn't measure the right things.*

BACK TO THE DRAWING BOARD

Remember when we lumped all San Francisco's passing attempts into one glob? Well, think about it. Are all attempts the same? Of course not. And what is the biggest difference? The circumstances under which they are thrown! By treating every pass as though it was attempted under the same circumstances, we've lost much of our ability to measure its worth. We no longer know the *situation.* We don't know how many passes came on third downs, what yard lines were involved. We don't even know the score.

But wait, you say. Virtually every play comes under different circumstances: different downs, different yard lines, different quarters. Are we going to end up with a stat sheet that looks like a play-by-play?

We have to make a trade-off between specific data (play-by-plays) and generalized data (totals). Actually, the trade-off is made now—but on the side of generalized data. Let's try to shift toward a happy medium.

Suppose we come at this from the other end. Instead of thinking exclusively about what was done, think about what they were trying to do. And what constitutes a success?

Back to basics. What is the objective of an offensive football play? Score a touchdown? Ultimately, yes, but every play that does not score a touchdown is not a failure. Most successful plays do not even register a first down, but they contribute toward getting one. What we need to do is identify successful and unsuccessful plays and then quantify them.

WHAT ARE THESE PEOPLE TRYING TO DO?

The key is the down and yards-to-go.

On first-and-10 (1-10), a 4-yard-gain is the minimum needed for a "win." The theory is that a team can then do the same thing on the next two downs and gain a first down. Should a penalty cause a first-and-more-than-10 or a goal line cause a first-and-less-than-10, the yardage necessary for a "win" changes, but the ratio stays the same—the play must gain about 40 percent of the necessary yardage. For example: first-and-15 (1-15) means 6 yards are necessary.

On second down, a play must gain 60 percent of the yardage necessary for a first down to register a "win." Examples: second-and-6 (2-6), 4 yards; second-and-10 (2-10), 6 yards.

On third down, the only gain worthy of a win is enough to get a first down. It doesn't matter if it's third-and-1 (3-1) or third-and-20 (3-20).

Fourth down attempts, though rare, can be treated exactly the same as third down attempts.

Therefore a very simple *situational statistic* is to take a play-by-play and mark every run or pass as a "W" for "win" or "F" for "failure." If we used the term "loss," we'd confuse everybody because some gains are still "losses."

Here's that three-minute stretch from the San Francisco-New England game:

Franklin kicks off for NE to Ring at the 15, returns 15 yards to the 30 (Reynolds)

W	SF1-10	SF30	(8:59) Montana at QB. Cribbs runs left for 7-yard gain (McGrew)
F	SF2-3	SF37	Cribbs runs up middle for 1-yard loss (T Williams)
F	SF3-4	SF36	Montana's pass deflected at line by Rembert—incomplete
–	SF4-4	SF36	Runager punts for SF to Fryar at NE15, returns 12 yards to the 27 (Ferrari)—49-yard punt
F	NE1-10	NE27	(7:29) Collins runs draw for 3-yard loss (Turner)
F	NE2-13	NE24	Eason passes complete to Baty for 5-yard gain (Walter)
F	NE3-8	NE29	Eason scrambles left, passes right, intended for Fryar—incomplete
–	NE4-8	NE29	Camarillo punts for NE to Griffin at SF33, returns 6 yards to 39 (Tatupu)—38-yard punt

Notice that Eason's 5-yard completion to Baty is an "F." On second-and-13 (2-13), New England needed an 8-yard gain for a "W."

W-F is a rudimentary situational stat. Nevertheless, if we add up an offense's W's, we should get a pretty fair idea of its efficiency. We can even divide the W's by offensive plays to get an offensive efficiency percentage. We can also add the rushing W's and the passing W's to rate the parts of the offense. Remember San Francisco's first quarter passing?

W	SF1-10	SF32	Montana passes to Craig for 11 yards
F	SF3-3	50	Kemp passes short right to Rice—incomplete
W	SF2-11	NE38	Montana passes over middle to Rice for 22 yards
W	SF1-10	SF31	Montana passes complete to Craig for 11 yards
F	SF1-10	NE25	Montana passes left intended for Cribbs—incomplete

By the way, there is one type of play that shouldn't be considered for W's or F's. You've seen it time and again at the end of the game when the quarterback takes the snap, steps back, and takes a 2- or 3-yard loss. The object of the play is not to gain but to use up time. It's absurd to count these plays as rushing attempts. A strong team could have as many as 40 of these in a season. A weak team might never get a chance to use it. What will an extra 40 attempts (and perhaps 80 yards lost) do to an offensive average? Throw these plays out or put them into a special category.

Inevitably we'll use W's and F's to look at individual stats. It hurts the soul to credit a running back with a W on a 4-yard gain when the key to the play was an anonymous guard's block, but that's no worse than crediting the back with the 4-yard gain.

THERE'S W'S AND THEN THERE'S *W'S*

Once we've made the plunge and rated plays on their success or failure, we might as well go whole hog and quantify them. In other words, it's time to decide which W's were extra successful and by how much and which F's were really loathsome.

To start, we'll award every W a point.

A gain of 80 percent of the yardage necessary for a first down, on either first or second down, gets a bonus point (8 yards on 1-10; 4 yards on 2-5). It's reasonable; the effort was twice what might be hoped for in the situation.

We can award bonus points for particularly long gains on this basis: 11+ = 1 point; 21+ = 2; 41+ = 3. For example, a 35-yard gain on first or second down is awarded 4 points (1 for a W, 1 for 80 percent, and 2 for 21+). Before anyone suggests that we should award percentage points (35 yards = 2.45), let *us* suggest that we keep this simple.

Losses are harder to figure. We wouldn't subtract any points for a loss unless it's over 2 yards. For 3 or more yards lost, subtract a single point.

Finally, for a turnover—a fumble lost or an interception—subtract 4 points unless it occurs on fourth down inside the other team's 35 on a play that would not otherwise have registered a first down. If a team goes for a first down at the 24, a fourth-down fumble is essentially meaningless in itself; the ball is turned over on a failure anyway.

This probably sounds more complicated than it really is, but the chart below should make it clear.

POINTS	1ST DOWN	2ND DOWN	3RD or 4TH DOWN
−4	Turnover	Turnover	Turnover†
−1	−3 or more	−3 or more	−3 or more
0	Less than 40%	Less than 60%	Less than 100%
1	40 to 79%	60 to 79%	100%
2	80%	80%	——
3*	11+ yards	11+ yards	11+ yards
4*	21+	21+	21+
5*	41+	41+	41+

* Subtract 1 point if not a first down.

† Unless on 4th down inside opponent's 35 on play that would otherwise not have registered a first down.

PUTTING IT TO WORK

To examine our system in action, we'll look at San Francisco's offense (all the rushes and passes) in our subject game:

W/F	PTS	SITUATION			PLAY/RESULT
F	0	1-10	SF	13	Craig takes pitch left for 1-yard loss
F	0	2-11	SF	12	Cribbs runs up middle for 4-yard loss
F	0	3-7	SF	16	Craig runs up middle for 2-yard gain
W	3	1-10	SF	32	Montana passes complete to Craig for 11 yards—FD (first down)
F	0	1-10	SF	43	Cribbs runs up middle for 2-yard gain
W	1	2-8	SF	45	Montana scrambles left for 5-yard gain
F	0	3-3		50	Kemp passes short right to Rice—incomplete
W	1	1-10	P	49	Cribbs runs right for 6-yard gain
W	2	2-4	P	43	Cribbs runs up middle for 6-yard gain—FD
F	0	1-10	P	37	Cribbs runs sweep left for 1-yard loss
W	4	2-11	P	38	Montana passes over middle for Rice for 22-yard gain—FD
W	3	1-10	P	16	Craig runs up middle for 13-yard gain—FD
W	2	1-G	P	3	Cribbs runs sweep right for 3-yard TOUCHDOWN—FD
W	3	1-10	SF	31	Montana passes complete to Craig for 11-yard gain—FD
W	2	1-10	SF	42	Cribbs takes pitch left for 8-yard gain
W	4	2-2		50	Craig runs up middle for 25-yard gain—FD
F	0	1-10	P	25	Montana passes left intended for Cribbs—incomplete
W	2	1-10	P	25	Cribbs runs delay up middle for 10-yard gain—FD
F	0	1-10	P	15	Craig runs up middle for 2-yard gain
F	0	2-8	P	13	Craig takes pitch left for no gain
F	−4	3-8	P	13	Montana passes into end zone intended for Clark INTERCEPTED

W/F	PTS	SITUATION		PLAY/RESULT
W	5	1-10	SF 42	Montana passes complete to Craig for 48-yard gain—FD
W	1	1-G	P 10	Cribbs runs over left guard for 4-yard gain
F	0	2-G	P 6	Rathman runs delay up middle for no gain
F	0	3-G	P 6	Cribbs runs sweep right for 5-yard gain
F	0	4-G	P 1	Montana attempts to go over the top for no gain
W	3	1-10	P 33	Craig runs left for 17-yard gain—FD
F	0	1-10	P 16	Montana passes left intended for Frank—incomplete
W	3	2-10	P 16	Cribbs runs sweep right for 12-yard gain—FD
W	2	1-G	P 4	Craig runs up the middle for 3-yard gain
W	2	1-G	P 1	Craig runs over right guard for TOUCHDOWN—FD
W	4	1-10	P 44	Montana passes complete to Francis for 31-yard gain—FD
F	0	1-20	P 23	Montana passes right complete to Craig for 6-yard gain
F	0	2-14	P 17	Montana passes left intended for Cribbs—incomplete
F	0	3-14	P 17	Montana passes complete to Rice for 2-yard loss
F	0	1-10	P 47	Montana passes deep intended for Rice—incomplete
				(END OF FIRST HALF)
W	1	1-10	SF 30	Cribbs runs left for 7-yard gain
F	0	2-3	SF 37	Cribbs runs up middle for 1-yard loss
F	0	3-4	SF 36	Montana's pass deflected at line
F	0	1-10	SF 39	Montana passes over middle intended for Rice—incomplete
F	0	2-10	SF 39	Montana passes deep across field intended for Rice—incomplete
F	0	3-10	SF 39	Montana passes left intended for Clark—incomplete
W	3	1-10	SF 38	Cribbs sweeps right for 11-yard gain—FD
W	1	1-10	SF 49	Craig runs left for 5-yard gain
W	2	2-5	P 46	Cribbs runs up middle for 4-yard gain
F	0	3-1+	P 42	Cribbs runs over right guard for 1-yard gain
W	1	4-0+	P 41	Montana sneaks over right guard for 1-yard gain—FD
W	1	1-10	P 40	Montana scrambles left for 6-yard gain
W	3	2-4	P 34	Montana passes complete to Clark for 13-yard gain—FD
F	0	1-10	P 21	Craig runs draw up middle for 1-yard gain
W	2	2-9	P 20	Montana passes complete to Clark for 8-yard gain
F	0	3-1	P 13	Cribbs sweeps right for 1-yard loss
W	1	1-10	P 30	Craig runs sweep left for 4-yard gain
F	0	2-6	P 26	Montana attempts screen for Cribbs—incomplete
W	3	3-6	P 26	Montana passes complete to Craig for 13-yard gain—FD
W	1	1-10	P 13	Craig runs sweep right for 7-yard gain
W	2	2-3+	P 6	Cribbs runs draw up middle for 3-yard gain
W	1	3-0+	P 3	Montana passes complete to Rice for 2-yard gain—FD
F	0	1-G	P 1	Cribbs runs right for 1-yard loss
F	0	2-G	P 2	Montana passes into end zone intended for Frank—incomplete
F	0	3-G	P 2	Craig runs over left tackle for 1-yard loss
W	2	1-10	P 25	Cribbs runs sweep right for 9-yard gain
W	2	2-1	P 16	Craig runs up middle for 6-yard gain—FD
W	3	1-10	P 10	Cribbs runs sweep left for 10-yard TOUCHDOWN—FD (note 3 pts bonus)
F	0	1-10	SF 23	Cribbs runs up middle for 3-yard gain
F	0	2-7	SF 26	Montana passes complete to Craig for no gain
W	3	3-7	SF 26	Montana passes complete to Rice for 13-yard gain—FD
F	0	1-10	SF 39	Craig runs over right guard for 2-yard gain
F	0	2-8	SF 41	Cribbs runs sweep left for 3-yard gain
F	0	3-5	SF 44	Cribbs runs sweep right for 2-yard gain

At end of game Montana took 3 intentional losses for—7 yards

Now, let's add 'em up and see what we can learn about the San Francisco attack. We also did the same for New England to produce San Francisco's defensive record. (Abbreviations below that may be unfamiliar are: PC, pass completions; AvgG, average gain; S, sacks; FD, first downs; FM/IN, fumbles/interceptions; AvgP, average WIN points per play.)

SAN FRANCISCO STATISTICS VS. NEW ENGLAND, DECEMBER 14, 1986

OFFENSE	ATT	PC	PCT	GROSS YDS	AvgG	S	YDS LOST	NET YDS	AvgG	FD	TD	FM IN	WINS	PCT	PTS	AvgP
Rushing	45	—	—	207	4.60	—	—	—	—	12	3	—	25	55.5	48	1.07
Passing	25	14	56.0	202	8.08	0	0	202	8.08	10	0	1	10	40.0	27	1.08
Total	70	—	—	409	5.84	0	0	409	5.84	22	3	1	35	50.0	75	1.07

Intentional losses: Montana 3 for −7.

DEFENSE	ATT	PC	PCT	GROSS YDS	AvgG	S	YDS LOST	NET YDS	AvgG	FD	TD	FM IN	OPP WINS	PCT	OPP PTS	AvgP
Rushing	20	—	—	60	3.00	—	—	—	—	4	1	1	6	30.0	4	0.20
Passing	37	22	59.4	227	6.14	3	20	207	5.59	10	2	2	19	47.5	29	0.73
Total	57	—	—	287	5.03	3	20	267	4.68	14	3	3	25	41.7	33	0.55

San Francisco Individual Rushing

PLAYER	ATT	YDS	AvgG	FD	TD	FM	WINS	PCT	PTS	AvgP
Cribbs	24	109	4.54	5	2	0	13	54.2	26	1.08
Craig	16	86	5.38	5	1	0	9	56.3	19	1.19
Montana	4	12	3.00	2	0	0	3	75.0	3	0.75
Rathman	1	0	0.00	0	0	0	0	0.0	0	0.00

San Francisco Individual Passing

PLAYER	ATT	PC	PCT	GROSS YDS	AvgG	S	YDS LOST	NET YDS	AvgG	FD	TD	IN	WINS	PCT	PTS	AvgP
Montana	24	14	58.3	202	8.42	0	0	202	8.42	10	0	1	10	41.7	27	1.13
Kemp	1	0	00.0	0	0.00	0	0	0	0.00	0	0	0	0	0.0	0	0.00

It certainly would be nice if we could look at the WIN figures for this game and shout "Eureka!" but one example is certainly not enough to prove anything absolutely. We need many more samples before we draw any absolute conclusions.

However, it's worth noting that the traditional offensive and defensive stats indicate a rather one-sided San Francisco victory, but the WIN percentages for total offense are quite close (50.0/41.7), remembering that San Francisco's defensive record equals New England's offense.

The final score: San Francisco 29, New England 24.

6

Driving for Glory

Pay attention. We're going to get into why teams win and lose here. No, not the sports page stuff, like "our receivers have butterfingers" or "our coach is a cretin." This is Basic Analysis (and we'll capitalize it just to show how important we think it is).

Once we have the ideas in this chapter digested, we can go on to more plebeian stuff like strategy and game plans. And you'll know where we're coming from. The main point we want to make concerns what we'll call *Win Probability,* that is, the probability of a team winning a football game based on any given *game situation.* A game situation consists of the score, how much time is left, who has the ball, and where they have it. By tracing hundreds of games and thousands of different game situations, we can know what the mathematical probability of winning is for any team on any down in any game.

Wait! Don't call your bookie. We didn't say we knew who *would* win, only the *probability* of winning. But then that's quite a lot.

Right now, we'll come at you from left field by explaining another way football isn't baseball.

You probably never noticed this, but in baseball the game is never over until the last man is out. That's a hard-sell concept in Cleveland, but you can quote us. The reason is in the nature of a baseball game,

74

which is, in effect, a series of more or less unconnected incidents. Each at bat, indeed each pitch, is a unique happening unrelated to the previous one, except perhaps in the batter's and pitcher's minds.

As a result, sudden turnabouts occur frequently. A pitcher sails through five no-hit innings and is hammered to the showers in the sixth; a batter hits home runs in his first two at bats and then strikes out. If your team is down five runs in the ninth with two away, you can still dream of a rally until the umpire's thumb goes up for that final out.

Baseball is linear and one-dimensional, proceeding inexorably forward, from out to out, until both teams run out of, uh, outs.

Football doesn't work that way. Baseball is a thread; football is a fabric. Plays in a football game occur within a three-dimensional framework. Each dimension constantly affects the other two, and together they produce the game situation.

The first football dimension is *time*. It may take more than three hours of TV time to get a game played, but the time on the field boils down to a mere sixty minutes (assuming there's no overtime). The clock controls the game, and each team schemes to control the clock. The more time they use running off plays, the less time the other guys have left to run off theirs. The so-called "time of possession" is an overrated statistic, but only because some folks look at it as an end in itself. Obviously a team has to *do* something with its possessions. If it just imitates eleven guys trying to hatch a football, its own time of possession works against it once the other team scores.

Everything that happens on a football field is relative to time, but time in the game is not equal. Time increases in value in direct proportion to its decrease in availability. As there becomes less of it, it becomes more precious, just like first edition *Action Comics*.

As time increases in value, so too do the events that occur within it. Anything good (or bad) that happens late in a close game helps (or hurts) a team more than the same thing happening early. This is simply because *after* the happening there is even less time for *another* happening. If a team goes ahead by a touchdown early in the first quarter, everyone nods and mutters those immortal words: "There's plenty of time left." When a team goes ahead by a point thirteen minutes into the fourth quarter, you can hear the icy edge of doom when someone says: "Two minutes left!" In fact, late events usually seem so magnified in retrospect that we might get the idea that only the fourth quarter is important, like the old lady who got to the park midway through the final period; when she saw the game was scoreless, she said, "Good, I haven't missed anything."

That's not the way it works. The fourth quarter of a football game is like the top floors of the skyscraper. It's what you notice first. It has all the gingerbread. It gives the 'scraper its character. But take away the foundation of the building, or the early part of a football game, and all you have is rubble.

Which brings us to the second football dimension—the *score*. In baseball, runs cross the plate one at a time, but a team keeps batting until there are three outs. There's no limit on how many runs a baseball team can plate before it must let its opponents bat. Does an umpire say, "Okay, Mr. Herzog, that's your run for this inning; now let the Cubs bat"? In football, as soon as *those* Cardinals score a touchdown, the Bears get their chance. If the Cards are down by ten points, there's no way they can catch up without giving Chicago a shot at the ball.

No NFL coach has ever been clever enough to devise a way to score more than six points on a single play. (Okay, add the extra point and call it seven, but that's two plays!) There have been proposals to change that. Like, always allowing a trailing team to receive. Or like increasing the value of extra-long plays, awarding, say, nine points for a ninety-yard run. Such ideas get as much applause as Thanksgiving in the turkey coop. Six points for a touchdown, no more. It's been that way since 1912, which in football is like saying it came down from Mt. Horeb on a stone tablet.

The "take-turns" rule produces the classic interaction between time and score: what's the score and how much time is left to change it?

But that interaction is always affected by possession of the ball at a particular *field position*—the third dimension in our football trinity. Field position used to so dominate coaches' minds that they built their teams around their punters. That was sixty years ago when one touchdown usually meant the game. Then, just about the time high-powered autos let Babbitt move out to Levittown, high-powered pass attacks allowed teams to move the ball far and quickly. Because teams score more often now and often from long distances, field positions have changed in value, like suburban real estate. Downtown (near the other guy's goal) still has the most value, but the boondocks (near your goal) aren't being given away with boxtops anymore. Nowadays, teams don't punt on first down when they get the ball inside their twenty.

Field position is still important; it's just not treated with such reverence anymore.

Adding field position to our trinity produces the OOPS offensive equation (Opportunity = [O'clock + Position]/Score). In footballese: *what* you can do depends on the *time* left, *where* you are, and *how much* you need. Most of the decisions that get coaches and quarterbacks exalted or excoriated start with OOPS: when to pass, where to punt, whether to try a field goal.

Everything that happens in a football game (except for the high-fives, hi-moms, and high-handed "we're number ones") takes its meaning from the interplay of time, score, and field position. What's the score? Where are we? How much time is left? It's kind of like playing Life, except in that game we seldom know the answer to the last question. But on a football field, all we have to do is look at the scoreboard to find out what, where, and how much. Then, to be a perfect quarterback, all we have to do is understand the meaning of each possible game situation.

How many possible game situations are there? An average game has 130-140 plays, but that's not really much help in coming up with *all* the possibilities. Well, let's see, there are 60 minutes in a game, but let's think of it in 15-second intervals and say 240 time units. Multiply that by 29 score possibilities in a reasonably close game, figuring you can be up to 14 points ahead, 14 behind, or tied. That's 6,960. Then there are 99 usable yard lines on a 100-yard field. A mere 689,040 possible game situations. Piece of cake!

THE DRIVE CHART

If we gave you 689,040 analyses, you'd need a derrick to get this book off your shelf, but fortunately there is a simpler way to investigate all this. Our basic tool will be the Drive Chart. Hold that thought about all those game situations while we look at a Drive Chart.

Here's one from the New England Patriots-Miami Dolphins game of December 22, 1986. We like this one because it has a wide variety of situations in a close game.

	DR SE	GM PR	SCORE START	HOW OBTAINED PLAY	YDS	RET	SCRIMM. BEG	END	NET TOT	YDS PEN	NO PL	FD —	CLOCK START	TIME END	TIME POSS	HOW GIVEN UP PLAY	YDS	RET	SCORE END
MIA	1	1	0–0	ko	58	21	m28	p24	48	0	8	3	15:00	10:37	4:23	fum	−1	0	0–0
PAT	1	1	0–0	fum	−1	0	p25	p16	−9	0	4	0	10:37	9:07	1:30	punt	64	16	0–0
MIA	2	1	0–0	punt	64	16	m36	m45	9	0	4	0	9:07	6:42	2:25	punt	30	0	0–0

DR SE	GM PR	SCORE START	HOW OBTAINED PLAY	YDS	RET	SCRIMM. BEG	END	NET TOT	YDS PEN	NO PL	FD —	CLOCK START	TIME END	TIME POSS	HOW GIVEN UP PLAY	YDS	RET	SCORE END
PAT 2	1	0–0	punt	30	0	p25	m0	75	15	13	5	6:42	2:25	4:17	TD	22	0	7–0
MIA 3	1	0–7	ko	75	30	m20	m43	23	0	6	1	2:25	14:50	2:35	punt	–8	0	0–7
PAT 3	2	7–0	punt	–8	0	m35	m29	6	0	4	0	14:50	13:04	1:46	FG	29	0	10–0
MIA —	2	0–10	ko	40	5	m30	m30	0	0	0	0	13:04	13:04	0:00	fum	0	6	0–10
PAT 4	2	10–0	fum	5	0	m24	m23	1	0	2	0	13:04	11:58	1:06	fum	0	10	10–0
MIA 4	2	0–10	fum	0	10	m32	p25	42	0	6	2	11:58	9:34	2:24	FG	25	0	3–10
PAT 5	2	10–3	ko	75	30	p20	p40	20	0	6	1	9:34	6:13	3:21	punt	40	0	10–3
MIA 5	2	3–10	punt	40	0	m21	m42	21	0	3	1	6:13	5:51	0:22	int	23	21	3–10
PAT 6	2	10–3	int	23	21	m44	m27	17	0	7	1	5:51	3:41	2:10	FG	27	0	13–3
MIA 6	2	3–13	ko	53	23	m35	p0	65	0	11	6	3:41	0:41	3:00	TD	1	0	10–13
PAT 7	2	13–10	ko	61	19	p23	p29	6	0	1	0	0:41	0:00	0:41	EOH	0	0	13–10
PAT 8	3	13–10	ko	75	30	p20	m22	58	0	8	3	15:00	11:00	4:00	FGA	21	22	13–10
MIA 7	3	10–13	FGA	21	22	m22	p4	74	0	7	3	11:00	8:35	2:25	FG	4	0	13–13
PAT 9	3	13–13	ko	75	30	p20	p28	8	0	3	0	8:35	6:55	1:40	int	25	7	13–13
MIA 8	3	13–13	int	25	7	p46	p0	46	0	3	2	6:55	6:01	0:54	TD	32	0	20–13
PAT 10	3	13–20	ko	63	31	p33	m0	67	0	8	3	6:01	3:09	2:52	TD	7	0	20–20
MIA 9	3	20–20	ko	45	21	m41	m40	–1	0	4	0	3:09	1:01	2:08	punt	53	5	20–20
PAT 11	3	20–20	punt	53	5	p12	p20	8	0	4	0	1:01	0:00	1:01	punt	37	17	20–20

We're leaving out the fourth quarter to keep you in suspense. Suffice it to say that at the beginning of the final period, the score was tied, 20-20. Pique your interest?

Those of you who understand all about this chart can skip right on to the next section with no hard feelings. In the meantime, we'll try to explain the chart to the nonskippers, if only to prove we can.

This is a chart of the first 20 of the 26 "drives" (14 for the Patriots and 12 for the Dolphins) in the game. A "drive" encompasses all the plays in a "possession" from first down until the ball is given up. We count punts, but not punt returns or kickoff returns. If a return team fumbles away a kick (as Miami did in the second quarter), it doesn't count as a drive.

Here's the first drive of the game:

DR SE	GM PR	SCORE START	HOW OBTAINED PLAY	YDS	RET	SCRIMM BEG	END	NET TOT	YDS PEN	NO PL	FD —	CLOCK START	TIME END	TIME POSS	HOW GIVEN UP PLAY	YDS	RET	SCORE END
MIA 1	1	0–0	ko	58	21	m28	p24	48	0	8	3	15:00	10:37	4:23	fum	–1	0	0–0

DR/SE (drive/series) indicates Miami's first drive. GM/PR (game/ period) simply means that it started in the first quarter, and SCORE/ START shows the score as 0-0 at the beginning of the drive. HOW OBTAINED/PLAY YDS RET tells us that Miami received a 58-yard kickoff (at the 7-yard line) and returned it 21 yards.

Next, SCRIMM/BEG END means Miami began its drive on its own 28 and drove to the Patriot 24. That's 48 yards (NET/TOT). There were 0 yards in penalties (YDS/PEN), and the drive used 8 plays (NO/PL). Miami made 3 first downs (FD/—). The Dolphins gained possession at 15:00 and lost it at 10:37 of the quarter (CLOCK TIME/START END). The whole thing took 4:23 of the clock (TIME/POSS).

Miami lost the ball on a fumble, also losing a yard on the play but with no runback by New England (HOW GIVEN UP/PLAY YDS RET). The score was still 0-0 (SCORE/END).

Let's look at the next drive. It's going to show that the Patriots took their first possession at their 25. After losing 9 yards on three plays, they punted on fourth down (with 9:07 left in the quarter). The punt went for 64 yards, to the Miami 20, but was returned for 16. Elapsed time: 1:30. On the drive chart it looks like this.

DR SE	GM PR	SCORE START	HOW OBTAINED PLAY YDS RET	SCRIMM BEG END	NET YDS TOT	YDS PEN	NO PL	FD —	CLOCK START	TIME END	TIME POSS	HOW GIVEN UP PLAY YDS RET	SCORE END
PAT	1	1	0-0	fum −1 0	p25 p16	−9	0	4	0	10:37	9:07	1:30	punt 64 16	0-0

See how it works?

Miami, starting at its own 36, could only gain 9 yards on its second possession before punting (rather poorly) to the Patriots. Look what happened then.

DR SE	GM PR	SCORE START	HOW OBTAINED PLAY YDS RET	SCRIMM BEG END	NET YDS TOT	YDS PEN	NO PL	FD —	CLOCK START	TIME END	TIME POSS	HOW GIVEN UP PLAY YDS RET	SCORE END
MIA	2	1	0-0	punt 64 16	m36 m45	9	0	4	0	9:07	6:42	2:25	punt 30 0	0-0
PAT	2	1	0-0	punt 30 0	p25 m0	75	15	13	5	6:42	2:25	4:17	TD 22 0	7-0

That's right, New England drove 75 yards in 13 plays, aided by 15 yards in penalties, to go ahead, 7-0. The touchdown came on a 22-yard play. The drive took 4:17.

On the ensuing kickoff, the ball was not returned and was placed at the Miami 20 (ko 75 30). Miami's drive (23 yards on 6 plays) extended into the next quarter.

DR SE	GM PR	SCORE START	HOW OBTAINED PLAY YDS RET	SCRIMM BEG END	NET YDS TOT	YDS PEN	NO PL	FD —	CLOCK START	TIME END	TIME POSS	HOW GIVEN UP PLAY YDS RET	SCORE END
MIA	3	1	0-7	ko 75 30	m20 m43	23	0	6	1	2:25	14:50	2:35	punt −8 0	0-7

Right about now, some of you are probably scratching your heads and saying, so what? You already looked at a play-by-play account a few chapters back. Isn't a drive chart just a simplified version?

Yes. But . . .

HERE'S THE DIFFERENCE

Back to the game situation possibilities.

If we try to analyze what happens in a football game play-by-play, we're looking at about 130 plays related to 689,040 possible situations. Even after we go through a game—or a season—or a lifetime, we'll have a heck of a time extracting very many universal truths (except maybe that football isn't much fun anymore).

But if we consider the totality of a drive, rather than its individual parts, we can get the first part of our game equation down to about 30 for the number of drives. We can see right away that 30 is easier to work with than 130. Oh, about a hundred easier on a guess.

Moreover, because we're dealing in larger segments, we can do a little reduction on the other end. For example, suppose we take our 240 time units—remember the 15-second intervals?—and chop our game into 3-minute intervals. Now we're down to 20 time units. It's not quite as exact, but we're not doing heart surgery. Go through our multiplication routine and we end up with 57,420 game situations.

We still wouldn't like to figure things out on our fingers and toes, but for your garden-variety computer working with 57,420 different possibilities, it is no more difficult than for you or me to run through our six tables. Well, for you anyway.

Now suppose we took the drive charts from a whole passel of NFL games—more than five hundred, let's say—and ran them through our trusty computer, looking at every drive in relation to all those different possibilities. We could then see what the game situation (time left, score, field position) was at the beginning of a drive and what it was at the end of that drive. We'd get a pretty good idea of how much each drive increased or decreased a team's chance of winning the game— the value of the drive.

You don't have to suppose about it; we did it.

Okay, now what?

Very simple. If you take enough game situations—in our case, more than two NFL seasons' worth—and relate them to the final scores, you can project a team's probability of winning the game from any given game situation.

That's a heckuva statement. In fact, we'd better qualify it right away. We're *not* saying we can predict who will win as soon as we see how far a team returns the opening kickoff. We're only quoting odds. In other words, if a team gets the ball at *a*-yard line, with the score at *b*, and *c* time left, its probability of winning the game, based on past performances, is *d*. Then, at the end of the drive, when the ball is at *e*, the score *f*, and there's *g* time left, the win probability has become *h*.

Let's use some real numbers. Suppose the Jets are trailing in a game by 14-0 when they take over the ball at the Patriots' 42 with 7:30 left in the first half. Their probability of winning the game at that point is 145 out of 1,000. In other words, in all previous similar situations, the team trailing went on to lose 85.5 percent of the time. But this time, the Jets get a drive going and score a touchdown with 4:56 still on the first-half clock. After the extra point, the score is still 14-7 against the Jets, but they've improved their chance of winning to 266 out of a thousand. In the past, teams in their situation have come back to win about a fourth of the time.

We can estimate the value of the Jets' touchdown drive by comparing the Win Probability at the beginning of the drive (145) with the Win Probability at the end of the drive (266): 121 Win Probability points.

Of course, every touchdown isn't "worth" the same number of Win Probability points. In the same game, the Jets drove in for another touchdown that was worth absolutely nothing to them—zilch! On that one, they scored with 1:05 left to make the final score 48-17, Patriots. Seven points went up on the scoreboard, but the Jets' chance of winning the game increased not a whit, and so they received zero Win Probability points.

WIN PROBABILITY

Win Probability is not going to let you get rich by sitting in the stands and making bets with your buddies depending on time, score, and field position. To repeat, it's not a predictive tool, even though it uses a probability factor. Win Probability evaluates. It tells you what a football event like a drive or a punt or an interception is worth, how much it increased (or decreased) a team's *probability* (not certainty) of winning.

Suppose the Lions drive 63 yards in the second quarter and then lose the ball on downs. What was the drive worth, 63 yards? What's that have to do with victory? What *is* important is how much the Lions' use of time and the change in their field position changed their game situation. If we can show you that the drive increased the likelihood that the Lions would eventually win the game, we have proved its value. And if we can show *how much* it increased Detroit's chances, we know what that value is!

Even though the Lions may eventually lose the game because of later events, that 63-yard drive had a value *at the time it was made.*

The beauty of Win Probability is that it can be used to evaluate the contributions made in each game by a team's offense, defense, and special teams.

All right, a specific example. You're three minutes into a 0-0 game and you take over at your own 35. The probability of your winning the game is 518 out of a thousand. Not much of an edge, you say. True, but here's something else. Three minutes later, with the game still scoreless, you again get the ball at your 35. Your win probability has gone up—to 519 out of 1,000. One point! Well, what did you expect?

But suppose you get a drive going. Three minutes later you have a first down at *their* 35. Your probability of winning is 576. Maybe you fumble right there. Everything changes. Your Win Probability drops to 481. What's significant here is that we can assign a value to your drive and to your fumble by comparing the win probabilities. Your drive was worth 57 Win Probability points (576 − 519), but the fumble cost you 95 (576 − 481). Overall, your bumbling offense rates a − 38 because your offensive team was worse off when it left the field than when it went on. Conversely, give your opponent's defense a + 38.

The best part of Win Probability is that it adjusts as the game goes on. In other words, it treats time, score, and field position according to their relationship to the game's outcome. A good drive with the game on the line is worth more than the same drive in the first quarter. Yardage gained after a game is irretrievably lost is worth bupkis. A fumble at a key moment costs a lot more.

Picture your 35-to-35 drive late in a game when you're trailing by one point. There are two minutes left. You get the ball with a 66 (out of 1,000) probability of winning. You misfire on a pass, but then you hit two in a row to get to your opponent's 35-yard line. Now there's one minute left. You're still behind, but your Win Probability is up to 279. Your late drive has thus far improved your likelihood of winning by 213. But if you fumble now, your Win Probability plunges to 44—a loss of 235!

Traditional statistics would show this scenario as 30 yards gained on 4 plays, with a turnover. Win Probability tells you what it's worth.

On the next few pages, we show Win Probability in actual game situations.

WIN PROBABILITY IN ACTION

Now let's go back to that New England at Miami game we looked at earlier. Just as a point of interest, this was a really big game for the Patriots. They had to win or be eliminated from the playoffs. On the dark side, they'd won only one other game in Miami in twenty years. The oddsmakers had the Dolphins favored by 3½ points. None of this has anything to do with Win Probability, which is only concerned with events on the field, but we thought you'd like to know.

Here is the first half again, but with Win Probability figures added.

	DR SE	GM PR	SCORE START	HOW OBTAINED PLAY	YDS	RET	SCRIMM BEG	END	NET TOT	YDS PEN	NO PL	FD —	CLOCK START	TIME END	TIME POSS	HOW GIVEN UP PLAY	YDS	RET	SCORE END	WIN BEG	PROBAB END	NOR	WIN OFF	TEAM TYPE	WIN SPE
																							kor	7
MIA	1	1	0-0	ko	58	21	m28	p24	38	0	8	3	15:00	10:37	4:23	fum	−1	0	0-0	507	498	498	−9	—	0
PAT	1	1	0-0	fum	−1	0	p25	p16	−9	0	4	0	10:37	9:07	1:30	punt	64	16	0-0	502	479	457	−45	punt	22
MIA	2	1	0-0	punt	64	16	m36	m45	9	0	4	0	9:07	6:42	2:25	punt	30	0	0-0	521	498	507	−14	punt	−9
PAT	2	1	0-0	punt	30	0	p25	m0	75	15	13	5	6:42	2:25	4:17	TD	22	0	7-0	502	718	715	213	XP	3
																							kor	−8
MIA	3	1	0-7	ko	75	30	m20	m43	23	0	6	1	2:25	14:50	2:35	punt	−8	0	0-7	274	214	280	6	punt	−66
PAT	3	2	7-0	punt	−8	0	m35	m29	6	0	4	0	14:50	13:04	1:46	FG	29	0	10-0	786	806	755	−31	FG	51
																							kor	7
MIA	—	2	0-10	ko	40	5	m30	m30	0	0	0	0	13:04	13:04	0:00	fum	0	6	0-10	201	113	201	0	kor	−88
PAT	4	2	10-0	fum	5	0	p24	m23	1	0	2	0	13:04	11:58	1:06	fum	0	10	10-0	887	796	796	−91	—	0
MIA	4	2	0-10	fum	0	10	m32	p25	42	0	6	2	11:58	9:34	2:24	FG	25	0	3-10	202	264	223	21	FG	41
																							kor	−9
PAT	5	2	10-3	ko	75	30	p20	p40	20	0	6	1	9:34	6:13	3:21	punt	40	0	10-3	727	752	742	15	punt	10
MIA	5	2	3-10	punt	40	0	m21	m42	21	0	3	1	6:13	5:51	0:22	int	23	21	3-10	250	203	203	−47	—	0
PAT	6	2	10-3	int	23	21	m44	m27	17	0	7	1	5:51	3:41	2:10	FG	27	0	13-3	797	834	787	−10	FG	47
																							kor	17
MIA	6	2	3-13	ko	53	23	m35	p0	65	0	11	6	3:41	0:41	3:00	TD	1	0	10-13	183	393	390	207	XP	3
																							kor	−1
PAT	7	2	13-10	ko	61	19	p23	p29	6	0	1	0	0:41	0:00	0:41	EOH	0	0	13-10	606	615	615	9	—	0

You'll notice at the right WIN PROBAB/BEG END NOR. This stands for Win Probability at the beginning of the drive (BEG), at the conclusion of the drive (END), and what the Win Probability would be if we counted only the offense (NOR). *The latter allows us to rate the contributions of special teams.*

WIN/OFF tells us how many Win Probability points are credited to or subtracted from the offense. Remember that the defense receives the reverse number of points. In other words, when the Patriots' offense was penalized −9 points for fumbling away its first drive, the Miami defense received a +9.

The final two columns, TEAM/TYPE and WI/SPE, identify special teams (kickoff, kickoff return, punt, punt return, field goal, field goal return, extra point, and extra point return), and any Win Probability points earned by those teams on the drive. You'll notice that the kickoff return team, whose efforts are not considered part of the drive, is evaluated separately on the line of type above the drive line (kor).

Some interesting points:

The Patriots' second drive resulted in a touchdown, putting them in front, 7-0. Their offense received a nice +213. The extra point team added a +3 when they successfully converted.

Miami received the kickoff and after a short drive (+6) attempted to punt. The blocked kick cost their punting team −66.

Despite its great opportunity, New England's offense (DR/SE 3) wasn't able to gain a first down (WIN/OFF −31). However, the Pats added to their lead with a field goal, crediting the field goal team with +51.

Things really went bad for the Dolphins when they fumbled and lost the ensuing kickoff at their 30-yard line. The kickoff return team gets a +7 for getting the kick to the 30 but a −88 for the costly fumble.

Luckily for Miami, the Patriots fumbled the ball right back to them —a −91 for the Pats' offense.

Late in the half, the Dolphins had a fine 61-yard drive in eleven plays to pull within three points at 10-13. At the beginning of the drive, they had only a 183 (out of 1,000) probability of winning, but the touchdown brought them up to 393, a +207 for the Miami offense and a +3 for the extra point team.

Good game, huh? Let's look at the third quarter.

DR SE	GM PR	SCORE START	HOW OBTAINED PLAY	YDS	RET	SCRIMM BEG	END	NET TOT	YDS PEN	NO PL	FD —	CLOCK START	TIME END	TIME POSS	HOW GIVEN UP PLAY	YDS	RET	SCORE END	WIN BEG	PROBAB END	NOR	WIN OFF	TEAM TYPE	WIN SPE
																							kor	−11
PAT 8	3	13-10	ko	75	30	p20	m22	58	0	8	3	15:00	11:00	4:00	FGA	21	22	13-10	603	624	672	69	FG	−48
MIA 7	3	10-13	FGA	21	22	m22	p4	74	0	7	3	11:00	8:35	2:25	FG	4	0	13-13	374	497	487	113	FG	10
																							kor	−13
PAT 9	3	13-13	ko	75	30	p20	p28	8	0	3	0	8:35	6:55	1:40	int	25	7	13-13	490	421	421	−63	—	0
MIA 8	3	13-13	int	25	7	p46	p0	46	0	3	2	6:55	6:01	0:54	TD	32	0	20-13	579	798	794	215	XP	4
																							kor	16
PAT 10	3	13-20	ko	63	31	p33	m0	67	0	8	3	6:01	3:09	2:52	TD	7	0	20-20	218	496	490	272	XP	6
																							kor	46
MIA 9	3	20-20	ko	45	21	m41	m40	−1	0	4	0	3:09	1:01	2:08	punt	53	5	20-20	550	538	495	−55	punt	43
PAT 11	3	20-20	punt	53	5	p12	p20	8	0	4	0	1:01	0:00	1:01	punt	37	17	20-20	462	394	432	−30	punt	−38

Well, the cheese is binding, as Grandma used to say.

The Pats opened the third quarter with a good drive but missed the field goal. The Dolphins took over and drove 74 yards before they kicked a field goal to tie the game at 13-13.

New England quickly gave the ball back to Miami on an intercepted pass at the Pats' 46. From there, the Dolphins touchdowned in three plays, picking up 215 offensive points for the go-ahead drive. In eight plays, the Patriots went 67 yards to deadlock the game at 20-20. Notice the extra point netted them 6 Win Probability points because it was getting later in the game and they would still have been behind without it.

Although the quarter ended with the score tied, Miami began the final period with the ball at the Patriots' 40-yard line after a fine 17-yard punt return. Miami's Win Probability was 606. It may have seemed higher among Dolphin fans who knew about New England's Orange Bowl jinx. To make matters worse for the Pats, regular quarterback Tony Eason had been knocked out of the game in the second quarter. Win Probability doesn't consider injuries or jinxes, only the score, the time, and the field position.

DR SE	GM PR	SCORE START	HOW OBTAINED PLAY	SCRIMM YDS RET	NET BEG END	YDS TOT PEN	NO PL	FD —	CLOCK START	TIME END	TIME POSS	HOW GIVEN UP PLAY	SCORE YDS RET	WIN END	PROBAB BEG END NOR	WIN TEAM OFF TYPE	WIN SPE
MIA	10	4 20-20	punt	37	17 p40 m0	40	0	3 2	15:00	13:29	1:31	TD	19 0 27-20	606	849 844	238 XP	5

When Miami roared in for another touchdown to go ahead 27-20 with 13:29 left, things looked great for the Dolphins. Their probability of winning zoomed to 849 out of a thousand. To put it another way, a team in their shoes will win about 17 out of 20 times.

But the Patriots weren't finished.

DR SE	GM PR	SCORE START	HOW OBTAINED PLAY	SCRIMM YDS RET	NET BEG END	YDS TOT PEN	NO PL	FD —	CLOCK START	TIME END	TIME POSS	HOW GIVEN UP PLAY	SCORE YDS RET	WIN END	PROBAB BEG END NOR	WIN TEAM OFF TYPE	WIN SPE
																kor	2
PAT	12	4 20-27	ko	57	18 p26 m0	74	5	7 5	13:29	8:20	5:09	TD	12 0 27-27	153	491 479	326 XP	12
																kor	−5
MIA	11	4 27-27	ko	63	22 m24 p46	30	0	5 1	8:20	6:55	1:25	punt	32 0 27-27	504	544 539	35 punt	5

Under backup quarterback Steve Grogan, the Pats moved 74 yards to a touchdown. Notice the offense received 326 Win Probability points. The extra point to tie was a must, and Tony Franklin delivered (12 WP points). Miami had a short drive and punted out at the Pats' 14. There was 6:55 left.

And here it is. The drive of the game.

DR SE	GM PR	SCORE START	HOW OBTAINED PLAY	YDS	RET	SCRIMM BEG	END	NET TOT	YDS PEN	NO PL	FD —	CLOCK START	TIME END	TIME POSS	HOW GIVEN UP PLAY	YDS	RET	SCORE END	WIN BEG	PROBAB END	NOR	WIN TEAM OFF	TYPE	WIN SPE
PAT 13	4	27-27	punt	32	0	p14	m0	86	0	12	5	6:55	0:44	6:11	TD	31	0	34-27	456	994	993	537	XP	1

Grogan led the Pats 86 yards in 12 plays to a go-ahead TD, his 31-yard pass to Stanley Morgan producing the points. Almost as important as the touchdown itself was the fact that the drive consumed 6:11 of the clock, leaving Miami only 44 seconds to turn the game around.

At this point, New England had a 994 WP. If they were in this position in 500 games, they'd win 497 of them.

But remember, the Dolphins have Marino's arm, Shula's brain, and the Orange Bowl jinx.

DR SE	GM PR	SCORE START	HOW OBTAINED PLAY	YDS	RET	SCRIMM BEG	END	NET TOT	YDS PEN	NO PL	FD —	CLOCK START	TIME END	TIME POSS	HOW GIVEN UP PLAY	YDS	RET	SCORE END	WIN BEG	PROBAB END	NOR	WIN TEAM OFF	TYPE	WIN SPE
																							kor	−1
MIA 12	4	27-34	ko	69	24	m20	m20	0	0	1	0	0:44	0:36	0:08	int	13	3	27-34	5	4	4	−1	—	0
PAT 14	4	34-27	int	13	3	m30	m33	−3	0	3	0	0:36	0.00	0:36	EOG	0	0	34-27	996	1000	1000	4	—	0

They couldn't do it. Marino's first pass after the kickoff was his last of the '86 season and his twenty-third interception of the year. New England ran out the clock, gaining their final 4 WP points by safely downing the ball three times.

And that's how they got into the playoffs.

All those bettors who took the Pats and the 3½ points told their friends they knew it all the time.

SUMMING UP

Now let's look at the totals.

TEAM	PAT WP PTS	DOLPHIN WP PTS
Offensive	+1169	+709
Defensive	−709	−1169
Kickoff	+25	+16
Kickoff Return	−16	−25
Punting	−6	−27
Punt Return	+27	+6
Field Goal	+50	+51
Field Goal Return (or Block)	−51	−50

TEAM	PAT WP PTS	DOLPHIN WP PTS
Extra Point	+22	+12
Extra Point Return (or Block)	−12	−22
Totals	+499	−499

Win Probability points relate only to individual games. A winning team will usually total about +500; the loser −500. Both New England and Miami showed good offenses throughout this game. Adding up all the Patriots' offensive points we get a +1,169. The Dolphins get +709. Both teams fell down on defense, and the special teams were a mixed bag.

How do these statistics differ from the traditional attempt-yards kind of stats? Simply that they show the accumulated value of performances in game situations.

To make our point, we'll show you Win Probability in two very different kinds of games next.

DRIVEN TO EXTREMES

Remember the old pitchman: "Yuh say yer not satisfied. Yuh say yuh want more f'yer money. *Tell yuh what I'm gonna do!*"

Right now, you're probably saying to yourself: Sure, Win Probability worked fine for that close Patriot-Dolphin game. But will it always work? What about a blowout game? What about one of those weird games where the "wrong" team wins?

Let's look at a really one-sided game and see what Win Probability has to say.

Possibly the worst game ever played by the Los Angeles Raiders, certainly their lousiest performance since Al Davis began instilling pride and poise in the black and silver, came late in 1986. At the Seattle Kingdome before a national TV Monday-night audience, the Raiders got pillaged, 37-0.

It wasn't just that they went into the game favored by 2½ points when bettors needed the Raiders-and-39 to win. It wasn't just that they gave up 37 points; they've given up more than that and won. It wasn't just that they were shut out for the first time in five years. The humiliating part of this Monday Night Massacre was that the Raiders played so *badly*! The "turning point" of this game was when it was put on the schedule the previous spring. Los Angeles was never "in" it.

Aside from the Seahawks and their fans, the only people who liked this game were Cagney & Lacey, who benefited from a lot of channel switching.

Win Probability won't give you a whole lot of new information about a blowout like this, but it can show you at what point Los Angeles lost any conceivable chance of winning. It can also show one of the fallacies of traditional statistics.

Let's look at the traditional numbers first:

	LOS ANGELES	SEATTLE
FIRST DOWNS	10	21
Rushing	2	10
Passing	8	10
Penalty	0	1
TOTAL NET YARDS	138	407
Rushing	40	183
Passing	98	224
PASSES ATTEMPTED	29	21
Completed	13	14
Had Intercepted	3	0
Tackled Attempting to Pass . . .	11	2
Yards Lost Attempting to Pass . .	68	19
PUNTS	8	2
Average	43.0	37.0
PUNT RETURNS	1	6
Yards Returned	8	45
KICKOFF RETURNS	6	1
Yards Returned	81	9
PENALTIES	5	4
Yards Penalized	31	30
RUSHING PLAYS	13	45
Average Gain	3.1	4.1
TOTAL PLAYS	53	68
Average Gain	2.6	6.0
FUMBLES	0	6
Fumbles Lost	0	1
FIELD GOAL ATTEMPTS	0	4
Made	0	3
THIRD DOWN PLAYS	13	16
Converted to First Down	2	10
TIME OF POSSESSION	24:03	35:57

Well, there aren't any surprises here. The Raiders were outgained better than three-to-one, threw three interceptions, and were sacked eleven times. They couldn't convert third downs worth beans. They gave up over 400 yards. They averaged under 3 yards a play. Lose? They were lucky not to be condemned!

Here's the first half Drive Chart with Win Probability added.

DR SE	GM PR	SCORE START	HOW OBTAINED PLAY	YDS	RET	SCRIMM BEG	END	NET TOT	YDS PEN	NO PL	FD -	CLOCK START	TIME END	TIME POSS	HOW GIVEN UP PLAY	YDS	RET	SCORE END	WIN BEG	END	PROBAB NOR	WIN OFF	TEAM TYPE	WIN SPE
																							kor	-7
RAI	1	1 0-0	ko	68	23	r20	r26	6	0	7	1	15:00	10:55	4:05	punt	33	0	0-0	493	471	474	-19	punt	-3
SEA	-	1 0-0	punt	33	0	s42	s42	0	0	0	0	10:55	10:55	0:00	fum	0	-2	0-0	531	445	531	0	pr	-86
RAI	2	1 0-0	fum	0	-2	s43	r48	-9	0	4	0	10:55	9:36	1:19	punt	41	15	0-0	555	496	513	-42	punt	-17
SEA	1	1 0-0	punt	41	15	s26	r0	74	0	9	3	9:36	6:03	3:33	TD	10	0	7-0	504	711	708	204	XP	3
RAI	3	1 0-7	ko	67	22	r20	r21	1	0	3	0	6:03	5:16	0:47	int	29	14	0-7	281	226	226	-55	—	0
SEA	2	1 7-0	int	29	14	r36	r0	36	0	4	2	5:16	2:49	2:27	TD	5	0	14-0	774	882	880	105	XP	2
RAI	4	1 0-14	ko	61	15	r19	s47	34	-5	7	2	2:49	13:33	4:16	punt	37	12	0-14	112	112	121	9	punt	-9
SEA	3	2 14-0	punt	37	12	s28	s42	14	5	5	1	13:33	11:06	2:27	punt	40	8	14-0	894	895	898	4	punt	-3
RAI	5	2 0-14	punt	40	8	r26	r26	0	-6	4	0	11:06	8:35	2:31	punt	49	4	0-14	105	94	85	-20	punt	9
SEA	4	2 14-0	punt	49	4	s29	s28	43	0	8	2	8:35	4:08	4:27	FG	28	0	17-0	906	941	924	18	FG	17
																							kor	-8
RAI	6	2 0-17	ko	65	13	r13	r13	0	0	4	0	4:08	2:16	1:52	punt	49	0	0-17	51	54	47	-4	punt	7
SEA	5	2 17-0	punt	49	0	s38	r0	62	-10	6	3	2:16	0:39	1:37	TD	12	0	24-0	946	989	988	42	XP	1
																							kor	0
RAI	7	2 0-24	ko	59	16	r22	r41	19	0	5	1	0:39	0:01	0:38	int	25	18	0-24	11	11	11	0	—	0
SEA	6	2 24-0	int	25	18	r48	r48	0	0	1	0	0:01	0:00	0:01	EOH	0	0	24-0	989	989	989	0	—	0

As you can see, the Raiders finished the first half down 24-0. At that point they had an 11 in 1,000 chance of winning. About 1 in 100. Probably Al Michaels didn't mention that. Stay tuned . . . please!

It took the Seahawks ten minutes of the second half to get those last 11 WP points.

DR SE	GM PR	SCORE START	HOW OBTAINED PLAY	YDS	RET	SCRIMM BEG	END	NET TOT	YDS PEN	NO PL	FD -	CLOCK START	TIME END	TIME POSS	HOW GIVEN UP PLAY	YDS	RET	SCORE END	WIN BEG	END	PROBAB NOR	WIN OFF	TEAM TYPE	WIN SPE
																							kor	0
SEA	7	3 24-0	ko	52	9	s22	r33	45	0	12	3	15:00	9:03	5:57	FG	33	0	27-0	988	998	993	5	FG	5
																							kor	0
RAI	8	3 0-27	ko	52	13	r26	r16	-10	-5	4	0	9:03	7:38	1:25	punt	36	10	0-27	2	2	2	0	punt	0
SEA	8	3 27-0	punt	36	10	s42	s35	7	-5	4	0	7:38	5:01	2:37	FG	35	0	30-0	998	1000	998	0	FG	2
																							kor	0
RAI	9	3 0-30	ko	53	15	r27	r10	-17	-10	4	0	5:01	4:03	0:58	punt	35	0	0-30	0	0	0	0	punt	0
SEA	9	3 30-0	punt	35	0	r44	r31	14	-5	7	1	4:03	2:06	1:57	fga	31	32	30-0	1000	1000	999	-1	fg	1
RAI	10	3 0-30	fga	31	32	r32	s34	34	0	8	2	2:06	14:51	2:15	down	0	1	0-30	0	0	0	0	—	0
SEA	10	4 30-0	down	0	1	s35	s10	65	-10	10	5	14:51	7:26	7:25	TD	3	0	37-0	1000	1000	1000	0	XP	0
																							kor	0
RAI	11	4 0-37	ko	61	9	r13	r24	11	0	6	1	7:23	5:16	2:07	punt	47	4	0-37	0	0	0	0	punt	0
SEA	11	4 37-0	punt	47	4	s33	r49	18	0	7	1	5:16	1:43	3:33	punt	33	0	37-0	1000	1000	1000	0	punt	0
RAI	12	4 0-37	punt	33	0	r17	s34	49	0	5	3	1:43	0:49	0:54	int	7	1	0-37	0	0	0	0	—	0
SEA	12	4 37-0	int	7	1	s28	s24	-4	0	2	0	0:49	0:00	0:49	EOG	0	0	37-0	1000	1000	1000	0	—	0

Okay, with 5:01 left in the third period, Norm Johnson kicked his third field goal for the Seahawks, and the Raiders' Win Probability was zero. Now somewhere in the long history of pro football, a team may have come back after trailing by thirty points with only twenty minutes to go. Maybe in some minor league. Maybe in some fictional account.

But in the real world of the modern NFL, this game was over.

But they played on. ABC had contracted for sixty minutes, and the NFL rules concurred. Neither the further accomplishments of the Seahawks nor the continued ineptitude of the Raiders meant anything, but they played on. The announcers made desperate small talk, and they played on. Seattle added another touchdown and another hundred yards or so to its statistics during what was, at most, a practice session.

And, *that's* why we like Win Probability. It only considers those parts of a game that have some meaning.

As Seattle drew farther ahead, the number of WP points they could add to their total decreased. Why? Because well before the first half ended, the Seahawks merely had to avoid doing something catastrophically bad. Give them credit—small credit—because the 'Hawks didn't suddenly fall apart. And that's good, but they surely shouldn't be rewarded with a bathtub full of WP points (even though they continued to add plenty to their traditional statistics). Extra WP points for avoiding a string of fatal errors would be like your boss calling you in and saying, "We're giving you a raise, Fernley, because you didn't destroy our factory this week."

Here are the WP totals:

TEAM	L.A. WP pts	SEA. WP pts
Offensive	−378	+378
Defensive	−131	+131
Kickoff	0	+29
Kickoff Return	−29	0
Punting	73	−3
Punt Return	3	−73
Field Goal	0	+25
Field Goal Return (or Block)	−25	0
Extra Point	0	6
Extra Point Return (or Block)	−6	0
Totals	−493	+493

So even in a monumental blowout, the winning team will end up with about 500 WP points, and the losing team with about −500. They'll seldom hit 500 on the nose because of a small amount of rounding off along the way.

Seattle's +131 on defense is impressive. A good defensive performance for an NFL team will usually be around 0. But remember: 11 sacks, 3 interceptions, and only a 2.6 average gain against them.

About the only good thing on the Raiders' side was the punting of ancient Ray Guy, playing in his last season. Guy is probably the best punter ever in pro football, and he kept to his high standard while everything else was crashing down around Los Angeles.

Seahawk fans may be surprised to see the field goal team credited with only 25 WP points. After all, Norm Johnson booted field goals of 46, 51, and 53 yards (and missed one of 49) during this game. Shouldn't that kind of effort be rewarded? We agree it was a nice piece of kicking, but how much did his goals actually contribute to the victory? Remember, the Seahawks were ahead 14-0 before he kicked the first and scored another touchdown before he got his last two. Where was the pressure? A 16-yard field goal in the final seconds to pull a game out of the fire is worth *beaucoup* points. Johnson's kicks, impressive as they were, simply added the icing to the cake.

THE KANSAS CITY STEALERS

The Seahawk-Raider game was a blowout. A couple of weeks later, there was a blowup. In one of those weirdo affairs that make you believe in kismet, Kansas City defeated Pittsburgh, 24-19.

What's so odd about that, you ask? Weren't the Chiefs a wild-card playoff team in '86? Didn't the Steelers suffer through their worst season since long before they won all those Super Bowls? True. But coming up on the last game of the season, the at-home Steelers were on a roll with five victories in eight games while the beat-up Chiefs, despite close wins in their last two games, had a moribund offense, shaky defense, and a history of not coming through in big games. They needed this game to make the playoffs for the first time since 1971, but the oddsmakers had the Steelers favored by two.

Okay, you say, it could have gone either way. Again, true. But look at the traditional stats:

	KC	PIT
FIRST DOWNS	8	28
Rushing	2	10
Passing	6	17
Penalty	0	1
TOTAL NET YARDS	171	515
Rushing	38	175
Passing	133	340
PASSES ATTEMPTED	24	43
Completed	12	22
Had Intercepted	1	1
Tackled Attempting to Pass	2	1
Yards Lost Attempting to Pass	14	11
PUNTS	8	4
Average	37.4	29.8
PUNT RETURNS	2	4
Yards Returned	16	11
KICKOFF RETURNS	5	5
Yards Returned	179	59
PENALTIES	4	4
Yards Penalized	26	21
RUSHING PLAYS	21	40
Average Gain	1.8	4.4
TOTAL PLAYS	47	84
Average Gain	3.6	6.1
FUMBLES	1	3
Fumbles Lost	0	1
FIELD GOAL ATTEMPTS	1	5
Made	1	4
THIRD DOWN PLAYS	13	16
Converted to First Down	3	5
TIME OF POSSESSION	25:02	34:58

Regardless of what you might have expected going in, if you looked at these statistics in your Monday newspaper before you read the score, you'd probably think the Steelers blew the Chiefs back to Missouri: 515 net offensive yards and a 6.1 average to 171 and a 1.8 average—much worse than the Raiders against the Seahawks! Twenty-eight first downs to 8—that's 3½ to 1! This looks like 40-something to nothing. And yet the Chiefs won.

See what we mean by weird?

How did it happen? Let's look at the Drive Chart.

| DR | GM | SCORE | HOW OBTAINED | | | SCRIMM | | NET | YDS | NO | FD | CLOCK | TIME | TIME | HOW GIVEN UP | | | SCORE | WIN | PROBAB | | WIN | TEAM | WIN |
SE	PR	START	PLAY	YDS	RET	BEG	END	TOT	PEN	PL	—	START	END	POSS	PLAY	YDS	RET	END	BEG	END	NOR	OFF	TYPE	SPE
																							kor	−3
KC	1	1 0-0	ko	53	10	k22	k26	4	0	4	0	15:00	12:49	2:11	punt	51	3	0-0	497	496	474	−23	punt	22
PIT	1	1 0-0	punt	51	3	p26	k46	28	0	7	2	12:49	9:57	2:52	fum	−2	0	0-0	504	459	459	−45	—	0
KC	2	1 0-0	fum	−2	0	k48	p35	17	5	6	1	9:57	7:37	2:20	punt	34	0	0-0	541	545	517	−24	punt	28
PIT	2	1 0-0	punt	34	0	p1	p9	8	0	4	0	7:37	6:23	1:14	punt	0	9	0-7	455	289	443	−12	punt	−154

Neither Kansas City nor Pittsburgh could do much in its opening drive, but the Steelers' fumble at the Chiefs' 46 eventually came back to hurt them. KC drove down to the Pittsburgh 35 and then opted for a punt instead of a field goal. It was an interesting choice that put Pittsburgh into a hole at its own 1-yard line. Four plays later, Harry Newsome tried to punt out of the end zone. Albert Lewis blocked it and Deron Cherry recovered for a touchdown to put the Chiefs in front, 7-0. KC's offense had a −47, but its punting and punt return teams had accounted for +204.

| DR | GM | SCORE | HOW OBTAINED | | | SCRIMM | | NET | YDS | NO | FD | CLOCK | TIME | TIME | HOW GIVEN UP | | | SCORE | WIN | PROBAB | | WIN | TEAM | WIN |
SE	PR	START	PLAY	YDS	RET	BEG	END	TOT	PEN	PL	—	START	END	POSS	PLAY	YDS	RET	END	BEG	END	NOR	OFF	TYPE	SPE
																							kor	−10
PIT	3	1 0-7	ko	56	10	p19	p46	27	0	7	1	6:23	2:51	3:32	punt	40	6	0-7	279	289	291	12	punt	−2
KC	3	1 7-0	punt	40	6	k20	k43	23	5	3	1	2:51	0:50	2:01	int	10	11	7-0	711	665	665	−45	—	0
PIT	4	1 0-7	int	10	11	k42	k49	−7	0	4	0	0:50	14:54	0:56	punt	36	0	0-7	335	296	292	−43	punt	4
KC	4	2 7-0	punt	36	0	k13	k29	58	−5	8	2	14:54	10:44	4:10	FG	29	0	10-0	704	811	759	55	FG	52

Both teams exchanged the ball a couple of times. Pittsburgh couldn't take advantage of a pass interception. With six seconds left in the first quarter, the Chiefs started their best drive of the game: 58 yards to the Steelers' 29. This time KC went for the field goal, and Nick Lowery delivered (47 yards from placement) to widen the Chiefs' lead.

| DR | GM | SCORE | HOW OBTAINED | | | SCRIMM | | NET | YDS | NO | FD | CLOCK | TIME | TIME | HOW GIVEN UP | | | SCORE | WIN | PROBAB | | WIN | TEAM | WIN |
SE	PR	START	PLAY	YDS	RET	BEG	END	TOT	PEN	PL	—	START	END	POSS	PLAY	YDS	RET	END	BEG	END	NOR	OFF	TYPE	SPE
																							kor	13
PIT	5	2 0-10	ko	51	12	p26	k14	60	0	8	3	10:44	7:29	3:15	FG	14	0	3-10	190	256	235	45	FG	21
																							kor	0
KC	-	2 10-3	ko	62	97	—	—	—	—	—	—	7:29	7:29	0:00	TD	97	0	17-3	744	905	744	0	kor	161

Pittsburgh finally put some points on the board midway through the second quarter. A nice 60-yard drive pooped out at the KC 14. Gary Anderson went back to the 31 and popped a field goal to make it 10-3.

But on the ensuing kickoff, KC's Boyce Green zipped 97 yards through a Steeler kickoff team that looked as if it had its mind on other things. So it was 17-3, and another 161 WP points for the Chiefs' special teams. Incidentally, Green didn't really make his run in 0 seconds (7:29 to 7:29); it's a simplification in the system because a touchdown kick return is not counted as "drive time."

	DR SE	GM PR	SCORE START	HOW OBTAINED PLAY	YDS	SCRIMM RET	BEG	END	NET YDS TOT	PEN	NO PL	FD —	CLOCK START	TIME END	TIME POSS	HOW GIVEN UP PLAY	YDS	RET	SCORE END	WIN BEG	END	PROBAB NOR	WIN OFF	TEAM TYPE	WIN SPE
																								kor	13
PIT	6	2	3–17	ko	52	19	p37	k14	49	0	8	3	7:29	3:36	3:53	FG	14	0	6–17	108	133	121	13	FG	12
																								kor	−4
KC	5	2	17–6	ko	57	14	k22	k31	9	0	4	0	3:36	2:00	1:36	punt	44	0	6–17	863	879	873	10	punt	6
PIT	7	2	6–17	punt	44	0	p25	k3	72	0	9	3	2:00	0:26	1:34	fga	−19	78	6–24	121	41	183	62	FG	−142

Pittsburgh again put on a good drive, and again it fizzled in the shadow of the Kansas City goal line. Nothing so demonstrates that there are yards and there are *yards* than the fact that Pittsburgh spent the whole game driving down the field, gained 515 yards, yet scored only one touchdown. Anderson's second field goal made it 17-6, KC.

The Chiefs couldn't do anything with their possession, as usual. Also as usual, Pittsburgh came barreling down the field, this time for 72 yards. They reached the KC 3 before they tried for yet another field goal.

This one was a second-guesser's dream. A successful field goal would still leave Pittsburgh eight points behind. With only 26 seconds in the first half, the Steelers had to consider what kind of situation to shoot for at the top of the second half when they were scheduled to receive. They could kick the field goal and figure to start the second half at 189 WP points, assuming an average runback to the Pittsburgh 25. Should they go for the TD and fail, they could still start at 127 WP points, only 62 less. But if they make the touchdown and add the extra point, they would likely start the second half at 334 WP points, 145 better than the field goal could get them.

Of course, the "book" says play it safe and get something! Kick the field goal. After all, a sure 3 beats a maybe 7, and the field goal certainly looks like a sure thing.

So what happened? Anderson set up at the 19. KC nose tackle Bill Maas roared through the middle like the Superchief to block the kick. Lloyd Burruss grabbed the ball and dashed 78 yards to the third touchdown for the Kansas City special teams. Instead of 17-9, the score jumped to 24-6.

Pittsburgh was in shock.

DR SE	GM PR	SCORE START	HOW OBTAINED PLAY	YDS	RET	SCRIMM BEG	SCRIMM END	NET TOT	YDS PEN	NO PL	FD —	CLOCK START	TIME END	TIME POSS	HOW GIVEN UP PLAY	YDS	RET	SCORE END	WIN BEG	WIN END	PROBAB NOR	WIN OFF	TEAM TYPE	WIN SPE
PIT 8	2	6-24	ko	32	3	p36	p49	13	0	3	1	0:26	0:00	0:26	EOH	0	0	6-24	42	45	45	3	—	0
																							kor	1
PIT 9	3	6-24	ko	53	15	p27	p29	2	0	4	0	15:00	13:55	1:05	punt	43	10	6-24	43	35	36	-7	punt	-1
KC 6	3	24-6	punt	43	10	k38	p41	21	-5	7	1	13:55	10:37	3:18	punt	19	0	24-6	965	966	970	5	punt	-4
PIT 10	3	6-24	punt	19	0	p22	k0	78	0	10	5	10:37	5:47	4:50	TD	9	0	13-24	34	82	81	47	XP	1

It took the Steelers until nearly ten minutes into the third quarter to get a touchdown, QB Mark Malone running 9 yards for the 6. Kansas City was selling yardage for time.

DR SE	GM PR	SCORE START	HOW OBTAINED PLAY	YDS	RET	SCRIMM BEG	SCRIMM END	NET TOT	YDS PEN	NO PL	FD —	CLOCK START	TIME END	TIME POSS	HOW GIVEN UP PLAY	YDS	RET	SCORE END	WIN BEG	WIN END	PROBAB NOR	WIN OFF	TEAM TYPE	WIN SPE
																							kor	-5
KC 7	3	24-13	ko	68	23	k20	k23	3	0	4	0	5:47	4:07	1:40	punt	43	3	13-24	913	914	908	-5	punt	6
PIT 11	3	13-24	punt	43	3	p37	k13	50	0	9	0	4:07	14:39	4:28	FG	13	0	16-24	86	88	79	-7	FG	9
																							kor	11
KC 8	4	24-16	ko	61	29	k33	p36	31	0	9	2	14:39	10:29	4:10	punt	30	0	24-16	923	975	968	45	punt	7
PIT 12	4	16-24	punt	30	0	p6	k9	85	0	9	5	10:29	7:40	2:49	FG	9	0	19-24	25	180	153	128	FG	27

And they were doing it very well. Of course, Pittsburgh cooperated by taking the "safe" field goal twice after long drives. Nevertheless, with half of the fourth quarter left, the Steelers trailed by five and still had a chance.

Perhaps the "right" team might yet win.

DR SE	GM PR	SCORE START	HOW OBTAINED PLAY	YDS	RET	SCRIMM BEG	SCRIMM END	NET TOT	YDS PEN	NO PL	FD —	CLOCK START	TIME END	TIME POSS	HOW GIVEN UP PLAY	YDS	RET	SCORE END	WIN BEG	WIN END	PROBAB NOR	WIN OFF	TEAM TYPE	WIN SPE
																							kor	22
KC 9	4	24-19	ko	61	29	k33	k38	5	0	5	0	7:40	6:38	1:02	punt	37	1	24-19	842	822	818	-24	punt	4
PIT 13	4	19-24	punt	37	1	p26	k33	41	0	8	3	6:38	2:22	4:16	int	11	0	19-24	178	55	55	-123	—	0
KC 10	4	24-19	int	11	0	k22	k21	-1	-5	4	0	2:22	1:50	0:32	punt	41	4	24-19	945	931	921	-24	punt	10
PIT 14	4	19-24	punt	41	4	p42	k49	9	0	4	0	1:50	1:16	0:34	down	0	0	19-24	69	10	10	-59	—	0
KC 11	4	24-19	down	0	0	50	k42	-8	0	3	0	1:16	0:00	1:16	EOG	0	0	24-19	990	1000	1000	10	—	0

The last few minutes are a study in what makes a good defense. Pittsburgh closed down the Chiefs completely on their possession. After the punt, the Chiefs' defense slowly leaked yardage to the Steelers. It took Pittsburgh four minutes to get 41 yards. This was a mixed curse. If Pittsburgh scored a touchdown, there'd be almost no time for Kansas City to come back. But of course, Pittsburgh had to score a touchdown.

With 2:22 left, Albert Lewis—the same Chief who'd blocked the punt in the first quarter—intercepted Malone's pass at the KC 22. The Pittsburgh defense stuffed the KC offense again. There was still a little time left, but this time the Chiefs returned the favor and held the

Steelers on downs. Then Kansas City ran out the last 1:16, picking up their last 10 WP points by losing 8 yards.

The traditional statistics say the wrong team won. But did they?

An examination of the Win Probability totals shows where the game was won.

TEAM	KC WP pts	PIT WP pts
Offensive	−14	+14
Defensive	−21	+21
Kickoff	−6	−182
Kickoff Return	+182	+6
Punting	+79	−153
Punt Return	+153	−79
Field Goal	+52	−73
Field Goal Return (or Block)	+73	−52
Extra Point	0	1
Extra Point Return (or Block)	−1	0
Totals	+497	−497

Look at those special teams!

What may be surprising is Kansas City's rather good defensive rating. After all, they gave up 515 yards, and that shoved them down in the league defensive standings. Well, that's traditional stats for you!

Actually, the KC defense did the job. They were tough in close, holding the Steelers to only one touchdown. And they made 'em pay in time for the yardage.

In a sense, the game was a summary of the season for both teams. Pittsburgh's offense lacked the home run punch of the old Terry Bradshaw-Lynn Swann-Franco Harris days, and their special teams were an embarrassment all year. Kansas City never found an offense, but their defense and special teams pulled them through.

After the game, Kansas City Coach John Mackovic admitted as much: "We did it the way we have done it all year, with special teams and defense." A few weeks later, he was replaced as head man by Frank Gansz, his special teams coach.

Over the winter, Pittsburgh Coach Chuck Noll went out and hired a new special teams coach to replace the one who hadn't done the job all season—Chuck Noll.

7

You *Can* Get There from Here

In the seasons immediately before the National Football League was born, the championship of the professional football world was settled each year on Ohio gridirons. In 1919, it came down to a December meeting between the Canton Bulldogs and the Massillon Tigers. The Tigers went out and hired every former college All-American they could talk into coming to Ohio. One observer swore he saw more than seventy players in Massillon jerseys at game time, but he may have been using the old sheep count: add the legs and divide by four. The Bulldogs used their regular lineup, with Jim Thorpe at tailback. Thorpe was usually enough for Canton to cakewalk, but at kickoff Ol' Jim had a wrenched back that made things like running 99 yards, leaping tall buildings, or tying his shoelaces sheer agony.

The first half was scoreless. By the second half, Canton had a gusty tailwind kicking up behind them and Thorpe tried to ride it on a couple of long-distance field goal shots. His third try was the charm. With his buddy Pete Calac holding at the 40-yard line, Jim place-kicked true for a 3-0 Canton lead.

That got Massillon off its duff, and the Tigers moved into Bulldog territory as soon as they got the ball. When the drive fizzled, Massillon's Skip Gougler tried his foot at a goal, but the wind knocked the ball into the dirt and out of bounds at the Canton 15.

Now consider the situation from the standpoint of the Canton quarterback: time is running out in the third quarter; you've less than a touchdown lead with first-and-10 deep in your own realm; your offense has been moribund; your best player is hurting; and you're facing a team of All-Americans who will have the wind in the final period. What do you call?

Well, Thorpe went back and stood on his 5-yard line. When he got the snap, he gritted his teeth and punted the ball for all he was worth (which at the time was $250 a game). The Massillon safety waited back a respectable, even respectful, distance, but Thorpe's kick was a wind-caught line drive that sailed over the poor guy's head. The whole menagerie of 'Dogs and Tigers chased hell-for-leather after the football, but no one caught up until it had rolled over the goal line 95 yards from where Thorpe had started it.

And that was the ball game. Thorpe's kick had cut the heart out of the Tigers. Canton kept them bottled at the far end of the field through the whole fourth quarter to win, 3-0.

If you saw that one coming—the first down punt—you're either a Thorpe groupie or you know how to think 1919. It was proper strategy back then, mainly because offenses were at the buggy-whip stage. In a close game, a single touchdown or field goal might be the only score all afternoon. A winning team seldom needed two hands to count up its first downs. Under those circumstances, if you got the ball inside your own 20, you were more likely to make some disastrous mistake than to break out. So, you punted.

Of course, you couldn't depend on a Thorpean, 95-yard boot—but still, you gave the other guys the ball at midfield; odds were they'd waste three downs and punt back. If your punter was good enough and you didn't take any dumb chances like running the ball or, God forbid, passing it, sooner or later you'd have the other guys backed up. Then you waited for them to goof.

That's how it was done in 1919. If you tried to play the game that way today, you'd get clobbered every time you pulled on your lowcuts. Field position is still the name of the game, but today's offensive strategy has changed the odds of scoring from any particular spot on the field. And, because the odds are different, play selection changes.

CARTER COUNTRY

Remember Virgil Carter, a Brigham Young quarterback before every BYU signal caller was considered a potential All-American? Carter played professionally for nine years, with terms at Chicago, Cincinnati, San Diego, and one season in the World Football League. Nobody ever seemed to think Carter had the talent to be anything but a backup in the NFL, but just about every time the regular quarterback got hurt, Carter would go in and his team would do well. It was kind of embarrassing to the coaches who wanted him to stay on the bench.

Anyway, Carter may have had a minor league arm, but he had a major league mind. He gave a lot of serious thought to just what happens on a football field, without being bound by all the clichés his coaches swore by. After all, the same coaches said he belonged in another line of work. In 1971, along with Robert E. Machol, Carter published a study in *Operations Research* in which he suggested evaluating field position in terms of potential points. In other words, first-and-10 at x-yard line means a team has y chance of scoring next, and that can be expressed as z points.

Carter analyzed 2,852 first down situations and expressed his point potentials, or "expected values," to three decimal points. For example, a first-and-10 at an opponent's 45 had an expected value of 2.392. However, he never claimed his numbers were absolutely reliable beyond one tenth of a point.

Since his article there have been several important rule changes and even some attitude changes that make Carter's "exact" figures much more approximate. However, we ran a couple of seasons' worth of games and came to basically the same conclusions.

IT ALL DEPENDS ON WHERE YOU'RE COMING FROM

To take the most obvious example, a team with a first down an inch from the opponent's goal line is all but certain of scoring. If it *always* scored, we'd say it had a 7-point potential, but—allowing for the possibility of a heroic goal-line stand (or a missed extra point)—call it a rounded-off 6-point potential.

On the other hand, give a team first-and-10 only 1 inch out from its *own* goal line with 99 yards, 2 feet, 11 inches to go down the field, and its scoring potential is about -2. That doesn't mean that a safety is imminent (although it's a distinct possibility); what it really means is that in the normal course of events, the team on defense is more likely to score next.

In our study of 224 games in 1986, we found 771 first-down plays from the 50-yard line (plus or minus 2 yards). This did *not* include 27 drives started in the final two minutes of each half, which were disregarded because no points were scored before the half ran out.

Of these 771 first downs, the offense scored next in 467 cases (298 TDs, 165 field goals, and 4 safeties) for 2,589 points. The team on defense at the time was the next to score 191 times (126 TDs and 65 field goals) for 1,077 points. And 113 times neither team scored. Subtract 1,077 from 2,589, and you leave the offense with a plus of 1,512 points. Divide by 771. With a first-and-10 at midfield, the offense has a point potential of 1.96.

Remembering that the figures can never be absolute—one freakish field goal can mess up a decimal point—we still see a consistency in point potential, depending on field position. If you look at all the first down situations from anywhere on the field, you get a straight line which passes through −2 points at your own goal line, 0 at your 25, +2 at midfield, +4 at the far 25, and +6 at the other goal line.

Your point potential increases by about a point every 12.5 yards. That's not the same as saying that a team scores a point for every 12.5 yards it gains. Actually on average, it takes 15 or 16 yards to produce a point because most possessions result in only a few yards and no points at all. But what does happen is that every 12.5 yards you are nearer your opponent's goal for first down increases your likelihood *of being the next scorer*—translated into point potential—by about a point.

By "the next scorer," we don't mean that your team will necessarily score on that particular possession. Until you get down near your opponent's goal line, the odds of scoring on a particular possession are not very good. As a matter of fact, if a kickoff goes into the end zone and you take over at your own 20, there is no more likelihood that you will score next than that your opponent will. It's an even-money bet.

However, once you get past your own 35, the odds shift to about two-to-one that the next team to put points on the board will be yours (+1).

There's a logic to this, if you think about it. Remember, we're talking about two evenly matched teams. Let's put the Bears' 1985 Super

Bowl champs against the Giants' 1986 winners. We might as well think big.

Let's say the Bears start a drive at their own 38 and gain only 5 yards in 3 downs. Chicago's punter gets off an average punt with an average runback by the Giants; call it a net of 35 yards. New York will then be starting at its 22, 16 yards poorer in field position than the Bears started.

Five yards gained and an average punt by the Giants gives the Bears a *second* chance to start a drive from the 38. The teams can keep the same approximate field positions and make the same average punts through several exchanges, but the Bears will always need fewer yards to get a score and will always have an extra chance to start a drive (until the half ends, of course). The advantage translates into a $+1$ point potential.

The advantage for the Bears increases as they move up the field (the distance needed to score decreases while they maintain their drive opportunity advantage). But if Chicago starts its drive at the 25, its opportunity advantage is offset by its distance-needed disadvantage, producing a standoff.

You can also look at it from the defensive side by changing the plus and minus signs. Therefore, a team with a first down at midfield has a $+2$ point potential and its opposite number, the defense, has a -2. The chart below also shows why a first down at the 25 leaves both the offense and defense with an equal likelihood of scoring.

―――――――― *POTENTIAL POINTS/YARDLINES* ――――――――

BEARS OFFENSE	BALL AT	GIANTS DEFENSE
-2	Goal Line	$+2$
-1	12.5	$+1$
0	25	0
$+1$	37.5	-1
$+2$	50	-2
$+3$	37.5	-3
$+4$	25	-4
$+5$	12.5	-5
$+6$	Goal Line	-6

BUT WHAT IF WE GOOF?

Consideration of the defensive side is important. In choosing our strategy, we have to be aware of what happens if we turn the ball over. Lord knows, turnovers are *the* stat of the '80s. However, to see what happens with a turnover, we need to stop thinking in terms of an offense and a defense. Now we have to think in terms of two offenses because a turnover moves the point potential not from our offense to their defense, but from our offense to *their* offense:

Okay, here's the same chart, given in terms of two offenses; you can easily see the result of a turnover:

POTENTIAL POINTS/YARDLINES

BEARS OFFENSE	BALL AT	GIANTS OFFENSE	TURNOVER DIFFERENCE (A + B)
−2	Goal Line	+6	4
−1	12.5	+5	4
0	25	+4	4
+1	37.5	+3	4
+2	50	+2	4
+3	37.5	+1	4
+4	25	0	4
+5	12.5	−1	4
+6	Goal Line	−2	4

That's right. A turnover (with no change of line of scrimmage) causes a four-point change in point potential *no matter where it occurs on the field!*

On the face of it, this probably seems ridiculous. Everybody knows it's worse to fumble near your own goal line than to fumble in the other guy's territory. Well, it is if you're in one of those situations where it's necessary to hang on to the ball for dear life, such as when you're nursing a two-point lead with only seconds left in the half.

And we're only talking about a turnover that's a simple transfer of possession. If your scatter-armed quarterback throws the ball into a defender's arms and watches him run for a touchdown, it doesn't matter a whole hell of a lot where the turnover took place—you're down a TD.

But under most circumstances, there's no big yard line change. Then you have to balance the likelihood that you would have scored on your possession (which you lose on the turnover) with the likelihood of the other team scoring when they gain possession. At midfield you've gone from a +2 for you to a +2 for them, a swing of 4 potential points. If you lose a fumble on first-and-10 at your own 12, you've put them in a +5 situation, but you were already at −1. To put it another way, the odds already favored your opponent scoring next; you only increased them—by four potential points. At the other end of the field—well, you get the picture.

The real loss on a turnover (at the line of scrimmage) is the difference in point potential should you punt. A 50-yard punt from your 25 to their 25 leaves both teams with the same point potential they had before. Even a common 37.5 net yard punt makes you only one point worse off than you were at first-and-10, when you stood 37.5 yards back down the field.

GENERALIZING FOR THE FIELD GENERAL

Admittedly, we're generalizing here. This data varies some from situation to situation. For example, there is an overall league average that assumes each team is equal and typical of the league as a whole (certainly a difficult concept to grasp in Tampa Bay). We probably would see some differences if we developed data for match-ups between particular teams, though the reliability would be diminished because we'd have smaller samples.

We should also re-examine our data periodically because of rule changes and the "evolution of the game," a fine term for what books the coaches read, what clinics they attend, and how their ulcers are acting up.

And there is also a variation within a game due to the current score and time remaining. Such factors can be taken into account by developing a model which uses the scoring potential as input and outputs a probability of winning the game as a function of score, time, and field position.

But in spite of all the variations that may affect particular game situations, we can still reach some general conclusions.

For instance, traditional football wisdom dictates careful, conservative, walk-on-eggs play calling when a team has its butt backed up near its own goalpost. The idea is: don't take a chance on doing anything that might cause a turnover. As a consequence, of course, a team won't do anything that might cause a turn*around*. It's an "out-of-the-frying-pan" strategy. After three plunges, the team punts and here comes the enemy back at them, already in scoring territory.

This strategy only makes sense if a team can run out the clock before having to punt. Otherwise they're just tap-dancing until the other team scores. Remember, a turnover causes the same 4-point swing in point potential no matter where it happens, so why condemn your offense to failure by limiting your play selection on the off chance you *might* make a mistake? Call the play that will get you out of the hole!

Now that we have your attention with a fairly modest proposal, try this multiple-choice test:

You have the ball, fourth down and 1 at your opponents' 10-yard line. There are 6 minutes left, and you're trailing by 3 points. You should

> a. Go for it
> b. Try for a field goal
> c. Renegotiate your contract

Pretty easy, huh? Everybody kicks a field goal in this situation. Why, it's as normal as blueberry pie. Well, here's a little secret:

If you said *b* or *c*, you're wrong. No, that's not a misprint. You *should* go for it. We're not kidding.

Golly, we *wish* we had the time to explain exactly why, but that'll just have to wait until a later chapter. Don't worry, we'll get back to it.

THE MAJOR MEASURE

But right now we have to talk about the most important measurement of team effectiveness—one you won't find listed in the record manual.

Team rankings for offense and defense (or rushing and passing broken down separately) are usually done by total yards. Another method is to use average yards per attempt, rather than the total. Still a third way to look at offensive and defensive stats is to take the league average in yards gained for each type of play: rush, pass, punt, and the various types of return, and then see how many yards above and below average each team ranks overall.

All of these measures have their uses and tell us something about offenses and defenses. At different places in this book, we'll be using all of them to illustrate something or other. However, none of them measure the actual objective of the game, which is to move the ball down the field willy-nilly and to prevent your opponent from doing the same. In other words, if one of the cornerstones of a football game is field position, you doggone well better come up with an accurate way of measuring your ability to change that position for the better and your opponent's position for the worse.

When your guys have the ball and can choose what to do with it, you're on a drive. It follows then that there is one heck of an advantage to getting your hands on the ball—the drive opportunity. But the way football is set up, the number of drive opportunities each team gets in a game are going to be just about the same. Kickoffs, punts, and most turnovers move the ball from one team's grasp to the other but do not give either team *more* opportunities.

The only ways one team can get "extra" drive opportunities in the normal sixty minutes are (1) to be in possession of the ball at the end of the first half and then receive the kickoff to start the second half; (2) to have the other team turn the ball over on a kickoff or punt return; or (3) to let the other team score a touchdown on a turnover or kick return. All three ways give a team two consecutive opportunities, but the first accomplishes little, the second is fairly rare, and the third is something you don't even want to think about.

Generally, then, we can say that two teams will have about the same number of drive opportunities in a game, whether the final score is 0-0 or 45-7. As the old saying goes, it ain't whatcha got, it's whatcha do with it.

Different styles of play will cause all sorts of variations in the number of plays involved in a successful drive. One team may grind out the yardage and have a fairly low average gain, yet move the ball effectively. Another team might zing down the field lickety-split, using very few plays. The real objective for a team is to gain as many yards on a particular drive as possible—*regardless of the number of plays.*

Thus the best measure of team performance is yards per drive. In 1986, the number of drives per NFL team varied by about plus or minus 10 percent. Now, obviously some teams employ offensive systems that tend to cause a high number of drive opportunities in a game, both for themselves and for their opponents. Such teams usually gain scads of yards and give up equal amounts. They do not necessarily win.

"What profit a team that it gain a touchdown and lose two?"
                                                              —Rockne, V, 7

Meanwhile other, more conservative teams move at a slower pace. They and their opponents hold the ball longer, use up more time, and ultimately have fewer drive opportunities and gain fewer yards. They do not necessarily win, either.

"Render unto the runners the yards that are theirs and unto the passers an occasional flare pass."
                                                              —Hayes, IV, 9

The significant drive figure from 1986 was not the plus or minus 10 percent on the number of drives; it was the plus or minus 20 percent variation on total yards. Some teams were doing a whole lot more with their opportunities than others.

FIGURING DRIVES

Just finding the number of drives for a team can be a hassle. The NFL doesn't keep track of them. However, the number of drives can be reasonably well estimated from available data, with a couple of factors unknown. Here's how you do it: the number will be almost equal to opponents' punts, touchdowns, field goal attempts, safeties, interceptions, and fumbles lost, plus one extra drive for each game. *Explanation:* a team gets the ball to start a drive after each of these actions by an opponent; in addition, every team normally receives a kickoff at the beginning of one half or the other in each game. The number of times a team chooses to kick off after winning the coin toss is practically nonexistent, but overtime games have to be checked for additional kickoffs. There is one figure that isn't known, and that's how many times an opponent was stopped on downs (allowing the other team to take over and start a drive).

Three items should be subtracted from the total, but only one is known, the number of touchdowns a team scores on returns (punt, kickoff, interception, or fumble, and not counting any TDs scored by a team on its own fumbles). The reason these have to be taken out is you've already counted them up as starting drives, but if a team scores a touchdown on a kickoff return, for example, it won't actually start a drive; it will kick off and let the opponent start its drive.

Two figures are unknown in figuring the number of drives. One is when a team fumbles away a kick. If a team fumbles a kickoff, there's just no way, using published data, to know it. So you've credited them with a drive (because of the kickoff), but they don't actually get it. The other unknown is the number of times the clock ran out with a score or turnover as the last play. Again you've counted it as something that would precede a drive, but in fact none follows.

Never fear. In 1986 there were 173 turnovers on downs (not counting 27 interceptions and fumbles on fourth downs), 65 fumbles on returns, and 93 scores as time ran out. They balance out and can be ignored.

Something else to consider, if a drive is in progress at the end of a half, is that the total possible gain can't be realized. Again, these situations should even out by the end of a season. The data given below for 1986 is actual drive data and does not count any drive which was in progress at the end of a half or any yards gained on that drive.

What the data shows is that teams with fewer drives tend to improve their rank on offense but slip on defense compared to where they rank with the traditional system of just adding up the yards. The opposite is true for teams with higher numbers of drives.

OFFENSE

RNK	TEAM	DRIVES	GAIN	PTS	TOTAL		AVERAGE	
1	Miami	173	38	2.4	6324	(2)	6.26	(1)
2	Cincinnati	182	36	2.1	6490	(1)	6.20	(2)
3	Washington	184	34	2.0	5601	(5)	5.36	(6)
4	Minnesota	175	32	2.2	5651	(4)	5.51	(3)
5	San Francisco	191	31	1.7	6082	(3)	5.44	(4)
6	Buffalo	171	31	1.5	5017	(19)	5.21	(8)
7	Seattle	183	30	1.8	5409	(8)	5.38	(5)
8	San Diego	194	30	1.8	5356	(12)	4.84	(18)
9	Chicago	194	30	1.6	5459	(7)	5.22	(7)
10	New York Giants	192	30	1.9	5378	(10)	5.00	(13)
11	New York Jets	192	30	1.8	5375	(11)	5.00	(12)
12	Cleveland	186	29	1.9	5394	(9)	5.15	(10)
13	Denver	184	29	1.8	5216	(15)	5.01	(11)
14	Green Bay	185	28	1.2	5061	(18)	4.93	(17)

RNK	TEAM	DRIVES	GAIN	PTS	TOTAL		AVERAGE	
15	Houston	193	28	1.3	5149	(16)	4.72	(19)
16	L.A. Raiders	203	28	1.4	5299	(14)	4.96	(15)
17	New England	196	28	1.9	5327	(13)	4.96	(14)
18	Atlanta	179	28	1.4	5106	(17)	4.70	(20)
19	New Orleans	188	28	1.5	4742	(21)	4.96	(16)
20	Dallas	198	28	1.7	5474	(6)	5.19	(9)
21	Tampa Bay	180	27	1.3	4361	(27)	4.50	(24)
22	Detroit	183	26	1.5	4555	(24)	4.51	(23)
23	Indianapolis	190	26	1.2	4700	(22)	4.49	(25)
24	Pittsburgh	195	26	1.4	4811	(20)	4.48	(26)
25	L.A. Rams	193	25	1.4	4653	(23)	4.62	(21)
26	St. Louis	177	24	1.1	4503	(26)	4.53	(22)
27	Philadelphia	205	23	1.2	4542	(25)	4.07	(28)
28	Kansas City	197	23	1.5	4218	(28)	4.21	(27)
	League Average	188	29	1.6	5187.6		4.98	

Legend: RNK=NFL rank in average yards per drive; DRIVES=number of drives; GAIN= average yards gained per drive; PTS=average points per drive; TOTAL=total yards gained from scrimmage (NFL ranking in parentheses); AVERAGE=average yards gained per attempt (NFL ranking in parentheses).

DEFENSE

RNK	TEAM	DRIVES	GAIN	PTS	TOTAL		AVERAGE	
1	Chicago	193	22	0.8	4130	(1)	4.12	(1)
2	L.A. Rams	200	25	1.3	4871	(5)	4.69	(6)
3	L.A. Raiders	196	26	1.7	4804	(3)	4.79	(9)
4	New England	195	26	1.5	5181	(16)	5.02	(18)
5	Denver	192	26	1.6	4947	(9)	4.82	(11)
6	Kansas City	206	27	1.4	4934	(8)	4.49	(2)
7	New York Giants	189	27	1.2	4757	(2)	4.78	(8)
8	Philadelphia	200	27	1.4	5224	(17)	5.00	(15)
9	Dallas	191	27	1.6	4985	(10)	4.90	(12)
10	San Francisco	200	28	1.1	4880	(6)	4.60	(3)
11	St. Louis	181	28	1.9	4864	(4)	4.69	(5)
12	Atlanta	180	28	1.4	4908	(7)	5.09	(22)
13	Houston	196	28	1.5	5034	(13)	4.78	(7)
14	Pittsburgh	191	29	1.5	5252	(18)	5.00	(14)
15	New Orleans	183	29	1.5	5102	(14)	4.60	(4)
16	Green Bay	180	29	2.1	5015	(12)	4.82	(10)
17	Buffalo	180	30	1.9	5523	(24)	5.15	(24)
18	Cincinnati	182	30	3.0	5274	(20)	5.01	(17)
19	Minnesota	184	30	1.4	5012	(11)	4.95	(13)
20	Washington	188	30	1.6	5297	(21)	5.06	(20)
21	Cleveland	180	30	1.6	5269	(19)	5.03	(19)
22	San Diego	191	30	1.9	5366	(23)	5.13	(23)
23	Detroit	177	30	1.6	5149	(15)	5.00	(16)
24	Seattle	186	31	1.5	5341	(22)	5.07	(21)
25	Indianapolis	180	32	2.0	5701	(25)	5.42	(25)

RNK	TEAM	DRIVES	GAIN	PTS	TOTAL		AVERAGE	
26	New York Jets	194	34	1.9	6050	(26)	5.60	(26)
27	Miami	175	35	2.3	6050	(26)	5.71	(27)
28	Tampa Bay	176	36	2.5	6333	(28)	5.96	(28)
	League Average	188	29	1.6	5187.6		4.98	

Legend: RNK=NFL rank in average yards per drive; DRIVES=number of drives; GAIN= average yards gained per drive; PTS=average points per drive; TOTAL=total yards gained from scrimmage (NFL ranking in parentheses); AVERAGE=average yards gained per attempt (NFL ranking in parentheses).

Jim Kelly and his Buffalo offense picked up 13 spots as a result of having only 174 drives, 14 below average. The supposedly high-powered Dallas offense dropped 14 places, which certainly reflects their disappointing 7-9 record.

Buddy Ryan's Philadelphia Eagles picked up 9 spots on defense because they had 200 drives to defend against, no doubt at least in part due to their ineffective offense. The Patriots moved up 12 spots, and the Cardinals dropped 7. Reflect for a moment on what those numbers meant for those clubs' 1987 prospects and actual performance.

PART TWO

8

The Joy of Sacks, and Other Mistakes

Explaining about football by starting with the mistakes is kind of like opening a discussion of the *Titanic* with the story of icebergs. But we're on traditional ground here. Every coach starts his pregame interview with "If we can just avoid making mistakes . . ." And after the game, what happened, Coach? "Mistakes killed us!"

If you listen to the coaches, you get the idea that a football game has nothing to do with skill, size, talent, speed, or emotion; it's just a hundred-yard multiple-choice test. Choose the right answers, you win. So how come M.I.T. doesn't produce a lot of top draft choices?

The fact is that many, maybe most, of the "mistakes" made on a football field are really just examples of getting "whupped" by more talented opponents.

Oh, mistakes—real mistakes—happen. When the Vikings' Jim Marshall ran a fumble recovery all the way back to his own goal line, that was a mistake. When Abner Haynes said the Chiefs would kick rather than receive in the overtime championship game, that was a mistake. When the Steelers drafted Darryl Sims number one, *that* was a mistake. Denver's choice of vertically striped socks in 1960—hoo, boy! But these were all in situations where the protagonist had a choice and demonstrably chose wrong.

But if a 250-pound linebacker crunches a 200-pound running back with sufficient force to stun an Indian elephant, is the fumble that follows a "mistake" or simply a natural result of the preceding action? Some backs fumble less often than others, but not because they're smarter. Their ability to hold on to the football better than some of their contemporaries is part of their physical skill. To call a fumble a "mistake" is to denigrate the fumbler as slow-witted and completely ignore the contribution of his opponent.

What are the "mistakes" these coaches complain about? Well, they are almost never the kind where a team runs up the gut when it should throw a screen pass. Of course not. Coaches call the plays for most teams. So the areas where actual choices are made—play calling and defensive formations—are sacrosanct. No, when a coach talks about mistakes, he means those physical events that are outside the norm, things that aren't supposed to happen (but always do). Things like fumbles, interceptions, sacks, and penalties.

Now these things may be results of mistakes. A back may run the wrong route and collide with his quarterback. The fumble that follows was caused by his mistake, but it isn't the mistake itself. If a quarterback underthrows and is intercepted, his estimate of his own arm strength may have been in error. What if the receiver comes back and catches the ball anyway? Whose mistake is that? On a sack, a quarterback may get dumped on his can because his tackle forgot who to block, but if the tackle was simply outmuscled by the defender, let's not say he was "mistaken." Does a hill underestimate a bulldozer?

PENALTIES

Even that *bête-noir* of all coaches, the penalty, is often only a mistake because someone got caught. We checked nearly 2,300 penalties and found this distribution:

Delay of Game	141
Personal Foul	171
Pass Interference	213
Offside	367
Illegal Procedure	668
Holding (and illegal blocks on returns)	735

We're willing to believe that offside and illegal procedure penalties are almost always errors in judgment, otherwise known as mistakes. We'll even stipulate that most delay of game penalties are caused by confusion, although some few—particularly on fourth downs—are intentional.

You've seen the personal foul where one player creams another after the play is over before God, the cameras, and the zebras. Okay, mistake. He lost his head. But most personal fouls, although chalked up to overexuberance, are nothing of the kind. They are carefully calculated acts meant to intimidate, inhibit, or injure. Maybe one out of six is flagged.

Also usually intentional is pass interference. You almost never see a defender interfere with a receiver he has covered. Only when he's already beaten does a defensive back grab a handful of jersey. Ah, you say, isn't the fact that he got beat *prima facie* evidence that he made a mistake? Once in a while, maybe. But usually the defender just got flat-out beat because his reactions or his feet were slower than his opponent's. Give some credit to the receiver. Imagine a track story that begins: "Jones won the hundred-yard dash in 9.6 because the other five men in the race made the mistake of running 9.7."

Finally, we get to holding, the most common of penalties. It's generally agreed that holding takes place somewhere along the line on every play. Only the most flagrant acts get called. Did you ever notice how shocked an offensive lineman looks when he gets flagged? Sure, he's shocked; he's been doing the same thing all day, and *now* they call it! The rules governing blockers' use of their hands have been liberalized, but everybody still holds. Give 'em an inch . . . you know. The only way to eliminate holding penalties is to put 'em all in straitjackets. Not the blockers, the officials! To call holding a mistake is like calling a firing squad an accidental shooting.

But whether penalties are mistakes or intentional is really just terminology. Sorry, Coach. They're going to happen. But, on the bright side, *they don't make a whole lot of difference.* Over the course of a season, they tend to even out. For every drive-killing holding penalty, there's an interference call that keeps a drive going. You can't even show that the least penalized teams will be the most successful. Of the 1980's Super Bowl winners, two had more penalties called against them than the opposition, and three lost more penalty yardage.

		PEN / YDS	OPP / YDS	DIF / YDS
1987	Washington Redskins	82 / 691	98 / 801	+16 / +110
1986	New York Giants	96 / 738	119 / 988	+23 / +250
1985	Chicago Bears	104 / 912	118 / 944	+14 / +32
1984	San Francisco 49ers	100 / 884	91 / 723	−9 / −161
1983	Los Angeles Raiders	121 / 992	109 / 947	−12 / −45
* 1982	Washington Redskins	46 / 404	52 / 419	+6 / +15
1981	San Francisco 49ers	92 / 752	108 / 866	+16 / +114
1980	Oakland Raiders	98 / 929	102 / 922	+4 / −7

* Strike year

The '86 Giants were remarkable for the difference between their penalties and their opponents', but for the most part we don't see any clear connection between avoiding penalties and winning. The timing of a penalty may have an important bearing on an individual game, but so can the timing of anything else—a long run, a fumble, an injury. We can't prove that over the long haul penalties help or hinder teams.

We might theorize that a winning team tends to have a few more penalties called on it, simply because more penalties are called on the offense. Therefore, a winning team—one that spends a lot of time with the ball—may actually be a little ahead by breaking even on penalties. And a losing team that spends more time on defense may be a little behind if its penalties match those of its opponents.

Of course in the real world, losing teams tend to draw more illegal procedure and offside penalties (mistakes) and more holding and pass interference penalties (desperation) than do winning teams.

We broke down more than 2,800 penalties as to whether they were called on the offense or the defense. The results show an advantage for the defense.

	OFFENSE			DEFENSE			TOT	DIFFERENCE	
	PEN	YDS	AVG	PEN	YDS	AVG	PEN	YDS	AVG
Unknown	565	−3164	−5.6	244	1806	7.4	809	−1358	−1.7
Run	348	−2923	−8.4	182	1329	7.3	530	−1594	−3.0
Pass	388	−3337	−8.6	528	5597	10.6	916	2260	2.5
Punt	49	−255	−5.2	41	226	5.5	90	−29	−0.3
Field Goal	5	−35	−7.0	9	50	5.6	14	15	1.1
Kickoffs	105	−536	−5.1	43	314	7.3	148	−222	−1.5
Returns	269	−2609	−9.7	43	525	12.2	312	−2084	−6.7
Total	1729	−12859	−7.4	1090	9847	9.0	2819	−3012	−1.1
Per Game	7.6	−57.4	—	4.9	44.0	—	12.6	−13.4	—
Per Team	61.8	−459.3	—	38.9	351.7	—	100.6	−107.6	—
P/Tm-P/Gm	3.9	−28.7	—	2.4	22.0	—	6.3	−6.7	—

The yards in the chart above are given in relation to offensive yardage. Plus yards advance the ball and minus yards move it back. The "unknown" penalties represent those for delay of game (mostly called before a play was run), and those where the play-by-play account of the game did not say what kind of play was run when the penalty was called.

Perhaps the most interesting thing is not that the offense comes up short by 3,012 total yards. After all, that breaks down to a -6.7 for each team per game (P/Tm-P/Gm), and that's not much of a difference. But what is surprising—at first—is that the offense actually comes out ahead of the defense on pass plays by an average of 2.5 yards per penalty. When you think about it, though, it makes sense. The longest penalty for the offense would be holding; the defense is more likely to get hit by a long interference penalty or a nasty personal foul. Add in the fact that the defense is more likely to be offsides, and you can see why the defense gets penalized more often and for more yards on passes.

Is there a message here? Well, if you're a coach who's absolutely paranoid about penalties, have your team pass all the time. There are more penalties on pass plays, but many more are called on the defense. And if your quarterback throws a lot of interceptions, you can still start your Monday morning interview with "Mistakes killed us!"

FUMBLES AND INTERCEPTIONS

Turnovers are overrated. They're important, just not as important as everyone thinks. Early in the '87 season, one of those national college score shows (sorry, we can't tell them apart) led its story of Memphis State's upset of Alabama with the news that the 'Bama quarterback threw three interceptions. Ah-hah! we said, 'Bama lost on turnovers. But then the host of the show (sorry, we can't tell them apart) added that 'Bama three times drove to inside the Memphis State 5 yard line without scoring. In that Memphis State won by three points, we have a strong feeling that those three goal line stands might have had more to do with their win than the three interceptions. A little bit later in the same score show (whatever it was), the same host (whoever he was) raved about the "great day" by some western college quarterback (sorry . . .), but we noticed the guy's stats included two interceptions.

As nearly as we can see, turnovers are important sometimes because they're a way to explain away a loss. It's easier for a coach to say his team lacks concentration than talent. Every team has turnovers, but unless they get up to five or six in a game, a good team will win in spite of them. It's not that good teams don't make mistakes (if you want to call turnovers mistakes); it's just that good teams make up for them with other outstanding plays.

In 1986 the Bears had just as many giveaways as takeaways. But they also had a rock-solid defense that allowed the fewest points ever over a 16-game season. So when they gave the ball away, they had just gutted it up and stopped their opponents cold. If they exchanged turnovers all day long with a lesser team, they'd have beat the poor guys' brains out.

In the chart below, we list the takeaway/giveaway ratio for all NFL teams for three years, along with their won-lost records. Generally the teams with the better ratios have the better records and the poorer ratios go with the losers, just as you'd expect. As a general rule it is better to have fewer fumbles and interceptions than your opponents. All that proves is that better teams tend to come up on the right side of takeaway/giveaway (TG below). It's a symptom of success more than a cause of it.

But how do you explain the Raiders?

	1986		1985		1984		TOTALS	
	TG	W-L-T	TG	W-L-T	TG	W-L-T	TG	W-L-T
Chicago	0	14-2-0	+23	15-1-0	+3	10-6-0	+26	39- 9-0
San Francisco	+20	10-5-1	+1	10-6-0	+16	15-1-0	+37	35-12-1
Denver	+6	11-5-0	+5	11-5-0	+21	13-3-0	+32	35-13-0
Miami	−10	8-8-0	0	12-4-0	+8	14-2-0	−2	34-14-0
N.Y. Giants	+11	14-2-0	−1	10-6-0	+8	9-7-0	+18	33-15-0
Washington	−4	12-4-0	−6	10-6-0	+15	11-5-0	+5	33-15-0
L.A. Rams	+6	10-6-0	+11	11-5-0	+4	10-6-0	+21	31-17-0
L.A. Raiders	−11	8-8-0	−8	12-4-0	−14	11-5-0	−43	31-17-0
New England	+16	11-5-0	+5	11-5-0	−4	9-7-0	+17	31-17-0
Seattle	+9	10-6-0	−3	8-8-0	+24	12-4-0	+30	30-18-0
N.Y. Jets	+1	10-6-0	+13	11-5-0	−1	7-9-0	+13	28-20-0
Dallas	−6	7-9-0	+7	10-6-0	+1	9-7-0	+2	26-22-0
Cincinnati	−8	10-6-0	+9	7-9-0	+1	8-8-0	+2	25-23-0
Cleveland	+13	12-4-0	−9	8-8-0	−4	5-11-0	0	25-23-0
Kansas City	+14	10-6-0	+7	6-10-0	+4	8-8-0	+25	24-24-0
Pittsburgh	−3	6-10-0	−2	7-9-0	+2	9-7-0	−3	22-26-0
Green Bay	−13	4-12-0	−5	8-8-0	+5	8-8-0	−13	20-28-0
Minnesota	+13	9-7-0	−3	7-9-0	−12	3-13-0	−2	19-29-0
New Orleans	0	7-9-0	+1	5-11-0	−18	7-9-0	−17	19-29-0
San Diego	−12	4-12-0	−7	8-8-0	−2	7-9-0	−21	19-29-0

	1986		1985		1984		TOTALS	
	TG	W-L-T	TG	W-L-T	TG	W-L-T	TG	W-L-T
Philadelphia	+9	5-10-1	−8	7-9-0	−2	6-9-1	−1	18-28-2
St. Louis	−7	4-11-1	−7	5-11-0	−3	9-7-0	−17	18-29-1
Detroit	+4	5-11-0	−5	7-9-0	−11	4-11-1	−12	16-31-1
Atlanta	+3	7-8-1	+4	4-12-0	−9	4-12-0	−2	15-32-1
Houston	−11	5-11-0	−2	5-11-0	−7	3-13-0	−20	13-35-0
Indianapolis	−9	3-13-0	−1	5-11-0	−7	4-12-0	−17	12-36-0
Tampa Bay	−10	2-14-0	−8	2-14-0	−11	6-10-0	−29	10-38-0
Buffalo	−21	4-12-0	−17	2-14-0	−7	2-14-0	−46	8-40-0

Well, here's how we explain it. The Raiders run a high-risk offense. In simple terms, that means they take chances in order to pick up large chunks of territory. They can score fast and in great abundance. If they have to lose the ball sometimes, well, that's a risk they are willing to take. They'll give up one touchdown to score two.

The same "hell-fer-leather" approach probably wouldn't do at all for a team with different personnel. For example, San Francisco can control the ball for long stretches at a time. It's important to the 49ers that they hold their turnovers to a minimum because turnovers disrupt their offense much more than losing the ball disrupts the Raiders'.

If the 49ers invest ten plays in a drive and then lose the ball on a turnover, it will take them a while to get the ball back and put another drive together. There are only so many minutes in a football game, so they have to capitalize on their drives. The Raiders figure they can go eighty yards in three or four plays, so an occasional turnover isn't a major disaster. It's a matter of philosophy.

In other words, turnovers mean different things to different teams. They hurt conservative offenses more than they hurt high-risk ones. Therefore, a strong team with a conservative offense will concentrate on holding on to the ball and will normally have a high positive ratio in turnovers. A strong team with a high-risk offense will sometimes have more giveaways than takeaways and not worry about it.

So much for theory.

Now for a complaint. In its published statistics, the NFL lumps all its fumbles together, giving the impression that they all occurred on running plays. Well, you know better than that. You've seen fumbles on returns and completed passes. What you can't tell from the published stats is the likelihood of fumbling in different situations.

We tracked over 431 turnover fumbles, first throwing out 30 that occurred as bobbles on the snap because we couldn't know what kind of play would have followed. Of the 401 remaining turnovers, 177

(44.1 percent) came on running plays. That broke down to 1.3 fumbles lost for every 100 rushes. Nearly as many, 155 (38.7 percent) came on passing plays. Of these, 69 were made by the passer, either when he was sacked or flushed out of the pocket, and 86 were made by receivers after they caught passes. The remaining fumbles: 35 were on punt returns, 25 on kickoff returns, 5 on pass interception returns, and 4 on botched kicks.

Do fumbles occur more often on any particular down? Not really. We put the bobbles back in and counted up all the fumbles lost on ball-control plays. The numbers: first down, 151; second down, 126; third down, 78; fourth down, 7. The number of fumbles goes down, but that is only because there are more first downs run over a season than second downs, more seconds than thirds, and more thirds than fourths.

The most interesting information we can derive from this is an estimate of what a team loses on average each time it fumbles. By examining thousands of first downs, second downs, and so on, we can see a "net yards expected" for each situation—how far a team might expect to move the ball down the field under normal circumstances. The details are a little involved, so we'll explain how we arrived at the figure in a note at the end of this chapter. For now we'll simply tell you that a fumble costs a team 50 yards (in round numbers).

Surprisingly interceptions are slightly less expensive, although they are much more common. Our calculations indicate an interception will cost a team about 45 yards. Again a full explanation will be found in the note at the end. For now we'll simply say that an interception normally happens farther down the field than a fumble.

We found a slightly higher likelihood of an interception on third down than on first or second and a much higher chance of interception on fourth down. We took all the pass plays and intended pass plays (sacks and those times when the passer was forced to run) on each down and found the following interception percentages:

DOWN	PASS PLAYS	INT	PCT INT
1	6025	212	3.52
2	5188	174	3.35
3	4527	179	3.95
4	196	14	7.14
Total	15936	579*	3.63

* There were also 2 interceptions on fourth-down fake field goal attempts.

Truthfully we expected a higher discrepancy, figuring there would be many more risky passes tried on third and fourth downs. Apparently NFL quarterbacks are even more cautious than we expected.

Should they be? Well, we said turnovers were overrated. In the NFL, it takes about 12 yards of offense to add a point on the scoreboard. Figuring 50 yards for a fumble and 45 for an interception, that means a team must give the ball away two more times than its opponent to lose (about) one touchdown. For a weak team, that can be fatal. But a team strong in all other categories can easily survive a few turnovers.

SACKS

A sack used to be just an important defensive accomplishment. Maybe a teammate would pat the sacker on the rump and mumble, "Nice play." And everybody would get ready for the next play. But somewhere along the way the sack evolved into an occasion for a tribal ceremony, with the sacker leaping, gyrating, pointing, and dancing, while his fellow bacchants high-five all over the place. Supermarkets have opened with less fanfare.

Gee, guys, it's *only* a sack. The NFL even passed a rule that was supposed to limit sack celebrations. Maybe it limited them a little— kept them from passing out party hats or something. Assuming that the quarterback, hereafter known as the sackee, is able to get up after the play, what exactly has a sack accomplished? For example, suppose it's third and 10 at the 50. The sack moves the ball back 7 yards. How much more has the sack accomplished than a plain old incomplete pass? We'll tell you—seven yards. Big deal!

But sometimes the dancers are justified.

Actually the key to a sack's value is where it occurs, and to some extent when. Any sack perpetrated within the other guy's territory on third down is only worth the yards lost. He'll have to punt and you can deduct the sack yardage from what he can expect in the exchange. Seven or so yards is hardly an occasion for wild rejoicing.

On first or second down in the opponents' territory, the value of a sack goes up slightly because it limits the opponent's options. Example: on second-and-7 at his 30, he can call any number of different plays. He can run or pass. But if you sack him and he faces a third-and-14, what option is left? Pass. And you, the defense, know it. We can forgive you a small celebration.

A sack accomplished on your side of the 50 is worth a great deal more than just the yardage, particularly on third down.

A first- or second-down sack restricts your opponent's options; a third-down sack ends them. Sack him on third and he loses the chance to go for a first down; he must settle for a punt or a field goal, depending on the yard line. Either way, you've deprived him of points he was already mentally putting on the scoreboard. Go ahead, dance!

We wouldn't mind a rule limiting sack dances to only those sacks on the defender's side of the 50.

The real value of a pass rush isn't measured by its sacks. The real value is that it makes it harder for an offense to complete deep passes. A good pass rush makes the passer throw early, sometimes before a receiver is open. It will reduce his options because he won't have time to pick out his second or third receiver. Sacks are a kind of badge, and we assume a team with a high sack total has also hurried the rival passer the rest of the day.

But in point of fact, a pass rush could do an excellent job for an entire game without once sacking the passer. If they force an opponent into a short passing game, hurry the passer into a few interceptions, cause a couple of other passes to fall incomplete, they may never get to dance, but they're definitely calling the tune.

Another thing that should be mentioned about a rush line with a high sack total is that somebody in the defensive backfield is doing a heckuva good job. If the receivers are open, no NFL QB is going to get sacked. Sacks happen when the passer has to hold on to the ball for an extra second because he can't find an open receiver. So the defensive secondary deserves as much credit for a sack as the dancing bear who pummels the QB. If one is missing, they'll both be missing.

One thing we always wondered was whether sacks were more common at one end of the field than the other. This becomes more important when we realize that a sack in the defender's territory hurts an offense more than a sack at the other end of the field. It always seems that *our* quarterback gets sacked at the most inopportune moment. We wondered if there might not be a Bermuda Triangle for quarterbacks, an area of the field where he was more likely to disappear beneath enemy jerseys.

The answer appears to be no, allowing for the number of passes attempted. We set up the following chart to apply to all pass plays, not just those that get into the air. In the first column, we broke the field into five-yard segments, moving down the field toward the goal line.

The second column, PASS PLAYS, includes every play that started off as a pass: actual attempts, sacks, and those times the passer was forced to run. (The latter category is recorded as a rush officially because the passer gets past the line of scrimmage.) The next several columns give the totals for pass attempts, completions, touchdown passes, interceptions, sacks, and forced runs.

The final three columns are percentage of sacks and forces (%S-F), completion percentage, and interception percentage, *all related to the total pass plays rather than the pass attempts.*

YD-LN	PASS PLAYS	PASS ATT	COMP	TD	IN	SACK	FORCE RUN	%S-F	COMP PCT	INT PCT
0-5	100	97	55	0	8	2	1	3.0	55.0	8.0
6-10	250	235	135	0	8	11	6	6.8	54.0	3.2
11-15	459	408	231	1	15	46	5	11.1	50.3	3.3
16-20	1163	1052	633	6	40	83	28	9.5	54.4	3.4
21-25	1179	1069	631	3	44	88	22	9.3	53.5	3.7
26-30	1349	1201	694	8	51	110	38	11.0	51.4	3.8
31-35	1373	1241	741	11	42	103	29	9.6	54.0	3.1
36-40	1325	1187	661	5	35	113	25	10.4	49.9	2.6
41-45	1214	1025	578	11	46	87	26	9.3	47.6	3.8
46-50	1174	997	556	8	50	79	26	8.9	47.4	4.3
51-55	1138	964	526	20	33	74	36	9.7	46.2	2.9
56-60	878	776	435	21	27	82	20	11.6	49.5	3.1
61-65	860	790	421	31	32	56	14	8.1	49.0	3.7
66-70	739	669	342	32	31	54	15	9.3	46.3	4.2
71-75	730	657	329	32	33	62	12	10.1	45.1	4.5
76-80	590	535	293	53	19	43	12	9.3	49.7	3.2
81-85	561	524	269	79	19	30	7	6.6	48.0	3.4
86-90	456	422	188	79	22	29	5	7.5	41.2	4.8
91-95	393	359	140	92	17	26	8	8.7	43.3	4.3
96-100	215	204	106	90	7	11	0	5.1	49.3	3.3
	15936	14412	7964	582	579	1189	335	9.6	50.0	3.6

And what conclusions do we draw? Well, not much. The percentages do not yield any real surprises. The completion percentage drops slightly as a team moves down the field, but this probably means nothing more than that teams take a few more chances as they get away from their own goal line. A sack (or force) seems about as likely to happen at either 25-yard line.

On the other hand, the likelihood of a sack goes up with the down. On first down, 5.1 percent of pass plays end in sacks; on second down, 7.2 percent; third down, 9.3; and fourth down, 8.7. This is obviously because the later downs are more often "passing situations," and the defense reacts accordingly.

The yards to go are also part of a "passing situation." The chart below shows the sacks, pass plays (including sacks and forced runs), and the percentage sacks for different downs with yards-to-go broken into five-yard increments.

YDS TO GO	First and SAK	P-PL	PCT	Second and SAK	P-PL	PCT	Third and SAK	P-PL	PCT	Fourth and SAK	P-PL	PCT	Summary SAK	P-PL	PCT
1-5	5	110	4.5	53	915	5.8	103	1397	7.4	5	93	5.4	166	2515	6.6
6-10	283	5644	5.0	231	3201	7.2	200	2045	9.8	8	60	13.3	722	10950	6.6
11-15	8	111	7.2	56	683	8.2	68	637	10.7	3	21	14.3	135	1452	9.3
16-20	6	143	4.2	23	307	7.5	38	319	11.9	1	12	8.3	68	781	8.7
21-	3	15	20.0	8	78	10.3	11	128	8.6	0	10	0.0	22	231	9.5
	305	6023	5.1	371	5184	7.2	420	4526	9.3	17	196	8.7	1113	15929	7.0

TO REVIEW

Even though we haven't found the Great Truth about winning (and losing) football, we can draw some conclusions about the various values or penalties of the various "mistakes" that coaches cry over.

Penalties. Generally the offense is more often flagged and loses more yardage on penalties than the defense. This may sometimes have the curious effect of causing successful teams to be penalized more often than unsuccessful teams because strong teams are on offense more often. But over the long haul, it is likely that poor teams "goof" more often and negate the effect.

An exception to the rule that the offense is more often penalized occurs on pass plays, where the defense is more penalized.

Although a particular penalty may occur at a particular time, and may have some effect on a particular game, over the course of a season any advantage tends to even out.

Turnovers. Although overrated as a source of victory or defeat, turnovers do have a measurable effect: a fumble costs 50 yards; an interception, 45. In general, a positive ratio of two turnovers will make about a touchdown's difference. However, because of different offensive philosophies, turnovers do not affect all teams equally. Conservative offenses are hurt more by turnovers than high-risk offenses. And obviously, teams with weak defenses are hurt more.

Sacks. Despite the celebration that follows every sack, the value of the sack itself to the defense depends on where and when it occurs. A sack on the defense's side of the 50-yard line is more valuable, particularly on third down, than a sack on the far side of the 50. A sack on third down on the far side is worth slightly less than a sack on first or second down.

The frequency of sacks does not seem to be affected by the yard line. However, as the down number and yards-to-go increase, the sack frequency increases.

A NOTE ON NET YARDS EXPECTED

The figures for turnovers cited in this chapter are based on the Net Yards Expected Table that derives from our analysis of play-by-play data on the basis of down (first through fourth) and yardage to go (1 through 25). For those who are technically oriented, these 100 down/to-go situations are detailed in the table that concludes this note; for the rest of us folks, we'll concentrate on the last three columns, of which only the last is used in these calculations.

The "0 PTS" column gives the average number of yards gained from the down in question until a punt, missed field goal, or turnover ends a drive. For example, a situation of first down and 10 yards to go yields an average of 15.6 yards in a nonscoring drive.

The "+ PTS" column gives the average yards gained from the down in question for a drive that culminates in a touchdown or field goal. Here, we recorded 951 situations of second-and-7; those that eventually ended in scores averaged 30.9 yards.

The NET column is the important one here. It gives a weighted average of yards gained from the down and yards to go in question based on the following algorithm:

For a punt, the gain is: the number of yards subsequently gained from scrimmage; plus the average length of punts (41 yards); minus the average length of returns—including fair catches, touchbacks, etc. —(6 yards); or a net of 35.

For a missed field goal or turnover, just the number of yards gained from scrimmage is counted. The average scrimmage line on a missed field goal is the 26, and the average return (nearly all touchbacks) is 27.

Scores were a little more complicated. For a touchdown, we gave a credit of 12 yards per point, or 84 yards. We then subtracted 26 yards for the average field position after the kickoff. This gave a net of 58 yards in bonuses. We then added the actual yards gained on the drive from the present point to the score. For a field goal, we gave a 12 × 3 or 36-yard bonus; plus we added in 17 yards for the score (because an average successful field goal is from the 17-yard line), and then subtracted 26 for the kickoff return, making a total of 27 yards in bonuses, plus the yards gained from scrimmage.

Thus the average is the net yards gained from scrimmage plus 35 for each punt, 27 for each field goal, and 58 for each TD, all divided by the number of plays.

Looking at this on a down-by-down basis, you get about 55 yards on first down, 50 on second, 45 on third, and 30 on fourth. This includes any yards gained from scrimmage between the down in question and the end of the drive. Of course, this varies with the yards-to-go, with a higher number for fewer yards-to-go.

Fumbles tend to occur earlier in the sequence, but only slightly. The data shows fumbles on these downs (1-151, 2-126, 3-78, 4-7) and interceptions on these downs (1-212, 2-174, 3-179, 4-14). The average expected yards for each of them is close enough to 50 to use it as a round number.

For interceptions, the ball is thrown on an average 19 yards downfield. The average return is 13 yards, including touchbacks. A fumble is essentially turned over on the spot (average gain for the fumbling team before the fumble is $+2$ yards for a rushing play, -8 for a passer fumble, and $+11$ for a receiver fumble; the return for the recovering team averages one yard). Therefore, a fumble should be a -50 penalty; an interception -45.

NET YARDS EXPECTED TABLE

DOWN/TOGO	NO	YDS	1ST	TD	FG	MFG	PUNT	PEN	TD	FG	MFG	PUNT	TURN	OPTD	SAFE	TIME	0 PTS	+ PTS	NET
1 1	119	1.2	84.9	58	1	0	0	5	98	14	0	1	5	1	0	2	0.0	1.2	52.4
1 2	68	2.0	82.4	23	2	0	0	8	51	11	1	0	5	0	0	0	0.5	2.2	49.9
1 3	50	2.4	80.0	12	0	0	0	3	38	7	0	0	3	2	0	0	1.8	2.5	50.3
1 4	79	3.8	83.5	24	0	0	0	6	60	11	2	0	6	0	0	0	6.1	3.5	51.6
1 5	183	17.5	76.5	20	0	1	0	4	88	27	14	23	27	4	0	4	14.3	19.4	53.8
1 6	62	4.3	72.6	7	0	0	0	4	43	12	0	1	6	0	0	1	4.4	4.3	50.3
1 7	72	3.4	61.1	8	0	0	0	4	39	19	4	0	9	1	0	2	-2.1	4.7	41.9
1 8	88	6.6	59.1	8	0	0	0	4	49	20	2	0	17	0	0	0	7.2	6.5	45.1
1 9	68	5.1	57.4	4	1	0	0	5	36	23	2	0	7	0	0	2	0.0	5.9	44.9
1 10	11776	25.0	67.6	178	11	8	0	670	2938	1811	781	3760	2339	133	14	561	15.6	38.8	54.8
1 11	9	28.6	77.8	3	0	0	0	0	4	0	0	4	1	0	0	0	25.2	32.8	69.9
1 12	5	8.0	40.0	1	0	0	0	0	1	1	2	1	0	0	0	0	-2.3	23.5	32.0
1 13	5	31.0	60.0	0	0	0	0	0	3	0	0	2	0	0	0	1	3.5	49.3	79.8
1 14	9	23.4	44.4	0	0	0	0	1	2	4	0	1	2	0	0	0	12.3	29.0	52.2
1 15	166	22.7	50.6	1	0	1	0	8	34	25	9	68	28	1	1	5	14.0	38.5	53.0
1 16	8	31.8	62.5	0	0	0	0	0	2	2	0	2	1	1	0	0	19.8	43.8	61.8
1 17	6	2.3	0.0	0	0	0	0	0	0	0	0	4	1	1	0	1	2.3	0.0	25.7

			THIS PLAY						DRIVE END											
DOWN/TOGO	NO	YDS	1ST	TD	FG	MFG	PUNT	PEN	TD	FG	MFG	PUNT	TURN	OPTD	SAFE	TIME	0	PTS	+PTS	NET
1 18	14	20.4	42.9	0	0	0	0	0	0	4	0	8	2	0	0		0	15.5	32.8	48.1
1 19	11	12.2	27.3	0	0	0	0	1	0	4	0	7	3	0	0		0	12.2	12.0	36.9
1 20	203	25.6	47.8	1	0	0	0	9	36	31	17	73	44	2	0		8	16.8	43.3	52.5
1 21	4	20.3	25.0	0	0	0	0	0	0	1	0	3	0	0	0		0	8.7	55.0	53.3
1 22	2	24.0	50.0	0	0	0	0	0	0	1	0	1	0	0	0		0	31.0	17.0	55.0
1 23	1	24.0	100.0	0	0	0	0	0	0	0	0	1	0	0	0		0	24.0	0.0	24.0
1 24	2	12.0	50.0	0	0	0	0	0	1	0	1	0	0	0	0		0	−5.0	29.0	41.0
1 25	15	19.7	40.0	0	0	0	0	2	1	3	5	1	4	0	1		1	12.5	39.5	31.3

			THIS PLAY						DRIVE END											
DOWN/TOGO	NO	YDS	1ST	TD	FG	MFG	PUNT	PEN	TD	FG	MFG	PUNT	TURN	OPTD	SAFE	TIME	0	PTS	+PTS	NET
2 1	553	17.7	87.3	75	2	0	0	31	218	95	33	105	96	5	1		19	12.3	21.9	51.9
2 2	434	19.2	82.9	30	0	0	0	33	165	71	31	97	65	4	1		15	12.1	25.1	53.5
2 3	494	20.3	76.9	14	0	0	0	27	145	76	28	142	97	6	0		15	14.0	28.1	51.5
2 4	662	22.3	74.3	27	1	0	0	47	195	118	42	183	120	4	0		23	14.6	31.0	53.9
2 5	732	22.1	70.6	21	0	0	0	30	227	143	43	203	112	4	0		27	12.4	31.5	55.0
2 6	843	18.9	61.9	27	1	0	0	55	217	150	61	282	123	10	0		23	9.6	30.9	50.3
2 7	951	18.2	58.4	28	0	1	0	65	214	149	64	358	151	12	3		31	10.4	30.9	48.6
2 8	889	19.2	56.9	21	1	1	0	57	193	141	63	358	125	8	1		28	11.2	32.5	50.2
2 9	692	18.2	50.6	22	0	0	0	47	147	97	56	278	101	10	3		17	10.7	31.8	48.3
2 10	2239	19.3	50.4	41	7	4	0	150	439	317	134	841	469	38	0	1	74	12.2	33.3	47.6
2 11	334	18.8	49.1	7	0	0	0	17	69	51	18	149	42	4	1		16	9.2	35.8	50.5
2 12	211	17.9	47.4	1	0	0	0	15	40	39	12	93	26	1	0		32	9.1	32.6	49.3
2 13	172	17.9	45.3	3	0	0	0	12	34	22	8	75	31	2	0		10	9.8	34.7	48.1
2 14	127	16.1	33.9	2	0	0	0	7	16	16	10	58	27	0	0		5	10.4	33.0	42.8
2 15	153	15.6	36.6	7	1	0	0	6	21	17	5	78	29	1	2		1	10.1	32.2	44.4
2 16	82	19.2	42.7	4	0	0	0	8	17	16	7	38	7	1	0		4	7.6	36.5	52.7
2 17	88	15.8	31.8	1	0	0	0	5	10	14	4	48	11	1	0		2	8.7	34.7	45.8
2 18	78	16.7	30.8	1	0	0	0	5	11	8	3	40	15	1	0		5	9.6	38.7	45.6
2 19	65	21.2	35.4	1	0	0	0	2	6	10	6	26	17	0	0		1	15.7	38.1	44.7
2 20	126	20.1	34.9	3	0	0	0	17	22	7	9	61	25	2	0		0	13.0	43.8	48.7
2 21	28	17.1	32.1	1	0	0	0	2	4	2	1	15	6	0	0		0	11.3	38.7	46.1
2 22	11	7.5	0.0	0	0	0	0	2	0	0	0	10	1	0	0		3	7.5	0.0	39.3
2 23	11	15.6	18.2	0	0	0	0	0	0	4	0	5	2	0	0		0	17.9	11.8	41.4
2 24	13	14.8	30.8	0	0	0	0	1	2	2	2	5	2	0	0		0	3.2	40.8	41.3
2 25	56	11.5	10.7	0	0	0	1	5	3	5	5	32	10	0	1		1	9.7	22.3	37.0

			THIS PLAY						DRIVE END											
DOWN/TOGO	NO	YDS	1ST	TD	FG	MFG	PUNT	PEN	TD	FG	MFG	PUNT	TURN	OPTD	SAFE	TIME	0	PTS	+PTS	NET
3 1	720	15.7	74.3	62	2	1	0	56	202	109	29	235	139	6	0		18	11.3	21.6	47.5
3 2	513	15.4	61.0	26	1	1	0	47	127	95	29	184	80	8	0		11	7.9	25.4	46.7
3 3	463	13.5	53.1	24	2	0	0	33	102	92	30	176	57	6	0		11	6.7	23.0	45.0
3 4	471	14.1	54.1	27	3	0	0	32	98	86	30	185	65	7	0		7	8.3	23.2	44.9
3 5	484	13.8	46.5	19	1	1	0	37	104	74	28	206	64	8	0		18	6.7	26.0	45.3
3 6	524	14.0	43.1	20	1	0	0	42	103	94	31	238	53	4	1		14	5.9	27.4	46.1
3 7	474	12.1	37.1	16	0	0	0	41	58	77	41	238	59	1	0		11	6.4	26.3	41.1
3 8	467	11.4	33.8	12	2	1	0	41	65	76	35	222	61	7	1		3	5.5	24.9	40.5
3 9	359	12.1	33.4	9	0	0	0	25	46	50	29	186	44	2	2		8	6.2	28.4	41.4
3 10	663	11.2	29.9	18	3	3	0	50	79	98	40	298	136	12	0		21	6.6	23.8	37.8
3 11	229	11.7	31.0	3	1	0	0	28	27	40	11	123	25	2	1		3	4.8	28.6	42.1
3 12	184	12.5	32.6	11	2	0	0	15	30	30	14	90	17	3	0		2	5.1	28.0	43.5
3 13	153	9.6	22.2	6	0	0	0	16	15	19	8	90	18	1	2		9	5.3	25.0	39.3
3 14	131	10.4	21.4	2	2	1	0	16	13	19	13	67	17	1	1		7	6.3	23.0	38.0
3 15	124	8.8	17.7	3	0	1	0	12	11	18	9	75	9	1	1		4	2.9	28.3	39.1
3 16	111	8.1	18.0	1	0	0	0	13	8	10	11	72	9	1	0		1	4.1	29.3	37.5
3 17	72	9.0	18.1	2	0	0	0	6	5	6	1	52	8	0	0		1	4.9	32.0	40.6
3 18	68	8.8	11.8	1	0	0	0	9	4	5	4	44	10	0	1		2	5.8	29.0	36.9
3 19	75	10.2	17.3	1	1	0	0	8	5	7	6	44	12	1	0		2	6.4	29.9	37.1
3 20	79	9.8	17.7	1	0	0	0	7	4	9	4	51	10	1	0		1	6.8	24.8	38.4

DOWN/TOGO	NO	YDS	1ST	THIS PLAY					DRIVE END								0 PTS	+ PTS	NET
				TD	FG	MFG	PUNT	PEN	TD	FG	MFG	PUNT	TURN	OPTD	SAFE	TIME			
3 21	40	15.6	20.0	2	0	0	1	3	4	8	1	20	6	1	0	1	11.2	25.8	44.3
3 22	22	8.1	9.1	1	0	0	0	1	2	0	0	19	1	0	0	1	3.7	52.5	43.6
3 23	19	3.1	5.3	0	0	0	0	2	0	3	3	12	1	0	0	1	2.4	6.3	29.4
3 24	25	7.9	16.0	0	0	1	0	4	1	2	4	15	3	0	0	0	5.1	28.3	33.4
3 25	85	8.9	9.4	0	0	0	0	7	1	7	4	59	13	0	1	0	8.6	11.0	36.1

DOWN/TOGO	NO	YDS	1ST	THIS PLAY					DRIVE END								0 PTS	+ PTS	NET
				TD	FG	MFG	PUNT	PEN	TD	FG	MFG	PUNT	TURN	OPTD	SAFE	TIME			
4 1	385	5.4	30.4	17	40	11	149	28	64	64	15	170	72	0	0	5	1.4	13.4	34.9
4 2	260	2.8	10.4	3	43	12	146	24	14	49	10	155	27	5	0	3	0.8	9.1	31.9
4 3	229	1.8	7.4	2	47	12	131	16	5	51	15	138	20	0	0	2	1.7	2.4	30.2
4 4	228	0.6	5.3	2	50	15	133	16	5	52	16	136	15	4	0	0	-0.0	2.4	28.9
4 5	217	0.7	4.1	0	34	21	139	9	3	38	20	139	15	2	0	1	0.0	3.5	28.6
4 6	246	0.6	2.8	0	51	18	163	7	2	52	17	166	8	1	0	2	0.6	0.5	30.4
4 7	273	1.2	5.1	3	38	31	175	19	8	43	31	184	6	1	0	1	0.2	5.5	30.8
4 8	237	0.4	1.7	0	31	23	168	7	1	33	23	168	9	3	0	1	-0.0	3.1	29.2
4 9	208	1.0	4.3	1	28	16	148	8	3	30	17	149	8	1	0	0	0.4	4.0	30.8
4 10	280	1.0	2.9	2	44	15	185	9	2	43	16	187	27	5	0	2	1.1	0.8	29.0
4 11	125	0.6	1.6	0	18	9	90	7	0	20	9	91	2	1	2	0	-0.3	4.9	30.4
4 12	120	-0.2	2.5	0	19	8	82	7	2	20	7	85	5	0	1	0	-0.1	-0.2	30.1
4 13	111	0.9	0.9	0	8	11	86	3	0	8	11	84	6	2	0	4	1.0	0.0	29.4
4 14	91	0.5	2.2	0	12	7	65	5	0	12	7	70	2	0	0	1	0.5	0.0	30.9
4 15	91	0.5	1.1	0	13	5	64	2	0	13	5	64	6	3	0	1	0.6	0.0	29.0
4 16	85	0.6	2.4	0	4	11	63	3	1	4	11	65	4	0	0	0	0.0	11.0	29.4
4 17	63	0.6	1.6	0	2	4	50	3	0	3	4	53	3	0	0	0	-0.0	12.3	31.1
4 18	71	0.2	1.4	0	6	4	56	3	0	6	5	56	2	2	0	0	0.2	0.0	30.1
4 19	48	1.2	6.3	0	2	2	36	5	1	3	2	38	3	1	0	0	0.5	9.0	31.8
4 20	56	-0.1	0.0	0	6	4	43	3	0	6	4	43	1	2	0	0	-0.1	0.0	29.7
4 21	36	3.3	0.0	0	4	1	27	0	0	4	1	27	4	0	0	0	3.7	0.0	32.5
4 22	25	0.1	0.0	0	2	1	19	2	0	2	1	20	1	1	0	0	0.1	0.0	30.2
4 23	28	0.5	0.0	0	3	0	21	2	0	3	0	23	2	0	0	0	0.5	0.0	32.1
4 24	19	1.5	5.3	0	2	0	13	2	0	2	0	15	2	0	0	0	1.7	0.0	32.0
4 25	100	1.9	4.0	0	3	4	86	4	1	4	4	86	3	1	1	0	0.7	24.6	33.6

9

Special Teams

The special teams aren't on the field as long as the "regulars." The offense and defense are both out there for many more minutes, but the "teams" have such potential for success or disaster that they exert an influence on the final score far out of proportion to their actual playing time.

They used to be called "suicide squads," but the word around the NFL is "special"—as in out of the ordinary. One national magazine even went so far as to call the special teams the "secret weapon" of last season. Actually they're about as secret as a recipe for hamburger because coaches and fans alike have known about them for years. Every NFL team has a special teams coach. Teams have even begun drafting players for their special teams abilities. And some folks rate "the teams" as one-third of a club's strength (or weakness).

There are six "teams" that can be labeled as "special," although they involve mostly the same players. They pair up nicely into three groups, each having something to do with kicking. The kickers and kick returners are listed as "specialists," as are the holders (for place kicks) and the guys who snap the ball. Everyone else is a grunt.

The first matched set of special teams either kicks off or receives kickoffs. The second pair punts or catches them. We'll consider those four here and the other two—extra points/field goals and the team set to spoil them—in the next chapter.

THE KICKOFF

How important is a kickoff? Teams nearly always choose to receive when they win the coin toss. A rare decision to kick off instead of to receive usually means some sort of odd field condition like a heavy rain, a high wind, knee-deep snow, or an infestation of toads.

But does it really make any difference whether a team kicks or receives? Not much.

We checked 2,071 kickoffs to see which team scored first after the kick, and you know what? It was practically a wash!

Look at this:

	NUM	PCT	PTS
Total number of kickoffs	2,071	—	—
Receiving team scored first	854	41.2	4225
Touchdown	556	—	3336
Field Goal	293	—	879
Safety	5	—	10
Kicking team scored first	796	38.4	3952
Touchdown	521	—	3126
Field Goal	266	—	798
Safety	9	—	18
Neither scored before time ran out	421	20.3	—

When you figure in extra points, the receiving team scored an average of about 0.15 points per kickoff more than the kickers. (Receivers, 4781 points divided by 2071 kickoffs equals 2.31 points per; kickers, 4463 points divided by the same number equal 2.16 per.) Big deal! They have to receive 7 times to gain a point!

But it's not really even that good. Remember, time ran out before either team scored better than a fifth of the time. Who would have scored first had they kept on playing? Well, we have no crystal ball, but we can look at those kickoffs that came at the beginnings of halves, when there was a full thirty minutes for one side or the other to score.

	NUM	PCT	PTS
Total number of kickoffs	464	—	
Receiving team scored first	227	48.9	1123
Touchdown	148	—	888
Field Goal	77	—	231
Safety	2	—	4
Kicking team scored first	229	49.4	1146
Touchdown	154	—	924
Field Goal	72	—	216
Safety	3	—	6
Neither scored before time ran out	8	1.7	—

Here, the kicking team has a slight edge—0.063 points per kickoff—again, so little difference as to be meaningless.

The verdict: under any normal circumstances, winning the coin flip means absolutely nothing.

Speaking of normal circumstances, normally the kickers try to boot the ball into the end zone and force the receivers to start from the 20, a slight edge for the kicking team. But with the goal line 65 yards away, only a few kickers can do it consistently. Actually most kickoffs 2 or 3 yards into the end zone are run out because a fast returner can usually get 20 yards upfield before he meets up with the kicking team. In 1986, 347 kickoffs (about one out of six) weren't returned, with the average touchback 5.9 yards into the end zone. In computing kickoff return yardage, the NFL ignores the touchbacks, meaning that the kickoff man gets no credit at all when he does his job well.

It's possible that a team with a strong kicker can actually have a higher return average against it than a team with a lesser kicker. That's because return yardage is figured from where the ball is caught, not from the goal line. A kicker whose boots are consistently short will be giving the receivers the ball between the 10- and 15-yard lines a lot. By the time the returner gets to the 30-yard line, the kicking team is on him. The result is that the team with the strong kicker ends up with an average return against them of 20 to 22 yards, meaning that the opponents are normally starting from scrimmage at about the 20. The team with the poor kicker (if their coverage is good) might keep their opponents' average return at 17 to 19 yards. But the opponents have most of their first downs at the 30-yard line.

RETURNING THE KICKOFF

Any discussion of kickoff returns has to start with the burning question: what kind of kickoff? There are, after all, three kinds: normal kicks, on-side kicks, and free kicks, usually after safeties. The latter two kinds are not very common (about one out of every fifty kickoffs is an on-sider; fewer than one out of a hundred is a free kick), but they are so different from your normal kickoffs that they have some effect on return yardage.

Let's start with the numbers:

	NORM	ON-SIDE	FREE KICK	ALL
Total Kicks	2017	40	14	2071
Returned for TD	7	0	0	7
Average Yards Returned for TDs	94.7	—	—	94.7
Returned (Other Than TD)	1494	34	13	1541
Avg Yds Rtn (Other Than TD)	19.8	1.8	13.7	19.4
On-Side Kick Lost by Rec.	—	4	—	4
Not Returned (Touchback)	347	0	0	347
Avg Yards Gained on Touchback	25.9	—	—	25.9
* Out of Bounds	2	1	0	3
Fumbled and Lost	25	0	0	25
Avg Yards Gained Before Fum.	18.6	0	0	18.6
Penalty (Either Team)	142	1	1	144
Avg Yards Gained Before Pen.	17.9	−3.0	8.0	17.7

* Ball fumbled out of bounds by receiving team, no return.

First of all, there are two real surprises. The number of penalties (144) is much lower than we expected. It seems to the average TV watcher (and to us) as if there's a penalty on just about every kickoff. Not so. Only about 7 percent of all kickoffs have penalties actually stepped off. Notice, we didn't say called. No record is kept of penalties called and declined. But even if another whole 7 percent were declined, the total number of penalties called would be lower than we expected.

Second, we were almost as surprised to note the low number of fumbles lost. We knew fumbles weren't as common as penalties, but we would have guessed about 1 out of every 20 kickoffs is fumbled and half of those are lost, or about 2.5 percent. The actual figure is less than half of that—1.2 percent.

Another interesting figure is the low percentage of on-side kicks recovered by the kicking team. We did a survey of 50 games in 1970, and found 4 out of 14 recovered by the kicking team (28.6 percent), but we felt the sample was a little small. When we checked all the kickoffs in 1986, we got a much lower number of successful on-siders: 4 out of 40, or 10 percent. This isn't a surprise. Almost every on-side kick occurs in an "on-side kick situation," with the kicking team behind and nearly out of time. The receiving team knows what's coming and puts in its most sure-handed men to recover the kick. Actually, it's perhaps notable that even 10 percent of the on-siders are successful.

Of course, if a team called an on-side kick in a situation when it was not expected, say, on the opening kickoff of the game, it would likely surprise the hell out of the receiving team and, therefore, greatly increase its chance of recovering.

So why don't they do it?

Well, most normal kickoffs end up with the receiving team in possession somewhere between its own 20- and 30-yard lines. And anything in that range gives about a fifty-fifty chance for either team to score next. In other words, as we pointed out before, there's no particular advantage or disadvantage for either team in a normal kickoff normally handled.

An on-side kick, if recovered, will give the kicking team possession on about its own 50-yard line. How much good will that do it? It works out to be worth about 2 points. But if the kicking team gives the receiving team the ball at that same 50-yard line, the receivers get the 2-point value. The break-even mark is 50 percent, but you break even on a normal kickoff, so you have to be darned certain of recovering before you try it. Well, it might work the first time, but after that teams would look for it, and your chance of recovering goes down like a rock in chicken soup.

Part of the problem is this: any coach calling for an on-side kick at the opening of a game is telling his team, "Well, boys, these guys are a couple of parsecs better than us. We're going in the toilet if we play this one normally." Once he's instilled that kind of confidence in his team, he can forget any benefit derived from a successful on-sider.

The on-side kick is a desperation tactic that should be reserved for desperate situations.

Except for what happened at Sullivan Stadium back in 1983. The Cleveland Browns' coaches had picked up an interesting eccentricity in the Patriots' kick returning. As the opponent's kicker approached the ball, the front line blockers for the Pats would begin edging back to get into their blocking pattern. By the time the ball was kicked, they were in full retreat. So, early in the second quarter, the Browns scored on a 65-yard pass interception to take a 10-0 lead. When Cleveland kicked off, their kicker nudged the ball down the field about ten yards and most of the Pats were still moving backward when the Browns fell on the ball. From there they scored again and the final score was 30-0. Perhaps that successful on-side kick totally destroyed the Pats. More likely the Browns just added insult to injury against a foe they would have drubbed anyway.

Okay, there are exceptions to every rule, but losing an early on-side kick is not the worst thing that can happen to a receiving team. Nor is failing to recover it the worst thing possible for the kicking team.

The two most catastrophic things that can happen on a kickoff are (1) a return for a touchdown and (2) losing the ball on a fumble. Both are rare, but just for that reason either can be terribly demoralizing to the victim.

Out of 2071 kickoffs, only 7 were brought back all the way. That's 0.3 percent! It's just not something you expect to happen, and when it does, the kicking team is likely to get that "what's the use!" feeling. A long return of any kind hurts, but not nearly so much if it stops short of scoring. In 1986 Tim McGee of the Bengals somehow managed to go 94 yards against the Vikings and *not* score. Although the Vikings eventually lost, they were not destroyed by the return. In fact, they had Cincy holding on by their fingernails at the end.

Anyway, a lost fumble on a kickoff is only slightly less chilling for the receiving team than is a TD return for the kickers—and a lost fumble is nearly 4 times as common.

There's an obvious message there. The most important thing for your kickoff-return man to do is hang on to the ball! The difference between the very best kickoff returner in the league and a very ordinary returner will usually be 5 or 6 yards on the average. If they each return 30 kicks during the season, the top man will add about 150 Win Probability points to his team's total. But a fumble lost on a kickoff can cost a team 80 to 100 WP points. So, if the top man loses 2 fumbles during the year and the average guy doesn't lose any, you're ahead with the average guy. One more thing worth mentioning: when the kickoff goes into the end zone even a yard or so, it probably should not be returned by the receivers. The numbers say so.

We checked on returns out of the end zone. The average start was two yards deep. There were 168 returned, including one touchdown runback, for an average of 24.5 yards. However, 18 others resulted in penalties, netting an average of 17 (23 less 6 for the penalties) and 5 were lost on fumbles, with a return of 19 minus the 50-yard penalty for a turnover. This works out to an average of 22 yards out from the 2-yard-deep start. In other words, to the 20-yard line—exactly where they would have ended if they had taken the touchback.

Add in the fact that a disastrous fumble is 5 times as likely as a touchdown return, and you can see the folly of running the ball back once it's in the end zone.

Okay, in 1986, New Orleans' Mel Gray ran a kickoff back 101 yards to open the second half against San Francisco. It put the Saints temporarily in front, and we're reminded of all those baseball stories of guys who missed the bunt sign and hit a home run. Actually, Gray wasn't really going against the odds. His return average for his other 30 returns was 25.5, and he didn't fumble once. So we'll call him the exception that proves the rule.

We decided to look at individual kick returners in a slightly different way than the NFL. The league's way of identifying the top man in kickoff returns is to add up all the yards and divide by the number of attempts. Those with 20 or more returns qualify for the championship in order of average yards returned. In 1986 Dennis Gentry of Chicago won with exactly 20 returns; Detroit's Herman Hunter, who brought back 49 (the highest number), did not even qualify for the top ten.

Two things bothered us. First of all, because the total number of returns for any individual is so low, a single long return can skew the average by several yards. So the first thing we did was lop off everyone's longest return (as an anomaly) and divide by one less attempt, figuring this would give us a truer picture of the players' "average" return.

The other thing that bothered us was that there was no adjustment for fumbles, even though holding on to the ball is the returner's most important job. We decided to subtract 50 yards from a returner's yardage for every fumble lost.

Unfortunately, the NFL lumps all of a player's fumbles together and the only way we could get the ones that occurred on kickoff returns was to go through every play-by-play. Since we hate to waste the effort, here's a quick summary: there were 25 fumbles lost on kickoff returns in 1986. The Chargers led the league with 4; the Browns didn't lose any but forced 3 by opponents. The Bills managed to lose 2 in one game (November 2 vs. Tampa Bay; yes, they lost). Joe

Carter of Miami, Lionel James of San Diego, and Eric Richardson of Buffalo were the only players to lose more than one fumble on kick-offs.

Back to our adjusted kickoff return average. The formula is simple:

$$Adj\ Avg = (yards - [50 \times fumbles + long]) / (No. - 1)$$

Checking only the 1987 top ten returners, we got some shuffling in the order. Alas for Lupe Sanchez of Pittsburgh (the AFC leader)! The adjusted average drops him all the way from third to tenth among the original NFL top ten.

TOP TEN RETURNERS

1986 NFL	Rank	NO	YDS	AVG	LG	TD	FM	ADJ AVG
Dennis Gentry, Chicago	1	20	576	28.8	91t	1	0	25.52
Mel Gray, New Orleans	2	31	866	27.9	101t	1	0	25.50
Vai Sikahema, St. Louis	7	37	847	22.9	44	0	0	22.3
Ken Bell, Denver	6	23	531	23.1	42	0	0	22.2
Gene Lang, Denver	8	21	480	22.9	42	0	0	21.9
B.J. Edmonds, Seattle	10	34	764	22.5	46	0	0	21.8
Tim McGee, Cincinnati	4	43	1007	23.4	94	0	0	21.7
Bobby Humphery, NY Jets	5	28	655	23.4	96t	1	0	20.7
Rufus Bess, Minnesota	9	31	705	22.7	43	0	1	20.4
Lupe Sanchez, Pittsburgh	3	25	591	23.6	64	0	1	19.9

Of course, kick returning is not a one-man show. We're talking about special *teams* here, not special players. The NFL ranks its kick-off returns, both team and individual, by their average return. That's better than total yards which would normally find the team with the worst defense finishing on top because they'd be kicked to most often. On the other hand, a team with a low number of kicks received and one or two long runs has a terrific advantage.

Here are the 1986 Team Kickoff Returns, both offensive and defensive, with an added category. We figured the "+YARDS," which is how many more or fewer yards the team gained (or prevented) than would an average return or kicking team with the same number of chances. For example, New Orleans averaged 24.2 on 55 returns. Had an average team (19.8) returned 55 kickoffs, they would have gotten only 1089 yards instead of the Saints' 1332. That gives the Saints 243 +YARDS. One advantage of +YARDS is that it normalizes the results to the attempts. In other words, a team with a good kickoff return group may not receive as much benefit from it as a team with a slightly less effective team, if the second group returns many more kickoffs. "+YARDS" shows this. Note, for example, that Chicago's average return is better than that of either St. Louis or Cincinnati, but the Bears actually received slightly less value over the whole season because they returned fewer kickoffs than the Cards or Bengals.

OFFENSE

KO RETURNS	NO	YDS	AVG	LG	TD	+YARDS
New Orleans	55	1332	24.2	101t	1	243.0
St. Louis	70	1548	22.1	53	0	162.0
Cincinnati	63	1389	22.0	94	0	141.6
Chicago	50	1115	22.3	91t	2	125.0
Minnesota	56	1200	21.4	43	0	91.2
Seattle	64	1322	20.7	46	0	54.8
Denver	53	1094	20.6	42	0	44.6
Dallas	59	1208	20.5	56	0	39.8
Kansas City	56	1117	19.9	97t	1	8.2
New England	58	1147	19.8	52	0	−1.4
Pittsburgh	66	1304	19.8	64	0	−2.8
Detroit	67	1321	19.7	54	0	−5.6
Los Angeles Rams	59	1160	19.7	55	0	−8.2
Washington	60	1175	19.6	37	0	−13.0
Cleveland	62	1213	19.6	100t	1	−14.6
Buffalo	55	1074	19.5	49	0	−15.0
Los Angeles Raiders	64	1252	19.6	59	0	−15.2
Indianapolis	74	1443	19.5	37	0	−22.2
Houston	59	1139	19.3	48	0	−29.2
Atlanta	54	1035	19.2	35	0	−34.2
Green Bay	76	1470	19.3	57	0	−34.8
New York Jets	63	1189	18.9	96t	1	−58.4
San Francisco	42	757	18.0	34	0	−74.6
Miami	65	1185	18.2	41	0	−102.0
Philadelphia	53	945	17.8	51	0	−104.4
New York Giants	50	868	17.4	30	0	−122.0
San Diego	65	1137	17.5	35	0	−150.0
Tampa Bay	75	1302	17.4	33	0	−183.0

DEFENSE

KO RETURNS	NO	YDS	AVG	LG	TD	+YARDS
Los Angeles Raiders	63	1064	16.9	37	0	183.4
Seattle	59	1002	17.0	42	0	166.2
Kansas City	71	1278	18.0	58	0	127.8
New England	81	1480	18.3	39	0	123.8
St. Louis	50	886	17.7	56	0	104.0
San Diego	60	1088	18.1	46	0	100.0
Cleveland	78	1476	18.9	91t	1	68.4
Miami	53	997	18.8	40	0	52.4

DEFENSE KO RETURNS	NO	YDS	AVG	LG	TD	+YARDS
Green Bay	62	1181	19.0	64	0	46.6
Minnesota	79	1532	19.4	94	0	32.2
New Orleans	35	662	18.9	55	0	31.0
Indianapolis	43	827	19.2	41	0	24.4
New York Giants	70	1362	19.5	57	0	24.0
Detroit	56	1096	19.6	36	0	12.8
Denver	65	1299	20.0	51	0	−12.0
Los Angeles Rams	64	1282	20.0	84	0	−14.8
Washington	50	1005	20.1	59	0	−15.0
Atlanta	59	1190	20.2	48	0	−20.8
Cincinnati	80	1611	20.1	96t	1	−27.0
Philadelphia	62	1261	20.3	40	0	−33.4
Buffalo	56	1157	20.7	44	0	−48.2
Dallas	66	1358	20.6	38	0	−51.2
Houston	32	695	21.7	44	0	−61.4
New York Jets	62	1307	21.1	52	0	−79.4
Tampa Bay	46	1009	21.9	85t	1	−98.2
Chicago	64	1376	21.5	55	0	−108.8
San Francisco	71	1598	22.5	101t	1	−192.2
Pittsburgh	56	1362	24.3	100t	3	−253.2

PUNTING

The NFL giveth and the NFL taketh away. An interesting example of this is how they handle blocked punts in the individual charts.

It's all a question of degree: if the defenders blow in and tackle the punter, or if they force him to run or pass, or if he drops the snap, *or* if the snap is bad—if *any* of these things happen—they will not be recorded in either the team or individual punting tables. Things like that happened 17 times in our sample, but you won't find those aborted punts anywhere in the 2,311 "real" punts. Those 17 wouldn't do much to the overall average, of course, but the marks for some individuals would be hurt.

But suppose the punter kicks the ball and a defender gets a hand, an arm, or his face in front of the punt. Ah, a blocked punt, you say. Maybe not. If the ball stays behind the line of scrimmage, *that's* a blocked punt. And while such things are figured into the team averages, they are only recorded in a special column for the individual punters and not charged against each of their averages. However, if the ball, after being blocked, gets one inch beyond the line of scrimmage, it stops being a blocked punt in the charts and becomes just a plain old punt. And thereby just kills the punter's average.

So here's what you learn from the league stats if you're a punter: if you can't be good, be rotten. If you're good enough to get your punts away all the time, that's best. But if you're not that good, make sure you're really slow and you'll never get charged with your mistakes. The NFL said there were 28 blocked punts in our sample. We found 7 more that were partially blocked.

Well, let's summarize:

PUNTING SUMMARY

PUNT PLAYS	NUM	PCT	RESULT
Total Punts	2311	—	Average Return: 6.4
Normal Returns	999	43.3	Average Return: 8.1
Returned for TD	14	0.6	Average Return: 69.0
Fair Catch	371	16.1	No Return
Downed	270	11.6	No Return
Touchbacks	229	9.9	Returned to 20-Yard Line
Out of Bounds	213	9.2	No Return
Fumble Lost on Return . . .	35	1.5	Average Return: 2.6
Penalty on Play	145	6.3	Average Return: 5.2
Blocked Punts	35	1.5	Average Return: 4.5
Returned for TD	14		Average Return: 10.7
Normal	16		Average Return: 0.5
Downed	1		No Return
Blocked Out of Bounds . .	4		No Return

OTHER	NO	RESULT
Ball Not Punted	29	. . . . .
Fake Punt—Run	9	Average Gain: 14.8
Made First Down	6	Average Gain: 21.5
Failed on Fourth Down . .	3	Average Gain: 1.3
Fake Punt—Pass	3	Average Gain: 24.3
Made First Down	2	Average Gain: 36.5
Failed on Fourth Down . .	1	Average Gain: 0.0
Punter Forced to Run	10	Average Gain: 5.7
Made First Down	4	Average Gain: 21.0
Failed on Fourth Down . .	6	Average Gain: −4.5
Punter Forced to Pass	1	Failed
Fumble—Bad Snap	1	. . . . .
Fumble by Kicker	2	1 Returned 25 Yards for TD
Safety	3	. . . . .

Again we're astonished at the low number of penalties. It seems as though the last time we saw a punt play without a flag, the returner was Whizzer White. Actually, though, these only count penalties that were accepted and where the play was allowed to stand. All those times when they punt again or where the penalty results in a first down for the kicking team are washed out.

We're also a bit surprised that 14 of the 35 blocked kicks (counting partials) resulted in immediate touchdowns. It seems awfully high, but we double checked. You've got it—14!

Finally, note that fake punts worked 8 out of 12 times. And on the 17 occasions when the punter was forced to run (or pass), he gained a first down 4 times. Does this suggest to you that coaches call for the punt a little too readily?

Another interesting thing about punting (and we'll need another chart to demonstrate this) is that a punter's average decreases as he approaches his opponent's goal line. Well, it makes sense if you think about it; he has a shorter field to kick to.

Although it only confirms what we already knew, this chart is worth looking at. Another thing that it demonstrates is that the chance for a blocked punt does not go up just because the kicker is shoved up against his own goal.

PUNTING DISTANCE IN RELATION TO YARD LINE

YARD LINE	PUNT	AVG	BLK	AVG RET*
1-5	34	43.5	0	6.7
6-10	52	42.3	2	9.1
11-15	127	41.8	4	5.9
16-20	190	42.7	6	5.6
21-25	261	43.4	5	6.7
26-30	279	42.9	1	5.7
31-35	227	42.3	7	6.4
36-40	271	42.9	2	5.3
41-45	198	42.1	1	6.2
46-50	212	40.1	3	6.6
51-55	166	37.6	4	6.1
56-60	160	33.7	0	7.0*
61-65	83	32.5	0	10.4*
66-70	15	28.8	0	8.0*

* Includes touchbacks.

Incidentally, the NFL still awards its individual punting championship to the kicker with the highest gross average, that is, divide all the distance he kicked by his number of punts (but don't count the blocked kicks). Rohn Stark came out on top in 1986 with a 45.2 average, and he didn't have any kicks blocked anyway.

However, a lot of people think the *net average* is a better gauge of a punter's ability. Include us with "a lot of people." A punter's net average is figured by starting with his gross yardage, subtracting 20 yards for each touchback, and subtracting the return yardage. Then *that* number is divided by the total number of punts (including his blocked kicks). Mr. Stark had an excellent 37.2 net average, but Reggie Roby of Miami had 37.4.

The NFL publishes the net average, but doesn't use it to choose its punt leader. The argument is that the punter shouldn't be made responsible if his team has lead-footed punt coverage or blocks badly. We're not sure why he's not held responsible for the touchbacks; maybe punters have a strong union. Anyway, to the whole thing we say, *pshaw!* (We're careful not to say it with a mouthful of crackers, however.) Count the blocked punts against him because some punters are slower than others. And recognize the fact that a good punter adjusts to his coverage just as he adjusts to poor snaps, leaky protection, high winds, cold hands, and warm hearts. We say rank the punters by net average.

We may not find too many allies on that (at least among punters), but one thing we'll never understand is why *team* punting isn't ranked by net average.

Just to be inconsistent, the NFL includes blocked punts in the team's attempts, and thereby lowers the team gross average. As an example, Harry Newsome, who did *all* of Pittsburgh's punting in '86, had 3 punts blocked. His personal gross average (40.1) suffered not a whit. But the team gross average ended at 38.7. If nothing else, that's confusing.

Here are the team punting records for '86, ranked according to + YARDS in relation to the net average:

	TOTAL PUNTS	GROSS YARDS	LG	GROSS AVG	TB	BK	OPP RET	RET YDS	IN 20	NET AVG	+YARDS
New York Giants	79	3539	61	44.8	11	0	41	386	24	37.1	229.1
Indianapolis	81	3622	63	44.7	5	0	52	533	22	36.9	218.7
New Orleans	82	3456	66	42.1	11	1	37	234	17	36.6	196.8
Chicago	70	2850	59	40.7	8	1	23	110	20	36.9	189.0

	TOTAL PUNTS	GROSS YARDS	LG	GROSS AVG	TB	BK	OPP RET	RET YDS	IN 20	NET AVG	+YARDS
Miami	56	2476	73	44.2	9	0	23	200	13	37.4	179.2
Washington	75	3271	58	43.6	16	0	36	220	21	36.4	165.0
New York Jets	85	3353	55	39.4	6	0	36	165	27	36.1	161.5
Cleveland	83	3423	61	41.2	10	0	44	268	21	35.6	116.2
Houston	89	3659	66	41.1	9	0	40	303	27	35.5	115.7
Atlanta	79	3421	71	43.3	9	1	47	477	19	35.0	63.2
Buffalo	75	3031	57	40.4	9	0	32	260	14	34.5	22.5
Dallas	87	3498	58	40.2	10	1	41	301	28	34.4	17.4
San Francisco	85	3450	62	40.6	8	2	49	373	23	34.3	8.5
Minnesota	73	2922	69	40.0	4	1	40	356	15	34.1	−7.3
Los Angeles Raiders	90	3620	64	40.2	11	0	42	357	20	33.8	−36.0
Kansas City	99	4033	56	40.7	6	0	52	572	23	33.7	−49.5
Philadelphia	111	4547	62	41.0	10	1	63	634	20	33.5	−77.7
Seattle	79	3048	55	38.6	7	0	38	298	10	33.0	−94.8
New England	92	3746	64	40.7	7	3	60	565	16	33.1	−101.2
San Diego	79	3193	62	40.4	11	2	43	370	15	32.9	−102.7
Denver	86	3376	57	39.3	9	1	40	362	15	33.0	−103.2
Tampa Bay	78	3132	60	40.2	8	0	39	414	19	32.8	−109.2
St. Louis	92	3411	52	37.1	4	1	44	296	21	33.0	−110.4
Los Angeles Rams	98	3740	57	38.2	5	1	47	416	26	32.9	−127.4
Green Bay	75	2825	63	37.7	6	5	44	287	8	32.2	−150.0
Pittsburgh	89	3447	64	38.7	11	3	34	364	18	32.2	−178.0
Detroit	85	3389	60	39.9	10	2	39	517	18	31.4	−238.0
Cincinnati	59	1996	52	33.8	3	2	19	182	12	29.7	−265.5

Before leaving punting, we want to air a few thoughts about the quick kick. Back in the days of the single wing, quick kicks on second and third downs were common because (1) there was less chance of getting a long drive going with those grind-it-out offenses, and (2) the single wing tailback, who did most of his team's punting, was already set up for a direct snap in deep formation. Once all teams started using the T-formation, the quick kick disappeared because a T-quarterback was too close to the line of scrimmage to get a kick off.

At about this time, the *type* of punt preferred changed too, from an emphasis on distance to an emphasis on hang time. The idea was that a 40-yard punt with no return was better than a 50-yard punt with a 15-yard return.

When teams started using the shotgun formation, we expected to see the return of the quick kick. We were wrong.

In some cases, the quarterback in the shotgun can't punt worth a darn, but the main reason for not kicking on second or third down seems to be that teams just don't want to give up the ball.

We still think it's a pretty good play. If your kicker can line the ball over the defensive backs, you could pick up 60 yards or so with the roll. At least, that's the theory.

Our data shows the average distance to where the opponent will start his next drive (allowing for scores and turnovers as well as punts) varies from about 48 yards on third-and-1 to about 35 yards on third-and-25. The net gain from a conventional punt from your own territory is about 36 yards. We estimate that if you could gain an extra 5 yards on a quick kick, it would be a good play with 15 or more yards to go and a break even play with about 10 to go. Unfortunately we don't have any significant data on the degree of difficulty, number of shanks, number of blocks, or anything else. About all we can say with absolute certainty is that if a quick kick is blocked on third down and the punting team recovers, they can still try another punt on fourth down.

Philadelphia tried it twice in 1986, the only NFL team to do it at all. (Denver did it in 1987.) On one occasion, QB Randall Cunningham's kick was partially blocked and went only 15 yards; his second try traveled only an ordinary 39 yards.

The sample doesn't support our faith in the quickie, but the sample is too small to prove anything. Considering their dreadful punting and so-so offenses, we think teams like Pittsburgh and Detroit should give it a try.

PUNT RETURNS

The first thought that occurs to us about punt returners is that anyone with enough concentration to focus his attention on a high, turning football while several tons of angry beef are bearing down on him has a great future as a diamond cutter. Probably the second most dangerous thing you can do on a football field is return a punt (the most dangerous is call Lawrence Taylor bad names), and we'll bet when a punt returner walks into a room, all the insurance salesmen go out the windows. Well, it's a dirty job, but somebody has to do it; if it was us, though, we'd start calling for a fair catch in the pregame warmups.

Of course, when a punt returner calls for a fair catch, some fans will boo, figuring the guy for a lack of guts. In another life, these fans probably sat in the Colosseum and rooted for the lions. Actually, knowing whether to call for a fair catch, return the kick, or just let it bounce is the most important decision a returner makes. Fewer than half of the punts (49.5 percent) in the NFL are returned. Here are the figures from 1986:

	NUM	PCT
Total Punts	2311	—
Returned	1145	49.5
Fair Catches	389	16.8
Downed (No Return)	331	14.3
Touchbacks	233	10.1
Out of Bounds	213	9.2

All of which makes it a little odd that the NFL ranks its punt returning, both individual and team, by only their average return. Think about it. Suppose a team is punted to five times in a game and returns one for ten yards. The other four are fair catches or downed or like that. The team's average return is ten yards! All right, children, here's today's math lesson, according to the NFL: 10 / 5 = 10!

We think the punt-return average—the true average, that is—should reflect all of the returns. Here we show you the team returns for 1986. We give you the number of times each team was punted to, the number actually returned, the number of fair catches, the number downed (which includes touchbacks, punts out of bounds, and blocked punts). We're also including the percentage returned, yards returned, the NFL average return, the true average, long return, touchdowns, and your old friend +YARDS.

	TOT NO	NO RET	NO FC	NO DWN	PCT RET	YDS	NFL AVG	TRUE AVG	LG	TD	+YARDS
Denver	86	48	8	30	55.8	552	11.5	6.4	70t	2	189.2
St. Louis	83	45	16	22	54.2	528	11.7	6.4	71t	2	182.6
Washington	95	51	20	24	53.7	550	10.8	5.8	44	0	152.0
Detroit	68	43	9	16	63.2	420	9.8	6.2	81t	1	136.0
Seattle	81	39	14	28	48.1	457	11.7	5.6	75t	1	113.4
Los Angeles Raiders	97	56	16	25	57.7	484	8.6	5.0	70t	1	77.6
Chicago	100	57	9	34	57.0	482	8.5	4.8	35	0	60.0
New Orleans	78	47	15	16	60.3	377	8.0	4.8	39	0	46.8
Los Angeles Rams	96	42	22	32	43.8	361	8.6	3.8	32	0	38.4
Philadelphia	97	44	16	37	45.4	374	8.5	3.9	76t	1	29.1
Miami	64	40	11	13	66.7	297	7.4	4.6	71t	1	25.6
New York Jets	75	39	9	27	52.0	341	8.7	4.5	28	0	22.5
Green Bay	70	33	7	30	47.1	316	9.6	4.5	83t	1	21.0
San Francisco	91	43	19	29	47.3	397	9.2	4.4	76t	1	18.2
New England	90	42	12	36	46.7	396	9.4	4.4	59t	1	18.0

	TOT NO	NO RET	NO FC	NO DWN	PCT RET	YDS	NFL AVG	TRUE AVG	LG	TD	+YARDS
Cleveland	80	41	10	29	51.3	350	8.5	4.4	84t	1	16.0
San Diego	81	37	16	28	45.7	334	9.0	4.1	30	0	−8.1
Pittsburgh	82	36	13	33	43.9	310	8.6	3.8	41	0	−32.8
Indianapolis	67	35	13	19	52.2	250	7.1	3.7	24	0	−33.5
Atlanta	83	44	12	27	53.0	292	6.6	3.5	30	0	−58.1
Houston	94	43	15	36	45.7	341	7.9	3.6	25	0	−75.2
Kansas City	83	35	18	30	42.1	265	7.6	3.2	48	0	−83.0
Cincinnati	77	29	17	31	37.7	235	8.1	3.1	25	0	−84.7
New York Giants	89	41	20	28	46.1	287	7.0	3.2	22	0	−89.0
Minnesota	75	31	17	27	41.3	215	6.9	2.9	15	0	−97.5
Buffalo	83	32	13	38	38.6	247	7.7	3.0	49t	1	−99.6
Dallas	87	46	17	24	52.9	252	5.5	2.9	28	0	−113.1
Tampa Bay	59	26	5	28	44.1	110	4.2	1.9	12	0	−135.7

PUTTING THEM ALL TOGETHER

You knew we were going to do it, right? Okay, now we're going to add up all those +YARDS and get an overall special teams rating, ignoring for the moment field goals and extra points. But before we do that, we need a disclaimer. While we think the +YARDS idea gives a good picture of the individual value of each special team, we're not at all certain that the sum of the four is an accurate reflection of their total value. Piling them together like so many ore cars only works if all the ore cars are equally full. We're not at all certain that a kickoff return yard is as valuable as a punt yard or a punt return yard. That's something that needs further study. Perhaps the teams should be weighted.

For now, however, we'll proceed on the assumption that each team is equally important.

In the next chart, which we call "Total Special Teams' +Yards," you can see the +YARDS for each special team and the totals. And for fun we divided the +YARDS by 12 because it takes about that many yards to add a point to a team's total. The leader, New Orleans at 43.1, is 86.9 points better than Tampa Bay, the last-place team at −43.8. That seems like a lot, but if you prorate the difference over a 16-game season, it simply means that in a given game the Saints' special teams are worth about 5.4 points in the spread. And that doesn't seem particularly out of line.

The biggest surprise for us was the rather ordinary rating for Kansas City, whose special teams produced 6 touchdowns in '86. Then we remembered that the ratings do not show the Chiefs' proclivity for blocking field goals. Second, the ratings make no allowance for a particularly opportunistic group. We decided that Kansas City's special teams were excellent on kickoffs, substandard on punts, but alert all the time.

TOTAL SPECIAL TEAMS' +YARDS

	KICKOFF	RETURNS	PUNTING	RETURNS	TOTAL	POINTS
New Orleans	31.0	243.0	196.8	46.8	517.6	43.1
St. Louis	104.0	162.0	−110.4	182.6	338.2	28.2
Washington	−15.0	−13.0	165.0	152.0	289.0	24.1
Chicago	−108.8	125.0	189.0	60.0	265.2	22.1
Seattle	166.2	54.8	−94.8	113.4	239.6	20.0
Los Angeles Raiders	183.4	−15.2	−36.0	77.6	209.8	17.5
Indianapolis	24.4	−22.2	218.7	−33.5	187.4	15.6
Cleveland	68.4	−14.6	116.2	16.0	186.0	15.5
Miami	52.4	−102.0	179.2	25.6	155.2	12.9
Denver	−12.0	44.6	−103.2	189.2	118.6	9.8
New York Jets	−79.4	−58.4	161.5	22.5	46.2	3.9
New England	123.8	−1.4	−101.2	18.0	39.2	3.6
New York Giants	24.0	−122.0	229.1	−89.0	42.1	3.5
Minnesota	32.2	91.2	−7.3	−97.5	18.6	1.6
Kansas City	127.8	8.2	−49.5	−83.0	3.5	0.3
Atlanta	−20.8	−34.2	63.2	−58.1	−49.9	−4.2
Houston	−61.4	−29.2	115.7	−75.2	−50.1	−4.2
Detroit	12.8	−5.6	−238.0	136.0	−94.8	−7.9
Dallas	−51.2	39.8	17.4	−113.1	−107.1	−8.9
Los Angeles Rams	−14.8	−8.2	−127.4	38.4	−112.0	−9.3
Green Bay	46.6	−34.8	−150.0	21.0	−117.2	−9.7
Buffalo	−48.2	−15.0	22.5	−99.6	−140.3	−11.7
San Francisco	−192.2	−74.6	8.5	18.2	−240.1	−12.0
San Diego	100.0	−150.0	−102.7	−8.1	−160.8	−13.4
Philadelphia	−33.4	−104.4	−77.7	29.1	−186.4	−15.5
Cincinnati	−27.0	141.6	−265.5	−84.7	−235.6	−19.6
Pittsburgh	−253.2	−2.8	−178.0	−32.8	−466.8	−38.9
Tampa Bay	−98.2	−183.0	−109.2	−135.7	−526.1	−43.8

10

Kicking Up a Storm

It's about time someone reconsidered the extra point. No, this is not going to be another plea for the NFL to institute the two-point conversion. To our mind, the only thing sillier than a two-point conversion is the present one-pointer. And we don't think any right can come from adding the option of another wrong.

The extra point has been around since Walter Camp had acne. Except for the occasional two-point pitch, nobody thinks about it anymore. Lord knows, no one *watches* it. At least not on television. More sandwiches are buttered, more beers are opened, more toilets are flushed across America during extra point kicks than at any other moment during the game. The halftime-score show is more interesting, the coin flip has more suspense, and the commercials have more action.

If the cameras panned the crowd at the game, you'd probably see (if *you* watched) that most of the people there are looking at their game programs, looking at girls, looking at guys, looking at guys looking at girls—anything to avoid wasting eyesight on the extra point.

Everyone just assumes it will be good. And 96 percent of the time it is. Listen, 96 percent of anything in this world is a lock. If they told you there was a 96 percent chance you wouldn't get mugged, you'd

147

visit New York tomorrow. If there was a 96 percent chance it'd run next month, you'd buy a new car. "Do you swear to love, honor, and obey 96 percent of the time?" "I sure do!" Kick . . . that . . . point! 96 percent.

Even the kicker doesn't watch the ball once it's kicked. By the time it's between the uprights, he's halfway back to the Gatorade.

So three or four minutes of every game, counting set-up time and mandatory high-fives, are wasted on something that's going to work out 96 percent of the time.

'Twas not always so. The extra point used to be a real spellbinder. Back in the early days, when touchdowns were rare and the kicker was often a guy who did five other things better, there was a real risk involved, and 7-6 games were common. The extra point was the main way football teams avoided having four or five ties a season. And that was fair. Getting a touchdown against a strong foe took a supreme effort. The extra point was really something extra—the cherry on top —that would reward a team if it could only do just a little more.

But that was a long time ago. The extra point man is now a specialist who can do 96 percent in his sleep. Now the extra point isn't a reward; it's a penalty. Because 4 percent are not going to be good.

We tracked 1,069 extra points. Of these, 1,026 were (ho-hum) good; 43 weren't. Of the 28 NFL teams, 22 missed at least one extra point during the course of the season. Of those missed, 11 came on errors by someone other than the kicker, either bad snaps or fumbled holds. The point didn't get kicked. Of the remaining 32 that were kicked but missed, some of those were also caused by poor snaps or fumbled holds, and a very few were blocked.

The thing that bothers us is that there's really no logic to the misses. The very best kickers will shank maybe one out of a hundred. The best holders and snappers will mess up once in a while. The best line will miss a block somewhere in the season. But these goofs have nothing to do with the quality of the opposition. They're going to happen sometime, simply because the kicking team is not built by Apple.

Call it Fate. Roll the dice enough times and eventually you get snake-eyes.

Of the 43 fated misses, 42 made absolutely no difference on the outcome of the game. Maybe some of them upset a gambler or two because of the point spread, but they didn't change who won or lost.

One did, and a pretty important game it was. In week fifteen of the '86 season, Denver was two games up on Kansas City when they hosted Washington, only a game behind New York. Washington scored a first quarter touchdown and set up for the extra point while America yawned. The snap appeared to be off the mark, and Jay Schroeder rushed to get the hold. Max Zendejas kicked the ball just as Schroeder touched it down—and the kick missed.

After that, the Redskins scored again, but Denver took a 31-23 lead in the fourth quarter and the 'Skins fell short with a final touchdown, 31-30. The win cemented Denver in first place and ended Washington's hopes of finishing first.

After the game, Redskin linebacker Rich Minot said, "At least 80 percent of the time when a team misses an extra point, it comes back to haunt them."

Well, not exactly, Rich. By our calculations, 2.3 percent of the time it haunts them, which ain't exactly Amityville. Figuring that about 45 seconds is used up by each extra point attempt, the NFL wasted 12 hours and 40 minutes on extra points to get one—*one*—that made any difference!

A lot of things can be done in 12 hours and 40 minutes: The NFL could play four more games, you could build a model airplane, we could do all but the "Colombian copper center" of a crossword puzzle, Ronald Reagan could put in two months' work. A lot of things.

But we'll let those twelve-plus hours go. After all, we've wasted time on more frivolous things. We watched "Dynasty" once until our eyes got tired; we read James Michener once until our lips got tired; we sired a child. (Actually, James Michener was more fun than watching extra points, though less educational.) Anyway, we won't begrudge the NFL those twelve-plus. What we object to is the one miss that made a difference.

Should any game, much less an important game with division titles at stake, turn on what is essentially a whim of fate? Would not a fairer —and far more exciting—outcome to that Denver-Washington game have been a 31-31 tie at the end of regulation time? Unless you live in Denver, you've got to agree. Deciding a football game by a missed extra point is like deciding the World Series by how flat they sing the national anthem.

So our first suggestion is that we do away with extra points altogether and just start counting touchdowns as seven points. It's fair, it's easy, and it will save time.

And it will happen about the time they need earmuffs in Pago Pago. If you suggested to the NFL that they just award extra points and get on with it, they'd huff about removing the excitement. Then they'd puff about how it'd affect individual career scoring records. And then they'd luff about the integrity of the game. But all their huff, puff, and luff is guff. The reason they won't do it is because the TV people wouldn't like it. The set up time for the PAT is when they show all those replays of the touchdown. You know, "Here's the catch as you just saw it; here it is from the other side; from field level; from the blimp."

If they couldn't show 'em while the extra point is being set up, the TV people would have to cut into the commercials after the extra point. TV gives up commercials about as easily as the Russian army gave up Stalingrad.

So here's an idea that is more feasible. Return some suspense to the extra point by making it harder to kick. Simply move the ball back to the 20. We calculate that a team will make about two-thirds of its kicks from the 27-yard line. *Voilà!* Instant suspense. People might actually start watching extra points. Best of all, a team will once again have to earn its extra point. And if it should win on the basis of a successful conversion, the victory would be deserved rather than a trick of fate.

FIELD GOALS

Most of the things you can do on a football field are measured from the line of scrimmage. Field goals aren't. Field goals are measured from where the ball is kicked to the crossbar on the goalpost.

So, in the individual field goal tabulations, you get to see this:

1-19	20-29	30-39	40-49	50+
24-26	171-193	193-245	138-258	33-93
.923	.886	.788	.535	.355

Immediately your eye goes to the right—the long kicks. Wow! Better than one-third of the 50-plussers were good. You remember the legends of Jim Thorpe standing at the 50-yard line and drop-kicking first over one goalpost and then turning around and putting one over the other goalpost. Maybe you remember Lou Groza being good for three points as soon as the Browns passed the 50. How about Tom Dempsey?

Ahh, but remember, when those guys were kicking, the goalposts were on the goal line. Since 1974 they've been ten yards farther back on the end lines. Today's kickers boot 'em just as far as they did in the old days, maybe farther. They just have to get closer to do it.

What's really important, of course, is not how far the field goal travels, but how close the kicker has to be to have a reasonable chance to make it.

To kick a fifty-yard field goal, the offense has to get the ball to the 32- or 33-yard line. That's ten yards of end zone, 30-odd yards from goal line to line of scrimmage, and seven or eight more back to the holder. In evaluating field goals, then, we have to remember that we're not talking about a weapon that is usable from midfield. A team must be two-thirds of the way to a touchdown to kick a field goal.

If we measure only the distance from the line of scrimmage to the goal line, we'd see this:

1-2	3-12	13-22	23-32	33+
24-26	171-193	193-245	138-258	33-93
.923	.886	.788	.535	.355

And now your eye goes to the left. Yes, believe it or not, those big, strong NFL teams settled for dinky little field goal attempts 26 times after they were within two yards of the goal line. And missed two of 'em!

Well, there are all kinds of situations. Surely some of those dinky fielders came with the score tied or the team behind by a point or two and only seconds left in the game. In that kind of situation, any coach who doesn't opt for a field goal is starkers. Or suppose a team is five points up with four minutes to play? You'd have to go for a chance to get two scores ahead, right?

But we're willing to bet that out of those 26 point-blank field goal tries, at least a dozen were of the "come-away-with-something" ilk. You know the kind. A team drives down the field okay, but then has problems near the goal line, and all of a sudden it's fourth down. By golly, says the coach, we've gotta come away with something!

The idea that you-gotta-come-away-with-something is on page six of *The Coach's Book of Conventional Wisdom*, which every coach receives along with his first whistle on a lanyard. It's in red ink. Underneath it's explained that any team that gets close to the goal line and doesn't come away with a point or so will undergo a psychic shock roughly akin to being weaned.

So he ignores his offense, which has been doing a good job, ignores the fact that even the best field goal in the world is still worth less than half a touchdown, ignores the fact that the following kickoff will give the opponent halfway decent field position, and sends in his kicker. So for a few minutes, he has a 3-point lead.

And when he comes up a few points shy at the end of the game, he can talk about how "mistakes killed us."

But the biggest mistake was his, when he fell into the come-away-with-something trap. Suppose he had tried for the touchdown and failed; how bad would it have been? His opponent would have been bottled up a yard or two from his own goal line. If his defense is any good at all, his offense would have gotten the ball back in good field position (and if his defense can't stop an opponent from driving 98 yards, a field goal isn't going to do him much good anyway). On the other hand, if he's successful, he has a touchdown.

In 1987, Minnesota Coach Jerry Burns was castigated by ESPN's Pete Axthelm for skipping a point-blank field goal against the Bears while leading 24-23 and under five minutes on the clock. The Vikes were stopped four times inside the 2. When Chicago came back to win, 30-24, it was all Burns' fault for not opting for a field goal. Somehow those three points would have kept the Bears from scoring a subsequent touchdown, the "reasoning" went. And when Minnesota lost its next game, *that* was blamed on the field goal they didn't try the week before. Some sort of emotional block.

Utter nonsense! Burns was dead right. The field goal, as it turned out, would not have won the game—it still left Minnesota vulnerable to a touchdown—while a touchdown would have given them a sure win. And anyone who thinks the next loss came from a carry-over must figure the Vikings' psyches are like grandma's pie crust—flaky and easily crumbled.

What you never read about is all the points lost because the field goal option was taken. What if Denver, in Super Bowl XXII, had not turned conservative near the goal line on its second possession? Remember, the Broncos had burst out in front 7-0 before two minutes were gone in the first quarter, then only three minutes later found themselves with a first-and-10 on the Redskin 13. Determined to "come away with something," they ran three low-risk plays that fooled no one, then kicked the "automatic" field goal. Maybe, if they had scored another blitzkrieg touchdown, the Redskins would have been shaken to their moccasins. (Or maybe they would have won 42-14 instead of 42-10—who's to say for sure?)

Or what if Vikings' coach Jerry Burns hadn't heard Axthelm's carping: in the 1987 NFC championship against the 'Skins, he kicked a first-half field goal from in close when going for the TD was the right call. If he had had 14 points under his belt for his closing drive of the game, rather than the 10 he actually had, he might have been able to kick a field goal that really meant something, one that would have forced an overtime.

Or try this: Pittsburgh at Houston in a must-win game. In the first quarter, a pass interception puts the Steelers on the Oilers' ten. On fourth down, Pittsburgh kicks a field goal: 3-0. Second quarter, the ball is moved to the Oiler 18; again they settle: 6-0. When Houston gets a touchdown, they lead 7-6. A Houston field goal makes it 10-6 at the half. Both teams exchange touchdowns in the third quarter, but Pittsburgh's running game seems to be working. The Steelers, trailing 17-13, drive down to the Oiler 3 and then kick a third field goal, leaving them a point behind. When Houston scores another touchdown, the game is over: 24-16, Oilers.

Now, in order not to lose, you say, Pittsburgh would have had to have taken two of those three field goals in for touchdowns, an unlikely 66.7 percent. Not really. You're forgetting that had they failed on each occasion, they still would have left the Oilers in far worse field position than they were given on the ensuing kickoff. With that figured into the equation, Pittsburgh's chances of winning improve.

We can't prove that taking the chance would have won for Pittsburgh, but there's no doubt that they played it safe—and lost.

All right, let's take a really close look at this field goal situation. As we said, the goalposts were moved to the back of the end zone in 1974. We can divide all of the NFL's field goal kicking since then into three sections. In 1974-77 the success rate was about 61 percent (1,464 out of 2,418). In 1978-81 the success rate went up to 64 percent (1,880 out of 2,940). The number of field goals attempted per game was about the same in both periods, 1.6 per team.

Then, starting in 1982, the success rate shot up. For 1982-86 it was 71 percent (2,580 out of 3,653) and the number per game also went up —to 1.8. Long field goals have become much more common and so has the success rate. As a matter of fact, both the number of 50-yard-plus attempts and the success rate have doubled since the 1974-77 period. The early figures were 29/152 for 19 percent and about one attempt every 10 games. Now it's up to 137/363 for 38 percent and an attempt every 6 games.

Here are the distance figures for the whole 1982-86 period:

Length	Scrimmage	FGM/FGA	Percent
0-19	1-2	107/112	95.5
20-29	3-12	825/925	89.2
30-39	13-22	855/1116	76.6
40-49	23-32	656/1127	58.2
50+	33+	137/363	37.7
Total		2580/3653	70.6

Next, in order to calculate the desirability of attempting a field goal on a fourth down situation, as opposed to going for a first down or punting, we need this information (from 1986 play-by-plays):

Scrimmage	Punt Yards	Return Yards*	Net
goal-own 45	42	6	36
own 45-50	40	6	34
50-opp 45	38	6	32
opp 45-40	35	7	28
opp 40-35	32	10	22
opp 35-30	29	10	19

* Including turnovers.

Finally, we need to know the probability of making a first down, given fourth down and the number of yards to go. Unfortunately there's not enough data for anything except fourth-and-one; we'll have to make some assumptions from third down data. For third down, the success rate includes only the yards made on that down, not any conversion that might have happened on fourth down if the play on third down failed. The "use" figure in the following chart combines data from third and fourth downs. There is a possibility of about a 2 percent error in these numbers, but that doesn't really affect the results. And penalties are neglected.

To Go	3rd Down		4th Down		Use
1	464/659	70%	112/162	69%	70%
2	259/475	55%	20/38	53%	54%
3	212/439	48%	14/25	70%	50%
4	220/443	50%	4/14	29%	48%
5	202/463	44%	4/15	27%	43%
6	187/495	38%	4/9	44%	38%

With this information, and using our potential scoring method which gives −2 points on your own goal line, 0 at the 25, 2 at midfield, and 6 on the other team's goal line, we can figure strategy. The potential scoring chart shows the expected number of points to be scored by the team with the ball, given first-and-10 at each yard line. This scoring potential is found by taking the next score that occurs and crediting it to whichever team scores next. The net point figure is equal to the number of points scored by the team with the ball, less the number scored by the other team, all over the number of first downs.

1st-and-10	Points		1st-and-10	Points
own goal	−2.0		midfield	2.0
10	−1.2		40	2.8
20	−.4		30	3.6
25	.0		25	4.0
30	.4		20	4.4
40	1.2		10	5.2
			opp goal	6.0

The expected value for a good field goal will be three points times the success percentage. This assumes a following kickoff that will start the other team at its own 25 (usually), which has a potential of zero points. For a missed field goal from inside the 20-yard line, the expected value for the other team will be −0.4 points at the 20-yard-line because of the touchback. For a miss from farther out, the expected value for the other team will vary from zero at the 25-yard line to 2 points at midfield.

We're using the table on field goal success for 1982-86 to figure this. The fail points represent the scoring potential of the kicking team, which is just the opposite of the defending team.

Scrimmage	Good Points		Fail Points		Net
opp goal	95	2.85	5	0.02	2.87
opp 5	90	2.70	10	0.04	2.74
10	85	2.55	15	0.06	2.61
15	77	2.31	23	0.09	2.40
20	70	2.10	30	0.12	2.22
25	60	1.80	40	0.00	1.80
30	50	1.50	50	−0.20	1.30
35	40	1.20	60	−0.48	0.72
40	25	.75	75	−0.90	−0.15
45	10	.30	90	−1.44	−1.14
50	0	.00	100	−2.00	−2.00

We can come up with a similar table for punting. We'll skip the 1 percent of punts that are blocked and any of the fakes or forced plays that come up when the punter is rushed.

Scrimmage	Net Yards	New Scrimmage	Potential
opp 30	15	opp 15	0.8
40	25	15	0.8
midfield	33	17	0.6
own 40	36	24	0.1
30	36	34	−0.7
20	36	44	−1.5
10	36	own 44	−2.3
own goal	36	36	−3.1

If we go for it, we will assume the success rate in the table already shown, with a success being one more yard than the required distance and a failure to be no gain at all. The potential is the success rate times its scoring potential minus the failure rate times its potential. For one yard to go, the success rate will be assumed to be 70 percent, and inversely the failure rate, 30 percent.

So if you're on your opponent's 5-yard line with fourth-and-1, making it will put you on the 3, worth 5.8 potential points for you. We'd love to give you 7 points (for a touchdown and extra point), but you'll still have to negotiate those last three yards, and, as someone once said, "There's many a slip . . ." We think the guy who said it was either a football coach or a lingerie salesman.

Anyway, if you fail, what have you lost? Your opponent's scoring potential will be a −1.6 points (or, in effect, a +.6 for you). The net will be 0.7 (70 percent success rate) times 5.8 plus 0.3 (30 percent failure rate) times 1.6—or 4.5 points (the math working out to 4.06 + 0.48 = 4.54).

Scrimmage	1 to go (70% good)	2 to go (54% good)	4 to go (48% good)	6 to go (38% good)
opp 5	4.5	3.9	3.7	3.3
10	4.1	3.5	3.3	2.9
20	3.3	2.7	2.5	2.1
30	2.5	1.9	1.7	1.3
40	1.7	1.1	0.9	0.5
midfield	0.9	0.3	0.1	−0.3
own 40	0.1	−0.5	−0.7	−1.1

About now, you're asking, "When will we get to the point?"

Hey, do you think when they planned D-Day they just said "Let's all jump into some boats and cruise over to France"? We're on to something controversial here—the idea that teams hurt themselves by settling too often for field goals or punts. They think they're playing it safe when they're actually going against the odds.

If we just *said* that, you'd never believe us. Hell, *we* wouldn't believe us! So we have to give you all the facts so you can see where we're coming from. Pay attention and quit bitching!

Now—finally—we can line up all the numbers and make a decision. The numbers given are the offensive team's net scoring potential, based on the odds of success or failure, so choose the higher number.

Scrimmage	Go-1 to Go	Go-6 to Go	Field Goal	Punt
opp 5	4.5	3.3	2.7	—
10	4.1	2.9	2.6	—
20	3.3	2.1	2.2	—
30	2	2.5	1.3	0.8
40	1.7	0.5	−0.1	0.8
midfield	0.9	−0.3	—	0.6
own 40	0.1	−1.1	—	0.1
30	−0.7	−1.9	—	−0.7

Scrimmage	Go-1 to Go	Go-6 to Go	Field Goal	Punt
20	−1.5	−2.7	—	−1.5
10	−2.3	−3.5	—	−2.3
own goal	−3.1	−4.3	—	−3.1

You probably don't believe what you're seeing. That's right. The table shows you should NOT kick a field goal *unless you have six or more yards to go on fourth down*. And if you're inside your opponent's 10-yard line, you shouldn't kick no matter the distance.

The irony of the whole thing is that the better kicker a coach has in his arsenal, the quicker he'll call for a field goal in a short yardage situation. So in effect, a great kicker can actually cost his team points.

Remember, of course, we're not talking about a game where you're two points down with six seconds left. We're controversial, not suicidal. We'll explain how the time left and the score affect this in a minute.

Another thing the chart shows is that going for the yardage on fourth-and-1 from anywhere on the field is about the equivalent of a punt. The crossover point from trying for a field goal to punting is about the opponent's 35-yard line.

To make going for it worthwhile, a team needs about a two-thirds chance of making the yards. A pro team can make 1 yard about 70 percent of the time, 2 yards around 55. These odds are the same at the 1-yard line or the 11 or the 21. The reward for a touchdown is so much greater than for a field goal that a team really can't afford to settle for three points.

Out of 815 field goal tries in 1986, 49 were attempted on fourth-and-1 and 52 on fourth-and-2. Only 83 were good. That's a "mere" 82 percent. Had they gone for the yards, they figured to make at least two-thirds of the tries, about 71. Of those, about 50 would have ended as touchdowns under normal circumstances. That's 350 points. But 83 field goals are worth 249 points. Additionally, on the failed tries for a first down, the opponents would nearly always be in a worse field position than they would be on a kickoff after a successful field goal.

In other words, any time a team is faced with a fourth-and-1 or even fourth-and-2, it should go for the first down (except in obvious situations where time remaining and score make a field goal mandatory). Actually, this even applies to punting, but the coach who will call for a run in a close game with fourth-and-2 at his own 10 has never been born. Statistically, we can demonstrate that a team would come out ahead, but we can't factor in a coach's ulcers.

Demonstrating the advantage of going for a first down isn't that hard. Getting a coach to go against *The Coach's Book of Conventional Wisdom*, however, is like getting a rooster to swear off dawn.

On November 9, 1987, *USA Today* headlined: "Gamble Fails But Steelers Win 17-16." The story: "Steelers Coach Chuck Noll gambled at the end of the game, and it nearly cost the Steelers. Pittsburgh had the ball fourth-and-1 on the Kansas City 38 when Noll chose to go for a first down. Kansas City linebacker Dino Hackett stopped Walter Abercrombie for no gain, giving the Chiefs the ball with 1:17 to play."

There it is, the implication that Noll's reckless "gamble" nearly lost the game for Pittsburgh. Actually, Noll was going *with* the odds. Not only that, but he had some extras! Kansas City hadn't scored from scrimmage against Pittsburgh in two games, but they *had* scored on blocked kicks. In fact, in the third quarter, they came within inches of blocking one of Harry Newsome's punts. Anyone who knew the real situation expected Noll to call for the run. Gamble, schmamble!

Moreover, the fact that the Steelers didn't make the yardage and still won underlines the correctness of the decision.

Hindsight is one of the great blessings of being a fan or a sportswriter. We don't have all the information on fans, but as nearly as we can tell no sportswriter in the entire history of football has *ever* made a strategy error the day after a game was played. When we think of the magnitude of that accomplishment, we get all misty. Or is it musty?

Going for it won't succeed every time, of course. And when it doesn't, the coach who dared go against the conventional wisdom accumulated in thousands of losses can expect to be excoriated in more than a few paragraphs. In the same *USA Today* that criticized Noll briefly, an entire column was devoted to blasting Colts' Coach Ron Meyer for blowing a game with San Diego.

It seems the Colts held a 13-3 lead in the third quarter when they came up fourth-and-1 on their own 40. Meyer had gone successfully for the first down in an earlier game, and he called the same play here. This time it didn't work. The Chargers took over, drove 21 yards, and kicked a 37-yard field goal to make it 13-6. In the fourth quarter, San Diego scored a touchdown to tie; Eric Dickerson, the Colts' 5.6-million-dollar man, fumbled into the end zone to lose the winning TD; and the Chargers nailed a final field goal with twelve seconds left to win.

Somehow, *USA Today* managed to blame all that on Meyer's failure to punt in the third quarter.

Considering the flaying a coach is going to get if he defies conventional wisdom, is it any wonder most of them opt for the "safe" decision—even if it's wrong?

Just for the record, here's the punt/field-goal/go-for-it information from 1986. You can see that going for it on fourth down happens a lot less often than the calculations warrant. And the cases of trying to get a first down with more than a yard to go are as rare as Tuesday touchdowns.

Scrimmage	All Downs Punt	All Downs Field Goal	4th-and-1 Go	4th-and-1 Punt	4th-and-1 FG	4th-and-2 to 6 Go	4th-and-2 to 6 Punt	4th-and-2 to 6 FG
Own 46-50	217	0	6	16	0	8	64	0
Opp 49-45	171	2	13	11	0	3	46	0
44-40	165	5	20	8	0	14	61	0
39-35	86	38	12	4	0	11	28	13
34-30	16	110	17	0	4	15	6	39
29-25	0	148	13	0	4	8	0	42
24-20	0	109	14	0	6	8	0	22
19-15	0	133	9	0	4	2	0	45
14-10	0	113	7	0	4	3	0	45
9-5	0	113	10	0	13	10	0	59
5-1	0	60	29	0	15	8	0	38

Of course, the decision is also very much a function of the score and the time remaining in the game. We said we'd get back to that, and we haven't lied to you yet, right?

The calculation is done exactly the same way, except that the probability of winning is used instead of potential points. However, there is a different win probability table for each time situation throughout the game. We'll take a single example here.

It's fourth-and-4 on your opponent's 10-yard line. The strategy is to go for a first down every time if we ignore the time and score. In this case, we'll say there are six minutes to play. We know there's an 85 percent success rate for a field goal and a 48 percent success rate for going for first down, so we can calculate the expected win potential for each strategy, depending on the score. The winning potential table gives the following numbers:

Score	WIN PROB 6 Min. Left	FIELD GOAL Make	FIELD GOAL Fail	FIELD GOAL Net	GO FOR IT Make	GO FOR IT Fail	GO FOR IT Net
−8	14.1	14.5	1.5	12.6*	14.8	2.2	8.2
−7	33.5	14.7	8.8	13.8	36.5	11.3	23.4*
−6	53.6	18.3	16.3	18.0	58.6	20.6	38.8*
−5	54.3	21.7	16.4	20.9	59.2	20.7	39.2*
−4	56.4	21.7	16.6	20.9	61.5	21.0	40.4*
−3	66.5	49.0	20.5	44.7	70.1	25.6	47.0*
−2	74.6	76.2	24.2	68.4*	76.3	30.1	52.3
−1	74.6	76.2	24.2	68.4*	76.3	30.1	52.3
0	84.1	80.1	51.6	75.8*	85.5	56.9	70.6
1	93.6	84.1	78.9	83.3	94.7	83.6	88.9*
2	93.6	84.3	78.9	83.5	94.7	83.6	88.9*
3	94.1	84.4	82.3	84.1	95.2	87.2	91.0*
4	96.2	91.7	85.9	90.8	96.8	89.0	92.7*
5	97.8	99.0	86.1	97.1*	98.1	89.3	93.5
6	97.8	99.0	86.1	97.1*	98.1	89.3	93.5
7	98.8	99.3	92.7	98.3*	98.9	94.4	97.0
8	99.8	99.5	99.2	99.5	99.8	99.5	99.6*

* Asterisk denotes higher Win Probability.

Now take a look. Let's check the situation of two points behind. Suppose you kick the field goal. The win probability for a successful field goal is the one in which you are one point ahead and the other team has a first-and-10 on its own 25 (after the kickoff). It's 76.2 percent. On the other hand (foot?), a missed field goal will put your opponent on his own 20-yard line with a two point lead. That gives you a win probability of only 24.2. Since the expected success rate for a field goal is 85 percent, the net win potential is $(.85 \times 76.2) + (.15 \times 24.2)$, or 68.4. Going for it gives you only a 52.3 net win potential. In this case, kick the field goal.

The table shows that for the situation in question (fourth-and-1 at the 10 with six minutes left), it's better to try for the field goal if you are 1, 2, or 8 points behind, or if the score is tied, or if you are 5 to 7 points ahead. Otherwise, the strategy should be to try for a first down.

Probably the most surprising thing is that you don't try for a field goal to tie if you're three points behind. Can that be right? Well, you've seen it happen a hundred times; a team ties the game with five or six minutes left and then loses. The numbers say that going for a first down is a slightly better choice; the field goal is only worthwhile if it puts you ahead.

But imagine what *USA Today* (not to mention the hometown papers) would do if a coach eschewed a "sure" tie to go for the first down and failed! Thus conformity, not cowardice, doth make cowards of coaches.

11

The Glory, the Blame, and the Ratings

"Did ya hear about the guy who spent $10,000 sending his son through college and all he got was a *quarter back*! But I wanna tell ya . . ."

If you're old enough to remember that ancient wheeze, you're also old enough to remember when a son (or daughter) could get four years of higher education for $10,000. Maybe even old enough to remember when a top-notch quarterback might have to pay his own way through school just like a real student.

Now, of course, a $10,000 investment is a bargain if your kid turns out to be a high NFL draft choice at any position. If he's a quarterback, he's got a pipeline to Ft. Knox. He can take care of you in your old age. If he's a first-round draft choice QB, he can take care of Poland in its old age.

Quarterbacks are the stars in the weekly NFL dramas. Their names go up on the marquee. They worry about best-side profiles. They have all the best lines. But it takes sixteen weeks and the playoffs before you know which QB is in a melodrama and which ones are in tragedies. When the curtain comes down on the final catastrophe—as it will for 27 out of 28—the audience will be dead certain the fatal flaw is within the protagonist—too much *hubris* or too little arm strength. The villains are all the guys on the other team, but when the other guys win, the home folks hiss the hero—their quarterback.

A few things you already think you know:

- It takes five years in the NFL to make a good quarterback.
- A bad team is bad because it lacks an outstanding quarterback.
- No team can win a Super Bowl or even expect a playoff berth without a first-rate quarterback.
- The highest-paid, most visible, and most important player on any team is its quarterback.

Like most things you've learned during your stay in this vale of tears, all of these are partly right. And partly wrong. Let's take 'em in order.

FIVE YEARS

Young quarterbacks used to sit around on NFL benches or, more often, stand on the sideline with clipboards for season after season until they got to be old quarterbacks. *Wait till next year and we'll let you take a couple of snaps, kid.* Matt Cavanaugh has been waiting in the wings since Carter was President. *Here, kid, take this chisel and knock off some rust.* Steve Ramsey gave great clipboard. *Don't just do something. Stand there!* Before he ever played in an official game, Cliff Stoudt had earned his NFL pension!

It takes five years, the coaches said, to learn to play quarterback in the NFL. There are audibles to learn. And secondary receivers. And reading defenses and . . . uh . . . well, four years sometimes.

Trouble was, most of those guys who watched for eighty or so games still didn't have the hang of it once they got the ball. Probably they never had the real stuff; it just took forever to prove it.

The good part was that everybody (except for those fans who believed their team's P.R.) came out ahead. The quarterback got five years of high pay for doing next to nothing. The coach who finally cut him couldn't be blamed because he hadn't been around when they wasted a draft choice on the kid. After five years, the front office had some new wonder who "is gonna be great in a couple of years." And even the old coach who blew the choice would be drawing his X's and O's for a new team, so he'd miss the flack.

It was a beautiful system, but some guys came along and messed it up. Guys named Marino and Elway and McMahon and more. Instead of learning how to hold a clipboard, they just jumped right in and started playing quarterback almost as soon as they learned their teammates' names. To this day, you hand Dan Marino a clipboard, he'll have to ask somebody how to hold it.

You used to have to look for kid QB's in what the league statistics call "non qualifiers," which sounds like something you should report to the Antidefamation League but is actually a listing of passers who threw too few passes in a season to "qualify" for the league passing championship. You'd see all those "future greats" listed with 12's or 7's or 3's under attempts, and you knew their coaches risked all by playing them late in the fourth quarter with the score 43-7.

To qualify for the NFL passing championship these days, a passer has to make 224 attempts, an average of 14 throws a game. A quarterback who tosses that many isn't necessarily his team's number one man, but he's not just an observer charting plays on the sideline either.

A survey of the league's 1986 qualifiers shows that most of them topped that magic 224 in their first or second seasons.

Quarterback	Year Over 224	Total	Year in League
John Elway	1983	259	First
Jim Kelly	1986	480	First
Bernie Kosar	1985	248	First
Neil Lomax	1981	236	First
Dan Marino	1983	296	First
Warren Moon	1984	450	First
Jim Plunkett	1971	328	First
Phil Simms	1979	265	First
Jack Trudeau	1986	417	First
David Archer	1985	312	Second
Tony Eason	1984	431	Second
Boomer Esiason	1985	431	Second
Dan Fouts	1974	237	Second
Eric Hipple	1981	279	Second
* Jim McMahon	1982	295	Second
Joe Montana	1980	273	Second
Marc Wilson	1981	366	Second
Steve Young	1986	363	Second
Bill Kenney	1981	274	Third
Tommy Kramer	1979	566	Third

Quarterback	Year Over 224	Total	Year in League
Ken O'Brien	1985	488	Third
Steve Pelluer	1986	378	Third
Jay Schroeder	1986	541	Third
Randy Wright	1986	492	Third
Dave Krieg	1983	243	Fourth
Ron Jaworski	1977	346	Fifth
Mark Malone	1984	272	Fifth
* Danny White	1980	436	Fifth
Dave Wilson	1985	293	Fifth

* Injured, did not qualify in 1986, but considered regular.

Rookie Jim Everett of the Rams threw only 147 times in 1986, but he signed in midseason and only played in 6 games—an average of 24.5 attempts per game.

So what's all this guff about five years? Well, twenty or twenty-five years ago, it made some sense. The colleges were that far behind the pros in the passing game—*Golly, coach, yuh mean we're ALLOWED to throw on SECOND down?*—and it took a while for a kid QB to learn how to do things like a pro—things like reading defenses, picking out second and third receivers, calling audibles, and hosting local TV shows.

The gap isn't nearly so great now; plenty of college programs are as savvy about passing as the pros, in part because a lot of ex-pros are coaching in colleges. Even though the college game is predicated on the run, their passing has come a long way in sophistication. As a matter of fact, a strong-armed high school kid starts looking for a college with a "pro-style" offense when he sifts scholarship offers because he knows it'll give him a leg up on an NFL career. Most real quarterback prospects show up for their first pro camp already knowing most of the things they have to.

Then too, that stand-around-and-watch stuff was always overrated. The real top QBs have always been able to take over early in their careers. Tittle, Layne, Unitas, Graham, Van Brocklin, and so on. Nearly all of the great ones were regulars in their first or second seasons.

Rule of thumb: unless there's a Hall of Fame candidate ahead of him, any quarterback who is going to be outstanding will play regularly by his second season. If a quarterback isn't number one by his third year, either fire the quarterback or fire the coach.

None of this is to say that somebody like Elway isn't a *better* quarterback now than he was as a rookie. Of course he is. But even back in '83 he was the best on the Broncos and better than a lot of other starters around the league. His coach, Dan Reeves, knew it. So Reeves shoved Elway out on the field, let him take his lumps, and four years later Denver was in the Super Bowl.

If there's an exception to our rule of thumb, it's right where you're most likely to see a kid QB playing in his first season—with a really ghastly team. A dog team may not have a decent veteran quarterback sometimes, but it almost never has a line that can protect anybody. Under those circumstances, a coach who wants to have his kid QB able-bodied when he finally gets bodies able to keep him that way better keep the kid on clipboard for a couple of years.

The story is that's what happened to Jim Plunkett, who went straight from Stanford to starting for the Patriots, which—considering the Pats' inability to protect their passer at that time—was like playing dodgeball on the hand grenade range. Plunkett was as brave as the next guy, maybe braver, but he was thoroughly shell-shocked by the time they booed him out of New England. They say it took Jim four or five seasons and lots of TLC from the Raiders before he was ready to go out and win a Super Bowl.

SOMEONE TO BLAME

When a team is going badly, the first guy to be booed is the quarterback. Many fans believe that the best way to improve his performance is to call him names and direct ugly sounds at him. Sure, we all respond well to that, don't we?

Well, there's no getting around the fact that the lousiest teams have mostly lousy players (or fewer good players, if you want to think positively). But the quarterback can be the victim rather than the perp.

Here's a matching game. Put the team record with its regular quarterback:

Bobby Layne	1949 New York Bulldogs, 1-10-1
Y. A. Tittle	1950 Baltimore Colts, 1-11-0
Norm Van Brocklin	1958 Philadelphia Eagles, 2-9-1

Bart Starr	1958 Green Bay Packers, 1-10-1
Fran Tarkenton	1961 Minnesota Vikings, 3-11-0
Bob Griese	1969 Miami Dolphins, 3-10-1
Roman Gabriel	1975 Philadelphia Eagles, 4-10-0
Joe Namath	1975 New York Jets, 3-11-0
Dan Fouts	1975 San Diego Chargers, 2-12-0
Ken Anderson	1978 Cincinnati Bengals, 4-12-0
Joe Montana	1980 San Francisco 49ers, 6-10-0
Phil Simms	1980 New York Giants, 4-12-0

Okay, we couldn't fool you. You're right, the quarterback in each case belongs with the team opposite. The point is, that's a darned good batch of quarterbacks and a really rotten batch of teams. You figure any of those clubs would have been winners with somebody else under center? To turn those losers into winners would have taken a quarterback who could also turn water into wine.

A long time ago, Giant fans used to festoon the Polo Grounds (*Polo Grounds*? We SAID a long time ago, didn't we?) with signs and banners questioning everything about Charlie Conerly, from his talent to his ancestry. The consensus was that he should skeedaddle back to Mississippi on the next bus. Charlie was such a terrible quarterback that the Giants lost games as often as Donald Duck loses his temper. All his fault, of course. Well, a couple of seasons went by, and the Giants got a whole bunch of new players and went out and won the NFL championship—with Charlie Conerly at quarterback. 'Course by then, he was just about the best danged signal-caller who ever came north from Mississip. *Everybody* at the Polo Grounds said so. Amazing how much ol' Charlie learned in just a few years!

Those loyal Pittsburgh fans once watched their quarterback get blindsided, and while he was being carried off they booed him. Later —four Super Bowls later—the fans forgot all about that, but we'll bet Terry Bradshaw didn't.

Nobody's saying that the best quarterbacks are all on the worst teams, like they say the best books don't get published or the best TV shows get canceled. Give some losing QBs a good line in front, receivers who can catch, a defense to give 'em the ball, and they'd *still* be bums. But it's hard as hell to tell from the stands.

Sometimes you'll hear the analogy that a quarterback is like a baseball pitcher. Not quite. Sure, a pitcher on a crummy team gets charged with a lot of losses that aren't his fault, but the difference is that he can still look good losing. He can have a low ERA, *beaucoup* strikeouts, some low-hit games. He doesn't get charged with an incomplete pitch if his catcher drops the ball. His shortstop boots the ball, a pitcher gets an unearned run; a lineman boots a block and a quarterback gets an unearned concussion.

TO THE VICTOR

The other side of the coin is that a quarterback who plays for a winner comes off as a—well, a winner. And the bigger the winner, the better the quarterback. Hence the old saw that only a great quarterback can win a Super Bowl. Define "great quarterback." *One who wins a Super Bowl.* A catch-22 that has nothing to do with wide receivers.

Let's take a look. Quarterbacks who have started and won (but never lost) Super Bowls: Terry Bradshaw, Joe Montana, Jim Plunkett, Bart Starr, Jim McMahon, Joe Namath, Phil Simms, Ken Stabler, John Unitas, and Doug Williams.

Certainly an impressive group. But great? The main claim to fame for Bradshaw and Namath is that they won Super Bowls—Bradshaw four and Namath the one he guaranteed. Would they be "great" if they hadn't won those five games? It's a bit early to hang immortality on McMahon or Simms. Stabler and Plunkett were good, but don't look for their busts in the Hall of Fame. Montana maybe, if he stays healthy and has a couple more good seasons. Unitas is on everybody's list of great quarterbacks, but the irony is that he spent most of Super Bowl V on the bench with hurt ribs. Earl Morrall subbed for him. Scratch Unitas and the only certified great in the group is Starr.

On the other hand: Len Dawson, Bob Griese, Roger Staubach, and Joe Theismann all won *and* lost Super Bowls. If you put these four on a "great" scale, they might average out a couple of pounds more of great than the fellas who only won.

SB NO.	YEAR	WINNING SUPER BOWL QUARTERBACKS	YR	HT	WT	AGE	SCHOOL	*AP	†PB
I	1966	Bart Starr, GB	11	6-1	200	33	Alabama	X	X
II	1967	Bart Starr, GB	12	6-1	200	34	Alabama	—	—
III	1968	Joe Namath, NYJ	4	6-2	195	25	Alabama	X	X
IV	1969	Len Dawson, KC	13	6-0	190	35	Purdue	—	X
V	1970	John Unitas, Bal	15	6-1	196	37	Louisville	—	—
VI	1971	Roger Staubach, Dal	3	6-2	197	29	Navy	—	X

SB NO.	YEAR	WINNING SUPER BOWL QUARTERBACKS	YR	HT	WT	AGE	SCHOOL	*AP	†PB
VII	1972	Bob Griese, Mia	6	6-1	190	27	Purdue	—	—
VIII	1973	Bob Griese, Mia	7	6-1	190	28	Purdue	—	X
IX	1974	Terry Bradshaw, Pit	5	6-3	218	25	La. Tech	—	—
X	1975	Terry Bradshaw, Pit	6	6-3	218	26	La. Tech	—	X
XI	1976	Ken Stabler, Oak	7	6-3	215	30	Alabama	—	X
XII	1977	Roger Staubach, Dal	9	6-2	202	35	Navy	—	X
XIII	1978	Terry Bradshaw, Pit	9	6-3	215	29	La. Tech	X	X
XIV	1979	Terry Bradshaw, Pit	10	6-3	215	30	La. Tech	—	X
XV	1980	Jim Plunkett, Oak	10	6-3	205	32	Stanford	—	—
XVI	1981	Joe Montana, SF	6	6-2	200	25	Notre Dame	—	X
XVII	1982	Joe Theismann, Was	9	6-0	198	33	Notre Dame	—	X
XVIII	1983	Jim Plunkett, Oak	13	6-3	205	35	Stanford	—	—
XIX	1984	Joe Montana, SF	6	6-2	200	25	Notre Dame	—	X
XX	1985	Jim McMahon, ChiB	4	6-1	190	26	B.Y.U.	—	X
XXI	1986	Phil Simms, NYG	7	6-3	215	30	Morehead St.	X	—
XXII	1987	Doug Williams, Was	7	6-4	220	32	Grambling	—	—

SB NO.	YEAR	LOSING SUPER BOWL QUARTERBACKS	YR	HT	WT	AGE	SCHOOL	*AP	†PB
I	1966	Len Dawson, KC	10	6-0	190	32	Purdue	X	X
II	1967	Daryle Lamonica, Oak	5	6-2	215	26	Notre Dame	X	X
III	1968	Earl Morrall, Bal	13	6-1	206	34	Michigan St.	X	X
IV	1969	Joe Kapp, Minn	3	6-2	215	31	California	—	X
V	1970	Craig Morton, Dal	7	6-4	214	27	California	—	—
VI	1971	Bob Griese, Mia	5	6-1	190	26	Purdue	X	X
VII	1972	Billy Kilmer, Was	10	6-0	204	32	U.C.L.A.	—	X
VIII	1973	Fran Tarkenton, Minn	13	6-1	190	33	Georgia	X	—
IX	1974	Fran Tarkenton, Minn	14	6-1	190	34	Georgia	—	X
X	1975	Roger Staubach, Dal	7	6-2	197	33	Navy	—	X
XI	1976	Fran Tarkenton, Minn	16	6-1	190	36	Georgia	—	X
XII	1977	Craig Morton, Den	14	6-4	214	34	California	—	—
XIII	1978	Roger Staubach, Dal	10	6-2	202	36	Navy	—	X
XIV	1979	Vince Ferragamo, Rams	3	6-3	207	25	Nebraska	—	—
XV	1980	Ron Jaworski, Phi	8	6-2	196	29	Youngstown St	—	X
XVI	1981	Ken Anderson, Cin	11	6-1	212	32	Augustana	X	X
XVII	1982	David Woodley, Mia	3	6-2	202	24	L.S.U.	—	—
XVIII	1983	Joe Theismann, Was	10	6-0	198	34	Notre Dame	X	X
XIV	1984	Dan Marino, Mia	2	6-3	214	23	Pittsburgh	X	X
XX	1985	Tony Eason, NE	3	6-4	212	26	Illinois	—	—
XXI	1986	John Elway, Den	4	6-3	210	26	Stanford	—	X
XXII	1987	John Elway, Den	5	6-3	210	27	Stanford	X	X

* All-Pro in Super Bowl year
† Pro Bowl (or AFL All-Star Game) in Super Bowl year

On the *other* hand (how many hands is that?), Ken Anderson, Tony Eason, John Elway, Vince Ferragamo, Ron Jaworski, Joe Kapp, Billy Kilmer, Daryle Lamonica, Dan Marino, Earl Morrall, Craig Morton,

Fran Tarkenton, and David Woodley started in Super Bowls but never won (although Morrall won as Unitas' sub).

By definition they weren't great, right? The jury is still out on Eason, Elway, and Marino. Even though he owned most of the league career passing records, Tarkenton took a couple of tries to get into the Hall of Fame, and none of the others is likely to get there. The price of losing.

Of course a lot of very good quarterbacks who've played in the last two decades never got as far as the Big One: Steve Bartkowski, George Blanda, John Brodie, Joe Ferguson, Dan Fouts, Roman Gabriel, John Hadl, Jim Hart, Charlie Johnson, Bert Jones, Sonny Jurgensen, Archie Manning, Babe Parilli, Brian Sipe, and Norm Snead, to name a few.

What do you think might have happened in 1974, for example, if Ken Anderson had been on the Steeler roster? Or suppose John Brodie had somehow got to Miami in the early 1970s. What if the Jets had drafted Marino? We could play "what-if" forever. What if Clark had dropped that end zone pass against Dallas in the playoff? What if Walter Camp had gone to Vassar?

So what's the point? Simply that getting to a Roman Numeral Game, much less winning it, is often an accident of the draft. Get with the right team, you've got a shot. We honor the quarterbacks who bring it off, and forget about the ones who perhaps never had the horses.

When the Colts drafted Elway as Number One in 1983, he took a look at their track record and told everyone how much he liked playing baseball. Eventually the Colts traded his rights to Denver, a team with a recent history of winning, and John decided baseball wasn't his destiny. He didn't even say it was a hobby. A couple of years later, after a Super Bowl, John is on more magazine covers than Jackie Onassis ever thought of. Meanwhile, only ten people outside the state of Indiana know who plays quarterback for the Colts.

Rule of thumb: any hotshot college quarterback drafted by a perennial loser should buy a baseball glove and telephone John Elway to ask about his next move.

NUMBER ONE

Quarterbacks make the big bucks.

Before he agreed to throw the football for the Tampa Bay Bucs, Vinnie Testaverde signed a contract for $8.2 million spread over six years, which means if he spends $3,744 every day including Sundays he'll be broke when the pact is up. Maybe he can borrow rent money from Elway, who'll still have $4.4 million left.

Elway makes about $62,500 a game. So do Joe Montana and Marc Wilson. Buffalo pays Jim Kelly $68,750, which means if they all get together he buys lunch.

It's nothing new. The numbers keep going up, but the QBs are always on top. Back in the mid-'50s Otto Graham was the first NFL player to make it to $25,000.

When quarterbacks aren't collecting paychecks from their teams—like when they're on strike—they can always pull down some extra bucks endorsing whatever happens to be at hand. Here, Super Bowl appearances really count. In 1987 the only QBs with national endorsements other than footballs and shoes had played in Super Bowls. King of the hill by far is Jim McMahon, whose estimated $3 million from endorsements is more than the next four combined. Nevertheless, Phil Simms ($900,000), Montana ($850,000), Dan Marino ($700,000), and Elway ($250,000) probably never need to take bottles back to the store for the deposits.

Quarterbacks are the glamor guys. You can get eyestrain searching for a football magazine with someone other than a quarterback on the cover. Maybe one out of ten has a running back; you could go blind looking for a lineman.

In no other team sport does one position dominate so completely in the public's mind. There are fans—or at least people who think of themselves as fans—who can't name any other player on their team except the quarterback. But that's nothing. How about the people who tell you they hate football? *They* can name a half dozen quarterbacks! Ask someone who hates arithmetic to name just one mathematician.

The adulation is not entirely undeserved. A quarterback handles the ball on every one of his team's ball-control plays. He does just about all of the passing. Hardly any quarterbacks choose the plays called in the huddle anymore, but they *do* call audibles at the line of scrimmage. There's no doubt that the QB is the single most important player on any team.

But that doesn't mean that the *quarterbacking* is the key to a team's success. If the defense is solid, the running game works, and the special teams perform, a team can get by with just average quarterbacking. That may sound sacrilegious. It's not. The average, ordinary, middle-level, generic NFL quarterback is a perfectly capable individual. If the rest of the team is good enough his main concern will be to avoid messing up. But remember, when the team wins, their fans will swear the quarterback was terrific.

On average, the difference between an outstanding quarterback and your common, garden-variety QB is three or four plays a game.

Where'd he get that, Mildred?

I think he's making it up.

No, not at all. We're not counting how well he calls his audibles. No statistics are kept on them, but we have faith that the cleverest quarterbacks call the best audibles because they have the most horses on the field.

On the mechanical side—the nuts and bolts physical part of playing quarterback—three or four plays separate the men from the boysenberries. Figure it this way. A typical game has about 175 plays of all kinds. Runs, passes, punts, kickoffs, field goal attempts, and extra points. On half of those the other team has the ball. The number one QB will also be on the sideline for everything but ball-control plays, so cross off all the kicks. That leaves about 33-35 runs and 38-40 passes. Forget about the runs, too. The QB has to hand off, but there's not much to choose between the ordinary and the outstanding among NFL ball handlers. The difference comes down to those 38-40 passes.

A lot of things have to happen on a successful pass: receivers have to get open and then hang on to the ball, the line has to block, and the QB has to get the ball there. How much of the play should we credit him with? We'll be generous and say 50 percent. That means the quarterback is responsible for 20 passes a game (the other 20 we'll credit to the receivers and the line).

Now of those 20—and by the way, they're not all completions; some might be intentional incompletions just to avoid interceptions, and some even the very best will miss—what's the difference between an outstanding QB and an average one? Well, in the NFL Passer Rating System (which we'll complain about in a few pages) the leader is usually about 20 points higher than the middle of the pack, or about 20 percent. And 20 percent of those 20 passes makes 4.

So what we're saying is that in a game between two otherwise equal teams, a really outstanding QB will pull off 4 plays that the average QB on the other side won't. He might avoid an interception, or keep a drive going, or pick up a first down. Whatever. It might make the difference.

But it might not.

Don't forget. Though the man is the single most important player, his *position* accounts for just part of what a team needs to do to win. If the defense collapses, or the special teams fall apart, or the runners don't run and the blockers don't block, he'll never get his picture on a magazine.

And when fans start talking about what's wrong with this awful team, they'll start with the quarterback.

The glory and the blame . . . and the money.

No one is paraphrasing Willie with *Mommas, don't let yore babies grow up to be QB's*. If your kid goes into medicine, you want him to be a surgeon instead of an emptier of bedpans. If he goes into law, you'd prefer a lawyer to a bailiff. If he's into football, hope for a quarterback. They get the most gravy with their lumps.

RANTING AT THE RATING SYSTEM

The only NFL thing badmouthed more often than a losing quarterback is the league's Passer Rating System.

There are folks out there who'd rather see the NFL's PRS canceled than get their taxes cut. They believe deep down that the passing of the Passer Rating System would bring universal peace and brotherhood, economic stability, and their favorite NFL quarterback to the top of the career list.

It seems that nobody has much good to say about the NFL's way of ranking its passers, and that's too bad because the present system is certainly a "long bomb" ahead of every other way they tried to do it previously.

But while we don't want to have the PRS exiled to Elba, we definitely have our reservations. Something is fishy, and we've reserved the end of this chapter for our carping.

But first we'll explain how we got to this point.

THE LESSONS OF HISTORY

For the first dozen years that the NFL existed, from 1920 through 1931, the league ignored the idea of statistics altogether. There weren't that many people showing up for games, and the league's leaders probably figured that no one cared about league leaders.

Then, in 1932, the NFL decided to start counting up its players' accomplishments. The decision to keep track of the numbers seems to have had little to do with Ultimate Truth, Revealed Verisimilitude, or the Reality of Sweat. It was just that the NFL headmen decided they might sell a few more tickets if they could say that one of the players on the visiting team was the leading something or other.

The revelation that statistics can sell tickets is one of the great discoveries of the twentieth century, ranking just behind pop-top cans and ahead of penicillin. However, a codicil to the law of capitalistic stats is that your numbers have to be believable. In other words, your stats somehow have to reflect the reality the fan feels in his gut before he'll ante up the price of admission.

Rushing, receiving, and scoring were easy: total yards, total passes caught, and total points scored. Those things reflected what fans saw and read. If the league said Beattie Feathers was the top rusher, fans could remember that he made a lot of long runs. Bronko Nagurski wasn't the leading rusher, but that was okay. Fans could believe that all his short gains didn't add up to Feathers' total. The stats reflected the perceived reality. Fans bought tickets to watch Feathers run—not very many tickets in those days, but a few. Enough to make it worthwhile to keep adding up rushing stats.

But passing was another kettle of fish. When a player hurled a pass, four different things might happen. The ball could bounce off the turf for an incompletion, and that was bad. It could be caught for some yards, and that was good. It could be caught for a touchdown, and that was terrific. Or it could be intercepted by an opponent, and that was terrible. Fans tended to remember their passers by the number of terrific and terrible things they did. From the start, the perception of passers was more subjective than that of any other major stat.

From 1932 through 1937, the NFL ignored all the philosophical implications and simply added up the yards as though passing were just another kind of rushing. Anyone reading the stat lists from those days may be a bit confused. After all, a lot of passers threw a lot of passes into the ground—or to opponents—and still ended up near the top of the league charts by completing a few long ones. Anyone throwing enough passes could eventually lead the league.

Green Bay's Arnie Herber threw often and deep. He was proud of his ability to hurl a football farther than some people could walk without packing a lunch. One time a couple of teammates bet him he couldn't throw the ball the length of the field if they allowed him the roll. Arnie chuckled and took the bet. Standing on one goal line, he unloaded toward the other. The ball arched high over midfield and came down at about the 15-yard line. To Arnie's chagrin, the angle of fall was so great that the ball hit and bounced back toward him, just as his teammates figured it would.

Although he lost the bet, Arnie won three NFL passing championships between 1932 and 1936. He seldom completed more than a third of his tosses. Nevertheless, when he connected, it was usually for a ton. Of course, having receivers who could run like Hall of Famers Don Hutson and Johnny Blood didn't hurt his yardage any.

Nevertheless long-throwing Arnie was generally perceived as the best passer around. His passing titles mirrored a reality that most fans could accept.

Then in 1937, Sammy Baugh came to the NFL. He showed he could throw both long and short. And he could usually complete about half of his throws, no matter what length. Accuracy became the name of the game. Hence the famous story where the coach says, "When the receiver breaks, Sam, hit him in the eye with the ball." And Baugh asks, "Which eye?"

Pass reality had changed.

So from 1938 through 1940, they determined the champ by completion percentage. And after a couple of injury-plagued seasons, Baugh won the passing title in 1940. He could do it all, but some of the league's best passers were getting blitzed by this method of ranking. Now the glove was on the other hand. The advantage was with the occasional passer who had surprise on his side. The heavy-duty passers—what few there were in those years—suffered because, as their attempts increased, their completion percentage tended to decrease.

Once more, change was in order. From 1941 through 1948, the league went for a more sophisticated method by using an inverse ranking system in which the best mark in a category got one point, the second best mark two points, and so on. Once all the points were added up, the winner was the man with the lowest total. In 1941-43 they "inversed" completions and completion percentage, but that gave all the advantage to the sharpshooters and gave nothing to the bombers.

In 1944-48, they tried to make everyone happy by rewarding both the heavy-duty tossers and the low-attempt/high-efficiency throwers with their mixture of categories. For the busy throwers, they counted total completions, yards gained, touchdowns, and interceptions. For the occasional hurler, percentages of completions and of interceptions. This went pretty well. People like Sammy Baugh, Cecil Isbell, and Bob Waterfield ended up at the top of the list. However, there were some disadvantages. In 1949 they dropped the number of interceptions from the list as a category favoring the less active passers.

The biggest problem for the inverse rating system of the '40s was that no one could figure it out unless he had all the stats from all the passers. Even then, it took hours in those noncalculator days to compute who ranked where and to add everything up. The average fan was lost. Moreover, by mixing totals and percentages, there was always the chance that some second- or third-team thrower would sneak into the top of the rankings. Finally, they had no logical way to figure a career mark. The NFL longed for a simpler system.

They thought they'd found it in 1950. They established the idea of a minimum number of attempts to qualify for the championship (100) and ranked everyone qualifying by average yards gained per pass. So in that first year, Pittsburgh tailback Joe Geri, who had generally awful stats but a high average gain, finished third in the league. Either he did it with mirrors or defensive backs regularly fell on their faces laughing when they saw one of his flutterballs. Nevertheless, the NFL stayed doggedly with average gain per pass as its only criterion until 1959. Result: six of the ten league passing champs threw fewer than 200 passes.

They knew something was wrong in 1957 when Tommy O'Connell, the Cleveland quarterback, finished on top. Tommy had taken over as Cleveland QB after Otto Graham retired, but no one ever got the two confused. Paul Brown, the legendary Cleveland coach, was critical as all-get-out about Tommy's inadequacies and generally gave the impression that O'Connell would stay on as his quarterback only until someone else applied. Almost anyone! Reading the writing on the wall better than he ever read a defense, O'Connell, the "best" passer in the league, retired before the next season began.

Meanwhile quarterbacks like Johnny Unitas and Bobby Layne won championship games, all-pro honors, but nary a passing title. Clearly the best quarterbacks in the league were being sacked by the system.

Back to the drawing board. In 1960 and 1961, the NFL returned to the inverse ranking system, using six categories: total completions, total yards, total TD passes, percentage of completions, percentage of interceptions, and average gain per attempt. They also insisted that the qualifiers had to average 10 attempts per game—120 total in 1960, 140 in 1961.

This was fine by Milt Plum, the Clevelander who succeeded Tommy O'Connell at QB. The new system melded so well with his limited skills that he finished both years at the top of the standings. Plum's primary passing ability was to dump short, safe screens to Jim Brown, and then watch the Hall of Fame fullback barrel for long gains. It made for great stats, but you either had to believe that Plum was the best passer in the world or that the system was short-sheeting the likes of Johnny Unitas, Y. A. Tittle, and Bart Starr.

In 1962 the league cut the categories down to four: percentage of completions, total touchdown passes, percentage of interceptions, and average gain per attempt. Despite some rumblings about including one total (touchdowns) in with three percentages, this system held through 1971. In 1972 they substituted percentage of touchdowns for total touchdowns. (Curiously the record manual to this day has no listing for season or career records in TD percentage.) People like Tittle, Starr, and Sonny Jurgensen did well in this system. They should have; just about everyone agreed they were the best.

Unfortunately there were still some real clinkers in this method. First of all, you still had to have every qualifier's numbers to figure *one* qualifier's rank. Worse, you couldn't really see what a passer was doing from year to year. Because he was ranked against every other full-time passer in the league, a passer might finish on top one season and the next year finish fifth with the same kind of stats. It looked as if he had slipped when in truth four others had improved.

TO THE RESCUE

Ah, but relief was in sight! For three years, a special study committee had been looking into ways of solving the problems. This group, headed by Don R. Smith of the Pro Football Hall of Fame, Seymour Siwoff of the Elias Sports Bureau, and Don Weiss, NFL Public Relations Director, and including Jan Van Duser, Curt Mosher, Tom Grimes, Bill McGrane and Jack Horrigan, spent three years studying the stats of all qualifying passers back to 1960. Eventually they settled on a system that was Smith's brainchild.

First, they kept the big four categories: percentage of completions, percentage of touchdowns, percentage of interceptions, and average gain per pass attempt. But instead of ranking a passer's marks against every other passer, the wrinkle that was at the root of what looked like the Last of the Big Problems, they ranked him against a set scale.

To try to visualize this, imagine yourself as a school teacher with two classes of twenty students each. You give each class the same test.

One class is graded against itself—the old NFL system. The kids with the highest marks get A's, the kids with the lowest marks get F's, and the ones in the middle get C's. It doesn't matter what the numbers are; if the whole class is full of dunderheads and the highest mark is only a 36, that student will still get an A. If, on the other hand, the class is made up of geniuses and the *lowest* mark is 96, that genius will fail! Boy, are the mommies going to scream! School boards being what they are, expect to be looking for another job in June.

You grade the second class against a previously determined scale. Let's say, A = 90 or better, B = 80 or better, etc. Now, imagine you've been teaching for twenty years and have given the same test every year. You've discovered that your best students always score above 90 and your worst can't make it to 60. All things considered, you'd have to say that this was the better way to rate the members of the class. It has fairness and continuity. Best of all, there's a built-in safety factor. If one year you have a whole lot of students who can't pass the test, and the school board starts getting antsy, the test is wrong! Change the test and you get rehired.

This is what the present NFL system does. It rates its passers on a previously determined scale. And if the passers aren't "passing" their test, the NFL changes the rules—er—test. More on that later; right now let's look at the system-to-end-all-systems—the final option that first saw the light of day in 1973.

By studying thirteen years of qualifying passers, the committee determined that an average passer completed 50.0 percent of his passes, threw 5 touchdowns for every 100 passes, had 11 out of every 200 tosses intercepted, and gained 7 yards per attempt on average. They awarded zero points for a really lousy job, one point for every average performance, and two for a record performance. There were plenty of increments. For example, here's part of the chart on completion percentage:

PCT	PTS	PCT	PTS
49.3	0.965	50.0	1.000
49.4	0.970	50.1	1.005
49.5	0.975	50.2	1.010
49.6	0.980	50.3	1.015
49.7	0.985	50.4	1.020
49.8	0.990	50.5	1.025
49.9	0.995	50.6	1.030

The total number of points (or fractions of points) earned by each passer in all four categories are then added together. Next that total is matched to a scale that goes from 0 to 158.3. An "average" grade in all four categories will give a passer a 66.6 rating. Only a scattered few have ever scored better than 100.

According to NFL P.R., the new system had four major pluses over all the other ways they'd tried before.

First, once a passer's rating had been established, whether for a season or a completed career, it was permanent. Thus both career and season records were easily determined and more meaningful. In the previous system, ranking passers against other passers, a career rating bobbed up and down every year like a Halloween apple, even for retired passers, depending on what all active qualifying passers did.

The second advantage was that an individual passer's rating could be determined independently of any other passer. Now you could figure out what Fran Tarkenton was doing without first having to know the record of Roger Staubach (and every other passer with a qualifying number of passes).

Third, passers who didn't throw the required number of passes could still be rated for either a season or a career. Before, the only throwers who counted were those with X-number of passes; all the subs were nowhere.

And finally, if you had all the tables to determine the points and convert the totals, computing the ratings was rapid and easy.

So everyone lived happily ever after, right?

Wrong!

THE SYSTEM UNDER SIEGE

The wonderful NFL Passer Rating System has turned out to be about as popular as the proverbial wet dog in a warm room.

From the start, some people screamed that you couldn't figure a passer's rating without a degree from M.I.T. That wasn't really fair, but it was true that you needed a copy of the NFL's little book of conversion tables. And most fans didn't have one. *And,* it was easier to complain about it than to write to the NFL and ask for one.

Other people were terribly upset when their favorite quarterback still finished well down in the rankings, even though they *knew* he was the best. The answer to that, of course, is that "best" is a subjective term applied to quarterbacks and includes many unmeasurables like ball handling, leadership, play calling, and courage. The system rated only how efficiently a passer threw the football. Even though most passers were quarterbacks and all quarterbacks were passers, the terms were not synonymous.

A scattered few felt that the numerical rating was too far divorced from any understandable concept (like total yards or average gain) to be meaningful. This, however, was only a matter of education. Once you've looked at a few tables of passer ratings, you begin to get the message that 88.7 is quite good and 37.4 puts a guy on the waiver wire.

While we reject the arguments that the system is too complicated or esoteric, and efficiency seems to us a rather likely criterion, we're not completely sold on the system. She's a terrific conversationalist with a great personality but . . .

For one thing, it's a little fuzzy on the edges. No matter how bad a passer is, he can't get less than 0 points. The bottom line is 30 percent completions, an average gain per pass of 3.00 yards, no touchdown passes (0.0 percent), and a 9.5 interception percentage. That's pretty bad, of course. His rating comes up 0.0. But if he'd completed only 20 percent for a zero average gain and had every other pass intercepted, he'd still be at 0.0. He should be drawn and quartered. Actually, we're not bothered much if the Passer Rating System is a bit soft-hearted with the the bottom of the scale. Anyone that incredibly awful needs all the help he can get.

We're more bothered by the top end. A maximum rating of 2.375 is set for each category. That's 77.5 percent completions, 12.50 yards per pass, 11.9 percent touchdowns, and no interceptions. If anyone does better than that, there's no bonus. 2.375 and that's it. You won't see those kinds of figures for a season very often (maybe never), but let's admit the possibility. Actually, Sid Luckman had 28 TD passes in only 202 attempts back in 1943. That's a 13.9 average, but because he only gets credit for 11.9, his 1943 rating is only sixth all-time instead of first.

Okay, you say you can't get very worked up that the PRS cheats the super elite and is kind to dumb animals. To tell the truth, neither can we. However, talking about the extremes is a start toward talking about the QB's the PRS really misrepresents—everyone else.

HOW IT REALLY WORKS—AND WHY IT DOESN'T

In very simple terms, the system looks like this:

Category/Rating	RATING POINTS			
	0	1	2	2.375
Percent Completions	30.0	50.0	70.0	77.5
Average Gain	3.00	7.00	11.00	12.50
Percent Touchdowns	0.0	5.0	10.0	11.9
Percent Interceptions	9.5	5.5	1.5	0.0

And from this we can see what's at the base of the PRS point system, how they calculate it. (And, incidentally, how you can work it out if you don't have the NFL's little booklet.) Look at "Percent Completions." All you have to do to figure out how they arrive at the number of points a passer receives for his percentage is subtract 30 (the bottom line on percentage) from his actual percentage and divide by 20 (the difference between the bottom line and the midpoint, or "average" score).

If a passer completes 50.0 of his passes, it's $50 - 30 = 20$, then $20 / 20 = 1$ point.

Here are some real examples, using NFL leaders:

YEAR	PASSER	COMP	ATT	PCT.	POINTS
1986	Tommy Kramer	208	372	$(55.91 - 30) / 20 =$	1.296
1985	Ken O'Brien	297	488	$(60.86 - 30) / 20 =$	1.543
1984	Dan Marino	362	564	$(64.18 - 30) / 20 =$	1.709
1981	Ken Anderson	300	479	$(62.63 - 30) / 20 =$	1.632
1979	Roger Staubach	267	461	$(57.92 - 30) / 20 =$	1.396

The points a passer receives for his average gain are figured in much the same way: start with his AvgG and subtract 3.0 (because that's the "0 number"); then divide by 4 (the difference between the "0 number" and the average, or "1-point number").

If a passer has a 7.00 AvgG, it's $7 - 3 = 4$, then $4 / 4 = 1$ point.

Here's what the same passers got for their AvgG's:

YEAR	PASSER	YDS	ATT	AvgG	POINTS
1986	Tommy Kramer	3000	372	$(8.065 - 3.0) / 4 =$	1.266
1985	Ken O'Brien	3888	488	$(7.967 - 3.0) / 4 =$	1.242
1984	Dan Marino	5084	564	$(9.014 - 3.0) / 4 =$	1.504
1981	Ken Anderson	3754	479	$(7.837 - 3.0) / 4 =$	1.209
1979	Roger Staubach	3586	461	$(7.779 - 3.0) / 4 =$	1.195

The points a passer receives for his percentage of touchdown passes are the easiest to calculate. Simply divide his TD% by 5 (the "1-point number"). You don't have to subtract anything because the "0 number" for TD% is actually 0.

So if a passer has a 5.0 TD% (say, 15 TDs in 300 attempts), it's $5.0 / 5 = 1$ point.

Once more our chosen five:

YEAR	PASSER	TD	ATT	TD%	POINTS
1986	Tommy Kramer	24	372	$6.452 / 5 =$	1.290
1985	Ken O'Brien	25	488	$5.123 / 5 =$	1.025
1984	Dan Marino	48	564	$8.511 / 5 =$	1.702
1981	Ken Anderson	29	479	$6.054 / 5 =$	1.211
1979	Roger Staubach	27	461	$5.857 / 5 =$	1.171

For the points a passer receives on his interception percentage, we have to do something slightly different because, unlike the other three numbers where higher is better, the best score is the *lowest* score here.

In this case, you subtract the passer's IN% from the "0 number" of 9.5, then divide by 4 (the difference between 9.5 and the "1-point number" of 5.5).

A passer with a 5.5 IN%—say, 22 interceptions in 400 attempts, comes out like this: $9.5 - 5.5 = 4.0 / 4 = 1$ point.

And once more, the five:

YEAR	PASSER	IN	ATT	IN% POINTS
1986	Tommy Kramer	10	372	9.5 − 2.688 / 4 = 1.703
1985	Ken O'Brien	8	488	9.5 − 1.639 / 4 = 1.965
1984	Dan Marino	17	564	9.5 − 3.014 / 4 = 1.622
1981	Ken Anderson	10	479	9.5 − 2.088 / 4 = 1.853
1979	Roger Staubach	11	461	9.5 − 2.386 / 4 = 1.779

Once you have all those points calculated, all you have to do is add them up and you can see who the leader is, but the NFL converts it to a "100 scale" by dividing by 6 and multiplying by 100. Neither step really means anything; they just make the ratings easier to read.

For our five:

	Kramer	O'Brien	Marino	Anderson	Staubach	
Comp%	1.296	1.543	1.709	1.632	1.396	
AvgG	1.266	1.242	1.504	1.209	1.195	
TD%	1.290	1.025	1.702	1.211	1.171	
IN%	1.703	1.965	1.622	1.853	1.779	
POINTS	5.555	5.775	6.537	5.905	5.541	/ 6 × 100
RATING	92.58	96.25	108.95	98.42	92.35	

Piece of cake!

If you'd like to see the whole formula all at once, it looks like this:

$$RATE = 100 \times [(Comp\% - 30) / 20 + (AvgG - 3) / 4 + TD\% / 5 + (9.5 - IN\%) / 4] / 6$$

(Note: starting in 1983, the NFL used the equation rather than the ratings charts. Until then, all the numbers had to be rounded off to get the right answer. Kramer's 1986 TD% of 6.452 would have been counted as 6.5. The equation is more accurate.)

Now direct your attention back to where we added up the point totals for the chosen five and we'll show you something odd. Do you see it? Almost everyone agrees that the average gain is the single most important statistic for any passer. (God knows, Joe Geri agrees!) In fact, for a decade it was the *only* determiner of pass rankings. Yet in the five leaders we show, the AvgG is never the highest point-getter. In fact, it's the lowest on three and second-lowest on the other two.

We're not stacking the deck; honest, you'd find the same thing on just about any passer you'd care to rate. But what it means is that the most important rating criterion counts the least, and the leaders—if they really are the leaders—are up front for the wrong reason!

Why is that?

We think we can show you. You see, although no one ever thinks of it this way, the Passer Rating System is really a yards-per-attempt formula, with bonuses for completions and touchdown passes, and penalties for interceptions.

Let's break the Passer Rating System down. What we'll do is manipulate the four rating categories to convert everything to yards. This gets a little complicated, so we'll put the explanation of how it's done at the end of this chapter. Right now, we'll just give you the formula:

$$RATE = 100 \, / \, 24 \times (com \times 20 + yards + TD \times 80 - int \times 100) \, / \atop att + 50 \, / \, 24$$

Now we can see what the various bonuses and penalties are worth.

AvgG stays just at whatever it is.

Each completion gets a 20-yard bonus.

Each touchdown pass gets an 80-yard bonus.

And each interception receives a 100-yard penalty.

Now remember, these bonuses and penalties are not something we're making up; they are simply another way of arriving at the same answer that the Passer Rating System gives—just as in school when you used to "prove" your long division answers by multiplying. The difference is that this way of proving shows us what the parts are really worth.

BUILDING A BETTER SYSTEM

How do you feel about giving a 20-point bonus for each completion? Not sure? Think of this. If one passer throws 2 passes and completes them both for 10 yards each, he'll have 60 points. Another passer misses his first toss and then hits his second for 40 yards. He also has 60 points. Both passers rate the same *even though the second guy moved his team twice as far*!

The NFL system favors the high-percentage, nickel passer. It always did, but that wasn't nearly so obvious until lately, when several teams began to use short passes out in the flat as, in effect, running plays. If Joe Montana dumps off to Roger Craig and the play loses 5 yards, Joe still gets 15 points.

Now how do you feel about it?

In building a better system, the first thing we'd do is get rid of completion percentage as any part of it. A completion in and of itself means absolutely nothing. Here's an extreme example: starting from his own 20, Joe Accurate completes three passes in a row, each for exactly 3 yards. It's fourth-and-1 at the 29. A long punt. Danny Bomb takes over at *his* 20. He throws 2 passes into the artificial turf and then hits a long one for 48 yards. It's first-and-10 at his opponent's 32. Which passer has the higher rating after 3 passes?

Joe Accurate, 69 to 68.

If one passer completes 6 for 10 for 70 yards and another completes 7 for 10 for 70 yards, their ratings would be—and should be—the same.

Okay, scratch the completion percentage.

Awarding an 80-yard bonus for a touchdown pass makes no sense either. It's like treating every TD toss as though it were an 80-yard bomb. Yet, the majority of touchdown passes are from inside the 25-yard line.

It's not the bonus we're objecting to—after all, the whole point of throwing a pass is to get the ball into the end zone—but the size of the bonus is way out of kilter. We advocate a 10-yard bonus for each touchdown pass. It's still higher than the yardage on a lot of TD tosses, but it allows for the fact that yardage is a lot harder to get once a team gets inside the opponent's 25.

Also way too much is that 100-yard penalty for an interception. Penalize 'em, sure; it's a turnover. But don't crucify 'em. What did it really cost? Actually about 45 yards on average, allowing for substitution of a punt and runback.

The average interception return is run back about 11 or 12 yards. Most interceptors don't get the ball back to the original line of scrimmage. Sometimes a deep interception is as good or even better than a punt. An interception at the end of a half doesn't really cost anything. A perfect system would take each individual interception (and touchdown) into account, but that would be far too complicated for the average fan. We'll still go with a −45, but we have a feeling it's still a couple of yards more than it should be.

Okay, so far we have a rating made up of the yardage, plus 10 for each touchdown, and minus 45 for each interception. Naturally it all gets divided by the total attempts.

We'll call it the New Rating System.

Before standing back and admiring our creation, we'd like to add one more twist. We want to subtract a passer's sack losses from his total yards gained—the New *Improved* Rating System. Now wait. Before you scream, consider this: sacks are a part—a risk, if you will—of passing. Some passers are sacked more often than others, and not entirely because they have poor lines. Dan Fouts could play behind tissue paper and still get most of his passes away. So could Marino. There are others, mercifully nameless here, who are just too slow in delivering. Or panic. Or can't find the open man. Why should they be rewarded by giving them all the pass gains and not charging them for their losses due to sacks?

Sack losses for individual quarterbacks aren't listed in the league passing charts, but you can find them if you look at the individual team stats. They also list the number of sacks, and these should be added to the pass attempts. The only real drawback that we see is that we can't figure out some of the old greats because their times sacked weren't kept anywhere until about twenty years ago.

Okay, here's the formula for our New Rating System:

$$RATE = (yards + TD \times 10 - int \times 45) / att$$

And for our New *Improved* Rating System:

$$RATE = (yards - sack\ yards + TD \times 10 - int \times 45) / (att + sacks)$$

LET'S SEE IF IT'LL FLY

Well, you can build a better mousetrap and still catch your finger if you're not careful. So let's check out our systems.

Here's the chosen five again, as they rank with the regular NFL Rating System, our New Rating System, and our New Improved System.

YEAR	PASSER	NFL RATE	NEW RATE	NEW IMPROVED
1986	Tommy Kramer	92.6	7.50	6.48
1985	Ken O'Brien	96.7	7.74	6.14
1984	Dan Marino	108.9	8.51	8.11
1981	Ken Anderson	98.5	7.50	6.85
1979	Roger Staubach	92.4	7.29	6.28

Not much help, is it? There's been some reordering, but whether that reflects truth or illusion isn't clear. What we really need to do is look at a whole season.

Well, no sooner said . . . Here's what happens with all the qualifiers from 1986:

NFL PASSER RATING SYSTEM		NEW RATING SYSTEM		NEW IMPROVED RATING SYSTEM	
PASSER	RATE	PASSER	NEWS	PASSER	NIRS
Tommy Kramer, Minn	92.6	Tommy Kramer, Minn	7.50	Boomer Esiason, Cin	6.55
Dan Marino, Mia	92.5	Boomer Esiason, Cin	7.32	Tommy Kramer, Min	6.48
Dave Krieg, Sea	91.0	Dave Krieg, Sea	7.03	Dan Marino, Mia	6.30
Tony Eason, NE	89.2	Tony Eason, NE	6.85	Bernie Kosar, Cle	5.79
Boomer Esiason, Cin	87.7	Jim Plunkett, Raid	6.83	Dave Krieg, Sea	5.74
Ken O'Brien, NYJ	85.8	Bernie Kosar, Cle	6.73	Joe Montana, SF	5.69
Bernie Kosar, Cle	83.8	Dan Marino, Mia	6.66	Tony Eason, NE	5.56
Jim Kelly, Buf	83.3	Jim Kelly, Buf	6.35	Jay Schroeder, Was	5.45
Jim Plunkett, Raid	82.5	Ken O'Brien, NYJ	6.31	Jim Plunkett, Raid	5.40
Joe Montana, SF	80.7	Joe Montana, SF	6.22	John Elway, Den	5.33
John Elway, Den	79.0	Jay Schroeder, Was	6.17	Jim Kelly, Buf	5.20
Eric Hipple, Det	75.6	John Elway, Den	6.13	Ken O'Brien, NYJ	5.15
Phil Simms, NYG	74.6	Dave Archer, Atl	5.79	Phil Simms, NYG	4.58
Neil Lomax, StL	73.6	Phil Simms, NYG	5.78	Dan Fouts, SD	4.50
Jay Schroeder, Was	72.9	Steve Pelluer, Dal	5.40	Dave Archer, Atl	4.43
Dave Archer, Atl	71.6	Neil Lomax, StL	5.16	Eric Hipple, Det	4.17
Dan Fouts, SD	71.4	Dan Fouts, SD	5.12	Bill Kenney, KC	4.14
Bill Kenney, KC	70.8	Bill Kenney, KC	5.06	Dave Wilson, NO	4.11
Ron Jaworski, Phi	70.2	Warren Moon, Hou	5.02	Randy Wright, GB	4.07
Steve Pelluer, Dal	67.9	Eric Hipple, Det	4.96	Warren Moon, Hou	4.00
Marc Wilson, Raid	67.4	Ron Jaworski, Phi	4.96	Ron Jaworski, Phi	3.97
Randy Wright, GB	66.2	Dave Wilson, NO	4.94	Steve Pelluer, Dal	3.95
Dave Wilson, NO	65.8	Steve Young, TB	4.90	Mark Malone, Pit	3.85
Steve Young, TB	65.5	Marc Wilson, Raid	4.86	Neil Lomax, StL	3.79
Mark Malone, Pit	62.5	Randy Wright, GB	4.84	Steve Young, TB	3.54
Warren Moon, Hou	62.3	Mark Malone, Pit	4.20	Marc Wilson, Raid	3.43
Jack Trudeau, Ind	53.5	Jack Trudeau, Ind	3.59	Jack Trudeau, Ind	2.87

As you can see, there has been some shifting. Esiason, for example, moved up. Ken O'Brien slipped a bit. No huge changes, though. We're not going to suddenly see the lowest rated passer (NFL-style) leap to the top, or a passer ranked high by the NFL suddenly tumble to the bottom. If that happened, we wouldn't believe our own system.

However, we believe that both the New Rating System and the New *Improved* Rating System give more accurate readings of passer efficiency than the old NFL system.

What you believe is up to you. But if you prefer the old NFL system, just remember, the next time a quarterback gets an easy completion by flipping to a back out into the flat—even though the play gains no yardage—the passer has just made 20 points.

CHANGING THE NFL RATINGS INTO YARDS

Original formula:

$RATE = 100 \times (COMP\ RATE + GAIN\ RATE + TD\ RATE + INT\ RATE) / 6$
  Example: if all rates were exactly average, they would be 1's.
  $RATE = 100 \times (1 + 1 + 1 + 1 + 1) / 6 = 66.7$

Now we want to combine terms. Remember that COMP PCT = COMP / ATT, TD PCT = TD / ATT, INT PCT = INT / ATT, AVG GAIN = YDS / ATT. So we can use the number of attempts as the common denominator.

For COMPLETION PERCENTAGE, we get
$$\frac{CMP / ATT - .30}{.20} = 5 \times COMP / ATT - 1.5$$

For AVERAGE GAIN, we get $\dfrac{YDS / ATT - 3}{\begin{array}{c}ATT - .75\\4\end{array}} = .25 \times YDS / ATT$

For TD PERCENTAGE, we get $\dfrac{TD / ATT}{.05} = 20 \times TD / ATT$

For INT PERCENTAGE, we get
$$\frac{.095 - INT / ATT}{.04} = 2.375 - 25 \times INT / ATT$$

Combining terms, we get

$5 \times CMP / ATT - 1.5 + .25 \times YDS / ATT - .75 + 20 \times TD / ATT + 2.375 - 25 \times INT / ATT$

Next we want to multiply top and bottom by 4 to get rid of the .25 in yards per attempt and combine constants and put in attempts as the denominator.

$$\frac{4\,(5 \times CMP + .25 \times YDS + 20 \times TD - 25 \times INT)}{4 \times ATT} + 2.375 - 1.5 - .75$$

This multiplying out, we get
$$\frac{(20 \times CMP + YDS + 80 \times TDS - 100 \times INT)}{4\ X\ ATT} + .125$$

Now, converting to NFL RATE by multiplying by 100 and dividing by 6:

$$RATE = \frac{100\ (20 \times CMP + YDS + 80 \times TDS - 100 \times INT)}{6 \times 4 \times ATT} + \frac{100 \times .125}{6}$$

This gives the final figure of

$$RATE = 4.16667\ \frac{(20 + CMP + YDS + 80 \times TDS - 100 \times INT)}{ATT} + 2.08333$$

4.16667 is 100 / 24 and 2.08333 is (100 × .125) / 6

$$\boxed{12}$$

The Running Game

That "you have to establish the run in order to pass" ranks as a ten on the cliché scale. We've heard it so often that we don't even listen anymore. "Yeah," we mumble, "establish the run and brush after every meal."

Did you ever ask yourself why you don't have to establish the pass in order to run? Well, as a matter of fact, that's true too; it's just not so obvious. If you can't pass at all, your opponent will concentrate on closing down your running game. By the second quarter, you'll be a couple of touchdowns behind and then you'll have to pass anyway. And when that still doesn't work, everyone will say it was because you couldn't run in the first quarter.

Escaping from a cliché like this one is harder than escaping from Devil's Island.

But there are a couple of reasons usually given as to why the run has more effect on the passing attack than vice versa.

One that you always hear is that your team feels better and your opponent develops all sorts of nervous ticks if you beat him on the ground. We have no real way of evaluating a linebacker's psyche—we heard that if you show 'em ink blots they smile and say "quarterback" —so we won't argue the point.

191

Another favorite is that a defense, as opposed to an offense, gets tired more quickly when they're out on the field for a long time. We never quite understood this. It always seemed to us that time spent shoving a 260-pound opponent around is equally exhausting whether you have the ball or not. We say "seemed" because we don't really know. We considered pushing some human mountain around for an afternoon in the interest of research, but then we thought better of it; you know, controlled environment and scientific neutrality and all that. So we decided to let the world's strongmen off easy—this time. We'll just assume the defense gets more tired. Maybe the cliché experts pulled a sweaty down lineman aside and asked, "Hey, are you more fatigued than that chipper wide receiver doing high fives in the end zone?" And the lineman said, "Yeah, man, I'm beat." Anyway, it is true that running plays keep the defense on the field longer than passing plays, and maybe the defenders get so tired tackling runners that they just let the receivers run willy-nilly.

But if you pinned us down as to a reason why establishing the run is more useful than establishing the pass, we'd suggest direction. Basically a secondary playing the pass moves backward from the line of scrimmage to keep the receivers in front of them. Meanwhile the down linemen charge in hell-for-leather to dump the passer. If the play called turns out to be a run, the linemen have a good shot at rushing flush into the rusher. And if the linemen don't get him, the secondary defenders are still between the runner and the goal line.

On the other hand, a defense playing the run either moves forward or holds its position. The tendency to hold its position will increase if the offense fakes a run first and then passes, the famous "play-action pass" celebrated every Sunday afternoon and Monday night by people who get paid to tell you what you're looking at. With the defense freezing or moving toward the line, a receiver can whip past and be open for a long gain or a touchdown.

Ergo: a defense playing pass is vulnerable to short running plays, but a defense playing run can be burned on long passes. And although either short gains or long gains can eventually score touchdowns, it takes many more short ones to do the job, allowing plenty of opportunity for fumbles and penalties to stop a drive. So the strategy is very simple: establish the run to the point that the defense looks for it and then burn them with a pass.

One thing about clichés is that they're often true. Tell the truth, did you ever see Mick Jagger gathering moss?

Speaking of clichés, how many times have you heard that "when so-and-so gains 100 yards rushing, his team wins 90 (or 93 or 96) percent of its games"? We love that one. It's like saying that when the rooster crows, the sun comes up 90 percent of the time. C'mon, guys! Cause and effect! The team didn't win because the guy gained 100 yards; the guy gained 100 because his team won!

It's really very simple. When does a team run? Usually in the first quarter to establish the you-know-what. By the second and third quarters, the running sloughs off, unless the team has gotten way ahead. When we reach the final quarter, we normally have two teams going in very different directions; the trailing team passing on almost every down trying to catch up, and the leading team running like crazy to eat up the clock. The wider the margin, the more the leader runs. And since most teams today depend on one back to do 70 percent of the running, the guy who plays with a strong team ends up with 100 or more yards.

Understand, we're not saying the 100-yard back doesn't make a very real contribution to winning. We're only saying that the likelihood of his gaining his yards is dependent upon the score, not the other way around.

In tracking several hundred games, we found the following: If a team was ahead by more than 7 points at the end of the game, it rushed (on average) 46 percent of the time in the first half and 61 percent in the second half, which is a blueprint for a 100-yard game by the team's main runner. On the other hand, if the lead was seven or less by the end of the game, the second half rushing was only 52 percent.

Meanwhile, the team trailing by more than seven at the end ran 42 percent in the first half and a mere 27 percent in the second. The lower first half figure is because the teams often trailed early and went heavily to the pass by the second quarter. When the game was close (7 points or less), the first half showed 46 percent running, the same as the leading team, but in the second half the figure dropped off to 37 percent.

You can see it a little better in this chart:

PERCENT OF RUSHING PLAYS

	SMALL LEAD		LARGE LEAD	
	1st Half	2nd Half	1st Half	2nd Half
Team Ahead	46	52	46	61
Team Behind	46	37	42	27

From looking at this, you'd think that a runner on a losing team racking up high yardage is as likely as Al Davis mentioning Pete Rozelle in his will. Actually since the NFL split into the American and National Conferences in 1970, nine men have led their conferences in rushing while playing for losing teams. Four did it twice:

Floyd Little, Denver 1970 Walter Payton, Chicago 1978
Larry Brown, Washington 1970 Walter Payton, Chicago 1980
Floyd Little, Denver 1971 Earl Campbell, Houston 1981
John Brockington, Green Bay 1971 George Rogers, New Orleans 1981
O. J. Simpson, Buffalo 1972 Earnest Jackson, San Diego 1984
John Brockington, Green Bay 1973 Gerald Riggs, Atlanta 1985
O. J. Simpson, Buffalo, 1976

It's almost a who's-who of runners. There were various reasons for their ability to gain despite their team's ineptitude. Some of these teams had exceptionally weak passing attacks and ran the ball in situations where almost any other team would pass. Some had incredibly poor defenses that couldn't hold leads. And in some cases, the teams got so far behind early, they ran the ball just to keep the other team from running up the score. The significant thing is that all of these guys were superior runners and continued to excel when they played for better teams.

Great runners generally find a way.

If you were a novelist and spent a hundred years trying to come up with the perfect name for a character who was to epitomize the rugged fullback of yesteryear, you'd never do better than "Bronko Nagurski." It's a name that reeks of down-in-the-mud, blood-on-the-elbow, leather-helmet, bone-jarring, CRUNCHING FOOTBALL. Of course, it's been done, so you'd have to think for another hundred years.

Anyway, the names of great running backs used to sound like— well, the names of great running backs. Bronko Nagurski, Ken Strong, Cliff Battles, Pat Harder, Eddie Price: they sound like they were born to smash off tackle. And if some misguided parent chose the wrong Christian name, there were always nicknames: Alphonse Leemans became "Tuffy," Clarence Manders became "Pug," Paul Younger was transformed into "Tank." The good old days may not always have been good, but they certainly were descriptive.

Today we have Eric Dickerson and Walter Payton and Marcus Allen. These are names for accountants! They don't even do nicknames right anymore. "Juice?" "Sweetness?" Are these runners or flavors?

Understand, there's nothing wrong with the players. We know full well that a rose by any other name would gain as many yards. No coach would bench a guy just because his name was Percy Puffmellow or something. Walter, Eric, Curt, Marcus, Gerald, and the others are terrific runners. Would that they sounded as good as they played!

One thing that's true is that today's runners rack up a lot more yardage than the well-named stars of yesterday. Why, back in 1941, a year that will live in infamy, ol' Pug Manders led the NFL in rushing with 486 yards. 486! That would be an ordinary month for Eric Dickerson. If you didn't know better, you might think that ol' Pug was running with one leg tied behind his back.

Well, in a way he was. See, these new guys have several advantages over the old-timers when it comes to gaining great gobs of yards. And it's only fair that we take a few moments to put things in proper perspective.

You probably think we're going to cavil about artificial turf and indoor stadiums, but we assume you already know that it's easier to cut on AstroTurf than on mud and easier to romp through climate control than through snowdrifts.

The most important advantage is that the new guys get to run more often than the old guys used to.

First of all, the new guys play more games. Ol' Pug did his plugging in an eleven-game season; from '43 to '45, teams played only 10 games. Today they play 16 games. It is reasonable to assume that someone playing 16 games is likely to gain a few more yards than someone who plays only two-thirds as many.

Remember all the fuss in baseball when Roger Maris hit 61 home runs in 162 games and so many people screamed that Babe Ruth hit his 60 in 154 games? Big deal! Not even 4 percent more games! Do you realize that Eric Dickerson gets the chance to play *33 percent* more games than Steve Van Buren could in 1949?

And in those extra games, a team's main runsmith gets to pack the pigskin (now *there's* a cliché!) a lot more often. The number of runs per team has in fact declined by about 20 percent since ol' Pug's day, from about 37-38 to around 30. But Pug played in the one-platoon days, which meant that he played offense and defense and, because he was human, sat out about a quarter of every game. Even when Pug went on the field on offense, he had to share the ball with a couple of other runners in his backfield.

By the 1950s two-platoon football was in, but teams used a full deck backfield for most of the decade. Every backfield had three runners saying "Gimme the ball." Y. A. Tittle once quarterbacked a backfield of Joe Perry, Hugh McElhenny, and John Henry Johnson. Probably when they all got in the huddle, he told them to take a number and wait.

Through the '60s and '70s, just about everybody used a pro-set with two running backs, but more and more merged into one main runner and his assistant. In 1984 James Wilder had 407 rushing attempts for Tampa Bay. His whole team only had 483. When a team's main runner gets the ball 70-80 percent of the time, he is going to get a lot of yards.

Pug Manders ran only 742 times in a nine-year career!

Here are the league leaders for the '40s with their actual records and what those project to over a 16-game schedule:

YEAR	RUNNER, TEAM	ACTUAL		16-GAMES	
		ATT	YDS	ATT	YDS
1940	Whizzer White, Detroit	146	514	212	825
1941	Pug Manders, Brooklyn	111	486	161	707
1942	Bill Dudley, Pittsburgh	162	696	236	1012
1943	Bill Paschal, New York Giants	147	572	235	915
1944	Bill Paschal, New York Giants	196	737	314	1179
1945	Steve Van Buren, Philadelphia	143	832	229	1331
1946	Bill Dudley, Pittsburgh	146	604	212	879
1947	Steve Van Buren, Philadelphia	217	1008	289	1344
1948	Steve Van Buren, Philadelphia	201	945	268	1260
1949	Steve Van Buren, Philadelphia	263	1146	351	1528

Even projected, most of the attempt totals look pretty trifling. Most of these guys did 30-40 percent of their team's running. Nevertheless to a modern eye, the projected YDS column looks a lot better than those wimpy actual numbers. Of course only Steve Van Buren in 1949 would stand a shot at leading a conference in rushing, but even ol' Pug has some decent numbers.

The problem with projections is that you have to assume that everything will keep trucking along at the same rate. Sometimes things don't. If you could project marriages from honeymoons, there'd be few divorces. We can only guess the player projected would continue to play at the same rate. For all we really know, ol' Pug would have played his eleventh game and never gained another inch.

Van Buren was really something special. Until he broke a thousand yards (actual) in 1947, only Beattie Feathers in 1934 had ever done that—and Feathers was a one-year wonder, playing behind the best line in the league and against some weak opponents, in an offense designed to take advantage of his breakaway speed. He never came close again—and there are statisticians who'll argue that he didn't do it in '34, that there were mistakes in his record.

But back to Van Buren. When he cracked 1,000 in '47, the NFL had just gone from an 11-game to a 12-game schedule. He wouldn't have made it without that extra game. Well, the next year, 1948, he came up 55 yards short. The funny thing was that he ran even better in '48. But in the next-to-last game of the season, the Eagles played Boston, and everyone knew Philadelphia could have phoned in the win. Besides, the Birds had already won their division and only had to stay healthy for the Championship Game. So Van Buren's coach sat him down and beat Boston black and blue with his other stars.

Van Buren had averaged 84 yards a game for 12 games in 1947, to break a thousand. But he averaged 86 yards a game for 11 games in 1948.

We're not suggesting that the NFL keep its rushing records according to how many games an individual runner plays. Van Buren's case is unusual, but if everything went on a per-game-played basis, sooner or later some guy would gain 200 yards in the first half of the opening game and then break his leg on the second-half kickoff.

The only reasonable way to make any comparison is to first look at the PSG record—Per Scheduled Game. Simply divide the yards, attempts, and touchdowns by the number of games on a team's schedule. If a runner is knocked out of a couple of games, he's not of any use to his team and the PSG record allows for that.

Look at this. Here are five different rushing seasons arranged in order of total yards.

YEAR	PLAYER, TEAM	ATT	YDS	AVG	TD
1984	Eric Dickerson, Los Angeles Rams	379	2105	5.6	14
1973	O. J. Simpson, Buffalo	332	2003	6.0	12
1980	Earl Campbell, Houston	373	1934	5.2	13
1963	Jim Brown, Cleveland	291	1863	6.4	12
1977	Walter Payton, Chicago	339	1852	5.5	14

But, if we look at the figures according to PSG, we get a very different order.

YEAR	PLAYER, TEAM	GM	ATT	YDS	AVG	TD
1973	O. J. Simpson, Buffalo	14	23.71	143.07	6.03	0.85
1963	Jim Brown, Cleveland	14	20.79	133.07	6.40	0.85
1977	Walter Payton, Chicago	14	24.21	132.29	5.46	1.00
1984	Eric Dickerson, Los Angeles Rams	16	23.69	131.56	5.55	0.88
1980	Earl Campbell, Houston	16	23.31	120.88	5.18	0.81

In other words, as well as Dickerson ran in 1984, he still didn't quite match the earlier efforts of Simpson, Brown, and Payton.

People have suggested that the Average Gain per Attempt figure be used to rank runners. The problem there is that there's always someone with only a few attempts and a long run. In 1944, Bulldog Turner was listed as 1 attempt for 48 yards! How Turner, one of the great centers, happened to be running the ball we don't know, but we're reasonably certain he wasn't the best running back in the league in 1944 or any other year.

Nevertheless we think the Average Gain is a useful figure, especially when compared with the League Average. For example, in 1986, Eric Dickerson ran the ball 404 times. He gained 1,821 yards, but my grandmother could gain a fair number of yards if they gave her the ball 404 times. The question is, how many more yards can be gained by handing off to Dickerson than by handing off to an average back (no, not my grandmother)? Easy. The league rushing average for 1986 was 3.936, so an average back would gain 3.936 × 404, or 1,590.1 yards. Dickerson was worth 230.9 extra yards. Curt Warner, who led the American Conference with 1,481 yards, ran 319 times. The math: 3.936 × 319 = 1255.6 for an average back. Warner made 225.4 extra yards on nearly 100 fewer attempts.

This is particularly useful in looking at team rushing. In 1986 the top five teams in total rushing yards were (in order) Chicago, Cincinnati, Atlanta, Los Angeles Rams, and Seattle. On the other hand, the Average Gains for these five put them in a different order: Cincinnati, Seattle, Chicago, Atlanta, and the Rams. The problem is, how to equate two very different sets of figures. Well, if we compare the Average Gains with the league average and figure out what an average team would have gained, the problem vanishes.

Team	ATT	YDS	AVG	AVG TEAM	DIFF
Cincinnati	521	2533	4.9	2050.7	482.3
Chicago	606	2700	4.5	2385.2	314.8
Seattle	513	2300	4.5	2019.2	280.8
Atlanta	578	2524	4.4	2275.0	249.0
Los Angeles Rams	578	2457	4.3	2275.0	182.0

We'll say some more about this way of looking at individuals later. Right now, we want to look at the Per Scheduled Game system.

We wanted to make some comparisons of individuals, so we worked out the PSG marks for attempts, yards, and touchdowns for the top five runners in each NFL year and then averaged the figures for longer periods. When we hit 1970, we started using the top five in each conference. The Average Gain figures were only averaged.

PER SCHEDULED GAME MARKS FOR LEADING NFL RUNNERS

YEARS	PSG ATT	PSG YDS	AVG	PSG TD
1932-35	10.86	49.00	4.51	0.35
1936-40	11.73	49.17	4.19	0.35
1941-45	11.33	51.87	4.58	0.50
1946-50	12.21	57.10	4.67	0.42
1951-55	12.74	63.24	4.97	0.51
1956-60	15.28	75.04	4.91	0.62
1961-65	15.79	74.96	4.75	0.61
1966-70	14.90	67.09	4.50	0.46
1971-75	17.26	77.66	4.50	0.47
1976-80	18.43	80.67	4.38	0.55
1981-86	18.92	82.76	4.38	0.57

You'll notice the attempts keep going up at about the same rate as the yards. But the Average Gain has actually declined a smidge since the 1950s. The indication is that the quality of running hasn't changed much over the years; the record yardage totals are simply a matter of increased rushing attempts.

Score one for ol' Pug.

13

Opus for the Unsung

You can tell what kind of football fans the guys at the end of the bar are by what they're arguing about.

Casual fans ("I always go to at least one game a year if my cousin gets me a ticket.") argue about teams.

Involved fans ("I never miss a game on TV if my mother-in-law doesn't come over.") argue about quarterbacks.

Rabid-but-unsophisticated fans ("When do the Dolphins play Notre Dame?") argue about running backs.

Literate fans ("Pro football is really a metaphor for the human condition.") discuss receivers.

Beer drinkers debate defenses. At the tops of their lungs. Watch out; they tend to gesticulate a lot.

But if you ever hear two guys outshouting each other about the best blocking linemen, you can bet your autographed copy of *Instant Replay* that you're listening to a couple of Pat-Dyed-in-the-wool, down-in-the-Dirt-Winston, do-or-die-for-dear-Joe-Rutgens *football fans*. That, of course, is irrespective of the fact that neither of them knows what the hell he's talking about.

The warts-and-all truth is that no one knows for sure who the very best blocking lineman is—or was—or will be. Lord! It's hard to find anyone who cares! The runners and passers whose health the linemen preserve care. Ask almost any runner and he'll tell you how much he owes to "what's-his-name and those other guys." When he wakes up on Monday morning with his head still where it was at kickoff on Sunday, he has at least a vague idea of what his linemen did for him. He may not recognize them face to face, but then again he doesn't usually have that view of them in a game.

"Offensive linemen" is the answer to the question Butch and Sundance kept asking. But who are the best?

We can be darned certain that guys like Bill Fralic, Russ Grimm, Anthony Munoz, Jim Colbert, and Dwight Stephenson are first-rate. But are they better than, say, Dennis Harrah, Keith Bishop, Jackie Slater, Brad Benson, Jay Hilgenberg, or Chris Hinton?

And what about Cody Risien, Roy Foster, Mike Webster, Ray Donaldson? What about Joe Jacoby? Mike Munchak?

Everyone says he has an opinion, but it's more like an act of faith. What can they base their opinions on? Runners, passers, catchers, and even defenders have some sort of statistical hook to hang their reputations on. Linemen not only lack stats, they lack visibility. It's probably not true that Jimmy Hoffa has been hiding out as an NFL guard all these years, but you'd have a tough time proving it. No one—and that's *no one*—watches a guard all the time a game is going on. Not a fan. Not a zebra. Not even the defender on the other side of the line. Oh, a down lineman will watch a guard as long as he's being blocked by him, but let the guard pull out and the fickle defender starts seeking cheap thrills with the opposing quarterback. If a guard were a TV show, his Nielsen would get him canceled before the first commercial.

Actually a team's line coach may watch our guard on film through an entire game. He'll even grade him. After a couple of games, any good line coach can tell you who the most effective blocker on his own team is. And who's not doing the job. But he can't make more than a rough estimate of the best in the whole league because he never sees all of the teams. And the only team he sees for all 16 games is his own.

If you talk to enough coaches and players, you can get a pretty good idea of the top blockers. Maybe a nice group of ten or twenty. Just don't expect them to settle on a number one.

Wait a minute, you say in your most Maddenesque manner, why don't we get all the grade sheets from the line coaches, put them together, and average out a winner?

Well, in the first place, we can't. Most line coaches guard their grade sheets as if they were Sigourney Weaver's unlisted telephone number. If their charges guarded quarterbacks as well, the word "sack" would be archaic. The idea seems to be that if a guy grades low, don't tell the opposition; if he grades high, don't tell his agent.

Even if we got hold of all the grade sheets, we couldn't average them out. Different coaches use different rating systems. A "near-perfect 9" becomes an "excellent 88.5" or "37/38" or whatever code means something to the coach. Some coaches give so much for "form"; others just want to know if the opponent was taken out of the play. Rating blockers is like rating ice skaters: one coach's "6" is another's "4.5."

If you check with a Bulgarian line coach, you'll think every lineman grades out a point low.

So let's give up and move on to another chapter, right? Wrong. In fact, there are some pretty good statistics readily available for telling us about blockers. We'll tell you about them as soon as we deliver a little lecture on offensive lines.

THEORY OF THE STRONGEST LINK

Suppose, just for the sake of argument, you had the best blocking tackle anyone ever dreamed of playing on your line. This guy can run-block Godzilla on its tail. He can pass-block the Johnstown Flood away from the quarterback. He's voted into the Hall of Fame at his first training camp. He makes the word "perfect" seem faint praise.

How much do you think the guy is worth on the hoof?

By himself—nothing. Well, maybe not zero, but close to it. Call it, next to *nada*.

By himself no blocking lineman has any real bearing on a game's outcome. He can deliver a key block, but if he's the only one doing it, the play will fail. He can flatten opponents all day and his team could still not gain an inch. It takes a whole line. An offensive line must work as a unit. *Everyone* has to be adequate.

Take what is probably the most famous block of all time. All right, the List of Famous Blocks is about as long as the List of Famous Aardvarks, but the block that most people bring up is the one Packer Jerry Kramer laid on Cowboy Jethro Pugh to allow Bart Starr to quarterback-sneak the winning touchdown in the 1966 NFL Championship Game, the so-called "Freezer Bowl." You recall there were 16 seconds left in 13-below temperatures when Starr followed Kramer into the end zone.

Now *that* was a key block! It won the title, put Green Bay in the first Super Bowl, and no doubt helped Kramer on his way to becoming a bestselling author. Everybody remembers it.

But how many remember that both Kramer *and* center Ken Bowman blocked Pugh? You can bet Jethro remembers. Did you ever wonder why Dallas's Bob Lilly—as tough a defensive tackle as ever crunched a quarterback—didn't do something heroic to stop Starr? Answer: Green Bay tackle Bob Skoronski wouldn't let him. Where was Cowboy Willie Towns? Answer: Forrest Gregg.

The point is that if every man along the Packers' offensive line didn't do his job on that play (and for the whole game, for that matter), Kramer would have had to write *Instant DOWNplay*.

It may be an overstatement (which never stopped us before) to say that an offensive line is only as strong as its weakest link, but it certainly can't be as good as its strongest link.

Because an offensive line is so interdependent, you seldom find a rookie able to move in there and improve a team's performance. There are a few—Atlanta's Fralic comes to mind—but most of the time it takes even very good blockers a season or two to fit in. Usually when a rookie is in the line, some veteran is hurt.

Rookies start at running back, at receiver, even at quarterback. Very few start at guard.

Which brings up a weird footnote on terminology. Runners and passers and catchers are always referred to as playing the "skill positions." Linemen, of course, are "unskilled." The idea seems to be that you need an apprenticeship, six sponsors, and a union card before you're allowed to touch the football, but any brainless lummox can shove Rosey Taylor around for an afternoon. It sounds as if you could make an offensive line by counting off the first five winos in an alley. Odd. Have you ever noticed how many NFL head coaches used to be offensive linemen?

THE LINE STAT LINE

To return to statistics. While it's true the NFL doesn't keep individual blocking stats, there are some numbers that indicate how well a whole line does. They're just never thought about as "line stats."

Think about what offensive linemen have to do. Just two things: run-block and pass-block.

If you look at the Team Average Rushing Gain Per Attempt, you'll get a good idea of how well a line run-blocks. The problem is very few fans think of it that way. They see a low average and decide their team needs new runners. If the average is high, they want to hear who ran the ball.

You know that game story that began, "Eric Dickerson ran for 154 yards today in leading to . . ." Just once we'd like to see "Jackie Slater, Dennis Harrah, Doug Smith, Tom Newberry, and Irv Pankey blocked for 154 yards today . . ."

It makes just as much sense. Probably the newspapers don't do it that way just to save newsprint.

The second important line stat is the Sacks column. Here fans usually look at the defensive side—"Hey, we sacked them seven times. Great!" It's equally valid to say something like: "Wow! Our lead-footed quarterback got off 34 passes and our line only let them tackle him twice!"

Maybe the klutz only got three of his tosses on target and the iron-handed receivers dropped two of those, but the line did a heckuva job.

If you take the average rushing gain and the percentage of sacks to attempts (including sacks which are attempts that didn't get attempted), you'll have a fair idea of how good (or bad) a line performs. Oh, sure, there are other factors. It helps to have runners like Dickerson or Payton who can take advantage of the opportunities provided. And a quarterback like Marino gets rid of the ball a lot quicker than, say, Randall Cunningham. But that just gets us back to the truism that all football stats are really team statistics. As long as we're going to look at Gerald Riggs's rushing stats (and evaluate his ability by them), it's every bit as logical to check out his line the same way.

Incidentally the NFL doesn't actually show Sack Percentage in its end-of-year stats. They just give the raw data: so many pass attempts, so many sacks. You have to add the sacks and pass attempts together yourself and then divide the sacks by the total.

On the next couple of pages, we've ranked the last few years of line play in the NFL, according to Rushing Average and Sack Percentage. We've also changed the raw averages for each into grades, using 120 as the high score. A team has to perform at record caliber to get that high. For example, the Cleveland Browns' 1963 record rushing average of 5.74 translates into 119.8. The New York Jets sack percentage of 1.72 (9 sacks in 523 pass attempts) in 1966 comes out to 120.1. An "average grade," a comfortable "C," is about 83.

The grades don't make the numbers any more "right"; they just make them easier to read. Otherwise you have to compare a rushing average (which is better as it goes up) with a sack percentage (which is better as it goes down).

Finally we averaged both grades together (using the percentages of rushes and passes for each team) to produce a total grade.

1984 PASS

Team	Rush Att	Rush Avg	Rush Grade*	+ Sak Att	Tot. Sak	Pct. Sak	Sak Grade†	Pos. Plays	Total Grade‡
L.A. Rams	541	5.29	110.4	390	32	8.21	88.8	931	101.35
Miami	484	3.96	82.6	586	14	2.39	116.7	1070	101.27
San Francisco	534	4.62	96.4	523	27	5.16	103.4	1057	99.86
Kansas City	408	3.74	78.1	626	33	5.27	102.9	1034	93.12
San Diego	456	3.63	75.8	698	36	5.16	103.4	1154	92.49
Green Bay	461	4.38	91.4	548	42	7.66	91.4	1009	91.40
Denver	508	4.09	85.4	510	35	6.86	95.2	1018	90.31
Chicago	674	4.41	92.0	426	36	8.45	87.6	1100	90.30
St. Louis	488	4.28	89.3	615	49	7.97	90.0	1103	89.69
New Orleans	523	4.15	86.6	521	45	8.64	86.7	1044	86.65
Cincinnati	540	4.03	84.1	541	45	8.32	88.2	1081	86.15
N.Y. Jets	504	4.34	90.6	540	52	9.63	81.9	1044	86.10
Dallas	469	3.65	76.2	653	48	7.36	92.8	1121	85.85
Tampa Bay	483	3.68	76.8	607	45	7.41	92.6	1090	85.60
Pittsburgh	574	3.80	79.3	478	35	7.32	93.0	1052	85.52
Detroit	446	4.52	94.3	592	61	10.30	78.7	1038	85.40
Buffalo	398	4.13	86.2	648	60	9.24	83.8	1046	84.71
Washington	588	3.87	80.8	533	48	9.00	85.0	1121	82.79
Houston	433	3.82	79.7	536	48	9.00	85.0	1121	82.79
Minnesota	444	4.15	86.6	597	64	10.72	76.7	1041	80.93
Philadelphia	381	3.51	73.3	666	60	9.01	00.9	1047	80.68
Seattle	495	3.32	69.3	539	42	7.79	90.8	1034	80.51
New England	482	4.22	88.1	566	66	11.66	72.2	1048	79.59
L.A. Raiders	516	3.66	76.4	545	54	9.91	80.6	1061	78.56
N.Y. Giants	493	3.37	70.3	580	55	9.48	82.7	1073	77.00
Atlanta	489	4.07	84.9	545	67	12.29	69.2	1034	76.62
Cleveland	489	3.47	72.4	550	55	10.00	80.2	1039	76.52
Indianapolis	510	3.97	82.9	469	58	12.37	68.8	979	76.15

* Rushing Grade (RG) = 120 × (Avg/5.75)
† Sack Grade   (SG) = 1.20 × {100 − [4 × (Pct − 1.70)]}
‡ Total Grade   (TG) = %r × RG + %p × SG

1985 PASS

Team	Rush Att	Rush Avg	Rush Grade*	+ Sak Att	Tot. Sak	Pct. Sak	Sak Grade†	Pos. Plays	Total Grade‡
Indianapolis	485	5.03	105.0	503	35	6.96	94.6	988	99.70
Miami	444	3.89	81.2	595	19	3.19	112.8	1039	99.30
San Francisco	477	4.68	97.7	592	42	7.09	94.1	1069	95.70
Cincinnati	503	4.34	90.6	559	41	7.33	93.0	1062	91.86
San Diego	440	3.78	78.9	671	39	5.81	100.3	1111	91.82
Pittsburgh	541	4.02	83.9	545	33	6.06	99.1	1086	91.53
Green Bay	470	4.70	98.1	563	50	8.88	85.5	1033	91.23
Denver	497	3.72	77.6	655	38	5.80	100.3	1152	90.51
Chicago	610	4.53	94.5	475	43	9.05	84.7	1085	90.21
L.A. Raiders	532	4.25	88.7	549	43	7.83	90.6	1081	89.66
Cleveland	533	4.29	89.5	450	36	8.00	89.8	983	89.63
New England	565	4.13	86.2	496	39	7.86	90.4	1061	88.16
Washington	571	4.42	92.2	564	52	9.22	83.9	1135	88.07
Dallas	462	3.77	78.7	631	44	6.97	94.7	1093	87.94
Buffalo	412	3.91	81.6	559	42	7.51	92.1	971	87.64
Minnesota	406	3.73	77.8	621	45	7.25	93.4	1027	87.24
Tampa Bay	434	3.79	79.1	548	40	7.30	93.1	979	87.18
N.Y. Giants	581	4.22	88.1	549	52	9.47	82.7	1130	85.48
Philadelphia	428	3.81	79.5	622	55	8.84	85.7	1050	83.18
Kansas City	428	3.47	72.4	554	43	7.76	90.9	982	82.84
Seattle	462	3.56	74.3	628	53	8.44	87.6	1090	81.96
N.Y. Jets	564	4.10	85.6	559	62	11.09	74.9	1123	80.27
St. Louis	417	4.73	82.3	599	65	10.85	78.5	1016	80.06
New Orleans	431	3.90	81.4	566	58	10.25	79.0	997	80.04
Atlanta	560	4.40	91.8	531	69	12.99	65.8	1091	79.15
Houston	428	3.67	76.6	570	58	10.18	79.3	998	78.14
L.A. Rams	503	4.09	85.4	460	57	12.39	68.7	963	77.43
Detroit	452	3.40	71.0	515	53	10.29	78.8	967	75.16

* Rushing Grade (RG) = $120 \times (Avg/5.75)$
† Sack Grade (SG) = $1.20 \times \{100 - [4 \times (Pct - 1.70)]\}$
‡ Total Grade (TG) = $\%r \times RG + \%p \times SG$

1986 PASS

Team	Rush Att	Rush Avg	Rush Grade*	+ Sak Att	Tot. Sak	Pct. Sak	Sak Grade†	Pos. Plays	Total Grade‡
Miami	349	4.43	92.4	662	17	2.57	115.8	1011	107.73
Cincinnati	521	4.86	101.5	525	28	5.33	102.6	1046	102.06
Chicago	606	4.46	93.0	439	24	5.47	101.9	1045	96.74
San Francisco	510	3.89	81.3	608	26	4.28	107.6	1118	95.61
Pittsburgh	564	3.94	82.3	511	20	3.91	109.4	1075	95.18
L.A. Rams	578	4.25	88.7	430	27	6.28	98.0	1002	93.23
New Orleans	505	4.11	85.7	452	27	5.97	99.5	957	92.21
Seattle	513	4.48	93.6	492	39	7.93	90.1	1005	91.89
Green Bay	424	3.81	79.4	602	37	6.15	98.6	1026	90.66
San Diego	471	3.35	69.8	636	32	5.03	104.0	1107	89.45
Washington	474	3.65	76.3	570	28	5.91	99.8	1044	89.13
Denver	455	3.69	77.0	587	38	6.47	97.1	1042	88.32
Buffalo	419	3.95	82.4	544	45	8.27	88.5	963	85.84
Dallas	448	4.40	91.7	606	59	9.74	81.4	1054	85.78
Cleveland	470	3.51	73.3	577	39	6.76	95.7	1047	85.64
Detroit	470	3.77	78.6	509	39	7.66	91.4	979	85.25
Minnesota	461	3.77	78.7	563	44	7.82	90.6	1024	85.24
N.Y. Giants	558	4.02	84.0	518	46	8.88	85.5	1076	84.72
Atlanta	578	4.36	91.1	508	56	11.02	75.3	1084	83.87
Indianapolis	407	3.66	76.5	639	53	8.29	88.4	1046	83.77
St. Louis	419	4.26	89.0	575	59	10.26	78.9	994	83.16
N.Y. Jets	490	3.53	73.7	582	45	7.73	91.0	1072	83.09
Houston	490	3.47	72.4	599	48	8.01	89.7	1089	81.92
Tampa Bay	455	4.09	85.5	515	56	10.87	76.0	970	80.46
Kansas City	432	3.40	70.9	571	50	8.76	86.1	1003	79.56
New England	469	2.93	61.1	604	47	7.79	90.8	1073	77.82
L.A. Raiders	475	3.77	78.7	594	64	10.77	76.5	1069	77.48
Philadelphia	499	4.01	83.7	618	104	16.83	47.4	1117	63.61

* Rushing Grade (RG) = $120 \times (Avg/5.75)$
† Sack Grade (SG) = $1.20 \times \{100 - [4 \times (Pct - 1.70)]\}$
‡ Total Grade (TG) = $\%r \times RG + \%p \times SG$

WHO ARE THOSE GUYS?

On the next couple of pages you'll see so many names you never saw before, you'll think you're reading the Dresden telephone directory. What they are is the starting offensive linemen in the NFL in 1984–86 by team.

Look closely. Unless some of them go into bank robbing, you may never see their names again.

No, we haven't included tight ends. Some teams use their tight end primarily as a receiver. Some use him as a third tackle. Mostly it's a mix. They block on runs and catch on passes. To include all, some, or part would be confusing, so we dropped them.

We marked players selected to the Pro Bowl or All-Pro teams.

You may have heard of some of them. And we marked rookies and "regulars" who played in only 12 or fewer games because these tend to disrupt the line's efficiency.

Keys to the 28 team tables that follow: *Before name*: # = Pro Bowl selection; * = Named to at least one All-Pro Team (AP, NEA, FWA, UPI). *After name:* -r = rookie; -X = started 12 or fewer games.

ATLANTA FALCONS

Team	Rush Att	Rush Avg	Rush Grade	Pass +Sak Att	Tot Sak	Pct Sak	Sak Grade	Pos Plays	Total Grade
1984	489	4.07	84.9	545	67	12.29	69.2	1034	76.62
1985	560	4.40	91.8	531	69	12.99	65.8	1091	79.15
1986	578	4.36	91.1	508	56	11.02	75.3	1084	83.87

	1984	1985	1986
T	# Mike Kenn	Mike Kenn-X	Mike Kenn
	Brett Miller	Brett Miller-X	Brett Miller
G	John Scully	John Scully-X	John Scully
	R. C. Thielemann	Bill Fralic-r	#* Bill Fralic
C	Jeff Van Note	Jeff Van Note	Wayne Radloff

1986: It's easy to credit Fralic with the steady improvement, but health is probably as much a factor.

BUFFALO BILLS

Team	Rush Att	Rush Avg	Rush Grade	Pass +Sak Att	Tot Sak	Pct Sak	Sak Grade	Pos Plays	Total Grade
1984	398	4.13	86.2	648	60	9.24	83.8	1046	84.71
1985	412	3.91	81.6	559	42	7.51	92.1	971	87.64
1986	419	3.95	82.4	544	45	8.27	88.5	963	85.84

	1984	1985	1986
T	Joe Devlin	Joe Devlin	Joe Devlin
	Ken Jones	Ken Jones	Ken Jones
G	Jon Borchardt	Tim Vogler	Will Wolford-r
	Jim Ritcher	Jim Ritcher	Jim Ritcher
C	Will Grant	Will Grant	Kent Hull-r

When O.J. Simpson was running for Buffalo, he used to take his linemen out to dinner. Smart man.

CHICAGO BEARS

Team	Rush Att	Rush Avg	Rush Grade	Pass +Sak Att	Tot Sak	Pct Sak	Sak Grade	Pos Plays	Total Grade
1984	674	4.41	92.0	426	36	8.45	87.6	1100	90.30
1985	610	4.53	94.5	475	43	9.05	84.7	1085	90.21
1986	606	4.46	93.0	439	24	5.47	101.9	1045	96.74

	1984	1985	1986
T	Jim Covert	#* Jim Covert	#* Jim Covert
	Keith Van Horne	Keith Van Horne	Keith Van Horne
G	Kurt Becker	Tom Thayer-r	Tom Thayer
	Mark Bortz	Mark Bortz	Mark Bortz
C	Jay Hilgenberg	#* Jay Hilgenberg	# Jay Hilgenberg

The Bears emphasize the run and their line blocks for the run as well as any in the league. McMahon wants them to learn to stop sacks that occur five minutes after the play is over.

CINCINNATI BENGALS

Team	Rush Att	Rush Avg	Rush Grade	Pass +Sak Att	Tot Sak	Pct Sak	Sak Grade	Pos Plays	Total Grade
1984	540	4.03	84.1	541	45	8.32	88.2	1081	86.15
1985	503	4.34	90.6	559	41	7.33	93.0	1062	91.86
1986	521	4.86	101.5	525	28	5.33	102.6	1046	102.06

	1984	1985	1986
T	Mike Wilson	Mike Wilson	Joe Walter
	#* Anthony Munoz	#* Anthony Munoz	#* Anthony Munoz
G	Max Montoya	Max Montoya	# Max Montoya
	Brian Blados-r	Brian Blados	Bruce Kozerski
C	Dave Rimington	Dave Rimington	Dave Rimington

Munoz is one of the few "name" linemen. He deserves it; so do his Bengal *amigos.*

CLEVELAND BROWNS

Team	Rush Att	Rush Avg	Rush Grade	Pass +Sak Att	Tot Sak	Pct Sak	Sak Grade	Pos Plays	Total Grade
1984	489	3.47	72.4	550	55	10.00	80.2	1039	76.52
1985	533	4.29	89.5	450	36	8.00	89.8	983	89.63
1986	470	3.51	73.3	577	39	6.76	95.7	1047	85.64

	1984	1985	1986
T	Rickey Bolden-r,X	Cody Risien-X	# Cody Risien
	Bill Contz-X	Paul Farren	Paul Farren
G	Joe DeLamielleure	George Lilja	Larry Williams-r
	Robert Jackson	Dan Fike	Dan Fike
C	Mike Baab	Mike Baab	Mike Baab

Risien missed all of 1984 with an injury.

DALLAS COWBOYS

Team	Rush Att	Rush Avg	Rush Grade	Pass +Sak Att	Tot Sak	Pct Sak	Sak Grade	Pos Plays	Total Grade
1984	469	3.65	76.2	652	48	7.36	92.8	1121	85.85
1985	462	3.77	78.7	631	44	6.97	94.7	1093	87.94
1986	448	4.40	91.7	606	59	9.74	81.4	1054	85.78

	1984	1985	1986
T	Phil Pozderac	Chris Schultz-X	Mark Tuinei
	Jim Cooper-X	Jim Cooper	Jim Cooper
G	Kurt Peterson	Kurt Peterson	Crawford Ker
	Glen Titensor	Glen Titensor	Glen Titensor
C	Tom Rafferty	Tom Rafferty	Tom Rafferty

With injuries and all, the '86 line was described as "patchwork." It was interesting to see how Herschel Walker's yardage leaped as things stabilized in '87.

DENVER BRONCOS

Team	Rush Att	Rush Avg	Rush Grade	Pass +Sak Att	Tot Sak	Pct Sak	Sak Grade	Pos Plays	Total Grade
1984	508	4.09	85.4	510	35	6.86	95.2	1018	90.31
1985	497	3.72	77.6	655	38	5.80	100.3	1152	90.51
1986	455	3.69	77.0	587	38	6.47	97.1	1042	88.32

	1984	1985	1986
T	Ken Lanier	Ken Lanier	Ken Lanier
	Dave Studdard	Dave Studdard	Dave Studdard
G	Keith Bishop	Keith Bishop	# Keith Bishop
	Paul Howard	Paul Howard	Paul Howard
C	Billy Bryan	Billy Bryan	Billy Bryan

The run-blocking was spotty in '86, but they protected Elway, and that got the Broncs to the Super Bowl.

DETROIT LIONS

Team	Rush Att	Rush Avg	Rush Grade	Pass +Sak Att	Tot Sak	Pct Sak	Sak Grade	Pos Plays	Total Grade
1984	446	4.52	94.3	592	61	10.30	78.7	1038	85.40
1985	452	3.40	71.0	515	53	10.29	78.8	967	75.16
1986	470	3.77	78.6	509	39	7.66	91.4	979	85.25

	1984	1985	1986
T	Keith Dorney	* Keith Dorney	Rich Strenger
	Don Laster-X	Lomas Brown-r	Lomas Brown
G	Chris Dieterich	Chris Dieterich-X	Keith Dorney
	Don Greco	Don Greco-X	Harvey Salem
C	Amos Fowler-X	Steve Mott	Steve Mott

1986: Not much depth, and some of these guys have been accused of loafing.

GREEN BAY PACKERS

Team	Rush Att	Rush Avg	Rush Grade	Pass +Sak Att	Tot Sak	Pct Sak	Sak Grade	Pos Plays	Total Grade
1984	461	4.38	91.4	548	42	7.66	91.4	1009	91.40
1985	470	4.70	98.1	563	50	8.88	85.5	1033	91.23
1986	424	3.81	79.4	602	37	6.15	98.6	1026	90.66

	1984	1985	1986
T	Greg Koch	Greg Koch	Ken Ruettgers
	Karl Swanke	Karl Swanke	Alan Veingrad-r
G	Ron Hallstrom	Ron Hallstrom	Ron Hallstrom
	Tim Huffman	Keith Uecker-X	Tom Neville-r
C	Larry McCarren	Rich Moran-r,X	Rich Moran

Considering Coach Gregg's housecleaning in '85 and an unusually high number of injuries, the Pack has been well served by its linemen.

HOUSTON OILERS

Team	Rush Att	Rush Avg	Rush Grade	Pass +Sak Att	Tot Sak	Pct Sak	Sak Grade	Pos Plays	Total Grade
1984	433	3.82	79.7	536	49	9.14	84.3	969	82.24
1985	428	3.67	76.6	570	58	10.18	79.3	998	78.14
1986	490	3.47	72.4	599	48	8.01	89.7	1089	81.92

	1984	1985	1986
T	Bruce Matthews	Bruce Matthews	Bruce Matthews
	Harvey Salem	Harvey Salem	Dean Steinkuhler
G	# Mike Munchak	# Mike Munchak	Jay Pennison
	D. Steinkuhler-r,X	John Schuhmacher	Kent Hill
C	Jim Romano-X	Jim Romano	Jim Romano

Matthews, Steinkuhler, and Munchak were all first round draft choices, making this the league's most disappointing group. Munchak was out with injuries in '86.

INDIANAPOLIS COLTS

Team	Rush Att	Rush Avg	Rush Grade	Pass +Sak Att	Tot Sak	Pct Sak	Sak Grade	Pos Plays	Total Grade
1984	510	3.97	82.9	469	58	12.37	68.8	979	76.15
1985	485	5.03	105.0	503	35	6.96	94.6	988	99.70
1986	407	3.66	76.5	639	53	8.29	88.4	1046	83.77

	1984	1985	1986
T	Jim Mills	#* Chris Hinton	# Chris Hinton
	Steve Wright	Karl Baldischwiler	Karl Baldischwiler
G	Ron Solt-r	Ron Solt	Ron Solt
	Ben Utt	Ben Utt	Ben Utt-X
C	Ray Donaldson	Ray Donaldson	# Ray Donaldson

Hinton may never live down being traded for John Elway, but he's a fine one; so is the whole group. Of the 53 sacks in '86, 27 came in four games.

KANSAS CITY CHIEFS

Team	Rush Att	Rush Avg	Rush Grade	Pass +Sak Att	Tot Sak	Pct Sak	Sak Grade	Pos Plays	Total Grade
1984	408	3.74	78.1	626	33	5.27	102.9	1034	93.12
1985	428	3.47	72.4	554	43	7.76	90.9	982	82.84
1986	432	3.40	70.9	571	50	8.76	86.1	1003	79.56

	1984	1985	1986
T	Matt Herkenhoff	Matt Herkenhoff-X	Irv Eatman
	David Lutz-X	David Lutz	Rich Baldinger
G	Brad Budde	Brad Budde-X	Brad Budde
	Tom Condon	Bob Olderman	Mark Adickes-r
C	Bob Rush	Bob Rush	Rich Donnalley

The word is that this is an average line with a below-average backfield. Maybe.

LOS ANGELES RAIDERS

Team	Rush Att	Rush Avg	Rush Grade	Pass +Sak Att	Tot Sak	Pct Sak	Sak Grade	Pos Plays	Total Grade
1984	516	3.66	76.4	545	54	9.91	80.6	1061	78.56
1985	532	4.25	88.7	549	43	7.83	90.6	1081	89.66
1986	475	3.77	78.7	594	64	10.77	76.5	1069	77.48

	1984	1985	1986
T	Bruce Davis	Bruce Davis	Bruce Davis
	# * Henry Lawrence	Henry Lawrence	Henry Lawrence
G	Charley Hannah-X	Charley Hannah	Charley Hannah
	Don Mosebar-X	Mickey Marvin	Mickey Marvin
C	Dave Dalby	Don Mosebar	# Don Mosebar

When does "veteran" become "aging veteran"? Hint: in 1987.

LOS ANGELES RAMS

Team	Rush Att	Rush Avg	Rush Grade	Pass +Sak Att	Tot Sak	Pct Sak	Sak Grade	Pos Plays	Total Grade
1984	541	5.29	110.4	390	32	8.21	88.8	931	101.35
1985	503	4.09	85.4	460	57	12.39	68.7	963	77.43
1986	578	4.25	88.7	430	27	6.28	98.0	1002	93.23

	1984	1985	1986
T	Bill Bain	# Jackie Slater	# Jackie Slater
	Irv Pankey-X	Irv Pankey-X	Irv Pankey
G	Dennis Harrah	# * Dennis Harrah-X	# * Dennis Harrah
	# Kent Hill	# Kent Hill	Tom Newberry-r
C	# Doug Smith	Doug Smith	# Doug Smith

1985: The big news was Eric Dickerson's holdout, but the reason for the drop in the line grade was due to QB Dieter Brock's proclivity for being sacked (51). Also, wasn't it odd how Dickerson went to the Colts and Charles White became an "overnight" star?

MIAMI DOLPHINS

Team	Rush Att	Rush Avg	Rush Grade	Pass +Sak Att	Tot Sak	Pct Sak	Sak Grade	Pos Plays	Total Grade
1984	484	3.96	82.6	586	14	2.39	116.7	1070	101.27
1985	444	3.89	81.2	595	19	3.19	112.8	1039	99.30
1986	349	4.43	92.4	662	17	2.57	115.8	1011	107.73

	1984	1985	1986
T	Jon Giesler	Jon Giesler	Jeff Dellenbach
	Cleveland Green	Cleveland Green-X	Greg Koch
G	Roy Foster	# * Roy Foster	# Roy Foster
	# * Ed Newman	Ronnie Lee	Ronnie Lee
C	# * Dwight Stephenson	# * Dwight Stephenson	# * Dwight Stephenson

Knock 15 points off the sack grade because Marino can set up and throw quicker than a whip can raise a welt; it's still a fine line.

MINNESOTA VIKINGS

Team	Rush Att	Rush Avg	Rush Grade	Pass +Sak Att	Tot Sak	Pct Sak	Sak Grade	Pos Plays	Total Grade
1984	444	4.15	86.6	597	64	10.72	76.7	1041	80.93
1985	406	3.73	77.8	621	45	7.25	93.4	1027	87.24
1986	461	3.77	78.7	563	44	7.82	90.6	1024	85.24

	1984	1985	1986
T	Tim Irwin	Tim Irwin	Tim Irwin
	Steve Riley	Terry Tausch	Gary Zimmerman-r
G	Curtis Rouse	Curtis Rouse	Jim Hough
	Terry Tausch	Boyd Brent	Terry Tausch
C	Ron Sams-r,X	Dennis Swilley	Dennis Swilley

Only so-so in '86, but Zimmerman showed he is a comer.

NEW ENGLAND PATRIOTS

Team	Rush Att	Rush Avg	Rush Grade	Pass +Sak Att	Tot Sak	Pct Sak	Sak Grade	Pos Plays	Total Grade
1984	482	4.22	88.1	566	66	11.66	72.2	1048	79.59
1985	565	4.13	86.2	496	39	7.86	90.4	1061	88.16
1986	469	2.93	61.1	604	47	7.79	90.8	1073	77.82

	1984	1985	1986
T	# Brian Holloway	# Brian Holloway	* Brian Holloway
	Darryl Haley	Steve Moore	Steve Moore
G	#* John Hannah	#* John Hannah	Paul Fairchild
	Ron Wooten	Ron Wooten	Ron Wooten
C	Pete Brock-X	Guy Morriss	Pete Brock

1986: The drop in rushing average is astounding even given Hannah's retirement. It necessitated a trade for Sean Farrell.

NEW ORLEANS SAINTS

Team	Rush Att	Rush Avg	Rush Grade	Pass +Sak Att	Tot Sak	Pct Sak	Sak Grade	Pos Plays	Total Grade
1984	523	4.15	86.6	521	45	8.64	86.7	1044	86.65
1985	431	3.90	81.4	566	58	10.25	79.0	997	80.04
1986	505	4.11	85.7	452	27	5.97	99.5	957	92.21

	1984	1985	1986
T	Stan Brock	Stan Brock	Stan Brock
	Chris Ward-X	Dave Lafary-X	Bill Contz
G	Kelvin Clark	Ralph Williams	Joel Hilginberg
	Brad Edelman-X	Brad Edelman-X	Chuck Commisskey
C	Steve Korte	Steve Korte-X	Steve Korte

The grades are higher than you might expect. So is the injury rate in the Superdome.

NEW YORK GIANTS

Team	Rush Att	Rush Avg	Rush Grade	Pass +Sak Att	Tot Sak	Pct Sak	Sak Grade	Pos Plays	Total Grade
1984	493	3.37	70.3	580	55	9.48	82.7	1073	77.00
1985	581	4.22	88.1	549	52	9.47	82.7	1130	85.48
1986	558	4.02	84.0	518	46	8.88	85.5	1076	84.72

	1984	1985	1986
T	Bill Roberts-r	Brad Benson	# Brad Benson
	Karl Nelson	Karl Nelson	Karl Nelson
G	Bill Ard	Bill Ard	Bill Ard
	Brad Benson	Chris Godfrey	Chris Godfrey
C	Kevin Belcher	Bart Oates-r	Bart Oates

1986: Super Bowl winners always look good in every department. This isn't the greatest line ever, but they got the job done. Its fragile chemistry was revealed by the collapse that Karl Nelson's preseason loss triggered in 1987.

NEW YORK JETS

Team	Rush Att	Rush Avg	Rush Grade	Pass +Sak Att	Tot Sak	Pct Sak	Sak Grade	Pos Plays	Total Grade
1984	504	4.34	90.6	540	52	9.63	81.9	1044	86.10
1985	564	4.10	85.6	559	62	11.09	74.9	1123	80.27
1986	490	3.53	73.7	582	45	7.73	91.0	1072	83.09

	1984	1985	1986
T	Reggie McElroy	Reggie McElroy-X	Jim Sweeney
	Marvin Powell	Marvin Powell	Gordon King
G	Dan Alexander	Dan Alexander	Dan Alexander
	Stan Waldemore	Jim Sweeney	Ted Banker
C	Joe Fields	Joe Fields	Joe Fields

QB O'Brien raises the sack total by hanging on to the football like a security blanket, but this is only an ordinary group at best.

PHILADELPHIA EAGLES

Team	Rush Att	Rush Avg	Rush Grade	Pass +Sak Att	Tot Sak	Pct Sak	Sak Grade	Pos Plays	Total Grade
1984	381	3.51	73.3	666	60	9.01	84.9	1047	80.68
1985	428	3.81	79.5	622	55	8.84	85.7	1050	83.18
1986	499	4.01	83.7	618	104	16.83	47.4	1117	63.61

	1984	1985	1986
T	Dean Miraldi	Ken Reeves-r	Ken Reeves
	Leonard Mitchell	Leonard Mitchell	Joe Conwell-r
G	Ron Baker	Ron Baker	Ron Baker
	Steve Kenney-X	Steve Kenney	Nick Haden-r
C	Mark Dennard	Mark Dennard	Matt Darwin-r

1986: What can you expect with three rookies (two of whom weren't even on the training camp roster) and a second-year tackle? The coaches charged the line with only 41 of the record 104 sacks and blamed everyone but the water boy for the others.

PITTSBURGH STEELERS

Team	Rush Att	Rush Avg	Rush Grade	Pass +Sak Att	Tot Sak	Pct Sak	Sak Grade	Pos Plays	Total Grade
1984	574	3.80	79.3	478	35	7.32	93.0	1052	85.52
1985	541	4.02	83.9	545	33	6.06	99.1	1086	91.53
1986	564	3.94	82.3	511	20	3.91	109.4	1075	95.18

	1984	1985	1986
T	Tunch Ilkin	Tunch Ilkin	Tunch Ilkin
	Larry Brown-X	Ray Pinney-X	Ray Pinney
G	Blake Wingle-X	Terry Long	Terry Long
	Craig Wolfley-X	Craig Wolfley	Craig Wolfley
C	# Mike Webster	# Mike Webster	Mike Webster

This group protects the passers; so far the passers haven't shown they can take advantage of it.

ST. LOUIS CARDINALS

Team	Rush Att	Rush Avg	Rush Grade	Pass +Sak Att	Tot Sak	Pct Sak	Sak Grade	Pos Plays	Total Grade
1984	488	4.28	89.3	615	49	7.97	90.0	1103	89.69
1985	417	4.73	82.3	599	65	10.85	78.5	1016	80.06
1986	419	4.26	89.0	575	59	10.26	78.9	994	83.16

	1984	1985	1986
T	Luis Sharpe	Luis Sharpe	Luis Sharpe
	Tootie Robbins	Tootie Robbins-X	Tootie Robbins
G	Joe Bostic	Joe Bostic	Joe Bostic
	Terry Stieve	Doug Dawson	Derak Kennard-r
C	Randy Clark	Randy Clark	Randy Clark

They say QB Lomax lost confidence in '86. Maybe he read the sack totals.

SAN DIEGO CHARGERS

Team	Rush Att	Rush Avg	Rush Grade	Pass +Sak Att	Tot Sak	Pct Sak	Sak Grade	Pos Plays	Total Grade
1984	456	3.63	75.8	698	36	5.16	103.4	1154	92.49
1985	440	3.78	78.9	671	39	5.81	100.3	1111	91.82
1986	471	3.35	69.8	636	32	5.03	104.0	1107	89.45

	1984	1985	1986
T	Sam Claphan	Sam Claphan-X	Gary Kowalski
	Ed White	Jim Lachey	Jim Lachey
G	Dennis McKnight	Dennis McKnight	Dennis McKnight
	Doug Wilkerson	Ed White	Sam Clapham
C	Don Macek	Don Macek	Don Macek

Under Air Coryell their main job was pass blocking; it remains to be seen if they can adjust to Coach Saunders' intention of running the ball.

SAN FRANCISCO 49ERS

Team	Rush Att	Rush Avg	Rush Grade	Pass +Sak Att	Tot Sak	Pct Sak	Sak Grade	Pos Plays	Total Grade
1984	534	4.62	96.4	523	27	5.16	103.4	1057	99.86
1985	477	4.68	97.7	592	42	7.09	94.1	1069	95.70
1986	510	3.89	81.3	608	26	4.28	107.6	1118	95.61

	1984	1985	1986
T	Bubba Paris	Bubba Paris	Bubba Paris-X
	#* Keith Fahnhorst	Keith Fahnhorst	Keith Fahnhorst
G	# Randy Cross	* Randy Cross	Randy Cross
	John Ayers	John Ayers	John Ayers
C	# Fred Quillan	# Fred Quillan	Fred Quillan

This has been a great group, perhaps one of the strongest ever. Its best days may now be behind it.

SEATTLE SEAHAWKS

Team	Rush Att	Rush Avg	Rush Grade	Pass +Sak Att	Tot Sak	Pct Sak	Sak Grade	Pos Plays	Total Grade
1984	495	3.32	69.3	539	42	7.79	90.8	1034	80.51
1985	462	3.56	74.3	628	53	8.44	87.6	1090	81.96
1986	513	4.48	93.6	492	39	7.93	90.1	1005	91.89

	1984	1985	1986
T	Bob Cryder-X	Bob Cryder	Ron Mattes-r
	Ron Essink	Ron Essink-X	Mike Wilson
G	Reggie McKenzie-X	Edwin Bailey	Edwin Bailey
	Robert Pratt	Bryan Millard-X	Bryan Millard
C	Blair Bush	Blair Bush	Blair Bush-X

Can anyone outside of the Northwest name a Seahawk lineman? Possibly in Cincinnati, where Bush and Wilson began as pros.

TAMPA BAY BUCCANEERS

Team	Rush Att	Rush Avg	Rush Grade	Pass +Sak Att	Tot Sak	Pct Sak	Sak Grade	Pos Plays	Total Grade
1984	483	3.68	76.8	607	45	7.41	92.6	1090	85.60
1985	434	3.79	79.1	548	40	7.30	93.1	979	87.18
1986	455	4.09	85.5	515	56	10.87	76.0	970	80.46

	1984	1985	1986
T	Gene Sanders	George Yarno-X	Rob Taylor-r
	Ron Heller-r	Ron Heller	Ron Heller
G	Steve Courson-X	Steve Courson	George Yarno
	Sean Farrell	Sean Farrell	Sean Farrell
C	Steve Wilson	Randy Grimes	Randy Grimes

Did Testaverde know how many sacks the Bucs gave up before he signed? Did he know Farrell would be in New England?

WASHINGTON REDSKINS

Team	Rush Att	Rush Avg	Rush Grade	Pass +Sak Att	Tot Sak	Pct Sak	Sak Grade	Pos Plays	Total Grade
1984	588	3.87	80.8	533	48	9.00	85.0	1121	82.79
1985	571	4.42	92.2	564	52	9.22	83.9	1135	88.07
1986	474	3.65	76.3	570	28	5.91	99.8	1044	89.13

	1984	1985	1986
T	#* Joe Jacoby	# Joe Jacoby-X	# Joe Jacoby
	Mark May	Mark May	Mark May
G	#* Russ Grimm	#* Russ Grimm	#* Russ Grimm
	Ken Huff-X	Ken Huff	R.C. Thielemann
C	Jeff Bostic-X	Rick Donnalley	Jeff Bostic

Considering their reputation, it seems like their record should be better. Maybe they just get up for the big games.

14

Three Minutes
to Fat Lady

Roger Staubach, the Dallas quarterback, was famous for bringing the Cowboys from behind at the end of the game. After he did it about a million times (when we checked the numbers, it turned out to be 23 fourth-quarter comebacks, 14 in the last two minutes or in overtime; golly, it *seemed* like a million), they started calling him "Captain Comeback." Those of us not enthralled by the Dallas mystique wondered why such a great leader let his team get behind by the fourth quarter so often?

Perhaps we just mistook what worked for Dallas—a mystique mistake.

Anyway, there is something to be said for a quarterback who can rally the troops and put on a last-ditch drive. In fact, far too much has been said about it. It's not the *only* mark of a top leader. There's something very comforting in having a QB who goes out there and buries the opposition in the first quarter and then coasts. Most of us who are fans of a particular team like the games our heroes win 42-7. No drama, no anxiety, no palpitations. Our kind of game!

Nevertheless the two-minute drill has been the stuff of legends ever since it was invented, probably by Bobby Layne, the quarterback who "never lost, just ran out of time." Or maybe by Frank Merriwell.

It's called the "two-minute" drill because that time-out taken with two minutes on the clock makes a nice bookmark, but the truth is that trailing teams go into it a minute, sometimes two, before the final gun. And their use of the clock just *before* the time out is sometimes more important than what they do in those final 120 seconds. We could look at the final five minutes or even ten, but we'll settle on the final three as the most important most often.

Let's take a look at the final three minutes of all the 1986 games where the team with the ball (a) enjoyed a lead of seven points or less; (b) was tied; or (c) trailed by seven points or less. There were 202 drives in that period in 97 different games.

The breakdown:

	WIN	LOSE	TIE
Team ahead has the ball	76 (1)*	3 (1)	1 (1)
Score is tied	14 (9)	12 (10)	5 (5)
Team behind has the ball	18 (5)	72 (3)	1 (1)

* Numbers in parentheses are for overtime games.

So if the team ahead has the ball, it looks pretty dull. Only three times all year did a team with a lead of one to seven points lose the game if they had the ball with three minutes or less to go. In other words, all those people who headed for the exits early were right 95 percent of the time.

On September 21, Miami scored at 12:04 of the final period to go ahead of the Jets, 45-38. But the Jets came back, completed an 80-yard drive to tie at 13:56, and won in overtime on a 43-yard, O'Brien to Wesley Walker touchdown pass.

The same day, Seattle blocked a New England punt and recovered in the end zone to tie the score at 31-31, with 12:48 gone in the fourth quarter. After the ensuing kickoff, the Seahawks forced the Patriots to punt. With 1:14 left, Krieg hit Ray Butler with a 67-yard strike to win the game, 38-31.

The third example came on November 16. Philadelphia led Detroit, 11-10, when Eagle quarterback Randall Cunningham fumbled at his own 37 with 1:44 left. Twelve seconds were still on the clock when Eddie Murray kicked a 41-yard field goal to win for the Lions.

One other example nearly qualifies. On October 19, San Francisco led Atlanta, 10-3, when they punted to the Falcons with only 1:44 to play. Eleven seconds later, David Archer passed 39 yards to Sylvester

Stamps to tie the score. Neither team could score in the overtime period.

In two of the three cases where the leading team lost after having the ball with three minutes or less to go, the crucial play was a mistake by the offense—New England let a punt be blocked and Philadelphia fumbled. Yet rare as come-from-behind victories may be, they boil Freudianly in fans' subconscious memories to produce the Yogi Syndrome—the game ain't over till it's over.

Winning a game that is tied or coming from behind when in control of the football is not at all the same thing, of course. A team that is within seven points of winning has a reasonably good chance of doing so *if* they enter the final three minutes with the ball nestled snugly in their big sweaty hands. In 1986 that happened almost twice a week— 28 times. On four different occasions, the trailing or tied team entered the three-minute crucible with the ball, lost it, and then got it back to win.

One such occasion was that Detroit-Philadelphia game of November 16. The Lions actually had the ball but lost it on an interception before the Eagle fumble. The Bears did the same thing against the poor Eagles in the big Mike Ditka-Buddy Ryan grudge match of September 14, missing a chance to win in regulation time, but taking the victory in overtime.

Looking at a more detailed breakdown of each situation, we see that the team ahead usually just killed the clock to win. On these occasions, those diehard fans were treated to their favorite offensive play, the dreaded quarterback kneel! If the team behind got the ball, more often than not they either turned the ball over (usually on an interception) or they simply ran out of time or downs (or ambition) before they could become the stuff of legends. The category of TIME RET indicates when there was a kickoff or turnover during which the clock ran out on the return or recovery so that no subsequent play could be run from scrimmage.

TEAM WITH BALL		KILL	PUNT	TIME RET	TD	FG	MISS FG	BLK PUNT	TURN OVER	4TH DOWN	NO TIME
AHEAD	80										
Win	76	47	17	8	2	–	–	–	2	–	–
Lose	3	–	1	–	–	–	–	1	1	–	–
Tie	1	–	1	–	–	–	–	–	–	–	–
TIED	31										

Win	14	2	2	–	1	3	2	–	3	1	–
Loss	12	2	2	1	–	–	–	–	3	4	–
Tie	5	2	3	–	–	–	–	–	–	–	–
BEHIND	91										
Win	18	–	–	–	11	5	–	–	1	–	1
Loss	72	–	–	–	1	3	4	–	28	24	12
Tie	1	–	–	–	1	–	–	–	–	–	–

TIME WAITS

Just how effective the last-gasp drive can be depends on how well (or poorly) a team uses its time-outs. Everyone knows this in principle, but some teams seem unaware of the nuts and bolts and waste precious seconds.

The official scoresheets give the time for the start of every play in the final two minutes of every half. (If only they would give all the starting times!) In addition to this, about three-quarters of the scoresheets indicate when time-outs were called. Apparently a fourth of the official scorers figure it's none of their business.

Looking at this data, it appears that a team trying to run out the clock can take about 36 seconds per play, if its players don't run out of bounds, have a penalty, or throw an incomplete pass. For a detailed description of the kind of player who would do any of these three while his team is trying to kill the big Timex, look under "bonehead" in your dictionary. But if the defensive team calls a time-out after the play, only about 6 seconds go by—saving 30 seconds each time.

On the other side of the football, a team trying to score at the end of the game can run a hurry-up offense and get a play off and completed in 18 seconds, if they don't manage to run out of bounds, throw an incomplete pass, or have a penalty. The actual running time of the play itself (you know, from "Hup" to "Umph") is 6 seconds. Thus calling a time-out on offense saves a team all of 12 seconds—although it does give the quarterback time to come to the sideline and plan what to do next or renegotiate his contract. Anyway, if you've been paying attention, you'll note that a defensive time-out saves 30 seconds and an offensive time-out saves only 12. Hold that thought.

Hey, what about field goals?

Glad you asked. We've all seen time run out on a team while its field goal team runs onto the field like first-graders going for the lavatory. How long does it take to set up and snap for the kick? Darned if we know. There were 17 field goal attempts in the final seconds in the 1986 scoresheets, but every last one of the suckers was preceded by an incomplete pass, a time-out, or a penalty. On a guess (dare we say "educated guess"?) we put the time to get the kick into the air at 27 seconds. Certainly, it takes a few seconds less than it takes a team *trying* to use up time to run a play.

The point is you can save 18 more seconds by using your time-outs while you're on defense over what you'll save if you use them on offense. Not only that, but there's always the chance that you won't *need* the time-outs on offense. You might run out of bounds, throw an incomplete pass, have a penalty, or do something really drastic like score. But if you don't score, you're going to look pretty silly running out of time with time-outs still in your quiver. You don't get to carry them over to the next game.

We found 59 games with time-out information available in which the team behind by seven or less had one or more drives in the final three minutes. There were 167 time-outs available (10 had been used earlier for somesuch). Of the 167, 39 were called just before the two-minute warning—33 while the opponents had the ball. A big 95 were called after the warning, but substantially less than a half—61—when the opponents were on offense. There were five time-outs that couldn't be determined from the data, but 28 (for shame!) were left over when the game finished.

Despite 39 hopeful signs, there's a definite reluctance among coaches to use a time-out before the two-minute mark, perhaps in the hope that they'll breed.

It's easy as shooting fish in a barrel to show mathematically that you can gain up to ten seconds per time-out by calling them earlier. Actually we've never shot a fish in a barrel (or in our pajamas either), so let's just say it's easier to show the advantage of an early time-out.

Okay, here's the sitch: the other team leads and has the ball with 2:35 remaining. If you don't call a time-out, they'll run one stinking play and chuckle through the two-minute warning. After everybody gets back to work, they run second down and you call a time-out. When they run third down, you're Johnny-on-the-mop with another time-out. They punt and you've got the ball with 1:40 left and one time-out left. That final time-out may never be used. It's nice to have it sitting around so you can run a draw play or a pass over the middle. It can be useful if you absolutely have to take a time-out to get your field goal team on the field, but that applies only if you're behind by three or less. That last time-out is a pleasant luxury. Would you trade it for an extra 30 seconds on the clock? Does a kitty litter?

If you call a time-out after the first down play by your opponent and then use up your other two time-outs after second and third downs, you can get the ball back (after the punt) with as much as 2:20 left to play. A full 30 secs! If your captain is slow as the rent check, you can still have an extra 20 seconds. You're out of time-outs, but you've still got the two-minute admonitory, and, if all else fails, we'll bet your quarterback knows how to throw an incomplete pass.

Incidentally, some QBs apparently didn't have the hang of it, so in 1987 the rules makers made it easier for the more slow-witted by allowing them to throw the ball straight down into the astroturf in the last two minutes without being charged with intentional grounding. We can't wait for the day some clod bounces the ball off his foot and into a linebacker's hands.

But back to the facts (ma'am). In about a third of the cases we tracked, the catch-up team could have had more time left had they called time-outs earlier (not including the 10 called well before the final part of the game). We can only assume that what was at work was that terminal coach's syndrome *upthecreekus interruptus*, characterized by the paralyzing fear of being caught naked at a football game without a time-out.

SEVERAL TONS OF PREVENTION

No discussion of the far end of a football game would be complete without some mention of the hated *prevent defense.* It used to be you could get gales of grins by saying the only thing it prevents is winning. Nowadays you just get nods of approval, gnashed teeth, and white knuckles.

If you've just come out of a twenty-year coma and don't know whereof we speak, the prevent defense is designed for the leading team to sell yardage for time. They let—nay, encourage!—the trailing team to complete short passes o'er the middle while the clock goes tickety-tock. They plan for the trailing team to run out of time before they score. Alas, in the immortal words of Robert Burns, "The best-laid plans of mice and men aftimes gang to hell in a handbucket." Or maybe it was Jerry Burns.

All too *af*-ten the trailing team *does* score and the erstwhile leaders have no time left to catch up. Curse you, Prevent!

Actually there's nothing wrong with the theory. But the way it's handled has left many a coach, when asked about his team's execution, to opt for before dawn with no blindfold.

The first glaring error is to go into it too early. We've seen teams start a semiprevent with six minutes left! The last time that made any sense was the 1940 Bears-Redskins championship game. There's nothing to be done for coaches who call for a prevent that early except keep them comfortable and under sedation.

The second—and more common error—is to call for a prevent when your secondary can't do what it has to do, namely keep the ball on the field. If a team can run 8-yard sideline passes one after another, it can move from its own 20 into field goal territory in 36 seconds at 6 seconds a play. But if it has to throw over the middle, even at 15 yards per completion, it will use the same amount of time just getting past the 50. No defense can stop every sideline pass, but a 50 percent ratio will usually force a throw in the middle. A coach simply has to know his secondary's capabilities.

There also has to be some semblance of a rush put on the passer. Nothing makes a prevent look sillier than a long completion down the middle. When such things happen, it's almost always because the passer had so much time that a receiver broke his route and slipped free. Again, a coach has to know his people. If he can't get some pressure on the passer with a prevent, he'd better not use it.

Assuming a coach believes his prevent can cut off half the sideline throws and apply some small pressure, to prevent or not to prevent comes down to simple math—how big the lead is, how much territory is expendable, and how much time is left.

Then figure 4-6 seconds for incomplete passes, 5-6 seconds for 6-8-yard completions that stop the clock out of bounds, 16-20 seconds for 10-15 yard passes in the middle. Factor in any time-outs the opposition has left, and you know whether to call for a prevent.

Please note: the management is not responsiple for games lost by free safeties who trip over yard markers. For further elaboration, see Robert Burns. Or Jerry.

(15)

Profile of a Winner

We wanted to do a good deed. We thought about saving whales, but we knew we'd end up spending them as fast as we got them, so we decided instead to figure out what it is that makes football teams win.

Okay, so coaches have been trying to do that ever since Alonzo first went stag. But we weren't looking for an answer like speed or big tackles or good halftime pep talks. We didn't plan to *build* a winning football team; we just wanted to develop some sort of profile of victory by using various available stats.

What makes a team win? Well, obviously, scoring more points than its opponents, and because football is divided into offense and defense, there are two ways to accomplish this: either score more points than the enemy or keep the enemy from scoring as many points as you do. Ideally a team will do both, score buckets of points and blank their opponents. In real life, though, most teams tend to do one better than the other, that is, they are either offense- or defense-minded.

Nevertheless there are limits. A football game is played within a specific time period (sixty minutes) and a scoring team must immediately kick off to its opponent. The best offense must be accompanied by a little bit of defense or it will be outscored. The stingiest defense will eventually allow a few points, so it must have some offensive help.

So the answer to why teams win is a little more complicated. What it really comes down to is identifying the ratio between offense and defense that will produce victory. To put it simply, using the famous scale of ten, if an offense is an "eight," a defense of "two" may suffice; a "four" offense needs a "six" defense to win.

And *that* wouldn't be so difficult to figure if every opponent had a generic offense and defense—"fives." Of course they don't. Opponents come in various degrees of ability, and they interact with each other. What really happens is that an "eight" offense suddenly slips to a "six" when confronted by a particularly strong defense, say, an "eight." But the "eight" defense is also down to a lower number because it's faced with a super offense. And none of this takes into consideration the accomplishments of special teams.

So we could say that a team wins when its degrees of strength or weakness on offense and defense interact with the degrees of strength or weakness on its opponent's offense and defense so as to produce a situation where it will score more points than its opponent—assuming that the special teams don't screw things up.

None of which helps us know who will win the next Super Bowl but at least begins to define the problem.

In theory every offensive play drawn up by a coach can go for a 99-yard touchdown if everything works perfectly. In the entire history of the National Football League there have been a grand total of seven 99-yard TDs from scrimmage. So much for theory. In the real world, some plays have legitimate possibilities of going all the way, some long passes, for example. Other plays have lesser expectations. For instance, a trap off tackle might be a great success if it gains 7 yards.

The fact that long passes often fall incomplete and off-tackle traps occasionally are broken for 40 yards has nothing to do with expectation. Such outcomes are more a matter of timing and execution. And luck.

An offense has to go after the 80-or-whatever yards it needs for touchdowns as a fat boy goes after pies in a pie-eating contest. If the fat boy takes only dinky little dainty bites, the other fat boys are going to eat all the pies before he gets to the first curly brown crust-edge. But if he tries to keep cramming whole pies into his mouth at once, he's going to choke. So his strategy is to keep taking healthy fat-boy bites for the most part and then, when the timing's right, gobble as big a chunk as he can. Some fat boys can scarf down more pies whole than other fat boys, but the contest is judged by the total pies eaten.

The difference between the fat boy and a football offense is that the fat boy doesn't have other fat boys trying to take the pies away from him the way an offense opposed by a defense on a football field does. Defenses, in theory, want to stop offenses cold, but of course they can't. So they end up being like diets. Some are crash diets; they fight the fat boys for every crumb of pie and even try their darnedest to steal a pie or two away from the pile. Other diets are moderate; they just keep edging the pies away from the fat boys, figuring the fat boys will waste so much energy getting to the pie they won't be able to eat much.

So what we have is a contest that pays off in pies but is won by bites. Or—in gridironese—a game pays off in touchdowns and field goals, but it is won by yardage. It follows then (as doth the night the day) that we ought to be able to understand winning and losing in terms of yards. We should be able to say x number of yards will give us y number of points, just like x number of bites will give our fat boy y number of pies. We sure ought.

We studied the relationships between various team stats and points by using a method called *multivariate linear regression*. (Geez, we love that kind of talk!) Well, it sounds a lot more complicated than it is. What you do is take a whole passel of independent variables (like the yards gained on different kinds of plays) and relate them to a dependent variable (like how many points were scored). You need at least as many samples (teams) as you have variables.

What the method does is create an equation which minimizes the difference between the value of the estimate of the dependent variable using the equation and its actual value. Or to put *that* in English, we ended up with an equation that would take all the weird numbers into account and give us the closest general prediction.

It looks like this:

$$Points = (Yards)/14.03 + [(Net\ Turnovers) \times 2.08 - 38.7]$$

Right away you probably want to know where we got the 14.03, the 2.08, and the 38.7. Well, if you take 560 samples (28 teams for 10 years on offense and the same number on defense), the numbers that give you the right answer—or actually, the most right answers and close-to-right answers—are those. They are ratio numbers and don't represent anything else.

The equation says that a team with a total offense (rushing and passing minus sack yards) of 6,324 yards and a net of -10 turnovers should score $(6324 / 14.03) - (10 \times 2.08 - 39)$, or 391 points. Miami had the 6,324 yards and -10 turnovers in 1986, and they scored 430 points, or 39 more than predicted. That's reasonably close, but most teams will come within 25 points, which is darned good.

Using total yards on other plays, such as punts, punt returns, kick-off returns, and interception returns didn't add much to the accuracy of the prediction. The reason all those extra numbers had so little effect is that they aren't really independent. If the variables are not really independent, the method isn't valid. Using all kinds of yardage reduced the error in the equation by only two yards, but it *also* increased the work by about tenfold. Frankly, the candle wasn't worth the cost.

A good team will have less punt yardage and kickoff return yardage and more punt return yardage and interception return yardage because a good team punts less often and kicks off more often. It also intercepts more passes because it is more likely to be ahead and have the other team passing to catch up.

We also checked average yards in all categories and net yards above the average, but it didn't improve the equation.

Figuring the relationship between points and wins is pretty easy. All you have to do is get the point differential (points scored minus points allowed) for about ten years of football games and relate it to the number of wins over .500.

Of course, there will be variations from team to team. You can even find examples of teams that gave up more points than they scored yet still had winning records. The New York Jets in '86 won ten of their first eleven games, some by close scores. After those eleven games, they had scored 303 points and allowed 203. Then the bottom dropped out of their year. They lost their last five games by an aggregate 61-183. They ended with a winning record (10-6) but a losing point differential (364-386).

The Jets weren't the first team to have this kind of mark, but they were hardly the norm. Most winning teams score more points than they give up, and most losing teams give up more than they score. If you get enough teams figured in, you get a solid picture. It turned out that over the last fifty years an extra 40 points scored or a fewer 40 points allowed provided one more win over the course of a season.

Well, that was nice, but we didn't see a whole lot of use to predicting what a team needs in 1988 from what it needed in 1948 (and not just because '48 was a bad year for predictions; remember Dewey?). When we looked at 1977-86, we found that the difference was down to 34 points per win. That might have something to do with the NFL's oft-trumpeted parity, but we have a hunch it's more because teams have played 16-game seasons since 1978.

Here's the way it breaks down:

1935–40	58 teams	37 points/win
1941–50	132 teams	43 points/win
1951–66	263 teams	42 points/win
1967–76	261 teams	39 points/win
1977–86	280 teams	34 points/win

Actually we can cut that a little finer by calculating the offensive-minded teams separately from the defensive-minded teams, using 38 points scored by both teams as the cutoff. Those teams whose games averaged 38 or more points (both teams, remember) in 1977-86 needed 36 points per win; the teams whose games averaged fewer than 38 points for the total score needed only 32 points per win. Splitting the difference gets us back to 34 points, which is the best figure to work with considering the various match-ups possible.

Really, adding 34 points over a whole season to register one win isn't much. Figure that represents six scores—say, four touchdowns and two field goals. Remember, they won't all come in one game. A couple of the "additional" scores would probably come in games already won; two others might occur in games lost by more than one score. That leaves 6 to 14 points to be added to close losses, and about a third of the 1986 games were decided by less than 6 points. Somewhere in there should be an extra win.

As a team's record moves away from .500, the actual number of points to register one more win (or loss) tends to decrease. For example, a 13-3 team (five games over .500) wouldn't necessarily have to score 170 (5 × 34) more points than its opponent. Nor would a 3-13 team have to score 170 points less than the opposition. This goes back to what we said about "additional" scores. As the won-lost record moves in the direction of many wins or many losses, there are fewer "wasted" scores.

This idea of a +34 points scoring differential equaling a win can lead us to some shaky predictions. For example, if a team is rolling through a season winning most of its games but with a very narrow total scoring differential, you might expect it to have some trouble toward the end of the schedule. Conversely a team with a high total scoring differential but a near .500 record could be one to watch for a late-season rush.

But predictions like that are, as we said, shaky. We might do better if we looked for some other signs.

How about this? Can we translate the needed number of *points* for an extra win into the necessary *yards* for an extra win? We know that over the course of a season teams will score 1 point for every 12 yards they gain. That's an average, of course. We don't mean that *every* team will do that. So take 12 × 34 and what do you get? 408. Therefore, over the course of a whole season, we can say a team must add 400

EMOTION

Betcha they'd have won one if they never heard of the Gipper. The importance of emotion is overrated in football.

Whenever there's a winner and a loser, somebody is sure to say that the winning team "wanted it more." That's ridiculous!

We aren't really upset if a player, all sweaty and bloody after a game, crows about his team's determination on the field after a victory. Or even when a loser credits his opponent with extra gumption. We don't believe it, but if it makes them feel better to look at the game result in that light, well, what the hell. It's easier to say "I didn't try hard enough this time, but I will next game" than to say "I really don't have the skills to play in this league, and I'm taking the owner's money under false pretenses."

If you lost *only* because of a breakdown in determination, you can fix it by next week.

We do get irked at the guy who sits in front of his TV gulping beer and insisting his team lacks the courage, the guts, to try hard. That same guy will call in sick on Monday because he's hung over.

Just suppose you could quantify the "will to win" on both 45-man rosters and find 44 on one team 3 percent higher than 44 on the other team. Ah, but the forty-fifth guy is the punt returner who brings the winning TD back 77 yards. Or the receiver who breaks free to make that victorious diving catch. Where's your old emotion then?

How many coaches have prated about "the team that won't be beaten can't be beaten" or "the size of the fight in the dog"?

Granted, if a team is 2-13, it may well just go through the motions in late December. We're not talking about them. What we hate is when a team struggles through a whole season, gets to a game that really means something, loses, and then is verbally tarred and feathered for not "wanting it enough to win." Somebody had to lose. But it wasn't a test of manhood. More likely it was a test of linebackers.

Think about it a minute. Suppose you're not talking about football players; suppose you're considering accountants. One day your accountant comes into work on a real emotional high. He's never been so fired up in his life. He can't wait to get at the books!

So what does he do? Well, he sets a new per-minute record for adding up columns of figures. He also misses seven entries, and costs his company fourteen million dollars. When they fire him, what're they going to say? The other accountants *wanted* it more?

It's like that in any line of work you can think of. If you're too emotionally charged, you make stupid mistakes. Why should football be any different?

Now, remember, we said emotion was overrated. We didn't say it didn't count for something.

We figure that by the time two decent teams take the field, the players have plenty of incentive: the thrill of victory, the agony of defeat, the prospect of continuing to earn six-figure salaries. The problem on game day is keeping all that "wanting it" under control.

But in the week before the game or, for that matter, starting in training camp—the times when a player has to muster that extra desire to get ready—emotion is critical. A coach who's a superior motivator doesn't give speeches in the locker room at halftime. That stuff went out with Rockne. What he really does is get his guys to *want* to spend extra time in the weight room, or on the blocking sled, or with the projector.

Playoff games are won by "wanting it" in August.

yards to its offense or lop 400 yards off its defense (or some combination thereof) to improve its record by one win.

That may seem like an awful lot of yards to get one lousy win, especially when you remember that no team in 1986 averaged 400 yards per game. Miami led the league with about 395 yards per outing. But if you think of it in terms of a season, it simply means boosting the offensive average or cutting into the defensive average by about 25 yards per game.

Take a look at Miami in '86: the Dolphins finished 8-8 and, sure enough, there was less than a 400-yard difference between the offense and defense—6,324 to 6,050. Actually it's kind of an amazing record when you think about it. How could an offense gain so many yards when its own defense kept it off the field so much? Or in other words, how can a defense find the time to give up so many yards when its offense must surely have controlled the ball most of the time? You sort of figure Dolphin fans sitting in the Orange Bowl must have looked more like a tennis crowd, swiveling their attention from one end of the field to the other.

Maybe there's no way the Dolphins could have gained 400 more yards as long as their defense was playing easy-come/easy-go, but if their defense had given up a "mere" 5,650 yards, they would have surely been 9-7.

Why, maybe they'd have gone to 10-6, you say, because the offense would have had more opportunities, and the way things were in Miami in '86, they'd have gotten more points. Well, don't count on it. We couldn't find any real relationship between yards allowed on defense and points scored on offense—or between yards gained on offense and points allowed on defense.

That sort of surprised us. We always figured that a team that scored a ton of points would automatically cut down on an opponent's yardage and vice versa. You know, "the best defense is a good offense" and that sort of thing.

Turnovers made a difference, of course, but just holding down an opponent's yardage didn't necessarily add points to a team's offensive total. We used the turnover equation and found 1 point scored for every 12.9 more yards gained on offense but it took 135 yards less on defense to add a point to the offense. It took almost a 1,000-yard improvement on defense to add one touchdown to the offense!

However, as we said, turnovers do have an effect on points scored. If we want to get a scoring differential from a yardage differential, we have to throw turnovers into our equation. Try this:

Net Points Scored and Allowed = [(Net Yards Gained − Net Yards Allowed)/12] + 4 × (Turnovers Gained − Turnovers Allowed)

We figure each turnover should increase or decrease the point total by 4 points. That's because when a team recovers a turnover it increases its own total by 2 and decreases its opponent's total by 2. And 2 and 2 are—well, you probably know about that already. Anyway, 4 points is consistent with our previously calculated figure of 50-45 yards for a turnover: 50/12 = 4 (rounded off). It also agrees with our potential scoring model which shows, for example, a net of +2 at midfield. If the ball is turned over at the 50, the potential for the team that loses the ball changes from +2 to −2, a net loss of 4. Actually, a turnover anywhere on the field results in a net loss of 4 points.

Here's Miami in 1986. As we said, they gained 6,324 net yards and gave up 6,050. That was the good news. The bad news was that they had 10 more turnovers than their opponents: 23 interceptions and 14 fumbles for the Dolphins as against only 13 interceptions and 14 fumbles for the other guys.

Let's see if we can predict what Miami's point differential should have been:

$$\frac{(6324 - 6050) + 4\,(-10)}{12} = 22.8 + (-40) = -17.2 \ point \ differential$$

Well, shucks! The Dolphins were supposed to give up 17 more points than they scored. What they actually did was score 25 more than they gave up, 430-405. In other words, our prediction was off by 42 points.

Okay, 42 points is a pretty big spread for a single game, but not much for a whole season—only about 2½ points a game. When we checked out all the teams in 1977-86, we found that two out of every three fell within that 42-point margin.

Some were really close. The 1986 Lions had a −594 total yards and a zero turnover advantage. Divide −594 by 12 and add 0 (for a 4 × 0 turnover advantage) and you get a −50. Detroit's actual scoring differential was −49, only one point off.

On the other hand, Green Bay in '86 was the farthest off of any team in the whole ten-year period. They had a predicted scoring differential of −48 but a real differential of −164, a difference of 116 points.

We found six other teams in the 1977-86 time period with more than a 100-point gap between their predicted and actual scoring differentials. Significantly, in five of those six cases the teams' won-lost records the next season moved in the direction of the predicted scoring differential.

For example, in 1980 the Cincinnati Bengals were 6-10 with a −68 scoring differential but their predicted differential was +42, a 110-point difference. In other words, the Bengals seemed to be a much stronger team than either their won-loss record or real scoring differential indicated. We might have gone way out on a limb and predicted a dramatic improvement in their 1981 fortunes, and in this case we would have been right. In 1981 the Bengals were in the Super Bowl.

Using yardage to predict points scored, even with a turnover factor included, has too many variables to have much more than a two-thirds correlation. For one thing, the season is so short—only 16 games—that only a few odd bounces of the ball can make a heckuva difference in whether a goal line gets crossed.

It's not the same as in baseball where hits, walks, and total bases correlate reasonably well with runs scored and the scoring differential is usually within eight games of the real won-lost record. In baseball the defense can't ever score. In baseball a team scores one point (run) at a time. Baseball has a season ten times as long as football.

Nevertheless we've learned some generalities; we have a rough outline for our profile of a winning team. We can demonstrate a definite correlation between point differential and winning. We can show a slightly lesser correlation between yards gained and points scored. And we can show a correlation between yardage differential plus turnover advantage and scoring differential. Therefore, a football team that outgains its opponent will usually win, particularly if it keeps its turnovers to about the same number as its opponents.

And from all that, we can suggest some general numbers. Over the course of a season, a team must gain about 400 yards more than its opponents and score about 34 more points than its opponents to have a won-lost record one game above .500 (9-7) for a season.

Finally, because we know those particular numbers apply in general, we can look at teams that do not correspond to the norm and make some predictions of their future success or failure.

1987

In about twenty years, NFL historians are going to look back at the 1987 season and decide if it was a "pivotal year" or a "watershed season" or—more likely—just one of those times that earns a few asterisks. Depending on their particular bent, the historians will probably label the whole mess either "interesting" or "tragic." The strike did it.

The strike made everything first tentative, then tabled, and finally tainted.

Question: can players prepare for the season's first two weeks when they expect to walk on a picket line in the third? Answer: some can and some can't. Conclusion: results of the prestrike games did not necessarily prove anything.

Question: could wins and losses in the third week—the one that was never played—have changed the playoff teams at the end of the season? Answer: you betcher bird! Conclusion: there's nothing wrong with a 15-game season unless you've scheduled one for 16 games.

Question: should the replace-scab games have been counted? Answer: the decision to count them was a *political* solution made by the NFL to (a) tell fans they really *had* paid to see official games—honest!—and (b) to tell the real players it was *their* fault if they lost games *in absentia*. Big, important entities make political decisions all the time. Remember when they split Indo China into North and South Viet Nam, Cambodia, and Laos? Remember how well that worked? Conclusion: for the first time since 1947 people wondered if a good college team could beat a pro team and were pretty sure they knew.

Question: after a month's layoff, during which some players worked out diligently and others drank beer and burped, and considering lots of simmering player resentment of owners and teammates, should *any* of the poststrike games have been counted? Answer: sure, but let's not pretend everything went back to normal once the players dragged in. Conclusion: well, shucks! *every* season has its usual distractions, injuries, digressions, and oddball happenings. The 1987 season just had a little more than usual. We might not be able to take any particular part of it as "normal," but the finale—the Redskin Super Bowl win—was right on target. After all, Washington *always* wins in strike years, doesn't it?

The day after the Big Game, just about everyone (outside of D.C.) made a point of referring to the "Super Bore." Okay, sure, it was the fifth straight blowout, but the first half was terrific. Close games are okay, but they can be boring, too. Remember SB V? 16-13, but what a yawner! The Super Bowl isn't really a game anyway; it's a spectacle. Except for a few hundred thousand followers of the involved teams, no one cares *who* wins, so long as there's plenty of action. You turn on the Super Bowl the way you watch a DeMille movie: You don't root for Moses or the Egyptians; you stay with it until the Red Sea parts. If you stopped watching after the first half of XXII and switched over to the "Murder, She Wrote" rerun, you saw one of the best SBs ever.

The turning point, according to most of the rehashes, was either when the 'Skins put on longer spikes or when Williams hit Sanders for 80 to make it 10-7. Sorry, guys, that wasn't it. The real turning point came at 5:51 of the first quarter, when Karlis kicked the field goal that boosted Denver to a 10-point lead.

You've seen it again and again. A team scores an early touchdown and then comes driving down the field, just as Denver did. It looks like it'll be 14-0 any second. You expect it. The *teams* expect it! And then something goes a little out of sync, and there the Broncos are: fourth-and-4 at the 7.

We think the world and all of Dan Reeves, but *we* knew—at least we strongly suspected—that if Karlis came on the field, the Broncos were in deep *guano*. Of course, we had one advantage Reeves didn't. We'd already read this book.

PART THREE

16

The Draft Dodge

There are several good things about the NFL draft. For example, the draft enables 336 healthy young men to fulfill Andy Warhol's prophecy of fifteen minutes of fame. Many of those who have achieved the equivalent of a fifth-grade education by spending four years on a college payroll will never know another moment of coast-to-coast notoriety unless they hijack the airplane taking them home from training camp.

Another good thing about the draft—the real reason the NFL needs it—is that it holds ticket prices down to a reasonably exorbitant price. If the teams had to bid competitively for each year's college crop, they'd have to sell their seats in a range that only fans with six-figure incomes could sit down. As long as a Testaverde can dicker only with Tampa Bay, he'll have to sign for no more than the gross national product of Paraguay. In an open market the only team that could afford him would be Monaco.

The third nice thing about the draft is that it makes it possible to field teams in some of our lesser garden spots. Really, can anyone find forty or so healthy young men who *prefer* freezing their hip pads off in Buffalo to lolling on a California beach?

Try lolling on the shore of Lake Erie some Decembrrrr! You'll have the bluest lolly you ever saw.

So the draft manages temporarily to delude 336 muscular kids into thinking they're as important as beer at a frat house and then brings them back to earth by forcing them to play for less scratch than their agents tell them they're worth. And some end up in places they'd never visit sober. We love it!

Admittedly we're a bit cynical about the way the draft treats 336 young footballers every year. It's not that we can't work up much sympathy for guys who are paid more for sixteen workdays than we are for sixteen workyears.

It's just that we always love a good rip-off. Our favorite pet is a rock, we still drink Hadacol, and we voted for Jim and Tammy for Couple of the Year. We've got a kid named Billy Sol (although she prefers "Kathy").

In the category of rip-offs, the NFL draft is certainly not in the Robert Vesco league. In fact, "rip-off" may be a little strong. Try "minor con." "Little scam." It's *The Sting* without Redford and Newman.

The draft is more one of those pleasant delusions that keep us going through gray days and brighten our darkest nights. Like when you were a kid and even after you spied the wrapped packages in the back of the closet, you still thought—hoped—that, well, maybe there just might really be a Santa Claus anyway. Or like now, when you tell your secret self, if all else goes kaflooey, you can still live by your wits.

To get through another day, we all need our hopes, our dreams— our illusions. Next year we'll all lose twenty pounds, quit smoking, be discovered, win the lottery, find love. And for the NFL fan saddled with a home club whose only chance for the playoffs is if twenty other teams disband, hope springs eternal in the NFL draft.

Next year we'll have that quarterback, that runner, that linebacker, and all will be well. We begin anticipating next year's draft in September—about the time we discover last year's draft wasn't the answer.

By bleak December when the fumbles, the missed tackles, the flubbed field goals, the interceptions, and the penalties have piled play-off hopes into a compost heap, we can take solace in each defeat because it improves our draft position. The most confirmed pro fan begins looking at college hotshots as possible draftees.

And then comes that magical spring morning when Rozelle walks to the mike and announces to the world what college star will save our franchise next year.

For several years the Tuesday ESPN broadcast of the draft was responsible for more sudden deaths of long-lost relatives than daytime World Series games used to cause. Draft Day ranks just below Thanksgiving as a national holiday. In '87, the NFL switched the broadcast to Sunday, to the relief of employers and the plague of churches. More fans watched their team draft than paid to see it play, a clear triumph of hope over expectation.

The first draft was held in 1936, the year Berlin had the Olympics, Spain had a Civil War, the Yankees had DiMaggio, and Margaret Mitchell had *Gone With the Wind*. Bert Bell, who later was a great success as NFL commissioner, was then busy being a great failure as owner of the Philadelphia Eagles. All the best college players were gravitating to the NFL's best places—in those days New York and Chicago—which could afford to pay a fair dollar for a fair game's work. Bell's Eagles were getting the leftovers—and being paid more than Bert could afford. He reasoned that no bright young college players would want to come to Philadelphia if they'd read W. C. Fields (at that time many college players could read), so he needed some sort of gimmick.

Bell convinced the other team owners to set up the draft, giving each team exclusive rights to deal with their player choices—certainly the only way Bell and several others could have a chance for some of the available college stars. The argument that convinced the Giants and Bears to go along (aside from the firm belief that it would save them a few bucks) was that the draft would improve the weakest teams and make them better box office draws when they visited New York and Chicago.

On February 8, 1936, Bell made the first selection—Chicago University All-America Jay Berwanger, the Testaverde of his time.

It was a setup. Bell could no more offer Berwanger a realistic contract than he could have signed President Roosevelt. But he traded the *rights* to sign Berwanger to the Bears for a couple of ordinary linemen whom he could afford. As it turned out, Chicago never got to sign Berwanger either, but they did get a pair of Hall of Fame linemen— Joe Stydahar and Danny Fortmann—on their own picks. New York got the best back who did play—another Hall-of-Famer, Tuffy Leemans. Bell made eight picks after Berwanger—and *not one* of them chose to play pro football!

Aside from Berwanger, the only other 1936 first-round choice who completely skipped pro football was Pittsburgh's—we kid you not—William Shakespeare. No, not *that* one. Over the years, Pittsburgh was often the league's laughing stock for their droll draft picks, but this was a Notre Dame halfback who ran plays, probably read some, but—as far as we know—never wrote any.

Even though it didn't do Bell much good, the NFL liked the draft and kept it. It began to catch on with the public too. After a couple of years, the season's choices were announced in the papers. Pretty soon there were predraft stories and everything.

Draft lore is awash with anecdotes of the rampant ineptitude in the days when owners came to the draft meeting carrying Street and Smith magazines as their scouting reports. There were incredibly bad choices: tackles with the bulk of Michael Jackson, quarterbacks with the arms of the Venus di Milo, guys who had to "hut" on "one" or they lost count. There were ineligible choices: Washington drafted a back one year, found out he was ineligible, drafted him the next year, and still couldn't sign him.

Nevertheless the draft prospered and multiplied. At this late date—considering all the time, sweat, and hoopla—it seems a little spoilsportish to point out that it doesn't do what it's supposed to do—namely, guarantee a competitive balance. Even if every team drafted perfectly, it wouldn't work. Consider:

Under the current way of doing things, each team has twelve selections, taken in order from the lowest ranked team to the Super Bowl champ—28 picks on each of 12 rounds, 336 players in all.

Now, just for the sake of argument, let's assign a point value to each player drafted, from 336 points for the first player down to 1 point for the last player. Remember, every team in this imaginary construct drafts perfectly, so the team with the first draft choice gets a "336 player" for its first choice, a "308 player" on the second round, a "280" on the third, and so on. Add up all twelve rounds, and they receive 2,184 points "worth" of players. The next-to-weakest team (with the second overall draft position) will total 2,172—12 points less. Meanwhile last year's Super Bowl winner, drafting twenty-eighth, can total only 1,860—324 points less.

But of course that would be so only if every player drafted ended up on the season roster. Actually, in this "perfect draft" it's unrealistic to count any players after the first four rounds. True, in real drafts some later draft choices sometimes become stars, but those are scouting mistakes. We don't have any scouting mistakes in our perfect draft.

Using only the first four rounds, we get a 1,176 total for the team that drafts first and a 1,068 total for the champs—a 108-point difference.

Now suppose we rate the entire average for the roster of the champs at the same level as the final fourth-round draft choice—225. (We know that's ridiculously low, but we're making a point.) $45 \times 225 = 10,125$. The 108 points for the last-place team represents its improvement—about 10 percent. In other words, if the same team keeps drafting perfectly and finishing last, they will improve to the level of champions after ten years.

All right, we were having a little fun here. The situation we've described is absurd—but the effect isn't. Change the numbers all you like, it's going to take too many years for the bottom team to rise to the top.

Think of it another way. In each draft, the champs are not eligible to choose the (theoretically) top 27 college players. But the draft of all the remaining players starts with the twenty-eighth choice. If the 27 top players all went to one lousy team, it would get competitive quicker than Billy Boy could bake a cherry pie. Instead, they're dispersed among 27 different teams. The net result is that the last-place team improves itself by about one player—if it made a good choice. The player has yet to be born who can single-handedly move a 2-14 team to .500.

Joe Horrigan, the curator/historian at the Pro Football Hall of Fame, has been watching drafts since the early 1960s, when he and his brothers were used as runners for a secret American Football League draft. He suggests that a way of improving the lot of the losers would be to start with five "bonus" picks, awarded to the five teams with the poorest records. These nontradable picks would be drawn for by the five weaklings. Once they had made those selections, the regular draft would begin, with the lowest ranked team picking first.

The NFL had a "bonus pick" arrangement in the 1950s, but every team was eligible once until they'd all had a bonus choice. In 1956 the Steelers made the most controversial pick when they chose Gary Glick, an obscure defensive back from Colorado A & M. Glick stuck around in the NFL for a few years, but he was never a star.

Several "draft-fixers" have suggested giving the bottom teams extra picks in the early rounds. If the NFL was sincere about equalizing competition, it might go that route. Ask an owner with a winning team if he'd be willing to let the losers have the top 20-25 players in the draft, and he'd probably answer, "Har-rumph!"

Under the present system, eventually—*e-v-e-n-t-u-a-l-l-y*—the draft will make a difference. Teams that draft well will sooner or later become competitive, may even win a championship. Teams that draft poorly will in the long run slip into crummydom. The sticking point is that teams that draft well have bright leadership all the way down the line. They sign the right free agents, make clever trades, fill gaps, think ahead. Let's face it, they'd win under any circumstances—and probably a lot quicker if they weren't constrained by the draft.

Rather than a way to equalize competition, the draft tends to preserve the status quo. However, the best and the brightest will eventually win in spite of it.

We can see this by tracing the progress of the eight expansion teams since 1960. These teams started with nothing or next to it and built through the draft. The chart below shows that it takes about six to seven years to put a successful program together.

EX YR	DALLAS YR RECORD	MINNESOTA YR RECORD	ATLANTA YR RECORD	MIAMI YR RECORD	NEW ORLEANS YR RECORD	CINCINNATI YR RECORD	SEATTLE YR RECORD	TAMPA BAY YR RECORD	WINNING TEAMS	TOTAL RECORD	WIN PCT
1	60 0-11-1	61 3-11-0	66 3-11-0	66 3-11-0	67 3-11-0	68 3-11-0	76 2-12-0	76 0-14-0	0	17-92-1	.159
2	61 4- 9-1	62 4-10-0	67 1-12-1	67 4-10-0	68 4- 9-1	69 4- 9-1	77 5- 9-0	77 2-12-0	0	26-81-5	.254
3	62 5- 8-1	63 5- 8-1	68 2-12-0	68 5- 8-1	69 5- 9-0	70* 8- 6-0	78* 9- 7-0	78 5-11-0	2	44-69-3	.392
4	63 4-10-0	64* 8- 5-1	69 6- 8-0	69 3-10-1	70 2-11-1	71 4-10-0	79 9- 7-0	79* 10- 6-0	3	46-67-3	.409
5	64 5- 8-1	65 7- 7-0	70 4- 8-2	70* 10- 4-0	71 4- 8-2	72 8- 6-0	80 4-12-0	80 5-10-1	3	47-63-6	.431
6	65* 7- 7-0	66 4- 9-1	71* 7- 6-1	71 10- 3-1	72 2-11-1	73 10- 4-0	81 6-10-0	81 9- 7-0	5	55-57-4	.491
7	66 10- 3-1	67 3- 8-3	72 7- 7-0	72 14- 0-0	73 5- 9-0	74 7- 7-0	82 4- 5-0	82 5- 4-0	5	55-43-4	.559
8	67 9- 5-0	68 8- 6-0	73 9- 5-0	73 2- 2-0	74 5- 9-0	75 11- 3-0	83 9- 7-0	83 2-14-0	6	65-51-0	.560
9	68 12- 2-0	69 12- 2-0	74 3-11-0	74 11- 3-0	75 2-12-0	76 10- 4-0	84 12- 4-0	84 6-10-0	5	68-48-0	.586
10	69 11- 2-1	70 12- 2-0	75 4-10-0	75 10- 4-0	76 4-10-0	77 8- 6-0	85 8- 8-0	85 2-14-0	5	59-56-1	.509

* First nonlosing season.

Cincinnati and Seattle won in their third seasons but then slipped back and had to regroup. The most successful teams were Dallas and Miami, which started slowly but built solidly. Minnesota was nearly as effective once they settled down. Cincinnati and Seattle did okay. Atlanta, Tampa Bay, and New Orleans didn't, though the Saints are showing some signs of salvation.

A similar study of baseball expansion teams showed it took about nine years to reach a success level. This may be simply because baseball players are often drafted out of high school and take longer to develop into major league quality.

The draft, in and of itself, doesn't guarantee a winner. But a smart team can benefit from it. Here are some suggestions as to how:

1. Know what you're drafting. You think this goes without saying? You haven't been reading the choices made by some of the confirmed losers for the last dozen years.

All but two teams belong to one of the big scouting combines, either Blesto or the National Football Scouting Service, but that is only the beginning. The winning teams take the input from the services and run it through their own scouting people to refine and sharpen it. It's just like in school; the kids who sit there everyday and only rely on what the teacher gives them never excel. It's the kids who do their homework and a little extra who come out on top.

2. Check your philosophy. Once a team has the best possible information, it can consider philosophy. Around Draft Day you hear a lot of teams blathering about "the best available athlete." Their idea is to pick the highest rated football player left on the board, regardless of his position. Other teams "draft for need." This means, if they're desperate for linebackers, they'll pick the top linebacker on the board, even though there may be two dozen running backs, offensive linemen, quarterbacks, and so forth who are better at their positions.

Finally, although they never admit it, a few teams still "draft for show." That's drafting a "name" college star just so the season ticket holders think they got a coup. Drafting for show is sheer suicide and needn't be seriously considered.

However, the other two philosophies have merits. The tendency is for winning teams to draft the best available athlete and for losers to draft for need. Frankly, this is bass-ackwards.

Losing teams have so many needs that trying to fill them with the draft becomes like a Dutch boy with the leakiest dike—he runs out of fingers before he runs out of cracks. One year they take a few ordinary linebackers because of a gaping hole. The next year they try to do something about the offensive line. The following year it's the pass rush. But even if they can finally get a complete roster of adequates, they'll finish 7-9. That's the "adequate" level. At this point, they realize they're only a couple of great players away from a winner—but they're no longer drafting first, second, or third.

A losing team with one of the first three draft choices should always try to pick a future Hall-of-Famer, regardless of position. If by doing that, the team ends up with a surplus at any position, it can trade.

Meanwhile, the winners who usually draft the best available, etc., are kidding themselves. By the twenty-fifth pick, the odds are stacked against finding a gem. They should decide where weaknesses are likely to occur two or three seasons from now and jump on them now. However, they must draft a projected starter on the first round.

For the majority of in-between teams, the fallacy is deciding on a philosophy before the opportunity. They have to look at what's available and what they need when their turn comes.

3. Be lucky. Branch Rickey, the baseball genius, used to say that luck was the residue of design. Maybe in baseball; with football, we're not so sure.

Obviously projecting what a player may become is no easy task. It always comes back to how good your information is. Even the best front offices will make a mistake, but sometimes fate takes a hand. An injury or worse can make a front office wrong, even when it's right.

And once a first- or second-round choice is wasted, the cracks in the dike come rapidly because draft choices that could have been used to shore up other weaknesses have to be used to fix the gap produced by the wasted choice.

A good example is what happened to Pittsburgh when their number one choice of 1983 was paralyzed in an off-the-field traffic accident. They'd projected Gabe Rivera as the anchor of the defensive line for the next ten years—sort of the Second Coming of Mean Joe Greene. Because of his career-ending injury, Pittsburgh used another first-round pick in 1985 for Darryl Sims, a huge Wisconsin lineman. But whereas Rivera had been a raging bull before his injury, Sims was like Ferdinand, the old storybook character who preferred to peacefully smell flowers. So in 1986, the Steelers used still another high choice—their second-round selection—on Gerald Williams, who so far has been no more than a journeyman. That's three major picks and the damned thing's still broke!

4. Trade as soon as the mileage hits 28. If you're at the bottom, it could take six or seven years to build a juggernaut. Keeping your few good veteran players in hopes of winning six games next season is foolish if they are not likely to be there down the road. Bite the bullet.

Trade any player 28 or older for as many draft choices as you can get, the higher the better.

The Steelers, the team that immortalized Gary Glick and Darryl Sims, built four Super Bowl winners with the draft from 1969 through 1974. In those years, there were seventeen rounds to each draft. How many players did the Steelers select? 1969, 17; 1970, 19; 1971, 22; 1972, 19; 1973, 20; 1974, 21. That's 16 "extra" picks acquired by trading off deadwood—nearly the equivalent of an extra draft! With extra picks, Pittsburgh chose: half of their "Steel Curtain" defensive line in Dwight White and "Fats" Holmes; Larry Brown, who became a regular at tight end and later at offensive tackle; wide receiver John Stallworth; and several lesser players who became useful subs.

Most coaches will tell you they'd rather have "live players" than draft choices. Sure. Their jobs depend on improving the team's record next year. But the team itself must look to the future, and when it's in deep buzzard *guano* it can't simply hope to get a *poco* better. Combing the hair different won't do; a whole facelift is needed.

Regrettably, too many teams stay constipated at 6-10 and 7-9 for season after season instead of swallowing the 2-14 that would lead to playoff regularity.

5. Check all the oysters. It's hard to believe that there's a football player under any rock that pro scouts haven't turned over. Nevertheless it's worth noting that some of Dallas' success in the 1960s was due to their discovering excellent free agents who had been passed over in the draft. Pittsburgh's "good" drafts in the '70s were possible in part because they had a better line than most other teams on the athletes in black colleges. Until the Cowboys and Steelers exploited those sources, no one realized their potential.

No, we can't tell somebody where to look now. Perhaps the growth of American football in England and Europe may produce some NFL stars down the line. Or maybe there's an untapped cache of ability closer to home. If a team looks hard enough—with an open mind—it may find itself suddenly a step up on everybody else.

For all its warts, the NFL draft will continue to fascinate fans for a few more years. It's the one day when everybody can delude himself into thinking he's a winner.

However, even a first-year law student knows it's illegal as all hell. A first-year *anything* student knows that! In this country, you just can't go around telling people they can only work at their chosen trade in one place.

Imagine a widget-maker being told, "You can't make widgets at our Malibu Widget Plant, even though there's an opening, *and* even though you're the best one to fill it. You see, our competitors—the Widgeteers of Muddy Bottom, North Dakota—have already claimed your services. They won't pay you as much as we would and the working conditions aren't as nice. But that's the luck of the draw. So just go over to Van Nuys, get your family, and head north."

One of these days, some judge is going to listen to the NFL lawyers explain all about keeping a competitive balance. And then Hizzoner is going to break his neck when he falls off the bench laughing.

17

Wanna Bet?

Several *billion* dollars are bet on football games every year. Some of that could be yours.

There's a lot of money to be made through football betting. For instance, bookies make a pretty good living. Guys who write books and sell services that tell you how to bet your money do well, too. Rumor has it that there are a few professional gamblers around who make enough each year to buy Nebraska.

Where do all these solid citizens get their profits? From you.

Which brings us to the first important maxim about betting on football.

Don't.

It's illegal in most places and immoral everywhere. Worse, you're almost certain to lose.

Don't.

Sure, your buddy tells you he's "a little ahead." He's also been driving the same car for five years.

Don't.

Okay, you're probably going to ignore that one, but we had to try.

And assuming that you're going to go right ahead and invest in the NFL instead of blowing your hard-earned wages on junk like rent and food, we have a few ideas to throw your way. They may help.

HOW THE THING WORKS

It certainly might help to know what you're up against. Even if you've already placed a few bets, you may not be sure about how everything works. So we'll start from scratch.

First of all, you're not going to bet on who wins the game. If it was that easy, even your worthless brother-in-law would get rich betting on football. Almost anyone who reads a sports page knows that the Bears, Broncos, and Redskins are going to win most of the time and Tampa Bay isn't. What you bet on in a football game isn't *who* but *how much they'll do it by*, the margin of victory, called the "point spread," or "spread."

Here's how it works. Let's say the Bears are playing the Falcons at Atlanta. You decide Chicago will probably win. They've got Singletary and Dent and Perry. And they've got Payton and McMahon and Gault. Atlanta has red uniforms. You *know* Chicago will win. But by how much? A touchdown? Two touchdowns?

By Tuesday the week of the game, just about every newspaper in the country prints the "Line," which is sometimes called the "Las Vegas Line," although it supposedly originates in Miami. The line is what very astute handicappers—the best in the world—think the margins, or spreads, will be in that week's games. If Hamlet was a handicapper, he'd ask: "2½ or not 2½; that is the question." To look at it from the other side, the purpose of the spread is to make every game appear "even," no matter how strong one team may be. The Line on some games may change during the week, usually because of heavy money bet on one team or sometimes because of late injuries to key players. Also, an individual bookmaker may quote a slightly different line on a game if he wants to encourage bets on one side. For example, a Chicago bookmaker may make the Bears heavier favorites if he can't find many Chicagoans willing to put their money on the Falcons.

In this scenario, the Bears are favored by 7 points—written either as Chicago −7 or Atlanta +7. The Bears are called the "favorites," and the Falcons are "underdogs," or, for bettors in a hurry, "dogs." But the spread theoretically makes the dog as strong as the favorite. A game really rated even, with no points given, is called a "Pick-'em."

You can think of it as betting on the teams if you want to, but you're really betting on the spread and your bookie doesn't much care which way you go, so long as he finds somebody who'll bet the other side. If you bet on the Bears, they not only have to win, they have to win by more than 7 points for you to collect. If you bet on Atlanta and they lose by 6, you win because you had an extra 7 points to add to the Falcons' score. Let's say the real score was 14-9, Chicago. The betting score, with the spread, was 14-16, Atlanta. Those who bet on Atlanta won despite the actual score.

Of course, if the actual score had been 14-7 (14-14 with the spread), everybody gets his money back. A spread-induced tie is called a "push," and no one likes it. To eliminate ties, most spreads have a half point, like 2½ or 5½. Half points make the bets more attractive by killing the push. Sometimes a bookie will sell you a half point and increase his cut.

His cut is in the "vigorish." Lovely word. It sounds like something sweet and sticky. Well, it is: sweet for him and sticky for you.

See, if you go out in your back yard and bet your neighbor $10 on the game, with or without the spread, one of you will end up with another $10 and the other will be out an equal amount. Not so if you bet with a bookie. With him, you have to bet $11 on Chicago to win $10. Meanwhile, somebody else has bet $11 on Atlanta. When the 14-9 score comes in, the bookie passes $10 of your money on to the Atlanta guy and keeps a dollar for himself. Thus the bookie takes in $22 and pays out $21 to the winner, keeping a dollar (4.5 percent of the total) for himself. That's the vigorish. Another name for it is "juice."

Now think a minute. If you make ten $10 bets and win half of them, you may think you're even. You're not. You're out $5. You made $50 on your winning teams and lost $55 on your losing teams (assuming you didn't buy a half point somewhere along the way, which usually puts the vigorish up to 12-10). That's why you must win eleven of twenty-one bets (52.4 percent) just to break even.

And that's why a bookie doesn't care which way you bet. As long as he can keep his bettors balanced on either side, he'll make money. As a matter of fact, he's called a bookmaker because he strives to keep his "book" balanced and thereby be guaranteed a profit.

UNDAUNTED . . .

For you to break even, you have to be right 52.4 percent (which is 11/21) of the time.

Well, you say, that doesn't sound very hard. You read the sports pages, maybe *The Sporting News*, perhaps a magazine or two. That certainly readies you to do battle against the handicappers who do this full time 365 days a year, study every available piece of football information under a microscope, squeeze every statistic until it burps, and no doubt have someone with an inside pipeline to the teams. Just how smart are you? Because make no mistake, to win you have to outsmart the guys who make the spread, and they're very smart.

But not perfect. For example, let's look at the Bears in '86. They were coming off a Super Bowl season, and a lot of experts predicted they'd repeat. Before the season started, they figured to be favored every game they played. Sure enough, they won 14 out of 16 games for a fine season. But let's see how they did against the spread.

GAME	OPPONENT	SPREAD	SCORE	RESULT
1	Cleveland	-11	41-31	Loss
2	Philadelphia.....	-16	13-10	Loss
3	at Green Bay....	-11½	25-12	Win
4	Cincinnati	-4½	44-7	Win
5	Minnesota	-13	23-0	Win
6	at Houston......	-13½	20-7	Loss
7	at Minnesota	-9	7-23	Loss
8	Detroit	-15	13-7	Loss
9	L.A. Rams......	-9	17-20	Loss
10	at Tampa Bay ...	-10½	23-3	Win
11	at Atlanta.......	-7	13-10	Loss
12	Green Bay	-14½	12-10	Loss
13	Pittsburgh	-10	13-10	Loss
14	Tampa Bay	-17	48-14	Win
15	at Detroit	-9½	16-13	Loss
16	at Dallas........	-3½	24-10	Win

The Bears won with the spread only 6 times. If you had made your $10 bets all season against the Bears, you could have made a nice $34 profit (ten wins for +$100 and six losses for −$66). Ah, had you but known!

Before you get all excited, we should mention that the Bears won 12 out of 16 with the spread in 1985. That could have cost you $92.

All the Bears' inability to beat the spread in '86 does is explain why you heard all those stories coming out of Chicago about how disappointed their fans were with the team. Many of them were giving the points, taking the Bears, and losing their shirts.

There may be some logic to betting for or against a team in every game, but it escapes us.

BETTING SYSTEMS

We should distinguish between handicapping systems and betting systems. A handicapping system tries to pick winners by evaluating, or handicapping, the teams. A betting system tries to win by placing the bets in such a way that the results must produce a profit.

Whenever we hear of a betting system, we think of Walter. One day Walter announced he was going to make his living playing the horses. Seeing as how Walter knew nothing about horses beyond that they ate oats and had two more legs than he did, we all wondered how he planned to divine which pony would run faster than the others.

"Nothing to it," quoth Walter. He would not do the picking. He'd leave that to one of the inexpensive handicapping sheets available at the track, in this case, Wheeling Downs, ensconced on an island in the middle of the Ohio River. His secret was in how he bet. "I have a system!" he said.

We found out later that the method of placing bets he planned is known by several names, the most common being "Doubling Up." At the time, we called it "Walter's System."

It was appealingly simple. After getting his choice of oat-eater from his handicapping sheet, Walter would wait by the betting windows at the track to get the last odds just at post time. Then he would quickly figure how much he needed to bet on his champion to win $100. Walter carried a very official-looking clipboard on which to make his last-second calculations.

Should his horse win the first race, Walter would pocket his $100 winnings and leave. Should he lose the first race, he would simply go through the same procedure for the second race, this time calculating what he had to bet to win his $100 *plus* whatever he'd lost on the first race. Should that steed also stumble, Walter would move on to the third race, aiming for $100 plus his first- and second-race losses. "Sooner or later," he explained, "I have to win."

It sounded reasonable to us, and when Walter came home after his first day at the track with his $100, it sounded even better. He modestly admitted it had taken three races. The next day, he won on the first race.

The third day, being a Saturday, we all accompanied Walter across the Ft. Henry Bridge to Wheeling Downs. We wanted to see his money machine in action. "Remember, we may only stay for the first race," he cautioned.

When he hadn't won by the fourth race, we discovered the glitch in his system. Each race required that higher and higher amounts of money be bet to allow for the increased amounts it was necessary to win to cover the earlier losses. By the fifth race, his bet was several hundred dollars. He'd gone through his previous winnings and was deep into his bankroll. For the seventh race, he had to bet all the money he had, and even then a win would not have got him square.

But of course he lost.

Give Walter credit. He had class. He was out more than a thousand dollars, but he didn't complain. Actually, he didn't say much of anything as we walked home over the Ft. Henry. But, right at the midpoint of the bridge, he stopped and with great determination sailed his clipboard far out and down into the Ohio River. It sank, too.

Should anyone be tempted to adapt Walter's System to football, he should be aware of the following:

To make $100 a week, your first week's bet is $110. Remember, you're only betting one game a week. You'd better win.

Your second week's bet goes up to $341.

By the fourth week, you'll bet $1,845 in hopes of coming out $400 ahead.

If you don't have a winner by the midpoint of the season, you have to bet $37,723—if you can find a bookie to handle it.

Certainly bettors have been known to lose fifteen in a row, but you can still get even and show a tidy $1,600 profit on the last week of the season. All you have to bet is $14,303,669.

Your total investment, counting your earlier losses, is over 27 million bucks. Instead of betting on a football team, why don't you buy one?

To summarize: betting systems are for suckers.

HANDICAPPING SYSTEMS

What most intelligent bettors (is that an oxymoron?) do is look over the spreads for the week and try to find one that doesn't look right. They don't care which team is favored. What they're searching for is a spread that seems all out of proportion to what they expect the final victory margin to be. That's called an "overlay."

Instead of going with gut feelings, these bettors usually look for patterns in past performances. Sometimes these can get pretty elaborate, like: bet on a home underdog that scored 10 points or less in each of its last 2 games. Or bet on a home underdog playing a nondivision game after a streak of 2 or more division games. Or bet against an NFC Central team as a road favorite versus a nondivisional opponent after a point-spread loss or tie.

Predicting the future with an example from the past can be intriguing but not always productive. Remember the girl you took out in high school because another guy said he'd gotten somewhere with her? She wouldn't even hold hands! You can find a pattern in anything if you look hard enough. Open your telephone book at random and look at the last four numbers of the first five listings on the page. Chances are you'll see some sort of pattern. There may be one, but it doesn't mean anything. You can't use it to predict the sixth number. Patterns often develop in football that have no true relationship to the real events on the field.

However, certain patterns do have some predictive power. If a team gives up a barrelful of points in three straight games against mediocre teams, don't expect them to imitate Gibraltar when they meet a good team. If a team that has shown a strong passing attack goes against a team that has proved itself vulnerable to the air, expect the pattern to continue.

The best-known pattern is the "home field advantage." It's an accepted fact in all sports that a team playing at home has an advantage which can be translated into points in the spread. Various studies bear this out, although the H.F.A. in pro football is thought to be smaller than in college football or any kind of basketball. There's some disagreement as to how much the H.F.A. is actually worth to a pro football team. It used to be figured at 3 points; some rate it as low as 2.1. We favor 2.2, but remember, it's only a general concept.

Among the many suggestions as to why a team has a home field advantage: familiarity, as in playing in Green Bay in December is easier for a Packer than a Ram; internal clocks, as in a 49er in a one o'clock game at Philadelphia is taking the field at his internal ten o'clock in the morning; and the home crowd, as in the visiting quarterback can't call his plays if the home fans scream loud enough. In his rookie year, Bernie Kosar sat up in a shotgun at Pittsburgh, but when the crowd drowned out his signals, he turned for help to an official. At that moment the Cleveland center snapped the ball. The fumble that resulted helped the Steelers win 10-9.

Incidentally, one theory as to why the home field advantage seems to be narrowing holds that artificial grass is responsible, making many fields more uniform. An offshoot of that is the theory that a team used to playing on one kind of surface will do poorly when they play on the other kind.

At any rate, knowledgeable bettors construct estimates of team's strength, usually called "power ratings." (We'll show you how to do that in a little bit.) Then they add in the home field advantage and often some other frills that they believe are important, and they come up with their own line. They compare it with the bookie's line, looking for overlays.

The best time to look for overlays is early in the season. At that point, even the line makers do some over- and underrating. If you spot a team on the rise or decline early, you may make a few bucks.

You may be surprised to learn that the best place to look for overlays is in the 6½ to 9½ range, but it makes sense if you think about it. A closer spread—say, 3½ points—indicates two teams that are near equals. If the game develops as billed, it may turn on one fluke play, wiping out all your careful analysis. Moreover, a close spread often indicates two strong teams. One of the strengths of a strong team is its consistency.

A big spread—say, 17 points—is a definite blowout but a shaky bet. You may be on the favorite, comfortably ahead by 21 points in the last minute, only to watch the leader's subs give up a "so-what" touchdown. If you're on the dog, trailing by only 14 in the fourth quarter, their desperation passes may end up as interception TD returns. Additionally, a favorite may relax a little and come out flat; or the dog may give up before they leave the locker room and really get murdered.

A middle ground spread—say, 7½ or 8½—shows two teams that are reasonably close to each other in ability. Here you can put your mind to work. If your analysis indicates a strength or weakness that you think the line makers may have missed, like the dog's excellent rush defense will offset the favorite's superior running, go with it. If you're right only 60 percent of the time, you'll make a profit.

PARLAYS AND CARDS

A large percentage of football betting is on parlays and parlay cards wherein the bettor tries to pick more than one winner because the payoff is higher. Bookies will seldom take parlays of more than four teams, but cards which seem to be available everywhere will go up to ten or more teams.

Most serious bettors sneer at parlays. They know how hard it is to pick one winner. They also know the odds of picking several—and the return.

To start at the long end, picking 10 winners usually pays 300-1. Big deal! The odds of having 10 right choices are 1,023-1. In other words, if you put $5 on a 10-game parlay on your best day ever, you win $1,500; in a completely fair world, you'd win $5,115!

Even at only 2 games, the odds are 18-5; the payoff is only 13-5. And on parlay cards, ties lose. The probability of a tie against the spread in any game is about 5 percent; the chances of picking ten games with no ties is only about 50-50 . . . so you'll lose half the time no matter what team you pick!

Here are the numbers for the other parlays:

GAMES	PAYS	ACTUAL ODDS
3	4-1	7-1
4	9-1	15-1
5	14-1	31-1
6	24-1	63-1
7	49-1	127-1
8	75-1 to 125-1	255-1
9	100-1 to 200-1	511-1

A variant parlay is a "Teaser," which teases the bettor by looking easier than it is. For example, you pick three teams that must not lose to the spread by *x* points. It looks like a cinch, and you'll probably keep coming oh-so close. If you ever win, you'll discover your payoff isn't at all close to the odds.

Another popular bet is the "over and under." Here you bet that the total number of points scored in a game by both teams will be over or under a specific number. It pays 11-10, just like a straight bet.

Finally, if you look hard enough, you can find a book who will take almost any kind of bet, from the halftime score to yards gained to how many times a linebacker will spit in the third quarter. The one constant is that the odds will be against you.

GETTING HELP

All kinds of people are available to help the determined bettor. We'd suggest a good psychiatrist.

Lacking that, a trip to your local library will reveal any number of books that will explain betting procedures in greater detail than we can give here. Most of them will also suggest some handicapping systems. Your newsstand probably has a whole rack of magazines, pamphlets, and sheets that will give you a veritable plethora of betting theories and "inside" information.

One writer promises: "I will make you $25,000 on any Saturday, Sunday, or Monday weekend in August or September absolutely free!" Another asks: "Would you spend $10 to make $10,000?"

We have two schools of thought. First, many of these writers do their homework. They must have some degree of success or they'd never stay in business. It's true you could go broke shopping around to see which ones give the best advice, but, extravagant claims aside, some of them might provide a careful bettor with an edge.

Our second thought is obvious: if these guys can pick so many winners so often, why are they wasting time writing when they could be off in the Bahamas spending their winnings? One thing is sure: the world has never had a shortage of people telling other people what to do with their money.

Each year *Pro Football Weekly* runs a handicapping contest for the various services. There are about 35 services picking around 80 games each. Just by using guesswork they should average about 50 percent correct picks, but by using what is called the binomial distribution we can get the expected variation due to chance. This shows that about two-thirds of the services should fall between 44 and 56 percent—even if they just threw darts at a board to make their picks. About one-sixth will be above 56 percent—the ones you'd want to listen to if only you knew who they were in advance. (And the existence of these four services was entirely predictable by the laws of chance, just as if you had flipped 35 coins 80 times each: you'd expect five or six of the coins to come up heads over 56 percent of the time, but you wouldn't think the coins had extra-special qualities.) And about a sixth will be below 44 percent—the ones you want to tell your dentist to use.

PFW lists only the leaders in its little contest, so there's no way to track the also-rans—no bad publicity. In 1986, four services finished above 56 percent, about what you'd expect. If you flipped 35 coins 80 times apiece, maybe 5 of them would come up heads more than 56 percent, but you wouldn't think those coins were any different from the others.

Similar results—a few over, a few under, and most in the middle— were obtained for the *PFW* contest in other years.

A curiosity: all these tip sheets are prominently displayed on news-stands in states where football betting is illegal . . . and no one seems to care. Would it bother anyone if a newsstand sold how-to primers on other crimes? What would happen if someone put out a sheet on how to murder your spouse? "I will dispose of 25,000 wives on any week-end in June absolutely free!"

The best use of a handicapper we ever heard of was detailed by David Feldman in his book *How to Win at Just About Everything.* Feldman insists he's done very well by scrutinizing the picks offered in the *New York Post* by one particular sportswriter and then betting *against* the scribe's choices.

Since we haven't checked Feldman's figures, we won't name his favorite sportswriter here—unless you read the *New York Post*, his name wouldn't mean very much to you anyway—but we like the idea. After all, a handicapper who's wrong more than 60 percent is every bit as useful as one who's right that often. All you need is consistency.

PRETESTING

If you're a veteran bettor, nothing we say here is going to change you. So good luck. If, on the other hand, you're a neophyte but deter-mined to get in on the exciting world of gambling, why not try a dry run?

Allow yourself an imaginary $1,000 stake. Use your newspaper for the spreads and make imaginary bets on paper for a few weeks, or better yet for a season. The games will still be there next year. If you don't do well on the dry run, you aren't likely to do any better with real money involved. If your imaginary $1,000 goes way up, maybe you have the knack.

But remember Erwin Trowbridge, the character in the popular 1930s comedy *Three Men on a Horse*. Every day on the bus to his job as a writer of greeting card verses, Erwin would dope out horses just for fun in his newspaper. And he never missed! Nine races, nine winners. Eventually, Erwin fell in with gamblers who held him captive while he picked horses for them. They were doing beautifully until they became suspicious that Erwin was suckering them to a fall. When they forced poor Erwin to make a bet himself, he lost his gift and had no idea which horse would win.

The message is clear: there's no pressure when all you can lose is paper.

SO YOU WANNA WIN SOME MONEY

All right, we warned you, but you're going to bet anyway. Somehow we knew you would.

Then let us suggest that you approach your selections scientifically. Sure, some people will tell you they pick winners on hunches, gut feelings, or by the quarterback's shoe size. Some people are nuts.

This is *your* money.

We think there are three steps to consider in doing your own handicapping. First, rank the teams from the strongest to the weakest. Second, adjust your evaluations for individual game situations. And third, look for mismatches in particular team areas.

Let's get at it.

AMV'S AND POWER RATINGS

The most popular way to rank teams is with Power Ratings based on points-for (PF) and points-against (PA). The popularity is deserved.

Innumerable studies have shown that the statistical category with the closest correlation to wins and losses is points-for and -against. Check it out. List all the NFL teams in order by their Average Margin of Victory (points-for minus points-against divided by games), or AMV, and then put their won-lost records next to them.

1986

	PF PA	AMV	W L T
Chicago	352-187	10.31	14- 2-0
New York Giants	371-236	8.44	14- 2-0
San Francisco	374-247	7.94	10- 5-1
Minnesota	398-273	7.81	9- 7-0
New England	412-307	6.56	11- 5-0
Cleveland	391-310	5.06	12- 4-0
Seattle	366-293	4.56	10- 6-0
Washington	368-296	4.50	12- 4-0
Denver	378-327	3.19	11- 5-0
Los Angeles Rams	309-267	2.63	10- 6-0
Kansas City	358-326	2.00	10- 6-0
Miami	430-405	1.56	8- 8-0
Cincinnati	409-394	0.94	10- 6-0
Dallas	346-337	0.56	7- 9-0
New Orleans	288-287	0.06	7- 9-0
Atlanta	280-280	0.00	7- 8-1
New York Jets	364-386	−1.38	10- 6-0
Los Angeles Raiders	323-346	−1.44	8- 8-0
Pittsburgh	307-336	−1.81	6-10-0
Detroit	277-326	−3.06	5-11-0
Houston	274-329	−3.44	5-11-0
Philadelphia	256-312	−3.50	5-10-1
Buffalo	287-348	−3.81	4-12-0
San Diego	335-396	−3.81	4-12-0
St. Louis	218-351	−8.31	4-11-1
Green Bay	254-418	−10.25	4-12-0
Indianapolis	229-400	−10.69	3-13-0
Tampa Bay	239-473	−14.63	2-14-0

You won't get a perfect correlation, of course. (If you did, why bother figuring the Average Margin of Victory?) There are always overachievers and underachievers. But if you line up offensive-yard and defensive-yard margins, takeaway and giveaway margins, or any other important stats you can think of, you'll normally get a much smaller correlation. Allowing for the vagaries of football, it's always possible that in some freak season an alphabetical list of teams will match up perfectly with their won-lost records. It's possible that you can kiss a toad and he'll turn into a prince, but we're betting on warty lips.

Another advantage of using the Average Margin of Victory (the first advantage is that it works) is that it's the same thing as saying the point difference. And remember, when you bet, you're looking for the point difference.

Let's say A is favored over B by 6½. A's AMV is +2.63. B's AMV is −3.06. The difference of 5.69 indicates that you should take B and the points, all other things being equal. We hasten to add that all other things are *never* equal, so keep your money in your wallet until we get all the way through this.

We're only trying to show you the general outline right now.

Rather than figuring with all those pluses and minuses, most handicappers convert the Average Margin of Victory into Power Ratings by adding a certain number of points to all AMV's so that they all become positive numbers. You could add 20 or 50 or 71.9874, just so long as you add the same number to every team's AMV. We'll use 100, which is the easiest of all. Team A's +2.63 becomes 102.63 and B's −3.06 becomes 96.94. The differences stay the same; this just makes for a simpler math problem when you're figuring those differences.

You can set this up for all twenty-eight NFL teams in only a few minutes. For that matter, you could do it for a couple of hundred college teams if you wanted, but it would take a lot longer and frankly the correlation wouldn't be nearly so good.

To illustrate how Power Ratings work, we'll imagine a tiny NFL with only four imaginary teams representing the imaginary cities of Atlanta, Buffalo, Chicago, and Denver.

In the season's first week, the scores were Atlanta over Buffalo, 24-10, and Chicago over Denver, 21-17.

The second week: Atlanta 24, Chicago 14; and Buffalo 14, Denver 12.

Week three: Denver 23, Atlanta 17, and Buffalo 17, Chicago 14.

As we go into week four, when Atlanta will play Buffalo again and Denver will oppose Chicago, we want to determine the Power Ratings before we bet.

BASE POWER RATINGS USING SCORING MARGIN

Teams W-L	ATLANTA (2-1-0)	BUFFALO (2-1-0)	CHICAGO (1-2-0)	DENVER (1-2-0)
Opp.	Buf 24-10	Atl 10-24	Den 21-17	Chi 17-21
&	Chi 24-14	Den 14-12	Atl 14-24	Buf 12-14
Scores	Den 17-23	Chi 17-14	Buf 14-17	Atl 23-17

PF-PA	65-47	41-50	49-58	52-52
Diff.	+18	−9	−9	0

AMV	(+18/3 = +6)	(−9/3 = −3)	(−9/3 = −3)	(0/3 = 0)
PR	106.00	97.00	97.00	100.00

According to this simple system, Atlanta should be favored by 9 and Denver by 3.

But wait a minute! There's something we haven't figured in. Schedule difficulty. In college football, where the differences are immense, this simple Power Rating can be a couple of touchdowns off. With the real NFL (the one with twenty-eight teams) schedule difficulty can change the Power Ratings by several points. And it's points that you are betting on. Even in our little imaginary league, our four teams haven't played schedules of equal difficulty. For example, Atlanta didn't play itself; therefore, it had a weaker schedule than the other three.

Figuring in a schedule-difficulty factor isn't that hard, but it will take some effort on your part, especially if you're working with only a hand calculator. For starters, all you do is add up the Power Ratings of a team's opponents, divide by the number of games, and add to or subtract from the Base Power Ratings.

First Adjusted Power Ratings
(Using Base Power Ratings of Opponents)

ATLANTA		BUFFALO		CHICAGO		DENVER	
Buf	97.00	Atl	106.00	Den	100.00	Chi	97.00
Chi	97.00	Den	100.00	Atl	106.00	Buf	97.00
Den	100.00	Chi	97.00	Buf	97.00	Atl	106.00
	294.00/3		303.00/3		303.00/3		300.00/3
	98.00		101.00		101.00		100.00
	(−2.00)		(+1.00)		(+1.00)		(0.00)
	106.00		97.00		97.00		100.00
	−2.00		+1.00		1.00		+0.00
	104.00		98.00		98.00		100.00

By doing this, we can see that Atlanta (which had the easiest schedule) dropped 2 points in its Power Rating. Buffalo and Chicago (with the most difficult schedules) went up a point each. Denver (with a middling-difficult slate) stayed the same.

Well, you probably feel pretty good about this. That wasn't so hard, was it?

Unfortunately you're nowhere near finished. Because now all the Power Ratings (PRs) have changed, and that's what you were basing your figures on! In other words, you have to go through the whole thing again with the reAdjusted Power Ratings (APRs). Then, when *they* are changed, you do it again. And again. It'll take about five or six runs before the numbers stabilize, which is why it's a darn sight easier to do this with a computer than a hand calculator. Of course, you don't *have* to be exact. It's *only* money.

For the record:

Second Adjusted Power Ratings
(Using First Adjusted Power Ratings of Opponents)

ATLANTA		BUFFALO		CHICAGO		DENVER	
Buf	98.00	Atl	104.00	Den	100.00	Chi	98.00
Chi	98.00	Den	100.00	Atl	104.00	Buf	98.00
Den	100.00	Chi	98.00	Buf	98.00	Atl	104.00
	296.00/3		302.00/3		302.00/3		300.00/3
	98.66		100.67		100.67		100.00
	(−1.33)		(+.67)		(+.67)		(0.00)
	106.00		97.00		97.00		100.00
	−1.33		+.67		+.67		+0.00
	104.67		97.67		97.67		100.00

Third Adjusted Power Ratings
(Using Second APR of Opponents)

ATLANTA		BUFFALO		CHICAGO		DENVER	
Buf	97.67	Atl	104.67	Den	100.00	Chi	97.67
Chi	97.67	Den	100.00	Atl	104.67	Buf	97.67
Den	100.00	Chi	97.67	Buf	97.67	Atl	104.67
	295.34/3		302.34/3		302.34/3		300.01/3
	98.45		100.78		100.78		100.00
	(−1.55)		(+.78)		(+.78)		(0.00)
	106.00		97.00		97.00		100.00
	−1.55		+.78		+.78		+0.00
	104.45		97.78		97.78		100.00

Fourth Adjusted Power Ratings
(Using Third APR of Opponents)

ATLANTA		BUFFALO		CHICAGO		DENVER	
Buf	97.78	Atl	104.45	Den	100.00	Chi	97.78
Chi	97.78	Den	100.00	Atl	104.45	Buf	97.78
Den	100.00	Chi	97.78	Buf	97.78	Atl	104.45
	295.56/3		302.23/3		302.23/3		300.01/3
	98.52		100.74		100.74		100.00
	(−1.48)		(+.74)		(+.74)		(0.00)
	106.00		97.00		97.00		100.00
	−1.48		+.74		+.74		+0.00
	104.52		97.74		97.74		100.00

Fifth Adjusted Power Ratings
(Using Fourth APR of Opponents)

ATLANTA		BUFFALO		CHICAGO		DENVER	
Buf	97.74	Atl	104.52	Den	100.00	Chi	97.74
Chi	97.74	Den	100.00	Atl	104.45	Buf	97.74
Den	100.00	Chi	97.74	Buf	97.74	Atl	104.52
	295.48/3		302.26/3		302.26/3		300.00/3
	98.49		100.75		100.75		100.00
	(−1.51)		(+.75)		(+.75)		(0.00)
	106.00		97.00		97.00		100.00
	−1.51		+.75		+.75		+0.00
	104.49		97.75		97.75		100.00

Sixth (Final) Adjusted Power Ratings
(Using Fifth APR of Opponents)

ATLANTA		BUFFALO		CHICAGO		DENVER	
Buf	97.75	Atl	104.49	Den	100.00	Chi	97.75
Chi	97.75	Den	100.00	Atl	104.49	Buf	97.75
Den	100.00	Chi	97.75	Buf	97.75	Atl	104.49
	295.50/3		302.24/3		302.24/3		299.99/3
	98.50		100.75		100.75		100.00
	(−1.50)		(+.75)		(+.75)		(0.00)

106.00	97.00	97.00	100.00
−1.50	+.75	+.75	+0.00
104.50	97.75	97.75	100.00

Here's the difference:

Using Base Power Ratings

Atlanta	106.00	Denver	100.00
Buffalo	97.00	Chicago	97.00
	9.00		3.00

Atlanta −9 over Buffalo   Denver −3 over Chicago

Using Final Adjusted Power Ratings

Atlanta	104.50	Denver	100.00
Buffalo	97.75	Chicago	97.75
	6.75		2.25

Atlanta −6.75 over Buffalo   Denver −2.25 over Chicago

Power Ratings can be refined in many different ways. One popular handicapper divides the league teams into 3 classes: 9 strong teams, 10 average-strength teams, and 9 weak teams—A, B, and C. His idea is that the stronger the opposition, the smaller the scoring margin tends to be, which is true enough. A Class A team will usually score a lot better against a Class C than it will against another Class A.

It seems to us there'd be little difference between the lowest "Class A" and the highest "Class B," making for a built-in inexactitude. What happens in a season where there are only 5 strong teams and 14 bums? Still, this system could be useful in spotting such tendencies as a high-rated team that really lays it on the weaklings.

Some bettors look for trends, trying to spot teams on the rise or slipping. Instead of following Power Ratings for a whole season, they'll figure only the last 4 or 5 games. This is tricky because the quality of opponents is much harder to figure for the short haul.

Now that you understand Power Ratings, you're ready for the next step in making an intelligent bet: adjusting to individual game situations.

HOME FIELD AND OTHER ADVANTAGES

If you have never heard of the Home Field Advantage, you've been living on the moon for a long time. Worse, you didn't read the first part of this chapter. We have no particular animus toward moon dwellers.

To review: teams (in all sports) tend to win more often at home than on the road. There are various theories why, but we needn't concern ourselves with them further, so long as we recognize that there is an advantage in being the home team. We *are* concerned with how many points the advantage is worth. In pro football, most studies show that it's worth between 2 and 2½ points. Here we'll split the difference and call it 2.25.

The simplest way to use it with Power Ratings is to add 2.25 to the home team's PR. Therefore, in our imaginary league, the Atlanta-Buffalo game changes like this.

At Atlanta			*At Buffalo*		
Atlanta	104.50 + 2.25 =	106.75	Atlanta		104.50
Buffalo		97.75	Buffalo	97.75 + 2.25 =	100.00
		9.00			4.50

And that's a swing of 4.5 points, not 2.25. So be careful.

Of course, if you have the time, it's better to go through each team and figure its individual home field advantage.

Here's what the '86 champion Giants did:

Home Points-For	220	Away Points-For	151
Home Points-Against	108	Away Points-Against	128
	112/8		23/8

PR (Home) 114.00
Base PR   108.44
PR (Away) 102.88

However, the difference is not as great as it appears. They played home-and-away against the other teams in their division (Washington, Dallas, Philadelphia, and St. Louis). But at home only they had San Diego, New Orleans, Denver, and Green Bay. Away they played the Raiders, Seattle, Minnesota, and San Francisco, a much tougher group. To be really accurate, *you should figure the Power Ratings of all the visiting and host teams.*

In addition to Home Field Advantage, some teams play better or worse depending on the surface. Generally this goes along with what kind of surface they're used to on their home field; if they play on grass at home, they are better equipped to deal with grass on the road. There are exceptions, of course, but it's worth knowing the kind of surface a team normally plays on.

TEAM	STADIUM	SURFACE
Atlanta Falcons	Atlanta Fulton County Stadium	Natural
Buffalo Bills	Rich Stadium	Artificial
Chicago Bears	Soldier Field	Artificial
Cincinnati Bengals	Riverfront Stadium	Artificial
Cleveland Browns	Municipal Stadium	Natural
Dallas Cowboys	Texas Stadium	Artificial
Denver Broncos	Mile High Stadium	Natural
Detroit Lions	Pontiac Silverdome	Artificial
Green Bay Packers	Lambeau Field and	Natural
	Milwaukee County Stadium	Natural
Houston Oilers	Astrodome	Artificial
Indianapolis Colts	Hoosierdome	Artificial
Kansas City Chiefs	Arrowhead	Artificial
Los Angeles Raiders	Los Angeles Memorial Coliseum	Natural
Los Angeles Rams	Anaheim Stadium	Natural
Miami Dolphins	Joe Robbie Stadium	Natural
Minnesota Vikings	Hubert H. Humphrey Metrodome	Artificial
New England Patriots	Sullivan Stadium	Artificial
New Orleans Saints	Louisiana Superdome	Artificial
New York Giants/Jets	Giants Stadium	Artificial
Philadelphia Eagles	Veterans Stadium	Artificial
Pittsburgh Steelers	Three Rivers Stadium	Artificial
St. Louis Cardinals	Busch Memorial Stadium	Artificial
San Diego Chargers	Jack Murphy Stadium	Natural
San Francisco 49ers	Candlestick Park	Artificial
Seattle Seahawks	Kingdome	Artificial
Tampa Bay Buccaneers	Tampa Stadium	Natural
Washington Redskins	Robert F. Kennedy Stadium	Natural

The weather can be a factor, although much less so than it was before domes mushroomed. Until they moved into the Humphrey

Dome, the Vikings were famous for ambushing California teams in December. Even though it don't rain in Indianapolis in the autumntime, you can still get a heckuva snowstorm in Buffalo. But to use weather information to your advantage, you need up-to-date reports. There are people who won't bet until they've called the weather bureau in the game city on the morning of the game. You also have to be a little lucky. Suppose team *x* falls apart in heavy rainstorms. Until it plays in its first monsoon, you won't know that. You could grow old waiting for the clouds to roll in again, and then, like as not, the opponent will be equally aquaphobic.

Injuries are one of the trickiest game-day factors. News that a key player is out or at less than 100 percent can make a team a more or less attractive bet. Bettors search for an edge on the injury lists, announced every week and dutifully published by the press, as an attempt by the NFL to keep everything equal among the wagering fraternity. Years ago teams were deluged with spies looking for "inside" information, so the league went to an open policy, figuring that if everyone knew, no one would benefit. The NFL wasn't looking to help anyone; they just didn't want to trip over a covey of 007s in the trainer's room.

Well, it was a nice idea. But it didn't work, and for several reasons.

In the first place, with no dishonesty intended, one coach will report a guard with a paper cut as only "probable." Another coach will consider "probable" to mean any player whose pupils respond to light. Additionally, any coach who figures he can get away with it will try to keep his opponent from learning about any injury that might be exploited.

The various categories are vague anyway. Not only do most "probables" usually play, so do many "possibles," and an astonishing number of "definitely outs." Does a "definitely out" get upgraded to "probable" if he plays?

Some handicappers talk about an "injury grapevine," a secret source of inside information on injuries. Just how bad is that noncommittal "shoulder" listed for the "probable" linebacker in the weekly report? Is that wide receiver's knee really okay? Those in on the grapevine swear by it, but whether any edge they gain is in their bankbooks or just in their heads is debatable.

Moreover, any "definitely in" can be definitely outed on the first play of the game. Hall of Fame tackle Turk Edwards blew out his knee on the pregame coin flip and never played another down.

All things considered, the injury angle is overrated. For example, a sidelined quarterback can set some bettors all atwitter. They want to write off the team using a backup. What they forget is that NFL teams don't have stumblebums on their rosters. The guy who steps in for the downed man is usually a more than competent player. With a week to get ready, most subs can do the job. And often, when a player is out, his teammates compensate by playing at a higher level. It happens. Something may be lost, but is it worth a point in the spread? That's all you need concern yourself with. Injuries during a game have a far greater impact on its outcome, but knowing that isn't any help at all in placing a bet on Saturday.

In general, unless you know that the injured regular is definitely out —like, if they're calling for last rites—and that his sub is only on the roster because he's the owner's nephew, don't let a single injury affect your handicapping. Now, several injuries, particularly at one position, can be a very different matter. A team that has to go to a third-string quarterback is *in extremis*. Losing two men out of the secondary or a couple off the offensive line can also hurt a lot more than having a gimpy running back.

However, because bettors usually overreact to injury reports, you'll sometimes see the spread moving during the week as the bookies try to balance. We'd suggest you go against the stream here. If the spread opens at +3 and moves to +4, stick with the dog.

Actually, this bettor overreaction and the usual human quality of playing the favorite tends to edge the spread up a little higher than it should be. As a result, over a long period of time, you can do all right by just betting the underdogs. From 1977 to 1986, in 2,114 games, the underdog won 1093, the favorites 875, and 56 were ties. That's about the coveted 55 percent, and it may not be as long-term an investment as it seems—check out the tips at the end of this chapter.

To summarize, in adjusting your evaluations to particular game situations, the home field advantage is an automatic 2.25. But be very careful about going overboard on weather, field surface, or injuries.

ONE ZONE EQUALS TWO BOMBS

No doubt the most slippery area for a handicapper is trying to match two specific teams in hope of spotting a strength lined up against a weakness that will cause one team to perform better or worse against this particular opponent than it would against another foe of equal strength.

A simple example: Kansas City has excellent special teams that have produced a half dozen scores in earlier games, while Pittsburgh's special teams have already given up several scores. You don't have to be a genius to figure there's a good chance the Chiefs will profit by this. Unfortunately for you, the guys making the spread know this too and have factored it into their calculations. So what we really have here is not something that you gain an edge by knowing; it's an edge *they* have if you don't know. Additionally, the Pittsburgh coaches know about the situation and have been working all week to do something about it. All of which tends to leave you nowhere.

You can drive yourself crazy trying to match up individual players. Aha! you say. Their tackle can't control our defensive end. Our guy will be all over their quarterback! Then you watch them trap our end all the way down the field.

Even matching generalities is dangerous. For example, your team may stuff the run (the other team's best suit) only to be bombed by an unexpectedly strong passing attack.

An area that may prove fruitful is to look at matches produced by different coaching philosophies. The coach's is sometimes based on his desire to hide or compensate for some weakness. For example, a team favoring a grind-it-out running style may do so because it lacks a valid passing threat. No coach ever wants to take a risk just for the thrill of it, but most of them will take chances if they think that's the only way to victory.

Here are the possibilities on offense:

Low-risk, ground-based attack. You won't find any team using the old Woody Hayes three-yards-and-a-cloud-of-dust philosophy, but some will stay on the ground more than others. The Green Bay Packers of Vince Lombardi were the prototype, but they had the defense to make it work. This is not a good "catch-up" offense. Look for a preference for long, time-consuming drives with a limited number of offensive plays, few fumbles, and occasional short, "safe" passes. The tight end will probably be more of a blocker than a receiver. A risk-taking defense, one that can overpower the running attack, can do well against this attack.

Low-risk, pass-based attack. Bill Walsh's 49ers do this about as well as anyone, but they have plenty of imitators. These teams control the ball with quick, safe, sideline passes. Although they complete a high percentage, most of them are for under 10 yards. Often the team's leading receiver is a back. When they run, it's likely to be a quick handoff up the gut. This attack does very well against a defense that specializes in stopping the run. However, a defense that can handle the run with only its line, leaving the linebackers and secondary free to cover, can give this offense trouble.

High-risk, ground-based attack. Designed to exploit the talent of a great running back, this offense may work against a defense that lays back and gives him the first move or one that is just weak against the run. However, an aggressive run-stopping defense can close it down and force it to go to the pass. You won't find many teams using this sort of attack and winning.

High-risk, pass-based attack. This offense needs a strong-armed quarterback, deep-threat receivers, and a big line that can give the plays time to develop. Does that sound like the Bengals? The average gain per pass is high, but so is the percentage intercepted. The accompanying ground game is usually the short-yardage, big-back type because extra horses are needed in the backfield for more blocking. The obvious defense is to rush the passer off his feet. Moreover, this is one place where a quarterback injury can really hurt.

High-risk, multiple offense. This attack, which is practically synonymous with the Dallas Cowboys, needs speed and execution. It produces plenty of big runs, big passes, and big mistakes. When it works, it can look brilliant, but a defense that plays conservatively can hold it in check until it self-destructs. Although the backs get the headlines, the offensive linemen in this kind of attack must be quick and experienced. Many of the Cowboys' troubles in the last couple of years were caused by lack of experience (and talent) in their offensive line.

If you can spot a mismatch in the offenses and defenses of two opponents, you can use that as a key to decide which side of the spread to come down on. But it *is* slippery. Teams are seldom so committed to one philosophy or another that they can't make some adjustments. A coaching change, even among the assistants, may herald a whole new philosophy. Losers are very likely to change, even in midseason.

The best approach is to start with careful Power Ratings, taking the home field advantage into account. Then look at other particular game situations like the weather, the field surface, and injuries. Finally, analyze the attacks and defenses, looking for mismatches.

It's a lot of work, but it's important. To make it worthwhile, you have to bat .550 in this league.

AN EDGE FOR THE EXPERTS

If you think a standard deviation describes an evangelist's bedroom escapade, abandon hope, all ye who enter here. The road is going to get tough . . . but you football fans know what to do when the going gets tough.

We have plotted the actual outcomes of games against the point spread and found—eureka!—that this yields a normal (or bell-shaped) distribution with a mean of zero (the actual point spread) and a range (or standard deviation, also known as sigma) of 13.5 points.

The standard deviation is a basic tool of statistical analysis. It is calculated by taking the sum of the squares of the differences between the predicted scores of the games and the actual scores, dividing by the number of games, and then taking the square root. Theory states that about two thirds of all the games (actually, 68.26 percent) will fall within one sigma of the average—that is, within 13.5 points of the point spread. Moreover, 95 percent will fall within two sigma, and 99.75 percent within three. What this says is if a team is favored by 7 points over another team, there is still a one-third chance that they will either win by more than 20 or lose by more than 6. This difference, due purely to chance or luck, is larger than most people would expect. From 1977 to 1986, in 2,114 regular season games, the difference from the spread was more than 13 points 640 times, or about 30 percent.

This information is meaningful. Let's say you feel that a 55 percent rate of success is reasonably achievable. Accordingly, if you bet about three games a week, plus playoffs for a total of sixty, you would hope to win thirty-three. At $110 a game, you would bet $6,600. Winning thirty-three times, you would take in $210 × 33, or $6,930. Your profit of 5 percent would come to $330.

Now, let's say you had a perfect handicapping system, one that gave the exact likelihood of winning for any game. Based on the assumption that the figure your system produces is correct and the line is wrong, here are your chances of success.

Error in line	Your chance of winning	Error in line	Your chance of winning
0 points	50.0 percent	4 points	61.2 percent
1	52.8	5	64.0
2	55.7	6	66.6
3	58.5	7	69.2

This data derives from the table for a normal distribution. The 2-point figure is the probability of the result being better than 2/13.5 of one standard deviation below the expected result. This looks like great news for you, crafty bettor: to meet your goal of a 55 percent success rate, all you have to do is perfectly recognize a 2-point error in the line!

But let's be real. Sometimes when you think you're right and the Vegas folks are wrong, it's actually the other way around. So let's say that half the time you're right and half the time they are. This means you have to be able to spot an error of 4 or more points, so that you'll win 61.2 percent of the time when you're right and 50.0 percent when you're wrong, for an average of a little over 55 percent.

Now the line doesn't miss the public perception of the correct figure by 4 points very often, if at all. The spread changes during the week if too much money is put on one side or the other, but this change is rarely more than 2 points, let alone 4. This looks like bad news for you.

However, remember that the bookie is handicapping the public's *opinion* of the relative strengths of the teams, not the true difference. And because the public shows a documented preference for betting on favorites, the line must be increased slightly to get an equal amount bet on each team. Thus underdogs tend to win more often than you would expect. As mentioned earlier in the chapter, from 1977 to 1986, in 2,114 games, the underdog won 1,093, the favorites 875, and 56 were ties. This amounts to about 55 percent by simply picking against the favorite. Even in 1986 underdogs won 119 of 221 games (3 were ties), or 54 percent. The teams tend to be more evenly matched than the public thinks.

Another useful tool in evaluating handicapping is knowing the binomial distribution. This accurately describes results of coin-flipping exercises, such as the probability of getting heads three times in five flips. What we want to look at is the expected variation due to chance. The standard deviation, remember, is equal to the square root of the product of the probability of success times the probability of failure times the number of samples. For our example of 60 bets with an expected success rate of 55 percent, that means a failure rate of 45 percent. We know the expected number of successes is .55 times 60 or 33. But the standard deviation is the square root of (.55 × .45 × 60), or a little less than 4. This means that two-thirds of the time we would expect to win between 29 and 37 games. The break even point is 52.4 percent or 31½ games, only 1½ below our expected number. So again, going to our normal distribution table (which applies to binomial distributions as well if the sample size is large) this says we are 1.5/4, or about 0.4 sigma from even money. This should be exceeded about 65 percent of the time, so even with our 4-point advantage, we should lose money about every third year.

The Home Field Advantage is another factor which is useful to know, but it provides much less of an edge than is commonly supposed. Earlier we mentioned that it could be counted as 2.25 points; here is the basis for that figure.

In the 1977-86 period, the average advantage in the point spread for the home team was 2.4 points, while the actual score was a little larger, 2.8 points. Before looking at the team data, let's figure out what the expected variation in Home Field Advantage should be. That advantage is measured by taking the average difference per game at home minus the average difference per game on the road, all divided by 2. If two teams were evenly matched, then team A would expect to win by 2 at home, team B by 2 on the road, so the overall difference would be four.

Now, we know that the average variation in point differential is about 13.5 points. However, since we have about 75 home games per team, this is reduced by the square root of 75, which is 8.7. Dividing 13.5 by 8.7, we get about 1.5 points. But there is also a variation of 1.5 points in road games. Assuming these are independent, statistical theory states the expected difference between home and road score differentials is the square root of 1.5 squared plus 1.5 squared, which is just about 2 points. Therefore we should expect about two thirds of the teams to have a Home Field Advantage between 1 and 5 points, and about one third outside that range. However, the advantage as reflected by the point spread should be a much tighter distribution, since this is based on expected rather than actual results.

And the results do show a tighter distribution than would be expected by chance. For points per game, we get two thirds between 1.4

and 4.4 points, a variation of only 3, not 4. For spreads, we get two thirds in the small range of 2.2 to 2.7 points. Thus, if there is any real difference in home advantage from one team to the next, *it is too small to measure in a ten-year sample.*

The data:

Team	Actual scores	Point spread	Team*	Actual scores	Point spread
Atlanta	2.2	2.5	Baltimore	0.4	2.5
Chicago	3.2	2.3	Buffalo	4.3	2.4
Dallas	3.8	2.2	Cincinnati	4.0	2.1
Detroit	4.9	2.7	Cleveland	1.7	2.4
Green Bay	3.1	1.9	Denver	3.1	2.2
Los Angeles Rams	1.8	2.3	Houston	3.7	2.0
Minnesota	2.2	2.3	Indianapolis	3.2	2.4
New Orleans	0.2	2.3	Kansas City	4.3	2.7
New York Giants	2.7	2.1	Los Angeles Raiders	1.1	2.9
Philadelphia	2.2	2.9	Miami	3.7	2.6
St. Louis	2.8	2.0	New England	2.5	2.2
San Francisco	1.3	2.2	New York Jets	2.7	2.2
Tampa Bay	2.8	2.9	Oakland Raiders	2.7	2.4
Washington	2.1	2.4	Pittsburgh	4.8	2.7
			San Diego	2.9	1.8
			Seattle	4.1	3.1

* Note that the Colts and Raiders appear twice in the list of American Football Conference teams, reflecting their separate Home Field Advantages in, respectively, Baltimore/Indianapolis and Oakland/Los Angeles.

18

The Theory of Relativity

One Sunday last season, NBC entertained itself on its "NFL Live!" pregame show by asking viewers to call in and vote for the greatest running back of all time. The choices were Jim Brown, Walter Payton, Gale Sayers, and O. J. Simpson. Host Bob Costas apologized that those were the only choices, admitting that there were a few others worthy of mention. Each telephone vote cost the caller fifty cents. During the program all four candidates were interviewed. They and nearly everyone who spoke made it clear, without actually saying so, that a vote for anyone but Brown was like electing a pit bull as Easter Bunny.

So the callers went right ahead and voted Walter Payton the greatest runner ever.

Brown might be criticized for his blocking, his acting, or his penchant for punching women, but when it comes to running a football, nearly everyone who saw him in action came away breathless. So our guess is that there's the rub—a lot of callers voted who never saw Brown run.

Well, it figures. Daddy pays the phone bill and thinks twice about investing fifty cents in his opinion; while Junior, who only started watching football games a couple of years ago, just votes and votes and lets Daddy pay for it. In electing Payton, the little tyke simply reinforces the view secretly held by all the young—that the world started when they were born. Ask them to vote which fighter had the best knockout punch and they'll skip over Dempsey to elect Sean Penn.

On the other hand, that attitude is no more unrealistic than the old-timer's belief that the world has gone to hell in a handbucket since he started shaving every day. If NBC had polled only retirement homes, Red Grange would have won hands down.

Every era has its "greatest." The votes may not be unanimous—Mantle over Mays, Chamberlain over Russell, Gretzky over Lemieux, Laurel over Hardy—but generally you can get some sort of consensus vote for the nonpareil within a given time period. The real problem comes when you try to pick the greatest "ever." The simple fact is that comparing stars from one era to those of another is tied to subjective impressions that we can never sort out.

The next step is to try to "prove" those subjective opinions with statistics. Most of us learn pretty early how to interpret season stats. It doesn't take a genius to figure out that Dan Marino is a better passer than Mark Malone. But when we start comparing statistics from one era to those of another, we have to take care. The stats are like satellite photos—the truth is there, but it takes some interpreting.

A popular baseball example is to cite the many high batting averages achieved between the two World Wars. It just happened to be a time of high batting averages when so-so hitters were regularly cranking out .300 batting averages. The "cure" is to normalize the league averages of the 1920s and '30s to those of today and then apply that knowledge to individual players. It works pretty well (although we once saw Ty Cobb "normalized" into a .240 hitter) because baseball, compared with most things, has changed little since the 1920s.

The same is not true of football. Although football stats can be trusted only from the mid-'30s, a little over fifty years, the changes in the game that affect them are far greater than those affecting more than a hundred years of baseball stats. There are any number of cosmetic changes that have made some small impact on football statistics. Artificial turf, indoor stadiums, and new equipment are always cited.

THE BIG FOUR

But four changes have had, according to some, a night-and-day effect. Before making any cross-era comparisons, we'd better go into them.

Expansion. In 1956 the NFL had 12 teams, each with 33 players on its roster. On any given Sunday, there were 396 NFL players, 264 of them offensive or defensive regulars. In 1986, the NFL had 28 teams, each with a 45-man roster. That's 1,260 players and 616 regulars. To put it another way, there are 220 men starting in the NFL today who would have been unemployed in 1956!

One could simply argue that today's stars excel against watered-down competition. Overall the talent in 1956 was better by a factor of 3.18.

However, there are at least three mitigating circumstances. While we cannot produce exact figures for any of them, taken together they tend to offset much of the talent dilution caused by expansion.

The male population in the U.S. has increased by nearly a third since 1956, so logically the number of potential NFL-quality players has gone up by a similar amount. Additionally we could theorize that the increase in NFL prestige and pay has turned many young men toward pro football careers who, in an earlier era, would have been content to settle for being brain surgeons or somesuch.

Second, opportunities for blacks (and other minorities) have greatly increased since the 1950s. During the Eisenhower years only a trickle of black athletes made it to colleges where they could receive the training to prepare for an NFL career. Throughout the era, one NFL team—the Washington Redskins—did not have a single black player. Today more than half of the NFL players are black. Why, there's even talk of having a black head coach in the league!

A third factor offsetting some of the expansion dilution is that out-standing players tend to play longer today. Of the 56 players who played in more than 200 games during their careers (as of 1986), 54 played all or part of their careers since 1970. This is due in small part to better training and medical techniques and in large part to better salaries and pensions. In the 1950s, it wasn't at all unusual for a player to quit at his peak when a better opportunity beckoned. Both Otto Graham and Norm Van Brocklin led their teams to championships and retired. That just isn't likely with today's economics.

Nevertheless the guy who argues that only the cream played in the

1950s and today's league is homogenized does have a point. Not a 3.18 point, however.

Platooning. We've discussed this before, but the point is worth making again that the switch to offensive and defensive units in the late 1940s changed football in several ways. Platooning brought on bigger players who could only play in short spurts, and all but eliminated the all-around player in favor of the specialist.

In discussing a running back from the 1940s, we have to remember that he had to play defense half the time, and as a consequence, was often rested for a quarter or more each game. This obviously cut into his yardage.

On the other hand, we think the size factor can be ignored in cross-era comparisons. What's important is that the size ratio from linemen to backs has stayed relatively constant. The linemen got bigger, but so did the backs. If anyone wants to argue that a Bill Dudley, at 175 pounds, would be too small for today's game, we'll simply point out that a "Bill Dudley" forty years later would have today's diet and weight training and would probably weigh 210—and run a couple of seconds faster.

Games Played. For some reason that we'll never understand, the NFL seems almost oblivious to the fact that they played 10 or 11 games a season until 1947, 12 games a year until 1961, 14 until 1978, and 16 since (when there wasn't a strike). And then the league gets all misty-eyed when somebody gains more whatevers while getting a fourth more opportunities.

Here's Steve Hirdt in *Gameday*, Vol. XVII, No. 9, talking about Walter Payton's career rushing record: "Obviously Payton has played more years, appeared in more games, and toted the ball more times than [Jim] Brown, but to focus on those things is to miss the true significance of Payton's achievement: the career record for rushing yardage is a monument to the man's durability as well as his consistency and brilliance."

Well, we're all for consistency and brilliance, and Payton has certainly had that. For that matter, Steve Hirdt is often brilliant and generally consistent. But in this case he's skirting. He's so intent on citing Payton for his excellent play over a long period of time that he misses the *true significance* of Brown's record. Payton's 16,193 yards (as of Hirdt's writing) were set in 181 scheduled Bear games. That's an average of 89.5 yards per scheduled game. Brown's 12,312 rushing yards came in 118 scheduled Cleveland games—an average of 104 yards. And that's even more consistent and more brilliant.

We can't prove that Brown would have gained 18,824 yards had he played 4 additional seasons or more games in those seasons. We strongly suspect he would have; he never missed a game, never was knocked out by injury, and retired after leading the league in rushing for the eighth time.

We're not trying to belittle Walter Payton. Far from it. In fact, if we were looking for the best *back* ever, we would consider his blocking, his pass receiving, and his team play. And if we did that, we just might choose Payton. Perhaps he's even the best football *player* ever, as Hub Arkush insisted in one issue of *Pro Football Weekly*. But the greatest *runner*? Jim Brown.

Admittedly you can't sell tickets or boost ratings with decades-old records. And intellectual honesty isn't a game-plan prerequisite when you're trying to win fans and influence Nielsen. But let's not ignore the obvious: more games means higher totals.

In his book *The 135 Greatest Running Backs*, written when the NFL still played 14-game schedules, David Shapiro dealt with this by projecting the top earlier runners' records into 14-game seasons. For example, Steve Van Buren's 10-game 832 yards rushing in 1945 translates to 1,165 yards for 14 games (and 1,331 yards in 16 games). Although some objected to Shapiro's crediting projected yards that were not actually gained, his point was made—older runners were getting shortchanged by the length of their seasons.

A more valid objection to Shapiro's method is that every time the number of games changes, all the old records have to be refigured. Indeed, his book came out just as the league went to a 16-game schedule.

We can take care of this when we make cross-era comparisons by using the PSG approach; we simply put all cumulative stats into the per scheduled game format we described in the chapter on the running game.

Van Buren's 1945 record—10 games, 143 attempts, 832 yards, 15 touchdowns—becomes 14.3 APSG (attempts per scheduled game), 83.2 YPSG (yards), and 1.5 TPSG (touchdowns).

Strategy. The hardest hurdle in making cross-era comparisons is taking into account the changes in strategy. Obviously, matching a modern T-formation against an old single wing creates all sorts of comparison problems, but it's the less obvious changes that kill you.

As an example, in 1956 NFL teams averaged 37.9 rushing attempts PSG and 22.8 passing attempts. In 1986 they had 30.3 rushing attempts PSG and 32.3 passing attempts PSG.

We can make some adjustments for the passers because that job was handled then and now by one man. But running and receiving drive us up the wall. Most teams today use one dominant running back and a second who blocks far more often than he runs. They use two wide-outs and a tight end most of the time but often go to three wide receivers. In 1956 most teams still used three running backs and two wide receivers. There wasn't even a tight end position! How does all that affect the number of rushing attempts and passes caught for a modern-day player over an old-timer?

Now try following this. In 1951 the Giants' Eddie Price set the record for rushing attempts that held until 1959: 21.9 APSG. In doing this, he carried 60.4 percent of his team's running plays. In 1984, when Tampa Bay's James Wilder set the current attempt record, he had 25.4 APSG—only 3.5 attempts more than Price—but he carried on 81.7 of the Bucs' runs.

In simple terms, teams are running less, but certain backs are running more often.

For receivers, we have to remember that more receivers are catching more passes. That's easy enough, but with more receivers on the field, won't the passes be divided into smaller portions? And how do you account for the tight ends and running backs who catch so many of the short passes that used to cut into the receivers' average yards?

CROSSING THE RUBICON

All right, we have enough disclaimers to fill a shelf of patent medicines. So are we saying you absotively possilutely can't do cross-era comparisons without looking like a darned fool?

No.

Here's what we think. If—and it's a big *if*—you can establish the top whatever for a season, you can also establish where he ranks among all the other whatevers during his career. And once you can rank him against his contemporaries, you can validly say where he ranks in another era by seeing how close he was to the top (or by how far he was *on* top) during his own era and comparing that rank with the ranks of players in other eras.

Instead of rating directly across eras, find how much the "greatest" of one era exceeded the others of his own time. Do this for one era after another. Then, when you're ready to cross eras, the verdict goes to that player who most outdistanced his contemporaries.

Before you say "huh?" let's use an example. Suppose the top-rated runner in any given season is always ranked at 100. The rest of the runners in that year are ranked by what percentage they duplicate the top mark. So you have a scale that might look like this: #1 = 100.0, #2 = 88.7, #3 = 85.9, #4 = 85.8, and so on.

Here are the top five runners for 1956 ranked according to their ADJUSTED YPSG (we'll explain that in a moment). Casares, the top man, has a RATE of 100.0 for his 103.8 YPSG. Matson was second in total yards, but McElhenny's ADJ YPSG was a tad higher. McElhenny's RATE is figured by dividing his ADJ YPSG (83.0) by Casares' (103.8). McElhenny's 83.0 ADJ YPSG is 80.0 percent of Casares' 103.8.

1956

Player, Team	Sg	Att	Yds	Avg	Td	Adj Ypsg	Rate
Rick Casares, Bears	12	*234	*1126	4.8	12	103.8	100.0
Hugh McElhenny, SF	12	185	916	5.0	8	83.0	80.0
Ollie Matson, Cards	12	192	924	4.8	5	81.7	78.7
Alan Ameche, Balt.	12	178	858	4.8	8	78.2	75.3
Frank Gifford, NY	12	159	819	5.2	5	72.4	69.7

* Led league.

Next, by adding up all the individuals' ranks year by year and dividing, we can get a career average. And *that* can be compared to the career averages of other runners in other eras, without worrying about the differing circumstances. So if you find a certain runner who had a career rank only 10 points away from a perfect 100 against his contemporaries, you can compare him with a runner from another era who was 16 points below 100 versus *his* contemporaries.

SHOW ME!

All right, we're going to look at the careers of five different running backs from different eras. We'll use the four from "NFL Live!": Payton, Simpson, Brown, and Sayers, and we'll add in Steve Van Buren for a runner from an earlier era.

Our ratings are going to be based on ADJUSTED YPSG. You know that YPSG means Yards Per Scheduled Game; the ADJUSTED means that we added a 10-point bonus for each touchdown, similarly to what we did with the New Passer Rating System we described earlier. We'll start with Van Buren:

Steve Van Buren

YEAR	TEAM	LG	SG	ATT	YDS	AVG	TD	ADJ YPSG	RATE	RAW
1944	Philadelphia	N	10	80	444	5.6	5	49.4	59.7	4778.7
1945	Philadelphia	N	10	143	*832	5.8	*15	98.2	100.0	14300.0
1946	Philadelphia	N	11	116	529	4.6	5	52.6	91.3	10593.7
1947	Philadelphia	N	12	*217	*1008	4.5	*13	94.8	100.0	21700.0
1948	Philadelphia	N	12	*201	*945	4.7	*10	87.1	100.0	20100.0
1949	Philadelphia	N	12	*263	*1146	4.4	*11	104.7	100.0	26300.0
1950	Philadelphia	N	12	*188	629	3.3	4	55.8	79.6	14972.9
1951	Philadelphia	N	12	112	327	2.9	6	32.3	37.2	4163.7
			91	1320	5860	4.4	69	72.0	88.6	116908.9

* Led league.

Okay, let's take the legend line across and see if we know what everything is. SG = Scheduled Games; YDS = Yards Rushing; AVG = Average Yards Rushing per Attempt; TD = Touchdowns. So far, so good. ADJ YPSG = Adjusted Yards Per Scheduled Game (explained above). RATE = how Van Buren's ADJ YPSG rated against those of his contemporaries. For example, 4 times he was top man (100.0), but in 1950 we divide his 55.8 against leader Marion Motley's 70.0 (810 yards and 3 TDs) to get a 79.6 RATE. And RAW is a simple multiplication of RATE by attempts (ATT) that will produce a raw total that yields a *weighted career RATE*: that is, dividing the RAW total by lifetime attempts gives the average rate.

(To get a rusher's adjusted career rating, we simply multiply his rate each year by the number of rushes he attempted that season. For example, in Steve Van Buren's case, look at his line for 1946, when his attempts numbered 116 and his rate was 91.3: multiplying the two, we get a raw total of 10,593.7, a total that means nothing in itself because it is dependent upon his number of attempts; if he had had more rushes, he would have had a higher point total. However, if we add up all his yearly point totals and divide by his total number of rush attempts, we will have a rusher's rate for his career that *is* meaningful for purposes of comparing one player with another.)

So what do we know about Van Buren? Reading the bottom line, we can see he was scheduled for 91 games (in case you're interested, he actually played in 83). His 2,320 career attempts and 5,860 yards don't look all that impressive today, but they were the NFL's top marks at one time. His 4.4 average gain and 69 touchdowns were also much more to write home about thirty years ago. The same can be said for his career ADJ YPSG of 72.0. Which brings us to the point. Look at that 88.6 average RATE! That's the one to compare with Payton, Brown, Simpson, and Sayers. It tells us that over eight seasons, including his poor final year when he was operating on one leg, he was still better than three-fourths perfect!

In effect, we're throwing out all the factors and circumstances that make one year so different from another. Some of them can't be accounted for mathematically. Some that can be accounted for take a formula that looks like the plan for a nuclear bomb. Instead, we're saying, "This is how good Van Buren was in his time. How good were others in *theirs?*"

Jim Brown

YEAR	TEAM	LG	SG	ATT	YDS	AVG	TD	ADJ YPSG	RATE	RAW
1957	Cleveland	N	12	202	*942	4.7	*9	86.0	100.0	20200.0
1958	Cleveland	N	12	*257	*1527	5.9	*17	141.4	100.0	25700.0
1959	Cleveland	N	12	*290	*1329	4.6	*14	122.4	100.0	29000.0
1960	Cleveland	N	12	215	*1257	5.8	9	112.3	100.0	21500.0
1961	Cleveland	N	14	*305	*1408	4.6	8	106.3	100.0	30500.0
1962	Cleveland	N	14	230	996	4.3	13	80.4	67.7	15563.7
1963	Cleveland	N	14	*291	*1863	*6.4	*12	141.6	100.0	29100.0
1964	Cleveland	N	14	*280	*1446	*5.2	7	108.3	100.0	28000.0
1965	Cleveland	N	14	*289	*1544	5.3	*17	122.4	100.0	28900.0
			118	2359	12312	5.2	106	113.3	96.8	228463.7

* Led league.

No runner ever dominated his position to the extent that Brown dominated his. He was simply in a class alone. When he retired to go into the movie star biz, he was still the best. However, that brings up a point that affects all averages, including our RATE. Most stars slow down toward the ends of their careers, pulling down their averages. Brown didn't. But consider this: if he'd played 3 more seasons *and not gained a yard*, he would have had a RATE over 70!

Gale Sayers

YEAR	TEAM	LG	SG	ATT	YDS	AVG	TD	YPSG	RATE	RAW
1965	Chicago	N	14	166	867	5.2	14	71.9	58.8	9752.7
1966	Chicago	N	14	229	*1321	5.4	8	93.6	100.0	22900.0
1967	Chicago	N	14	186	880	4.7	7	67.9	7.2	13437.3
1968	Chicago	N	14	138	856	*6.2	2	62.6	62.6	8641.0
1969	Chicago	N	14	*236	*1032	4.4	8	79.4	100.0	23600.0
1970	Chicago	N	14	23	52	2.3	0	3.7	4.4	101.8
1971	Chicago	N	14	13	38	2.9	0	2.7	3.2	41.4
			98	991	4956	5.0	39	54.6	79.2	78474.2

* Led league.

Gale Sayers' fans will immediately shout "Foul!" when they see that his yearly YPSG and RATE are being computed as though he played full seasons in 1970 and '71, when in fact he played only 4 games over those 2 years. The counter argument holds that a sidelined player should not be rated only on the games he played but also on the ones he missed. To use Games Played as a measure would be equally "unfair" to a player knocked out on the opening kickoff or rested during the second half. Durability certainly is one factor in evaluating any player. However, his lifetime rate is weighted by attempts, so he is not penalized for trying to play.

Versatility is another important factor in discussing a player, and Sayers was certainly versatile: he ran from scrimmage, caught passes, and returned kicks brilliantly. But here we are only concerned with his running from scrimmage.

Sayers' RATE was a hefty 82.0 for his 5 full seasons, but we could take the five best seasons for each of the other backs discussed here and get higher RATES yet. His 79.2 for his whole 7 years only looks ordinary because of the company he's in.

O. J. Simpson

YEAR	TEAM	LG	SG	ATT	YDS	AVG	TD	ADJ YPSG	RATE	RAW
1969	Buffalo	N	14	181	697	3.9	2	51.2	76.8	13909.6
1970	Buffalo	N	14	120	488	4.1	5	38.4	45.8	5494.4
1971	Buffalo	N	14	183	742	4.1	5	56.6	66.4	12148.9
1972	Buffalo	N	14	292	*1251	4.3	6	93.6	100.0	29200.0

YEAR	TEAM	LG	SG	ATT	YDS	AVG	TD	ADJ YPSG	RATE	RAW
1973	Buffalo	N	14	*332	*2003	6.0	*12	151.6	100.0	33200.0
1974	Buffalo	N	14	*270	1125	4.2	3	82.5	77.2	20831.7
1975	Buffalo	N	14	*329	*1817	*5.5	*16	141.2	100.0	32900.0
1976	Buffalo	N	14	290	*1503	5.2	8	113.1	100.0	29000.0
1977	Buffalo	N	14	126	557	4.4	0	39.8	28.0	3523.2
1978	San Francisco	N	16	161	593	3.7	1	37.7	38.2	6144.4
1979	San Francisco	N	16	120	460	3.8	3	30.6	26.0	3116.1
			158	2404	11236	4.7	61	75.0	78.8	189468.4

* Led league.

Early in Simpson's pro career, Buffalo Coach John Rauch wanted to turn him into a receiver. He didn't really become a superstar pro until his fourth season. And he would look more impressive if he'd retired three years earlier. For a five-year period, however, he was really something. His per-game average in 1973, when he gained 2,003 yards, is the best ever. But we're trying to evaluate a whole career, not just the best parts.

Some critics have contended that Buffalo actually hurt itself by using a run-oriented offense showcasing Simpson during those years. We can't buy that. The Bills had the best runner and not a whole lot more. So they ran Simpson. During his best five seasons, the Bills finished on the plus side of .500 three times. Without him, they might have finished in the Continental League.

Walter Payton

YEAR	TEAM	LG	SG	ATT	YDS	AVG	TD	ADJ YPSG	RATE	RAW
1975	Chicago	N	14	196	679	3.5	7	53.5	37.9	7425.6
1976	Chicago	N	14	*311	1390	4.5	13	108.6	96.0	29862.3
1977	Chicago	N	14	*339	*1852	*5.5	*14	142.3	100.0	33900.0
1978	Chicago	N	16	*333	1395	4.2	11	94.1	99.3	31719.3
1979	Chicago	N	16	*369	1610	4.4	14	109.4	92.8	34221.0
1980	Chicago	N	16	317	1460	4.6	6	95.0	73.6	23345.0
1981	Chicago	N	16	339	1222	3.6	6	80.1	71.0	24090.8
1982	Chicago	N	9	148	596	4.0	1	67.3	71.6	10601.4
1983	Chicago	N	16	314	1421	4.5	6	92.6	71.6	23392.0
1984	Chicago	N	16	381	1684	4.4	11	112.1	79.9	30446.1
1985	Chicago	N	16	324	1551	4.8	9	102.6	87.8	28447.5
1986	Chicago	N	16	321	1333	4.2	8	88.3	73.2	23489.0
1987	Chicago	N	15	146	533	3.7	4	38.2	38.6	5637.3
			119	3838	16726	4.4	110	91.9	79.9	306577.3

* Led league.

The reason both the baseball and pro football Halls of Fame have a five-year waiting period after retirement before a player can be elected is to add the perspective of distance. Payton is a good case in point because without the mandatory wait, he'd probably be enshrined in Canton right now. A fair question is: What could he possibly do in the next five years to keep him out? Okay, just suppose that four years after he retires we suddenly learn that he's a serial killer, that he sold government secrets to a foreign power, and he hasn't paid his cable-TV bill. Moreover, he knocks down little old ladies, hates kids, and makes obscene phone calls to Bette Midler. What then?

Well, *then* the vote might be close.

Now we can look at these five runners in three ways: total YARDS, YPSG, and RATE. By ranking these five against only their contemporaries, we have the following order:

	YARDS	YPSG	RATE
Jim Brown	12312	113.3	96.8
Steve Van Buren	5860	72.0	88.6
Walter Payton	16276	91.9	79.9
Gale Sayers	4956	50.6	79.2
O. J. Simpson	11236	75.0	78.8

Note that Van Buren's YPSG is only fourth best, but his RATE compensates for the different circumstances he played under and edges him past Payton when ranked against his contemporaries.

Space won't permit our tracing every great running back (including your personal favorite), but we'll do the next best thing: we'll give you all the yearly leaders so you can work out the career marks for any other runners.

LEAGUE LEADER—ADJUSTED YPSG

Year	Player, Team	LG	SG	Att	Yds	Avg	TD	Adj YPSG
1932	Cliff Battles, Bos	N	10	*148	*576	3.9	3	60.6
1933	Jim Musick, Bos	N	12	*173	*809	4.7	5	71.6
1934	Beattie Feathers, Brs	N	13	117	*1004	*8.6	8	83.4
1935	Ernie Caddel, Det	N	12	87	450	5.2	*6	42.5
1936	Ace Gutowsky, Det........	N	12	192	827	4.3	6	73.9
1937	Cliff Battles, Was	N	11	*216	*874	4.0	*5	84.0
1938	Whizzer White, Pit	N	11	*152	*567	3.7	4	55.2

Year	Player, Team	LG	SG	Att	Yds	Avg	TD	Adj YPSG
1939	Bill Osmanski, Brs.........	N	11	121	*699	5.8	7	69.0
1940	Johnny Drake, Cle.........	N	11	134	480	3.6	*9	51.8
1941	Pug Manders, Bkn.........	N	11	111	*486	4.4	6	49.6
1942	Bill Dudley, Pit	N	11	*162	*696	4.3	5	67.8
1943	Bill Paschal, NYG.........	N	10	*147	*572	3.9	*10	67.2
1944	Bill Paschal, NYG.........	N	10	*196	*737	3.8	*9	82.7
1945	Steve Van Buren, Phi	N	10	143	*832	5.8	*15	98.2
1946	Bill Dudley, Pit	N	11	*146	*604	4.1	3	57.6
	Spec Sanders, NYY........	A	14	*140	*709	5.1	*6	54.9
1947	Steve Van Buren, Phi	N	12	*217	*1008	4.5	*13	94.8
	Spec Sanders, NYY........	A	14	*231	*1432	6.2	*18	115.1
1948	Steve Van Buren, Phi	N	12	*201	*945	4.7	*10	87.1
	Marion Motley, Cle........	A	14	157	*964	6.1	5	72.4
1949	Steve Van Buren, Phi	N	12	*263	*1146	4.4	*11	104.7
	Joe Perry, SF	A	12	115	*783	*6.8	*8	71.9
1950	Marion Motley, Cle........	N	12	140	*810	5.8	3	70.0
1951	Eddie Price, NYG	N	12	*271	*971	3.6	7	86.8
	Rob Goode, Was	N	12	208	951	4.6	*9	86.8
1952	Dan Towler, LA	N	12	156	*894	5.7	*10	82.8
1953	Joe Perry, SF	N	12	*182	*1018	5.3	*10	93.2
1954	Joe Perry, SF	N	12	*173	*1049	6.1	8	94.1
1955	Alan Ameche, Balt	N	12	*213	*961	4.5	*9	87.6
1956	Rick Casares, Brs..........	N	12	*234	*1126	4.8	*12	103.8
1957	Jim Brown, Cle	N	12	202	*942	4.7	*9	86.0
1958	Jim Brown, Cle	N	12	*257	*1527	5.9	*17	141.4
1959	Jim Brown, Cle	N	12	*290	*1329	4.6	*14	122.4
1960	Jim Brown, Cle	N	12	215	*1257	5.8	9	112.3
	Abner Haynes, Dal	A	14	*156	*875	5.6	*9	68.9
1961	Jim Brown, Cle	N	14	*305	*1408	4.6	8	106.3
	Billy Cannon, Hou	A	14	200	*948	4.7	6	72.0
1962	Jim Taylor, GB	N	14	*272	*1474	5.4	*19	118.9
	Cookie Gilchrist, Buf	A	14	214	*1096	5.1	*13	87.6
1963	Jim Brown, Cle	N	14	*291	*1863	*6.4	*12	141.6
	Clem Daniels, Oak	A	14	214	*1099	5.1	3	80.6
1964	Jim Brown, Cle	N	14	*280	*1446	*5.2	7	108.3
	Cookie Gilchrist, Buf	A	14	*230	*981	4.3	*6	74.4
1965	Jim Brown, Cle	N	14	*289	*1544	5.3	*17	122.4
	Paul Lowe, SD	A	14	222	*1121	*5.1	*7	85.1
1966	Gale Sayers, Brs...........	N	14	229	*1231	5.4	8	93.6
	Jim Nance, Bos	A	14	*299	*1458	4.9	*11	112.0

Year	Player, Team	LG	SG	Att	Yds	Avg	TD	Adj YPSG
1967	Leroy Kelly, Cle	N	14	*235	*1205	*5.1	*11	93.9
	Jim Nance, Bos	A	14	*269	*1216	4.5	7	91.9
1968	Leroy Kelly, Cle	N	14	*248	*1239	5.0	*16	100.0
	Paul Robinson, Cin	A	14	*238	*1023	4.3	*8	78.8
1969	Gale Sayers, Brs...........	N	14	*236	*1032	4.4	8	79.4
	Dickie Post, SD	A	14	182	*873	4.8	6	66.6
1970	Larry Brown, Was	N	14	237	*1125	4.7	5	83.9
1971	Floyd Little, Den..........	N	14	*284	*1133	4.0	6	85.3
1972	O. J. Simpson, Buf.........	N	14	*291	*1251	4.3	6	93.6
1973	O. J. Simpson, Buf.........	N	14	*332	*2003	6.0	*12	151.6
1974	Otis Armstrong, Den	N	14	263	*1407	*5.3	9	106.9
1975	O. J. Simpson, Buf.........	N	14	*329	*1817	*5.5	*16	141.2
1976	O. J. Simpson, Buf.........	N	14	*290	*1503	5.2	8	113.1
1977	Walter Payton, Brs	N	14	*330	*1852	*5.5	*14	142.3
1978	Earl Campbell, Hou	N	16	302	*1450	4.8	13	98.8
1979	Earl Campbell, Hou	N	16	368	*1697	4.6	*19	117.9
1980	Earl Campbell, Hou	N	16	*373	*1934	*5.2	*13	129.0
1981	George Rogers, NO........	N	16	*378	*1674	4.4	*13	112.8
1982	Freeman McNeil, NYJ	N	9	151	*786	*5.2	6	94.0
1983	Eric Dickerson, LA........	N	16	*390	*1808	4.6	18	124.3
1984	Eric Dickerson, LA........	N	16	379	*2105	5.6	*14	140.3
1985	Marcus Allen, Raid........	N	16	380	*1759	4.6	11	116.8
1986	Eric Dickerson, LA........	N	16	*404	*1821	4.5	11	120.7
1987	Charles White, LA	N	15	*324	*1374	4.2	*11	98.9

* Led or tied for league leadership.

PASSING

We explained our New Rating System for passers earlier, but to remind you: it's a yards per *attempt* average, with a 10-point bonus for touchdowns and a 45-point penalty for interceptions.

A good question here might be "Why do you rate rushers on (scheduled) game averages but passers on attempt averages?" Good question; glad you asked. The answer is simple enough: everybody (you, us, and your chiropodist) rates runners on *how many yards* they get but rates passers on *how efficiently* they use their attempts. If we rated runners by efficiency, we'd usually have a team's third or fourth most productive runner leading. If we rated passers by total yards, we'd have too many losing-team quarterbacks who threw for 250 yards (and 3 interceptions) in the fourth quarters of long-lost games.

Here are the leading passers through the years, according to our system (NEWS), as detailed in an earlier chapter, "The Glory, the Blame, and the Ratings." In order to qualify, a passer needed 50 attempts in 1932-37, 8.33 attempts per game in 1938-60, 10 attempts per game in 1961-76, and 14 attempts per game from 1977-to date. When the leader is someone other than the passer ranked first by one of the NFL's several systems, there is a # symbol marked before the year.

LEADING PASSERS—NEW RATING SYSTEM (NEWS)

YEAR	PLAYER, TEAM	LG	ATT	COM	YDS	TD	IN	NEWS
#1932	Keith Molesworth, ChiB	N	54	22	475	4	6	4.54
#1933	Keith Molesworth, ChiB	N	50	19	421	5	4	5.82
1934	Arnie Herber, GB	N	*115	*42	*799	*8	12	2.95
#1935	Arnie Herber, GB	N	106	40	729	8	6	5.08
1936	Arnie Herber, GB	N	*173	*77	*1289	*11	13	4.41
#1937	Bernie Masterson, ChiB	N	72	26	615	8	7	5.28
#1938	Bernie Masterson, ChiB	N	112	46	848	7	9	4.58
#1939	Arnie Herber, GB	N	139	57	1107	8	9	5.63
1940	Sammy Baugh, Was	N	177	111	*1367	*12	10	5.86
#1941	Sid Luckman, ChiB	N	119	68	1181	9	6	8.41
1942	Cecil Isbell, GB	N	268	*146	*2021	*24	14	6.09
#1943	Sid Luckman, ChiB	N	202	110	*2194	*28	12	9.57
1944	Frankie Filchock, Was	N	147	*84	1139	*13	9	5.88
1945	Sammy Baugh, Was	N	182	*128	1669	11	4	8.79
#1946	Sid Luckman, ChiB	N	220	110	*1826	17	16	5.57
	Otto Graham, Cle	A	174	95	1834	*17	5	10.22
1947	Sammy Baugh, Was	N	*354	*210	*2938	*25	15	7.10
	Otto Graham, Cle	A	269	163	*2753	*25	11	9.32
#1948	Ray Mallouf, Crds	N	143	73	1160	13	6	7.13
#	Y. A. Tittle, Balt	A	289	161	2522	16	9	7.88
#1949	Tommy Thompson, Phi	N	214	116	1727	16	11	6.50
	Otto Graham, Cle	A	285	*161	*2785	19	10	8.86
1950	Norm Van Brocklin, LA	N	233	127	2061	18	14	6.91
1951	Bob Waterfield, LA	N	176	88	1566	13	10	7.08
#1952	Tobin Rote, GB	N	157	82	1268	13	8	6.61
1953	Otto Graham, Cle	N	258	167	*2722	11	9	9.41
1954	Norm Van Brocklin, LA	N	260	139	*2637	13	21	7.01
1955	Otto Graham, Cle	N	185	98	1721	15	8	8.17
1956	Ed Brown, ChiB	N	168	96	1667	11	12	7.36
1957	Tommy O'Connell, Cle.	N	110	63	1229	9	8	8.72
#1958	Bobby Layne, Det-Pit.	N	294	145	2510	14	12	7.18
1959	Charlie Conerly, NYG	N	194	113	1706	14	4	8.59
1960	Milt Plum, Cle	N	250	151	2297	21	5	9.13
#	Tom Flores, Oak	A	252	136	1738	12	12	5.23
#1961	John Brodie, SF	N	283	155	2588	14	12	7.73
	George Blanda, Hou	A	362	187	*3330	*36	22	7.46

YEAR	PLAYER, TEAM	LG	ATT	COM	YDS	TD	IN	NEWS
1962	Bart Starr, GB	N	285	178	2438	12	9	7.55
	Len Dawson, KC	A	310	189	2759	*29	17	7.37
1963	Y. A. Tittle, NYG	N	367	221	3145	*36	14	7.83
	Tobin Rote, SD	A	286	170	2510	20	17	6.80
#1964	Johnny Unitas, Balt	N	305	158	2824	19	6	9.00
	Len Dawson, KC	A	354	199	2879	30	18	6.69
#1965	Johnny Unitas, Balt	N	282	164	2530	23	12	7.87
#	Len Dawson, KC	A	305	163	2262	*21	14	6.04
1966	Bart Starr, GB	N	251	156	2257	14	3	9.01
	Len Dawson, KC	A	284	159	2527	*26	10	8.23
#1967	Fran Tarkenton, NYG	N	377	204	3088	29	19	6.69
	Daryle Lamonica, Oak	A	425	220	3228	*30	20	6.18
#1968	Bart Starr, GB	N	171	109	1617	15	8	8.23
	Len Dawson, KC	A	224	131	2109	17	9	8.37
#1969	Craig Morton, Dal	N	302	162	2619	21	15	7.13
	Greg Cook, Cin	A	197	106	1854	15	11	7.66
#1970	Craig Morton, Dal	N	207	102	1819	15	7	7.99
1971	Roger Staubach, Dal	N	211	126	1882	15	4	8.78
#1972	Earl Morrall, Mia	N	150	83	1360	11	7	7.70
#1973	Fran Tarkenton, Minn	N	274	169	2113	15	7	7.11
1974	Ken Anderson, Cin	N	328	213	2667	18	10	7.31
1975	Ken Anderson, Cin	N	377	228	*3169	21	11	7.65
#1976	Bert Jones, Balt	N	343	207	*3104	24	9	8.57
#1977	Craig Morton, Den	N	254	131	1929	14	8	6.73
1978	Roger Staubach, Dal	N	413	231	3190	25	16	6.59
1979	Roger Staubach, Dal	N	461	267	3586	27	11	7.29
#1980	Ron Jaworski, Phi	N	451	257	3529	27	12	7.23
1981	Ken Anderson, Cin	N	479	300	3754	29	10	7.50
#1982	Dan Fouts, SD	N	330	204	2883	*17	11	7.75
#1983	Joe Theismann, Was	N	459	276	3714	29	11	7.64
1984	Dan Marino, Mia	N	*564	*362	*5084	*48	17	8.51
1985	Ken O'Brien, NYJ	N	488	297	3888	25	8	7.74
1986	Tommy Kramer, Minn	N	372	208	3000	24	10	7.50
1987	Bernie Kosar, Cle	N	389	241	3033	22	9	7.32

* Led or tied for league leadership.

Frankly, we were surprised that Tommy O'Connell *still* led the league in passing in 1957, even under our system. Maybe the answer is simply that for one season he really was the best. One thing is clear. He got the best out of his talent. There's probably no higher compliment, for anybody doing anything.

The list of quarterbacks someone has nominated as the "greatest of all time" is longer than the list of agents looking to represent next year's Heisman winner, but the following five are among the most commonly named.

Sammy Baugh

Year	Team	Lg	ATT	COM	YARD	TD	IN	NEWS	RATE	RAW
1937	Was	N	*171	*81	*1127	8	14	3.37	63.9	10926.9
1938	Was	N	128	63	853	6	11	3.27	71.3	9139.2
1939	Was	N	96	53	518	6	9	1.80	32.0	3072.0
1940	Was	N	177	111	*1367	*12	10	5.86	100.0	17700.0
1941	Was	N	193	106	1236	10	19	2.49	29.6	5712.8
1942	Was	N	225	132	1524	16	11	5.28	86.8	19530.0
1943	Was	N	*239	*133	1754	23	19	4.72	49.4	11806.6
1944	Was	N	146	82	849	4	8	3.62	61.6	8993.6
1945	Was	N	182	*128	1669	11	4	8.79	100.0	18200.0
1946	Was	N	161	87	1163	8	17	2.97	53.3	8581.3
1947	Was	N	*354	*210	*2938	*25	15	7.10	100.0	35400.0
1948	Was	N	*315	*185	*2599	22	23	5.66	79.4	25011.0
1949	Was	N	255	145	1903	18	14	5.70	87.7	22363.5
1950	Was	N	166	90	1130	10	11	4.43	64.1	10640.6
1951	Was	N	154	67	1104	7	17	2.66	37.5	5775.0
1952	Was	N	33	20	152	2	1	3.85	58.2	1920.6
			2995	1693	21886	188	203	4.89	71.7	214773.1

* Led league.

Baugh was the NFL's most famous passer from the day he put on a Redskin uniform. He started as a single-wing tailback and only switched to the T-formation around 1945. Curiously the Redskins' best seasons came before 1946 but most of Baugh's best statistical totals came after that year.

Obviously there's a connection. The Redskins were a good team when Baugh joined them. His presence—he was also a good defensive back and one of the best punters ever—made them a dynasty, as they won five division titles and two championships in 1937-45. But everybody got old. Baugh was left with little help after the war and tried to make up the difference with his passes.

Ironically he ended with career totals that were the best for his time. Had his team been more impressive in his final years, his totals would have been lower, but his averages would no doubt have been much better.

Otto Graham

Year	Team	Lg	ATT	COM	YARD	TD	IN	NEWS	RATE	RAW
1946	Cle	A	174	95	1834	*17	5	10.22	100.0	17400.0
1947	Cle	A	269	163	*2753	*25	11	9.32	100.0	26900.0
1948	Cle	A	333	173	*2713	25	15	6.87	87.2	29037.6
1949	Cle	A	285	*161	*2785	19	10	8.86	100.0	28500.0
1950	Cle	N	253	137	1943	14	20	4.68	67.7	17128.1
1951	Cle	N	265	147	2205	17	16	6.25	88.2	23373.0
1952	Cle	N	364	*181	*2816	*20	24	5.32	80.5	29302.0
1953	Cle	N	258	167	*2722	11	9	9.41	100.0	25800.0
1954	Cle	N	240	142	2092	11	17	5.99	85.4	20496.0
1955	Cle	N	185	98	1721	15	8	8.17	100.0	18500.0
			2626	1464	23584	174	135	7.33	90.0	236436.7

* Led league.

Graham, like Jim Brown, retired at his peak.

The only knock anyone hears about Graham is that he didn't call his own plays. You don't hear it so often now, of course, because almost every quarterback today gets his calls sent in. In a few years, Graham will be *praised* as a pioneer in receiving instructions from the bench!

His most impressive record is taking his team to 10 championship games and winning 7. Nevertheless in those phony ratings where they give things like 4.2 for arm strength and 5.3 for sobriety, Graham is sometimes penalized for leadership because he didn't call those plays. Good grief! What did he have to do to get a high leadership rating? Win the Korean War?

Johnny Unitas

Year	Team	Lg	ATT	COM	YARD	TD	IN	NEWS	RATE	RAW
1956	Balt	N	198	110	1498	9	10	5.75	78.1	15463.8
1957	Balt	N	301	172	2550	24	17	6.73	77.2	23237.2
1958	Balt	N	263	136	2007	19	7	7.16	99.7	26221.1
1959	Balt	N	367	193	2899	32	14	7.05	82.1	30130.7
1960	Balt	N	378	190	3099	25	24	6.00	65.7	24834.6
1961	Balt	N	420	229	2990	16	24	4.93	68.8	26796.0
1962	Balt	N	389	222	2967	23	23	5.56	73.6	28630.4
1963	Balt	N	410	237	3481	20	12	7.66	97.8	40098.0
1964	Balt	N	305	158	2824	19	6	9.00	100.0	30500.0
1965	Balt	N	282	164	2530	23	12	7.87	100.0	28200.0
1966	Balt	N	348	195	2748	22	24	5.43	60.2	20949.6
1967	Balt	N	436	255	3428	20	16	6.67	99.7	43469.2
1968	Balt	N	32	11	139	2	4	−0.66	−8.0	−255.2
1969	Balt	N	327	178	2342	12	20	4.78	67.0	21909.0
1970	Balt	N	321	166	2213	14	18	4.81	60.2	19324.2

Year	Team	Lg	ATT	COM	YARD	TD	IN	NEWS	RATE	RAW
1971	Balt	N	176	92	942	3	9	3.22	36.7	6459.2
1972	Balt	N	157	88	1111	4	6	5.61	72.9	11445.3
1973	SD	N	76	34	471	3	7	2.45	34.4	2614.4
			5186	2830	40239	290	253	6.12	77.1	400027.5

* Led league.

By the mid-1960s Johnny U. was being rated the "best ever." His later seasons, spoiled by injuries and the fact that he hung on a little too long, didn't add anything to that assessment and may have hurt it.

Of all the records set and reset by various players, Unitas has the one that seems least likely ever to be broken—47 consecutive games throwing a touchdown pass. No one has come within a season's worth of tying it. It's the pro football equivalent of DiMaggio's hitting streak.

What should be remembered is that Unitas' Colts won two championships and were in the title race every year while he was setting the record (1956-60). You have to assume that most of those 47 touchdowns were needed. He didn't nickel-and-dime his TDs either. The average length of the 102 TD passes he threw during his streak was 25.5 yards. Two-thirds were over 10 yards, including 2 of more than 80. His shortest TD toss was a one-yarder against the Bears on October 18, 1959, but he already had a 25-yarder that day.

Fran Tarkenton

Year	Team	Lg	ATT	COM	YARD	TD	IN	NEWS	RATE	RAW
1961	Minn	N	280	157	1997	18	17	5.04	65.2	18256.0
1962	Minn	N	329	163	2595	22	25	5.14	68.0	22372.0
1963	Minn	N	297	170	2311	15	15	6.01	76.8	22809.6
1964	Minn	N	306	171	2506	22	11	7.29	81.0	24786.0
1965	Minn	N	329	171	2609	19	11	7.00	89.0	29281.0
1966	Minn	N	358	192	2561	17	16	5.62	67.3	22303.4
1967	NYG	N	377	204	3088	29	19	6.69	100.0	37700.0
1968	NYG	N	337	182	2555	21	12	6.60	80.2	27027.4
1969	NYG	N	409	220	2918	23	8	6.82	95.6	39100.4
1970	NYG	N	389	219	2777	19	12	6.24	78.1	30380.9
1971	NYG	N	386	*226	2567	11	21	4.48	51.1	19724.6
1972	Minn	N	378	215	2651	18	13	5.94	77.2	29181.6
1973	Minn	N	274	169	2113	15	7	7.11	100.0	27400.0
1974	Minn	N	351	199	*2598	17	12	6.35	86.8	30466.8
1975	Minn	N	*425	*273	*2994	*25	13	6.26	81.8	34765.0
1976	Minn	N	412	*255	*2961	17	8	6.73	78.5	32342.0
1977	Minn	N	258	155	1734	9	14	4.63	68.8	17750.4

Year	Team	Lg	ATT	COM	YARD	TD	IN	NEWS	RATE	RAW
1978	Minn	N	572	345	3468	25	32	3.98	60.4	34548.8
			6467	3686	47003	342	266	5.95	77.4	500239.4

* Led league.

This point has been made many times, so we'll just give you the short version: Tarkenton never won a Super Bowl (Boo!); Tarkenton got his team into three Super Bowls (Yay!).

A more important thing to think about: virtually no one on this planet ever suggested that Tarkenton was the best passer around during any one of his seasons; but he holds all the *total* pass records. Let's hear it from the consistency-durability contingent!

Roger Staubach

Year	Team	Lg	ATT	COM	YARD	TD	IN	NEWS	RATE	RAW
1969	Dal	N	47	23	421	1	2	7.26	101.8	4784.6
1970	Dal	N	82	44	542	2	8	2.46	30.8	2525.6
1971	Dal	N	211	126	1882	15	4	8.78	100.0	21100.0
1972	Dal	N	20	9	98	0	2	0.40	5.2	104.0
1973	Dal	N	286	179	2428	*23	15	6.93	97.5	27885.0
1974	Dal	N	360	190	2552	11	15	5.52	75.5	27180.0
1975	Dal	N	348	198	2666	17	16	6.08	79.5	27666.0
1976	Dal	N	369	208	2715	14	11	6.40	74.6	27527.4
1977	Dal	N	*361	*210	*2620	*18	9	6.63	98.6	35594.6
1978	Dal	N	413	231	3190	*25	16	6.59	100.0	41300.0
1979	Dal	N	461	267	3586	*27	11	7.29	100.0	46100.0
			2958	1685	22700	153	109	6.53	88.5	261767.2

* Led league.

All the hoopla about Staubach bringing his team back in the final quarter shouldn't obscure the fact that he was a remarkably consistent passer. Like Graham, he retired while still in his prime, statistically after his most productive season.

He was also a role model for anybody who used to read the Hardy Boys. Somebody should take a poll to see how Staubach fans rate Jim McMahon. We'll bet the Bears' quarterback would get higher marks from people who used to cheer for Bobby Layne.

This time, we figure the career average RATE by using the RAW (ATT × RATE) divided by the number of attempts because we're talking about efficiency per pass instead of a per scheduled game rate. In this case we have to adjust for "short" seasons; otherwise a 1-pass year and a 500-pass year would have the same weight. We don't want seasons like Staubach's injury-ruined 1972 to have the same "weight" as a normal year.

Ranked against their contemporaries, the five passers' career averages line up as follows: Graham 90.0, Staubach 88.5, Tarkenton 77.4, Unitas 77.1, and Baugh 71.7. Of the top ten lifetime passers, listed below, four are active and can expect their RATEs to decline from current levels.

Dan Marino, 90.1	Dan Fouts, 82.3
Otto Graham, 90.0	Ken Anderson, 82.0
Joe Montana, 88.5	Sid Luckman, 81.3
Roger Staubach, 88.5	Neil Lomax, 80.7
Len Dawson, 83.6	Dave Krieg, 80.1

Of course, that's their passing. As for which one ranks as the greatest quarterback, we'll leave that to those who feel qualified to rate such areas as "leadership," "ball handling," "poise," and all the other intangibles.

You can work out your favorite QB's RATE for a year or career by using the season leader chart.

PASS RECEIVING

To be able to rate anything, whether football players or pizza, it's best if you can hang everything on one standard. Otherwise you can spend the day proving Salerno's has the best crust, then have the guys for Luigi's bring up anchovies and you have to start all over. The four categories of importance with pass receivers are Number of Receptions, Yardage, Average Gain, and Touchdowns.

The NFL has always awarded its pass receiving championship to the player with the most receptions. Now they publish the yardage leader in the weekly stats, so it may be only a matter of time before the title goes to that guy. We hope so. With passers tossing little flat passes to running backs like confetti at a birthday party, reception totals don't mean that much anymore.

Average Gain is interesting but can be misleading. Would you rather have someone catch two passes for 30 yards or one pass for 16? Too often the leader in this category catches a significantly smaller number of passes than the league's top man. We believe (in our heart of hearts) that total yardage is the single most important stat for a receiver, and to compare across eras, you should use the YPSG figure.

Naturally some credit should be given to touchdown passes—say, ten yards per. Does this sound familiar?

You're right. We're going to rate receivers in the same way we rated runners: ADJ YPSG.

Here are the yearly leaders:

LEADING PASS RECEIVERS—ADJUSTED YPSG

Year	Player, Team	LG	SG	Att	Yds	Avg	TD	Adj YPSG
1932	Ray Flaherty, NYG	N	12	*21	*350	*16.7	*5	33.3
1933	Paul Moss, Pit	N	11	13	*383	*29.5	2	36.6
1934	Joe Carter, Phi	N	11	*16	238	14.9	4	25.3
1935	Don Hutson, GB	N	12	18	420	23.3	*6	40.0
1936	Don Hutson, GB	N	12	*34	*536	15.5	*8	51.3
1937	Gaynell Tinsley, Crds	N	11	36	*675	18.8	5	65.9
1938	Don Hutson, GB	N	11	32	*548	17.1	*9	58.0
1939	Don Hutson, GB	N	11	*34	*846	24.9	6	82.4
1940	Don Looney, Phi	N	11	*58	*707	12.2	4	67.9
1941	Don Hutson, GB	N	11	*58	*738	12.7	*10	76.2
1942	Don Hutson, GB	N	11	*74	*1211	16.3	*17	125.6
1943	Don Hutson, GB	N	10	*47	*776	16.5	*11	88.6
1944	Don Hutson, GB	N	10	*58	*866	14.9	*9	95.6
1945	Jim Benton, Cle	N	10	45	*1067	23.7	8	114.7
1946	Jim Benton, Cle	N	11	*63	*981	15.6	6	94.6
	Dante Lavelli, Cle	A	14	*40	*843	21.1	8	65.9
1947	Mal Kutner, Crds	N	12	43	*944	21.9	7	84.5
	Mac Speedie, Cle	A	14	*67	*1146	17.1	6	86.1
1948	Mal Kutner, Crds	N	12	41	*943	23.0	*14	90.3
	Bill Hillenbrand, Balt	A	14	50	*970	19.4	6	73.6
1949	Tom Fears, LA	N	12	*77	1013	13.2	*9	91.9
	Mac Speedie, Cle	A	12	*62	*1028	16.6	7	91.5
1950	Tom Fears, LA	N	12	*84	*1116	13.3	7	98.8
1951	Elroy Hirsch, LA	N	12	*66	*1495	*22.7	*17	138.8
1952	Billy Howton, GB	N	12	53	*1231	23.2	13	113.4
1953	Pete Pihos, Phi	N	12	*63	*1049	16.7	*10	95.8
1954	Bob Boyd, LA	N	12	53	*1212	22.9	6	106.0
1955	Pete Pihos, Phi	N	12	*62	*864	13.9	7	77.8
1956	Billy Howton, GB	N	12	55	*1188	21.6	*12	109.0
1957	Raymond Berry, Balt	N	12	47	*800	17.0	6	71.7
1958	Del Shofner, LA	N	12	51	*1097	21.5	8	98.1

Year	Player, Team	LG	SG	Att	Yds	Avg	TD	Adj YPSG
1959	Raymond Berry, Balt	N	12	*66	*959	14.5	*14	91.6
1960	Raymond Berry, Balt	N	12	*74	*1298	17.5	10	116.5
	Bill Groman, Hou	A	14	72	*1473	20.5	12	113.8
1961	Tommy McDonald, Phi ...	N	14	64	*1144	17.9	*13	91.0
	Charlie Hennigan, Hou....	A	14	82	*1746	21.3	12	133.3
1962	Bobby Mitchell, Was	N	14	*72	*1384	19.2	11	106.7
	Art Powell, NYT.........	A	14	64	*1130	17.7	8	86.4
1963	Bobby Mitchell, Was	N	14	69	*1436	20.8	7	107.6
	Art Powell, Oak..........	A	14	73	*1304	17.9	*16	104.6
1964	Johnny Morris, ChiB	N	14	*93	*1200	12.9	*10	92.9
	Charlie Hennigan, Hou....	A	14	*101	*1546	15.3	8	116.1
1965	Dave Parks, SF	N	14	*80	*1344	16.8	*12	104.6
	Lance Alworth, SD	A	14	69	*1602	*23.2	*14	124.4
1966	Bob Hayes, Dal	N	14	64	1232	19.3	*13	97.3
	Lance Alworth, SD	A	14	*73	*1383	18.9	*13	108.7
1967	Ben Hawkins, Phi	N	14	59	*1265	21.4	10	97.5
	Don Maynard, NYJ	A	14	71	*1434	20.2	10	109.6
1968	Paul Warfield, Cle	N	14	50	1067	21.3	*12	84.8
	Lance Alworth, SD	A	14	*68	*1312	19.3	10	100.9
1969	Harold Jackson, Phi	N	14	65	*1116	17.2	9	86.1
	Warren Wells, Oak........	A	14	47	*1260	*26.8	*14	100.0
1970	Gene Washington, SF	N	14	53	*1100	20.8	12	87.1
1971	Otis Taylor, KC..........	N	14	57	*1110	19.5	7	84.3
1972	John Gilliam, Minn.......	N	14	47	1035	*22.0	7	78.9
1973	Harold Carmichael, Phi ...	N	14	*67	*1116	*16.7	9	86.1
1974	Cliff Branch, Oak	N	14	60	*1092	18.2	*13	87.3
1975	Ken Burrough, Hou	N	14	53	*1063	20.1	8	81.6
1976	Cliff Branch, Oak	N	14	46	1111	24.2	*12	87.9
1977	Ken Burrough, Hou	N	14	43	*816	19.0	8	64.0
1978	Wesley Walker, NYJ	N	16	48	*1169	24.4	8	78.1
1979	Steve Largent, Sea	N	16	66	*1237	18.7	9	82.9
1980	John Jefferson, SD........	N	16	82	*1340	16.3	*13	91.9
1981	Alfred Jenkins, Atl	N	16	70	*1358	19.4	*13	93.0
1982	Wes Chandler, SD	N	9	49	*1032	21.1	*9	124.7
1983	Mike Quick, Phi..........	N	16	69	*1409	20.4	13	96.2
1984	Roy Green, St.L.	N	16	78	*1555	19.9	*12	104.7
1985	Mike Quick, Phi..........	N	16	73	1247	17.1	11	84.8
1986	Jerry Rice, SF............	N	16	86	*1570	18.3	*15	107.5
1987	Jerry Rice, SF............	N	15	65	1078	16.6	*22	86.5

* Led league.

To show you this method in action, we'll give you the records of five of the many great receivers who've sparkled in the last fifty years: Don Hutson, Elroy "Crazylegs" Hirsch, Raymond Berry, Lance Alworth, and Steve Largent.

Don Hutson

YEAR	TEAM	LG	SG	NO	YDS	AVG	TD	ADJ YPSG	RATE	RAW
1935	Green Bay	N	12	18	420	23.3	*6	40.0	100.0	1800.0
1936	Green Bay	N	12	*34	*536	15.8	*8	51.3	100.0	3400.0
1937	Green Bay	N	11	*41	552	13.5	*7	56.5	85.7	3517.5
1938	Green Bay	N	11	32	*548	17.1	*9	58.0	100.0	3200.0
1939	Green Bay	N	11	*34	*846	24.9	6	82.4	100.0	3400.0
1940	Green Bay	N	11	45	664	14.8	*7	66.7	98.2	4421.7
1941	Green Bay	N	11	*58	*738	12.7	*10	76.2	100.0	5800.0
1942	Green Bay	N	11	*74	*1211	16.4	*17	125.6	100.0	7400.0
1943	Green Bay	N	10	*47	*776	16.5	*11	88.6	100.0	4700.0
1944	Green Bay	N	10	*58	*866	14.9	*9	95.6	100.0	5800.0
1945	Green Bay	N	10	*47	834	17.7	9	92.4	80.6	3786.4
			120	488	7991	16.4	99	74.8	96.8	47225.4

* Led league.

Hutson was to pass receiving what Freud was to psychoanalysis. Before him there were just a lot of guys clomping around trying to get the job done. After him they knew how. He invented or perfected just about every technique and maneuver that became s.o.p.

The amazing thing is how long it took them to catch up. If you add up the receptions by all the runners-up in the eight years he led the league and add the three ends who finished ahead of him in 1935, 1938, and 1940, they total 391 catches to his 488. In 1941 and '42, he more than doubled the totals of the second-place finishers. And when he retired in 1945, the next highest career total was Jim Benton—298 behind.

Among Hutson's many innovations, he practiced—for hours—catching *bad* passes. He was blessed through his first eight years with two fine passers in Arnie Herber and Cecil Isbell, but three of his best seasons came catching the throws of their very ordinary successors.

Elroy Hirsch

YEAR	TEAM	LG	SG	NO	YDS	AVG	TD	ADJ YPSG	RATE	RAW
1946	Chicago	AAC	14	27	347	12.9	3	26.9	40.8	1102.8
1947	Chicago	AAC	14	10	282	28.2	3	22.3	25.9	258.7
1948	Chicago	AAC	14	7	101	14.4	1	7.9	10.8	75.4
1949	Los Angeles	N	12	22	326	14.8	4	30.5	33.2	730.0
1950	Los Angeles	N	12	42	687	16.4	7	63.1	63.8	2680.8
1951	Los Angeles	N	12	*66	*1495	*22.7	*17	138.8	100.0	6600.0
1952	Los Angeles	N	12	25	590	23.6	4	52.5	46.3	1157.2
1953	Los Angeles	N	12	61	941	15.4	4	81.8	85.4	5208.1
1954	Los Angeles	N	12	35	720	20.6	3	62.5	59.0	2063.7
1955	Los Angeles	N	12	25	460	18.4	2	40.0	51.4	1284.8
1956	Los Angeles	N	12	35	603	17.2	6	55.3	50.7	1774.1
1957	Los Angeles	N	12	32	477	14.9	6	44.8	62.4	1998.1
			150	387	7029	18.2	60	50.9	64.4	24933.8

* Led league.

After a spectacular college and service career, Hirsch spent his first four pro seasons as an often-injured halfback, three with the dreadful Chicago Rockets of the AAFC. He started to come on as a receiver in 1950 when the Rams moved him out to flanker, and in 1951 had arguably the best single season of any pass catcher ever. He had the most catches, most yards, highest average, and most touchdowns. No other modern pass receiver has done that. And 10 of his 17 touchdowns came on long-distance passes.

He made a couple of movies, including one in which he played himself in his life story. As an actor, he ranked ahead of Red Grange, Johnny Mack Brown, and Terry Bradshaw, even with Jim Brown, Alex Karras, and O. J. Simpson, and behind Ed Marinaro and Burt Reynolds. On the football field, partly because of injuries, he never matched his '51 season. But then neither did any healthy receiver.

Raymond Berry

YEAR	TEAM	LG	SG	NO	YDS	AVG	TD	ADJ YPSG	RATE	RAW
1955	Baltimore	N	12	13	205	15.8	0	17.1	21.9	285.3
1956	Baltimore	N	12	37	601	16.2	2	51.8	47.5	1756.7
1957	Baltimore	N	12	47	*800	17.0	6	71.7	100.0	4700.0
1958	Baltimore	N	12	*56	794	14.2	*9	73.7	75.1	4205.9
1959	Baltimore	N	12	*66	*959	14.5	*14	91.6	100.0	6600.0
1960	Baltimore	N	12	*74	*1298	17.5	10	116.5	100.0	7400.0
1961	Baltimore	N	14	75	873	11.6	0	62.4	68.5	5139.3
1962	Baltimore	N	14	51	687	13.5	3	51.2	48.0	2447.6
1963	Baltimore	N	14	44	703	16.0	3	52.4	48.7	2141.6

YEAR	TEAM	LG	SG	NO	YDS	AVG	TD	ADJ YPSG	RATE	RAW
1964	Baltimore	N	14	43	663	15.4	6	51.6	55.6	2391.4
1965	Baltimore	N	14	58	739	12.7	7	57.8	55.3	3205.1
1966	Baltimore	N	14	56	786	14.0	7	61.1	62.8	3519.5
1967	Baltimore	N	14	11	167	15.2	1	12.6	13.0	142.6
			70	631	9275	14.7	68	58.6	69.6	43935.1

* Led league.

Berry was Don Hutson without the talent but every bit as much dedication. He was too light, too short, and too slow to play in the NFL. But he spent countless hours practicing patterns and many more studying defenders on film until he made himself a star.

Never the breakaway threat Hutson or Hirsch were, Raymond ("Don't call me Ray") was the master of the precise pattern for ten or fifteen yards. In one of the best lessons in determination since the Little Engine That Could, Berry moved past Hutson in career catches in 1964 and finished three years later with the then-record total.

During his eleven years in the NFL, he fumbled exactly once. Well, nobody's perfect.

Lance Alworth

YEAR	TEAM	LG	SG	NO	YDS	AVG	TD	ADJ YPSG	RATE	RAW
1962	San Diego	A	14	10	226	22.6	3	18.3	21.2	211.6
1963	San Diego	A	14	61	1205	*19.8	11	93.9	89.8	5479.2
1964	San Diego	A	14	61	1235	20.2	*13	97.5	83.9	5120.8
1965	San Diego	A	14	69	*1602	*23.2	*14	124.4	100.0	6900.0
1966	San Diego	A	14	*73	*1383	18.9	*13	108.1	100.0	7300.0
1967	San Diego	A	14	52	1010	19.4	9	78.6	71.7	3778.8
1968	San Diego	A	14	*68	*1312	19.3	10	100.9	100.0	6800.0
1969	San Diego	A	14	*64	1003	15.7	4	74.5	74.5	4768.0
1970	San Diego	N	14	35	608	17.4	4	46.3	53.1	1859.0
1971	Dallas	N	14	34	487	14.3	2	36.2	43.0	1460.8
1972	Dallas	N	14	15	195	13.0	2	15.4	19.5	2918.6
			154	542	10267	18.9	85	72.2	68.8	43920.1

* Led league.

Alworth is the receiver most commonly compared with Hutson. He was fortunate in that he joined the pro team that was most progressive in its use of the pass, Sid Gillman's San Diego Chargers. He'd been a running back in college, and a good one, but Gillman turned him into the Chargers' knockout punch. For a record seven straight seasons, he gained over 1,000 yards receiving.

Though nicknamed "Bambi" because of his youthful looks, speed, and leaping ability, he was "stag" in the end zone 85 times and brought more groans to opponents than this sentence did to readers. In 1978, he became the first former American Football League player to be named to the Pro Football Hall of Fame.

Of the four retired receivers we rated, Alworth's 81.0 career RATE is ahead of Berry's 69.6 and Hirsch's 64.4. Hutson, of course, was so dominant in his time that no one ranks near his 96.7—or is ever likely to. We were surprised, however, that an active receiver is within hailing distance.

Steve Largent

YEAR	TEAM	LG	SG	NO	YDS	AVG	TD	ADJ YPSG	RATE	RAW
1976	Seattle	N	14	54	705	13.0	4	53.2	60.5	3268.1
1977	Seattle	N	14	33	643	19.4	10	53.1	83.0	2736.5
1978	Seattle	N	16	71	1168	16.5	8	78.0	99.9	7094.3
1979	Seattle	N	16	66	*1237	18.7	9	82.9	100.0	6600.0
1980	Seattle	N	16	66	1064	16.1	6	70.3	76.5	5046.5
1981	Seattle	N	16	75	1224	16.3	9	82.1	88.3	6623.0
1982	Seattle	N	9	34	493	14.5	3	58.1	46.6	1584.8
1983	Seattle	N	16	72	1074	14.9	11	74.0	76.9	5539.2
1984	Seattle	N	16	74	1164	15.7	12	80.3	76.7	5672.6
1985	Seattle	N	16	79	*1287	16.3	6	84.2	99.3	7841.8
1986	Seattle	N	16	70	1070	15.3	9	72.5	67.4	4720.9
1987	Seattle	N	15	58	912	15.7	8	66.1	76.4	4437.7
			180	752	12041	16.0	95	72.2	81.3	61160.4

* Led league.

Largent goes quietly on his way catching pass after pass. He holds the record for most consecutive games catching one or more passes, and the way he's going he'll end up holding every "total" receiving record. Still, if he sat down next to them in a beanery, few fans outside Seattle would recognize him. Seattle isn't exactly a U.S. media center. If he played in New York, they'd put up a statue of him out in the harbor, a football under one arm and the other arm raised in victory.

Largent doesn't need a statue. He's got statistics.

Amid all the huzzahs for Jerry Rice in 1987, we were happy to see a few words of sanity from columnist Dan Daly, writing in the January 8, 1988 edition of *Pro Football Weekly*. Daly pointed out that Rice's 22 touchdown receptions, while an NFL record, did not automatically constitute the greatest season ever for a receiver. In the first place, there are other categories by which a receiver may be rated—number of catches, yardage, and average yards, to name only the traditional stats. But Daly went a step farther to show that there are touchdown receptions and then there are *touchdown receptions*! He checked the yardage on Rice's TDs and found that 8 of them were for less than 10 yards and his average yardage per TD catch was 23.4. Now, 23.4 is nice yardage, but consider:

When Don Hutson caught 17 TDs in 10 games in 1941, 6 were of less than 10 yards and his average per TD was 26.0.

When Mark Clayton caught 18 in 16 games (he only played in 15) in 1984, only 4 were less than 10 yards; he averaged 28.1.

When Bill Groman caught 17 in 14 games in 1961, a mere 2 were under 10 yards; his average was a whopping 34.9 per TD catch.

But to quote a famous American mammy's-boy, you ain't heard nothin' yet!

In 1951, Elroy Hirsch caught 17 touchdowns for the Rams in 12 games. Two were for less than 10 yards, but his yardage on those 17, according to Daly, totaled 812. That included bombs of 51, 54, 70, 73, 76, 79, 81, and 91 yards. Hirsch's average was a breathtaking 47.8 yards per touchdown!

Now THAT'S a receiver!

19

Great Performances

About the only time you ever hear about some records is when someone comes near to breaking them. The rest of the time they just sit around in the record book, waiting to be challenged. Records are made to be broken, we say. Some people say the same thing about rules.

Maybe it should be a rule that once a year we all sit down by a roaring fire with our families and read the record book out loud. When we come across something truly significant or mind-boggling— a super record—we can all ooh! and ahh! and pause to reflect together.

Lacking a handy record book or a roaring fire and if the rest of the family wants to watch MTV, this is the short version.

LONGEVITY

George Halas coached the Bears for 40 years in four different shifts: 1920-29, 1933-42, 1946-55, and 1958-67. That he won his first championship in 1921 and his last in 1963 proves that he had a knack for it. Still, we tend to look at his 40 years sort of the same way we view Connie Mack's 50 years as manager of baseball's Philadelphia A's— it's easier to get rehired if you own the team.

We're most impressed with Tom Landry's 28 years as head coach at Dallas, which is only third in the record book behind Halas' 40 and Curly Lambeau's 33. But we wouldn't give the trophy to Landry; we'd award it to his boss Tex Schramm, who not only realized he had a great coach from the start but managed to (a) keep him and (b) keep from panicking and firing him when the Cowboys played badly. Has any other front office gone that long without making a disastrously precipitous coaching change? Even Halas fired Halas a couple of times.

On the playing field, the longevity record is easily George Blanda's. As every schoolboy knows, it's 26 seasons. And most schoolboys know he set it over 27 years, from 1949 to 1975; he was "retired" in 1959. What those precocious schoolboys may not know is that Blanda would never have had the chance to stick around so long had he been a better linebacker. Back in his rookie year, 1949, he was only the Bears' third-team quarterback and second-line kicker, so they had him help out backing up the line once in a while. Now imagine if you will what would have happened if he'd been terrific. He'd never again have been allowed to take a snap. The limit for linebackers appears to be about 15 years, not even close to quarterbacks and kickers.

Earl Morrall, a quarterback, and Lou Groza, a tackle for a while but a kicker always, played 21 years each. But think about Charlie Joiner, who ran pass patterns—good ones—for 18 seasons. And he was still a regular in his eighteenth. Most of us couldn't run 18 pass patterns without needing a couple of years off to recuperate.

Nevertheless the absolute champ of longevity by our lights is Jim Marshall, the Minnesota defensive end. Jim weighed about 235-240 while taking on tackles who had 40 pounds on him. He did it for 20 seasons (1960-79), which might be impressive enough, but what really turns the mind to peanut butter is that he never missed a game! For 282 consecutive regular-season games, he lined up at defensive end. Not counting exhibitions and playoffs, he figures to have been blocked (or blocked *at*) more than 18,000 times by bigger and usually younger ruffians.

SCORING

Blanda holds the all-time total scoring record with 2,002 points. Of course, if you kick extra points and field goals for 26 seasons, you're going to end up with a pile of points. As a matter of fact, the top twenty-five career scorers in pro football history are all kickers.

Nine out of ten of the top season scorers on a per game basis are kickers who also did something else that added some touchdowns to their totals. Paul Hornung has the record, with 176 points in 1960 for a 14.7 per game average. He did that with 41 extra points kicked out of 41 attempts, 15 field goals out of 28 tries, and 15 touchdowns, 13 on rushes.

The only nonkicker in the top ten is Steve Van Buren, who scored 18 touchdowns in 1945. Even *he* kicked 2 extra points to bring his total to 110, but the impressive part is his 18 TDs. He ran from scrimmage for 15, caught 2 touchdown passes, and scored 1 on a kickoff return—all in 10 games. His 1.8 touchdowns per game is unmatched; O. J. Simpson's 1.64 in 1975 (23 TDs in 14 games) is second.

The record for single-game scoring was set back in 1929 by Ernie Nevers of the then Chicago Cardinals. On Thanksgiving Day, he blitzed the Bears for 6 touchdowns and 4 PATs, scoring all the Cards' points in a 40-6 win that helped convince Halas to take his first coaching sabbatical. The Bears weren't very successful all that season, only 4-9-2, but their defense was decent most of the time. In the other 14 games they gave up only an average of 12.8 points.

In 1951 Halas had a bout of *déjà vu* as Cleveland's Dub Jones tied Nevers's touchdown record with 6 against the Bears. This was a better Bear team, 7-5, but the defense allowed a 21.8 average except when they went against Jones. Nevers scored his 6 touchdowns on line plunges, but Dub got his by both running and catching passes.

At last in 1965, Halas was on the right sideline. Gale Sayers scored six times for him against the 49ers. San Francisco had a porous defense (26.2 points in their other games) but a winning record: 7-6-1. All things considered, Sayers's day should have an asterisk putting him a step up on Nevers and Jones.

He opened in the first quarter with an 80-yard TD on a screen pass from Rudy Bukich. In the second quarter, he scored on runs of 21 and 7 yards. Came the third quarter, Sayers ran 50 yards for his fourth touchdown and plunged a yard for his fifth. So you could expect that when they got into the fourth quarter, the Bears might work the ball down to the one-millimeter line and then hand it to Gale for the record. Forget it. His sixth touchdown was on a twisting, 85-yard punt return. Moreover, when Chicago got down to the San Francisco two a little later, they gave the ball to Jon Arnett to score.

Most of the famous field goals in pro football history have been memorable because they won games in the final seconds. New Orleans' Tom Dempsey's boot in 1970 beat Detroit, but the big news was its length—63 yards. The Lions' defensive tackle Alex Karras said later that the Detroiters laughed when the Saints lined up to kick. Even so, the champion of coast-to-coast kicking is probably Steve Cox, who since 1983 has had three of the longest boots ever: 57, 58, and 60 yards.

RUSHING

Harry Newman was the New York Giants' quarterback in 1934. Not a T-quarterback, of course. Harry played tailback in the Giants' single wing, called the signals, and did their passing. But Harry entered the NFL record book for a rushing feat. On November 11 of '34 against Green Bay, Harry set a record for rushing attempts that stood for 39 years—an appropriate number because his attempts were originally marked at 39 (later reviewed and dropped to 38). Harry always said that he kept calling other backs' signals, but they refused to carry the ball because the Packers were beating the daylights out of them. Sure, Harry. The Giants won 17-3.

Two years later, on November 28, 1936, George Grosvenor of the Cardinals made a stab at Harry's record with 32 carries in one of the Cards' infrequent wins over the Bears. One week later he came closer, with 35 attempts during a scoreless tie with Green Bay.

In 1973, O. J. Simpson broke Newman's record with 39 carries. And in '76 Franco Harris lifted the mark to 41. Butch Woolfolk of the Giants set the current standard with 43 against Philadelphia in 1983. Tampa Bay's James Wilder tied that the next season in an overtime game against the Packers, but no one ever ran as many times over a whole season as Wilder did that year—407. He also holds the per game record with 25.4.

Eric Dickerson set a new total yardage mark with 2,105 the same year Wilder ran so often, but his per-game average of 133.1 was 10 yards short of O.J.'s 143.1 in '73 when he gained 2,003 in two fewer outings. Simpson set a new NFL record for one-game yardage with

250 against the Patriots and upped it to 273 against Detroit three years later. Then a year after that, in 1977, Walter Payton gained 275 in 40 attempts against Minnesota, and that's held since.

Arguably a better day was Marion Motley's in 1950. The old Cleveland fullback gained "only" 188 on October 29 against the Steelers, but he did it on a mere 11 carries, a 17.09 average!

When Beattie Feathers gained 1,004 yards for the Bears in 1934, he was the first back to top the magic thou, but historians have argued ever since whether he had the officially listed 101 attempts or an actual 117. Big deal! He has the season average gain record whether it's 9.9 or 8.6. Skeets Quinlan of the Rams came closest to Feathers' record in 1953 with 7.3 (705 yards, 97 carries), but our personal favorite is Bobby Douglass, who averaged 6.9 for the Bears in 1972 (968 yards, 141 carries). Douglass was a T-quarterback!

Another rushing record of note is Van Buren's 1945 average of 1.5 touchdowns per game (15 TDs in 10 games). The amazing part is that he did it without any single big game, never getting more than three in one day.

PASSING

Elsewhere we've belabored the NFL's Passer Rating System, but we haven't mentioned what passer holds the record for the highest mark under that system. It's a passer who wasn't in the NFL when he did it: Otto Graham in 1946 with the Browns in the old All-America Football Conference. Otto had a 112.1 mark (he didn't know it at the time because the system didn't come out until 1973), and the next season passed for 109.9, the fourth highest rating. The official all-time NFL record is held by another Cleveland quarterback, Milt Plum, with 110.4 in 1960. Sammy Baugh's 109.9 for 1945 ranks second in the NFL and third overall.

The best rating since the NFL instituted the system and the fifth best all-time is Dan Marino's 108.9 in 1984. Because he threw more than twice as many passes in his season than did the first four on the list, we tend to regard Marino's year as the best ever. He set the season records for yards gained (5,084) and touchdowns (48) that season. His 317.8 yards per game is also a record.

You've heard that a passer who gains a lot of yardage in a game usually loses. Often that's true. The tip-off is usually in his number of attempts; if he throws 50 times to gain 300 yards, that's not so good.

When the Rams' Norm Van Brocklin gained an incredible 554 yards against the New York Yanks in 1951, he threw 41 passes for an average gain of 13.5 yards and his team won 54-14. Baugh had the best average gain of all—18.6—in beating Boston, 59-21, in 1948 with 446 yards on 24 throws. Incidentally, Boston in '48 and the Yanks of '51 are the same porous franchise.

As we just mentioned, Marino set the TD pass record in 1984 with 48. His 3.0 touchdowns per game also broke Sid Luckman's 41-year-old per-game record of 2.8 on 28 TDs in 10 games during the 1943 season. Sid was helped along by 7 in one game against the Giants that year. Four other passers have thrown 7 in a single game: Adrian Burk, Philadelphia 1954; George Blanda, Houston 1961; Y. A. Tittle, Giants 1962; and Joe Kapp, Minnesota 1969.

In the previous chapter, we discussed Johnny Unitas' consecutive-game streak of touchdown passes, possibly the best performance by a passer over an extended period.

The worst performance by a passer may have been by Jim Hardy of the Cards, who was intercepted by the Eagles 8 times while losing 45-7 in 1950. He also fumbled once to set up an Eagle touchdown. Hardy wasn't exactly a poor quarterback, just inconsistent. In his next game, he threw 6 touchdown passes!

Even after his interception day, Hardy probably felt better than Bert Jones of Baltimore on October 26, 1980, or Warren Moon of Houston on September 29, 1985. Each was sacked a record 12 times. The 10 quarterbacks who were sacked 11 times in games include Hall-of-Famer Bart Starr and current politician Jack Kemp.

PASS RECEIVING

When Hardy threw his 6 touchdown passes in a 1950 game, he directed 5 of them to end Bob Shaw. Shaw also caught 4 in a game for Los Angeles in 1949 to tie a record first set in 1934 by Philadelphia's Joe Carter in a 64-0 win over Cincinnati. You may not remember that Cincinnati had an NFL team in the early '30s. And 1934 was the Reds' second year in the league, but after Philadelphia beat them on November 4, they folded up and quit football for less humiliating activities.

About two dozen men have caught 4 TD's in one game over the years, but only Shaw had caught 5 until Kellen Winslow of the Chargers duplicated that against Oakland in 1981.

Tom Fears of the Rams gets the record for most catches in a single game with 18 back in 1950. It happened to be the last scheduled game of the season for the Rams, and Fears' 18 catches gave him 84, breaking the record of 77 he'd set the year before. He gained 189 yards and scored 2 touchdowns that day, as the Rams beat the Packers 51-14. Since Fears set his single game record, 8 players have caught 14 to 17 in a game, but 4 of them were running backs catching mostly swing passes.

Stephone Paige of the Chiefs carved a new single-game yardage mark when he gained 309 on only 8 receptions against the Chargers in 1985. The old record, 303 by the Rams' Jim Benton, had held since 1945.

When Benton set the mark, he broke a record held by Don Hutson (1935-45). Ten days later, Hutson played his last game and retired, owning (or being tied for) every other pass receiving record in the book except for the longest completed pass. The only Hutson records that remain today are those for consecutive years leading in receptions, yardage, and touchdowns, and for career touchdown passes. And the career TD mark is due to be broken by Steve Largent of Seattle early in 1988.

Barring injury, Steve Largent will retire holding the career receiving marks in catches, yards, and touchdowns, but Hutson could tell him: *sic transit gloria.*

INTERCEPTIONS

One of those truisms like saying that a 300-yard game means a losing quarterback and a 100-yard rusher means victory is that the league leader in pass interceptions isn't a very good defender, or they wouldn't throw so often in his territory. Like the first two statements, the one about interceptions has a grain of truth—smart quarterbacks pick on the weakest defensive backs. But if that were all there was to it, you'd expect a rookie to be the interception leader every year, and that's only happened twice since 1967.

One league-leading rookie who certainly was no weakling was Dick "Night Train" Lane with the Rams in 1952. He grabbed 14 enemy tosses that year in only 12 games, both the total and per-game record (1.17 PG). Lane went on to a Hall of Fame career (1952-65) and ranks third all-time in interceptions with 68.

The career leader is Paul Krause (1964-79) with 81, followed by Emlen Tunnell (1948-61) at 79.

Several defenders have snatched 13 passes in a season, the last being Everson Walls of Dallas in 1981, but the second best season on a per-game basis belongs to—you'd never guess—Sammy Baugh! Remembered today for his passing, Baugh was a two-way player for the first part of his career, and a darned good one. In 1943 he intercepted 11 passes in only 10 games, for a 1.10 PG rate. In one game against Detroit that year, Sam got 4. No one has topped that in a single game since, but seventeen have tied it.

The newest interception record belongs to Vencie Glenn of San Diego, who ran one back against Denver for a record 103 yards last season. (And wouldn't you like to know Coach Al Saunders's thoughts when he saw Glenn starting out of the end zone?) Counting Glenn, fourteen players have returned pass interceptions for 100 yards or more, but Butch Kottler of Pittsburgh has a singular honor: his 99-yard return in 1933 scored the franchise's first NFL touchdown. It won him a spot in the hearts of Pittsburghers but not a job; after one more game, he was cut.

PUNTING

Any punting records set in Denver are a little suspect. The ball slices unimpeded through mile-high air. In 1986 Bronco punters averaged 41.29 yards at home and 37.78 on the road; opponents were 43.84 at Denver and only 41.76 at their own stadiums. All the same you've got to hand it to Steve O'Neal of the Jets, who unleashed a monster kick in Denver on September 21, 1969. When it stopped rolling, it measured 98 yards.

Until 1975 the NFL record book listed the second longest punt as a 94-yarder by Pete Henry in 1923, and some reports have credited Joe Guyon with a 95-yard kick in 1920. Both players were with the Canton Bulldogs when they supposedly made their long punts, but Canton newspaper accounts of the games in question do not support the claims. Time has a way of reducing hair, widening waistlines, and increasing punt yards.

The highest punting average for a season was by—here he is again—Sammy Baugh in 1940. On 35 kicks, Baugh averaged 51.4 yards. Unfortunately there's no way to figure his net yards at this late date.

PUNT RETURNS

No one in NFL history has ever returned a punt end zone to end zone, but three men have brought boots back 98 yards for TDs. The first was Gil LeFebvre for the Cincinnati Reds (remember them?) in 1933. Charlie West of Minnesota equalled that in 1968, and then Dennis Morgan of Dallas made it three in 1974.

Possibly the most remarkable punt returner was Jack Christiansen with Detroit from 1951-57, who is tied with Denver's Rick Upchurch (1975-83) for most touchdown returns with 8. Christiansen had the third highest career average, 12.75 yards, and the third highest single season average, 21.5 in 1952. It was that '52 season that was the interesting one. He scored four of his career TD's (Upchurch scored four in 1976) in only two games: on October 14 against the Rams, he became the first player to return two punts for TD's in one game; and then on November 22 against the Packers, he became the *second* man to get a pair. Since then, four others, including Upchurch, have returned two in a game for touchdowns, but no one else has done it twice.

KICKOFF RETURNS

Christiansen is in the Hall of Fame as a defensive back. The record for career touchdowns on kickoff returns is held by Travis Williams (1967-71) and two other Hall-of-Famers, Gale Sayers (1965-71) and Ollie Matson (1952, 1954-66). Sayers has the highest career average, with 30.6, one full yard ahead of Lynn Chandnois (1950-56).

Williams had the best kickoff return season ever as a Green Bay rookie in '67, returning 18 punts for a 41.1 average. Four of his efforts went for touchdowns. The longest return of his career, however, came for the Rams in his last season—105 yards.

Al Carmichael of Green Bay (1956), Noland Smith of Kansas City (1967), and Roy Green of St. Louis (1979) all brought kickoffs back 106 yards for touchdowns.

Most records are broken sooner or later, although Tony Dorsett's 99-yard run from scrimmage against Minnesota in 1983 seems likely to stay in the NFL book. Even if some runner ties his yardage, Dorsett should be listed first on a yards-per-blocker basis; he only had nine teammates on the field at the time.

20

Rumblings in the Pantheon

Pro football has its Hall of Fame. You can find it by driving to Canton, Ohio, and then following the signs. You can't miss it. It's housed in one of the darndest-looking buildings you've ever seen. Designed (we think) to look as if a giant football has crashed into the roof, it comes off more like a big scoop of vanilla ice cream on top of a snare drum (or some say an orange-juice squeezer). Although the building is eccentric architecturally (to say the least), we'll hazard an opinion that of the various players, coaches, and contributors enshrined within it, you'll find fewer clinkers than you would see walking through baseball's Hall of Fame.

Which doesn't mean we'll rubber-stamp everyone who's in. Or out.

Which brings us to Bill James, who may never have been to Canton and certainly never will be enshrined there.

Bill James writes about baseball. So far as we know, he's never expressed a football opinion in print (or, for that matter, an opinion on roller derby, hurling, water polo, or arm wrestling). James's often controversial ideas are usually supported by statistical evidence, though he doesn't make a fetish of it.

In one of his essays, James tried to determine the parameters of baseball's Hall of Fame by looking at the records of those enshrined and suggesting other players who might fit inside or outside the limits. He was able to identify some overlooked stars and also pinpoint a few who belonged in the Hall the way bacon belongs at a Bar Mitzvah. We thought he had a great idea and turned to applying the same system to the Pro Football Hall of Fame.

Right away we were in trouble. Most football players either in, or eligible and reasonably under consideration for enshrinement, don't have any statistics at all. Those players for whom we do have numbers must have them interpreted in a wide variety of ways—much wider and more various than in baseball.

Undaunted, we went on, knowing that "going on" was a virtue for Columbus and a vice for lemmings.

We've always said that all-pro teams are the statistics of linemen. That also applies to any other players who have few or no stats. And it so happened that we were sitting on the world's most complete list of all-pro teams.

Some people say that all-pro teams don't mean very much because they're "just based on someone's opinion." Well, shucks! Who gets drafted, who stays on the roster, who starts, who gets to run the ball, and—lest we forget—whether someone was holding on the play are all based on *someone's* opinion. We prefer to say that all these things are based on *someone's perception*.

And that's how players get into the Hall of Fame: they are *perceived* by thirty qualified and perceptive selectors as being several giant steps better than other players.

All-pro teams have the advantage of immediacy. They tell you how good a player was perceived to have been in a particular season *when he played*—not how he's remembered ten or twenty years later. Memory is selective and self-serving. It's easy to look back two decades and say, "Why, sure! My ol' buddy Joe was the very best that ever played at his position." It doesn't go down so smooth when we look and find that ol' Joe was never named first-team all pro in all the ten years he played.

It can work the other way too. One of the things that mitigates against linemen getting into the Hall is that, having no statistics to look at, selectors have to rely more heavily on the say-so of former opponents.

"How was Smith?" they ask.

"Oh, he was pretty good," allows the old pro.

"A strong blocker, was he?"

And the old pro fills with pride. "Well, he could never block *me!*"

Maybe not, but if Smith was picked year after year as the top guard, he must have been blocking someone!

Using our collection of all-pro teams does present one problem. We actually have access to more "teams" than the Hall of Fame selectors. We had originally intended to look at the information available to the selectors and find our HOF parameters there. Instead, we decided to use everything at our disposal and see which enshrinees are justified by the facts. And which *excludniks* may have better claims.

Modern-day HOF selectors have based their perceptions of distant stars for the most part on only the most reprinted all-pro squads. For example, until recently, the earliest all-NFL team was thought to be the "Official Team" chosen in 1931 by coaches and team officials. In point of fact, the first selection was made in 1920, the first year of the league's existence, by Bruce Copeland, the sports editor of the *Rock Island Argus.* He had seen every team but Buffalo in action, Copeland said, and he'd also talked to various coaches and players around the league.

We haven't found any 1921 selections, but in 1922 George Halas in Chicago and Guy Chamberlin in Canton both made all-NFL selections. Each was a playing coach. Halas put Chamberlin on his first team, but Guy didn't return the favor.

Starting in 1923, the *Green Bay Press-Gazette* began polling coaches, team, and game officials and producing an end-of-season all-league team that was continued annually into the 1930s. Comments by sportswriters of the time indicate that the Green Bay poll was accepted as a valid indication of the league's best, making it the best source on who-was-who in the 1920s. But several other newspapers in league cities announced all-league teams intermittently through the decade. These vary in quality, but here we've only considered those that have strong "pedigrees." Remember, a sportswriter like former pro player Wilfrid Smith, who was based in Chicago, got to see all the top teams in action.

Naming an "official team" began in 1931, but so did selections by United Press that appear just as valid. The New York *Daily News* published a poll of sportswriters from league cities, starting in 1937. I.N.S. also published its first "all" team that year. The Associated Press began selecting in 1940, although you'll seldom see the first ten years published. *The Sporting News* and N.E.A. began choosing teams in the 1950s.

Starting with 1970, we used only the teams listed in the league record manual plus *The Sporting News*. We have more than enough "teams" to calculate. Too many to list them all.

In the charts that follow, we tried to present all the information you need to make some reasonable choices. We separated pro players into two major groups. Pre-1950 players are listed as "two-way players," in five charts by position because they played offense and defense both. A few players who played the bulk of their seasons before 1950—mainly quarterbacks—are listed in the next section as "one-way players" because their reputations were earned mostly by what they did with the ball. There are eleven "position charts" for one-way players.

Reading across a chart, you'll see the player's name and the years he played. Only the first and last years are listed; many players missed seasons during their careers. The number of seasons played is under YR. Those players who missed seasons because of military service are marked with "+." Longevity is a factor in selecting for the Hall, although there's no official minimum number of seasons played. No one with fewer than five seasons played was considered for our study, but we surmise that the Hall considers eight seasons a norm for pre-1950 enshrinees and ten seasons for post-1950. The only elected exceptions have been players with overpowering credentials.

The next piece of information is accumulated all-pro selections. Under "C" are Consensus Seasons, meaning the player was picked on the majority of teams chosen in a given year. We found some surprises here. Some players we'd assumed were consensus choices several times were never actually tagged by the majority. Under "1" are the number of seasons a player was picked as a first-team selection on at least one important all-pro team but was not a consensus pick. (Incidentally we counted any Pro Bowl selection as a first team pick). Under "2" are the number of seasons the player showed up as at least a second-team choice. Although some all-pro teams did not make second-team picks and some (we think) were never published, we believe this is important information in rounding out the picture.

Under "PTS," you'll find the most controversial piece of information. We wanted a quick reference, so we awarded points for all-pro selections on the following basis: 8 = consensus, 5 = first-team, and 3 = second-team. This seemed to us to be about the weight and ratio that many HOF selectors gave to selections. If you want to weight them differently for your own amusement, you have the number of each kind of selection. We listed players in order of their "points."

One word of caution. We believe that some selectors may downgrade selections from the war years (1942-45), the old All-America Football Conference (1946-49), or the first few years of the American Football League (1960-63). There doesn't seem to be any consistency to it, but it may explain why a few players have failed to gain entrance to the Hall.

Under "CH" are the number of Championship Games (1932-65) or Super Bowls (1966-86) played in. The split indicates wins-losses. Like it or not, a player is helped into the Hall of Fame by playing for a winner. With quarterbacks, this seems to be the most important single factor.

"ST" is a cumulative point total for leading the league in rushing, passing, receiving, or scoring (4 points), interceptions (3 points), kick returns (2 points), or punting (1 point). One-point bonuses were added for leading a major category in yardage or touchdowns or in field goals. Certain accomplishments have more impact, but we decided not to weight them. For example, O. J.'s 2,003 yards rushing in 1973 meant more to selectors than Floyd Little's league-leading total of 1,133 in 1971.

The players on each chart are divided into three groups.

The first group represents those players who would seem to have all the necessities for Hall of Fame selection. We'll call them the Hall of Greatest. Alas, you'll see many players not yet enshrined and who may never be.

The second group, which we'll call the Hall of Just Great, lists some fine players who may for one reason or another fall just short of HOF quality. Those in this group who have been elected have—hopefully—some extra qualifications not accounted for in our system that have pushed them over the top.

The third group—the Hall of Very Good—would be called the Hall of Definitely Outs except that there's a surprising number of "Ins" in this group. Some of them were elected as coaches. A couple, we think, were mistakes. But a few actually have virtues that properly lift them to a higher plane.

After each chart we discuss some of the more interesting choices.

Before we get to the charts, we want a last word on all-pro teams. We stuck to them ruthlessly except for 1921 where there was no team selected. Because there were several enshrinees and potential enshrinees playing in that year, we had to do something about it or cheat them. We read newspaper accounts of every game from that season and as many pregame stories as we could find and then asked this question: if three all-league teams had been selected in 1921, is it likely that this player would have been named to two of them? If our judgment was yes, we marked a consensus choice; if we weren't sure but thought maybe, we gave him a **1**. These are marked after the players' names as # = consensus and † = **1**.

Whew! Enough explanation! Let's get to the fun!

TWO-WAY PLAYERS (1920-49)

Two-Way Ends

Player	Career	Yr	C	1	2	Pts	Ch	St
*Don Hutson	1935-45	11	7	2	2	72	3-2	72
Lavie Dilweg	1926-34	9	5	2	1	53	3-0	0
*Bill Hewitt	1932-43	9	4	2	0	42	2-1	1
*Guy Chamberlin#	1919-27	9	3	1	0	29	5-0	0
*Ray Flaherty	1927-35	8	2	2	1	29	1-2	5
*Red Badgro	1927-36	8	3	1	0	29	1-2	4
Jim Poole	1937-46	+7	2	1	1	28	1-2	0
Perry Schwartz	1938-46	+7	2	1	1	24	0-1	0
Luke Johnsos	1929-38	9	1	2	1	21	2-1	0
Jim Benton	1938-47	9	2	0	1	19	2-0	6
Bill Karr	1933-38	6	1	0	2	14	1-1	0
Tillie Voss	1921-29	9	1	0	2	14	0-0	0
Harry Ebding	1931-37	8	0	1	1	8	1-1	1
*George Halas	1920-28	9	0	0	1	3	1-0	1
*Wayne Millner	1936-45	+7	0	0	1	3	1-3	0

To no one's surprise, Hutson outdistances everyone; he has the statistics, all-league selections, good teams, and two Most Valuable Player years. We can't help but wonder how much his brilliance has caused selectors to forget Lavie Dilweg, who was the premier Green Bay end in the era before Hutson. Dilweg couldn't compare with Hutson as a receiver, but in his day an end was judged by his blocking and tackling. From his pile of honors, there's no doubt that Dilweg's contemporaries considered him the best.

The least likely Hall of Fame end (perhaps the least likely Hall of Famer) is Wayne Millner, who was an outstanding college star at Notre Dame but only a competent pro. In 1937 I.N.S. named him to its second-team all-NFL.

Halas, in our humble opinion the single most important person in
pro football history, would never have made it into the Hall of Fame
as an end. However, because of a lack of accurate information about
the early years of the NFL, later ages have often assumed that men
who went on to become outstanding coaches must have been the best
players of their day. Hence Halas, Curly Lambeau, Steve Owen, and
Jim Conzelman were remembered as *players* over men who were far
better.

Chamberlin, however, was the premier end of the NFL's first half
dozen years *and* the most successful coach, winning four championships in five years with Canton, Cleveland, and Frankford (a suburb of
Philadelphia).

Ray Flaherty was elected mostly for his success as Washington's
coach in the Baugh years, but he and Red Badgro were the best pair of
ends in the league when they played for the Giants. Badgro was
elected in 1981, forty-five years after he retired, the longest wait for
any enshrinee. He was an excellent defender with a knack for making
big plays.

Two-Way Tackles

Player	Career	Yr	C	1	2	Pts	Ch
Albert Wistert	1943-51	9	5	2	1	53	2-1
*Turk Edwards	1932-40	9	4	3	1	50	1-0
*Bruiser Kinard	1938-47	+9	4	3	1	50	0-1
*Ed Healey†	1920-27	8	4	3	0	47	0-0
*Cal Hubbard	1927-36	9	5	1	0	45	3-0
*Pete Henry#	1920-28	8	4	0	1	35	2-0
Duke Slater	1922-31	10	2	2	3	35	0-0
*Joe Stydahar	1936-46	+9	4	0	1	35	3-2
*Link Lyman	1922-34	11	2	1	3	30	4-2
George Christensen	1931-38	8	2	2	1	29	1-1
Bob Reinhard	1946-50	5	2	1	1	24	0-1
Gus Sonnenberg	1923-31	6	3	1	0	23	1-0
Baby Ray	1938-48	11	1	2	1	21	2-1
Lee Artoe	1940-48	+7	1	0	4	20	2-1
Bull Behman	1924-31	8	2	0	1	19	1-0
Fred Davis	1941-51	+9	1	1	2	19	2-2
Frank Cope	1938-47	10	0	2	2	16	2-3
*Steve Owen	1924-33	9	1	1	1	16	1-0
Vic Sears	1941-53	12	1	1	3	16	2-1

Player	Career	Yr	C	1	2	Pts	Ch
Willie Wilkin	1938-43	6	2	0	0	16	1-2
Jim Barber	1935-41	7	1	1	0	13	1-2
Bill Lee	1935-46	+9	0	0	1	3	1-1

We never met Al Wistert. Maybe there's something awful about him that we don't know. But golly! He was the top lineman—among several excellent guards and tackles—on one of the NFL's dynasties, the postwar Eagles. Could it be that everyone gets him confused with his two brothers, Francis and Alvin, who were also All-Americans at Michigan?

Early 1920s tackles Pete Henry and Ed Healey are often listed on "best ever" teams. They rank behind several others here, in part because their careers were not overlong.

Duke Slater was a terrific tackle on mostly bad teams in the 1920s. He was also black. Considering that prejudice was more overt in that period, his all-league record is more remarkable.

Steve Owen was an okay tackle, but his brother Bill may have been just as good. Stout Steve is in the Hall, and deservedly, as a coach.

Two-Way Guards

Player	Career	Yr	C	1	2	Pts	Ch
*Danny Fortmann	1936-43	8	6	1	1	56	3-2
*Mike Michalske	1926-37	11	6	1	0	53	3-0
Riley Matheson	1939-48	10	4	2	2	48	1-0
Ox Emerson	1931-38	8	4	2	0	42	1-1
Ray Bray	1939-52	+11	3	2	0	34	3-1
Buster Ramsey	1946-51	6	3	0	2	30	1-1
Jim McMillen	1924-28	5	2	2	1	29	0-0
Swede Young-strom#	1920-27	8	3	0	1	27	1-0
*George Musso	1933-44	12	2	0	3	25	4-3
Joe Kopcha	1929-36	6	2	1	1	24	2-1
Len Younce	1941-48	+6	1	2	1	21	0-1
Lon Evans	1933-37	5	2	0	1	19	1-0
*Walt Kiesling	1926-38	13	1	1	2	19	1-1
Russ Letlow	1936-46	+8	2	0	2	18	2-1
Zuck Carlson	1929-37	9	1	0	3	17	2-1
Butch Gibson	1930-34	5	1	1	1	14	1-1

Player	Career	Yr	C	1	2	Pts	Ch
Duke Osborn	1921-28	8	0	1	1	8	3-0
Rudy Comstock	1923-33	11	0	1	0	5	3-0

Guys like Joe Kopcha and Buster Ramsey were probably better players than Walt Kiesling and maybe George Musso, but they only played half as long. Kopcha, for example, took 1930-31 off to study medicine and then left pro football altogether to practice as soon as he became a full-fledged doctor. No doubt the world and Kopcha were both better off when Joe turned to doctoring, but it cost him a spot in the Hall of Fame.

Danny Fortmann, who was an even better guard than Kopcha, managed to get in eight seasons before turning to medicine. We have no rating for either of them as doctors, but it brings up an interesting point. One of the criticisms leveled at the *College* Football Hall of Fame, whether merited or not, has always been that it recognizes some players for their postfootball careers instead of sticking to how well they played the game. The Pro Hall has avoided such criticism, but a player's chance for enshrinement drops if he has a brush with the law and increases if he stays in the public eye after he retires from playing. Such influences would seem to be the result of having enshrinees chosen by people rather than machines.

Fortmann and Michalske are almost automatically selected as the best of the two-way guards. Both benefited by playing linebacker on defense, increasing their visibility.

Bray, Matheson, and Emerson are all underrated. The Bears had so many good linemen through his time that Bray gets lost in the crowd. Matheson was a terrific guard but is downrated because several of his best seasons came during the war. Emerson was a quiet sort who was more reliable than spectacular. It probably didn't help that he played part of his career in Portsmouth, Ohio—hardly a media hotbed.

Kiesling, on the other hand, is a questionable selection. He was the biggest guard of his time, but seldom was considered the best. His later coaching record of 30-55-5 in three sessions with Pittsburgh doesn't help. He was in charge of the Steelers when they cut Johnny Unitas. Now *there's* a claim to fame!

Two-Way Centers

Player	Career	Yr	C	1	2	Pts	Ch	St
*Mel Hein	1931-45	15	7	1	4	73	2-4	0
*Bulldog Turner	1940-52	13	7	2	1	69	4-1	3
*George Trafton†	1920-32	12	3	2	1	37	2-0	0
Nate Barrager	1930-35	5	2	0	3	25	1-0	0
Charlie Brock	1939-47	9	1	1	2	19	2-0	0
Frank Bausch	1934-41	8	0	2	1	13	1-2	0
*Alex Wojciechowicz	1938-50	13	0	1	1	8	2-1	0
Ki Aldrich	1939-47	+7	0	0	2	6	1-2	0

For a period of about twenty years, Hein and Turner owned the all-league center slot. The only question was which one was better. Old-timers still disagree. Perhaps Hein's Most Valuable Player award in 1938 gives him an edge. How many linemen can be MVP?

We'd feel a lot more comfortable with Wojciechowicz' selection if he'd finished second to Hein or Turner in the all-pro voting more often. He played linebacker exclusively for the Eagle champs in the late '40s when there were no offense-defense selections, and that might have cost him some honors. Incidentally, remember the character Wojo on TV's *Barney Miller* and how everyone struggled to spell his name? Now you know how.

Two-Way Backs

Player	Career	Yr	C	1	2	Pts	Ch	St
*Paddy Driscoll#	1919-29	11	7	1	1	64	1-0	14
*Dutch Clark	1931-38	7	6	0	0	48	1-1	14
*Clarke Hinkle	1932-41	10	3	4	3	41	2-1	6
*Ernie Nevers	1926-31	5	5	0	0	40	0-0	5
*Ken Strong	1929-47	12	4	1	1	40	1-5	7
Verne Lewellen	1924-32	9	4	0	2	38	3-0	6
*Bronko Nagurski	1930-43	9	3	2	1	37	3-1	1
Benny Friedman	1927-34	8	4	0	1	35	0-0	4
*Cliff Battles	1932-37	6	3	1	1	32	1-1	9
*Bill Dudley	1942-53	+9	2	1	2	27	0-0	13
*Tuffy Leemans	1936-43	8	2	0	3	25	1-2	4
*Red Grange	1925-34	9	2	1	1	24	2-1	0
*Ace Parker	1937-46	+7	2	1	1	24	0-1	3

Player	Career	Yr	C	1	2	Pts	Ch	St
Cecil Isbell	1938-42	5	2	0	2	22	2-1	10
Ward Cuff	1937-47	11	1	2	1	21	1-3	2
Jack McBride	1925-34	10	2	1	0	21	2-1	10
Ed Danowski	1934-41	7	2	0	1	19	2-2	9
Glenn Presnell	1931-36	6	1	1	2	19	1-1	5
Joey Sternaman	1922-30	9	2	0	1	19	0-0	5
*Arnie Herber	1930-45	13	1	2	0	18	4-2	14
Andy Farkas	1938-45	8	1	1	1	14	1-2	7
*George McAfee	1940-50	+8	1	0	2	14	3-0	2
*Tony Canadeo	1941-52	+11	0	2	1	13	1-0	0
Ted Fritsch	1942-50	9	1	1	0	13	1-0	6
Bill Paschal	1943-48	6	1	1	0	13	0-1	10
Fritz Pollard†	1919-26	8	1	1	0	13	1-0	4
Ace Gutowsky	1932-39	8	0	0	4	12	2-1	0
Pug Manders	1939-47	9	1	0	1	11	0-1	4
*Curly Lambeau	1921-29	9	0	0	3	9	0-0	0
*Johnny Blood	1925-38	14	0	1	1	8	4-0	6
*Joe Guyon†	1919-27	8	0	1	1	8	1-0	0
*Jim Thorpe	1915-28	11	1	0	0	8	0-0	1
*Jimmy Conzelman	1920-29	10	0	0	1	3	1-0	2
Marshall Goldberg	1938-48	+9	0	0	1	3	1-1	7

How can Jim Thorpe rank so low? Easy. He was a great player from 1915 to 1920; after that, he was a great *attraction*. He is the only person in the Pro Football Hall of Fame who got there for what he did *before* there was a league. From the time he joined the Canton Bulldogs in 1915 until the end of the 1919 season, the team lost only twice and claimed the mythical U.S. pro championship four times. Newspaper accounts from those years simply took it for granted that he was the best player in the world.

Guyon was in the same backfield as Thorpe much of the time from 1919 through 1924. His greatest claim to fame seems to be that some men who played against them both thought Joe was better than Jim. He probably was from 1921 on, but he actually played very little, only a few games in three of his seasons.

Johnny Blood was a legendary character, and some have suggested that's what got him into the HOF. He played all the backfield positions but mostly at wingback in a single wing. He was widely regarded as the best pass receiver in the league until Hutson came along. Catching passes, of course, wouldn't have won a back all-league honors in those days.

Ernie Nevers had the shortest career of anyone in the Hall, but he was regarded as the best or second-best player in pro football in each of his seasons. Except for scoring, we have only partial statistics from pre-1932, but what we have support the view that Nevers was outstanding in every phase of the game.

The two '20s backs most hurt by our lack of stats are Verne Lewellen and Benny Friedman. Both were triple-threat tailbacks but each was regarded as the best in football at one part of the triad. Lewellen was a fabled punter in an age when punting was often the most important part of a "game plan." Friedman was pro football's first "name" passer, but all we can say for certain is that he led the league in throwing TD passes four straight years.

Fortunately for Arnie Herber, the league started keeping statistics in 1932, allowing him to win three passing titles. He's often called "the NFL's first great passer," but he was more like its first *proven* good passer.

Friedman, by the way, probably lost any chance he ever had of getting into the Hall by telling everyone who would listen how much he belonged there. He thought they should have named it after him. If we were HOF selectors and a player told us we were a dunderheaded ninny if we didn't elect him, we'd find ten good reasons to keep him out before he could say *"J'accuse!"*

There's a widely held belief that Red Grange was a flop as a pro. After breaking in with much fanfare and a coast-to-coast tour in 1925, he was the centerpiece of his own short-lived league in 1926. He was such a national hero that his presence on the pro gridiron greatly enhanced the sport's status. For that reason alone, he deserves a Hall of Fame niche. He tore up a knee in 1927 and sat out 1928. In later years, he insisted he was "just another runner" after the injury. That's modesty. He was a consensus all-pro in 1930-31 and a useful member of the 1932-33 Bear champions. If you picked an all-star backfield from the 1920s, basing it solely on what they did on the field, Grange would be on the second team, but that ain't chopped liver.

Bill Dudley, George McAfee, Ace Parker, and to a lesser extent Tony Canadeo are hurt in their rankings here because they were at their peak during World War II. The Hall of Fame selectors, to their credit, enshrined them anyway.

Dudley twice led the NFL in rushing and finished up as a Pro Bowl defensive back. McAfee was the league's most effective breakaway runner before the war. Parker won an MVP award for his all-around play (as did Dudley), and Canadeo after years of steady play became, in 1949, the third NFL player in history to gain over 1,000 yards rushing.

Fritz Pollard has received some support for the Hall on the basis that he was the NFL's first black star. He was a very good halfback in the early years, but most contemporary accounts laud Duke Slater as the best black player of the 1920s.

ONE-WAY PLAYERS (1950-)

Receivers

Player	Career	Yr	C	1	2	Pts	Ch	St
*Paul Warfield	1964-77	13	6	2	0	58	3-1	3
*Lance Alworth	1962-72	11	7	0	0	56	2-2	14
*Pete Pihos	1947-55	9	5	2	2	52	2-1	15
*Charley Taylor	1964-77	13	3	5	1	46	0-1	8
Mac Speedie	1946-52	7	5	1	0	45	5-2	18
*Fred Biletnikoff	1965-78	14	2	4	1	39	2-1	4
*Dante Lavelli	1946-56	11	3	3	2	39	7-3	5
*Raymond Berry	1955-67	13	3	3	1	36	2-1	17
*Elroy Hirsch	1946-57	12	2	3	1	34	2-3	10
Charley Hennigan	1960-66	7	3	2	0	34	2-1	5
Del Shofner	1957-67	11	4	0	0	32	0-3	1
Billy Wilson	1951-60	10	2	3	0	31	0-0	13
Tommy McDonald	1957-68	12	0	6	0	30	1-0	3
Harold Jackson	1968-83	16	3	1	0	29	0-0	6
Drew Pearson	1973-83	11	3	1	0	29	1-2	6
Ahmad Rashad	1972-82	10	3	1	0	29	0-1	9
Lionel Taylor	1959-68	10	3	1	0	29	0-0	20
Art Powell	1959-68	10	1	4	0	28	0-0	4
Cliff Branch	1972-85	14	2	2	0	26	2-0	3
Harold Carmichael	1971-84	14	2	2	0	26	0-1	8
Mel Gray	1971-82	12	2	2	0	26	0-0	2
Billy Howton	1952-63	12	2	2	0	26	0-0	2
*Bobby Mitchell	1958-68	11	2	2	0	26	0-0	7
Otis Taylor	1965-74	10	2	2	0	26	1-1	2
*Tom Fears	1948-56	9	2	1	1	24	2-3	14
Harlon Hill	1954-62	9	3	0	0	24	0-1	2
Lynn Swann	1974-82	9	3	0	0	24	4-0	1

Player	Career	Yr	C	1	2	Pts	Ch	St
John Gilliam	1967-77	11	1	3	0	23	0-1	0
Bob Hayes	1965-75	11	1	3	0	23	2-1	3
*Don Maynard	1958-73	15	0	4	1	23	1-0	2
Roy Jefferson	1965-76	12	1	2	1	21	0-1	1
Gene Washington	1969-79	10	2	1	0	21	0-0	2
Gary Collins	1962-71	10	1	2	0	18	1-0	1
Gordie Soltau	1950-58	9	1	2	0	18	0-0	8
Ken Kavanaugh	1940-50	+8	1	1	1	16	3-0	2
Carroll Dale	1960-73	14	0	3	0	15	3-1	0
Charlie Joiner	1969-86	18	0	2	1	13	0-0	0
Jim Phillips	1958-67	10	1	1	0	13	0-0	4
Bobby Walston	1951-62	12	0	2	1	13	1-0	4
Bobby Joe Conrad	1958-69	12	0	2	0	10	0-0	4
Boyd Dowler	1959-71	12	0	2	0	10	5-1	0

Once you get past Raymond Berry, just about anybody on this list could go into the Hall without stinking up the joint. The trick is finding something special to set one receiver above a talented group. Hirsch, for example, had the single best season of any receiver ever. And Fears was one of the first receivers to catch ridiculously large numbers of passes.

Still there have been so many good wide receivers that they could fill a Hall of Fame all by themselves. One who has apparently been forgotten in the crowd is Mac Speedie, the top pass catcher for the Browns in their early years. He hurt his HOF chances by jumping to the Canadian Football League in 1953. His running mate Dante Lavelli, who stayed in Cleveland, has been an enshrinee since 1975, but when they were in tandem, Speedie got more passes, yards, and all-pro votes.

If we only count Alworth's consensus years, he'd rank just ahead of Warfield, which is how most critics put them.

Bobby Mitchell and Don Maynard rank lower here than you might expect. That's partly because there were so many good receivers playing at the same time. Notice that Alworth is the only receiver whose career was predominantly in the 1960s who really jumps out from the rest. Maynard is the Franco Harris of wide receivers; he was probably never in any year the very top at his position, but he was very good for a very long time and his cumulative numbers were excellent. When he retired, he held the top career marks in both catches and yardage.

Bobby Mitchell is a good example of a player whose career can't be calculated completely here. In his first four seasons, he was a running back in Jim Brown's shadow at Cleveland. Nevertheless he had good yardage totals, returned punts and kickoffs for high averages, and went to the Pro Bowl once. Traded to Washington in 1962, he exploded as a receiver. For two years he was the best in the NFL, catching 141 passes for over 2,800 yards. He followed that with four steady years of 58-60 passes. All told, he scored 91 touchdowns and gained 14,078 all-purpose yards.

Tight Ends

Player	Career	Yr	C	1	2	Pts	Ch	St
*Mike Ditka	1961-71	12	3	2	1	37	2-1	0
John Mackey	1963-72	10	3	2	0	34	0-2	0
Jackie Smith	1963-78	16	1	4	0	28	0-1	0
Dave Casper	1974-84	11	2	2	0	26	2-0	0
Pete Retzlaff	1956-66	11	1	4	0	28	1-0	1
Ted Kwalick	1969-77	9	2	1	0	21	1-0	0
Jerry Smith	1965-77	13	1	1	0	13	0-1	0
Ron Kramer	1957-67	10	0	1	1	8	2-1	0
Bob Tucker	1970-80	11	0	1	0	5	0-0	4

Thirty years ago there was no such position as tight end, and Ditka was the first elected to the Hall of Fame. Ditka's coaching success with Chicago may have helped his chances by reminding selectors how good he was. He played a little longer and caught many more passes than John Mackey, who is rated by some as better.

Offensive Tackles

Player	Career	Yr	C	1	2	Pts	Ch	St
*Rosey Brown	1953-65	13	8	2	1	77	1-5	0
*Ron Mix	1960-71	11	9	0	0	72	1-2	0
Jim Tyrer	1961-74	14	7	3	0	71	2-1	0
*Forrest Gregg	1956-71	+15	6	4	0	68	5-1	0
*Lou Groza	1946-67	21	5	4	2	66	8-4	10
Lou Creekmur	1950-59	10	6	3	0	63	3-1	0
Ron Yary	1968-82	15	7	1	0	61	0-4	0
Bob Brown	1964-73	10	6	1	1	56	0-0	0
Art Shell	1968-82	15	6	1	0	53	2-0	0

Player	Career	Yr	C	1	2	Pts	Ch	St
*Mike McCormack	1951-62	+10	1	8	1	51	2-1	0
Dan Dierdorf	1971-83	13	5	1	0	45	0-0	0
George Kunz	1969-80	11	3	4	0	44	0-0	0
Winston Hill	1963-77	15	2	4	2	42	1-0	0
Bob St. Clair	1953-63	11	1	5	3	42	0-0	0
Rayfield Wright	1967-79	13	4	2	0	42	2-1	0
Dick Schafrath	1957-71	15	2	4	1	39	1-1	0
Russ Washington	1968-82	15	1	5	1	36	0-0	0
Lou Rymkus	1943-51	+7	4	0	1	35	5-2	0
Bob Vogel	1963-72	10	0	7	0	35	0-2	0
Ernie McMillen	1961-75	15	1	4	2	34	0-0	0
Leon Gray	1973-83	11	3	2	0	34	0-0	0
Ralph Neely	1965-77	13	3	1	0	29	2-1	0

Lou Groza became a very good offensive tackle, but it's no secret that he's in the Hall because of his kicking. Later kickers have surpassed most of his records, but probably no booter ever had so much impact. For years the Browns could score three points from ten or twenty yards farther out than any other team, and that translated into a heck of an edge.

The other Browns tackle enshrined, McCormack, was a better blocker than Groza (and a whole lot of other people). He's the kind of player who gets in for long and consistent service. His stint as an NFL head coach and then his move into the Seattle front office no doubt helped selectors remember him in a rosey light.

Speaking of Rosey (how's that for a segue?), Brown gets the top rank here, but Forrest Gregg is usually tabbed as the best tackle ever. Vince Lombardi called him the best football *player* he had. Not so much now, but a decade ago everything Lombardi ever said was being chiseled in stone.

Creekmur, who won all-NFL honors at both guard and tackle, is largely forgotten today. He was an important part of the Bobby Layne Lions in the early 1950s.

Dierdorf, who's highly visible on "Monday Night Football" (and that won't hurt him a bit), is figured a shoo-in at Canton when he becomes eligible. Of course, there may be a little hometown pride involved—he's *from* Canton, but the only real mark against him is that he played for teams that absolutely refused to win championships.

We think it all depends on how much of the blame for the Cardinals' dedicated ineptitude can be placed on one exceptional offensive tackle.

Offensive Guards

Player	Career	Yr	C	1	2	Pts	Ch
John Hannah	1973-85	13	9	1	1	80	0-1
Tom Mack	1966-78	13	7	3	0	71	0-0
*Jim Parker	1957-67	11	7	2	0	66	2-1
*Gene Upshaw	1967-81	15	5	5	0	65	2-1
Larry Little	1967-80	14	5	2	1	53	2-1
Billy Shaw	1961-69	9	4	4	0	52	2-1
Ed Budde	1963-76	14	2	7	0	51	2-1
Joe DeLamielleure	1973-85	13	6	0	1	51	0-0
Dick Barwegan	1947-54	8	5	2	0	50	0-1
Walt Sweeney	1963-75	13	4	3	0	47	1-0
Stan Jones	1954-66	13	3	4	0	44	1-1
John Niland	1966-75	10	3	3	1	42	1-2
Ken Gray	1958-70	13	2	5	0	41	0-0
Jerry Kramer	1958-68	11	4	1	1	40	5-1
Dick Stanfel	1952-58	7	5	0	0	40	2-1
Bruno Banducci	1944-54	11	4	1	2	43	0-1
Bob Talamini	1960-68	9	4	1	1	40	2-1
Gene Hickerson	1958-73	15	3	3	0	39	1-0
Jim Ray Smith	1956-64	9	3	2	1	37	0-1
Bucko Kilroy	1943-55	12	1	4	2	34	2-1
Duane Putnam	1952-62	11	3	2	0	34	0-1
Ed White	1969-85	17	2	3	1	34	0-4
Harley Sewell	1952-63	11	0	5	2	31	3-1
Bob Kuechenberg	1970-83	14	0	6	0	30	2-2
Abe Gibron	1949-59	11	2	2	1	29	3-2
Art Spinney	1950-60	+9	0	3	0	15	2-0

If you're an offensive guard, it's easier to get into the Kremlin than into the Hall of Fame, but they'd probably need the whole KGB to keep John Hannah out. Mack is not such a sure shot, despite his high all-league totals. Most of them were actually all-NFC, while Upshaw and Little or DeLamielleure picked up the all-NFLs.

The total number of offensive guards in the Hall is really only one and a half, since Parker was a tackle until 1962. When the Colts moved him to guard, it was noted that he was taking on a more demanding job. Don't you think some of the HOF selectors should recognize how important the job is? Don't *you* think there should be more guards in the Hall?

We've been impressed with the position ever since our high school football days when we played—uh—never mind.

Centers

Player	Career	Yr	C	1	2	Pts	Ch
*Jim Otto	1960-74	15	12	1	0	101	0-1
*Jim Ringo	1953-67	15	6	4	1	71	2-1
Mick Tinglehoff	1962-78	17	7	0	0	56	0-4
*Jim Langer	1970-81	12	5	1	0	45	2-2
Ray Wietecha	1953-62	10	1	6	0	38	1-4
Tom Banks	1971-80	10	4	1	0	37	0-0
*Frank Gatski	1946-57	12	4	1	0	37	8-3
Bob DeMarco	1961-75	15	0	5	1	28	4-0
Bill Walsh	1949-54	6	1	3	1	26	0-0

Somewhere Mick Tingelhoff is muttering, "What did I have to do?"

Jim Otto's record looks like a misprint. It isn't. He was the consensus pick at center in every one of the American Football League's ten years, then added a couple of all-AFCs. The thing that impresses us most is that he was the consensus choice in the first couple of years of the Raiders' existence when the team was so bad it was the league joke.

Jim Ringo also got many of his honors before the Packers became a winning team.

Langer made it into the Hall just in time. As good as he was, after Dwight Stephenson retires no one will remember the Dolphins ever had another center.

The main differences between Frank Gatski and a lot of other good centers is that he anchored the middle of the line for eight championship teams (seven with Cleveland) and Otto Graham had the cleanest pants in the league for ten years.

Quarterbacks

Player	Career	Yr	C	1	2	Pts	Ch	St
*Otto Graham	1946-55	10	9	1	0	77	7-3	28
*Johnny Unitas	1956-73	18	5	6	0	70	2-2	8

Player	Career	Yr	C	1	2	Pts	Ch	St
*Sammy Baugh	1937-52	16	5	3	2	61	2-3	37
*Fran Tarkenton	1961-78	18	2	9	0	61	0-3	9
*Sid Luckman	1939-50	12	5	1	2	51	4-1	8
*Y. A. Tittle	1948-64	17	3	4	0	44	0-3	6
*Norm Van Brocklin	1949-60	12	1	7	0	43	2-3	12
Bob Griese	1967-80	14	2	4	1	39	2-1	9
*Roger Staubach	1969-79	11	4	1	0	37	2-1	25
*Len Dawson	1957-75	19	2	4	0	36	2-1	18
*Bob Waterfield	1945-52	8	3	2	0	34	2-2	13
Ken Anderson	1971-86	16	2	3	0	31	0-1	13
John Hadl	1962-77	16	1	5	1	31	1-2	9
*Bobby Layne	1948-62	15	1	4	1	31	3-1	7
Ken Stabler	1970-84	15	2	2	0	31	1-0	9
*Joe Namath	1965-77	13	2	2	1	29	1-0	4
*Sonny Jurgensen	1957-74	18	1	4	0	28	1-1	19
*Bart Starr	1956-71	16	1	3	1	26	5-1	12
Roman Gabriel	1962-77	16	1	3	0	23	0-0	2
*George Blanda	1949-75	26	1	2	0	18	1-3	6
Terry Bradshaw	1970-83	14	1	2	0	18	4-0	5
John Brodie	1957-73	17	1	2	0	18	0-0	11
Tobin Rote	1950-66	13	1	2	0	18	2-0	6
Joe Theismann	1971-85	15	2	0	0	16	2-1	4
Charlie Conerly	1948-61	14	0	3	0	15	2-3	4
Earl Morrall	1956-76	21	1	1	0	13	1-1	9

All-pro selections don't mean much here. Neither do statistics. The first and generally last question is "Did he win?" Starr doesn't grade out all that well in all-pro picks, but five championships put him in rarefied company. When you say "Bradshaw," what do you think of? Four Super-whats?

Tarkenton and Tittle (say that five times fast!) never won the Big One, but they got their teams there three times each. Namath only won once, but it was the BIG Big One, the Super Bowl that showed the American Football League wasn't creamed corn.

The amazing guy is Sonny Jurgensen. He was with the champion Eagles in 1960, but on the bench. In '72, Billy Kilmer was in charge when the Redskins made it to the Super Bowl. So just because Sonny was probably the most perfect passer who ever spiraled a football for all the years in between, is that any reason to put him in the Hall of

Fame? Well, we think it's darned nice that there's yet hope for some QB even if he's saddled with a poor team. He can still get to Canton if he's just good enough. How good was Jurgensen? If he'd had a team like the Packers of the 1960s behind him, the above quarterback list could be titled "Jurgensen *et al.*"

Tarkenton, incidentally, took a couple of years to get into the Hall, and some of his fans were pretty irate about it. How could the passer with the highest cumulative stats be left out? Well, of the dozen quarterbacks with the most total yardage, only Jurgensen, Tittle, Unitas, and Tarkenton have been elected. Of the others—Joe Ferguson, Roman Gabriel, Norm Snead, John Brodie, Ken Anderson, John Hadl, Jim Hart, and Dan Fouts—only two have a real shot of ever getting in.

Running Backs

Player	Career	Yr	C	1	2	Pts	Ch	St
*Jim Brown	1957-65	9	8	1	0	69	1-1	41
*Lenny Moore	1956-67	12	5	3	0	65	2-1	5
*Ollie Matson	1952-66	14	4	4	0	52	0-0	6
Franco Harris	1972-84	13	2	7	0	51	4-0	2
*Steve Van Buren	1944-51	8	5	1	1	48	2-1	30
*Frank Gifford	1952-64	12	4	3	0	47	1-2	0
*O. J. Simpson	1969-79	11	5	1	0	45	0-0	22
*Gale Sayers	1965-71	7	5	0	0	40	0-0	15
Leroy Kelly	1964-73	10	3	3	0	39	1-0	22
Chuck Foreman	1973-80	8	4	1	0	37	0-3	6
Pat Harder	1946-53	8	3	2	1	37	3-1	13
Floyd Little	1967-75	9	3	2	1	37	0-0	12
*Marion Motley	1946-55	9	4	1	0	37	3-1	8
*Doak Walker	1950-55	6	4	1	0	37	2-1	8
*Hugh McElhenny	1952-64	13	2	4	0	36	0-1	0
Earl Campbell	1978-85	8	3	2	0	34	0-0	14
*Larry Csonka	1968-79	11	3	2	0	34	2-1	0
*Joe Perry	1948-63	16	3	2	0	34	0-1	14
*Jim Taylor	1958-67	10	1	5	0	33	4-1	10
Don Perkins	1961-68	8	0	6	0	30	0-0	0
Larry Brown	1969-76	8	3	1	0	29	0-1	8
Rick Casares	1955-66	12	1	4	0	28	1-1	5
Lawrence Mc-Cutcheon	1972-81	10	1	4	0	28	0-1	4

Player	Career	Yr	C	1	2	Pts	Ch	St
Alan Ameche	1955-60	6	1	3	1	26	2-0	5
Calvin Hill	1969-81	12	2	2	0	26	2-1	0
Dan Towler	1950-55	6	2	2	0	26	1-2	5
*Paul Hornung	1957-66	9	2	0	1	19	4-1	13
*Charlie Trippi	1947-55	9	1	1	2	19	2-1	3
*John Henry Johnson	1954-66	13	0	3	1	18	1-0	0
Chuck Muncie	1976-84	9	1	2	0	18	0-0	1
John Riggins	1974-85	11	1	1	0	13	1-1	11
Wilbert Montgomery	1977-85	9	1	1	0	13	0-1	3

We've been telling you that Jim Brown dominated his era, so we're not surprised to find him at the top of this list. By the time all the votes are in, Payton will probably slip in just behind.

Actually this is another place where all-pro selections are not the most important ranking device. They're useful for people like Moore, Matson, Gifford, and Sayers, who do a lot of things well, but statistics seem to be the most important thing here. Riggins, for example, is a strong candidate because he (a) stuck around long enough to accumulate high numbers and (b) had one year with an outlandish 24 touchdowns.

Franco Harris is the Don Maynard of running backs.

The HOF selectors got a bad rap when they took their good sweet time in putting Paul Hornung in. A lot of media types said it was because he was suspended for gambling for the 1963 season. A few suggested there was a "Packer backlash" because so many of Lombardi's players were already enshrined. Perhaps some selectors thought twice about those things, but Hornung's big problem was that his numbers were shaky.

If those who lobbied so hard for him had taken the time to look, they would have noted that he never ran for 700 yards and only twice topped 600. He caught 28 passes one season and was under 20 in all the others. He led the league in scoring three times—twice with remarkable totals of 176 and 146 points—but more than half of that was from kicking, and his distance was only fair on field goals. His best stat was his number of championships, but that counts mostly for quarterbacks.

We don't mind having Hornung in the Hall of Fame. On balance, we'd put him there. But if he hadn't been named, we wouldn't miss a wink of sleep over it.

Why are Charlie Trippi and John Henry Johnson in the Hall of Fame?

Trippi was one of those do-everything backs and ended up as the Cardinals' quarterback for a couple of years because he was the best passer they had. He was also, at various times, the Cards' best defensive back, best kicker, and best kick returner. When the Cardinals were a good team in 1947-48, he played running back and was a sensation.

John Henry Johnson spent part of his career in that Tittle-Perry-McElhenny backfield that the 49ers had in the early '50s. Then he had his thousand-yard seasons in the 1960s with the Steelers just when Brown and Jim Taylor were getting all the attention. But John Henry was considered the most devastating blocking back of his day, and the only runner whose blocking has compared to his is Payton.

The back who jumps right out at you that has yet to be elected is Leroy Kelly. He had all the stats anyone could need but he was doubly cursed in his choice of time and place. First, he had his best years while Gale Sayers was the toast of Chicago. Second—and worst—he succeeded Jim Brown in Cleveland's backfield. It makes him kind of a trivia question, like who was the Yankee rightfielder *after* Babe Ruth? Who played 007 after Sean Connery? Who earned money the old-fashioned way after John Houseman?

As the years go by and more runners accumulate higher career yardage, and they will under the circumstances existing, it will get harder each year for Kelly to get elected. But the Hall could do a lot worse.

Defensive Ends

Player	Career	Yr	C	1	2	Pts	Ch
*Gino Marchetti	1952-66	14	7	4	0	76	2-1
Carl Eller	1964-79	16	6	2	1	61	0-4
*Andy Robustelli	1951-64	14	3	6	2	60	2-5
Jack Youngblood	1971-84	14	6	2	0	58	0-1
*Deacon Jones	1961-74	14	6	2	0	58	0-0
*Doug Atkins	1953-69	17	2	7	0	51	1-1
Claude Humphrey	1968-71	14	4	2	3	51	0-1
*Willie Davis	1958-69	12	4	2	1	45	5-1
Jerry Mays	1961-70	10	2	5	1	44	2-1
*Len Ford	1948-58	11	4	1	2	43	3-3

Player	Career	Yr	C	1	2	Pts	Ch
Bill Stanfil	1969-76	8	4	2	0	42	2-1
Elvin Bethea	1968-83	16	2	5	0	41	0-0
Gene Brito	1951-60	10	4	1	1	40	0-0
L. C. Greenwood	1969-81	13	3	3	0	39	4-0
Lee Roy Selmon	1976-85	10	3	3	0	39	0-0
Jim Katcavage	1956-68	13	3	2	0	34	1-5
Ed Sprinkle	1944-55	12	1	4	0	28	4-0
Gerry Philbin	1964-73	10	2	0	1	19	1-0
Jim Marshall	1960-79	20	0	3	1	18	0-2
Harvey Martin	1973-83	11	1	2	0	18	1-2

You could sack a lot of quarterbacks with Gino Marchetti, Andy Robustelli, and Deacon Jones. It's too bad the NFL didn't keep records of sacks when they played.

Are we wrong, or is it somehow just a little harder to get into the Hall of Fame if you played for the Vikings? We can think of a half dozen good candidates waiting. Eller's chances may have been set back by his much-publicized drug problem. But he conquered it, and that's a lot harder than sacking a quarterback.

Doug Atkins played forever and had some good years, but, given his physical equipment, he always seemed to be a little disappointing.

Defensive Tackles

Player	Career	Yr	C	1	2	Pts	Ch
*Merlin Olsen	1962-76	15	7	7	0	91	0-0
*Joe Greene	1969-81	13	9	2	0	82	4-0
*Alan Page	1967-81	15	7	4	0	76	0-4
*Bob Lilly	1961-74	14	8	1	0	69	2-1
*Leo Nomellini	1950-63	14	5	4	2	66	0-0
*Bill Willis	1946-53	8	5	3	0	55	5-2
*George Connor	1948-55	8	6	1	0	51	0-0
Alex Karras	1958-70	12	4	2	3	51	0-0
Buck Buchanan	1963-75	13	4	3	1	50	1-1
*Ernie Stautner	1950-63	14	0	8	2	46	0-0
*Art Donovan	1950-61	12	4	2	1	45	2-0
Bob Gain	1952-64	+12	1	6	2	44	3-2
*Arnie Weinmeister	1948-53	6	5	0	1	43	0-0
Henry Jordan	1957-69	13	3	3	0	39	4-1

Player	Career	Yr	C	1	2	Pts	Ch
Bud McFadin	1952-65	11	3	2	1	37	0-1
Bob Toneff	1952-64	+12	1	4	3	37	0-0
Houston Antwine	1961-71	11	2	4	0	36	1-1
Dale Dodrill	1951-59	9	2	3	1	34	0-0
Gene Lipscomb	1953-62	10	2	3	0	31	2-1
Don Colo	1950-58	9	0	4	2	26	2-2
Les Bingaman	1948-54	7	2	1	1	24	2-1
Tom Sestak	1962-68	7	2	0	2	22	2-0
Thurman McGraw	1950-54	5	1	2	0	18	2-1

According to this chart, the four best defensive tackles in the history of football were in the NFL from 1969 to 1974. In this case, the chart may be right on the nose.

But the Fab Four weren't the *only* good ones.

Leo Nomellini used to screw up his face and huff and grunt before the snap. If that didn't intimidate the offense, he'd use his 280 pounds to flatten them.

Ernie Stautner played with the disastrous Steeler teams of the 1950s, yet managed to impress enough to be an early Hall of Fame selection. His all-pro points here are lower than several, but he got them with very little help from his Steeler team, which was pretty awful for most of his career.

George Connor of the Bears and Bill Willis of the Browns had relatively short careers. That reduces their scores here, but did not hurt them with HOF selectors. Connor was a consensus all-pro in different seasons at offensive tackle, defensive tackle, and linebacker. Willis was an undersized but cat-quick defensive guard who would play linebacker today.

When Arnie Weinmeister was elected to the Hall in 1984, it lifted a few eyebrows because he only played six seasons, two in the AAFC and four in the NFL with the Giants. But those who saw him play weren't surprised at all. One of the strongest men in the league and certainly the fastest tackle, he may have made more tackles behind the line of scrimmage *per game* than any lineman ever.

With exceptional players like Connor, Willis, and Weinmeister, the best way to use this chart is to figure their average all-pro points per season.

Linebackers

Player	Career	Yr	C	1	2	Pts	Ch
Ted Hendricks	1969-83	15	6	5	0	73	3-0
*Joe Schmidt	1953-65	13	7	3	0	71	2-1
*Chuck Bednarik	1949-62	14	7	2	1	69	3-1
*Bill George	1952-66	15	7	2	0	66	2-0
Jack Lambert	1974-84	11	7	2	0	66	4-0
*Jack Ham	1971-82	12	7	1	1	64	4-0
Nick Buoniconti	1962-76	14	6	3	0	63	2-2
*Bobby Bell	1963-74	12	7	1	0	61	1-2
*Dick Butkus	1965-73	9	6	2	0	58	0-0
Larry Grantham	1960-72	13	3	4	1	57	1-0
Chuck Howley	1958-73	15	4	4	0	52	1-1
*Willie Lanier	1967-77	11	4	4	0	52	1-1
Maxie Baughan	1960-74	15	2	7	0	51	1-0
Robert Brazile	1975-84	10	5	2	0	50	0-0
Andy Russell	1963-76	12	3	4	1	48	2-0
Bill Bergey	1969-80	12	5	1	1	48	0-1
Mike Stratton	1962-73	12	4	3	0	47	2-0
Randy Gradishar	1974-83	10	2	6	0	46	0-2
Dave Wilcox	1964-74	11	3	3	2	45	0-0
*Sam Huff	1956-69	13	2	5	1	44	1-5
Les Richter	1954-62	9	0	8	0	40	0-1
Bill Forester	1953-63	11	4	1	0	37	2-1
*Ray Nitschke	1958-72	15	3	0	4	36	4-1
Joe Fortunato	1955-66	12	2	2	1	29	1-1
Jim Houston	1960-72	13	0	4	3	29	1-0
Mike Curtis	1965-78	14	1	4	0	28	1-0
Tommy Nobis	1966-76	11	1	4	0	28	0-0
Lee Roy Jordan	1963-76	14	1	3	1	26	1-1
Dave Robinson	1963-74	12	2	2	0	26	3-0
Wayne Walker	1958-72	15	2	1	1	24	0-0
George Webster	1967-76	10	3	0	0	24	0-0
Dan Currie	1958-66	9	1	2	1	21	2-1
Larry Morris	1955-66	11	0	0	1	3	1-1

Outside linebackers get almost as much attention at the Hall as guards. That will change in a few years, as folks like Lawrence Taylor, Wilber Marshall, and Ted Hendricks become eligible for induction. It's not that the players have gotten better; it's just that the shift to the 3-4 defense has given the outside linebacker a pass rushing responsibility that makes him more spectacular than some of the earlier stars like Chuck Howley, Maxie Baughan, and Mike Stratton.

For years, the middle backer in a 4-3 was the star of the show. We have the feeling that guys like Sam Huff and Ray Nitschke were a little overrated because of the defense they played, but we wouldn't fight about it. Certainly not with Huff or Nitschke.

Dick Butkus suffers a bit here because of his injury-shortened career, but not nearly as much as Tommy Nobis, who had both injuries and a more publicized Butkus to contend with. There are people who say that when he had both his legs under him Nobis was the best ever. Frankly, all we know is that Butkus got the votes for the all-pro teams.

Well, Van Gogh couldn't sell a painting while lesser artists got rich. On the other hand, the French media didn't cover the art scene then the way the American media covers the NFL now.

Quick trivia question: how many linebackers have been MVP in a Super Bowl?

Answer: one; Chuck Howley of Dallas in SB V. And remember, he played *outside* backer.

Defensive Backs

Player	Career	Yr	C	1	2	Pts	Ch	St
*Ken Houston	1967-80	14	6	6	0	78	0-0	3
Paul Krause	1964-79	16	6	3	1	66	0-4	6
Willie Wood	1960-71	12	5	5	0	65	5-1	4
*Emlen Tunnell	1948-61	14	5	5	0	65	2-3	0
Johnny Robinson	1960-71	12	6	3	0	63	2-1	3
*Larry Wilson	1960-73	14	6	2	0	58	0-0	3
*Dick Lane	1952-65	14	4	5	0	57	0-0	6
Mel Renfro	1964-77	14	2	8	0	56	2-2	3
*Yale Lary	1952-64	+11	3	6	0	54	4-0	2
*Willie Brown	1963-78	15	6	1	0	53	1-1	0
Roger Wehrli	1969-82	14	6	1	0	51	0-0	0
*Herb Adderley	1961-72	12	3	5	0	49	6-2	0
Cornell Green	1962-74	13	4	3	0	47	1-1	0
*Jack Christiansen	1951-58	8	5	1	0	45	3-1	8
Goose Gonsoulin	1960-67	8	3	4	0	44	0-0	3
Erich Barnes	1958-71	14	1	7	0	43	0-3	0
Bobby Dillon	1952-59	8	5	0	1	43	0-0	0
Eddie Meador	1959-70	12	0	8	1	43	0-0	0
Jim Patton	1955-66	12	5	0	1	43	1-5	3

Player	Career	Yr	C	1	2	Pts	Ch	St
Lem Barney	1967-77	11	3	3	1	42	0-0	3
Cliff Harris	1970-79	10	4	2	0	42	2-1	0
Jimmy Johnson	1961-76	16	3	2	2	40	0-0	0
Mel Blount	1970-83	14	3	2	1	39	4-0	3
Jake Scott	1970-78	9	3	3	0	39	2-1	0
Abe Woodson	1958-66	9	4	1	0	37	0-0	6
George Saimes	1963-72	10	4	1	0	37	1-0	0
Jack Tatum	1971-80	10	2	4	0	36	1-0	0
Bobby Boyd	1960-68	9	3	2	0	34	0-1	3
Jack Butler	1951-59	9	3	2	0	34	0-0	3
Pat Fischer	1961-77	17	1	4	2	34	0-1	0
Don Doll	1949-54	6	2	3	0	31	0-1	2
Louis Wright	1975-85	11	3	1	0	29	0-1	0
Jim David	1952-59	8	1	5	0	28	3-1	0
Jerry Norton	1954-64	11	1	4	0	28	0-0	0
Dick Anderson	1968-77	10	3	0	0	24	2-1	3
Andy Nelson	1957-64	8	1	3	0	23	2-0	3
Warren Lahr	1949-59	11	1	1	3	22	4-4	0
Bill Bradley	1969-77	9	2	1	0	21	0-0	6
Will Sherman	1952-61	+9	1	2	1	21	0-1	3
Jimmy Hill	1955-66	12	0	4	0	20	0-1	0
Richie Petitbon	1959-72	14	0	4	0	20	1-1	0
Bert Rechichar	1952-61	10	0	3	1	18	2-1	0

* Career interruption.

We were astonished that Herb Adderley wasn't in the top four on all-pro points, and we had a recount. He didn't move up. All right, no system is perfect.

On the other hand, Willie Wood's high total bears out what we've always said about him. It brings up the idea that we alluded to earlier, the possibility of a Packer backlash. It's true that a lot of Lombardi's Packers have entered the Hall of Fame: Bart Starr, Jim Taylor, Paul Hornung, Jim Ringo, Forrest Gregg, Herb Adderley, Willie Davis, Ray Nitschke, and Lombardi himself. But they *were* the dominant team of the 1960s (and some would say the best ever). They didn't win five championships with a few good men; they had a lot of them. What about Jerry Kramer, Henry Jordan, Dave Robinson, Boyd Dowler, Carroll Dale, and—yes—Willie Wood?

Paul Krause holds the career interception title with 81, but so far it hasn't gotten him an invite to Canton. The knock seems to be that he didn't tackle as hard as, say, Dick "Night Train" Lane. We're not certain that pound-for-pound anyone ever tackled as hard as Lane.

All right, you knew it was coming. Who is out that we think should be in? Contributors like commissioners, owners, and coaches are outside this study. We used our all-pro points (with, admittedly, a dash of interpretation) and limited our list to only those players who have been passed over for at least ten years.

Here are ten that we'd like to see enshrined in Canton (in order of preference):

Al Wistert	Carl Eller
Lavie Dilweg	Verne Lewellen
Mac Speedie	Duke Slater
Leroy Kelly	Mick Tingelhoff and
Willie Wood	*any* offensive guard.

We really don't want to see anybody tossed out of the Hall into the cold Ohio snow. When you're in, you're in. On the other hand, we think our survey shows some enshrinees as a little light on credentials. We'd be remiss if we didn't list what appear to be the shakiest "ins" among the players.

Here they are, ranked from a slight tremor down to full-fledged quivering:

Doug Atkins	Joe Namath
George Musso	Paul Hornung
Jim Langer	Joe Guyon
Johnny Blood	Al Wojciechowicz
Walt Kiesling	Wayne Millner

To be fair, we should add that the most-criticized selections are owners and coaches.

And finally, for all you young readers who hope to grow up to be Hall of Famers, here are:

TEN RULES FOR GETTING INTO THE HALL OF FAME

During your career:

1. Don't be an offensive lineman, especially a guard. You've got a better chance getting to Canton by winning a lottery, buying a team, and going in as an owner.

2. Contrive to play for a team that wins many championships but has almost no stars except you.

3. Don't play next to a superstar. His glare may dim your light.

4. Don't succeed a superstar at your position. No one remembers George Selkirk.*

5. Have a long career, but don't stick around so long they'll remember only the shadow. Leave 'em wanting more.

After you retire:

6. Stay alive. The last deceased Hall of Famer to be named after his death was in 1976.

7. Don't let a superstar succeed you at your position. Can you get that in your final contract?

8. Stay in the limelight after you retire; coach, join a front office, make movies, or get behind a mike.

9. Don't get busted. Which ain't bad advice even if you never play football.

10. Let others tell how good you were. If you say it, no one will believe you and you'll be a bore. On the other hand, don't be too self-deprecating; they *may* believe you. Keep your mouth shut and smile.

---

* Selkirk was the New York Yankee rightfielder in 1935; George Lazenby struck out as James Bond in *On Her Majesty's Secret Service*, and Leo McKern now pitches for Smith-Barney.

PART FOUR

The Tables

ANY GIVEN SUNDAY

How much has pro football changed over the years? One way to tell is to look at the raw numbers produced by a "typical" game in each season. The chart below does just that.

L	PTS	1DR	1DP	1PN	RA	RY	RTD	PA	PC	PY	PS	PSY	PTD	PI	PNT	PAV	PR	PRY	KR	KRY	IRY	PN	PNY	FUM	FML	XPA	XPM	FGA	FGM
N	16	6	4	1	37	119	1	20	9	122	—	—	1	2	6	41	3	41	3	64	28	4	38	2	1	2	2	1	0

All the numbers shown in the example—a typical game from the 1941 NFL season—have been rounded to the nearest whole number for simplicity. And remember, these are the stats for one team and would be doubled to produce a game total.

Reading from left to right: L = League. PTS = Points Scored. We can see that the average number of points scored each game by a 1941 NFL team was 16. 1DR = First Downs Rushing (6), 1DP = First Downs Passing (4), 1PN = First Downs by Penalty (1).

RA = Rushing Attempts (37), RY = Rushing Yards (119), RTD = Rushing Touchdowns (1).

PA = Passing Attempts (20), PC = Pass Completions (9), PY = Passing Yards (122), PS = Passing Sacks (blank; no figures were available until 1961), PSY = Passing Sack Yards (blank; no figures were available on this until 1949), PTD = Passing Touchdowns (1), PI = Pass Interceptions (2).

PNT = Number of Punts (6), PAV = Punt Average (41), PR = Punt Returns (3), PRY = Punt Return Yards (41).

KR = Kickoff Returns (3), KRY = Kickoff Return Yards (64).

IRY = Interception Return Yards (28).

PN = Penalties (4), PNY = Penalty Yards (38).

FUM = Number of Fumbles (2), FML = Fumbles Lost (1).

XPA = Extra Point Attempts (2), XPM = Extra Points Made (2).

FGA = Field Goals Attempted (1), FGM = Field Goals Made (0).

351

YEAR	L	PTS	1DR	1DP	1PN	RA	RY	RTD	PA	PC	PY	PS	PSY	PTD	PI	PNT	PAV	PR	PRY	KR	KRY	IRY	PN	PNY	FUM	FML	XPA	XPM	FGA	FGM
1935	N	11	9	(Total)		41	116	1	15	5	80			1	2				36					20	2	2	1	1	0	0
1936	N	12	11	(Total)		39	142	1	15	6	83				2				39					26	2	2	2	1	0	0
1937	N	13	10	(Total)		39	127	1	17	8	93			1	2				42					25	2	2	2	1	0	0
1938	N	13	11	(Total)		38	125	1	18	7	106			1	2	6	40		34		59	24		26	3	1	2	1	1	0
1939	N	15	11	(Total)		37	121		20	9	129				2	6			38					25			2	2	1	0
1940	N	15	11	(Total)		37	120	1	20	9	125			1	2	6			39					31	2	1	2	2	1	0
1941	N	16	6	4	1	37	119	1	20	9	122			1	2	6	41	3	41	3	64	28	4	38	2		2	2	1	0
1942	A	16	6	5	1	37	125	1	20	9	124			1	2	6	39	3	39	3	64	25	5	40	2	1	3	2	1	0
1943	N	19	6	5	1	37	118	1	22	10	141			1	2	6	38	3	36	3	70	29	5	45	2	2	3	3	1	0
1944	A	18	6	5	1	37	119	1	21	9	129			1	2	6	37	3	35	3	71	32	7	54	3	1	3	3	1	0
1945	N	18	6	5	1	36	123	1	21	10	144			1	2	5	38	3	34	3	69	26	6	57	3	1	3	2	1	0
1946	N	19	8	6	1	38	126	1	21	10	143			1	2	5	41	3	34	4	75	30	8	67	3	2	3	2	1	0
1946	A	20	6	4		35	120	1	20	10	135	2	18	1	2	5	41	3	41	4	80	25	4	33	3	2	3	3	1	0
1947	N	22	8	7	2	36	139	1	25	12	181	3		1	1	5	42	3	42	3	79	29	4	69	3	1	3	3	1	0
1947	A	21	7	5		35	151	1	21	10	148	3	20	2	2	4	40	3	35	4	87	24	4	31	2	2	3	3	1	0
1948	N	23	8	6	1	38	151	1	26	12	174	3	21	2	2	6	41	3	40	4	80	29	8	68	3	1	3	3	1	0
1948	A	23	8	6	1	35	162	1	25	12	177	3	26	2	2	5	41	3	37	4	78	24	6	48	3		3	3	1	0
1949	N	22	8	8		39	151	1	27	13	179	2	19	1	2	6	41	3	39	4	75	29	6	56	2		3	3	1	1
1949	A	21	7	5	1	36	153	1	23	11	166	2	19	1	2	5	40	3	36	3	74	23	5	40	3	2	3	3	1	0
1950	N	23	8	7	1	37	154	1	28	13	186	2	16	1	2	6	40	3	36	4	84	30	7	61	3		3	3	1	1
1951	N	22	9	8	2	38	152	1	27	13	184	2	14	1	2	6	40	3	31	4	79	26	7	59	2		3	3	1	1
1952	N	22	7	8	1	35	134	1	28	13	186	2	18	2	2	6	41	3	35	4	88	29	6	58	3		3	3	2	1
1953	N	22	8	8	1	33	134	1	30	14	193	2	19	1	2	6	41	4	21	4	85	30	6	49	3	1	3	3	2	1
1954	N	21	7	9	1	33	132	1	29	15	211	2	19	1	2	5	41	3	20	4	84	27	6	54	3	1	3	3	2	1
1955	N	22	8	8	1	37	147	1	27	13	176	2	16	1	2	5	41	3	19	4	82	23	5	46	3	1	3	2	2	1
1956	N	20	9	7	1	38	156	1	23	12	161	2	14	2	2	5	41	3	21	4	80	24	5	44	3	1	2	2	2	1
1957	N	20	7	8	1	36	140	1	23	12	172	2	18	2	2	5	41	3	18	3	78	24	6	47	2	1	3	2	2	1
1958	N	23	8	9	1	33	141	1	27	14	196	2	16	1	2	5	41	3	19	4	78	22	5	48	2		3	3	2	1
1959	N	21	8	8		34	144	1	26	13	187	2	17	1	2	5	43	3	20	3	70	20	4	41	2		3	3	2	1
1960	N	22	7	10	2	33	133	1	26	13	191	3	20	2	2	5	42	2	14	4	86	22	5	49	2	1	3	3	2	1
1960	A	24	7	9	1	31	105	1	33	16	218			1	2	5	38	2	17	4	92	22	5	48	2		3	3	2	1
1961	N	24	7	9	1	31	131	1	27	14	202	3	22	2	2	4	43	2	19	4	88	24	4	40	2	1	3	3	2	1
1961	A	24	6	9	1	29	115	1	32	15	217	3	22	2	2	5	41	2	20	4	85	31	5	47	2	1	3	3	2	1

YEAR	L	PTS	1DR	1DP	1PN	RA	RY	RTD	PA	PC	PY	PS	PSY	PTD	PI	PNT	PAV	PR	PRY	KR	KRY	IRY	PN	PNY	FUM	FML	XPA	XPM	FGA	FGM
1962	N	22	7	9	1	31	126	1	27	15	215	3	21	2	2	4	42	2	15	4	94	22	4	44	2	1	3	3	2	1
1962	A	23	6	9	1	29	126	1	31	15	210	2	20	2	2	5	40	2	17	4	93	28	5	48	2	1	3	3	2	1
1963	N	22	6	9	1	31	126	1	28	14	208	3	22	2	2	5	43	2	22	4	88	25	5	46	2	1	3	3	2	1
1963	A	23	6	10	1	27	113	1	32	15	224	3	24	2	2	5	41	2	23	4	95	26	5	46	2	1	3	3	2	1
1964	N	22	7	9	1	31	124	1	28	14	199	3	25	2	1	5	43	2	21	4	91	21	5	50	2	1	3	3	2	1
1964	A	23	6	10	1	28	110	1	33	16	236	3	24	2	2	5	41	2	23	4	95	32	5	45	2	1	3	3	2	1
1965	N	23	7	9	1	31	121	1	28	14	206	3	22	2	2	5	42	2	17	4	90	22	5	48	2	1	3	3	2	1
1965	A	21	6	9	1	29	109	1	33	15	208	2	19	1	2	5	43	2	23	4	88	26	5	52	2	1	2	3	2	1
1966	N	22	6	9	1	31	121	1	32	15	201	3	23	2	2	5	41	2	15	4	91	23	5	50	2	1	3	3	2	1
1966	A	23	7	9	1	29	116	1	32	15	215	2	18	2	2	5	42	2	18	4	93	24	6	48	2	1	3	3	2	1
1967	N	22	7	9	1	31	120	1	29	15	200	2	20	1	2	5	40	2	14	4	90	22	5	56	2	1	3	3	2	1
1967	A	23	6	9	1	29	116	1	31	15	206	3	23	2	2	5	42	3	24	4	88	30	5	48	2	1	2	3	2	1
1968	N	21	7	8	1	32	127	1	27	14	188	2	19	1	1	5	40	2	15	4	84	19	5	52	2	1	2	2	2	1
1968	A	22	6	9	1	32	126	1	29	14	199	2	22	1	2	6	42	3	24	4	83	24	5	49	2	1	3	2	2	1
1969	N	21	7	9	1	30	122	1	28	15	198	3	20	1	1	5	40	2	15	4	80	18	5	54	2	1	2	2	2	1
1969	A	21	6	8	1	30	120	1	27	14	200	2	21	2	2	5	42	3	19	4	83	26	6	54	2	1	2	2	2	1
1970	N	19	6	9	1	31	120	1	27	14	181	2	20	1	1	6	41	3	20	4	78	19	7	60	2	1	2	2	2	1
1971	N	19	7	8	1	32	130	1	26	13	174	2	18	2	1	5	41	2	17	4	84	22	6	54	2	1	2	2	2	1
1972	N	20	8	8	1	34	139	1	25	13	169	2	17	1	1	4	41	2	15	4	81	17	5	47	2	1	2	2	2	1
1973	N	19	8	7	1	36	144	1	24	13	159	2	18	1	1	5	40	2	20	3	78	19	5	47	2	1	2	2	2	1
1974	N	18	8	8	1	34	133	1	26	14	171	2	18	1	1	5	39	3	33	4	85	19	5	47	2	1	2	2	2	1
1975	N	21	8	9	1	36	145	1	27	14	183	3	20	1	1	6	40	3	28	4	91	21	6	52	2	1	2	3	2	1
1976	N	19	8	8	1	37	151	1	26	14	173	2	21	1	1	6	39	3	29	4	84	16	7	56	2	1	2	2	2	1
1977	N	17	8	8	1	37	144	1	25	13	162	2	20	1	1	6	38	2	28	4	75	20	6	56	2	1	2	2	2	1
1978	N	18	8	8	2	36	142	1	26	14	178	2	19	1	1	5	39	3	25	4	78	18	6	58	2	1	2	2	2	1
1979	N	20	8	9	1	34	136	1	29	16	199	2	19	1	1	5	39	3	21	3	81	19	6	54	2	2	2	2	2	1
1980	N	20	7	10	1	32	128	1	31	17	214	2	18	1	1	5	40	3	22	4	78	17	6	53	2	1	2	2	2	1
1981	N	21	8	10	2	32	130	1	32	17	223	2	18	1	1	5	41	3	23	4	77	20	6	54	2	1	2	2	2	1
1982	N	20	7	10	1	31	118	1	25	18	221	3	21	1	1	5	41	3	22	4	78	16	6	51	2	1	2	2	2	1
1983	N	22	8	10	1	32	130	1	31	18	225	3	21	1	1	5	41	3	24	4	78	19	6	53	2	1	3	2	2	1
1984	N	21	7	11	1	31	124	1	32	18	228	3	22	1	1	5	41	3	23	4	77	19	6	54	2	1	2	2	2	1
1985	N	22	7	11	1	30	125	1	32	18	227	3	22	1	1	5	41	3	24	4	81	16	6	50	2	1	3	2	2	1
1986	N	21	7	11	2	30	119	1	32	18	226	3	20	1	1	5	40	3	22	4	75	15	6	52	2	1	2	2	2	1
1987	N	22	7	11	2	31	124	1	32	18	224	3	20	1	1	5	39	3	24	4	78	16	7	55	2	1	3	2	2	1

YEARLY AVERAGES

The following chart lists the averages in various statistical categories season by season.

Again, from left to right: L = League. YD/RUSH = Yards Gained per Rushing Play.

COM PCT = Pass Completion Percentage, YD/PASS = Yards Gained per Pass Attempt, TD PCT = Touchdown Pass Percentage, INT PCT = Pass Interception Percentage, NY/PASS = Net Yards per Pass Attempt, including Sacks when known (Pass Yards − Sack Yards)/(Attempts + Sacks), LG RATE = NFL Passer Rating, NW RATE = New Passer Rating (Yards + 10 × TD − 45 × Interceptions)/Attempts.

YD/PRET = Yards per Punt Return.

YD/KRET = Yards per Kickoff Return.

YD/IRET = Yards per Interception Return.

FUM PCT = Percent of Fumbles Lost.

XP PCT = Extra Point Percentage, FG PCT = Field Goal Percentage.

YEAR	L	YD/RUSH	COM PCT	YD/PASS	TD PCT	INT PCT	NY/PASS	LG RATE	NW RATE	YD/PRET	YD/KRET	YD/IRET	FUM PCT	XP PCT	FG PCT
1935	N		34.3	5.28	4.0	13.7	5.28	26.30	−0.48				92.5	77.5	
1936	N	3.48	36.5	5.41	4.2	12.9	5.41	29.57	0.02				87.7	81.9	
1937	N	3.27	38.4	5.64	5.0	11.3	5.64	34.71	1.03				69.4	82.4	40.6
1938	N	3.29	40.6	5.73	4.6	10.8	5.73	35.49	1.32				45.5	82.3	38.8
1939	N	3.25	42.5	6.33	4.4	9.3	6.33	39.89	2.59				41.2	82.1	39.6
1940	N	3.24	42.9	6.12	4.4	9.8	6.12	38.56	2.13			11.71	50.6	85.5	
1941	N	3.21	44.3	6.06	4.5	10.0	6.06	39.57	2.03	12.69	22.35	14.14	49.2	88.2	39.8
1942	N	3.38	43.8	6.05	4.8	9.7	6.05	40.25	2.15	12.15	21.96	12.69	50.0	92.8	35.5
1943	N	3.21	44.4	6.53	6.6	10.5	6.53	48.64	2.46	11.54	22.36	12.59	40.9	91.7	23.5
1944	N	3.20	42.9	6.11	5.5	11.1	6.11	42.14	1.69	11.59	21.74	13.62	44.6	87.6	33.3
1945	N	3.39	45.4	6.81	5.2	9.1	6.81	47.40	3.21	11.23	20.66	13.48	39.4	90.9	45.3
1946	N	3.32	44.8	6.72	5.4	9.1	6.72	47.64	3.18	11.79	21.02	15.60	52.1	92.8	42.7
1946	A	3.40	48.4	6.68	5.9	8.3	6.68	55.36	3.54	13.72	22.11	15.19	49.2	92.9	48.5
1947	N	3.90	47.0	7.25	6.3	8.4	7.25	57.60	4.11	12.92	19.99	13.99	54.5	92.4	44.5
1947	A	4.33	49.0	7.19	6.4	7.1	7.19	64.50	4.62	13.38	22.93	16.71	46.6	90.4	43.9
1948	N	4.00	48.1	6.70	6.3	7.4	6.70	60.00	3.98	12.06	21.09	14.75	55.2	93.4	40.9
1948	A	4.57	48.8	7.05	6.0	6.7	7.05	64.22	4.64	13.69	21.13	14.10	47.4	93.8	42.7
1949	N	3.89	46.6	6.55	5.1	7.5	5.46	53.88	3.66	11.91	21.11	13.90	53.8	94.4	45.6
1949	A	4.23	47.4	7.09	5.3	7.3	7.09	58.42	4.34	12.66	21.46	13.72	57.3	97.1	40.8
1950	N	4.16	46.6	6.74	5.1	8.0	5.49	52.88	3.67	11.14	22.57	13.71	56.4	93.9	44.2
1951	N	4.05	46.6	6.82	5.2	7.4	5.50	55.62	4.00	10.08	21.99	12.91	59.7	95.1	51.6
1952	N	3.81	46.3	6.66	5.4	7.4	5.13	55.70	3.88	10.13	22.70	14.23	59.4	93.3	43.0
1953	N	4.00	47.3	6.52	4.4	7.2	5.42	53.59	3.74	6.06	22.79	14.17	56.7	95.7	46.6
1954	N	3.98	50.4	7.18	5.0	6.9	6.02	61.72	4.55	5.82	21.80	13.26	58.4	95.7	53.6
1955	N	3.99	47.9	6.62	4.7	6.8	5.61	57.13	4.05	5.63	23.07	12.73	64.5	93.2	46.0
1956	N	4.11	50.5	7.08	4.9	7.3	6.02	59.62	4.28	6.73	22.59	14.18	59.9	94.1	51.1
1957	N	3.90	50.5	7.41	5.1	6.9	6.02	63.16	4.81	5.44	22.64	14.84	56.7	95.8	52.2

YEAR	L	YD/RUSH	COM PCT	YD/PASS	TD PCT	INT PCT	NY/PASS	LG RATE	NW RATE	YD/PRET	YD/KRET	YD/IRET	FUM PCT	XP PCT	FG PCT
1958	N	4.23	49.4	7.16	5.3	6.2	6.12	65.29	4.93	5.74	22.32	13.11	57.5	95.6	46.9
1959	N	4.22	50.0	7.25	5.3	6.0	6.08	66.86	5.10	6.45	21.42	13.24	56.9	95.6	46.8
1960	N	4.08	50.2	7.23	5.4	6.7	5.91	64.18	4.77	6.72	21.80	12.73	54.3	96.8	56.2
1960	A	3.22	48.5	6.61	5.0	5.9	6.61	62.10	4.44	9.30	23.10	11.33	52.6	93.9	44.2
1961	N	4.22	52.1	7.48	5.4	6.3	6.08	68.51	5.20	9.46	23.38	14.42	57.4	97.0	48.1
1961	A	3.99	46.8	6.70	5.0	6.4	5.59	59.10	4.33	10.99	21.51	14.94	54.8	94.2	42.6
1962	N	4.07	53.3	7.85	5.6	6.1	6.48	72.59	5.68	8.20	23.70	13.41	59.8	95.4	49.5
1962	A	4.31	47.6	6.80	5.1	7.0	5.74	57.87	4.16	8.59	22.95	13.12	54.7	93.1	53.1
1963	N	4.05	51.5	7.52	5.6	5.6	6.15	71.74	5.57	9.37	23.40	15.94	55.3	95.0	49.6
1963	A	4.11	48.7	7.09	5.4	6.0	5.83	65.30	4.94	10.38	22.38	13.50	60.9	96.5	47.1
1964	N	4.00	51.4	7.16	5.1	4.8	5.64	71.69	5.50	9.13	23.35	15.39	54.3	95.1	53.1
1964	A	3.96	49.0	7.05	5.1	6.4	5.87	62.63	4.69	9.60	22.55	15.04	52.5	97.0	52.9
1965	N	3.92	51.3	7.46	5.7	5.1	6.08	73.51	5.72	7.81	23.22	15.85	53.8	95.6	53.8
1965	A	3.80	45.3	6.37	4.5	5.6	5.43	58.05	4.31	9.52	21.77	14.50	55.4	100.0	54.5
1966	N	3.90	51.6	6.91	4.6	5.2	5.59	67.44	5.03	6.34	22.06	14.89	54.3	96.3	55.7
1966	A	4.01	46.3	6.81	5.0	5.4	5.87	62.97	4.86	8.69	22.39	14.17	51.6	97.0	52.8
1967	N	3.92	51.0	6.94	5.0	5.7	5.75	66.65	4.89	6.08	22.58	13.45	56.6	96.9	49.2
1967	A	3.92	47.6	6.70	4.9	5.9	5.49	61.60	4.55	9.15	22.06	16.42	47.0	97.0	53.5
1968	N	4.02	51.6	7.02	5.1	5.5	5.77	68.65	5.08	7.05	21.32	12.81	59.8	95.1	55.6
1968	A	3.97	47.5	6.91	4.7	5.6	5.69	62.62	4.85	8.64	21.56	15.02	54.4	98.3	58.7
1969	N	4.00	52.6	6.99	5.1	4.9	5.76	71.60	5.29	6.38	21.67	12.63	55.3	97.7	52.7
1969	A	4.03	49.8	6.96	4.8	5.8	5.74	64.49	4.84	7.79	23.11	15.84	59.3	97.6	57.8
1970	N	3.83	51.1	6.73	4.4	5.2	5.51	65.55	4.82	7.36	22.06	13.37	56.1	96.9	59.4
1971	N	4.02	50.9	6.72	4.1	5.8	5.57	62.17	4.53	7.02	22.99	14.45	53.1	97.5	58.7
1972	N	4.14	51.7	6.82	4.5	5.3	5.66	66.32	4.87	7.14	23.06	13.12	48.4	96.5	61.1
1973	N	4.06	52.0	6.56	4.3	5.3	5.29	64.88	4.59	8.10	22.46	14.67	50.6	96.8	63.1
1974	N	3.88	52.5	6.49	3.9	5.2	5.35	64.22	4.54	9.79	22.17	13.91	49.0	90.6	60.6
1975	N	4.01	52.5	6.68	4.3	5.3	5.45	65.82	4.71	9.13	22.43	14.47	51.0	90.9	64.2
1976	N	4.08	52.2	6.63	4.2	4.8	5.28	67.01	4.87	9.03	21.44	12.96	55.0	89.8	59.5
1977	N	3.85	51.3	6.50	4.0	5.7	5.18	61.21	4.31	8.82	21.39	14.07	53.3	91.1	58.3

YEAR	L	YD/ RUSH	COM PCT	YD/ PASS	TD PCT	INT PCT	NY/ PASS	LG RATE	NW RATE	YD/ PRET	YD/ KRET	YD/ IRET	FUM PCT	XP PCT	FG PCT
1978	N	3.95	53.1	6.73	4.0	5.4	5.54	65.01	4.69	8.38	21.38	12.96	52.0	92.0	63.1
1979	N	4.00	54.1	6.87	4.1	4.6	5.76	70.45	5.21	7.65	20.28	13.97	52.6	90.3	63.1
1980	N	3.97	56.2	7.00	4.4	4.6	5.96	73.74	5.38	8.29	19.92	12.25	48.2	94.0	63.6
1981	N	4.02	54.6	7.03	4.2	4.3	6.02	72.90	5.52	8.56	20.29	14.59	52.8	94.4	65.9
1982	N	3.82	56.4	7.02	4.0	4.4	5.84	73.43	5.44	8.13	20.09	11.87	50.0	93.9	68.2
1983	N	4.09	56.9	7.18	4.4	4.4	6.01	75.88	5.64	8.61	19.55	13.52	51.6	95.2	71.5
1984	N	4.02	56.4	7.14	4.3	4.1	5.90	76.12	5.73	8.63	19.81	14.60	49.0	96.3	71.7
1985	N	4.10	54.8	7.04	4.1	4.2	5.83	73.55	5.57	9.28	20.99	12.16	52.4	95.7	72.2
1986	N	3.94	55.4	6.99	4.1	4.0	5.88	74.13	5.59	8.58	19.75	11.62	47.4	96.0	68.6
1987	N	3.95	54.8	6.96	4.5	4.0	5.87	75.18	5.61	9.11	19.43	12.44	49.9	95.5	69.8

SEASON-BY-SEASON

With the charts on the following pages, you can see what happened to your favorite teams for every season since 1935. We started there because no reliable statistical information was available for earlier years.

At the left you'll find the team's season record (W, L, T) and the number of points it scored (PTS) and gave up (OPP). You can also follow the team's playoff record with this code:

\# alone means a team lost out on a playoff berth by the league's tie-breaking procedure. A letter after \# means that a team won a playoff berth on a tie-breaker; the letter indicates the kind of playoff game, as follows:

P = Playoff Round of top teams (1949 AAC and 1982 NFL only).
W = Wild Card Playoff.
D = Divisional Championship Playoff.
C = Conference Championship Game.
L = League Championship Game, replaced by S in 1970 to date.
S = Super Bowl.

A letter after the indicated game means the team won and advanced to the next round. An asterisk (*) at the end means the team won the final game and was the league champion.

The statistical record following the team's seasonal record is as follows:

NET = Net Point (PTS − OPP), P-W = Predicted Net Wins (derived from net points over 40), D-W = Delta Net Wins (actual net wins minus predicted net wins; net wins is wins minus losses over two).

Y-O = Total Yards on Offense (including laterals through 1949, except for 1940 when no data was published), Y-D = Total Yards Allowed on Defense, Y-N = the net difference between the two.

T-O = Offensive Turnovers (fumbles lost and interceptions), T-D = Defensive Takeaways, T-N = Net Turnovers (turnovers minus takeaways). Interceptions were estimated for 1935 only based on league average times attempts. Fumbles lost for 1935–40 on offense were estimated from total fumbles based on league average fumbles lost.

P-NP = Predicted Net Points (Net Yards over 12, plus Net Turnovers × four), D-NP = Delta Net Points (actual minus predicted).

PR-O = Passer Rating Offense in Yards (Rating is yards, including sack yards when known, plus 10 times TD's, minus 45 times interceptions), PR-D = Passer Rating Defense, PR-N = Passer Rating Net (PR-O − PR-D). Defensive yards were not separated into rushing and passing from 1935–40 so PR-D and PR-N cannot be figured for those years.

YD-O = Yards per Drive Offense, YD-D = Yards per Drive Defense. This is total net yards divided by estimated number of drives. Drives are estimated as opponents' punts, plus opponents' scores, plus opponents' turnovers, plus for receiving a kickoff at the opening of one half for each game—all of which give a team possession and allow it to start a drive. The number of drive for 1935–40 could not be estimated because no punting data was available.

1935 N.F.L.

EASTERN DIVISION	W	L	T	PCT		PTS	OPP	NET	P-W	D-W	Y-O	Y-D	Y-N	T-O	T-D	T-N	P-NP	D-NP	PR-O
NEW YORK GIANTS	9	3	0	.750	L	180	96	84	2.1	0.9	2445	2019	426	39	45	6	60	24	0.9
BROOKLYN DODGERS	5	6	1	.455		90	141	−51	−1.3	0.8	1876	2960	−1084	53	64	11	−46	−5	−1.8
PITTSBURGH PIRATES	4	8	0	.333		100	209	−109	−2.7	0.7	1557	3204	−1647	60	48	−12	−185	76	−1.7
BOSTON REDSKINS	2	8	1	.200		65	123	−58	−1.5	−1.5	2086	1982	104	52	46	−6	−15	−43	−1.7
PHILADELPHIA EAGLES	2	9	0	.182		60	179	−119	−3.0	−0.5	2028	2669	−641	48	52	4	−37	−82	−0.5

WESTERN DIVISION	W	L	T	PCT		PTS	OPP	NET	P-W	D-W	Y-O	Y-D	Y-N	T-O	T-D	T-N	P-NP	D-NP	PR-O
DETROIT LIONS	7	3	2	.700	L*	191	111	80	2.0	0.0	2756	2023	733	38	36	−2	53	27	1.1
GREEN BAY PACKERS	8	4	0	.667		181	96	85	2.1	−0.1	2979	2161	818	58	48	−10	28	57	0.6
CHICAGO CARDINALS	6	4	2	.600		99	97	2	0.1	0.9	2256	2068	188	43	47	4	32	−30	−1.2
CHICAGO BEARS	6	4	2	.600		192	106	86	2.2	−1.2	3462	2337	1125	62	67	5	114	−28	0.3

1936 N.F.L.

EASTERN DIVISION	W	L	T	PCT		PTS	OPP	NET	P-W	D-W	Y-O	Y-D	Y-N	T-O	T-D	T-N	P-NP	D-NP	PR-O
BOSTON REDSKINS	7	5	0	.583	L	149	110	39	1.0	0.0	2612	2181	431	50	54	4	52	−13	0.5
PITTSBURGH PIRATES	6	6	0	.500		88	187	−99	−2.5	2.5	2225	3032	−807	58	51	−7	−95	−4	−0.6
NEW YORK GIANTS	5	6	1	.455		115	163	−48	−1.2	0.7	2744	2841	−97	49	43	−6	−32	−16	1.2
BROOKLYN DODGERS	3	8	1	.273		92	161	−69	−1.7	−0.8	1932	2798	−866	46	51	5	−52	−17	−3.1
PHILADELPHIA EAGLES	1	11	0	.083		51	196	−145	−3.6	−1.4	2068	2857	−789	64	44	−20	−146	1	−5.5

WESTERN DIVISION	W	L	T	PCT		PTS	OPP	NET	P-W	D-W	Y-O	Y-D	Y-N	T-O	T-D	T-N	P-NP	D-NP	PR-O
GREEN BAY PACKERS	10	1	1	.909	L*	248	118	130	3.3	1.3	3323	2664	659	39	50	11	99	31	3.7
CHICAGO BEARS	9	3	0	.750		222	94	128	3.2	−0.2	3416	3000	416	42	59	17	103	25	1.9
DETROIT LIONS	8	4	0	.667		235	102	133	3.3	−1.3	3701	2489	1212	40	34	−6	77	56	−0.8
CHICAGO CARDINALS	3	8	1	.273		74	143	−69	−1.7	−0.8	2654	2725	−71	55	59	4	10	−79	0.2

1937 N.F.L.

EASTERN DIVISION	W	L	T	PCT		PTS	OPP	NET	P-W	D-W	Y-O	Y-D	Y-N	T-O	T-D	T-N	P-NP	D-NP	PR-O
WASHINGTON REDSKINS	8	3	0	.727	L*	195	120	75	1.9	0.6	2915	2123	792	46	41	−5	46	29	2.4
NEW YORK GIANTS	6	3	2	.667		128	109	19	0.5	1.0	2611	2158	453	28	44	16	102	−83	3.1
PITTSBURGH PIRATES	4	7	0	.364		122	145	−23	−0.6	−0.9	2386	2232	154	49	40	−9	−23	0	−1.3
BROOKLYN DODGERS	3	7	1	.300		82	174	−92	−2.3	0.3	2001	2821	−820	42	37	−5	−88	−4	0.0
PHILADELPHIA EAGLES	2	8	1	.200		86	177	−91	−2.3	−0.7	1766	3150	−1384	36	36	0	−115	24	−0.7

WESTERN DIVISION	W	L	T	PCT		PTS	OPP	NET	P-W	D-W	Y-O	Y-D	Y-N	T-O	T-D	T-N	P-NP	D-NP	PR-O
CHICAGO BEARS	9	1	1	.900	L	201	100	101	2.5	1.5	2693	2255	438	31	38	7	65	36	4.1
GREEN BAY PACKERS	7	4	0	.636		220	122	98	2.5	−1.0	3203	2297	906	38	33	−5	56	42	1.8
DETROIT LIONS	7	4	0	.636		180	105	75	1.9	−0.4	2707	2102	605	30	42	12	98	−23	−1.2
CHICAGO CARDINALS	5	5	1	.500		135	165	−30	−0.8	0.8	2450	2526	−76	42	45	3	6	−36	2.1
CLEVELAND RAMS	1	10	0	.091		75	207	−132	−3.3	−1.2	1791	2702	−911	42	30	−12	−124	−8	−0.9

1938 N.F.L.

EASTERN DIVISION	W	L	T	PCT		PTS	OPP	NET	P-W	D-W	Y-O	Y-D	Y-N	T-O	T-D	T-N	P-NP	D-NP	PR-O
NEW YORK GIANTS	8	2	1	.800	L*	194	79	115	2.9	0.1	2692	2029	663	29	48	19	131	−16	2.1
WASHINGTON REDSKINS	6	3	2	.667		148	154	−6	−0.2	1.6	2986	2174	812	47	28	−19	−8	2	1.7
BROOKLYN DODGERS	4	4	3	.500		131	161	−30	−0.8	0.8	2231	2958	−727	19	37	18	11	−41	4.1
PHILADELPHIA EAGLES	5	6	0	.455		154	164	−10	−0.3	−0.3	1927	3270	−1343	25	33	8	−80	70	1.1
PITTSBURGH PIRATES	2	9	0	.182		79	169	−90	−2.3	−1.3	2358	2626	−268	39	22	−17	−90	0	−2.7

WESTERN DIVISION	W	L	T	PCT		PTS	OPP	NET	P-W	D-W	Y-O	Y-D	Y-N	T-O	T-D	T-N	P-NP	D-NP	PR-O
GREEN BAY PACKERS	8	3	0	.727	L	223	118	105	2.6	−0.1	3037	2594	443	28	33	5	57	48	3.6
DETROIT LIONS	7	4	0	.636		119	108	11	0.3	1.2	2640	2199	441	24	36	12	85	−74	0.4
CHICAGO BEARS	6	5	0	.545		194	148	46	1.1	−0.6	2979	3020	−767	44	39	−5	−84	0	2.7
CLEVELAND RAMS	4	7	0	.364		131	215	−84	−2.1	0.6	2253	3020	−767	43	38	−5	46	0	−0.3
CHICAGO CARDINALS	2	9	0	.182		111	168	−57	−1.4	−2.1	2512	2558	−46	41	28	−13	−56	−1	0.9

1939 N.F.L.

EASTERN DIVISION	W	L	T	PCT		PTS	OPP	NET	P-W	D-W	Y-O	Y-D	Y-N	T-O	T-D	T-N	P-NP	D-NP	PR-O
NEW YORK GIANTS	9	1	1	.900	L	168	85	83	2.1	1.9	2257	2482	−225	20	45	25	81	2	3.1
WASHINGTON REDSKINS	8	2	1	.800		242	94	148	3.7	−0.7	3490	2116	1374	32	36	4	131	17	5.8
BROOKLYN DODGERS	4	6	1	.400		108	219	−111	−2.8	1.8	2352	3113	−761	29	28	−1	−67	−44	2.0
PHILADELPHIA EAGLES	1	9	1	.100		105	200	−95	−2.4	−1.6	2160	2954	−794	34	30	−4	−82	−13	2.2
PITTSBURGH PIRATES	1	9	1	.100		114	216	−102	−2.6	−1.5	2236	3100	−864	44	22	−22	−160	58	−1.7

WESTERN DIVISION	W	L	T	PCT		PTS	OPP	NET	P-W	D-W	Y-O	Y-D	Y-N	T-O	T-D	T-N	P-NP	D-NP	PR-O
GREEN BAY PACKERS	9	2	0	.818	L*	233	153	80	2.0	1.5	3445	2770	675	22	35	13	108	-28	5.4
CHICAGO BEARS	8	3	0	.727		298	157	141	3.5	-1.0	3988	2604	1384	32	42	10	155	-14	6.0
DETROIT LIONS	6	5	0	.545		145	150	-5	-0.1	0.6	2905	2603	302	31	26	-5	5	-10	2.3
CLEVELAND RAMS	5	5	1	.500		195	164	31	0.8	-0.8	2683	2785	-102	33	37	4	8	23	2.3
CHICAGO CARDINALS	1	10	0	.091		84	254	-170	-4.3	-0.3	2027	2998	-971	47	22	-25	-181	11	-1.1

1940 N.F.L.

EASTERN DIVISION	W	L	T	PCT		PTS	OPP	NET	P-W	D-W	Y-O	Y-D	Y-N	T-O	T-D	T-N	P-NP	D-NP	PR-O
WASHINGTON REDSKINS	9	2	0	.818	L	245	142	103	2.6	0.9	3289	2847	442	42	27	-15	-23	126	4.4
BROOKLYN DODGERS	8	3	0	.727		186	120	66	1.6	0.9	2813	2836	-23	25	32	7	26	40	4.3
NEW YORK GIANTS	6	4	1	.600		131	133	-2	-0.1	1.0	2512	2219	293	29	34	5	44	-46	2.6
PITTSBURGH PIRATES	2	7	2	.222		60	178	-118	-3.0	0.5	1977	2742	-765	40	23	-17	-132	14	-1.6
PHILADELPHIA EAGLES	1	10	0	.091		111	211	-100	-2.5	-2.0	2153	2780	-627	27	25	-2	-60	-40	2.8

WESTERN DIVISION	W	L	T	PCT		PTS	OPP	NET	P-W	D-W	Y-O	Y-D	Y-N	T-O	T-D	T-N	P-NP	D-NP	PR-O
CHICAGO BEARS	8	3	0	.727	L*	238	152	86	2.2	0.3	3219	2750	469	33	38	5	59	27	4.8
GREEN BAY PACKERS	6	4	1	.600		238	155	83	2.1	-1.1	3400	2532	868	37	47	10	112	-29	2.8
DETROIT LIONS	5	5	1	.500		138	153	-15	-0.4	0.4	2634	2357	277	40	49	9	59	-74	0.2
CLEVELAND RAMS	4	6	1	.400		171	191	-20	-0.5	-0.5	2724	3102	-378	38	39	1	-28	8	2.3
CHICAGO CARDINALS	2	7	2	.222		139	222	-83	-2.1	-0.4	2227	2783	-556	45	42	-3	-58	-25	-2.6

1941 N.F.L.

EASTERN DIVISION	W	L	T	PCT	PTS	OPP	NET	P-W	D-W	Y-O	Y-D	Y-N	T-O	T-D	T-N	P-NP	D-NP	PR-O	PR-D	PR-N	YD-O	YD-D
NEW YORK GIANTS	8	3	0	.727L	238	114	124	3.1	-0.6	2400	2378	22	26	42	16	66	58	4.2	-0.2	4.4	16.1	16.3
BROOKLYN DODGERS	7	4	0	.636	158	127	31	0.8	0.7	2887	2379	508	28	28	0	42	-11	1.9	1.7	0.1	22.0	18.3
WASHINGTON REDSKINS	6	5	0	.545	176	174	2	0.1	0.4	2675	2448	227	41	35	-6	-5	7	1.2	1.9	-0.7	18.7	17.7
PHILADELPHIA EAGLES	2	8	1	.200	119	218	-99	-2.5	-0.5	2317	2867	-550	42	31	-11	-90	-9	1.0	2.3	-1.3	16.0	20.6
PITTSBURGH STEELERS	1	9	1	.100	103	276	-173	-4.3	0.3	1881	2718	-837	49	27	-22	-158	-15	-4.9	2.2	-7.1	12.6	16.8

WESTERN DIVISION	W	L	T	PCT	PTS	OPP	NET	P-W	D-W	Y-O	Y-D	Y-N	T-O	T-D	T-N	P-NP	D-NP	PR-O	PR-D	PR-N	YD-O	YD-D
CHICAGO BEARS	10	1	0	.909DL*	396	147	249	6.2	-1.7	4399	2539	1860	30	48	18	227	22	8.7	0.1	8.6	32.1	18.8
GREEN BAY PACKERS	10	1	0	.909D	258	120	138	3.5	1.0	3296	2564	732	24	48	24	157	-19	5.2	1.3	3.9	23.5	18.7
DETROIT LIONS	4	6	1	.400	121	195	-74	-1.9	0.9	1871	3009	-1138	31	30	-1	-99	25	-0.0	3.5	-3.6	12.9	21.2
CHICAGO CARDINALS	3	7	1	.300	127	197	-70	-1.8	-0.3	2767	2606	161	32	31	-1	9	-79	3.2	3.6	-0.4	20.8	18.1
CLEVELAND RAMS	2	9	0	.182	116	244	-128	-3.2	-0.3	2353	2972	-619	43	26	-17	-120	-8	-0.4	4.3	-4.8	15.8	20.2

1942 N.F.L.

EASTERN DIVISION	W	L	T	PCT	PTS	OPP	NET	P-W	D-W	Y-O	Y-D	Y-N	T-O	T-D	T-N	P-NP	D-NP	PR-O	PR-D	PR-N	YD-O	YD-D
WASHINGTON REDSKINS	10	1	0	.909L*	227	102	125	3.1	1.4	3121	1950	1171	30	26	-4	82	43	3.9	1.3	2.5	22.9	13.8
PITTSBURGH STEELERS	7	4	0	.636	167	119	48	1.2	0.3	2606	2388	218	21	28	7	46	2	1.3	1.6	-0.2	19.0	16.9
NEW YORK GIANTS	5	5	1	.500	155	139	16	0.4	-0.4	2178	2897	-719	21	34	13	-8	24	2.9	3.4	-0.5	16.6	22.5
BROOKLYN DODGERS	3	8	0	.273	100	168	-68	-1.7	-0.8	2249	2824	-575	34	26	-8	-80	12	-2.1	3.2	-5.3	17.3	21.4
PHILADELPHIA EAGLES	2	9	0	.182	134	239	-105	-2.6	-0.9	2551	3026	-475	28	28	0	-40	-65	3.4	3.1	0.3	18.1	22.9

WESTERN DIVISION	W	L	T	PCT	PTS	OPP	NET	P-W	D-W	Y-O	Y-D	Y-N	T-O	T-D	T-N	P-NP	D-NP	PR-O	PR-D	PR-N	YD-O	YD-D
CHICAGO BEARS	11	0	0	1.000L	376	84	292	7.3	-1.8	3930	1703	2227	44	51	7	214	78	4.5	-0.8	5.4	26.7	10.8
GREEN BAY PACKERS	8	2	1	.800	300	215	85	2.1	0.9	3690	3086	604	26	48	22	138	-53	5.7	0.3	5.4	24.9	22.0
CLEVELAND RAMS	5	6	0	.455	150	207	-57	-1.4	0.9	2573	3563	-990	35	33	-2	-91	34	1.8	3.3	-1.5	19.3	24.6
CHICAGO CARDINALS	3	8	0	.273	98	209	-111	-2.8	0.3	2453	2997	-544	40	33	-7	-73	-38	0.6	2.5	-1.9	16.1	21.3
DETROIT LIONS	0	11	0	.000	38	263	-225	-5.6	0.1	2206	3123	-917	56	28	-28	-188	-37	-2.7	4.7	-7.4	14.8	21.7

1943 N.F.L.

EASTERN DIVISION	W	L	T	PCT	PTS	OPP	NET	P-W	D-W	Y-O	Y-D	Y-N	T-O	T-D	T-N	P-NP	D-NP	PR-O	PR-D	PR-N	YD-O	YD-D
WASHINGTON REDSKINS	6	3	1	.667DL	229	137	92	2.3	-0.8	2909	2358	551	31	34	3	58	34	4.6	-0.3	4.9	20.8	16.7
NEW YORK GIANTS	6	3	1	.667D	197	170	27	0.7	0.8	2196	2738	-542	14	28	14	11	16	2.9	4.7	-1.8	15.7	21.9
PHIL-PITT	5	4	1	.556	225	230	-5	-0.1	0.6	2878	2301	577	35	30	-5	28	-33	2.0	2.5	-0.5	20.7	16.4
BROOKLYN DODGERS	2	8	0	.200	65	234	-169	-4.2	1.2	1629	3122	-1493	30	24	-6	-148	-21	0.4	4.7	-4.3	12.2	22.5

WESTERN DIVISION	W	L	T	PCT	PTS	OPP	NET	P-W	D-W	Y-O	Y-D	Y-N	T-O	T-D	T-N	P-NP	D-NP	PR-O	PR-D	PR-N	YD-O	YD-D
CHICAGO BEARS	8	1	1	.889L*	303	157	146	3.7	-0.2	4042	2262	1780	35	30	-5	128	18	8.0	-0.1	8.1	31.3	16.4
GREEN BAY PACKERS	7	2	1	.778	264	172	92	2.3	0.2	3351	2707	644	25	51	26	158	-66	5.0	-1.3	6.3	24.1	20.4
DETROIT LIONS	3	6	1	.333	178	218	-40	-1.0	-0.5	2408	2837	-429	42	31	-11	-80	40	-1.1	4.0	-5.1	17.0	19.0
CHICAGO CARDINALS	0	10	0	.000	95	238	-143	-3.6	-1.4	1854	2933	-1079	44	28	-16	-154	11	-2.7	5.5	-8.3	14.8	23.8

1944 N.F.L.

EASTERN DIVISION	W	L	T	PCT	PTS	OPP	NET	P-W	D-W	Y-O	Y-D	Y-N	T-O	T-D	T-N	P-NP	D-NP	PR-O	PR-D	PR-N	YD-O	YD-D
NEW YORK GIANTS	8	1	1	.889L	206	75	131	3.3	0.2	2389	2318	71	24	45	21	90	41	1.5	-0.8	2.3	18.5	17.4
PHILADELPHIA EAGLES	7	1	2	.875	267	131	136	3.4	-0.4	2621	1943	678	32	37	5	77	59	3.6	0.1	3.5	19.1	14.2
WASHINGTON REDSKINS	6	3	1	.667	169	180	-11	-0.3	1.8	2930	2695	235	29	28	-1	16	-27	4.8	2.1	2.6	23.4	21.7
BOSTON YANKS	2	8	0	.200	82	233	-151	-3.8	0.8	1506	2723	-1217	30	27	-3	-113	-38	0.5	3.1	-2.6	11.3	21.4
BROOKLYN TIGERS	0	10	0	.000	69	166	-97	-2.4	-2.6	2021	2410	-389	37	19	-18	-104	7	-1.3	4.8	-6.1	15.4	18.3

WESTERN DIVISION	W	L	T	PCT	PTS	OPP	NET	P-W	D-W	Y-O	Y-D	Y-N	T-O	T-D	T-N	P-NP	D-NP	PR-O	PR-D	PR-N	YD-O	YD-D
GREEN BAY PACKERS	8	2	0	.800L*	238	141	97	2.4	0.3	2492	2417	607	31	41	10	91	6	2.1	0.1	2.0	24.2	19.5
CHICAGO BEARS	6	3	1	.667	258	172	86	2.2	-0.7	3250	2006	1244	32	34	2	112	-26	4.7	0.3	4.3	25.6	15.3
DETROIT LIONS	6	3	1	.667	216	151	65	1.6	-0.1	2655	2673	-18	36	42	6	23	42	1.8	1.7	0.1	20.6	19.9
CLEVELAND RAMS	4	6	0	.400	188	224	-36	-0.9	-0.1	2411	2887	-476	41	44	3	-28	-8	1.1	1.8	-0.8	17.2	21.2
CARD-PITT	0	10	0	.000	108	328	-220	-5.5	0.5	2282	3017	-735	53	28	-25	-161	-59	-2.0	5.3	-7.2	16.5	22.2

1945 N.F.L.

EASTERN DIVISION	W	L	T	PCT	PTS	OPP	NET	P-W	D-W	Y-O	Y-D	Y-N	T-O	T-D	T-N	P-NP	D-NP	PR-O	PR-D	PR-N	YD-O	YD-D
WASHINGTON REDSKINS	8	2	0	.800L	209	121	88	2.2	0.8	3549	2208	1341	20	22	2	120	-32	6.4	2.3	4.1	37.4	22.5
PHILADELPHIA EAGLES	7	3	0	.700	272	133	139	3.5	-1.5	3016	2073	943	24	26	2	87	52	4.2	2.4	1.8	25.6	17.0
NEW YORK GIANTS	3	6	1	.333	179	198	-19	-0.5	-1.0	2366	3083	-717	25	27	2	-52	33	4.8	0.1		20.4	26.6
BOSTON YANKS	3	6	1	.333	123	211	-88	-2.2	0.7	1897	2857	-960	36	38	2	-72	-16	0.7	0.8	-0.1	14.7	22.1
PITTSBURGH STEELERS	2	8	0	.200	79	220	-141	-3.5	0.5	1709	3040	-1331	29	27	-2	-119	-22	-1.8	6.1	-7.9	14.5	26.7

WESTERN DIVISION	W	L	T	PCT	PTS	OPP	NET	P-W	D-W	Y-O	Y-D	Y-N	T-O	T-D	T-N	P-NP	D-NP	PR-O	PR-D	PR-N	YD-O	YD-D
CLEVELAND RAMS	9	1	0	.900L*	244	136	108	2.7	1.3	3546	2510	1036	38	44	6	110	-2	5.2	1.2	4.0	28.6	19.6
DETROIT LIONS	7	3	0	.700	195	194	1	0.0	2.0	2485	2548	-63	46	33	-13	-57	58	0.3	3.3	-3.0	18.4	18.3
GREEN BAY PACKERS	6	4	0	.600	258	173	85	2.1	-1.1	2869	3116	-247	31	41	10	19	66	2.7	3.1	-0.4	21.7	23.8
CHICAGO BEARS	3	7	0	.300	192	235	-43	-1.1	-0.9	3382	2756	626	22	21	-1	48	-91	6.0	3.6	2.3	31.3	27.3
CHICAGO CARDINALS	1	9	0	.100	98	228	-130	-3.3	-0.8	2263	2891	-628	31	23	-8	-84	-46	2.1	5.9	-3.8	18.9	24.7

1946 N.F.L.

EASTERN DIVISION	W	L	T	PCT	PTS	OPP	NET	P-W	D-W	Y-O	Y-D	Y-N	T-O	T-D	T-N	P-NP	D-NP	PR-O	PR-D	PR-N	YD-O	YD-D
NEW YORK GIANTS	7	3	1	.700L	236	162	74	1.9	0.1	2927	3134	-207	41	45	4	-1	75	2.4	4.1	-1.7	21.1	22.7
PHILADELPHIA EAGLES	6	5	0	.545	231	220	11	0.3	0.2	2917	2490	427	47	44	-3	24	-13	4.1	1.4	2.7	18.8	16.0
WASHINGTON REDSKINS	5	5	1	.500	171	191	-20	-0.5	0.5	3132	2451	681	44	34	-10	17	-37	3.3	1.7	1.6	22.7	18.2
PITTSBURGH STEELERS	5	5	1	.500	136	117	19	0.5	-0.5	2313	2719	-406	28	31	3	-22	41	2.6	2.3	0.4	17.8	20.6
BOSTON YANKS	2	8	1	.200	189	273	-84	-2.1	-0.9	2699	3586	-887	37	31	-6	-98	14	3.6	4.5	-0.9	19.1	24.7

WESTERN DIVISION	W	L	T	PCT	PTS	OPP	NET	P-W	D-W	Y-O	Y-D	Y-N	T-O	T-D	T-N	P-NP	D-NP	PR-O	PR-D	PR-N	YD-O	YD-D
CHICAGO BEARS	8	2	1	.800L*	289	193	96	2.4	0.6	3695	2689	1006	34	49	15	144	-48	5.2	2.1	3.1	24.5	18.0
LOS ANGELES RAMS	6	4	1	.600	277	257	20	0.5	0.5	3793	3525	268	44	38	-6	-2	22	3.7	5.0	-1.4	26.7	24.7
GREEN BAY PACKERS	6	5	0	.545	148	158	-10	-0.3	0.8	2618	2661	-43	29	52	23	88	-98	0.4	1.3	-0.9	17.9	19.6
CHICAGO CARDINALS	6	5	0	.545	260	198	62	1.5	-1.0	3572	2882	690	49	45	-4	42	20	4.6	2.3	2.3	24.6	18.8
DETROIT LIONS	1	10	0	.091	142	310	-168	-4.2	-0.3	2169	3698	-1529	45	29	-16	-191	23	1.0	6.4	-5.3	15.1	25.7

1946 A.A.F.C

EASTERN DIVISION	W	L	T	PCT	PTS	OPP	NET	P-W	D-W	Y-O	Y-D	Y-N	T-O	T-D	T-N	P-NP	D-NP	PR-O	PR-D	PR-N	YD-O	YD-D
NEW YORK YANKEES	10	3	1	.769L	270	192	78	2.0	1.5	3490	2619	871	45	34	-11	29	49	3.0	3.9	-0.8	20.5	14.9
BROOKLYN DODGERS	3	10	1	.231	226	339	-113	-2.8	-0.7	3275	4535	-1260	40	38	-2	-113	0	4.3	6.8	-2.5	17.9	25.2
BUFFALO BISONS	3	10	1	.231	249	370	-121	-3.0	-0.5	3413	4445	-1032	58	51	-7	-114	-7	2.1	5.5	-3.4	18.3	22.8
MIAMI SEAHAWKS	3	11	0	.214	167	378	-211	-5.3	1.3	2573	4124	-1551	56	44	-12	-177	-34	1.2	3.9	-2.8	15.4	23.8

WESTERN DIVISION	W	L	T	PCT	PTS	OPP	NET	P-W	D-W	Y-O	Y-D	Y-N	T-O	T-D	T-N	P-NP	D-NP	PR-O	PR-D	PR-N	YD-O	YD-D
CLEVELAND BROWNS	12	2	0	.857L*	423	137	286	7.2	-2.2	4244	2933	1311	37	64	27	217	69	9.2	-1.5	10.7	25.1	15.7
SAN FRANCISCO 49ERS	9	5	0	.643	307	189	118	3.0	-1.0	3896	3023	873	42	47	5	93	25	3.8	3.8	0.0	22.1	18.0
LOS ANGELES DONS	7	5	2	.583	305	290	15	0.4	0.6	4142	3457	685	43	37	-6	33	-18	3.2	4.8	-1.6	23.1	20.7
CHICAGO ROCKETS	5	6	3	.455	263	315	-52	-1.3	0.8	3439	3336	103	47	53	6	33	-85	2.5	1.6	0.9	16.6	17.5

1947 N.F.L.

EASTERN DIVISION	W	L	T	PCT	PTS	OPP	NET	P-W	D-W	Y-O	Y-D	Y-N	T-O	T-D	T-N	P-NP	D-NP	PR-O	PR-D	PR-N	YD-O	YD-D
PHILADELPHIA EAGLES	8	4	0	.667DL	308	242	66	1.6	0.4	3760	3769	-9	33	36	3	11	55	4.9	4.7	0.2	24.1	22.8
PITTSBURGH STEELERS	8	4	0	.667D	240	259	-19	-0.5	2.5	3358	3488	-130	35	32	-3	-23	4	3.1	5.1	-1.9	22.4	22.2
BOSTON YANKS	4	7	1	.364	168	256	-88	-2.2	0.7	2719	4064	-1345	35	45	10	-72	-16	2.5	3.1	-0.6	17.0	25.2
WASHINGTON REDSKINS	4	8	0	.333	295	367	-72	-1.8	-0.2	4679	4033	646	39	29	-10	14	-86	6.7	6.2	0.6	28.9	27.8
NEW YORK GIANTS	2	8	2	.200	190	309	-119	-3.0	-0.0	3201	3908	-707	42	39	-3	-71	-48	3.4	3.6	-0.2	18.5	24.9

WESTERN DIVISION	W	L	T	PCT	PTS	OPP	NET	P-W	D-W	Y-O	Y-D	Y-N	T-O	T-D	T-N	P-NP	D-NP	PR-O	PR-D	PR-N	YD-O	YD-D
CHICAGO CARDINALS	9	3	0	.750L*	306	231	75	1.9	1.1	4351	3971	380	41	45	4	48	27	4.8	3.7	1.1	28.3	25.8
CHICAGO BEARS	8	4	0	.667	363	241	122	3.1	-1.0	5053	3879	1174	58	47	-11	54	68	4.8	4.2	0.6	30.8	24.9
GREEN BAY PACKERS	6	5	1	.545	274	210	64	1.6	-1.1	3873	3396	477	32	51	19	116	-52	4.1	2.1	2.0	23.9	20.3
LOS ANGELES RAMS	6	6	0	.500	259	214	45	1.1	-1.1	3831	3659	172	48	48	0	14	31	1.8	3.7	-1.8	23.1	20.7
DETROIT LIONS	3	9	0	.250	231	305	-74	-1.9	-1.1	3771	4429	-658	52	43	-9	-91	17	3.3	4.9	-1.6	23.4	26.8

1947 A.A.F.C

EASTERN DIVISION	W	L	T	PCT	PTS	OPP	NET	P-W	D-W	Y-O	Y-D	Y-N	T-O	T-D	T-N	P-NP	D-NP	PR-O	PR-D	PR-N	YD-O	YD-D
NEW YORK YANKEES	11	2	1	.846L	378	239	139	3.5	1.0	4725	3147	1578	35	29	-6	108	31	5.3	4.3	1.0	29.3	20.0
BUFFALO BISONS	8	4	2	.667	320	288	32	0.8	1.2	4108	4147	-39	40	32	-8	-35	67	4.1	4.8	-0.7	26.5	26.9
BROOKLYN DODGERS	3	10	1	.231	181	340	-159	-4.0	0.5	2996	4646	-1650	30	36	6	-114	-45	1.4	6.1	-4.7	18.7	28.0
BALTIMORE COLTS	2	11	1	.154	167	377	-210	-5.3	0.8	3498	4456	-958	47	39	-8	-112	-98	3.9	5.6	-1.6	20.9	27.0

WESTERN DIVISION	W	L	T	PCT	PTS	OPP	NET	P-W	D-W	Y-O	Y-D	Y-N	T-O	T-D	T-N	P-NP	D-NP	PR-O	PR-D	PR-N	YD-O	YD-D
CLEVELAND BROWNS	12	1	1	.923L*	410	185	225	5.6	-0.1	5547	3888	1659	28	51	23	230	-5	9.2	1.2	7.9	36.5	23.9
SAN FRANCISCO 49ERS	8	4	2	.667	327	264	63	1.6	0.4	4760	4133	627	37	45	8	84	-21	4.6	5.0	-0.4	29.6	27.2
LOS ANGELES DONS	7	7	0	.500	328	256	72	1.8	-1.8	3907	4044	-137	39	37	-2	-19	91	4.0	5.0	-1.0	23.3	23.8
CHICAGO ROCKETS	1	13	0	.071	263	425	-162	-4.1	-1.9	3878	4958	-1080	52	39	-13	-142	-20	4.2	5.4	-1.2	22.2	28.8

1948 N.F.L.

EASTERN DIVISION	W	L	T	PCT	PTS	OPP	NET	P-W	D-W	Y-O	Y-D	Y-N	T-O	T-D	T-N	P-NP	D-NP	PR-O	PR-D	PR-N	YD-O	YD-D
PHILADELPHIA EAGLES	9	2	1	.818L*	376	156	220	5.5	-2.0	4651	3169	1482	34	39	5	144	76	6.0	3.1	2.8	29.1	18.6
WASHINGTON REDSKINS	7	5	0	.583	291	287	4	0.1	0.9	4479	3933	546	43	42	-1	42	-38	5.4	3.7	1.7	29.9	26.6
NEW YORK GIANTS	4	8	0	.333	297	388	-91	-2.3	-0.3	3847	4673	-826	36	50	14	-13	-78	5.6	2.9	2.7	22.0	27.3
PITTSBURGH STEELERS	4	8	0	.333	200	243	-43	-1.1	-0.9	3478	3707	-229	46	31	-15	-79	36	1.1	5.7	-4.5	22.9	24.4
BOSTON YANKS	3	9	0	.250	174	372	-198	-4.9	1.9	2522	4858	-2336	54	42	-12	-243	45	-0.4	5.4	-5.8	14.1	26.5

WESTERN DIVISION	W	L	T	PCT	PTS	OPP	NET	P-W	D-W	Y-O	Y-D	Y-N	T-O	T-D	T-N	P-NP	D-NP	PR-O	PR-D	PR-N	YD-O	YD-D
CHICAGO CARDINALS	11	1	0	.917L	395	226	169	4.2	0.8	4705	4058	647	28	47	19	130	39	6.4	5.1	1.3	28.0	23.3
CHICAGO BEARS	10	2	0	.833	375	151	224	5.6	-1.6	4405	2931	1474	40	46	6	147	77	4.4	1.2	3.1	27.0	16.7
LOS ANGELES RAMS	6	5	1	.545	327	269	58	1.5	-1.0	4576	3794	782	42	43	1	69	-11	4.8	4.8	0.0	26.3	22.7
GREEN BAY PACKERS	3	9	0	.250	154	290	-136	-3.4	0.4	3135	3848	-713	48	44	-4	-75	-61	0.5	1.7	-1.2	18.1	22.9
DETROIT LIONS	2	10	0	.167	200	407	-207	-5.2	1.2	3735	4562	-827	46	33	-13	-121	-86	4.1	5.9	-1.9	22.2	29.8

1948 A.A.F.C

EASTERN DIVISION	W	L	T	PCT	PTS	OPP	NET	P-W	D-W	Y-O	Y-D	Y-N	T-O	T-D	T-N	P-NP	D-NP	PR-O	PR-D	PR-N	YD-O	YD-D
BUFFALO BISONS	7	7	0	.500L	360	358	2	0.1	-0.1	5421	4812	609	39	40	1	55	-53	4.7	5.9	-1.2	31.2	29.2
BALTIMORE COLTS	7	7	0	.500	333	327	6	0.2	-0.2	5065	4960	105	34	36	2	17	-11	7.4	4.5	2.9	31.9	29.3
NEW YORK YANKEES	6	8	0	.429	265	301	-36	-0.9	-0.1	3943	4782	-839	39	43	4	-54	18	3.3	5.1	-1.8	23.6	28.6
BROOKLYN DODGERS	2	12	0	.143	253	387	-134	-3.3	-1.7	4311	5131	-820	47	42	-5	-88	-46	3.1	3.7	-0.6	26.1	31.9

WESTERN DIVISION	W	L	T	PCT	PTS	OPP	NET	P-W	D-W	Y-O	Y-D	Y-N	T-O	T-D	T-N	P-NP	D-NP	PR-O	PR-D	PR-N	YD-O	YD-D
CLEVELAND BROWNS	14	0	0	1.000L*	389	190	199	5.0	2.0	5366	3616	1750	27	40	13	198	1	6.8	3.3	3.6	34.8	22.3
SAN FRANCISCO 49ERS	12	2	0	.857	495	248	247	6.2	-1.2	5767	4521	1246	35	52	17	172	75	6.2	3.8	2.4	34.5	27.6
LOS ANGELES DONS	7	7	0	.500	258	305	-47	-1.2	1.2	4051	4929	-878	40	40	0	-73	26	4.0	4.7	-0.7	24.0	28.5
CHICAGO ROCKETS	1	13	0	.071	202	439	-237	-5.9	-0.1	4009	5182	-1173	65	33	-32	-226	-11	2.3	6.1	-3.9	23.6	31.6

1949 N.F.L.

EASTERN DIVISION	W	L	T	PCT	PTS	OPP	NET	P-W	D-W	Y-O	Y-D	Y-N	T-O	T-D	T-N	P-NP	D-NP	PR-O	PR-D	PR-N	YD-O	YD-D
PHILADELPHIA EAGLES	11	1	0	.917*	364	134	230	5.8	-0.8	4448	2472	1976	26	43	17	233	-3	5.2	0.2	5.1	28.7	16.2
PITTSBURGH STEELERS	6	5	1	.545	224	214	10	0.3	0.3	3437	3759	-322	27	31	4	-11	21	2.2	2.8	-0.6	23.7	25.2
NEW YORK GIANTS	6	6	0	.500	287	298	-11	-0.3	0.3	3373	3928	-555	33	40	7	-18	7	3.0	3.5	-0.5	20.7	24.4
WASHINGTON REDSKINS	4	7	1	.364	268	339	-71	-1.8	0.3	4110	4533	-423	42	31	-11	-79	8	3.4	4.7	-1.4	26.2	28.3
NEW YORK BULLDOGS	1	10	1	.091	153	368	-215	-5.4	0.9	2878	4430	-1552	45	28	-17	-197	-18	1.8	5.4	-3.5	18.1	27.9

WESTERN DIVISION	W	L	T	PCT	PTS	OPP	NET	P-W	D-W	Y-O	Y-D	Y-N	T-O	T-D	T-N	P-NP	D-NP	PR-O	PR-D	PR-N	YD-O	YD-D
LOS ANGELES RAMS	8	2	2	.800L	360	239	121	3.0	-0.0	4415	3549	866	45	48	3	84	37	4.4	1.7	2.7	26.3	21.1
CHICAGO BEARS	9	3	0	.750	332	218	114	2.8	0.2	4748	3196	1552	48	43	-5	109	5	4.5	2.8	1.7	29.1	19.1
CHICAGO CARDINALS	6	5	1	.545	360	301	59	1.5	-1.0	3747	4296	-549	42	54	12	2	57	1.9	2.7	-0.8	21.5	24.8
DETROIT LIONS	4	8	0	.333	237	259	-22	-0.6	-1.5	3350	3462	-112	49	49	0	-9	-13	2.0	0.9	1.1	20.3	21.2
GREEN BAY PACKERS	2	10	0	.167	114	329	-215	-5.4	1.4	3119	3999	-880	45	35	-10	-113	-102	-0.6	3.5	-4.1	17.5	23.0

1949 A.A.F.C

	W	L	T	PCT	PTS	OPP	NET	P-W	D-W	Y-O	Y-D	Y-N	T-O	T-D	T-N	P-NP	D-NP	PR-O	PR-D	PR-N	YD-O	YD-D
CLEVELAND BROWNS	9	1	2	.900PL*	339	171	168	4.2	−0.2	4611	3582	1029	33	42	9	122	46	8.8	1.5	7.3	31.8	23.0
SAN FRANCISCO 49ERS	9	3	0	.750PL	416	227	189	4.7	−1.7	4793	3313	1480	42	47	5	143	46	4.8	2.1	2.7	28.5	21.0
NEW YORK YANKEES	8	4	0	.667P	196	206	−10	−0.3		2.3	3175	3323	−148	42	41	−1	−16	6	0.5	3.9	−3.5	19.7	20.9
BUFFALO BISONS	5	5	2	.500P	236	256	−20	−0.5	0.5	3920	3725	195	34	31	−3	4	−24	4.8	6.7	−1.9	26.7	26.0
CHICAGO HORNETS	4	8	0	.333	179	268	−89	−2.2	0.2	3089	4041	−952	47	52	5	−59	−30	2.9	5.8	−2.9	19.4	25.1
LOS ANGELES DONS	4	8	0	.333	253	322	−69	−1.7	−0.3	3566	4562	−996	40	38	−2	−91	22	2.7	5.8	−3.1	23.5	29.8
BALTIMORE COLTS	1	11	0	.083	172	341	−169	−4.2	−0.8	3639	4247	−608	43	30	−13	−103	−66	4.6	5.6	−1.0	25.3	29.1

1950 N.F.L.

AMERICAN CONFERENCE	W	L	T	PCT	PTS	OPP	NET	P-W	D-W	Y-O	Y-D	Y-N	T-O	T-D	T-N	P-NP	D-NP	PR-O	PR-D	PR-N	YD-O	YD-D
CLEVELAND BROWNS	10	2	0	.833CL*	310	144	166	4.2	−0.2	3768	2963	805	33	55	22	155	11	3.0	0.2	2.7	23.5	18.0
NEW YORK GIANTS	10	2	0	.833	268	150	118	3.0	1.0	3407	2969	438	30	54	24	133	−15	3.4	1.5	1.9	20.4	18.2
PHILADELPHIA EAGLES	6	6	0	.500	254	141	113	2.8	−2.8	4014	3049	965	43	48	5	100	13	1.9	0.5	1.4	24.2	19.1
PITTSBURGH STEELERS	6	6	0	.500	180	195	−15	−0.4	0.4	3305	3321	−16	58	38	−20	−81	66	1.7	1.6	0.1	21.5	20.5
CHICAGO CARDINALS	5	7	0	.417	233	287	−54	−1.4	0.4	3588	4040	−452	45	46	1	−34	−20	1.9	3.6	−1.7	21.7	23.8
WASHINGTON REDSKINS	3	9	0	.250	232	326	−94	−2.3	−0.7	3758	4004	−246	47	31	−16	−85	−9	3.2	3.9	−0.8	23.6	25.3

NATIONAL CONFERENCE	W	L	T	PCT	PTS	OPP	NET	P-W	D-W	Y-O	Y-D	Y-N	T-O	T-D	T-N	P-NP	D-NP	PR-O	PR-D	PR-N	YD-O	YD-D
LOS ANGELES RAMS	9	3	0	.750CL	466	309	157	3.9	−0.9	5240	4161	1079	44	46	2	98	59	5.5	2.7	2.8	29.1	21.8
CHICAGO BEARS	9	3	0	.750C	279	207	72	1.8	1.2	4095	3357	738	41	32	−9	26	46	2.4	3.3	−0.8	25.0	19.9
NEW YORK YANKEES	7	5	0	.583	366	367	−1	−0.0	1.0	4485	4968	−483	39	44	5	−20	19	4.6	3.1	1.5	25.8	27.6
DETROIT LIONS	6	6	0	.500	321	285	36	0.9	−0.9	4030	3677	353	47	55	8	61	−25	2.9	2.8	0.2	21.8	20.2
GREEN BAY PACKERS	3	9	0	.250	244	406	−162	−4.1	1.1	3210	4473	−1263	57	42	−15	−165	3	−0.1	4.0	−4.0	17.0	23.8
SAN FRANCISCO 49ERS	3	9	0	.250	213	300	−87	−2.2	−0.8	3505	3703	−198	46	43	−3	−29	−58	1.5	3.2	−1.7	21.1	24.4
BALTIMORE COLTS	1	11	0	.083	213	462	−249	−6.2	1.2	3526	5246	−1720	52	48	−4	−159	−90	2.4	3.6	−1.3	18.9	29.8

1951 N.F.L.

AMERICAN CONFERENCE	W	L	T	PCT	PTS	OPP	NET	P-W	D-W	Y-O	Y-D	Y-N	T-O	T-D	T-N	P-NP	D-NP	PR-O	PR-D	PR-N	YD-O	YD-D
CLEVELAND BROWNS	11	1	0	.917L	331	152	179	4.5	0.5	3610	3002	608	36	51	15	111	68	4.2	1.7	2.4	22.4	16.6
NEW YORK GIANTS	9	2	1	.818	254	161	93	2.3	1.2	2900	2974	−74	39	53	14	50	43	0.5	0.8	−0.3	16.1	16.5
WASHINGTON REDSKINS	5	7	0	.417	183	296	−113	−2.8	1.8	3555	4050	−495	43	33	−10	−81	−32	1.5	4.2	−2.7	24.2	28.3
PITTSBURGH STEELERS	4	7	1	.364	183	235	−52	−1.3	−0.2	2952	3345	−393	43	46	3	−21	−31	1.2	0.9	0.3	17.3	20.0
PHILADELPHIA EAGLES	4	8	0	.333	234	264	−30	−0.8	−1.3	3052	3294	−242	47	37	−10	−60	30	1.1	2.6	−1.5	18.3	19.0
CHICAGO CARDINALS	3	9	0	.250	210	287	−77	−1.9	−1.1	3847	3753	94	44	43	−1	4	−81	2.5	2.6	−0.1	23.2	23.5

NATIONAL CONFERENCE	W	L	T	PCT	PTS	OPP	NET	P-W	D-W	Y-O	Y-D	Y-N	T-O	T-D	T-N	P-NP	D-NP	PR-O	PR-D	PR-N	YD-O	YD-D
LOS ANGELES RAMS	8	4	0	.667L*	392	261	131	3.3	−1.3	5409	3879	1530	37	29	−8	96	35	6.4	2.6	3.8	34.5	22.8
DETROIT LIONS	7	4	1	.636	336	259	77	1.9	−0.4	4188	3864	324	33	31	−2	19	58	4.2	4.6	−0.4	28.5	24.3
SAN FRANCISCO 49ERS	7	4	1	.636	255	205	50	1.3	0.3	4013	3650	363	39	42	3	42	8	2.9	2.0	0.9	24.2	24.2
CHICAGO BEARS	7	5	0	.583	286	282	4	0.1	0.9	4364	4046	318	35	42	7	55	−51	3.4	3.6	−0.2	27.4	25.3
GREEN BAY PACKERS	3	9	0	.250	254	375	−121	−3.0	0.0	3753	4470	−717	44	35	−9	−96	−25	2.9	4.6	−1.7	21.9	29.0
NEW YORK YANKEES	1	9	2	.100	241	382	−141	−3.5	−0.5	3675	4991	−1316	36	34	−2	−118	−23	2.8	4.9	−2.1	21.1	29.7

1952 N.F.L.

AMERICAN CONFERENCE	W	L	T	PCT	PTS	OPP	NET	P-W	D-W	Y-O	Y-D	Y-N	T-O	T-D	T-N	P-NP	D-NP	PR-O	PR-D	PR-N	YD-O	YD-D
CLEVELAND BROWNS	8	4	0	.667L	310	213	97	2.4	−0.4	4352	3075	1277	37	36	−1	102	−5	4.0	2.2	1.7	26.4	17.8
NEW YORK GIANTS	7	5	0	.583	234	231	3	0.1	0.9	3028	3481	−453	36	45	9	−2	5	1.8	2.9	−1.1	16.5	20.4
PHILADELPHIA EAGLES	7	5	0	.583	252	271	−19	−0.5	1.5	3335	3150	185	41	39	−2	7	−26	3.1	2.6	0.5	18.1	17.3
PITTSBURGH STEELERS	5	7	0	.417	300	273	27	0.7	−1.7	3395	4289	−894	37	40	3	−63	90	3.4	4.0	−0.6	19.5	24.2
CHICAGO CARDINALS	4	8	0	.333	172	221	−49	−1.2	−0.8	2959	3353	−394	45	43	−2	−41	−8	1.0	2.4	−1.4	17.6	19.8
WASHINGTON REDSKINS	4	8	0	.333	240	287	−47	−1.2	−0.8	3395	3397	−2	38	34	−4	−16	−31	3.0	2.9	0.1	21.9	21.8

NATIONAL CONFERENCE	W	L	T	PCT	PTS	OPP	NET	P-W	D-W	Y-O	Y-D	Y-N	T-O	T-D	T-N	P-NP	D-NP	PR-O	PR-D	PR-N	YD-O	YD-D
DETROIT LIONS	9	3	0	.750CL*	344	192	152	3.8	−0.8	3988	3245	743	38	57	19	138	14	3.0	1.9	1.1	22.7	17.8
LOS ANGELES RAMS	9	3	0	.750C	349	234	115	2.9	0.1	4103	3496	607	48	56	8	83	32	3.1	0.9	2.2	23.6	19.6
SAN FRANCISCO 49ERS	7	5	0	.583	285	221	64	1.6	−0.6	3880	3204	676	36	35	−1	52	12	2.9	2.7	0.2	23.1	19.9
GREEN BAY PACKERS	6	6	0	.500	295	312	−17	−0.4	0.4	3859	3269	590	56	41	−15	−11	−6	4.0	2.4	1.6	21.4	17.5
CHICAGO BEARS	5	7	0	.417	245	326	−81	−2.0	1.0	3278	4012	−734	51	46	−5	−81	0	1.8	3.9	−2.1	17.8	21.8
DALLAS TEXANS	1	11	0	.083	182	427	−245	−6.1	1.1	2781	4382	−1601	55	46	−9	−169	−76	0.4	3.1	−2.7	15.1	24.9

1953 N.F.L.

EASTERN CONFERENCE	W	L	T	PCT	PTS	OPP	NET	P-W	D-W	Y-O	Y-D	Y-N	T-O	T-D	T-N	P-NP	D-NP	PR-O	PR-D	PR-N	YD-O	YD-D
CLEVELAND BROWNS	11	1	0	.917L	348	162	186	4.7	0.3	4391	3575	816	24	41	17	136	50	7.7	2.4	5.3	28.1	22.5
PHILADELPHIA EAGLES	7	4	1	.636	352	215	137	3.4	-1.9	4811	2998	1813	46	41	-5	131	6	4.1	2.3	1.8	28.1	17.7
WASHINGTON REDSKINS	6	5	1	.545	208	215	-7	-0.2	0.7	3234	3638	-404	47	44	-3	-46	39	1.1	1.6	-0.6	21.0	21.7
PITTSBURGH STEELERS	6	6	0	.500	211	263	-52	-1.3	1.3	3399	3381	18	35	35	0	2	-54	2.3	3.9	-1.6	19.3	20.7
NEW YORK GIANTS	3	9	0	.250	179	277	-98	-2.5	-0.5	2760	3741	-981	43	37	-6	-106	8	0.9	4.0	-3.1	16.2	21.6
CHICAGO CARDINALS	1	10	1	.091	190	337	-147	-3.7	-0.8	3042	4026	-984	48	36	-12	-130	-17	1.8	3.9	-2.1	17.5	22.6

WESTERN CONFERENCE	W	L	T	PCT	PTS	OPP	NET	P-W	D-W	Y-O	Y-D	Y-N	T-O	T-D	T-N	P-NP	D-NP	PR-O	PR-D	PR-N	YD-O	YD-D
DETROIT LIONS	10	2	0	.833L*	271	205	66	1.6	2.3	3958	3545	413	42	53	11	78	-12	3.3	1.0	2.3	23.7	20.6
SAN FRANCISCO 49ERS	9	3	0	.750	372	237	135	3.4	-0.4	4398	3425	973	38	40	2	89	46	4.4	2.6	1.7	28.9	22.4
LOS ANGELES RAMS	8	3	1	.727	366	236	130	3.3	-0.8	4713	3452	1261	40	43	3	117	13	5.8	1.7	4.1	26.6	19.3
CHICAGO BEARS	3	8	1	.273	218	262	-44	-1.1	-1.4	3628	4152	-524	51	37	-14	-100	56	2.8	4.9	-2.1	20.3	24.1
BALTIMORE COLTS	3	9	0	.250	182	350	-168	-4.2	1.2	2716	4486	-1770	48	56	8	-116	-52	0.5	3.1	-2.6	15.1	25.1
GREEN BAY PACKERS	2	9	1	.182	200	338	-138	-3.5	-0.0	3220	3851	-631	48	47	-1	-57	-81	0.3	2.9	-2.6	17.5	22.0

1954 N.F.L.

EASTERN CONFERENCE	W	L	T	PCT	PTS	OPP	NET	P-W	D-W	Y-O	Y-D	Y-N	T-O	T-D	T-N	P-NP	D-NP	PR-O	PR-D	PR-N	YD-O	YD-D
CLEVELAND BROWNS	9	3	0	.750L*	336	162	174	4.3	-1.3	4124	2658	1466	39	42	3	134	40	4.6	2.2	2.3	25.3	16.3
PHILADELPHIA EAGLES	7	4	1	.636	284	230	54	1.4	0.1	3803	2747	1056	52	50	-2	80	-26	3.5	1.4	2.1	20.7	15.2
NEW YORK GIANTS	7	5	0	.583	293	184	109	2.7	-1.7	3808	3348	460	37	55	18	110	-1	4.6	1.6	2.9	22.3	19.8
PITTSBURGH STEELERS	5	7	0	.417	219	263	-44	-1.1	0.1	3455	4370	-915	43	50	7	-48	4	2.8	3.1	-0.2	21.3	27.8
WASHINGTON REDSKINS	3	9	0	.250	207	432	-225	-5.6	2.6	3120	4793	-1673	55	36	-19	-215	-10	0.7	6.0	-5.3	19.6	29.6
CHICAGO CARDINALS	2	10	0	.167	183	347	-164	-4.1	0.1	3274	4326	-1052	53	43	-10	-128	-36	1.0	5.2	-4.2	19.8	26.4

WESTERN CONFERENCE	W	L	T	PCT	PTS	OPP	NET	P-W	D-W	Y-O	Y-D	Y-N	T-O	T-D	T-N	P-NP	D-NP	PR-O	PR-D	PR-N	YD-O	YD-D
DETROIT LIONS	9	2	1	.818L	337	189	148	3.7	-0.2	4433	3746	687	32	42	10	97	51	5.2	2.6	2.6	28.8	22.4
CHICAGO BEARS	8	4	0	.667	301	279	22	0.6	1.5	4246	4105	141	50	45	-5	-8	30	3.9	2.8	1.2	24.0	23.7
SAN FRANCISCO 49ERS	7	4	1	.636	313	251	62	1.5	-0.0	4704	4020	684	25	37	12	105	-43	4.8	4.8	-0.1	30.7	26.4
LOS ANGELES RAMS	6	5	1	.545	314	285	29	0.7	-0.2	5187	4182	1005	41	29	-12	36	-7	6.4	4.1	2.3	33.9	28.3
GREEN BAY PACKERS	4	8	0	.333	234	251	-17	-0.4	-1.6	3487	4350	-863	31	33	2	-64	47	3.2	4.5	-1.3	23.2	28.2
BALTIMORE COLTS	3	9	0	.250	131	279	-148	-3.7	0.7	2934	3930	-996	34	30	-4	-99	-49	2.1	4.3	-2.1	19.8	26.4

1955 N.F.L.

EASTERN CONFERENCE	W	L	T	PCT	PTS	OPP	NET	P-W	D-W	Y-O	Y-D	Y-N	T-O	T-D	T-N	P-NP	D-NP	PR-O	PR-D	PR-N	YD-O	YD-D
CLEVELAND BROWNS	9	2	1	.818L*	349	218	131	3.3	0.2	3970	2841	1129	29	40	11	138	-7	6.2	2.0	4.2	24.8	17.6
WASHINGTON REDSKINS	8	4	0	.667	246	222	24	0.6	1.4	3348	3190	158	42	43	1	17	7	1.8	3.3	-1.5	20.8	19.5
NEW YORK GIANTS	6	5	1	.545	267	223	44	1.1	-0.6	3453	3808	-355	31	39	8	2	42	4.1	3.8	0.3	21.6	23.7
CHICAGO CARDINALS	4	7	1	.364	224	252	-28	-0.7	-0.8	2971	3910	-939	45	47	2	-70	42	1.2	2.2	-1.0	17.0	22.2
PHILADELPHIA EAGLES	4	7	1	.364	248	231	17	0.4	-1.9	3789	3231	558	45	36	-9	11	6	3.7	3.3	0.4	22.7	19.1
PITTSBURGH STEELERS	4	8	0	.333	195	285	-90	-2.3	0.3	3671	3109	562	47	29	-18	-25	-65	2.8	3.8	-1.0	20.9	18.4

WESTERN CONFERENCE	W	L	T	PCT	PTS	OPP	NET	P-W	D-W	Y-O	Y-D	Y-N	T-O	T-D	T-N	P-NP	D-NP	PR-O	PR-D	PR-N	YD-O	YD-D
LOS ANGELES RAMS	8	3	1	.727L	260	231	29	0.7	1.8	4004	3933	71	28	46	18	78	-49	3.7	2.9	0.8	26.0	24.9
CHICAGO BEARS	8	4	0	.667	294	251	43	1.1	0.9	4316	4157	159	41	34	-7	-15	58	3.2	3.4	-0.2	26.8	26.3
GREEN BAY PACKERS	6	6	0	.500	258	276	-18	-0.4	0.4	3662	3862	-200	44	49	5	3	-21	2.9	1.6	1.3	22.9	24.1
BALTIMORE COLTS	5	6	1	.455	214	239	-25	-0.6	0.1	3464	4122	-658	30	33	3	-43	18	2.6	3.9	-1.3	24.9	28.8
SAN FRANCISCO 49ERS	4	8	0	.333	216	298	-82	-2.1	0.0	3651	4008	-357	46	34	-12	-78	-4	2.5	3.1	-0.6	22.8	25.5
DETROIT LIONS	3	9	0	.250	230	275	-45	-1.1	-1.9	3887	4015	-128	41	39	-2	-26		3.8	5.2	-1.4	23.7	24.9

1956 N.F.L.

EASTERN CONFERENCE	W	L	T	PCT	PTS	OPP	NET	P-W	D-W	Y-O	Y-D	Y-N	T-O	T-D	T-N	P-NP	D-NP	PR-O	PR-D	PR-N	YD-O	YD-D
NEW YORK GIANTS	8	3	1	.727L*	264	197	67	1.7	0.8	3696	3081	615	27	33	6	75	-8	4.0	3.0	0.9	25.8	21.4
CHICAGO CARDINALS	7	5	0	.583	240	182	58	1.5	-0.5	3422	3599	-177	35	45	10	25	33	3.8	0.4	3.4	23.9	24.3
WASHINGTON REDSKINS	6	6	0	.500	183	225	-42	-1.0	1.0	2961	3199	-238	35	34	-1	-24	-18	2.3	3.7	-1.4	20.3	21.5
CLEVELAND BROWNS	5	7	0	.417	167	177	-10	-0.3	-0.8	3020	3135	-115	30	26	-4	-26	16	2.0	1.5	0.5	23.4	24.0
PITTSBURGH STEELERS	5	7	0	.417	217	250	-33	-0.8	-0.2	3016	3186	-170	34	40	6	10	-43	2.4	3.0	-0.8	18.9	20.4
PHILADELPHIA EAGLES	3	8	1	.273	143	215	-72	-1.8	-0.7	2654	3226	-572	38	27	-11	-92	20	0.4	2.9	-2.4	18.1	22.4

WESTERN CONFERENCE	W	L	T	PCT	PTS	OPP	NET	P-W	D-W	Y-O	Y-D	Y-N	T-O	T-D	T-N	P-NP	D-NP	PR-O	PR-D	PR-N	YD-O	YD-D
CHICAGO BEARS	9	2	1	.818L	363	246	117	2.9	0.6	4537	3676	861	29	38	9	108	9	5.3	3.7	1.6	28.4	23.9
DETROIT LIONS	9	3	0	.750	300	188	112	2.8	0.2	4206	3408	798	34	40	6	91	21	4.2	2.4	1.8	28.4	22.3
SAN FRANCISCO 49ERS	5	6	1	.455	233	284	-51	-1.3	0.8	3813	4162	-349	31	34	3	-17	-34	3.6	4.5	-0.9	27.0	27.8
BALTIMORE COLTS	5	7	0	.417	270	322	-52	-1.3	0.3	4123	4176	-53	32	28	-4	-20	-32	4.0	5.9	-1.9	27.1	27.8
GREEN BAY PACKERS	4	8	0	.333	264	342	-78	-2.0	-0.0	3819	4710	-891	29	27	-2	-82	4	4.8	5.2	-0.5	26.3	33.6
LOS ANGELES RAMS	4	8	0	.333	291	307	-16	-0.4	-1.6	4397	4106	291	46	28	-18	-48	32	3.8	4.5	-0.7	29.1	26.2

1957 N.F.L.

EASTERN CONFERENCE	W	L	T	PCT	PTS	OPP	NET	P-W	D-W	Y-O	Y-D	Y-N	T-O	T-D	T-N	P-NP	D-NP	PR-O	PR-D	PR-N	YD-O	YD-D
CLEVELAND BROWNS	9	2	1	.818L	269	172	97	2.4	1.1	3670	2802	868	24	31	7	100	−3	5.6	2.0	3.6	25.3	19.3
NEW YORK GIANTS	7	5	0	.583	254	211	43	1.1	−0.1	3749	3171	578	32	32	0	48	−5	6.2	3.5	26.8	21.4
PITTSBURGH STEELERS	6	6	0	.500	161	178	−17	−0.4	0.4	2890	2791	99	32	42	10	48	−65	3.4	2.5	0.9	19.1	18.0
WASHINGTON REDSKINS	5	6	1	.455	251	230	21	0.5	−1.0	3494	3595	−101	30	28	−2	−16	37	5.3	5.3	0.0	25.5	25.9
PHILADELPHIA EAGLES	4	8	0	.333	173	230	−57	−1.4	−0.6	2737	3683	−946	39	36	−3	−91	34	0.9	4.8	−3.9	17.5	24.9
CHICAGO CARDINALS	3	9	0	.250	200	299	−99	−2.5	−0.5	3217	4108	−891	37	25	−12	−122	23	3.1	6.2	−3.1	21.3	28.1

WESTERN CONFERENCE	W	L	T	PCT	PTS	OPP	NET	P-W	D-W	Y-O	Y-D	Y-N	T-O	T-D	T-N	P-NP	D-NP	PR-O	PR-D	PR-N	YD-O	YD-D
DETROIT LIONS	8	4	0	.667CL*	251	231	20	0.5	1.5	3840	3365	475	35	43	8	72	−52	3.1	2.7	0.4	25.6	22.3
SAN FRANCISCO 49ERS	8	4	0	.667C	260	264	−4	−0.1	2.1	3658	4248	−590	32	34	2	−41	37	4.0	4.8	−0.9	25.4	29.5
BALTIMORE COLTS	7	5	0	.583	303	235	68	1.7	−0.7	4123	3406	717	31	40	9	96	−28	5.2	3.0	2.2	26.9	22.4
LOS ANGELES RAMS	6	6	0	.500	307	278	29	0.7	−0.7	4143	3725	418	37	25	−12	−13	42	3.6	4.1	−0.5	27.3	23.6
CHICAGO BEARS	5	7	0	.417	203	211	−8	−0.2	−0.8	3454	3116	338	43	30	−13	−24	16	1.9	3.3	−1.4	21.6	19.4
GREEN BAY PACKERS	3	9	0	.250	218	311	−93	−2.3	−0.7	3232	4197	−965	41	47	6	−56	−37	2.4	2.6	−0.3	19.6	26.7

1958 N.F.L.

EASTERN CONFERENCE	W	L	T	PCT	PTS	OPP	NET	P-W	D-W	Y-O	Y-D	Y-N	T-O	T-D	T-N	P-NP	D-NP	PR-O	PR-D	PR-N	YD-O	YD-D
NEW YORK GIANTS	9	3	0	.750DL	246	183	63	1.6	1.4	3330	3418	−88	26	40	14	49	14	4.3	3.5	0.9	23.3	22.6
CLEVELAND BROWNS	9	3	0	.750D	302	217	85	2.1	0.9	4107	3660	447	22	34	12	85	0	4.7	5.1	−0.4	28.3	26.5
PITTSBURGH STEELERS	7	4	1	.636	261	230	31	0.8	0.7	4273	3383	890	42	42	0	74	−43	5.6	2.5	3.0	27.0	21.3
WASHINGTON REDSKINS	4	7	1	.364	214	268	−54	−1.4	−0.1	3673	4402	−729	33	38	5	−41	−13	3.7	6.9	−3.2	25.9	31.9
CHICAGO CARDINALS	2	9	1	.182	261	356	−95	−2.4	−1.1	4030	4760	−730	49	31	−18	−133	38	3.7	6.0	−2.2	24.9	29.0
PHILADELPHIA EAGLES	2	9	1	.182	235	306	−71	−1.8	−1.7	3790	4047	−257	43	27	−16	−85	14	4.7	5.5	−0.8	25.6	27.3

WESTERN CONFERENCE	W	L	T	PCT	PTS	OPP	NET	P-W	D-W	Y-O	Y-D	Y-N	T-O	T-D	T-N	P-NP	D-NP	PR-O	PR-D	PR-N	YD-O	YD-D
BALTIMORE COLTS	9	3	0	.750L*	381	203	178	4.4	−1.4	4539	3284	1255	22	52	30	225	−47	5.9	1.3	4.6	27.8	21.1
CHICAGO BEARS	8	4	0	.667	298	230	68	1.7	0.3	3581	3066	515	43	40	−3	31	37	2.6	2.5	0.2	20.9	18.1
LOS ANGELES RAMS	8	4	0	.667	344	278	66	1.6	0.4	4406	3828	578	49	41	−8	16	50	4.4	2.4	1.9	25.9	22.0
SAN FRANCISCO 49ERS	6	6	0	.500	257	324	−67	−1.7	1.7	4111	4010	101	40	31	−9	−28	−39	3.2	4.0	−0.8	28.4	27.1
DETROIT LIONS	4	7	1	.364	261	276	−15	−0.4	−1.1	3229	3837	−608	33	38	5	−31	16	4.1	3.8	0.3	21.0	24.9
GREEN BAY PACKERS	1	10	1	.091	193	382	−189	−4.7	−0.3	3241	4615	−1374	44	32	−12	−163	−26	2.0	6.4	−4.5	21.0	29.6

1959 N.F.L.

EASTERN CONFERENCE	W	L	T	PCT	PTS	OPP	NET	P-W	D-W	Y-O	Y-D	Y-N	T-O	T-D	T-N	P-NP	D-NP	PR-O	PR-D	PR-N	YD-O	YD-D
NEW YORK GIANTS	10	2	0	.833L	284	170	114	2.8	1.2	4173	2843	1330	33	38	5	131	−17	6.7	2.1	4.6	27.1	18.2
CLEVELAND BROWNS	7	5	0	.583	270	214	56	1.4	−0.4	4015	3764	251	14	30	16	85	−29	5.4	5.1	0.3	31.6	30.6
PHILADELPHIA EAGLES	7	5	0	.583	268	278	−10	−0.3	1.3	3887	3938	−51	25	40	15	56	−66	5.6	3.6	2.0	25.9	27.3
PITTSBURGH STEELERS	6	5	1	.545	257	216	41	1.0	−0.5	3595	3342	253	33	34	1	25	16	3.5	3.2	0.3	22.9	20.9
WASHINGTON REDSKINS	3	9	0	.250	185	350	−165	−4.1	1.1	3487	4644	−1157	40	27	−13	−148	−17	1.9	6.2	−4.3	24.9	33.2
CHICAGO CARDINALS	2	10	0	.167	234	324	−90	−2.3	1.8	3172	4015	−843	55	30	−25	−170	80	2.8	5.8	−3.0	19.0	24.5

WESTERN CONFERENCE	W	L	T	PCT	PTS	OPP	NET	P-W	D-W	Y-O	Y-D	Y-N	T-O	T-D	T-N	P-NP	D-NP	PR-O	PR-D	PR-N	YD-O	YD-D
BALTIMORE COLTS	9	3	0	.750L*	374	251	123	3.1	−0.1	4458	3899	559	23	49	26	151	−28	6.2	1.8	4.3	28.2	25.8
CHICAGO BEARS	8	4	0	.667	252	196	56	1.4	0.6	3511	3676	−165	31	39	8	18	38	4.5	2.9	1.6	23.4	23.4
GREEN BAY PACKERS	7	5	0	.583	248	246	2	0.1	0.9	3739	3552	187	33	29	−4	0	2	4.3	3.6	0.7	26.0	23.1
SAN FRANCISCO 49ERS	7	5	0	.583	255	237	18	0.4	0.6	3388	4018	−630	32	36	4	−37	55	2.4	4.2	−1.8	23.5	25.9
DETROIT LIONS	3	8	1	.273	203	275	−72	−1.8	−0.7	3456	3656	−200	46	33	−13	−69	−3	1.4	5.2	−3.8	20.9	23.4
LOS ANGELES RAMS	2	10	0	.167	242	315	−73	−1.8	−2.2	4260	3794	466	41	21	−20	−41	−32	4.2	6.2	−1.9	27.3	24.8

1960 N.F.L.

EASTERN CONFERENCE	W	L	T	PCT	PTS	OPP	NET	P-W	D-W	Y-O	Y-D	Y-N	T-O	T-D	T-N	P-NP	D-NP	PR-O	PR-D	PR-N	YD-O	YD-D
PHILADELPHIA EAGLES	10	2	0	.833L*	321	246	75	1.9	2.1	3950	4027	−77	30	45	15	54	21	6.3	2.0	4.3	25.6	25.8
CLEVELAND BROWNS	8	3	1	.727	362	217	145	3.6	−1.1	3974	3806	168	17	45	28	126	19	6.8	2.7	4.1	27.6	26.4
NEW YORK GIANTS	6	4	2	.600	271	261	10	0.3	0.8	3694	3100	594	49	34	−15	−11	21	4.2	3.2	1.0	22.8	19.0
ST. LOUIS CARDINALS	6	5	1	.545	288	230	58	1.5	−1.0	4167	3029	1138	47	44	−3	83	−25	2.9	3.1	−0.3	26.2	19.1
PITTSBURGH STEELERS	5	6	1	.455	240	275	−35	−0.9	0.4	4045	4284	−239	35	29	−6	−44	9	5.7	5.7	−0.1	28.1	28.2
WASHINGTON REDSKINS	1	9	2	.100	178	309	−131	−3.3	−0.7	2744	4066	−1322	38	34	−4	−126	−5	1.5	6.1	−4.6	17.5	27.8

WESTERN CONFERENCE	W	L	T	PCT	PTS	OPP	NET	P-W	D-W	Y-O	Y-D	Y-N	T-O	T-D	T-N	P-NP	D-NP	PR-O	PR-D	PR-N	YD-O	YD-D
GREEN BAY PACKERS	8	4	0	.667L	332	209	123	3.1	−1.1	4025	3442	583	25	37	12	97	26	4.7	3.4	1.3	27.2	23.1
DETROIT LIONS	7	5	0	.583	239	212	27	0.7	0.3	3392	3397	−5	30	30	0	0	27	2.1	3.6	−1.5	23.2	21.9
SAN FRANCISCO 49ERS	7	5	0	.583	208	205	3	0.1	0.9	3260	3405	−145	16	28	12	36	−33	3.1	3.3	−0.2	23.0	23.5
BALTIMORE COLTS	6	6	0	.500	288	234	54	1.4	−1.4	4245	3317	928	36	39	3	89	−35	5.1	1.3	3.8	27.2	21.8
CHICAGO BEARS	5	6	1	.455	194	299	−105	−2.6	−2.1	3465	3067	398	42	19	−23	−59	−46	1.4	3.1	−1.7	22.1	20.0
LOS ANGELES RAMS	4	7	1	.364	265	297	−32	−0.8	−0.7	3271	4073	−802	31	36	5	−47	15	2.7	4.2	−1.5	20.8	26.4
DALLAS COWBOYS	0	11	1	.000	177	369	−192	−4.8	−0.7	3153	4372	−1219	50	26	−24	−198	6	2.0	5.3	−3.3	20.5	28.8

1960 A.F.L.

EASTERN DIVISION	W	L	T	PCT	PTS	OPP	NET	P-W	D-W	Y-O	Y-D	Y-N	T-O	T-D	T-N	P-NP	D-NP	PR-O	PR-D	PR-N	YD-O	YD-D
HOUSTON OILERS	10	4	0	.714L*	379	285	94	2.3	0.7	4936	4901	35	45	51	6	27	67	5.3	5.4	-0.1	32.3	23.9
NEW YORK TITANS	7	7	0	.500	382	399	-17	-0.4	0.4	4794	4297	497	48	40	-8	9	-26	5.1	4.7	0.4	35.0	22.9
BUFFALO BILLS	5	8	1	.385	296	303	-7	-0.2	-1.3	3900	3854	46	44	49	5	24	-31	3.5	2.7	0.8	24.2	19.3
BOSTON PATRIOTS	5	9	0	.357	286	349	-63	-1.6	-0.4	4083	4471	-388	45	45	0	-32	-31	4.4	4.7	-0.3	20.5	24.0

WESTERN DIVISION	W	L	T	PCT	PTS	OPP	NET	P-W	D-W	Y-O	Y-D	Y-N	T-O	T-D	T-N	P-NP	D-NP	PR-O	PR-D	PR-N	YD-O	YD-D
LOS ANGELES CHAR-GERS	10	4	0	.714L	373	336	37	0.9	2.1	4713	4601	112	45	45	0	9	28	4.7	3.9	0.9	26.0	25.4
DALLAS TEXANS	8	6	0	.571	362	253	109	2.7	-1.7	4645	3982	663	37	48	11	99	10	4.9	3.5	1.4	25.1	21.8
OAKLAND RAIDERS	6	8	0	.429	319	388	-69	-1.7	0.7	4708	4983	-275	46	40	-6	-47	-22	4.0	5.3	-1.3	31.0	25.7
DENVER BRONCOS	4	9	1	.308	309	393	-84	-2.1	-0.4	4442	5132	-690	52	44	-8	-90	6	3.8	5.2	-1.5	30.4	26.6

1961 N.F.L.

EASTERN CONFERENCE	W	L	T	PCT	PTS	OPP	NET	P-W	D-W	Y-O	Y-D	Y-N	T-O	T-D	T-N	P-NP	D-NP	PR-O	PR-D	PR-N	YD-O	YD-D
NEW YORK GIANTS	10	3	1	.769L	368	220	148	3.7	-0.2	4597	3962	635	43	54	11	97	51	4.4	2.1	2.2	23.7	19.8
PHILADELPHIA EAGLES	10	4	0	.714	361	297	64	1.6	1.4	5112	4927	185	40	33	-7	-13	77	6.1	5.7	0.4	30.8	28.5
CLEVELAND BROWNS	8	5	1	.615	319	270	49	1.2	0.3	4537	4131	406	33	38	5	54	-5	5.8	4.5	1.3	28.2	26.7
ST. LOUIS CARDINALS	7	7	0	.500	279	267	12	0.3	-0.3	3378	3986	-608	41	44	3	-39	51	2.8	3.3	-0.5	18.2	21.2
PITTSBURGH STEELERS	6	8	0	.429	295	287	8	0.2	-1.2	4093	3909	184	56	45	-11	-29	37	2.8	3.3	-0.5	20.4	19.5
DALLAS COWBOYS	4	9	1	.308	236	380	-144	-3.6	1.1	4480	4592	-112	48	43	-5	-29	-115	3.7	4.3	-0.6	26.4	27.2
WASHINGTON REDSKINS	1	12	1	.077	174	392	-218	-5.4	-0.1	3247	4825	-1578	40	41	1	-128	-90	2.2	5.7	-3.5	17.8	28.7

WESTERN CONFERENCE	W	L	T	PCT	PTS	OPP	NET	P-W	D-W	Y-O	Y-D	Y-N	T-O	T-D	T-N	P-NP	D-NP	PR-O	PR-D	PR-N	YD-O	YD-D
GREEN BAY PACKERS	11	3	0	.786L*	391	223	168	4.2	-0.2	4714	4051	663	26	46	20	135	33	5.6	2.6	3.0	31.4	25.8
DETROIT LIONS	8	5	1	.615	270	258	12	0.3	1.2	4412	3938	474	42	41	-1	36	-24	3.4	2.9	0.5	24.8	23.0
BALTIMORE COLTS	8	6	0	.571	302	307	-5	-0.1	1.1	4922	3782	1140	42	24	-18	23	-28	3.6	3.4	0.2	31.2	22.9
CHICAGO BEARS	8	6	0	.571	326	302	24	0.6	0.4	4562	4449	113	38	37	-1	5	19	4.7	4.5	0.3	25.8	25.6
SAN FRANCISCO 49ERS	7	6	1	.538	346	272	74	1.9	-1.4	4904	4181	723	36	31	-5	40	34	5.6	4.2	1.3	30.5	24.7
LOS ANGELES RAMS	4	10	0	.286	263	333	-70	-1.8	-1.3	4295	4813	-518	32	39	7	-15	-55	3.5	4.2	-0.7	26.3	29.7
MINNESOTA VIKINGS	3	11	0	.214	285	407	-122	-3.1	-1.0	3886	5593	-1707	44	45	1	-138	16	2.7	5.6	-2.9	22.1	32.5

1961 A.F.L.

EASTERN DIVISION	W	L	T	PCT	PTS	OPP	NET	P-W	D-W	Y-O	Y-D	Y-N	T-O	T-D	T-N	P-NP	D-NP	PR-O	PR-D	PR-N	YD-O	YD-D
HOUSTON OILERS	10	3	1	.769L*	513	242	271	6.8	-3.3	6288	4025	2263	39	48	9	225	46	7.0	1.9	5.0	33.8	20.5
BOSTON PATRIOTS	9	4	1	.692	413	313	100	2.5	0.0	4214	4123	91	30	42	12	56	44	4.2	4.5	-0.4	23.0	22.8
NEW YORK TITANS	7	7	0	.500	301	390	-89	-2.2	2.2	4065	4677	-612	52	46	-6	-75	-14	2.3	3.9	-1.6	20.5	24.0
BUFFALO BILLS	6	8	0	.429	294	342	-48	-1.2	0.2	3950	4264	-314	42	44	2	-18	-30	2.7	4.0	-1.3	20.1	22.2

WESTERN DIVISION	W	L	T	PCT	PTS	OPP	NET	P-W	D-W	Y-O	Y-D	Y-N	T-O	T-D	T-N	P-NP	D-NP	PR-O	PR-D	PR-N	YD-O	YD-D
SAN DIEGO CHARGERS	12	2	0	.857L	396	219	177	4.4	0.6	4313	3720	593	44	66	22	137	40	4.2	0.6	3.6	22.3	19.5
DALLAS TEXANS	6	8	0	.429	334	343	-9	-0.2	-0.8	4759	4302	457	45	42	-3	26	-35	3.6	4.0	-0.4	26.3	24.0
DENVER BRONCOS	3	11	0	.214	251	432	-181	-4.5	0.5	3811	4418	-607	68	40	-28	-163	-18	1.5	4.1	-2.7	18.4	21.2
OAKLAND RAIDERS	2	12	0	.143	237	458	-221	-5.5	0.5	3285	5156	-1871	44	36	-8	-188	-33	2.1	4.5	-2.4	18.8	29.0

1962 N.F.L.

EASTERN CONFERENCE	W	L	T	PCT	PTS	OPP	NET	P-W	D-W	Y-O	Y-D	Y-N	T-O	T-D	T-N	P-NP	D-NP	PR-O	PR-D	PR-N	YD-O	YD-D
NEW YORK GIANTS	12	2	0	.857L	398	283	115	2.9	2.1	5005	4546	459	36	39	3	50	65	6.2	3.8	2.4	28.9	26.0
PITTSBURGH STEELERS	9	5	0	.643	312	363	-51	-1.3	3.3	4402	4625	-223	36	38	2	-11	-40	3.2	4.8	-1.6	25.3	25.7
CLEVELAND BROWNS	7	6	1	.538	291	257	34	0.9	-0.4	4306	3924	382	33	37	4	48	-14	5.0	2.8	2.2	29.1	25.8
WASHINGTON REDSKINS	5	7	2	.417	305	376	-71	-1.8	0.8	4311	5238	-927	44	48	4	-61	-10	4.9	6.1	-1.2	24.1	29.4
DALLAS COWBOYS	5	8	1	.385	398	402	-4	-0.1	-1.4	4912	5184	-272	36	36	0	-23	19	5.9	6.7	-0.8	26.7	29.1
ST. LOUIS CARDINALS	4	9	1	.308	287	361	-74	-1.9	-0.6	4798	4711	87	51	31	-20	-73	-1	4.1	6.0	-1.8	27.3	27.7
PHILADELPHIA EAGLES	3	10	1	.231	282	356	-74	-1.9	-1.6	4540	5046	-506	44	39	-5	-62	-12	4.8	5.1	-0.2	27.0	29.3

WESTERN CONFERENCE	W	L	T	PCT	PTS	OPP	NET	P-W	D-W	Y-O	Y-D	Y-N	T-O	T-D	T-N	P-NP	D-NP	PR-O	PR-D	PR-N	YD-O	YD-D
GREEN BAY PACKERS	13	1	0	.929L*	415	148	267	6.7	-0.7	4791	3277	1514	28	50	22	214	53	5.4	1.1	4.3	30.9	20.6
DETROIT LIONS	11	3	0	.786	315	177	138	3.5	0.5	4503	3217	1286	42	47	5	127	11	4.1	2.4	1.7	26.6	18.1
CHICAGO BEARS	9	5	0	.643	321	287	34	0.9	1.1	4549	4147	402	44	47	3	46	-12	4.4	2.9	1.5	23.7	22.1
BALTIMORE COLTS	7	7	0	.500	293	288	5	0.1	-0.1	4666	4123	543	44	42	-2	37	-32	4.8	4.2	0.7	26.4	23.4
SAN FRANCISCO 49ERS	6	8	0	.429	282	331	-49	-1.2	0.2	3941	4549	-608	33	26	-7	-79	30	3.7	6.1	-2.3	24.9	30.9
MINNESOTA VIKINGS	2	11	1	.154	254	410	-156	-3.9	-0.6	4080	5101	-1021	54	43	-11	-129	-27	2.6	5.4	-2.8	22.1	27.7
LOS ANGELES RAMS	1	12	1	.077	220	334	-114	-2.8	-2.7	3865	4981	-1116	35	37	2	-85	-29	3.5	5.6	-2.0	22.0	28.1

1962 A.F.L.

EASTERN DIVISION	W	L	T	PCT	PTS	OPP	NET	P-W	D-W	Y-O	Y-D	Y-N	T-O	T-D	T-N	P-NP	D-NP	PR-O	PR-D	PR-N	YD-O	YD-D
HOUSTON OILERS	11	3	0	.786L	387	270	117	2.9	1.1	4971	4130	841	57	52	-5	50	67	2.9	2.3	0.6	25.6	21.0
BOSTON PATRIOTS	9	4	1	.692	346	295	51	1.3	1.2	4736	4534	202	33	35	2	25	26	6.0	4.5	1.5	26.3	24.4
BUFFALO BILLS	7	6	1	.538	309	272	37	0.9	-0.4	4464	4429	35	38	50	12	51	-14	2.6	2.9	-0.3	24.8	24.1
NEW YORK TITANS	5	9	0	.357	278	423	-145	-3.6	1.6	3955	4655	-700	55	45	-10	-98	-47	2.4	3.5	-1.0	19.4	23.3

WESTERN DIVISION	W	L	T	PCT	PTS	OPP	NET	P-W	D-W	Y-O	Y-D	Y-N	T-O	T-D	T-N	P-NP	D-NP	PR-O	PR-D	PR-N	YD-O	YD-D
DALLAS TEXANS	11	3	0	.786L*	389	233	156	3.9	0.1	4862	3951	911	31	48	17	144	12	5.5	2.8	2.6	28.1	23.5
DENVER BRONCOS	7	7	0	.500	353	334	19	0.5	-0.5	4702	4538	164	54	46	-8	-18	37	3.1	3.8	-0.7	25.4	23.0
SAN DIEGO CHARGERS	4	10	0	.286	314	392	-78	-2.0	-1.0	4081	4518	-437	48	42	-6	-60	-18	2.6	3.6	-1.0	21.0	23.9
OAKLAND RAIDERS	1	13	0	.071	213	370	-157	-3.9	-2.1	3687	4703	-1016	49	47	-2	-93	-64	2.2	3.1	-0.8	18.4	24.9

1963 N.F.L.

EASTERN CONFERENCE	W	L	T	PCT	PTS	OPP	NET	P-W	D-W	Y-O	Y-D	Y-N	T-O	T-D	T-N	P-NP	D-NP	PR-O	PR-D	PR-N	YD-O	YD-D
NEW YORK GIANTS	11	3	0	.786L	448	280	168	4.2	-0.2	5024	3758	1266	34	50	16	170	-2	5.8	1.8	4.0	27.8	20.2
CLEVELAND BROWNS	10	4	0	.714	343	262	81	2.0	1.0	4856	4126	730	37	32	-5	41	40	4.6	3.8	0.8	30.0	25.2
ST. LOUIS CARDINALS	9	5	0	.643	341	283	58	1.5	0.5	4870	3954	916	39	37	-2	68	-10	5.0	3.6	1.4	27.4	22.5
PITTSBURGH STEELERS	7	4	3	.636	321	295	26	0.6	0.9	4913	4829	84	33	44	11	51	-25	5.2	5.2	0.0	28.1	27.1
DALLAS COWBOYS	4	10	0	.286	305	378	-73	-1.8	-1.2	4263	5325	-1062	36	37	1	-85	12	4.1	5.6	-1.5	24.4	30.6
WASHINGTON REDSKINS	3	11	0	.214	279	398	-119	-3.0	-1.0	4423	5077	-654	53	31	-22	-143	24	3.8	5.8	-2.0	24.8	29.2
PHILADELPHIA EAGLES	2	10	2	.167	242	381	-139	-3.5	-0.5	3852	4821	-969	47	30	-17	-149	10	3.0	6.0	-3.0	22.4	28.4

WESTERN CONFERENCE	W	L	T	PCT	PTS	OPP	NET	P-W	D-W	Y-O	Y-D	Y-N	T-O	T-D	T-N	P-NP	D-NP	PR-O	PR-D	PR-N	YD-O	YD-D
CHICAGO BEARS	11	1	2	.917L*	301	144	157	3.9	1.1	4172	3176	996	25	54	29	199	-42	4.8	0.6	4.3	24.7	19.0
GREEN BAY PACKERS	11	2	1	.846	369	206	163	4.1	0.4	4781	3599	1182	41	43	2	107	56	5.0	2.7	2.3	29.0	20.0
BALTIMORE COLTS	8	6	0	.571	316	285	31	0.8	0.2	4938	4036	902	37	32	-5	55	-24	6.2	4.5	1.7	28.4	23.1
DETROIT LIONS	5	8	1	.385	326	265	61	1.5	-3.0	4324	3761	563	40	35	-5	27	34	4.1	3.0	1.1	23.6	20.7
MINNESOTA VIKINGS	5	8	1	.385	309	390	-81	-2.0	0.5	4011	4731	-720	35	42	7	-32	-49	3.9	6.3	-2.4	22.0	27.0
LOS ANGELES RAMS	5	9	0	.357	210	350	-140	-3.5	1.5	3470	4538	-1068	39	32	-7	-117	-23	2.7	5.3	-2.6	19.4	25.9
SAN FRANCISCO 49ERS	2	12	0	.143	198	391	-193	-4.8	-0.2	3281	5447	-2166	30	27	-3	-193	0	2.5	6.3	-3.8	19.5	33.0

1963 A.F.L.

EASTERN DIVISION	W	L	T	PCT	PTS	OPP	NET	P-W	D-W	Y-O	Y-D	Y-N	T-O	T-D	T-N	P-NP	D-NP	PR-O	PR-D	PR-N	YD-O	YD-D
BOSTON PATRIOTS	7	6	1	.538DL	327	257	70	1.8	-1.3	4165	3639	526	41	41	0	44	26	3.2	2.7	0.5	21.8	18.3
BUFFALO BILLS	7	6	1	.538D	304	291	13	0.3	0.2	4895	4073	822	40	33	-7	41	-28	4.3	0.1		26.9	23.8
HOUSTON OILERS	6	8	0	.429	302	372	-70	-1.8	0.8	4431	4581	-150	57	48	-9	-49	-21	3.7	2.6	1.1	23.0	24.0
NEW YORK JETS	5	8	1	.385	249	399	-150	-3.8	2.3	3508	5166	-1658	44	36	-8	-170	20	2.8	5.3	-2.5	20.3	29.2

WESTERN DIVISION	W	L	T	PCT	PTS	OPP	NET	P-W	D-W	Y-O	Y-D	Y-N	T-O	T-D	T-N	P-NP	D-NP	PR-O	PR-D	PR-N	YD-O	YD-D
SAN DIEGO CHARGERS	11	3	0	.786L*	399	255	144	3.6	0.4	5153	4138	1015	36	44	8	117	27	5.7	3.1	2.6	31.0	23.1
OAKLAND RAIDERS	10	4	0	.714	363	282	81	2.0	1.0	4521	4055	466	38	52	14	95	-14	4.5	2.5	1.9	23.4	21.5
KANSAS CITY CHIEFS	5	7	2	.417	347	263	84	2.1	-3.1	4348	4187	161	38	45	7	41	43	4.2	3.5	0.6	24.4	23.3
DENVER BRONCOS	2	11	1	.154	301	473	-172	-4.3	-0.2	3995	5075	-1080	44	35	-9	-126	-46	2.8	7.2	-4.4	20.3	25.9

1964 N.F.L.

EASTERN CONFERENCE	W	L	T	PCT	PTS	OPP	NET	P-W	D-W	Y-O	Y-D	Y-N	T-O	T-D	T-N	P-NP	D-NP	PR-O	PR-D	PR-N	YD-O	YD-D
CLEVELAND BROWNS	10	3	1	.769L*	415	293	122	3.1	0.5	4486	4722	-236	26	40	14	36	86	4.7	4.7	-0.0	27.5	28.6
ST. LOUIS CARDINALS	9	3	2	.750	357	331	26	0.6	2.3	4517	4292	225	40	39	-1	15	11	4.1	3.7	0.4	24.7	23.6
PHILADELPHIA EAGLES	6	8	0	.429	312	313	-1	-0.0	-1.0	4400	4317	83	40	29	-11	-37	36	4.3	4.4	-0.1	24.2	23.5
WASHINGTON REDSKINS	6	8	0	.429	307	305	2	0.1	-1.0	3958	4060	-102	33	55	22	80	-78	4.9	2.0	3.0	20.2	20.4
DALLAS COWBOYS	5	8	1	.385	250	289	-39	-1.0	-0.5	3704	3750	-46	43	38	-5	-24	-15	2.2	3.9	-1.7	19.6	20.1
PITTSBURGH STEELERS	5	9	0	.357	253	315	-62	-1.5	-0.5	3960	4231	-271	41	26	-15	-83	21	2.5	4.4	-2.0	24.1	25.5
NEW YORK GIANTS	2	10	2	.167	241	399	-158	-4.0	-0.0	3879	4363	-484	49	33	-16	-104	-54	3.1	5.1	-2.0	20.6	24.2

WESTERN CONFERENCE	W	L	T	PCT	PTS	OPP	NET	P-W	D-W	Y-O	Y-D	Y-N	T-O	T-D	T-N	P-NP	D-NP	PR-O	PR-D	PR-N	YD-O	YD-D
BALTIMORE COLTS	12	2	0	.857L	428	225	203	5.1	-0.1	4779	3930	849	19	41	22	159	44	6.7	2.8	3.9	27.6	22.6
GREEN BAY PACKERS	8	5	1	.615	342	245	97	2.4	-0.9	4381	3179	1202	23	41	18	172	-75	5.4	2.9	2.6	25.3	18.8
MINNESOTA VIKINGS	8	5	1	.615	355	296	59	1.5	0.0	4306	4340	-34	30	35	5	17	42	4.8	5.1	-0.3	24.2	23.6
DETROIT LIONS	7	5	2	.583	280	260	20	0.5	0.5	3972	4062	-90	34	30	-4	-24	44	4.4	3.5	0.9	23.4	24.0
LOS ANGELES RAMS	5	7	2	.417	283	339	-56	-1.4	0.4	3908	4195	-287	39	30	-9	-60	4	3.6	4.5	-0.9	21.6	22.7
CHICAGO BEARS	5	9	0	.357	260	379	-119	-3.0	1.0	4007	4485	-478	33	30	-3	-52	-67	4.1	6.2	-2.1	23.3	27.0
SAN FRANCISCO 49ERS	4	10	0	.286	236	330	-94	-2.3	-0.7	4073	4404	-331	46	29	-17	-96	2	4.0	5.0	-1.1	21.9	23.4

1964 A.F.L.

EASTERN DIVISION	W L T	PCT	PTS	OPP	NET	P-W	D-W	Y-O	Y-D	Y-N	T-O	T-D	T-N	P-NP	D-NP	PR-O	PR-D	PR-N	YD-O	YD-D
BUFFALO BILLS	12 2 0	.857L*	400	242	158	4.0	1.0	5206	3878	1328	52	43	−9	75	83	4.2	3.4	0.8	27.8	19.2
BOSTON PATRIOTS	10 3 1	.769	365	297	68	1.7	1.8	4527	4360	167	39	48	9	50	18	4.5	3.6	0.9	22.6	21.8
NEW YORK JETS	5 8 1	.385	278	315	−37	−0.9	−0.6	3889	4916	−1027	40	44	4	−70	33	2.4	3.9	−1.5	20.8	26.3
HOUSTON OILERS	4 10 0	.286	310	355	−45	−1.1	−1.9	4874	5241	−367	44	38	−6	−55	10	3.9	4.7	−0.8	28.0	30.3

WESTERN DIVISION	W L T	PCT	PTS	OPP	NET	P-W	D-W	Y-O	Y-D	Y-N	T-O	T-D	T-N	P-NP	D-NP	PR-O	PR-D	PR-N	YD-O	YD-D
SAN DIEGO CHARGERS	8 5 1	.615L	341	300	41	1.0	0.5	4664	4040	624	46	45	−1	48	−7	4.4	2.7	1.8	25.8	21.8
KANSAS CITY CHIEFS	7 7 0	.500	366	306	60	1.5	−1.5	4700	3946	754	41	46	5	83	−23	4.9	3.5	1.5	25.1	20.8
OAKLAND RAIDERS	5 7 2	.417	303	350	−47	−1.2	0.2	4902	4743	159	51	36	−15	−47	0	3.8	4.3	−0.5	26.2	26.9
DENVER BRONCOS	2 11 1	.154	240	438	−198	−4.9	0.4	3332	4970	−1638	40	53	13	−85	−113	1.4	3.6	−2.2	16.7	26.2

1965 N.F.L.

EASTERN CONFERENCE	W L T	PCT	PTS	OPP	NET	P-W	D-W	Y-O	Y-D	Y-N	T-O	T-D	T-N	P-NP	D-NP	PR-O	PR-D	PR-N	YD-O	YD-D
CLEVELAND BROWNS	11 3 0	.786L	363	325	38	0.9	3.1	4398	4712	−314	25	32	7	2	36	4.4	4.5	−0.2	26.0	27.6
DALLAS COWBOYS	7 7 0	.500	325	280	45	1.1	−1.1	3995	4192	−197	35	38	3	−4	49	4.4	4.5	−0.2	22.2	23.0
NEW YORK GIANTS	7 7 0	.500	270	338	−68	−1.7	1.7	4081	4913	−832	30	36	6	−45	−23	5.2	5.6	−0.4	25.5	30.5
WASHINGTON REDSKINS	6 8 0	.429	257	301	−44	−1.1	0.1	3608	3870	−262	41	42	1	−18	−26	4.0	2.9	1.1	20.3	22.4
PHILADELPHIA EAGLES	5 9 0	.357	363	359	4	0.1	−2.1	5012	4418	594	36	36	0	50	−46	4.8	4.6	0.2	29.5	25.7
ST. LOUIS CARDINALS	5 9 0	.357	296	309	−13	−0.3	−1.7	4562	4297	265	32	32	0	22	−35	4.2	4.7	−0.5	26.4	25.1
PITTSBURGH STEELERS	2 12 0	.143	202	397	−195	−4.9	−0.1	3354	4530	−1176	57	27	−30	−218	23	1.2	5.6	−4.4	17.7	24.4

WESTERN CONFERENCE	W L T	PCT	PTS	OPP	NET	P-W	D-W	Y-O	Y-D	Y-N	T-O	T-D	T-N	P-NP	D-NP	PR-O	PR-D	PR-N	YD-O	YD-D
GREEN BAY PACKERS	10 3 1	.769CL*	316	224	92	2.3	1.2	3601	3969	−368	26	50	24	65	27	4.8	2.1	2.7	20.7	23.2
BALTIMORE COLTS	10 3 1	.769C	389	284	105	2.6	0.9	4598	4045	553	36	36	0	46	59	5.8	4.1	1.7	26.7	23.0
CHICAGO BEARS	9 5 0	.643	409	275	134	3.3	−1.3	4897	4268	629	28	44	16	116	18	6.3	4.2	2.1	28.1	24.7
SAN FRANCISCO 49ERS	7 6 1	.538	421	402	19	0.5	0.0	5270	4640	630	40	30	−10	13	6	6.1	5.8	0.3	29.6	25.6
MINNESOTA VIKINGS	7 7 0	.500	383	403	−20	−0.5	0.5	4824	4248	576	37	30	−7	20	−40	5.4	5.1	0.3	27.7	24.0
DETROIT LIONS	6 7 1	.462	257	295	−38	−0.9	0.4	3303	3557	−254	41	46	5	−1	−37	2.0	2.9	−0.9	17.7	19.5
LOS ANGELES RAMS	4 10 0	.286	269	328	−59	−1.5	−1.5	4179	4023	156	41	26	−15	−47	−12	4.2	6.1	−1.9	24.4	23.3

1965 A.F.L.

EASTERN DIVISION	W L T	PCT	PTS	OPP	NET	P-W	D-W	Y-O	Y-D	Y-N	T-O	T-D	T-N	P-NP	D-NP	PR-O	PR-D	PR-N	YD-O	YD-D
BUFFALO BILLS	10 3 1	.769L*	313	226	87	2.2	1.3	3749	4284	−535	38	57	19	31	56	3.1	3.6	−0.5	19.5	21.2
NEW YORK JETS	5 8 1	.385	285	303	−18	−0.4	−1.0	4065	4213	−148	40	38	−2	−20	2	3.8	3.5	0.3	21.4	22.9
BOSTON PATRIOTS	4 8 2	.333	244	302	−58	−1.5	−0.5	3624	4131	−507	41	30	−11	−86	28	2.7	4.0	−1.2	19.8	22.2
HOUSTON OILERS	4 10 0	.286	298	429	−131	−3.3	0.3	3988	5153	−1165	46	40	−6	−121	−10	2.6	3.3	−0.8	20.1	26.3

WESTERN DIVISION	W L T	PCT	PTS	OPP	NET	P-W	D-W	Y-O	Y-D	Y-N	T-O	T-D	T-N	P-NP	D-NP	PR-O	PR-D	PR-N	YD-O	YD-D
SAN DIEGO CHARGERS	9 2 3	.818L	340	227	113	2.8	0.7	5101	3262	1839	39	41	2	161	−48	5.1	2.1	2.9	27.0	17.5
OAKLAND RAIDERS	8 5 1	.615	298	239	59	1.5	0.0	3998	4188	−190	26	38	12	32	27	4.1	3.8	0.3	23.4	23.5
KANSAS CITY CHIEFS	7 5 2	.583	322	285	37	0.9	0.1	4295	3761	534	40	33	−7	17	20	4.3	3.4	0.9	23.3	20.2
DENVER BRONCOS	4 10 0	.286	303	392	−89	−2.2	−0.8	4469	4297	172	46	39	−7	−14	−75	2.9	4.4	−1.5	23.2	23.6

1966 N.F.L.

EASTERN CONFERENCE	W L T	PCT	PTS	OPP	NET	P-W	D-W	Y-O	Y-D	Y-N	T-O	T-D	T-N	P-NP	D-NP	PR-O	PR-D	PR-N	YD-O	YD-D
DALLAS COWBOYS	10 3 1	.769L	445	239	206	5.2	−1.7	5145	3558	1587	24	31	7	160	46	5.9	3.5	2.4	29.1	19.3
CLEVELAND BROWNS	9 5 0	.643	403	259	144	3.6	−1.6	5071	4266	805	25	49	24	163	−19	5.9	2.6	3.3	30.0	25.7
PHILADELPHIA EAGLES	9 5 0	.643	326	340	−14	−0.3	2.3	3759	4370	−611	39	35	−4	−67	53	2.5	4.2	−1.6	21.9	25.0
ST. LOUIS CARDINALS	8 5 1	.615	264	265	−1	−0.0	1.5	3541	3492	49	37	31	−6	−20	19	2.9	3.0	−0.2	18.4	18.1
WASHINGTON REDSKINS	7 7 0	.500	351	355	−4	−0.1	−0.8	4391	4692	−301	35	43	8	7	−11	5.1	4.5	0.6	23.9	25.4
PITTSBURGH STEELERS	5 8 1	.385	316	347	−31	−0.8	−0.7	3446	4291	−845	39	40	1	−66	35	3.3	3.9	−0.6	18.5	22.2
ATLANTA FALCONS	3 11 0	.214	204	437	−233	−5.8	1.8	3536	5272	−1736	44	32	−12	−193	−40	2.2	5.8	−3.6	20.7	31.2
NEW YORK GIANTS	1 12 1	.077	263	501	−238	−5.9	0.4	3932	4945	−1013	44	24	−20	−164	−74	2.6	6.5	−3.9	22.0	30.3

WESTERN CONFERENCE	W L T	PCT	PTS	OPP	NET	P-W	D-W	Y-O	Y-D	Y-N	T-O	T-D	T-N	P-NP	D-NP	PR-O	PR-D	PR-N	YD-O	YD-D
GREEN BAY PACKERS	12 2 0	.857LS*	335	163	172	4.3	0.7	4275	3603	672	24	42	18	128	44	7.3	1.8	5.6	26.4	22.0
BALTIMORE COLTS	9 5 0	.643	314	226	88	2.2	−0.2	4486	4091	395	39	40	1	37	51	4.6	3.2	1.4	25.5	24.1
LOS ANGELES RAMS	8 6 0	.571	289	212	77	1.9	−0.9	4282	3771	511	29	46	17	111	−34	3.8	3.2	0.6	24.6	20.3
SAN FRANCISCO 49ERS	6 6 2	.500	320	325	−5	−0.1	0.1	4782	4179	603	38	29	−9	14	−19	3.8	4.3	−0.5	26.1	22.6
CHICAGO BEARS	5 7 2	.417	234	272	−38	−0.9	−0.1	3699	3971	−272	35	38	3	−11	−27	2.3	4.2	−1.9	20.7	22.3
DETROIT LIONS	4 9 1	.308	206	317	−111	−2.8	0.3	3853	4414	−561	49	35	−14	−103	−8	2.5	3.8	−1.3	21.2	24.4
MINNESOTA VIKINGS	4 9 1	.308	292	304	−12	−0.3	−2.2	4639	3922	717	36	22	−14	4	−16	3.8	4.2	−0.4	26.4	23.1

1966 A.F.L.

EASTERN DIVISION	W	L	T	PCT	PTS	OPP	NET	P-W	D-W	Y-O	Y-D	Y-N	T-O	T-D	T-N	P-NP	D-NP	PR-O	PR-D	PR-N	YD-O	YD-D
BUFFALO BILLS	9	4	1	.692L	358	255	103	2.6	−0.1	4748	4109	639	36	38	2	61	42	4.2	4.0	0.3	26.5	21.3
BOSTON PATRIOTS	8	4	2	.667	315	283	32	0.8	1.2	4536	4491	45	34	37	3	16	16	4.4	4.9	−0.6	23.6	24.3
NEW YORK JETS	6	6	2	.500	322	312	10	0.3	−0.3	4906	4278	628	38	29	−9	16	−6	4.5	4.0	0.5	27.1	24.0
HOUSTON OILERS	3	11	0	.214	335	396	−61	−1.5	−2.5	4412	4995	−583	40	31	−9	−85	24	3.8	5.9	−2.1	23.8	26.7
MIAMI DOLPHINS	3	11	0	.214	213	362	−149	−3.7	−0.3	3458	4611	−1153	42	46	4	−80	−69	1.6	4.4	−2.9	17.6	26.2

WESTERN DIVISION	W	L	T	PCT	PTS	OPP	NET	P-W	D-W	Y-O	Y-D	Y-N	T-O	T-D	T-N	P-NP	D-NP	PR-O	PR-D	PR-N	YD-O	YD-D
KANSAS CITY CHIEFS	11	2	1	.846LS	448	276	172	4.3	0.2	5114	3970	1144	31	41	10	135	37	6.1	2.5	3.6	29.6	22.1
OAKLAND RAIDERS	8	5	1	.615	315	288	27	0.7	0.8	4571	3910	661	38	40	2	63	−36	4.6	2.8	1.8	25.1	20.7
SAN DIEGO CHARGERS	7	6	1	.538	335	284	51	1.3	−0.8	4553	4558	−5	22	35	13	52	−1	5.6	2.6	3.0	28.8	27.3
DENVER BRONCOS	4	10	0	.286	196	381	−185	−4.6	1.6	3168	4544	−1376	47	31	−16	−179	−6	1.7	5.1	−3.4	17.2	25.8

1967 N.F.L.

CAPITOL CONFERENCE	W	L	T	PCT	PTS	OPP	NET	P-W	D-W	Y-O	Y-D	Y-N	T-O	T-D	T-N	P-NP	D-NP	PR-O	PR-D	PR-N	YD-O	YD-D
DALLAS COWBOYS	9	5	0	.643CL	342	268	74	1.9	0.1	4699	3871	828	42	48	6	93	−19	4.0	3.2	0.7	25.4	20.8
PHILADELPHIA EAGLES	6	7	1	.462	351	409	−58	−1.5	1.0	4344	4972	−628	40	35	−5	−72	14	4.7	5.1	−0.4	24.7	28.9
WASHINGTON REDSKINS	5	6	3	.455	347	353	−6	−0.2	−0.3	4977	5255	−278	31	34	3	−11	5	6.0	5.4	0.6	27.0	28.6
NEW ORLEANS SAINTS	3	11	0	.214	233	379	−146	−3.7	−0.3	3790	4928	−1138	37	32	−5	−115	−31	3.2	4.8	−1.6	21.2	27.7

CENTURY CONFERENCE	W	L	T	PCT	PTS	OPP	NET	P-W	D-W	Y-O	Y-D	Y-N	T-O	T-D	T-N	P-NP	D-NP	PR-O	PR-D	PR-N	YD-O	YD-D
CLEVELAND BROWNS	9	5	0	.643C	334	297	37	0.9	1.4	4081	4666	−585	35	36	1	−45	82	3.6	4.2	−0.7	24.4	26.7
NEW YORK GIANTS	7	7	0	.500	369	379	−10	−0.3	0.3	4904	4284	620	30	32	2	60	−70	5.6	4.7	0.9	29.7	26.4
ST. LOUIS CARDINALS	6	7	1	.462	333	356	−23	−0.6	0.1	4780	4185	595	46	32	−14	−6	−17	3.4	5.3	−1.8	25.7	22.0
PITTSBURGH STEELERS	4	9	1	.308	281	320	−39	−1.0	−1.5	3908	3955	−47	45	39	−6	−28	−11	3.0	3.8	−0.9	21.0	21.9

CENTRAL CONFERENCE	W	L	T	PCT	PTS	OPP	NET	P-W	D-W	Y-O	Y-D	Y-N	T-O	T-D	T-N	P-NP	D-NP	PR-O	PR-D	PR-N	YD-O	YD-D
LOS ANGELES RAMS	11	1	2	.917TC	398	196	202	5.1	−0.1	4640	3526	1114	29	45	16	157	45	5.5	2.3	3.3	24.8	18.0
BALTIMORE COLTS	11	1	2	.917T	394	198	196	4.9	0.1	5008	3843	1165	25	40	15	157	39	5.8	2.6	3.2	30.4	23.2
SAN FRANCISCO 49ERS	7	7	0	.500	273	337	−64	−1.6	1.6	4418	4044	374	36	29	−7	3	−67	3.3	4.0	−0.7	24.3	22.2
ATLANTA FALCONS	1	12	1	.077	175	422	−247	−6.2	0.7	3013	5531	−2518	39	27	−12	−258	11	1.7	6.6	−4.9	17.0	32.0

COASTAL CONFERENCE	W	L	T	PCT	PTS	OPP	NET	P-W	D-W	Y-O	Y-D	Y-N	T-O	T-D	T-N	P-NP	D-NP	PR-O	PR-D	PR-N	YD-O	YD-D
GREEN BAY PACKERS	9	4	1	.692CLS*	332	209	123	3.1	−0.6	4279	3300	979	37	40	3	94	29	3.5	0.9	2.6	24.6	18.4
CHICAGO BEARS	7	6	1	.538	239	218	21	0.5	−0.0	3293	3406	−113	32	44	12	39	−18	2.4	1.8	0.6	18.2	19.7
DETROIT LIONS	5	7	2	.417	260	259	1	0.0	−1.0	3538	3528	10	40	33	−7	−27	28	2.4	2.3	0.1	19.7	19.0
MINNESOTA VIKINGS	3	8	3	.273	233	294	−61	−1.5	−1.0	3478	3856	−378	37	35	−2	−40	−21	1.9	3.4	−1.6	18.6	21.7

1967 A.F.L.

EASTERN DIVISION	W	L	T	PCT	PTS	OPP	NET	P-W	D-W	Y-O	Y-D	Y-N	T-O	T-D	T-N	P-NP	D-NP	PR-O	PR-D	PR-N	YD-O	YD-D
HOUSTON OILERS	9	4	1	.692L	258	199	59	1.5	1.0	3503	4055	−552	27	39	12	2	57	1.7	2.8	−1.1	21.1	24.9
NEW YORK JETS	8	5	1	.615	371	329	42	1.0	0.5	5152	3775	1377	37	33	−4	99	−57	5.2	2.4	2.7	27.8	20.9
BUFFALO BILLS	4	10	0	.286	237	285	−48	−1.2	−1.8	3588	3447	141	47	36	−11	−32	−16	1.9	1.9	0.1	18.9	18.7
MIAMI DOLPHINS	4	10	0	.286	219	407	−188	−4.7	1.7	3659	4980	−1321	44	36	−8	−142	−46	2.4	5.0	−2.6	21.4	29.8
BOSTON PATRIOTS	3	10	1	.231	280	389	−109	−2.7	−0.8	4027	4206	−179	54	34	−20	−95	−14	2.5	5.2	−2.8	21.1	22.1

WESTERN DIVISION	W	L	T	PCT	PTS	OPP	NET	P-W	D-W	Y-O	Y-D	Y-N	T-O	T-D	T-N	P-NP	D-NP	PR-O	PR-D	PR-N	YD-O	YD-D
OAKLAND RAIDERS	13	1	0	.929LS	468	233	235	5.9	0.1	5116	3294	1822	36	45	9	188	47	4.9	1.9	3.0	25.0	15.9
KANSAS CITY CHIEFS	9	5	0	.643	408	254	154	3.8	−1.8	4490	3944	546	27	49	22	134	20	4.5	2.5	2.0	25.8	22.3
SAN DIEGO CHARGERS	8	5	1	.615	360	352	8	0.2	1.3	5125	4705	420	34	23	−11	−9	17	5.5	5.7	−0.2	29.5	26.3
DENVER BRONCOS	3	11	0	.214	256	409	−153	−3.8	−0.2	2947	5201	−2254	30	41	11	−144	−9	2.4	4.5	−2.1	15.2	25.7

1968 N.F.L.

CAPITOL CONFERENCE	W	L	T	PCT	PTS	OPP	NET	P-W	D-W	Y-O	Y-D	Y-N	T-O	T-D	T-N	P-NP	D-NP	PR-O	PR-D	PR-N	YD-O	YD-D
DALLAS COWBOYS	12	2	0	.857C	431	186	245	6.1	−1.1	5117	3633	1484	33	41	8	156	89	5.7	3.1	2.6	30.1	19.9
NEW YORK GIANTS	7	7	0	.500	294	325	−31	−0.8	0.8	4324	4341	−17	30	40	10	39	−70	4.8	3.5	1.3	27.0	28.2
WASHINGTON REDSKINS	5	9	0	.357	249	358	−109	−2.7	0.7	3648	4683	−1035	37	35	−2	−94	−15	4.3	4.5	−0.2	21.1	27.4
PHILADELPHIA EAGLES	2	12	0	.143	202	351	−149	−3.7	−1.3	3561	4514	−953	42	20	−22	−167	18	2.5	5.7	−3.2	22.7	28.0

CENTURY CONFERENCE	W	L	T	PCT	PTS	OPP	NET	P-W	D-W	Y-O	Y-D	Y-N	T-O	T-D	T-N	P-NP	D-NP	PR-O	PR-D	PR-N	YD-O	YD-D
CLEVELAND BROWNS	10	4	0	.714CL	394	273	121	3.0	−0.0	4889	4090	799	30	46	16	131	−10	6.3	2.1	4.1	28.4	23.6
ST. LOUIS CARDINALS	9	4	1	.692	325	289	36	0.9	1.6	4183	4419	−236	31	21	−10	−60	96	3.5	5.7	−2.1	25.2	26.5
NEW ORLEANS SAINTS	4	9	1	.308	246	327	−81	−2.0	−0.5	3863	4291	−428	42	44	2	−28	−53	2.5	4.3	−1.7	20.5	23.1
PITTSBURGH STEELERS	2	11	1	.154	244	397	−153	−3.8	−0.7	4200	4785	−585	40	26	−14	−105	−48	3.1	6.1	−3.0	24.0	28.5

CENTRAL CONFERENCE	W	L	T	PCT	PTS	OPP	NET	P-W	D-W	Y-O	Y-D	Y-N	T-O	T-D	T-N	P-NP	D-NP	PR-O	PR-D	PR-N	YD-O	YD-D
BALTIMORE COLTS	13	1	0	.929CLS	402	144	258	6.4	−0.4	4681	3377	1304	34	41	7	137	121	5.6	1.7	3.8	29.1	20.1
LOS ANGELES RAMS	10	3	1	.769	312	200	112	2.8	0.7	4104	3118	986	29	44	15	142	−30	3.9	2.0	1.9	22.7	16.8
SAN FRANCISCO 49ERS	7	6	1	.538	303	310	−7	−0.2	0.7	4709	4020	689	37	31	−6	33	−40	4.8	3.4	1.4	27.2	23.0
ATLANTA FALCONS	2	12	0	.143	170	389	−219	−5.5	0.5	3164	5320	−2156	39	30	−9	−216	−3	2.2	6.6	−4.4	19.7	32.8

COASTAL CONFERENCE	W	L	T	PCT	PTS	OPP	NET	P-W	D-W	Y-O	Y-D	Y-N	T-O	T-D	T-N	P-NP	D-NP	PR-O	PR-D	PR-N	YD-O	YD-D
MINNESOTA VIKINGS	8	6	0	.571C	282	242	40	1.0	0.0	3606	3758	−152	31	38	7	15	25	3.2	3.6	−0.4	22.1	23.3
CHICAGO BEARS	7	7	0	.500	250	333	−83	−2.1	2.1	4058	4371	−313	37	30	−7	−54	−29	2.3	5.8	−3.5	22.8	25.6
GREEN BAY PACKERS	6	7	1	.462	281	227	54	1.4	−1.9	4024	3596	428	33	34	1	40	14	5.0	3.3	1.7	23.7	22.1
DETROIT LIONS	4	8	2	.333	207	241	−34	−0.9	−1.1	4022	3837	185	32	36	4	31	−65	4.3	3.2	1.1	24.2	23.3

1968 A.F.L.

EASTERN DIVISION	W	L	T	PCT	PTS	OPP	NET	P-W	D-W	Y-O	Y-D	Y-N	T-O	T-D	T-N	P-NP	D-NP	PR-O	PR-D	PR-N	YD-O	YD-D
NEW YORK JETS	11	3	0	.786LS*	419	280	139	3.5	0.5	5047	3363	1684	28	43	15	200	−61	6.1	2.4	3.7	25.4	17.4
HOUSTON OILERS	7	7	0	.500	303	248	55	1.4	−1.4	4352	3375	977	38	30	−8	49	6	3.6	2.3	1.3	24.0	18.1
MIAMI DOLPHINS	5	8	1	.385	276	355	−79	−2.0	0.5	4106	4884	−778	30	40	10	−25	−54	3.4	5.4	−2.0	23.9	29.2
BOSTON PATRIOTS	4	10	0	.286	229	406	−177	−4.4	1.4	3127	4415	−1288	53	40	−13	−159	−18	1.0	4.0	−3.0	15.0	21.0
BUFFALO BILLS	1	12	1	.077	199	367	−168	−4.2	−1.3	2870	4225	−1355	42	35	−7	−141	−27	0.3	3.8	−3.4	13.9	21.4

WESTERN DIVISION	W	L	T	PCT	PTS	OPP	NET	P-W	D-W	Y-O	Y-D	Y-N	T-O	T-D	T-N	P-NP	D-NP	PR-O	PR-D	PR-N	YD-O	YD-D
OAKLAND RAIDERS	12	2	0	.857DL	453	233	220	5.5	−0.5	5696	4061	1635	39	40	1	140	80	6.1	2.5	3.5	29.5	20.3
KANSAS CITY CHIEFS	12	2	0	.857D	371	170	201	5.0	−0.0	4503	4089	414	27	49	22	123	78	6.7	2.6	4.2	25.7	22.7
SAN DIEGO CHARGERS	9	5	0	.643	382	310	72	1.8	0.2	5388	4333	1055	45	35	−10	48	24	5.0	4.4	0.6	29.4	23.5
DENVER BRONCOS	5	9	0	.357	255	404	−149	−3.7	1.7	3971	5024	−1053	40	32	−8	−120	−29	2.8	5.5	−2.7	20.1	25.2
CINCINNATI BENGALS	3	11	0	.214	215	329	−114	−2.8	−1.2	3426	4717	−1291	21	19	−2	−116	2	3.4	5.5	−2.0	20.8	28.8

1969 N.F.L.

CAPITOL CONFERENCE	W	L	T	PCT	PTS	OPP	NET	P-W	D-W	Y-O	Y-D	Y-N	T-O	T-D	T-N	P-NP	D-NP	PR-O	PR-D	PR-N	YD-O	YD-D
DALLAS COWBOYS	11	2	1	.846C	369	223	146	3.7	0.8	5122	3707	1415	30	35	5	138	8	5.7	3.5	2.2	28.9	20.5
WASHINGTON REDSKINS	7	5	2	.583	307	319	−12	−0.3	1.3	4316	4476	−160	26	26	0	−13	1	4.7	4.0	0.7	26.8	26.6
NEW ORLEANS SAINTS	5	9	0	.357	311	393	−82	−2.1	0.0	4679	5018	−339	32	22	−10	−68	−14	4.8	7.4	−2.6	28.0	30.4
PHILADELPHIA EAGLES	4	9	1	.308	279	377	−98	−2.5	−0.0	4345	4978	−633	39	29	−10	−93	−5	3.5	5.6	−2.1	23.4	27.1

CENTURY CONFERENCE	W	L	T	PCT	PTS	OPP	NET	P-W	D-W	Y-O	Y-D	Y-N	T-O	T-D	T-N	P-NP	D-NP	PR-O	PR-D	PR-N	YD-O	YD-D
CLEVELAND BROWNS	10	3	1	.769CL	351	300	51	1.3	2.2	4428	4454	−26	35	41	6	22	29	4.9	4.2	0.6	25.7	26.2
NEW YORK GIANTS	6	8	0	.429	264	298	−34	−0.9	−0.1	4368	4208	160	23	33	10	53	−87	5.6	4.0	1.6	27.6	26.8
ST. LOUIS CARDINALS	4	9	1	.308	314	389	−75	−1.9	−0.6	4185	5176	−991	35	27	−8	−115	40	4.0	6.5	−2.5	23.3	28.9
PITTSBURGH STEELERS	1	13	0	.071	218	404	−186	−4.7	−1.3	3626	4401	−775	49	41	−8	−97	−89	2.1	4.1	−2.0	19.0	23.8

CENTRAL CONFERENCE	W	L	T	PCT	PTS	OPP	NET	P-W	D-W	Y-O	Y-D	Y-N	T-O	T-D	T-N	P-NP	D-NP	PR-O	PR-D	PR-N	YD-O	YD-D
LOS ANGELES RAMS	11	3	0	.786C	320	243	77	1.9	2.1	3934	4001	−67	18	38	20	74	3	5.7	3.2	2.5	22.5	22.7
BALTIMORE COLTS	8	5	1	.615	279	268	11	0.3	1.2	4477	4649	−172	39	25	−14	−70	81	4.3	5.6	−1.3	26.8	27.7
ATLANTA FALCONS	6	8	0	.429	276	268	8	0.2	−1.2	3811	4317	−506	31	46	15	18	−10	4.1	3.8	0.3	22.6	25.4
SAN FRANCISCO 49ERS	4	8	2	.333	277	319	−42	−1.0	−1.0	4694	4175	519	38	31	−7	15	−57	4.2	4.1	0.1	26.2	23.9

COASTAL CONFERENCE	W	L	T	PCT	PTS	OPP	NET	P-W	D-W	Y-O	Y-D	Y-N	T-O	T-D	T-N	P-NP	D-NP	PR-O	PR-D	PR-N	YD-O	YD-D
MINNESOTA VIKINGS	12	2	0	.857CLS	379	133	246	6.2	−1.2	4096	2720	1376	30	42	12	163	83	4.4	0.8	3.6	22.4	14.8
DETROIT LIONS	9	4	1	.692	259	188	71	1.8	0.7	3355	3084	271	30	42	12	71	0	2.5	2.7	−0.2	19.6	17.6
GREEN BAY PACKERS	8	6	0	.571	269	221	48	1.2	−0.2	4068	3827	241	38	26	−12	−28	76	5.1	2.8	2.3	25.1	23.6
CHICAGO BEARS	1	13	0	.071	210	339	−129	−3.2	−2.8	3568	3881	−313	38	27	−11	−70	−59	1.5	4.5	−3.0	20.9	22.8

1969 A.F.L.

EASTERN DIVISION	W	L	T	PCT	PTS	OPP	NET	P-W	D-W	Y-O	Y-D	Y-N	T-O	T-D	T-N	P-NP	D-NP	PR-O	PR-D	PR-N	YD-O	YD-D
NEW YORK JETS	10	4	0	.714D	353	269	84	2.1	0.9	4583	4082	501	33	45	12	90	−6	5.1	3.5	1.7	26.0	23.2
HOUSTON OILERS	6	6	2	.500D	278	279	−1	−0.0	0.0	4531	3773	758	48	40	−8	31	−32	3.0	3.4	−0.4	23.2	19.3
BOSTON PATRIOTS	4	10	0	.286	266	316	−50	−1.3	−1.8	3419	4810	−1391	28	34	6	−92	42	3.6	4.7	−1.1	21.1	28.3
BUFFALO BILLS	4	10	0	.286	230	359	−129	−3.2	0.2	3867	4334	−467	51	37	−14	−95	−34	2.4	4.6	−2.2	20.6	23.3
MIAMI DOLPHINS	3	10	1	.231	233	332	−99	−2.5	−1.0	3590	4126	−536	42	31	−11	−89	−10	1.9	4.8	−3.0	19.0	22.5

WESTERN DIVISION	W	L	T	PCT	PTS	OPP	NET	P-W	D-W	Y-O	Y-D	Y-N	T-O	T-D	T-N	P-NP	D-NP	PR-O	PR-D	PR-N	YD-O	YD-D
OAKLAND RAIDERS	12	1	1	.923DL	377	242	135	3.4	2.1	5036	3770	1266	33	42	9	142	−7	5.5	2.3	3.1	26.1	19.6
KANSAS CITY CHIEFS	11	3	0	.786DLS*	359	177	182	4.6	−0.6	4607	3163	1444	39	47	8	152	30	4.4	1.5	2.8	25.2	16.9
SAN DIEGO CHARGERS	8	6	0	.571	288	276	12	0.3	0.7	4611	4237	374	34	37	3	43	−31	3.8	3.5	0.3	25.9	24.4
DENVER BRONCOS	5	8	1	.385	297	344	−47	−1.2	−0.3	4161	4641	−480	31	28	−3	−52	5	3.8	5.2	−1.3	23.6	26.4
CINCINNATI BENGALS	4	9	1	.308	280	367	−87	−2.2	−0.3	3868	5337	−1469	38	36	−2	−130	43	5.2	4.8	0.4	20.7	28.4

1970 A.F.C.

EASTERN DIVISION	W	L	T	PCT	PTS	OPP	NET	P-W	D-W	Y-O	Y-D	Y-N	T-O	T-D	T-N	P-NP	D-NP	PR-O	PR-D	PR-N	YD-O	YD-D
BALTIMORE COLTS	11	2	1	.846DCS*	321	234	87	2.2	2.3	4134	3845	289	36	34	−2	16	71	4.5	2.9	1.6	22.7	21.6
MIAMI DOLPHINS	10	4	0	.714W	297	228	69	1.7	1.3	4039	4004	35	30	38	8	35	34	3.7	4.0	−0.3	25.6	25.3
NEW YORK JETS	4	10	0	.286	255	286	−31	−0.8	−2.2	3960	3655	305	33	34	1	29	−60	3.5	3.7	−0.2	22.6	20.6
BUFFALO BILLS	3	10	1	.231	204	337	−133	−3.3	−0.2	3895	3806	89	52	26	−26	−97	−36	3.1	4.7	−1.7	20.4	20.5
BOSTON PATRIOTS	2	12	0	.143	149	361	−212	−5.3	0.3	2626	4261	−1635	41	25	−16	−200	−12	0.9	5.6	−4.7	15.6	24.5

CENTRAL DIVISION	W	L	T	PCT	PTS	OPP	NET	P-W	D-W	Y-O	Y-D	Y-N	T-O	T-D	T-N	P-NP	D-NP	PR-O	PR-D	PR-N	YD-O	YD-D
CINCINNATI BENGALS	8	6	0	.571D	312	255	57	1.4	−0.4	3927	4178	−251	23	39	16	43	14	4.0	3.9	0.1	21.6	23.2
CLEVELAND BROWNS	7	7	0	.500	286	265	21	0.5	−0.5	4161	4244	−83	38	31	−7	−35	56	4.1	3.9	0.2	25.7	24.1
PITTSBURGH STEELERS	5	9	0	.357	210	272	−62	−1.5	−0.5	3752	3996	−244	48	38	−10	−60	−2	1.7	3.6	−1.8	19.0	21.4
HOUSTON OILERS	3	10	1	.231	217	352	−135	−3.4	−0.1	4062	4398	−336	38	26	−12	−76	−59	3.2	5.5	−2.3	22.0	23.8

WESTERN DIVISION	W	L	T	PCT	PTS	OPP	NET	P-W	D-W	Y-O	Y-D	Y-N	T-O	T-D	T-N	P-NP	D-NP	PR-O	PR-D	PR-N	YD-O	YD-D
OAKLAND RAIDERS	8	4	2	.667DC	300	293	7	0.2	1.8	4829	4116	713	30	27	−3	47	−40	5.0	3.8	1.2	27.1	22.7
KANSAS CITY CHIEFS	7	5	2	.583	272	244	28	0.7	0.3	3577	3667	−90	31	43	12	41	−13	3.5	1.7	1.7	19.5	20.1
SAN DIEGO CHARGERS	5	6	3	.455	282	278	4	0.1	−0.6	3953	4182	−229	25	24	−1	−23	27	4.3	4.9	−0.7	24.0	26.0
DENVER BRONCOS	5	8	1	.385	253	264	−11	−0.3	−1.2	3827	3705	122	41	32	−9	−26	15	2.0	4.3	−2.3	19.9	18.8

1970 N.F.C

EASTERN DIVISION	W	L	T	PCT	PTS	OPP	NET	P-W	D-W	Y-O	Y-D	Y-N	T-O	T-D	T-N	P-NP	D-NP	PR-O	PR-D	PR-N	YD-O	YD-D
DALLAS COWBOYS	10	4	0	.714DCS	299	221	78	2.0	1.0	4449	3569	880	28	39	11	117	−39	4.8	2.1	2.7	26.0	21.5
NEW YORK GIANTS	9	5	0	.643	301	270	31	0.8	1.2	4433	4063	370	26	30	4	47	−16	5.2	4.5	0.7	27.7	25.2
ST. LOUIS CARDINALS	8	5	1	.615	325	228	97	2.4	−0.9	4471	3869	602	33	35	2	58	39	4.3	3.1	1.1	25.5	22.1
WASHINGTON REDSKINS	6	8	0	.429	297	314	−17	−0.4	−0.6	4129	4333	−204	24	28	4	−1	−16	5.1	4.3	0.7	26.6	28.3
PHILADELPHIA EAGLES	3	10	1	.231	241	332	−91	−2.3	−1.2	3990	3953	37	39	28	−11	−41	−50	3.6	4.6	−1.0	23.2	23.1

CENTRAL DIVISION	W	L	T	PCT	PTS	OPP	NET	P-W	D-W	Y-O	Y-D	Y-N	T-O	T-D	T-N	P-NP	D-NP	PR-O	PR-D	PR-N	YD-O	YD-D
MINNESOTA VIKINGS	12	2	0	.857D	335	143	192	4.8	0.2	3815	2803	1012	31	44	13	136	56	4.4	0.6	3.8	21.7	15.6
DETROIT LIONS	10	4	0	.714W	347	202	145	3.6	−0.6	3984	3448	536	27	44	17	113	32	4.6	3.0	1.6	23.6	20.8
CHICAGO BEARS	6	8	0	.429	256	261	−5	−0.1	−0.9	3265	4067	−802	35	31	−4	−83	78	3.1	4.6	−1.6	17.6	21.6
GREEN BAY PACKERS	6	8	0	.429	196	293	−97	−2.4	1.4	3409	4055	−646	41	37	−4	−70	−27	2.1	3.6	−1.5	18.2	21.9

WESTERN DIVISION	W	L	T	PCT	PTS	OPP	NET	P-W	D-W	Y-O	Y-D	Y-N	T-O	T-D	T-N	P-NP	D-NP	PR-O	PR-D	PR-N	YD-O	YD-D
SAN FRANCISCO 49ERS	10	3	1	.769DC	352	267	85	2.1	1.4	4503	3972	531	25	42	17	112	−27	7.0	3.3	3.6	24.1	21.9
LOS ANGELES RAMS	9	4	1	.692	325	202	123	3.1	−0.6	4271	3548	723	30	35	5	80	43	4.7	3.4	1.2	24.1	19.4
ATLANTA FALCONS	4	8	2	.333	206	261	−55	−1.4	−0.6	3431	3876	−445	38	35	−3	−49	−6	2.7	3.7	−1.0	20.1	22.5
NEW ORLEANS SAINTS	2	11	1	.154	172	347	−175	−4.4	−0.1	3673	4952	−1279	40	38	−2	−115	−60	3.6	5.1	−1.5	21.0	28.3

1971 A.F.C.

EASTERN DIVISION	W	L	T	PCT	PTS	OPP	NET	P-W	D-W	Y-O	Y-D	Y-N	T-O	T-D	T-N	P-NP	D-NP	PR-O	PR-D	PR-N	YD-O	YD-D
MIAMI DOLPHINS	10	3	1	.769DCS	315	174	141	3.5	−0.0	4412	3661	751	23	31	8	95	46	5.4	3.4	2.1	29.0	23.6
BALTIMORE COLTS	10	4	0	.714WC	313	140	173	4.3	−1.3	4071	2852	1219	32	41	9	138	35	2.9	1.4	1.5	23.7	17.1
NEW ENGLAND PATRIOTS	6	8	0	.429	238	325	−87	−2.2	1.2	3556	4072	−516	32	29	−3	−55	−32	3.7	4.4	−0.7	20.6	23.1
NEW YORK JETS	6	8	0	.429	212	299	−87	−2.2	1.2	3267	4357	−1090	26	27	1	−87	0	2.7	4.4	−1.8	20.3	27.8
BUFFALO BILLS	1	13	0	.071	184	394	−210	−5.3	−0.8	3326	4604	−1278	48	22	−26	−211	1	1.5	5.4	−4.0	18.5	26.0

CENTRAL DIVISION	W	L	T	PCT	PTS	OPP	NET	P-W	D-W	Y-O	Y-D	Y-N	T-O	T-D	T-N	P-NP	D-NP	PR-O	PR-D	PR-N	YD-O	YD-D
CLEVELAND BROWNS	9	5	0	.643D	285	273	12	0.3	1.7	3857	4194	−337	45	40	−5	−48	60	3.1	2.8	0.3	22.2	23.0
PITTSBURGH STEELERS	6	8	0	.429	246	292	−46	−1.1	0.1	3882	4248	−366	42	35	−7	−59	13	2.4	4.9	−2.5	20.6	23.2
HOUSTON OILERS	4	9	1	.308	251	330	−79	−2.0	−0.5	3515	3795	−280	51	37	−14	−79	0	1.9	2.9	−1.0	18.3	20.0
CINCINNATI BENGALS	4	10	0	.286	284	265	19	0.5	−3.5	4266	3906	360	23	39	16	94	−75	4.4	3.0	1.4	24.7	22.8

WESTERN DIVISION	W	L	T	PCT	PTS	OPP	NET	P-W	D-W	Y-O	Y-D	Y-N	T-O	T-D	T-N	P-NP	D-NP	PR-O	PR-D	PR-N	YD-O	YD-D
KANSAS CITY CHIEFS	10	3	1	.769D	302	208	94	2.3	1.2	4190	3768	422	26	33	7	63	31	5.1	3.1	2.1	26.0	21.7
OAKLAND RAIDERS	8	4	2	.667	344	278	66	1.6	0.4	4258	4137	121	39	40	1	14	52	3.1	3.8	−0.7	24.9	23.9
SAN DIEGO CHARGERS	6	8	0	.429	311	341	−30	−0.8	−0.3	4738	4558	180	43	32	−11	−29	−1	4.5	3.9	0.6	27.2	26.5
DENVER BRONCOS	4	9	1	.308	203	275	−72	−1.8	−0.7	4158	3819	339	39	40	1	32	−104	2.4	3.2	−0.7	23.0	21.3

1971 N.F.C

EASTERN DIVISION	W	L	T	PCT	PTS	OPP	NET	P-W	D-W	Y-O	Y-D	Y-N	T-O	T-D	T-N	P-NP	D-NP	PR-O	PR-D	PR-N	YD-O	YD-D
DALLAS COWBOYS	11	3	0	.786DCS*	406	222	184	4.6	−0.6	5036	3468	1567	35	51	16	195	−11	6.0	2.8	3.2	29.1	19.1
WASHINGTON REDSKINS	9	4	1	.692W	276	190	86	2.2	0.3	4030	3523	507	35	41	6	66	20	4.9	2.1	2.8	22.6	20.0
PHILADELPHIA EAGLES	6	7	1	.462	221	302	−81	−2.0	1.5	3571	4622	−1051	35	47	12	−40	−41	3.7	4.2	−0.4	19.8	26.0
ST. LOUIS CARDINALS	4	9	1	.308	231	279	−48	−1.2	−1.3	4001	4365	−364	46	33	−13	−82	34	3.6	4.4	−0.8	24.0	25.7
NEW YORK GIANTS	4	10	0	.286	228	362	−134	−3.3	0.3	4175	4366	−191	45	30	−15	−76	−58	3.4	5.4	−1.9	24.1	26.5

CENTRAL DIVISION	W	L	T	PCT	PTS	OPP	NET	P-W	D-W	Y-O	Y-D	Y-N	T-O	T-D	T-N	P-NP	D-NP	PR-O	PR-D	PR-N	YD-O	YD-D
MINNESOTA VIKINGS	11	3	0	.786D	245	139	106	2.7	1.3	3350	3406	−56	30	45	15	55	51	2.6	1.6	1.0	19.0	18.4
DETROIT LIONS	7	6	1	.538	341	286	55	1.4	−0.9	4577	3859	718	33	33	0	60	−5	5.3	3.7	1.6	28.8	24.3
CHICAGO BEARS	6	8	0	.429	185	276	−91	−2.3	1.3	3336	4520	−1184	46	45	−1	−103	12	1.5	3.9	−2.4	17.6	24.7
GREEN BAY PACKERS	4	8	2	.333	274	298	−24	−0.6	−1.4	3914	4008	−94	44	32	−12	−56	32	2.7	4.8	−2.1	22.8	24.0

WESTERN DIVISION	W	L	T	PCT	PTS	OPP	NET	P-W	D-W	Y-O	Y-D	Y-N	T-O	T-D	T-N	P-NP	D-NP	PR-O	PR-D	PR-N	YD-O	YD-D
SAN FRANCISCO 49ERS	9	5	0	.643DC	300	216	84	2.1	−0.1	4706	3679	1027	42	30	−12	38	46	4.2	4.1	0.1	28.3	21.8
LOS ANGELES RAMS	8	5	1	.615	313	260	53	1.3	0.2	4233	4037	196	29	34	5	36	17	4.5	3.1	1.4	25.0	23.5
ATLANTA FALCONS	7	6	1	.538	274	277	−3	−0.1	0.6	3959	3787	172	36	38	2	22	−25	4.7	2.2	2.4	24.4	23.8
NEW ORLEANS SAINTS	4	8	2	.333	266	347	−81	−2.0	0.0	3666	4438	−772	25	45	20	16	−97	3.3	4.3	−1.0	21.3	26.4

1972 A.F.C.

EASTERN DIVISION	W	L	T	PCT	PTS	OPP	NET	P-W	D-W	Y-O	Y-D	Y-N	T-O	T-D	T-N	P-NP	D-NP	PR-O	PR-D	PR-N	YD-O	YD-D
MIAMI DOLPHINS	14	0	0	1.000DCS*	385	171	214	5.3	1.7	5036	3297	1739	28	46	18	217	−3	6.1	1.8	4.3	31.3	20.5
NEW YORK JETS	7	7	0	.500	367	324	43	1.1	−1.1	4787	4709	78	31	31	0	7	36	5.5	5.0	0.5	29.2	28.2
BALTIMORE COLTS	5	9	0	.357	235	252	−17	−0.4	−1.6	4187	4312	−125	34	36	2	−2	−15	4.7	4.3	0.4	24.9	26.1
BUFFALO BILLS	4	9	1	.321	257	377	−120	−3.0	0.5	3733	4192	−459	39	31	−8	−70	−50	1.9	3.4	−1.5	21.1	23.3
NEW ENGLAND PATRIOTS	3	11	0	.214	192	446	−254	−6.3	2.3	3659	5250	−1591	38	24	−14	−189	−65	2.1	6.8	−4.7	21.5	32.8

CENTRAL DIVISION	W	L	T	PCT	PTS	OPP	NET	P-W	D-W	Y-O	Y-D	Y-N	T-O	T-D	T-N	P-NP	D-NP	PR-O	PR-D	PR-N	YD-O	YD-D
PITTSBURGH STEELERS	11	3	0	.786DC	343	175	168	4.2	−0.2	4231	3771	460	26	48	22	126	42	3.6	2.0	1.7	24.2	21.2
CLEVELAND BROWNS	10	4	0	.714W	268	249	19	0.5	2.5	3709	4069	−360	28	29	1	−26	45	3.3	3.7	−0.4	22.3	23.7
CINCINNATI BENGALS	8	6	0	.571	299	229	70	1.8	−0.8	4317	3552	765	29	29	0	64	6	4.7	2.4	2.3	24.8	20.4
HOUSTON OILERS	1	13	0	.071	164	380	−216	−5.4	−0.6	3191	4734	−1543	33	24	−9	−165	−51	1.8	5.7	−4.0	18.4	28.9

WESTERN DIVISION	W	L	T	PCT	PTS	OPP	NET	P-W	D-W	Y-O	Y-D	Y-N	T-O	T-D	T-N	P-NP	D-NP	PR-O	PR-D	PR-N	YD-O	YD-D
OAKLAND RAIDERS	10	3	1	.750D	365	248	117	2.9	0.6	4745	3916	829	32	37	5	89	28	4.9	3.1	1.8	28.9	23.7
KANSAS CITY CHIEFS	8	6	0	.571	287	254	33	0.8	0.2	3953	4027	−74	32	43	11	38	−5	3.2	3.3	−0.1	23.0	23.3
DENVER BRONCOS	5	9	0	.357	325	350	−25	−0.6	−1.4	4472	3851	621	34	22	−12	4	−29	4.2	4.4	−0.2	26.3	22.9
SAN DIEGO CHARGERS	4	9	1	.321	264	344	−80	−2.0	−0.5	4299	3881	418	48	34	−14	−21	−59	3.0	3.4	−0.4	25.9	24.0

1972 N.F.C

EASTERN DIVISION	W	L	T	PCT	PTS	OPP	NET	P-W	D-W	Y-O	Y-D	Y-N	T-O	T-D	T-N	P-NP	D-NP	PR-O	PR-D	PR-N	YD-O	YD-D
WASHINGTON REDSKINS	11	3	0	.786DCS	336	218	118	3.0	1.0	4275	3595	680	26	32	6	81	37	5.9	3.0	2.9	26.1	21.8
DALLAS COWBOYS	10	4	0	.714WC	319	240	79	2.0	1.0	4466	3755	711	38	33	−5	39	40	3.7	4.1	−0.4	26.7	22.1
NEW YORK GIANTS	8	6	0	.571	331	247	84	2.1	−1.1	4483	4194	289	29	38	9	60	24	5.6	4.0	1.6	30.1	27.4
ST. LOUIS CARDINALS	4	9	1	.321	193	303	−110	−2.8	0.3	3267	4739	−1472	39	27	−12	−171	61	2.8	5.7	−2.9	20.3	29.1
PHILADELPHIA EAGLES	2	11	1	.179	145	352	−207	−5.2	0.7	3463	4738	−1275	38	27	−11	−150	−57	3.0	5.4	−2.5	21.9	30.4

CENTRAL DIVISION	W	L	T	PCT	PTS	OPP	NET	P-W	D-W	Y-O	Y-D	Y-N	T-O	T-D	T-N	P-NP	D-NP	PR-O	PR-D	PR-N	YD-O	YD-D
GREEN BAY PACKERS	10	4	0	.714D	304	226	78	2.0	1.0	3539	3474	65	19	36	17	73	5	4.2	3.4	0.8	21.8	20.6
DETROIT LIONS	8	5	1	.607	339	290	49	1.2	0.3	4155	4208	−53	25	27	2	4	45	4.6	4.9	−0.4	28.1	29.2
MINNESOTA VIKINGS	7	7	0	.500	301	252	49	1.2	−1.2	4263	3701	562	32	40	8	79	−30	5.2	1.9	3.3	24.9	22.0
CHICAGO BEARS	4	9	1	.321	225	275	−50	−1.3	−1.3	3468	3923	−455	35	35	0	−38	−12	2.6	3.8	−1.2	21.3	24.5

	W	L	T	PCT	PTS	OPP	NET	P-W	D-W	Y-O	Y-D	Y-N	T-O	T-D	T-N	P-NP	D-NP	PR-O	PR-D	PR-N	YD-O	YD-D
WESTERN DIVISION																						
SAN FRANCISCO 49ERS	8	5	1	.607D	353	249	104	2.6	−1.1	4351	4026	325	37	36	−1	23	81	4.8	3.6	1.2	25.2	22.4
ATLANTA FALCONS	7	7	0	.500	269	274	−5	−0.1	0.1	4011	3767	244	34	33	−1	16	−21	4.1	3.2	0.9	25.2	22.8
LOS ANGELES RAMS	6	7	1	.464	291	286	5	0.1	−0.6	4355	3907	448	31	27	−4	21	−16	3.3	4.0	−0.7	25.6	23.8
NEW ORLEANS SAINTS	2	11	1	.179	215	361	−146	−3.7	−0.8	3664	4491	−827	37	27	−10	−109	−37	3.4	5.1	−1.7	21.8	26.9

1973 A.F.C.

EASTERN DIVISION	W	L	T	PCT	PTS	OPP	NET	P-W	D-W	Y-O	Y-D	Y-N	T-O	T-D	T-N	P-NP	D-NP	PR-O	PR-D	PR-N	YD-O	YD-D
MIAMI DOLPHINS	12	2	0	.857DCS*	343	150	193	4.8	0.2	4103	3281	822	28	29	1	73	120	4.5	1.1	3.4	26.5	20.6
BUFFALO BILLS	9	5	0	.643	259	230	29	0.7	1.3	4085	3915	170	27	33	6	38	−9	1.7	4.0	−2.4	25.2	24.8
NEW ENGLAND PATRIOTS	5	9	0	.357	258	300	−42	−1.0	−1.0	3843	4188	−345	42	31	−11	−73	31	3.8	3.2	0.7	23.4	24.5
BALTIMORE COLTS	4	10	0	.286	226	341	−115	−2.9	−0.1	3506	4488	−982	38	37	−1	−86	−29	1.5	5.3	−3.8	21.5	27.9
NEW YORK JETS	4	10	0	.286	240	306	−66	−1.6	−1.4	3920	4178	−258	39	38	−1	−26	−40	3.0	4.0	−1.0	21.8	24.4

CENTRAL DIVISION	W	L	T	PCT	PTS	OPP	NET	P-W	D-W	Y-O	Y-D	Y-N	T-O	T-D	T-N	P-NP	D-NP	PR-O	PR-D	PR-N	YD-O	YD-D
CINCINNATI BENGALS	10	4	0	.714#D	286	231	55	1.4	1.6	4512	3705	807	26	34	8	99	−44	5.4	3.1	2.3	26.9	22.6
PITTSBURGH STEELERS	10	4	0	.714#W	347	210	137	3.4	−0.4	4070	3324	746	40	55	15	122	15	2.8	0.3	2.5	21.6	17.5
CLEVELAND BROWNS	7	5	2	.571	234	255	−21	−0.5	1.5	3341	3827	−486	37	21	−16	−105	84	1.6	4.0	−2.4	19.0	21.1
HOUSTON OILERS	1	13	0	.071	199	447	−248	−6.2	0.2	3307	4647	−1340	52	27	−25	−212	−36	1.8	4.9	−3.1	17.2	24.5

WESTERN DIVISION	W	L	T	PCT	PTS	OPP	NET	P-W	D-W	Y-O	Y-D	Y-N	T-O	T-D	T-N	P-NP	D-NP	PR-O	PR-D	PR-N	YD-O	YD-D
OAKLAND RAIDERS	9	4	1	.679DC	292	175	117	2.9	−0.4	4773	3160	1613	34	33	−1	130	−13	4.1	2.5	1.5	26.7	18.1
DENVER BRONCOS	7	5	2	.571	354	296	58	1.5	−0.5	4473	4235	238	29	29	0	20	38	4.5	4.6	−0.1	26.0	23.5
KANSAS CITY CHIEFS	7	5	2	.571	231	192	39	1.0	0.0	3536	3575	−39	31	39	8	29	10	3.6	2.2	1.4	19.8	20.0
SAN DIEGO CHARGERS	2	11	1	.179	188	386	−198	−4.9	0.4	3622	4518	−896	51	34	−17	−143	−55	1.4	4.7	−3.3	19.5	25.2

1973 N.F.C.

EASTERN DIVISION	W	L	T	PCT	PTS	OPP	NET	P-W	D-W	Y-O	Y-D	Y-N	T-O	T-D	T-N	P-NP	D-NP	PR-O	PR-D	PR-N	YD-O	YD-D
DALLAS COWBOYS	10	4	0	.714#DC	382	203	179	4.5	−1.5	4751	3466	1285	28	41	13	159	20	5.1	3.4	1.7	27.8	20.2
WASHINGTON REDSKINS	10	4	0	.714#W	325	198	127	3.2	−0.2	3797	3779	18	32	44	12	50	77	4.8	2.5	2.3	20.9	20.8
PHILADELPHIA EAGLES	5	8	1	.393	310	393	−83	−2.1	0.6	4789	5062	−273	28	30	2	−15	−68	5.2	5.6	−0.4	27.7	29.3
ST. LOUIS CARDINALS	4	9	1	.321	286	365	−79	−2.0	−0.5	4054	5149	−1095	29	27	−2	−99	20	4.4	6.3	−1.9	24.7	31.2
NEW YORK GIANTS	2	11	1	.179	226	362	−136	−3.4	−1.1	4039	4159	−120	40	32	−8	−42	−94	3.1	4.0	−1.0	24.6	24.8

CENTRAL DIVISION	W	L	T	PCT	PTS	OPP	NET	P-W	D-W	Y-O	Y-D	Y-N	T-O	T-D	T-N	P-NP	D-NP	PR-O	PR-D	PR-N	YD-O	YD-D
MINNESOTA VIKINGS	12	2	0	.857DCS	296	168	128	3.2	1.8	4231	3868	363	26	36	10	70	58	5.2	2.5	2.7	27.7	23.0
DETROIT LIONS	6	7	1	.464	271	247	24	0.6	−1.1	4046	3905	141	33	33	0	12	12	3.3	2.6	0.7	25.0	24.9
GREEN BAY PACKERS	5	7	2	.429	202	259	−57	−1.4	0.4	3256	3821	−565	28	33	5	−27	−30	2.1	3.7	−1.6	19.7	24.2
CHICAGO BEARS	3	11	0	.214	195	334	−139	−3.5	−0.5	3129	4183	−1054	42	33	−9	−124	−15	1.7	3.6	−2.0	17.2	23.1

WESTERN DIVISION	W	L	T	PCT	PTS	OPP	NET	P-W	D-W	Y-O	Y-D	Y-N	T-O	T-D	T-N	P-NP	D-NP	PR-O	PR-D	PR-N	YD-O	YD-D
LOS ANGELES RAMS	12	2	0	.857D	388	178	210	5.3	−0.3	4906	2951	1955	20	38	18	235	−25	5.9	2.4	3.6	28.9	17.4
ATLANTA FALCONS	9	5	0	.643	318	224	94	2.3	−0.3	4038	3559	479	33	37	4	56	38	4.4	1.6	2.9	22.9	20.2
NEW ORLEANS SAINTS	5	9	0	.357	163	312	−149	−3.7	1.7	3501	4580	−1079	34	30	−4	−106	−43	2.7	4.5	−1.8	20.4	26.3
SAN FRANCISCO 49ERS	5	9	0	.357	262	319	−57	−1.4	−0.6	4224	4329	−105	39	32	−7	−37	−20	2.9	4.3	−1.4	22.3	23.4

1974 A.F.C.

EASTERN DIVISION	W	L	T	PCT	PTS	OPP	NET	P-W	D-W	Y-O	Y-D	Y-N	T-O	T-D	T-N	P-NP	D-NP	PR-O	PR-D	PR-N	YD-O	YD-D
MIAMI DOLPHINS	11	3	0	.786D	327	216	111	2.8	1.2	4275	3806	469	31	33	2	47	64	4.6	4.0	0.7	27.4	23.5
BUFFALO BILLS	9	5	0	.643W	264	244	20	0.5	1.5	3586	3489	97	29	31	2	16	4	3.4	2.4	1.0	22.1	20.6
NEW ENGLAND PATRIOTS	7	7	0	.500	348	289	59	1.5	−1.5	4474	4067	407	38	38	0	34	25	3.9	3.8	0.1	25.4	22.5
NEW YORK JETS	7	7	0	.500	279	300	−21	−0.5	0.5	4061	4297	−236	32	26	−6	−44	23	4.0	3.8	0.2	24.5	25.7
BALTIMORE COLTS	2	12	0	.143	190	329	−139	−3.5	−1.5	3843	4126	−283	37	24	−13	−76	−63	2.2	5.6	−3.4	23.3	26.3

CENTRAL DIVISION	W	L	T	PCT	PTS	OPP	NET	P-W	D-W	Y-O	Y-D	Y-N	T-O	T-D	T-N	P-NP	D-NP	PR-O	PR-D	PR-N	YD-O	YD-D
PITTSBURGH STEELERS	10	3	1	.750DCS*	305	189	116	2.9	0.6	4375	3074	1301	40	47	7	136	−20	2.8	1.2	1.6	23.8	16.2
CINCINNATI BENGALS	7	7	0	.500	283	259	24	0.6	−0.6	4489	3942	547	31	20	−11	2	22	5.4	3.8	1.6	28.1	24.8
HOUSTON OILERS	7	7	0	.500	236	282	−46	−1.1	1.1	3338	4425	−1087	33	36	3	−79	33	3.1	3.6	−0.5	19.6	26.3
CLEVELAND BROWNS	4	10	0	.286	251	344	−93	−2.3	−0.7	3651	4440	−789	39	40	1	−62	−31	1.8	3.5	−1.6	19.0	24.4

WESTERN DIVISION	W	L	T	PCT	PTS	OPP	NET	P-W	D-W	Y-O	Y-D	Y-N	T-O	T-D	T-N	P-NP	D-NP	PR-O	PR-D	PR-N	YD-O	YD-D
OAKLAND RAIDERS	12	2	0	.857DC	355	228	127	3.2	1.8	4718	4219	499	28	41	13	94	33	5.2	2.5	2.6	27.6	24.4
DENVER BRONCOS	7	6	1	.536	302	294	8	0.2	0.3	4485	4391	94	30	33	3	20	−12	4.6	3.8	0.9	26.4	25.5
KANSAS CITY CHIEFS	5	9	0	.357	233	293	−60	−1.5	−0.5	3828	4464	−636	38	44	6	−29	−31	2.5	3.7	−1.2	20.6	24.9
SAN DIEGO CHARGERS	5	9	0	.357	212	285	−73	−1.8	−0.2	4415	4830	−415	33	28	−5	−55	−18	3.9	5.5	−1.7	27.9	30.2

1974 N.F.C

EASTERN DIVISION	W	L	T	PCT	PTS	OPP	NET	P-W	D-W	Y-O	Y-D	Y-N	T-O	T-D	T-N	P-NP	D-NP	PR-O	PR-D	PR-N	YD-O	YD-D
ST. LOUIS CARDINALS	10	4	0	.714#D	285	218	67	1.7	1.3	4314	4251	63	17	25	8	37	30	5.4	3.9	1.5	27.3	26.1
WASHINGTON REDSKINS	10	4	0	.714#W	320	196	124	3.1	-0.1	4245	3285	960	20	40	20	160	-36	5.8	2.0	3.8	25.6	19.3
DALLAS COWBOYS	8	6	0	.571	297	235	62	1.5	-0.5	4983	3463	1520	31	26	-5	107	-45	4.6	4.4	0.2	28.5	20.3
PHILADELPHIA EAGLES	7	7	0	.500	242	217	25	0.6	-0.6	3597	4270	-673	29	34	5	-36	61	3.2	3.8	-0.6	21.7	25.6
NEW YORK GIANTS	2	12	0	.143	195	299	-104	-2.6	-2.4	3689	4457	-768	36	25	-11	-108	4	2.8	4.7	-2.0	23.2	28.8

CENTRAL DIVISION	W	L	T	PCT	PTS	OPP	NET	P-W	D-W	Y-O	Y-D	Y-N	T-O	T-D	T-N	P-NP	D-NP	PR-O	PR-D	PR-N	YD-O	YD-D
MINNESOTA VIKINGS	10	4	0	.714DCS	310	195	115	2.9	0.1	4611	3907	704	22	33	11	103	12	5.7	3.3	2.4	28.8	24.0
DETROIT LIONS	7	7	0	.500	256	270	-14	-0.3	0.3	3653	4338	-685	25	30	5	-37	23	4.5	3.7	0.7	22.5	26.3
GREEN BAY PACKERS	6	8	0	.429	210	206	4	0.1	-1.1	3607	3641	-34	37	35	-2	-11	15	2.8	2.6	0.2	20.6	21.2
CHICAGO BEARS	4	10	0	.286	152	279	-127	-3.2	0.2	3200	3818	-618	37	32	-5	-72	-55	1.9	3.9	-2.0	18.4	23.0

WESTERN DIVISION	W	L	T	PCT	PTS	OPP	NET	P-W	D-W	Y-O	Y-D	Y-N	T-O	T-D	T-N	P-NP	D-NP	PR-O	PR-D	PR-N	YD-O	YD-D
LOS ANGELES RAMS	10	4	0	.714DC	263	181	82	2.1	1.0	4332	3404	928	27	25	-2	69	13	5.0	3.0	2.0	26.6	21.3
SAN FRANCISCO 49ERS	6	8	0	.429	226	236	-10	-0.3	-0.8	3988	3964	24	42	40	-2	-6	-4	2.3	3.2	-0.9	23.6	23.2
NEW ORLEANS SAINTS	5	9	0	.357	166	263	-97	-2.4	0.4	3744	3797	-53	33	35	2	4	-101	2.2	3.7	-1.5	22.0	22.7
ATLANTA FALCONS	3	11	0	.214	111	271	-160	-4.0	0.0	2800	4136	-1336	55	29	-26	-215	55	-0.1	2.8	-2.9	15.4	22.2

1975 A.F.C.

EASTERN DIVISION	W	L	T	PCT	PTS	OPP	NET	P-W	D-W	Y-O	Y-D	Y-N	T-O	T-D	T-N	P-NP	D-NP	PR-O	PR-D	PR-N	YD-O	YD-D
BALTIMORE COLTS	10	4	0	.714#D	395	269	126	3.2	-0.2	4498	4173	325	18	41	23	119	7	5.4	2.7	2.7	25.4	22.9
MIAMI DOLPHINS	10	4	0	.714#	357	222	135	3.4	-0.4	4509	3789	720	26	30	4	76	59	4.7	2.8	1.9	28.7	23.5
BUFFALO BILLS	8	6	0	.571	420	355	65	1.6	-0.6	5467	5073	394	34	45	11	77	-12	5.1	4.8	0.3	31.4	29.0
NEW ENGLAND PATRIOTS	3	11	0	.214	258	358	-100	-2.5	-1.5	4283	4464	-181	50	29	-21	-99	-1	3.0	4.6	-1.5	22.5	23.5
NEW YORK JETS	3	11	0	.214	258	433	-175	-4.4	0.4	4230	5456	-1226	41	28	-13	-154	-21	2.0	6.9	-4.9	25.6	34.3

CENTRAL DIVISION	W	L	T	PCT	PTS	OPP	NET	P-W	D-W	Y-O	Y-D	Y-N	T-O	T-D	T-N	P-NP	D-NP	PR-O	PR-D	PR-N	YD-O	YD-D
PITTSBURGH STEELERS	12	2	0	.857DCS*	373	162	211	5.3	-0.3	4887	3661	1226	32	37	5	122	89	5.2	1.6	3.6	28.6	20.8
CINCINNATI BENGALS	11	3	0	.786W	340	246	94	2.3	1.7	5060	3923	1137	34	44	10	135	-61	6.1	2.0	4.0	29.1	22.4
HOUSTON OILERS	10	4	0	.714	293	226	67	1.7	1.3	3937	4137	-200	34	43	9	19	48	3.3	3.3	-0.0	22.5	22.9
CLEVELAND BROWNS	3	11	0	.214	218	372	-154	-3.8	-0.2	3807	4623	-816	37	26	-11	-112	-42	2.1	6.1	-4.0	21.8	26.6

WESTERN DIVISION	W	L	T	PCT	PTS	OPP	NET	P-W	D-W	Y-O	Y-D	Y-N	T-O	T-D	T-N	P-NP	D-NP	PR-O	PR-D	PR-N	YD-O	YD-D
OAKLAND RAIDERS	11	3	0	.786DC	375	255	120	3.0	1.0	4964	3629	1335	48	41	-7	83	37	3.5	0.9	2.6	26.7	18.7
DENVER BRONCOS	6	8	0	.429	254	307	-53	-1.3	0.3	4534	4006	528	48	32	-16	-20	-33	2.4	3.9	-1.4	25.5	23.0
KANSAS CITY CHIEFS	5	9	0	.357	282	341	-59	-1.5	-0.5	4207	5236	-1029	34	42	8	-54	-5	4.0	5.1	-1.1	23.6	29.8
SAN DIEGO CHARGERS	2	12	0	.143	189	345	-156	-3.9	-1.1	3411	4952	-1541	29	34	5	-108	-48	2.4	4.3	-1.9	19.7	30.8

1975 N.F.C

EASTERN DIVISION	W	L	T	PCT	PTS	OPP	NET	P-W	D-W	Y-O	Y-D	Y-N	T-O	T-D	T-N	P-NP	D-NP	PR-O	PR-D	PR-N	YD-O	YD-D
ST. LOUIS CARDINALS	11	3	0	.786D	356	276	80	2.0	2.0	4955	4595	360	39	37	-2	22	58	5.1	3.9	1.2	29.1	26.0
DALLAS COWBOYS	10	4	0	.714WCS	350	268	82	2.1	1.0	5025	3739	1286	35	44	9	143	-61	4.9	2.7	2.2	27.5	20.2
WASHINGTON REDSKINS	8	6	0	.571	325	276	49	1.2	-0.2	4669	4483	186	46	37	-9	-21	70	4.0	4.2	-0.2	24.1	23.7
NEW YORK GIANTS	5	9	0	.357	216	306	-90	-2.3	0.3	3729	4789	-1060	37	24	-13	-140	50	3.3	4.7	-1.4	21.4	28.2
PHILADELPHIA EAGLES	4	10	0	.286	225	302	-77	-1.9	-1.1	4142	4771	-629	35	44	9	-16	-61	3.3	3.4	-0.1	23.1	26.8

CENTRAL DIVISION	W	L	T	PCT	PTS	OPP	NET	P-W	D-W	Y-O	Y-D	Y-N	T-O	T-D	T-N	P-NP	D-NP	PR-O	PR-D	PR-N	YD-O	YD-D
MINNESOTA VIKINGS	12	2	0	.857D	377	180	197	4.9	0.1	4955	3153	1802	26	42	16	214	-17	5.3	1.2	4.0	28.6	18.2
DETROIT LIONS	7	7	0	.500	245	262	-17	-0.4	0.4	4064	4000	64	30	37	7	33	-50	3.8	3.3	0.4	22.7	23.5
CHICAGO BEARS	4	10	0	.286	191	379	-188	-4.7	1.7	3492	4576	-1084	40	27	-13	-142	-46	2.3	4.9	-2.6	18.7	24.5
GREEN BAY PACKERS	4	10	0	.286	226	285	-59	-1.5	-1.5	3619	4511	-892	38	41	3	-62	3	2.7	4.2	-1.4	20.0	24.1

WESTERN DIVISION	W	L	T	PCT	PTS	OPP	NET	P-W	D-W	Y-O	Y-D	Y-N	T-O	T-D	T-N	P-NP	D-NP	PR-O	PR-D	PR-N	YD-O	YD-D
LOS ANGELES RAMS	12	2	0	.857DC	312	135	177	4.4	0.6	4566	3322	1244	25	40	15	164	13	4.3	2.1	2.2	26.7	19.8
SAN FRANCISCO 49ERS	5	9	0	.357	255	286	-31	-0.8	-1.2	4158	4026	132	44	27	-17	-57	26	3.8	4.1	-0.3	23.9	22.7
ATLANTA FALCONS	4	10	0	.286	240	289	-49	-1.2	-1.8	3861	4812	-951	48	37	-11	-123	74	2.2	3.3	-1.1	21.0	25.7
NEW ORLEANS SAINTS	2	12	0	.143	165	360	-195	-4.9	-0.1	3187	4317	-1130	40	39	-1	-98	-97	1.2	5.0	-3.8	17.4	24.1

1976 A.F.C.

EASTERN DIVISION	W	L	T	PCT	PTS	OPP	NET	P-W	D-W	Y-O	Y-D	Y-N	T-O	T-D	T-N	P-NP	D-NP	PR-O	PR-D	PR-N	YD-O	YD-D
BALTIMORE COLTS	11	3	0	.786#D	417	246	171	4.3	−0.3	5236	4187	1049	28	36	8	119	52	7.0	4.3	2.7	30.6	24.2
NEW ENGLAND PATRIOTS	11	3	0	.786#W	376	236	140	3.5	0.5	4694	4022	672	36	50	14	112	28	3.1	2.7	0.4	26.4	22.0
MIAMI DOLPHINS	6	8	0	.429	263	264	−1	−0.0	−1.0	4386	5081	−695	23	29	6	−34	33	4.6	6.5	−1.9	28.5	34.8
NEW YORK JETS	3	11	0	.214	169	383	−214	−5.3	1.3	3530	4916	−1386	53	32	−21	−200	−14	0.9	5.3	−4.4	19.6	27.8
BUFFALO BILLS	2	12	0	.143	245	363	−118	−3.0	−2.1	4404	4730	−326	43	42	−1	−31	−87	3.0	4.4	−1.4	22.9	24.8

CENTRAL DIVISION	W	L	T	PCT	PTS	OPP	NET	P-W	D-W	Y-O	Y-D	Y-N	T-O	T-D	T-N	P-NP	D-NP	PR-O	PR-D	PR-N	YD-O	YD-D
PITTSBURGH STEELERS	10	4	0	.714#DC	342	138	204	5.1	−2.1	4637	3323	1314	31	46	15	170	34	4.0	2.3	1.7	25.1	18.1
CINCINNATI BENGALS	10	4	0	.714#	335	210	125	3.1	−0.1	4300	3670	630	35	41	6	77	48	4.3	1.8	2.6	23.8	19.5
CLEVELAND BROWNS	9	5	0	.643	267	287	−20	−0.5	2.5	4542	3793	749	37	32	−5	42	−62	4.5	3.0	1.6	27.4	21.8
HOUSTON OILERS	5	9	0	.357	222	273	−51	−1.3	−0.7	3570	3987	−417	33	28	−5	−55	4	3.0	4.0	−1.0	18.5	20.8

WESTERN DIVISION	W	L	T	PCT	PTS	OPP	NET	P-W	D-W	Y-O	Y-D	Y-N	T-O	T-D	T-N	P-NP	D-NP	PR-O	PR-D	PR-N	YD-O	YD-D
OAKLAND RAIDERS	13	1	0	.929DCS*	350	237	113	2.8	3.2	5190	4379	811	29	25	−4	52	61	6.2	4.3	1.9	31.1	25.8
DENVER BRONCOS	9	5	0	.643	315	206	109	2.7	−0.7	4136	3734	402	34	37	3	46	63	3.4	2.4	1.0	22.0	20.2
SAN DIEGO CHARGERS	6	8	0	.429	248	285	−37	−0.9	−0.1	4456	4676	−220	31	31	0	−18	−19	4.1	4.7	−0.6	25.9	27.3
KANSAS CITY CHIEFS	5	9	0	.357	290	376	−86	−2.2	0.2	4802	5357	−555	33	43	10	−6	−80	5.0	4.3	0.7	26.2	29.8
TAMPA BAY BUC-CANEERS	0	14	0	.000	125	412	−287	−7.2	0.2	3006	4801	−1795	37	28	−9	−186	−101	1.6	5.9	−4.2	16.4	28.6

1976 N.F.C

EASTERN DIVISION	W	L	T	PCT	PTS	OPP	NET	P-W	D-W	Y-O	Y-D	Y-N	T-O	T-D	T-N	P-NP	D-NP	PR-O	PR-D	PR-N	YD-O	YD-D
DALLAS COWBOYS	11	3	0	.786D	296	194	102	2.6	1.5	4884	3730	1154	29	28	−1	92	10	5.5	3.0	2.5	29.2	22.1
WASHINGTON REDSKINS	10	4	0	.714#W	291	217	74	1.9	1.1	4096	4122	−26	43	47	4	14	60	3.1	2.2	1.0	20.5	19.9
ST. LOUIS CARDINALS	10	4	0	.714#	309	267	42	1.0	2.0	5136	4089	1047	37	39	2	95	−53	5.9	3.7	2.2	29.9	23.6
PHILADELPHIA EAGLES	4	10	0	.286	165	286	−121	−3.0	0.0	3572	4603	−1031	32	24	−8	−118	−3	1.9	5.5	−3.6	20.1	30.9
NEW YORK GIANTS	3	11	0	.214	170	250	−80	−2.0	−2.0	3696	4191	−495	36	27	−9	−77	−3	2.2	4.3	−2.1	21.6	25.9

CENTRAL DIVISION	W	L	T	PCT	PTS	OPP	NET	P-W	D-W	Y-O	Y-D	Y-N	T-O	T-D	T-N	P-NP	D-NP	PR-O	PR-D	PR-N	YD-O	YD-D
MINNESOTA VIKINGS	11	2	1	.821DCS	305	176	129	3.2	1.3	4858	3671	1187	29	32	3	111	18	5.4	2.2	3.3	29.4	21.3
CHICAGO BEARS	7	7	0	.500	253	216	37	0.9	−0.9	3843	4201	−358	28	47	19	46	−9	3.0	2.9	0.1	20.2	21.8
DETROIT LIONS	6	8	0	.429	262	220	42	1.0	−2.1	4353	3587	766	33	39	6	88	−46	4.3	2.1	2.2	23.8	19.8
GREEN BAY PACKERS	5	9	0	.357	218	299	−81	−2.0	0.0	3452	4123	−671	45	26	−19	−132	51	2.1	3.7	−1.6	19.5	22.5

WESTERN DIVISION	W	L	T	PCT	PTS	OPP	NET	P-W	D-W	Y-O	Y-D	Y-N	T-O	T-D	T-N	P-NP	D-NP	PR-O	PR-D	PR-N	YD-O	YD-D
LOS ANGELES RAMS	10	3	1	.750DC	351	190	161	4.0	−0.5	4869	3656	1213	36	48	12	149	12	5.3	1.7	3.6	25.2	19.0
SAN FRANCISCO 49ERS	8	6	0	.571	270	190	80	2.0	−1.0	4085	3562	523	33	25	−8	12	68	2.5	3.5	−1.0	22.0	18.5
ATLANTA FALCONS	4	10	0	.286	172	312	−140	−3.5	0.5	3103	4578	−1475	41	38	−3	−135	−5	1.1	3.5	−2.5	16.2	24.0
NEW ORLEANS SAINTS	4	10	0	.286	253	346	−93	−2.3	−0.7	3759	4491	−732	32	39	7	−33	−60	3.2	4.5	−1.4	19.1	23.4
SEATTLE SEAHAWKS	2	12	0	.143	229	429	−200	−5.0	0.0	4065	5400	−1335	48	26	−22	−199	−1	2.8	5.4	−2.6	22.5	29.5

1977 A.F.C.

EASTERN DIVISION	W	L	T	PCT	PTS	OPP	NET	P-W	D-W	Y-O	Y-D	Y-N	T-O	T-D	T-N	P-NP	D-NP	PR-O	PR-D	PR-N	YD-O	YD-D
BALTIMORE COLTS	10	4	0	.714#D	295	221	74	1.9	1.1	4588	3988	600	26	47	21	134	−60	5.0	2.2	2.8	24.9	22.3
MIAMI DOLPHINS	10	4	0	.714#	313	197	116	2.9	0.1	4327	3982	345	27	33	6	53	63	4.5	3.8	0.6	28.7	25.7
NEW ENGLAND PATRIOTS	9	5	0	.643	278	217	61	1.5	0.5	4310	3638	672	36	29	−7	28	33	3.9	3.2	0.6	26.8	21.9
NEW YORK JETS	3	11	0	.214	191	300	−109	−2.7	−1.3	3620	4648	−1028	40	28	−12	−134	25	2.5	5.3	−2.8	21.4	27.3
BUFFALO BILLS	3	11	0	.214	160	313	−153	−3.8	−0.2	4391	4453	−62	44	33	−11	−49	−104	3.2	3.8	−0.6	25.4	26.0

CENTRAL DIVISION	W	L	T	PCT	PTS	OPP	NET	P-W	D-W	Y-O	Y-D	Y-N	T-O	T-D	T-N	P-NP	D-NP	PR-O	PR-D	PR-N	YD-O	YD-D
PITTSBURGH STEELERS	9	5	0	.643D	283	243	40	1.0	1.0	4645	3692	953	49	44	−5	59	−19	4.4	1.9	2.5	25.8	20.5
HOUSTON OILERS	8	6	0	.571	299	230	69	1.7	−0.7	3864	3957	−93	38	54	16	56	13	2.9	2.7	0.2	20.7	21.0
CINCINNATI BENGALS	8	6	0	.571	238	235	3	0.1	0.9	4194	4124	70	32	39	7	34	−31	4.2	4.4	−0.2	24.8	25.5
CLEVELAND BROWNS	6	8	0	.429	269	267	2	0.1	−1.0	4375	4115	260	53	39	−14	−34	36	2.4	3.1	−0.6	25.7	23.2

WESTERN DIVISION	W	L	T	PCT	PTS	OPP	NET	P-W	D-W	Y-O	Y-D	Y-N	T-O	T-D	T-N	P-NP	D-NP	PR-O	PR-D	PR-N	YD-O	YD-D
DENVER BRONCOS	12	2	0	.857DCS	274	148	126	3.2	1.8	3906	3775	131	27	39	12	59	67	4.1	2.7	1.4	21.6	21.2
OAKLAND RAIDERS	11	3	0	.786WC	351	230	121	3.0	1.0	4736	3976	760	40	47	7	91	30	3.6	3.0	0.5	26.9	22.6
SAN DIEGO CHARGERS	7	7	0	.500	222	205	17	0.4	−0.4	4005	3652	353	31	31	0	29	−12	3.7	2.5	1.2	26.2	23.0
SEATTLE SEAHAWKS	5	9	0	.357	282	373	−91	−2.3	0.3	4292	4818	−526	46	36	−10	−84	−7	2.7	3.8	−1.1	24.8	28.0
KANSAS CITY CHIEFS	2	12	0	.143	225	349	−124	−3.1	−1.9	3936	4993	−1057	47	44	−3	−100	−24	2.4	3.4	−1.0	21.4	26.3

1977 N.F.C

EASTERN DIVISION	W	L	T	PCT	PTS	OPP	NET	P-W	D-W	Y-O	Y-D	Y-N	T-O	T-D	T-N	P-NP	D-NP	PR-O	PR-D	PR-N	YD-O	YD-D
DALLAS COWBOYS	12	2	0	.857DCS*	345	212	133	3.3	1.7	4812	3213	1599	24	31	7	161	−28	5.4	1.8	3.6	26.4	17.5
WASHINGTON REDSKINS	9	5	0	.643#	196	189	7	0.2	1.8	3615	4110	−495	30	33	3	−29	36	3.0	2.9	0.0	19.5	22.3
ST. LOUIS CARDINALS	7	7	0	.500	272	287	−15	−0.4	0.4	4541	4504	37	37	31	−6	−21	6	4.4	4.1	0.4	26.7	26.8
PHILADELPHIA EAGLES	5	9	0	.357	220	207	13	0.3	−2.3	3578	3793	−215	38	34	−4	−34	47	2.8	2.6	0.1	19.6	20.6
NEW YORK GIANTS	5	9	0	.357	181	265	−84	−2.1	0.1	3284	3870	−586	34	32	−2	−57	−27	1.3	4.6	−3.3	18.0	21.0

CENTRAL DIVISION	W	L	T	PCT	PTS	OPP	NET	P-W	D-W	Y-O	Y-D	Y-N	T-O	T-D	T-N	P-NP	D-NP	PR-O	PR-D	PR-N	YD-O	YD-D
MINNESOTA VIKINGS	9	5	0	.643#DC	231	227	4	0.1	1.9	4189	3799	390	46	29	−17	−36	40	3.7	3.0	0.8	24.1	20.8
CHICAGO BEARS	9	5	0	.643#	255	253	2	0.1	2.0	4655	4285	370	35	31	−4	15	−13	3.5	3.4	0.0	24.9	23.5
DETROIT LIONS	6	8	0	.429	183	252	−69	−1.7	0.7	3224	3772	−548	30	35	5	−26	−43	2.0	3.4	−1.5	17.4	20.8
GREEN BAY PACKERS	4	10	0	.286	134	219	−85	−2.1	−0.9	3212	4033	−821	30	24	−6	−92	7	2.4	3.5	−1.1	20.3	25.5
TAMPA BAY BUC-CANEERS	2	12	0	.143	103	223	−120	−3.0	−2.0	2693	3934	−1241	46	41	−5	−123	3	−0.1	2.6	−2.8	14.5	21.9

WESTERN DIVISION	W	L	T	PCT	PTS	OPP	NET	P-W	D-W	Y-O	Y-D	Y-N	T-O	T-D	T-N	P-NP	D-NP	PR-O	PR-D	PR-N	YD-O	YD-D
LOS ANGELES RAMS	10	4	0	.714D	302	146	156	3.9	−0.9	4591	3575	1016	28	41	13	137	19	4.6	2.1	2.5	26.5	20.5
ATLANTA FALCONS	7	7	0	.500	179	129	50	1.3	−1.3	3246	3242	4	25	48	23	92	−42	2.1	0.8	1.3	17.4	17.2
SAN FRANCISCO 49ERS	5	9	0	.357	220	260	−40	−1.0	−1.0	3594	3457	137	25	18	−7	−17	−23	2.7	4.4	−1.7	21.8	21.9
NEW ORLEANS SAINTS	3	11	0	.214	232	336	−104	−2.6	−1.4	3597	4622	−1025	32	25	−7	−113	9	2.1	5.0	−3.0	20.8	27.2

1978 A.F.C.

EASTERN DIVISION	W	L	T	PCT	PTS	OPP	NET	P-W	D-W	Y-O	Y-D	Y-N	T-O	T-D	T-N	P-NP	D-NP	PR-O	PR-D	PR-N	YD-O	YD-D
NEW ENGLAND PATRIOTS	11	5	0	.688#D	358	286	72	1.8	1.2	5965	4615	1350	46	43	−3	101	−29	4.4	4.3	0.1	32.1	24.7
MIAMI DOLPHINS	11	5	0	.688#W	372	254	118	3.0	0.0	4835	5169	−334	30	53	23	64	54	4.7	3.4	1.3	25.7	27.3
NEW YORK JETS	8	8	0	.500	359	364	−5	−0.1	0.1	4857	5524	−667	37	40	3	−44	39	3.6	4.3	−0.7	26.0	28.9
BUFFALO BILLS	5	11	0	.313	302	354	−52	−1.3	−1.7	4630	5188	−558	34	30	−4	−63	11	4.1	4.5	−0.5	26.2	28.2
BALTIMORE COLTS	5	11	0	.313	239	421	−182	−4.6	1.6	4107	5911	−1804	47	37	−10	−190	8	2.0	6.3	−4.2	20.1	29.9

CENTRAL DIVISION	W	L	T	PCT	PTS	OPP	NET	P-W	D-W	Y-O	Y-D	Y-N	T-O	T-D	T-N	P-NP	D-NP	PR-O	PR-D	PR-N	YD-O	YD-D
PITTSBURGH STEELERS	14	2	0	.875DCS*	356	195	161	4.0	2.0	4996	4168	828	39	48	9	105	56	4.9	2.6	2.3	26.9	22.7
HOUSTON OILERS	10	6	0	.625WDC	283	298	−15	−0.4	2.4	4814	4914	−100	38	34	−4	−24	9	4.4	4.8	−0.4	25.2	25.7
CLEVELAND BROWNS	8	8	0	.500	334	356	−22	−0.6	0.6	5347	5352	−5	50	45	−5	−20	−2	4.5	4.2	0.3	26.0	26.1
CINCINNATI BENGALS	4	12	0	.250	252	284	−32	−0.8	−3.2	4872	4632	240	49	37	−12	−28	−4	3.0	3.4	−0.4	23.1	21.7

WESTERN DIVISION	W	L	T	PCT	PTS	OPP	NET	P-W	D-W	Y-O	Y-D	Y-N	T-O	T-D	T-N	P-NP	D-NP	PR-O	PR-D	PR-N	YD-O	YD-D
DENVER BRONCOS	10	6	0	.625D	282	198	84	2.1	−0.1	4829	4449	380	34	44	10	72	12	4.1	2.5	1.6	25.7	22.7
OAKLAND RAIDERS	9	7	0	.563	311	283	28	0.7	0.3	4913	4894	19	43	43	0	2	26	3.2	3.4	−0.2	25.5	25.2
SEATTLE SEAHAWKS	9	7	0	.563	345	358	−13	−0.3	1.3	5511	5518	−7	41	39	−2	−9	−4	4.5	4.6	−0.1	29.8	30.0
SAN DIEGO CHARGERS	9	7	0	.563	355	309	46	1.1	−0.1	5471	4559	912	51	38	−13	24	22	4.5	3.2	1.3	26.4	22.9
KANSAS CITY CHIEFS	4	12	0	.250	243	327	−84	−2.1	−1.9	4820	4966	−146	34	35	1	−8	−76	3.0	4.6	−1.6	27.2	27.7

1978 N.F.C

EASTERN DIVISION	W	L	T	PCT	PTS	OPP	NET	P-W	D-W	Y-O	Y-D	Y-N	T-O	T-D	T-N	P-NP	D-NP	PR-O	PR-D	PR-N	YD-O	YD-D
DALLAS COWBOYS	12	4	0	.750DCS	384	208	176	4.4	−0.4	5959	4009	1950	35	36	1	167	9	5.5	2.8	2.7	29.8	20.6
PHILADELPHIA EAGLES	9	7	0	.563W	270	250	20	0.5	0.5	4653	4635	18	38	48	10	42	−22	3.7	3.6	0.1	23.9	24.3
WASHINGTON REDSKINS	8	8	0	.500	273	283	−10	−0.3	0.3	4647	4914	−267	37	32	−5	−42	32	3.7	3.4	0.3	22.1	23.4
ST. LOUIS CARDINALS	6	10	0	.375	248	296	−48	−1.2	−0.8	5125	4747	378	35	42	7	60	−108	4.5	2.9	1.6	25.8	23.9
NEW YORK GIANTS	6	10	0	.375	264	298	−34	−0.9	−1.1	4449	5042	−593	39	39	0	−49	15	2.5	3.3	−0.7	22.0	25.2

CENTRAL DIVISION	W	L	T	PCT	PTS	OPP	NET	P-W	D-W	Y-O	Y-D	Y-N	T-O	T-D	T-N	P-NP	D-NP	PR-O	PR-D	PR-N	YD-O	YD-D
MINNESOTA VIKINGS	8	7	1	.531#D	294	306	−12	−0.3	0.8	4779	4806	−27	51	43	−8	−34	22	3.2	3.9	−0.7	23.8	24.0
GREEN BAY PACKERS	8	7	1	.531#	249	269	−20	−0.5	1.0	4107	4963	−856	42	47	5	−51	31	3.5	2.9	0.6	20.5	24.1
DETROIT LIONS	7	9	0	.438	290	300	−10	−0.3	−0.8	4465	4483	−18	33	41	8	31	−41	3.5	3.7	−0.2	23.5	23.7
CHICAGO BEARS	7	9	0	.438	253	274	−21	−0.5	−0.5	4459	4680	−221	36	33	−3	−30	9	1.9	4.0	−2.1	23.7	24.4
TAMPA BAY BUC-CANEERS	5	11	0	.313	241	259	−18	−0.4	−2.6	3801	4328	−527	38	43	5	−24	6	2.5	2.4	0.0	18.3	21.5

WESTERN DIVISION	W	L	T	PCT	PTS	OPP	NET	P-W	D-W	Y-O	Y-D	Y-N	T-O	T-D	T-N	P-NP	D-NP	PR-O	PR-D	PR-N	YD-O	YD-D
LOS ANGELES RAMS	12	4	0	.750DC	316	245	71	1.8	2.2	5182	3893	1289	44	43	−1	103	−32	4.0	2.1	1.9	24.8	18.3
ATLANTA FALCONS	9	7	0	.563WD	240	290	−50	−1.3	2.3	4062	4431	−369	41	37	−4	−47	−3	2.9	3.9	−1.0	19.2	20.7
NEW ORLEANS SAINTS	7	9	0	.438	281	298	−17	−0.4	−0.6	4996	4884	112	31	41	10	49	−66	5.0	3.8	1.2	26.7	26.3
SAN FRANCISCO 49ERS	2	14	0	.125	219	350	−131	−3.3	−2.7	4047	5024	−977	63	45	−18	−153	22	0.9	4.6	−3.7	18.5	23.3

1979 A.F.C.

EASTERN DIVISION	W	L	T	PCT	PTS	OPP	NET	P-W	D-W	Y-O	Y-D	Y-N	T-O	T-D	T-N	P-NP	D-NP	PR-O	PR-D	PR-N	YD-O	YD-D
MIAMI DOLPHINS	10	6	0	.625D	341	257	84	2.1	−0.1	4950	4439	511	37	38	1	47	37	4.4	4.1	0.3	27.7	23.9
NEW ENGLAND PATRIOTS	9	7	0	.563	411	326	85	2.1	−1.1	5470	4323	1147	39	43	4	112	−27	4.7	3.4	1.3	25.9	20.2
NEW YORK JETS	8	8	0	.500	337	383	−46	−1.1	1.1	5244	5821	−577	38	40	2	−40	−6	4.1	5.9	−1.8	27.2	30.3
BUFFALO BILLS	7	9	0	.438	268	279	−11	−0.3	−0.7	4837	5011	−174	34	41	7	14	−25	5.3	3.9	1.4	23.5	24.9
BALTIMORE COLTS	5	11	0	.313	271	351	−80	−2.0	−1.0	4846	5074	−228	40	39	−1	−23	−57	4.1	4.4	−0.2	22.8	24.2

CENTRAL DIVISION	W	L	T	PCT	PTS	OPP	NET	P-W	D-W	Y-O	Y-D	Y-N	T-O	T-D	T-N	P-NP	D-NP	PR-O	PR-D	PR-N	YD-O	YD-D
PITTSBURGH STEELERS	12	4	0	.750DCS*	416	262	154	3.8	0.2	6258	4270	1988	52	42	−10	126	28	5.3	2.9	2.4	30.2	20.3
HOUSTON OILERS	11	5	0	.688WDC	362	331	31	0.8	2.2	4827	4990	−163	32	50	18	58	−27	3.5	2.7	0.8	24.3	24.8
CLEVELAND BROWNS	9	7	0	.563	359	352	7	0.2	0.8	5772	5650	122	44	32	−12	−38	45	4.3	4.9	−0.6	29.3	28.8
CINCINNATI BENGALS	4	12	0	.250	337	421	−84	−2.1	−1.9	4639	5911	−1272	29	44	15	−46	−38	3.7	5.8	−2.2	23.0	30.5

WESTERN DIVISION	W	L	T	PCT	PTS	OPP	NET	P-W	D-W	Y-O	Y-D	Y-N	T-O	T-D	T-N	P-NP	D-NP	PR-O	PR-D	PR-N	YD-O	YD-D
SAN DIEGO CHARGERS	12	4	0	.750D	411	246	165	4.1	−0.1	5583	4456	1127	35	46	11	138	27	5.3	2.7	2.6	30.7	22.5
DENVER BRONCOS	10	6	0	.625W	289	262	27	0.7	1.3	5142	4852	290	40	37	−3	12	15	4.3	4.5	−0.2	27.1	24.9
SEATTLE SEAHAWKS	9	7	0	.563	378	372	6	0.2	0.9	5557	5834	−277	36	33	−3	−35	41	5.5	5.3	0.1	30.0	31.7
OAKLAND RAIDERS	9	7	0	.563	365	337	28	0.7	0.3	5174	5486	−312	38	46	8	6	22	4.8	4.4	0.4	28.1	29.2
KANSAS CITY CHIEFS	7	9	0	.438	238	262	−24	−0.6	−0.4	3976	4971	−995	36	37	1	−79	55	2.3	4.1	−1.8	21.4	26.7

1979 N.F.C

EASTERN DIVISION	W	L	T	PCT	PTS	OPP	NET	P-W	D-W	Y-O	Y-D	Y-N	T-O	T-D	T-N	P-NP	D-NP	PR-O	PR-D	PR-N	YD-O	YD-D
DALLAS COWBOYS	11	5	0	.688#D	371	313	58	1.5	1.5	5968	4586	1382	34	23	−11	71	−13	6.1	4.4	1.7	31.1	23.6
PHILADELPHIA EAGLES	11	5	0	.688#WD	339	282	57	1.4	1.5	5031	4745	286	29	33	4	40	17	5.0	3.3	1.7	27.5	25.9
WASHINGTON REDSKINS	10	6	0	.625#	348	295	53	1.3	0.7	4904	5146	−242	25	47	22	68	−15	4.8	3.9	1.0	27.1	28.1
NEW YORK GIANTS	6	10	0	.375	237	323	−86	−2.2	0.2	3774	5378	−1604	40	38	−2	−142	56	2.4	4.4	−2.0	18.9	26.5
ST. LOUIS CARDINALS	5	11	0	.313	307	358	−51	−1.3	−1.7	5184	5077	107	45	37	−8	−23	−28	3.1	4.5	−1.4	24.7	25.4

CENTRAL DIVISION	W	L	T	PCT	PTS	OPP	NET	P-W	D-W	Y-O	Y-D	Y-N	T-O	T-D	T-N	P-NP	D-NP	PR-O	PR-D	PR-N	YD-O	YD-D
TAMPA BAY BUC-CANEERS	10	6	0	.625#DC	273	237	36	0.9	1.1	5049	3949	1100	41	38	−3	80	−44	3.7	3.3	0.3	24.9	19.9
CHICAGO BEARS	10	6	0	.625#W	306	249	57	1.4	0.6	4637	4506	131	29	43	14	67	−10	3.9	2.8	1.1	24.2	23.1
MINNESOTA VIKINGS	7	9	0	.438	259	337	−78	−2.0	1.0	4903	5223	−320	41	33	−8	−59	−19	3.8	4.1	−0.3	24.4	27.1
GREEN BAY PACKERS	5	11	0	.313	246	316	−70	−1.8	−1.3	4542	5647	−1105	44	32	−12	−140	70	3.7	4.6	−0.8	26.1	32.8
DETROIT LIONS	2	14	0	.125	219	365	−146	−3.7	−2.3	4013	4957	−944	46	26	−20	−159	13	2.5	4.4	−1.9	20.6	25.0

WESTERN DIVISION	W	L	T	PCT	PTS	OPP	NET	P-W	D-W	Y-O	Y-D	Y-N	T-O	T-D	T-N	P-NP	D-NP	PR-O	PR-D	PR-N	YD-O	YD-D
LOS ANGELES RAMS	9	7	0	.563DCS	323	309	14	0.3	0.6	5133	4553	580	49	41	−8	16	−2	3.1	3.3	−0.2	23.5	20.9
NEW ORLEANS SAINTS	8	8	0	.500	370	360	10	0.3	−0.3	5627	5535	92	36	42	6	32	−22	5.2	4.0	1.2	30.6	30.6
ATLANTA FALCONS	6	10	0	.375	300	388	−88	−2.2	0.2	4929	5759	−830	43	36	−7	−97	9	3.5	6.0	−2.5	25.4	29.1
SAN FRANCISCO 49ERS	2	14	0	.125	308	416	−108	−2.7	−3.3	5573	5393	180	39	34	−5	−5	−103	4.6	5.9	−1.2	29.5	30.1

1980 A.F.C.

EASTERN DIVISION	W	L	T	PCT	PTS	OPP	NET	P-W	D-W	Y-O	Y-D	Y-N	T-O	T-D	T-N	P-NP	D-NP	PR-O	PR-D	PR-N	YD-O	YD-D
BUFFALO BILLS	11	5	0	.688D	320	260	60	1.5	1.5	4972	4101	871	41	44	3	85	−25	4.4	2.9	1.5	26.9	21.8
NEW ENGLAND PATRIOTS	10	6	0	.625	441	325	116	2.9	−0.9	5435	4762	673	36	34	−2	48	68	5.1	4.2	1.0	27.7	24.7
MIAMI DOLPHINS	8	8	0	.500	266	305	−39	−1.0	1.0	4564	5224	−660	42	45	3	−43	4	3.3	4.1	−0.7	24.4	28.4
BALTIMORE COLTS	7	9	0	.438	355	387	−32	−0.8	−0.2	5206	5546	−340	37	34	−3	−40	8	4.3	5.5	−1.2	27.3	28.0
NEW YORK JETS	4	12	0	.250	302	395	−93	−2.3	−1.7	4882	5615	−733	41	32	−9	−97	4	3.5	5.1	−1.6	27.4	30.7

CENTRAL DIVISION	W	L	T	PCT	PTS	OPP	NET	P-W	D-W	Y-O	Y-D	Y-N	T-O	T-D	T-N	P-NP	D-NP	PR-O	PR-D	PR-N	YD-O	YD-D
CLEVELAND BROWNS	11	5	0	.688#D	357	310	47	1.2	1.8	5588	5626	−38	28	32	4	13	34	6.2	5.5	0.7	32.9	32.5
HOUSTON OILERS	11	5	0	.688#W	295	251	44	1.1	1.9	5642	4612	1030	47	39	−8	54	−10	3.9	3.7	0.2	31.2	25.5
PITTSBURGH STEELERS	9	7	0	.563	352	313	39	1.0	0.5	5554	5134	420	42	40	−2	27	12	5.3	4.5	0.8	29.7	27.3
CINCINNATI BENGALS	6	10	0	.375	244	312	−68	−1.7	−0.3	4884	4804	80	33	42	9	43	−111	3.4	4.6	−1.2	26.1	25.7

WESTERN DIVISION	W	L	T	PCT	PTS	OPP	NET	P-W	D-W	Y-O	Y-D	Y-N	T-O	T-D	T-N	P-NP	D-NP	PR-O	PR-D	PR-N	YD-O	YD-D
SAN DIEGO CHARGERS	11	5	0	.688#DC	418	327	91	2.3	0.7	6410	4691	1719	48	38	−10	103	−12	5.8	3.7	2.2	31.1	23.2
OAKLAND RAIDERS	11	5	0	.688#WDCS*	364	306	58	1.5	1.5	5045	5038	7	44	52	8	33	25	4.1	3.3	0.8	24.3	24.6
KANSAS CITY CHIEFS	8	8	0	.500	319	336	−17	−0.4	0.4	4321	5315	−994	30	43	13	−31	14	4.3	3.7	0.5	22.9	28.6
DENVER BRONCOS	8	8	0	.500	310	323	−13	−0.3	0.3	4642	5245	−603	37	28	−9	−86	73	3.5	5.3	−1.8	25.8	28.7
SEATTLE SEAHAWKS	4	12	0	.250	291	408	−117	−2.9	−1.1	4879	5177	−298	38	34	−4	−41	−76	3.9	4.8	−0.9	25.5	28.8

1980 N.F.C

EASTERN DIVISION	W L T	PCT	PTS	OPP	NET	P-W	D-W	Y-O	Y-D	Y-N	T-O	T-D	T-N	P-NP	D-NP	PR-O	PR-D	PR-N	YD-O	YD-D
PHILADELPHIA EAGLES	12 4 0	.750#DCS	384	222	162	4.1	-0.1	5519	4443	1076	28	35	7	118	44	6.4	3.2	3.2	30.0	23.3
DALLAS COWBOYS	12 4 0	.750#WDC	454	311	143	3.6	0.4	5482	5279	203	39	47	8	49	94	4.7	4.2	0.6	27.8	26.9
WASHINGTON REDSKINS	6 10 0	.375	261	293	-32	-0.8	-1.2	4854	4695	159	36	45	9	49	-81	4.2	2.0	2.2	25.4	24.5
ST. LOUIS CARDINALS	5 11 0	.313	299	350	-51	-1.3	-1.7	4859	5384	-525	37	34	-3	-56	5	3.4	4.7	-1.3	23.6	26.3
NEW YORK GIANTS	4 12 0	.250	249	425	-176	-4.4	0.4	4339	5752	-1413	43	41	-2	-126	-50	3.0	5.6	-2.6	21.8	29.1

CENTRAL DIVISION	W L T	PCT	PTS	OPP	NET	P-W	D-W	Y-O	Y-D	Y-N	T-O	T-D	T-N	P-NP	D-NP	PR-O	PR-D	PR-N	YD-O	YD-D
MINNESOTA VIKINGS	9 7 0	.563#D	317	308	9	0.2	0.8	5330	5856	-526	26	38	12	4	5	4.7	4.8	-0.2	30.1	32.4
DETROIT LIONS	9 7 0	.563#	334	272	62	1.5	-0.5	5540	4533	1007	31	34	3	96	-34	5.4	4.0	1.4	29.5	23.7
CHICAGO BEARS	7 9 0	.438	304	264	40	1.0	-2.0	4835	4907	-72	39	31	-8	-38	78	3.2	4.7	-1.5	27.0	27.0
TAMPA BAY BUC-CANEERS	5 10 1	.344	271	341	-70	-1.8	-0.8	5059	5405	-346	38	28	-10	-69	-1	4.8	5.2	-0.4	25.4	28.4
GREEN BAY PACKERS	5 10 1	.344	231	371	-140	-3.5	1.0	5097	5782	-685	41	27	-14	-113	-27	3.9	6.0	-2.2	27.0	31.4

WESTERN DIVISION	W L T	PCT	PTS	OPP	NET	P-W	D-W	Y-O	Y-D	Y-N	T-O	T-D	T-N	P-NP	D-NP	PR-O	PR-D	PR-N	YD-O	YD-D
ATLANTA FALCONS	12 4 0	.750D	405	272	133	3.3	0.7	5649	5264	385	26	42	16	96	37	5.6	4.4	1.2	29.3	27.7
LOS ANGELES RAMS	11 5 0	.688W	424	289	135	3.4	-0.4	6006	4546	1460	36	42	6	146	-11	5.2	3.0	2.2	30.3	22.2
SAN FRANCISCO 49ERS	6 10 0	.375	320	415	-95	-2.4	0.4	5320	5969	-649	40	34	-6	-78	-17	4.3	6.2	-2.0	28.3	32.3
NEW ORLEANS SAINTS	1 15 0	.063	291	487	-196	-4.9	-2.1	5010	6218	-1208	35	24	-11	-145	-51	4.8	6.1	-1.3	26.6	32.6

1981 A.F.C.

EASTERN DIVISION	W L T	PCT	PTS	OPP	NET	P-W	D-W	Y-O	Y-D	Y-N	T-O	T-D	T-N	P-NP	D-NP	PR-O	PR-D	PR-N	YD-O	YD-D
MIAMI DOLPHINS	11 4 1	.719D	345	275	70	1.8	1.8	5322	5363	-41	31	33	2	5	65	4.5	5.0	-0.5	29.1	27.8
NEW YORK JETS	10 5 1	.656W	355	287	68	1.7	0.8	5396	4871	525	31	36	5	64	4	5.0	3.9	1.1	27.7	24.7
BUFFALO BILLS	10 6 0	.625#WD	311	276	35	0.9	1.1	5640	4945	695	38	36	-2	50	-15	5.5	4.3	1.2	31.9	26.0
BALTIMORE COLTS	2 14 0	.125	259	533	-274	-6.8	0.8	4908	6793	-1885	37	30	-7	-185	-89	4.3	7.5	-3.2	26.5	38.8
NEW ENGLAND PATRIOTS	2 14 0	.125	322	370	-48	-1.2	-4.8	5623	5827	-204	50	33	-17	-85	37	4.2	5.1	-0.9	28.5	29.6

CENTRAL DIVISION	W L T	PCT	PTS	OPP	NET	P-W	D-W	Y-O	Y-D	Y-N	T-O	T-D	T-N	P-NP	D-NP	PR-O	PR-D	PR-N	YD-O	YD-D
CINCINNATI BENGALS	12 4 0	.750DCS	421	304	117	2.9	1.1	5968	5289	679	24	37	13	109	8	6.4	4.7	1.7	32.1	28.1
PITTSBURGH STEELERS	8 8 0	.500	356	297	59	1.5	-1.5	5598	5652	-54	41	46	5	16	43	5.4	4.5	0.8	28.0	28.8
HOUSTON OILERS	7 9 0	.438	281	355	-74	-1.9	0.9	4511	5726	-1215	44	31	-13	-153	79	4.1	5.1	-1.0	23.6	30.6
CLEVELAND BROWNS	5 11 0	.313	276	375	-99	-2.5	-0.5	5915	5367	548	53	35	-18	-26	-73	4.5	5.8	-1.3	29.4	27.2

WESTERN DIVISION	W L T	PCT	PTS	OPP	NET	P-W	D-W	Y-O	Y-D	Y-N	T-O	T-D	T-N	P-NP	D-NP	PR-O	PR-D	PR-N	YD-O	YD-D
SAN DIEGO CHARGERS	10 6 0	.625#D	478	390	88	2.2	-0.2	6744	6136	608	40	41	1	55	33	6.6	5.7	0.9	34.6	31.0
DENVER BRONCOS	10 6 0	.625#	321	289	32	0.8	1.2	5426	4878	548	39	46	7	74	-42	5.2	3.7	1.5	26.6	24.1
KANSAS CITY CHIEFS	9 7 0	.563	343	290	53	1.3	-0.3	5273	5373	-100	46	47	1	-4	50	4.0	4.4	-0.4	26.9	27.1
OAKLAND RAIDERS	7 9 0	.438	273	343	-70	-1.8	0.8	4977	5473	-496	48	32	-16	-105	35	3.1	5.6	-2.5	23.3	25.6
SEATTLE SEAHAWKS	6 10 0	.375	322	388	-66	-1.6	-0.4	5021	5940	-919	38	48	10	-37	-29	5.3	4.5	0.7	26.9	33.4

1981 N.F.C

EASTERN DIVISION	W L T	PCT	PTS	OPP	NET	P-W	D-W	Y-O	Y-D	Y-N	T-O	T-D	T-N	P-NP	D-NP	PR-O	PR-D	PR-N	YD-O	YD-D
DALLAS COWBOYS	12 4 0	.750DC	367	277	90	2.3	1.8	5880	5419	461	35	53	18	110	-20	5.8	3.4	2.4	28.8	26.8
PHILADELPHIA EAGLES	10 6 0	.625W	368	221	147	3.7	-1.7	5553	4447	1106	39	47	8	124	23	4.6	3.0	1.6	30.0	23.8
NEW YORK GIANTS	9 7 0	.563WD	295	257	38	0.9	0.1	4326	4825	-499	36	34	-2	-50	88	3.4	3.9	-0.5	20.8	22.9
WASHINGTON REDSKINS	8 8 0	.500	347	349	-2	-0.1	0.1	5623	5206	417	41	39	-2	27	-29	4.8	4.5	0.3	28.8	26.8
ST. LOUIS CARDINALS	7 9 0	.438	315	408	-93	-2.3	1.3	5077	5723	-646	44	38	-6	-78	-15	3.7	5.0	-1.3	26.6	30.1

CENTRAL DIVISION	W L T	PCT	PTS	OPP	NET	P-W	D-W	Y-O	Y-D	Y-N	T-O	T-D	T-N	P-NP	D-NP	PR-O	PR-D	PR-N	YD-O	YD-D
TAMPA BAY BUC-CANEERS	9 7 0	.563D	315	268	47	1.2	-0.2	5160	5312	-152	28	46	18	59	-12	6.1	3.2	2.9	27.3	28.9
DETROIT LIONS	8 8 0	.500	397	322	75	1.9	-1.9	5933	4846	1087	43	39	-4	75	0	4.8	4.5	0.2	31.6	24.7
GREEN BAY PACKERS	8 8 0	.500	324	361	-37	-0.9	0.9	4859	5185	-326	41	54	13	25	-62	4.2	3.5	0.6	24.3	26.7
MINNESOTA VIKINGS	7 9 0	.438	325	369	-44	-1.1	0.1	5845	5373	472	50	35	-15	-21	-23	4.5	5.6	-1.1	29.2	25.5
CHICAGO BEARS	6 10 0	.375	253	324	-71	-1.8	-0.2	4633	5394	-761	40	40	0	-63	-8	3.0	4.8	-1.8	21.5	24.9

WESTERN DIVISION	W L T	PCT	PTS	OPP	NET	P-W	D-W	Y-O	Y-D	Y-N	T-O	T-D	T-N	P-NP	D-NP	PR-O	PR-D	PR-N	YD-O	YD-D
SAN FRANCISCO 49ERS	13 3 0	.813DCS*	357	250	107	2.7	2.3	5484	4763	721	25	48	23	152	-45	5.8	3.3	2.5	28.4	24.1
ATLANTA FALCONS	7 9 0	.438	426	355	71	1.8	-2.8	5664	5354	310	41	46	5	46	25	4.9	4.8	0.0	25.4	24.1
LOS ANGELES RAMS	6 10 0	.375	303	351	-48	-1.2	-0.8	4793	5124	-331	47	33	-14	-84	36	2.4	4.4	-2.0	23.0	24.9
NEW ORLEANS SAINTS	4 12 0	.250	207	378	-171	-4.3	0.3	4705	5253	-548	47	34	-13	-98	-73	2.7	5.7	-3.0	25.9	30.9

1982 A.F.C.

AMERICAN DIVISION	W L T	PCT	PTS	OPP	NET	P-NW	D-NW	Y-OFF	Y-DEF	Y-NET	T-O	T-D	T-N	P-NP	D-NP	PR-O	PR-D	PR-N	YD-O	YD-D
LOS ANGELES RAIDERS	8 1 0	.889PD	260	200	60	1.5	2.0	2955	3066	−111	24	29	5	11	49	4.6	3.8	0.8	24.4	24.5
MIAMI DOLPHINS	7 2 0	.778PDCS	198	131	67	1.7	0.8	2658	2312	346	23	27	4	45	22	3.2	0.9	2.3	26.1	22.0
CINCINNATI BENGALS	7 2 0	.778P	232	177	55	1.4	1.1	3288	2893	395	16	20	4	49	6	6.1	4.7	1.4	34.6	29.5
PITTSBURGH STEELERS	6 3 0	.667P	204	146	58	1.5	0.0	2970	2874	96	25	25	0	8	50	4.2	4.0	0.2	26.1	24.8
SAN DIEGO CHARGERS	6 3 0	.667PD	288	221	67	1.7	−0.2	4048	3253	795	20	25	5	86	−19	7.4	5.0	2.4	40.5	30.7
NEW YORK JETS	6 3 0	.667PDC	245	166	79	2.0	−0.5	3218	2629	589	18	26	8	81	−2	5.5	3.1	2.4	29.8	24.6
NEW ENGLAND PATRIOTS	5 4 0	.556P	143	157	−14	−0.3	0.9	2633	2808	−175	17	23	6	9	−23	5.0	3.7	1.2	25.1	27.5
CLEVELAND BROWNS	4 5 0	.444#P	140	182	−42	−1.0	0.5	2718	3114	−396	24	28	4	−17	−25	3.4	4.0	−0.6	25.2	28.1
BUFFALO BILLS	4 5 0	.444#	150	154	−4	−0.1	−0.4	2927	2334	593	26	21	−5	29	−33	3.1	3.0	0.1	27.6	22.9
SEATTLE SEAHAWKS	4 5 0	.444#	127	147	−20	−0.5	0.0	2594	2794	−200	24	22	−2	−25	5	3.6	3.0	0.6	23.2	26.4
KANSAS CITY CHIEFS	3 6 0	.333	176	184	−8	−0.2	−1.3	2498	2732	−234	12	22	10	21	−29	4.3	4.5	−0.2	24.7	28.5
DENVER BRONCOS	2 7 0	.222	148	226	−78	−2.0	−0.5	2837	3169	−332	36	19	−17	−96	18	3.1	5.7	−2.6	24.7	27.1
HOUSTON OILERS	1 8 0	.111	136	245	−109	−2.7	−0.8	2373	3438	−1065	26	17	−9	−125	16	3.1	7.2	−4.0	21.8	31.3
BALTIMORE COLTS	0 8 1	.056	113	236	−123	−3.1	−0.9	2483	3296	−813	21	11	−10	−108	−15	3.5	6.9	−3.5	23.9	32.6

1982 N.F.C

NATIONAL DIVISION	W L T	PCT	PTS	OPP	NET	P-NW	D-NW	Y-OFF	Y-DEF	Y-NET	T-O	T-D	T-N	P-NP	D-NP	PR-O	PR-D	PR-N	YD-O	YD-D
WASHINGTON REDSKINS	8 1 0	.889PDCS*	190	128	62	1.5	2.0	2985	2560	425	16	24	8	67	−5	5.5	3.9	1.6	27.1	22.7
DALLAS COWBOYS	6 3 0	.667PC	226	145	81	2.0	−0.5	3199	2753	446	26	25	−1	33	48	5.0	3.6	1.4	28.8	25.0
GREEN BAY PACKERS	5 3 1	.611PD	226	169	57	1.4	−0.4	2910	2707	203	26	23	−3	5	52	4.3	3.8	0.4	26.0	22.9
MINNESOTA VIKINGS	5 4 0	.556PD	187	198	−11	−0.3	0.8	2879	2895	−16	17	21	4	15	−26	4.4	4.5	−0.1	24.2	24.5
ATLANTA FALCONS	5 4 0	.556P	183	199	−16	−0.4	0.9	2963	2848	115	21	25	4	26	−42	4.6	4.9	−0.4	28.0	27.1
ST. LOUIS CARDINALS	5 4 0	.556P	135	170	−35	−0.9	1.4	2542	2848	−306	16	15	−1	−30	−5	4.1	5.6	−1.4	23.1	27.4
TAMPA BAY BUC-CANEERS	5 4 0	.556P	158	178	−20	−0.5	1.0	2895	2442	453	23	21	−2	30	−50	4.8	3.5	1.3	27.3	23.0
DETROIT LIONS	4 5 0	.444#P	181	176	5	0.1	−0.6	2534	2722	−188	26	26	0	−16	21	2.6	3.7	−1.0	21.5	23.7
NEW ORLEANS SAINTS	4 5 0	.444#	129	160	−31	−0.8	0.3	2655	2607	48	24	22	−2	−4	−27	3.1	4.8	−1.7	24.4	25.1
NEW YORK GIANTS	4 5 0	.444#	164	160	4	0.1	−0.6	2729	2684	45	19	18	−1	0	4	5.0	4.1	0.9	24.2	23.8
SAN FRANCISCO 49ERS	3 6 0	.333	209	206	3	0.1	−1.6	3242	3035	207	21	13	−8	−15	18	5.9	5.4	0.6	29.2	26.9
CHICAGO BEARS	3 6 0	.333	141	174	−33	−0.8	−0.7	2493	2851	−358	19	20	1	−26	−7	3.8	4.6	−0.9	22.5	23.8
PHILADELPHIA EAGLES	3 6 0	.333	191	195	−4	−0.1	−1.4	2685	2938	−253	23	27	4	−5	1	4.4	4.4	0.0	24.0	27.7
LOS ANGELES RAMS	2 7 0	.222	200	250	−50	−1.3	−1.3	3024	3333	−309	24	18	−6	−50	0	4.7	6.0	−1.3	26.5	29.0

1983 A.F.C.

EASTERN DIVISION	W L T	PCT	PTS	OPP	NET	P-W	D-W	Y-O	Y-D	Y-N	T-O	T-D	T-N	P-NP	D-NP	PR-O	PR-D	PR-N	YD-O	YD-D
MIAMI DOLPHINS	12 4 0	.750D	389	250	139	3.5	0.5	5195	5039	156	27	43	16	77	62	6.1	3.8	2.3	27.6	27.1
NEW ENGLAND PATRIOTS	8 8 0	.500	274	289	−15	−0.4	0.4	5311	5576	−265	38	36	−2	−30	15	4.5	4.9	−0.4	28.9	30.1
BUFFALO BILLS	8 8 0	.500	283	351	−68	−1.7	1.7	4823	5809	−986	40	31	−9	−118	50	3.5	5.7	−2.2	24.7	29.2
BALTIMORE COLTS	7 9 0	.438	264	354	−90	−2.3	1.3	5018	5640	−622	33	36	3	−40	−30	3.4	5.5	−2.1	26.1	29.4
NEW YORK JETS	7 9 0	.438	313	331	−18	−0.4	−0.6	5493	5301	192	47	36	−11	−28	10	3.9	4.2	−0.3	27.9	26.6

CENTRAL DIVISION	W L T	PCT	PTS	OPP	NET	P-W	D-W	Y-O	Y-D	Y-N	T-O	T-D	T-N	P-NP	D-NP	PR-O	PR-D	PR-N	YD-O	YD-D
PITTSBURGH STEELERS	10 6 0	.625D	355	303	52	1.3	0.7	5014	4732	282	43	45	2	32	20	3.3	3.7	−0.4	25.3	23.4
CLEVELAND BROWNS	9 7 0	.563#	356	342	14	0.3	0.6	5583	5142	441	38	32	−6	13	1	4.5	4.6	−0.2	31.4	28.4
CINCINNATI BENGALS	7 9 0	.438	346	302	44	1.1	−2.1	5287	4327	960	33	39	6	104	−60	5.1	3.6	1.5	29.2	24.6
HOUSTON OILERS	2 14 0	.125	288	460	−172	−4.3	−1.7	4900	5632	−732	47	29	−18	−133	−39	3.3	5.4	−2.1	25.7	29.6

WESTERN DIVISION	W L T	PCT	PTS	OPP	NET	P-W	D-W	Y-O	Y-D	Y-N	T-O	T-D	T-N	P-NP	D-NP	PR-O	PR-D	PR-N	YD-O	YD-D
LOS ANGELES RAIDERS	12 4 0	.750DCS*	442	338	104	2.6	1.4	5686	4748	938	49	36	−13	26	78	4.8	4.2	0.6	27.1	21.8
SEATTLE SEAHAWKS	9 7 0	.563#WDC	403	397	6	0.2	0.9	5092	6029	−937	38	54	16	−14	20	4.9	5.3	−0.4	24.6	30.1
DENVER BRONCOS	9 7 0	.563#W	302	327	−25	−0.6	1.6	4811	5609	−798	41	47	6	−43	18	4.0	4.5	−0.5	23.8	28.6
SAN DIEGO CHARGERS	6 10 0	.375	358	462	−104	−2.6	0.6	6197	5955	242	55	33	−22	−68	−36	5.2	5.8	−0.6	31.6	30.5
KANSAS CITY CHIEFS	6 10 0	.375	386	367	19	0.5	−2.5	5595	5386	209	38	51	13	69	−50	3.7	1.8		26.1	25.2

1983 N.F.C.

EASTERN DIVISION	W L T	PCT	PTS	OPP	NET	P-W	D-W	Y-O	Y-D	Y-N	T-O	T-D	T-N	P-NP	D-NP	PR-O	PR-D	PR-N	YD-O	YD-D
WASHINGTON REDSKINS	14 2 0	.875DCS	541	332	209	5.2	0.8	6139	5264	875	18	61	43	245	−36	6.6	4.4	2.3	30.4	25.2
DALLAS COWBOYS	12 4 0	.750W	479	360	119	3.0	1.0	5959	5427	532	39	48	9	80	39	5.1	4.9	0.3	28.1	25.0
ST. LOUIS CARDINALS	8 7 1	.531	374	428	−54	−1.4	1.9	5145	5005	140	48	48	0	12	−66	4.3	3.7	0.5	23.8	23.1
PHILADELPHIA EAGLES	5 11 0	.313	233	322	−89	−2.2	−0.8	4534	5447	−913	36	23	−13	−128	39	4.7	5.6	−1.0	24.9	29.6
NEW YORK GIANTS	3 12 1	.219	267	347	−80	−2.0	−2.5	5285	4994	291	58	36	−22	−64	−16	3.6	4.6	−1.1	24.5	23.0

CENTRAL DIVISION	W	L	T	PCT	PTS	OPP	NET	P-W	D-W	Y-O	Y-D	Y-N	T-O	T-D	T-N	P-NP	D-NP	PR-O	PR-D	PR-N	YD-O	YD-D
DETROIT LIONS	9	7	0	.563D	347	286	61	1.5	-0.5	5136	5216	-80	39	37	-2	-15	76	3.9	4.2	-0.3	27.9	27.2
GREEN BAY PACKERS	8	8	0	.500	429	439	-10	-0.3	0.3	6172	6403	-231	50	31	-19	-95	85	5.7	5.6	0.2	30.7	30.9
CHICAGO BEARS	8	8	0	.500	311	301	10	0.3	-0.3	5830	5132	698	36	38	2	66	-56	4.6	4.3	0.3	28.6	25.4
MINNESOTA VIKINGS	8	8	0	.500	316	348	-32	-0.8	0.8	5019	5487	-468	32	48	16	25	-57	4.0	3.8	0.1	24.7	27.4
TAMPA BAY BUC-CANEERS	2	14	0	.125	241	380	-139	-3.5	-2.5	4477	5397	-920	37	41	4	-61	-78	3.9	4.6	-0.7	21.7	27.5

WESTERN DIVISION	W	L	T	PCT	PTS	OPP	NET	P-W	D-W	Y-O	Y-D	Y-N	T-O	T-D	T-N	P-NP	D-NP	PR-O	PR-D	PR-N	YD-O	YD-D
SAN FRANCISCO 49ERS	10	6	0	.625DC	432	293	139	3.5	-1.5	6054	5189	865	31	42	11	116	23	6.3	4.1	2.2	32.5	27.9
LOS ANGELES RAMS	9	7	0	.563WD	361	344	17	0.4	0.6	5474	5392	82	47	44	-3	-5	22	4.7	4.6	0.1	26.6	26.0
NEW ORLEANS SAINTS	8	8	0	.500	319	337	-18	-0.4	0.4	4938	4691	247	47	39	-8	-11	-7	3.2	3.4	-0.1	24.0	24.1
ATLANTA FALCONS	7	9	0	.438	370	389	-19	-0.5	-0.5	5628	5826	-198	29	30	1	-13	-6	5.7	6.0	-0.3	31.3	33.3

1984 A.F.C.

EASTERN DIVISION	W	L	T	PCT	PTS	OPP	NET	P-W	D-W	Y-O	Y-D	Y-N	T-O	T-D	T-N	P-NP	D-NP	PR-O	PR-D	PR-N	YD-O	YD-D
MIAMI DOLPHINS	14	2	0	.875DCS	513	298	215	5.4	0.6	6936	5420	1516	28	36	8	158	57	8.0	4.1	4.0	38.1	30.8
NEW ENGLAND PATRIOTS	9	7	0	.563	362	352	10	0.3	0.8	5263	5100	163	29	25	-4	-2	12	5.1	4.8	0.3	27.8	25.5
NEW YORK JETS	7	9	0	.438	332	364	-32	-0.8	-0.2	5148	5566	-418	34	33	-1	-39	7	4.1	5.5	-1.4	27.7	30.6
INDIANAPOLIS COLTS	4	12	0	.250	239	414	-175	-4.4	0.4	4132	5577	-1445	38	31	-7	-148	-27	2.7	5.5	-2.9	21.3	28.5
BUFFALO BILLS	2	14	0	.125	250	454	-204	-5.1	-0.9	4341	5582	-1241	44	37	-7	-131	-73	2.4	5.9	-3.5	21.5	28.8

CENTRAL DIVISION	W	L	T	PCT	PTS	OPP	NET	P-W	D-W	Y-O	Y-D	Y-N	T-O	T-D	T-N	P-NP	D-NP	PR-O	PR-D	PR-N	YD-O	YD-D
PITTSBURGH STEELERS	9	7	0	.563DC	387	310	77	1.9	-0.9	5420	4916	504	40	42	2	50	27	4.9	3.7	1.2	26.7	25.2
CINCINNATI BENGALS	8	8	0	.500	339	339	0	0.0	0.0	5480	5259	221	39	40	1	22	-22	4.6	4.3	0.2	30.1	28.4
CLEVELAND BROWNS	5	11	0	.313	250	297	-47	-1.2	-1.8	4828	4641	187	39	35	-4	0	-47	4.1	3.9	0.2	26.4	25.4
HOUSTON OILERS	3	13	0	.188	240	437	-197	-4.9	-0.1	4884	5968	-1084	31	24	-7	-118	-79	5.0	5.9	-0.9	27.1	34.3

WESTERN DIVISION	W	L	T	PCT	PTS	OPP	NET	P-W	D-W	Y-O	Y-D	Y-N	T-O	T-D	T-N	P-NP	D-NP	PR-O	PR-D	PR-N	YD-O	YD-D
DENVER BRONCOS	13	3	0	.813D	353	241	112	2.8	2.2	4935	5687	-752	34	55	21	21	91	4.5	4.1	0.5	24.2	27.3
SEATTLE SEAHAWKS	12	4	0	.750WD	418	282	136	3.4	0.6	5068	4963	105	39	63	24	105	31	4.8	2.9	1.9	24.0	22.8
LOS ANGELES RAIDERS	11	5	0	.688W	368	278	90	2.3	0.8	5244	4644	600	48	34	-14	-6	96	4.2	3.6	0.7	24.6	21.1
KANSAS CITY CHIEFS	8	8	0	.500	314	324	-10	-0.3	0.3	5095	5625	-530	37	41	4	-28	18	4.5	3.9	0.6	24.7	26.7
SAN DIEGO CHARGERS	7	9	0	.438	394	413	-19	-0.5	-0.5	6297	5936	361	38	36	-2	22	-41	5.7	6.2	-0.5	32.6	31.6

1984 N.F.C

EASTERN DIVISION	W	L	T	PCT	PTS	OPP	NET	P-W	D-W	Y-O	Y-D	Y-N	T-O	T-D	T-N	P-NP	D-NP	PR-O	PR-D	PR-N	YD-O	YD-D
WASHINGTON REDSKINS	11	5	0	.688D	426	310	116	2.9	0.1	5350	5361	-11	28	43	15	59	57	5.1	4.8	0.3	28.5	28.1
NEW YORK GIANTS	9	7	0	.563#WD	299	301	-2	-0.1	1.0	5292	5193	99	27	35	8	40	-42	5.2	4.7	0.4	26.6	26.2
ST. LOUIS CARDINALS	9	7	0	.563#	423	345	78	2.0	-1.0	6345	5094	1251	36	33	-3	92	-14	6.2	4.5	1.7	31.9	25.7
DALLAS COWBOYS	9	7	0	.563#	308	308	0	0.0	1.0	5320	5036	284	43	44	1	28	-28	4.0	3.0	1.0	24.7	22.6
PHILADELPHIA EAGLES	6	9	1	.406	278	320	-42	-1.0	-0.5	4698	5239	-541	33	31	-2	-53	11	4.2	4.3	-0.1	23.5	26.6

CENTRAL DIVISION	W	L	T	PCT	PTS	OPP	NET	P-W	D-W	Y-O	Y-D	Y-N	T-O	T-D	T-N	P-NP	D-NP	PR-O	PR-D	PR-N	YD-O	YD-D
CHICAGO BEARS	10	6	0	.625DC	325	248	77	1.9	0.1	5437	3863	1574	31	34	3	143	-66	4.5	3.3	1.2	28.2	20.3
GREEN BAY PACKERS	8	8	0	.500	390	309	81	2.0	-2.0	5449	5291	158	37	42	5	33	48	4.3	3.5	0.8	26.7	26.2
TAMPA BAY BUC-CANEERS	6	10	0	.375	335	380	-45	-1.1	-0.9	5321	5474	-153	43	32	-11	-57	12	4.5	5.0	-0.6	29.4	29.6
DETROIT LIONS	4	11	1	.281	283	408	-125	-3.1	-0.4	5318	5319	-1	36	25	-11	-44	-81	4.2	6.3	-2.0	29.1	29.9
MINNESOTA VIKINGS	3	13	0	.188	276	484	-208	-5.2	0.2	4716	6352	-1636	41	29	-12	-184	-24	3.2	7.1	-3.8	24.6	34.3

| | | | | | | | | P- | D- | Y- | Y- | | | | | | | | | | | |
WESTERN DIVISION	W	L	T	PCT	PTS	OPP	NET	NW	NW	OFF	DEF	Y-NET	T-O	T-D	T-N	P-NP	D-NP	PR-O	PR-D	PR-N	YD-O	YD-D
SAN FRANCISCO 49ERS	15	1	0	.938DCS*	475	227	248	6.2	0.8	6366	5176	1190	22	38	16	163	85	7.2	4.0	3.2	36.2	28.0
LOS ANGELES RAMS	10	6	0	.625W	346	316	30	0.8	1.3	5006	5266	-260	35	39	4	-6	36	3.9	5.1	-1.1	26.9	27.6
NEW ORLEANS SAINTS	7	9	0	.438	298	361	-63	-1.6	0.6	5008	4914	94	41	23	-18	-64	1	3.4	4.4	-1.0	26.4	27.3
ATLANTA FALCONS	4	12	0	.250	281	382	-101	-2.5	-1.5	5044	5279	-235	41	32	-9	-56	-45	4.2	5.9	-1.7	28.3	29.5

1985 A.F.C.

EASTERN DIVISION	W	L	T	PCT	PTS	OPP	NET	P-W	D-W	Y-O	Y-D	Y-N	T-O	T-D	T-N	P-NP	D-NP	PR-O	PR-D	PR-N	YD-O	YD-D
MIAMI DOLPHINS	12	4	0	.750DC	428	320	108	2.7	1.3	5843	5767	76	41	41	0	6	102	5.8	5.1	0.7	31.1	30.8
NEW YORK JETS	11	5	0	.688#W	393	264	129	3.2	-0.2	5896	4772	1124	29	42	13	146	-17	6.2	4.4	1.8	30.5	25.0
NEW ENGLAND PATRIOTS	11	5	0	.688#WDCS	362	290	72	1.8	1.2	5499	4714	785	42	47	5	85	-13	4.8	3.8	1.0	26.2	21.9
INDIANAPOLIS COLTS	5	11	0	.313	320	386	-66	-1.6	-1.4	5006	5599	-593	34	33	-1	-53	-13	3.6	5.5	-1.9	26.5	29.8
BUFFALO BILLS	2	14	0	.125	200	381	-181	-4.5	-1.5	4595	5540	-945	52	35	-17	-147	-34	3.0	4.8	-1.8	24.3	28.9

CENTRAL DIVISION	W	L	T	PCT	PTS	OPP	NET	P-W	D-W	Y-O	Y-D	Y-N	T-O	T-D	T-N	P-NP	D-NP	PR-O	PR-D	PR-N	YD-O	YD-D
CLEVELAND BROWNS	8	8	0	.500D	287	294	−7	−0.2	0.2	4921	4958	−37	36	27	−9	−39	32	4.9	4.5	0.5	26.0	27.9
CINCINNATI BENGALS	7	9	0	.438	441	437	4	0.1	−1.1	5900	5663	237	29	38	9	56	−52	6.2	5.5	0.7	30.7	30.3
PITTSBURGH STEELERS	7	9	0	.438	379	355	24	0.6	−1.6	5350	4659	691	36	34	−2	50	−26	4.0	4.0	0.0	27.3	22.7
HOUSTON OILERS	5	11	0	.313	284	412	−128	−3.2	0.2	4652	6155	−1503	37	35	−2	−133	5	4.0	5.9	−1.9	23.7	32.7

WESTERN DIVISION	W	L	T	PCT	PTS	OPP	NET	P-W	D-W	Y-O	Y-D	Y-N	T-O	T-D	T-N	P-NP	D-NP	PR-O	PR-D	PR-N	YD-O	YD-D
LOS ANGELES RAIDERS	12	4	0	.750D	354	308	46	1.1	2.8	5408	4603	805	38	30	−8	35	11	4.1	4.3	−0.1	25.8	21.9
DENVER BRONCOS	11	5	0	.688#	380	329	51	1.3	1.7	5496	5179	317	31	36	5	46	5	4.3	3.9	0.4	26.6	24.1
SEATTLE SEAHAWKS	8	8	0	.500	349	303	46	1.1	−1.1	5007	5160	−153	41	44	3	−1	47	4.2	4.4	−0.3	23.5	24.6
SAN DIEGO CHARGERS	8	8	0	.500	467	435	32	0.8	−0.8	6535	6265	270	49	42	−7	−6	38	5.8	5.4	0.4	32.0	29.6
KANSAS CITY CHIEFS	6	10	0	.375	317	360	−43	−1.1	−0.9	4877	5658	−781	34	41	7	−37	−6	4.7	4.1	0.6	25.0	28.4

1985 N.F.C

EASTERN DIVISION	W	L	T	PCT	PTS	OPP	NET	P-W	D-W	Y-O	Y-D	Y-N	T-O	T-D	T-N	P-NP	D-NP	PR-O	PR-D	PR-N	YD-O	YD-D
DALLAS COWBOYS	10	6	0	.625#D	357	333	24	0.6	1.4	5602	5608	−6	41	48	7	28	−4	4.8	4.0	0.7	27.7	27.6
NEW YORK GIANTS	10	6	0	.625#WD	399	283	116	2.9	−0.9	5884	4320	1564	38	37	−1	126	−10	5.0	3.2	1.8	28.6	20.9
WASHINGTON REDSKINS	10	6	0	.625#	297	312	−15	−0.4	2.4	5338	4480	858	40	34	−6	48	−63	3.5	3.7	−0.1	27.9	23.6
PHILADELPHIA EAGLES	7	9	0	.438	286	310	−24	−0.6	−0.4	5216	5135	81	40	32	−8	−25	1	4.0	4.3	−0.3	26.2	25.8
ST. LOUIS CARDINALS	5	11	0	.313	278	414	−136	−3.4	0.4	5086	5381	−295	34	27	−7	−53	−83	4.2	5.6	−1.4	25.9	28.0

CENTRAL DIVISION	W	L	T	PCT	PTS	OPP	NET	P-W	D-W	Y-O	Y-D	Y-N	T-O	T-D	T-N	P-NP	D-NP	PR-O	PR-D	PR-N	YD-O	YD-D
CHICAGO BEARS	15	1	0	.938DCS*	456	198	258	6.4	0.6	5837	4135	1702	31	54	23	234	24	5.3	2.5	2.9	29.9	20.8
GREEN BAY PACKERS	8	8	0	.500	337	355	−18	−0.4	0.4	5371	5173	198	45	40	−5	−4	−14	3.8	4.8	−1.0	26.5	25.6
MINNESOTA VIKINGS	7	9	0	.438	346	359	−13	−0.3	−0.7	5151	5464	−313	47	44	−3	−38	25	4.1	4.7	−0.6	26.7	28.5
DETROIT LIONS	7	9	0	.438	307	366	−59	−1.5	0.5	4476	5591	−1115	41	36	−5	−113	54	4.2	4.3	−0.1	24.2	30.1
TAMPA BAY BUC-CANEERS	2	14	0	.125	294	448	−154	−3.8	−2.2	4766	6108	−1342	48	40	−8	−144	−10	4.0	5.6	−1.7	23.7	30.5

WESTERN DIVISION	W	L	T	PCT	PTS	OPP	NET	P-W	D-W	Y-O	Y-D	Y-N	T-O	T-D	T-N	P-NP	D-NP	PR-O	PR-D	PR-N	YD-O	YD-D
LOS ANGELES RAMS	11	5	0	.688DC	340	277	63	1.6	1.4	4520	4648	−128	35	46	11	33	30	4.3	3.2	1.1	22.4	23.2
SAN FRANCISCO 49ERS	10	6	0	.625#W	411	263	148	3.7	−1.7	5920	5191	729	34	35	1	65	83	5.6	4.1	1.5	30.1	25.4
NEW ORLEANS SAINTS	5	11	0	.313	294	401	−107	−2.7	−0.3	4479	5815	−1336	36	37	1	−107	0	3.5	5.2	−1.7	22.1	29.5
ATLANTA FALCONS	4	12	0	.250	282	452	−170	−4.3	0.3	4960	5850	−890	30	34	4	−58	−112	3.2	5.4	−2.2	25.8	31.1

1986 A.F.C.

EASTERN DIVISION	W	L	T	PCT	PTS	OPP	NET	P-W	D-W	Y-O	Y-D	Y-N	T-O	T-D	T-N	P-NP	D-NP	PR-O	PR-D	PR-N	YD-O	YD-D
NEW ENGLAND PATRIOTS	11	5	0	.688D	412	307	105	2.6	0.4	5327	5181	146	24	40	16	76	29	6.1	4.2	1.9	26.5	24.6
NEW YORK JETS	10	6	0	.625#WD	364	386	−22	−0.6	2.6	5375	6050	−675	37	38	1	−52	30	5.1	6.1	−1.0	27.3	31.2
MIAMI DOLPHINS	8	8	0	.500	430	405	25	0.6	−0.6	6324	6050	274	37	27	−10	−17	42	6.4	6.2	0.2	35.9	34.0
BUFFALO BILLS	4	12	0	.250	287	348	−61	−1.5	−2.5	5017	5523	−506	39	18	−21	−126	65	5.0	5.9	−0.9	27.3	30.2
INDIANAPOLIS COLTS	3	13	0	.188	229	400	−171	−4.3	−0.7	4700	5701	−1001	44	35	−9	−119	−52	3.6	6.2	−2.6	24.5	30.7

CENTRAL DIVISION	W	L	T	PCT	PTS	OPP	NET	P-W	D-W	Y-O	Y-D	Y-N	T-O	T-D	T-N	P-NP	D-NP	PR-O	PR-D	PR-N	YD-O	YD-D
CLEVELAND BROWNS	12	4	0	.750DC	391	310	81	2.0	2.0	5394	5269	125	24	37	13	62	19	5.9	4.9	1.1	28.4	27.4
CINCINNATI BENGALS	10	6	0	.625#	409	394	15	0.4	1.6	6490	5274	1216	36	28	−8	69	−54	6.3	4.8	1.5	34.0	28.2
PITTSBURGH STEELERS	6	10	0	.375	307	336	−29	−0.7	−1.3	4811	5252	−441	36	33	−3	−49	20	3.6	4.7	−1.0	24.1	26.3
HOUSTON OILERS	5	11	0	.313	274	329	−55	−1.4	−1.6	5149	5034	115	43	32	−11	−34	−21	3.7	4.8	−1.2	25.6	25.6

WESTERN DIVISION	W	L	T	PCT	PTS	OPP	NET	P-W	D-W	Y-O	Y-D	Y-N	T-O	T-D	T-N	P-NP	D-NP	PR-O	PR-D	PR-N	YD-O	YD-D
DENVER BRONCOS	11	5	0	.688DCS	378	327	51	1.3	1.7	5216	4947	269	29	35	6	46	5	5.2	4.5	0.6	26.2	25.0
KANSAS CITY CHIEFS	10	6	0	.625#W	358	326	32	0.8	1.2	4218	4934	−716	35	49	14	−4	36	3.8	3.3	0.5	20.1	23.4
SEATTLE SEAHAWKS	10	6	0	.625#	366	293	73	1.8	0.2	5409	5341	68	27	36	9	42	31	5.5	4.8	0.7	28.9	27.8
LOS ANGELES RAIDERS	8	8	0	.500	323	346	−23	−0.6	0.6	5299	4804	495	49	38	−11	−3	−20	4.5	3.8	0.7	25.7	22.7
SAN DIEGO CHARGERS	4	12	0	.250	335	396	−61	−1.5	−2.5	5356	5366	−10	49	37	−12	−49	−12	3.9	5.7	−1.8	26.4	26.4

1986 N.F.C

EASTERN DIVISION	W	L	T	PCT	PTS	OPP	NET	P-W	D-W	Y-O	Y-D	Y-N	T-O	T-D	T-N	P-NP	D-NP	PR-O	PR-D	PR-N	YD-O	YD-D
NEW YORK GIANTS	14	2	0	.875DCS*	371	236	135	3.4	2.6	5378	4757	621	32	43	11	96	39	4.6	3.9	0.6	28.2	24.0
WASHINGTON REDSKINS	12	4	0	.750WDC	368	296	72	1.8	2.2	5601	5297	304	32	28	−4	9	63	5.4	4.9	0.6	29.5	27.6
DALLAS COWBOYS	7	9	0	.438	346	337	9	0.2	−1.2	5474	4985	489	41	35	−6	17	−8	4.3	4.3	0.0	27.0	24.9
PHILADELPHIA EAGLES	5	10	1	.344	256	312	−56	−1.4	−1.1	4542	5224	−682	27	36	9	−21	−35	3.2	4.1	−0.9	21.9	25.5
ST. LOUIS CARDINALS	4	11	1	.281	218	351	−133	−3.3	−0.2	4503	4864	−361	29	22	−7	−58	−75	3.5	5.0	−1.5	24.2	27.0

CENTRAL DIVISION	W L T	PCT	PTS	OPP	NET	P-W	D-W	Y-O	Y-D	Y-N	T-O	T-D	T-N	P-NP	D-NP	PR-O	PR-D	PR-N	YD-O	YD-D
CHICAGO BEARS	14 2 0	.875D	352	187	165	4.1	1.9	5459	4130	1329	47	47	0	111	54	4.0	2.4	1.6	27.7	20.0
MINNESOTA VIKINGS	9 7 0	.563	398	273	125	3.1	−2.1	5651	5012	639	29	42	13	105	20	6.3	4.3	2.0	30.5	26.9
DETROIT LIONS	5 11 0	.313	277	326	−49	−1.2	−1.8	4555	5149	−594	37	41	4	−34	−15	3.8	3.8	−0.0	24.1	27.5
GREEN BAY PACKERS	4 12 0	.250	254	418	−164	−4.1	0.1	5061	5015	46	45	32	−13	−48	−116	4.0	4.9	−0.9	26.8	27.3
TAMPA BAY BUC-CANEERS	2 14 0	.125	239	473	−234	−5.8	−0.2	4361	6333	−1972	42	32	−10	−204	−30	2.9	6.6	−3.7	23.3	35.4

WESTERN DIVISION	W L T	PCT	PTS	OPP	NET	P-W	D-W	Y-O	Y-D	Y-N	T-O	T-D	T-N	P-NP	D-NP	PR-O	PR-D	PR-N	YD-O	YD-D
SAN FRANCISCO 49ERS	10 5 1	.656D	374	247	127	3.2	−0.7	6082	4880	1202	29	49	20	180	−53	5.6	2.7	2.9	30.1	24.4
LOS ANGELES RAMS	10 6 0	.625W	309	267	42	1.0	1.0	4653	4871	−218	37	43	6	6	36	3.9	3.6	0.3	22.7	23.9
ATLANTA FALCONS	7 8 1	.469	280	280	0	0.0	−0.5	5106	4908	198	33	36	3	29	−29	3.9	4.6	−0.7	27.3	26.2
NEW ORLEANS SAINTS	7 9 0	.438	288	287	1	0.0	−1.0	4742	5102	−360	43	43	0	−30	31	3.7	4.1	−0.4	25.0	26.4

1987 A.F.C.

EASTERN DIVISION	W L T	PCT	PTS	OPP	NET	P-W	D-W	Y-O	Y-D	Y-N	T-O	T-D	T-N	P-NP	D-NP	PR-O	PR-D	PR-N	YD-O	YD-D
INDIANAPOLIS COLTS	9 6 0	.600D	300	238	62	1.5	−0.0	4995	4550	445	34	45	11	81	−19	4.9	3.8	1.1	30.6	29.9
NEW ENGLAND PATRIOTS	8 7 0	.533	320	293	27	0.7	−0.2	4454	4877	−423	31	42	11	9	18	4.4	4.1	0.3	27.7	29.2
MIAMI DOLPHINS	8 7 0	.533	362	335	27	0.7	−0.2	5538	5445	93	37	32	−5	−12	39	5.5	5.3	0.2	36.4	35.1
BUFFALO BILLS	7 8 0	.467	270	305	−35	−0.9	0.4	4741	4906	−165	43	31	−12	−62	27	4.1	4.9	−0.8	28.7	29.0
NEW YORK JETS	6 9 0	.400	334	360	−26	−1.0	−0.9	4630	5041	−411	34	29	−5	−54	28	4.2	5.2	−0.9	28.9	30.9

CENTRAL DIVISION	W L T	PCT	PTS	OPP	NET	P-W	D-W	Y-O	Y-D	Y-N	T-O	T-D	T-N	P-NP	D-NP	PR-O	PR-D	PR-N	YD-O	YD-D
CLEVELAND BROWNS	10 5 0	.667DC	390	239	151	3.8	−1.3	5200	4264	936	29	36	7	106	45	6.2	3.9	2.3	33.8	30.2
HOUSTON OILERS	9 6 0	.600WD	345	349	−4	−0.1	1.6	5223	4993	230	37	37	0	19	−23	4.9	4.5	0.4	32.6	31.4
PITTSBURGH STEELERS	8 7 0	.533	285	299	−14	−0.3	0.9	4410	4920	−510	33	44	11	2	−16	2.8	4.6	−1.8	27.9	31.7
CINCINNATI BENGALS	4 11 0	.267	285	370	−85	−2.1	−1.4	5377	4697	680	32	26	−6	33	−118	4.3	5.4	−0.5	35.4	32.6

WESTERN DIVISION	W L T	PCT	PTS	OPP	NET	P-W	D-W	Y-O	Y-D	Y-N	T-O	T-D	T-N	P-NP	D-NP	PR-O	PR-D	PR-N	YD-O	YD-D
DENVER BRONCOS	10 4 1	.700DCS	379	288	91	2.3	0.7	5624	4813	811	36	47	11	112	−21	5.4	3.5	2.0	33.7	31.1
SEATTLE SEAHAWKS	9 6 0	.600W	371	314	57	1.4	0.1	4735	5159	−424	36	38	2	−27	84	4.7	5.0	−0.3	32.7	34.2
SAN DIEGO CHARGERS	8 7 0	.533	253	317	−64	−1.6	2.1	4588	4953	−365	43	28	−15	−90	26	4.3	4.9	−0.6	28.1	29.8
LOS ANGELES RAIDERS	5 10 0	.333	301	289	12	0.3	−2.8	5267	4364	903	31	28	−3	63	−51	4.8	5.0	−0.1	35.8	30.1
KANSAS CITY CHIEFS	4 11 0	.267	273	388	−115	−2.9	−0.6	4418	5639	−1221	41	28	−13	−154	39	4.2	6.0	−1.8	32.0	38.1

1987 N.F.C

EASTERN DIVISION	W L T	PCT	PTS	OPP	NET	P-W	D-W	Y-O	Y-D	Y-N	T-O	T-D	T-N	P-NP	D-NP	PR-O	PR-D	PR-N	YD-O	YD-D
WASHINGTON REDSKINS	11 4 0	.733DCS*	379	285	94	2.3	1.2	5597	5022	575	37	34	−3	36	58	5.9	4.3	1.5	33.7	29.5
DALLAS COWBOYS	7 8 0	.467	340	348	−8	−0.2	−0.3	5056	5061	−5	40	43	3	12	−20	4.5	4.7	−0.2	30.3	29.9
ST. LOUIS CARDINALS	7 8 0	.467	362	368	−6	−0.2	−0.3	5326	5384	−58	27	33	6	19	−25	5.2	5.7	−0.6	32.5	35.7
PHILADELPHIA EAGLES	7 8 0	.467	337	380	−43	−1.1	0.6	5077	5249	−172	35	48	13	38	−81	4.4	4.8	−0.4	26.7	28.2
NEW YORK GIANTS	6 9 0	.400	280	312	−32	−0.8	−0.7	4659	4658	1	42	34	−8	−32	0	4.4	3.8	0.6	26.9	26.9

CENTRAL DIVISION	W L T	PCT	PTS	OPP	NET	P-W	D-W	Y-O	Y-D	Y-N	T-O	T-D	T-N	P-NP	D-NP	PR-O	PR-D	PR-N	YD-O	YD-D
CHICAGO BEARS	11 4 0	.733D	356	282	74	1.9	1.6	5044	4215	829	44	24	−20	−11	85	4.1	4.3	−0.1	33.4	27.0
MINNESOTA VIKINGS	8 7 0	.533WDC	336	335	1	0.0	0.5	4809	4824	−15	33	37	4	15	−14	4.0	4.0	−0.0	30.6	29.8
GREEN BAY PACKERS	5 9 1	.367	255	300	−45	−1.1	−0.9	4482	4923	−441	35	42	7	−9	−36	4.1	4.6	−0.5	28.0	30.2
TAMPA BAY BUC-CANEERS	4 11 0	.267	286	360	−74	−1.9	−1.6	4381	4987	−606	31	36	5	−31	−43	4.4	5.0	−0.5	28.8	31.2
DETROIT LIONS	4 11 0	.267	269	384	−115	−2.9	−0.6	4391	5273	−882	37	32	−5	−94	−21	3.6	5.1	−1.5	29.7	36.9

WESTERN DIVISION	W L T	PCT	PTS	OPP	NET	P-W	D-W	Y-O	Y-D	Y-N	T-O	T-D	T-N	P-NP	D-NP	PR-O	PR-D	PR-N	YD-O	YD-D
SAN FRANCISCO 49ERS	13 2 0	.867D	459	253	206	5.2	0.3	5987	4095	1892	26	38	12	206	0	6.7	3.0	3.8	41.6	25.3
NEW ORLEANS SAINTS	12 3 0	.800W	422	283	139	3.5	1.0	4964	4350	614	28	48	20	131	8	5.6	3.2	2.4	30.1	29.6
LOS ANGELES RAMS	6 9 0	.400	317	361	−44	−1.1	−0.4	4651	5121	−470	33	27	−6	−63	19	4.3	5.5	−1.2	28.9	32.6
ATLANTA FALCONS	3 12 0	.200	205	436	−231	−5.8	1.3	4066	5907	−1841	49	27	−22	−241	10	2.7	5.9	−3.1	26.9	35.8

LIFETIME RECORDS

Here are the lifetime records of 100 outstanding rushers, passers, and receivers. The following basic statistics are included:

LG = League Games Scheduled, G = Games Played, ATT = Rushing or Passing Attempts, NO = Number of Pass Receptions, COM = Completed Passes, YDS = Yards, AVG = Average Yards per Attempt or Reception, TD = Touchdowns, INT = Interceptions.

In addition to the basic statistics, we are adding the following adjusted figures for the basis of comparisons.

AYD/G = Adjusted Yards per Game for Rushers (for rushers and receivers, adjusted yards is Yards + (10 × TD), AYD/L = Adjusted Yards per Game divided by the league leader as a percent (so 100 means the player led the league), Y/14G = Net Yards adjusted to a 14-game schedule, N/14G = Net Receptions adjusted to a 14-game schedule, Y-RATE = our New Passer Rating, which is (Yards + 10 × TD − 45 × interceptions)/Attempts. L-RATE = passer rating (Y-RATE) compared to league leader and given as percent.

RUSHING

MARCUS ALLEN

	LG	G	ATT	YDS	AVG	TD	AYD/G	AYD/L	Y/14G
1982 LOS ANGELES RAIDERS(N)	9	9	160	697	4.36	11	89.7	95.4	1084
1983 LOS ANGELES RAIDERS(N)	16	15	266	1014	3.81	9	69.0	55.5	887
1984 LOS ANGELES RAIDERS(N)	16	16	275	1168	4.25	13	81.1	57.8	1022
1985 LOS ANGELES RAIDERS(N)	16	16	380	1759	4.63	11	116.8	100.0	1539
1986 LOS ANGELES RAIDERS(N)	16	13	208	759	3.65	5	50.6	41.9	664
1987 LOS ANGELES RAIDERS(N)	15	12	200	754	3.77	5	53.6	54.2	704
TOTAL 6 YEARS	*88*	*81*	*1489*	*6151*	*4.13*	*54*	*76.0*	*69.5*	*5900*

OTTIS ANDERSON

	LG	G	ATT	YDS	AVG	TD	AYD/G	AYD/L	Y/14G
1979 ST. LOUIS CARDINALS(N)	16	16	331	1605	4.85	8	105.3	89.3	1404
1980 ST. LOUIS CARDINALS(N)	16	16	301	1352	4.49	9	90.1	69.9	1183
1981 ST. LOUIS CARDINALS(N)	16	16	328	1376	4.20	9	91.6	81.3	1204
1982 ST. LOUIS CARDINALS(N)	9	8	145	587	4.05	3	68.6	72.9	913
1983 ST. LOUIS CARDINALS(N)	16	15	296	1270	4.29	5	82.5	66.4	1111
1984 ST. LOUIS CARDINALS(N)	16	15	289	1174	4.06	6	77.1	55.0	1027
1985 ST. LOUIS CARDINALS(N)	16	9	117	479	4.09	4	32.4	27.8	419
1986 ST. LOUIS CARDINALS(N)									
NEW YORK GIANTS(N)	16	12	75	237	3.16	3	16.7	13.8	207
1987 NEW YORK GIANTS(N)	15	6	2	6	3.00	0	0.4	0.4	6
TOTAL 9 YEARS	*136*	*113*	*1884*	*8086*	*4.29*	*47*	*62.9*	*67.8*	*7475*

WILLIAM ANDREWS

	LG	G	ATT	YDS	AVG	TD	AYD/G	AYD/L	Y/14G
1979 ATLANTA FALCONS(N)	16	15	239	1023	4.28	3	65.8	55.8	895
1980 ATLANTA FALCONS(N)	16	16	265	1308	4.94	4	84.3	65.3	1145
1981 ATLANTA FALCONS(N)	16	16	289	1301	4.50	10	87.6	77.7	1138
1982 ATLANTA FALCONS(N)	9	9	139	573	4.12	5	69.2	73.6	891
1983 ATLANTA FALCONS(N)	16	16	331	1567	4.73	7	102.3	82.3	1371
1986 ATLANTA FALCONS(N)	16	15	52	214	4.12	1	14.0	11.6	187
TOTAL 6 YEARS	*89*	*87*	*1315*	*5986*	*4.55*	*30*	*70.6*	*69.3*	*5628*

CLIFF BATTLES

	LG	G	ATT	YDS	AVG	TD	AYD/G	AYD/L	Y/14G
1932 BOSTON BRAVES(N)	10	8	148	576	3.89	3	60.6	100.0	806
1933 BOSTON REDSKINS(N)	12	12	146	737	5.05	3	63.9	89.3	860
1934 BOSTON REDSKINS(N)	12	12	103	511	4.96	6	47.6	52.7	596
1935 BOSTON REDSKINS(N)	12	7	84	310	3.69	1	26.7	62.7	362
1936 BOSTON REDSKINS(N)	12	11	176	614	3.49	5	55.3	74.9	716
1937 WASHINGTON REDSKINS(N)	11	10	216	874	4.05	5	84.0	100.0	1112
TOTAL 6 YEARS	*69*	*60*	*873*	*3622*	*4.15*	*23*	*55.8*	*84.0*	*4453*

JIM BROWN

	LG	G	ATT	YDS	AVG	TD	AYD/G	AYD/L	Y/14G
1957 CLEVELAND BROWNS(N)	12	12	202	942	4.66	9	86.0	100.0	1099
1958 CLEVELAND BROWNS(N)	12	12	257	1527	5.94	17	141.4	100.0	1782
1959 CLEVELAND BROWNS(N)	12	12	290	1329	4.58	14	122.4	100.0	1551
1960 CLEVELAND BROWNS(N)	12	12	215	1257	5.85	9	112.3	100.0	1467
1961 CLEVELAND BROWNS(N)	14	14	305	1408	4.62	8	106.3	100.0	1408
1962 CLEVELAND BROWNS(N)	14	14	230	996	4.33	13	80.4	67.7	996
1963 CLEVELAND BROWNS(N)	14	14	291	1863	6.40	12	141.6	100.0	1863
1964 CLEVELAND BROWNS(N)	14	14	280	1446	5.16	7	108.3	100.0	1446
1965 CLEVELAND BROWNS(N)	14	14	289	1544	5.34	17	122.4	100.0	1544
TOTAL 9 YEARS	*118*	*118*	*2359*	*12312*	*5.22*	*106*	*113.3*	*96.8*	*13155*

LARRY BROWN

	LG	G	ATT	YDS	AVG	TD	AYD/G	AYD/L	Y/14G
1969 WASHINGTON REDSKINS(N)	14	14	202	888	4.40	4	66.3	83.5	888
1970 WASHINGTON REDSKINS(N)	14	13	237	1125	4.75	5	83.9	100.0	1125
1971 WASHINGTON REDSKINS(N)	14	13	253	948	3.75	4	70.6	82.8	948
1972 WASHINGTON REDSKINS(N)	14	12	285	1216	4.27	8	92.6	98.9	1216
1973 WASHINGTON REDSKINS(N)	14	14	273	860	3.15	8	67.1	44.3	860
1974 WASHINGTON REDSKINS(N)	14	11	163	430	2.64	3	32.9	30.7	430
1975 WASHINGTON REDSKINS(N)	14	14	97	352	3.63	3	27.3	19.3	352
1976 WASHINGTON REDSKINS(N)	14	11	20	56	2.80	0	4.0	3.5	56
TOTAL 8 YEARS	*112*	*102*	*1530*	*5875*	*3.84*	*35*	*55.6*	*71.1*	*5875*

EARL CAMPBELL

	LG	G	ATT	YDS	AVG	TD	AYD/G	AYD/L	Y/14G
1978 HOUSTON OILERS(N)	16	15	302	1450	4.80	13	98.8	100.0	1269
1979 HOUSTON OILERS(N)	16	16	368	1697	4.61	19	117.9	100.0	1485
1980 HOUSTON OILERS(N)	16	15	373	1934	5.18	13	129.0	100.0	1692
1981 HOUSTON OILERS(N)	16	16	361	1376	3.81	10	92.3	81.8	1204
1982 HOUSTON OILERS(N)	9	9	157	538	3.43	2	62.0	66.0	837
1983 HOUSTON OILERS(N)	16	14	322	1301	4.04	12	88.8	71.5	1138
1984 HOUSTON OILERS(N)									
NEW ORLEANS SAINTS(N)	16	14	146	468	3.21	4	31.8	22.6	410
1985 NEW ORLEANS SAINTS(N)	16	16	158	643	4.07	1	40.8	34.9	563
TOTAL 8 YEARS	*121*	*115*	*2187*	*9407*	*4.30*	*74*	*83.9*	*80.5*	*8597*

LARRY CSONKA

	LG	G	ATT	YDS	AVG	TD	AYD/G	AYD/L	Y/14G
1968 MIAMI DOLPHINS(A)	14	11	138	540	3.91	6	42.9	54.4	540
1969 MIAMI DOLPHINS(A)	14	11	131	566	4.32	2	41.9	62.8	566
1970 MIAMI DOLPHINS(N)	14	14	193	874	4.53	6	66.7	79.5	874
1971 MIAMI DOLPHINS(N)	14	14	195	1051	5.39	7	80.1	94.0	1051
1972 MIAMI DOLPHINS(N)	14	14	213	1117	5.24	6	84.1	89.8	1117
1973 MIAMI DOLPHINS(N)	14	14	219	1003	4.58	5	75.2	49.6	1003
1974 MIAMI DOLPHINS(N)	14	12	197	749	3.80	9	59.9	56.0	749
1976 NEW YORK GIANTS(N)	14	12	160	569	3.56	4	43.5	38.5	569
1977 NEW YORK GIANTS(N)	14	14	134	464	3.46	1	33.9	23.8	464
1978 NEW YORK GIANTS(N)	16	16	91	311	3.42	6	23.2	23.5	272
1979 MIAMI DOLPHINS(N)	16	16	220	837	3.80	12	59.8	50.7	732
TOTAL 11 YEARS	*158*	*148*	*1891*	*8081*	*4.27*	*64*	*55.2*	*59.8*	*7938*

ERIC DICKERSON

	LG	G	ATT	YDS	AVG	TD	AYD/G	AYD/L	Y/14G
1983 LOS ANGELES RAMS(N)	16	16	390	1808	4.64	18	124.3	100.0	1582
1984 LOS ANGELES RAMS(N)	16	16	379	2105	5.55	14	140.3	100.0	1842
1985 LOS ANGELES RAMS(N)	16	14	292	1234	4.23	12	84.6	72.4	1080
1986 LOS ANGELES RAMS(N)	16	16	404	1821	4.51	11	120.7	100.0	1593
1987 LOS ANGELES RAMS(N)									
INDIANAPOLIS COLTS(N)	15	12	283	1288	4.55	6	89.9	90.8	1202
TOTAL 5 YEARS	*79*	*74*	*1748*	*8256*	*4.72*	*61*	*112.2*	*93.9*	*7299*

TONY DORSETT

	LG	G	ATT	YDS	AVG	TD	AYD/G	AYD/L	Y/14G
1977 DALLAS COWBOYS(N)	14	14	208	1007	4.84	12	80.5	56.6	1007
1978 DALLAS COWBOYS(N)	16	16	290	1325	4.57	7	87.2	88.3	1159
1979 DALLAS COWBOYS(N)	16	14	250	1107	4.43	6	72.9	61.8	969

TONY DORSETT

	LG	G	ATT	YDS	AVG	TD	AYD/G	AYD/L	Y/14G
1980 DALLAS COWBOYS(N)	16	15	278	1185	4.26	11	80.9	62.7	1037
1981 DALLAS COWBOYS(N)	16	16	342	1646	4.81	4	105.4	93.5	1440
1982 DALLAS COWBOYS(N)	9	9	177	745	4.21	5	88.3	94.0	1159
1983 DALLAS COWBOYS(N)	16	16	289	1321	4.57	8	87.6	70.5	1156
1984 DALLAS COWBOYS(N)	16	16	302	1189	3.94	6	78.1	55.6	1040
1985 DALLAS COWBOYS(N)	16	16	305	1307	4.29	7	86.1	73.7	1144
1986 DALLAS COWBOYS(N)	16	13	184	748	4.07	5	49.9	41.3	655
1987 DALLAS COWBOYS(N)	15	12	130	456	3.51	1	31.1	31.4	426
TOTAL 11 YEARS	166	157	2755	12036	4.37	72	76.8	69.0	11191

FRANCO HARRIS

	LG	G	ATT	YDS	AVG	TD	AYD/G	AYD/L	Y/14G
1972 PITTSBURGH STEELERS(N)	14	14	188	1055	5.61	10	82.5	88.1	1055
1973 PITTSBURGH STEELERS(N)	14	12	188	698	3.71	3	52.0	34.3	698
1974 PITTSBURGH STEELERS(N)	14	12	208	1006	4.84	5	75.4	70.5	1006
1975 PITTSBURGH STEELERS(N)	14	14	262	1246	4.76	10	96.1	68.1	1246
1976 PITTSBURGH STEELERS(N)	14	14	289	1128	3.90	14	90.6	80.1	1128
1977 PITTSBURGH STEELERS(N)	14	14	300	1162	3.87	11	90.9	63.9	1162
1978 PITTSBURGH STEELERS(N)	16	16	310	1082	3.49	8	72.6	73.5	947
1979 PITTSBURGH STEELERS(N)	16	15	267	1186	4.44	11	81.0	68.7	1038
1980 PITTSBURGH STEELERS(N)	16	13	208	789	3.79	4	51.8	40.2	690
1981 PITTSBURGH STEELERS(N)	16	16	242	987	4.08	8	66.7	59.1	864
1982 PITTSBURGH STEELERS(N)	9	9	140	604	4.31	2	69.3	73.8	940
1983 PITTSBURGH STEELERS(N)	16	16	279	1007	3.61	5	66.1	53.2	881
1984 SEATTLE SEAHAWKS(N)	16	8	68	170	2.50	0	10.6	7.6	149
TOTAL 13 YEARS	189	173	2949	12120	4.11	91	68.9	63.5	11803

CLARK HINKLE

	LG	G	ATT	YDS	AVG	TD	AYD/G	AYD/L	Y/14G
1932 GREEN BAY PACKERS(N)	14	11	95	331	3.48	3	25.8	59.6	331
1933 GREEN BAY PACKERS(N)	13	13	139	413	2.97	4	34.8	52.7	445
1934 GREEN BAY PACKERS(N)	13	12	144	359	2.49	1	28.4	34.0	387
1935 GREEN BAY PACKERS(N)	12	9	77	273	3.55	2	24.4	57.5	319
1936 GREEN BAY PACKERS(N)	12	12	100	476	4.76	5	43.8	59.3	555
1937 GREEN BAY PACKERS(N)	11	11	129	552	4.28	5	54.7	65.2	703
1938 GREEN BAY PACKERS(N)	11	11	114	299	2.62	3	29.9	54.2	381
1939 GREEN BAY PACKERS(N)	11	11	135	381	2.82	5	39.2	56.0	485
1940 GREEN BAY PACKERS(N)	11	11	109	383	3.51	2	36.6	70.7	487
1941 GREEN BAY PACKERS(N)	11	11	129	393	3.05	5	40.3	81.1	500
TOTAL 10 YEARS	119	112	1171	3860	3.30	35	35.4	58.6	4592

JOHN HENRY JOHNSON

	LG	G	ATT	YDS	AVG	TD	AYD/G	AYD/L	Y/14G
1954 SAN FRANCISCO 49ERS(N)	12	12	129	681	5.28	9	64.3	68.3	795
1955 SAN FRANCISCO 49ERS(N)	12	7	19	69	3.63	1	6.6	7.5	81
1956 SAN FRANCISCO 49ERS(N)	12	12	80	301	3.76	2	26.8	25.8	351
1957 DETROIT LIONS(N)	12	12	129	621	4.81	5	55.9	65.0	725
1958 DETROIT LIONS(N)	12	9	56	254	4.54	0	21.2	15.0	296
1959 DETROIT LIONS(N)	12	10	82	270	3.29	2	24.2	19.7	315
1960 PITTSBURGH STEELERS(N)	12	12	118	621	5.26	2	53.4	47.6	725
1961 PITTSBURGH STEELERS(N)	14	14	213	787	3.69	6	60.5	56.9	787
1962 PITTSBURGH STEELERS(N)	14	14	251	1141	4.55	7	86.5	72.8	1141

	LG	G	ATT	YDS	AVG	TD	AYD/G	AYD/L	Y/14G
1963 PITTSBURGH STEELERS(N)	14	12	186	773	4.16	4	58.1	41.0	773
1964 PITTSBURGH STEELERS(N)	14	14	235	1048	4.46	7	79.9	73.7	1048
1965 PITTSBURGH STEELERS(N)	14	1	3	11	3.67	0	0.8	0.6	11
1966 HOUSTON OILERS(A)	14	14	70	226	3.23	3	18.3	16.3	226
TOTAL 13 YEARS	*168*	*143*	*1571*	*6803*	*4.33*	*48*	*43.4*	*53.4*	*7273*

LEROY KELLY	LG	G	ATT	YDS	AVG	TD	AYD/G	AYD/L	Y/14G
1964 CLEVELAND BROWNS(N)	14	14	6	12	2.00	0	0.9	0.8	12
1965 CLEVELAND BROWNS(N)	14	13	37	139	3.76	0	9.9	8.1	139
1966 CLEVELAND BROWNS(N)	14	14	209	1141	5.46	15	92.2	98.5	1141
1967 CLEVELAND BROWNS(N)	14	14	235	1205	5.13	11	93.9	100.0	1205
1968 CLEVELAND BROWNS(N)	14	14	248	1239	5.00	16	99.9	100.0	1239
1969 CLEVELAND BROWNS(N)	14	13	196	817	4.17	9	64.8	81.6	817
1970 CLEVELAND BROWNS(N)	14	13	206	656	3.18	6	51.1	60.9	656
1971 CLEVELAND BROWNS(N)	14	14	234	865	3.70	10	68.9	80.9	865
1972 CLEVELAND BROWNS(N)	14	14	224	811	3.62	4	60.8	64.9	811
1973 CLEVELAND BROWNS(N)	14	13	132	389	2.95	3	29.9	19.7	389
TOTAL 10 YEARS	*140*	*136*	*1727*	*7274*	*4.21*	*74*	*57.2*	*77.5*	*7274*

TUFFY LEEMANS	LG	G	ATT	YDS	AVG	TD	AYD/G	AYD/L	Y/14G
1936 NEW YORK GIANTS(N)	12	11	206	830	4.03	2	70.8	95.8	968
1937 NEW YORK GIANTS(N)	11	9	144	429	2.98	0	39.0	46.4	546
1938 NEW YORK GIANTS(N)	11	11	121	463	3.83	4	45.7	82.9	589
1939 NEW YORK GIANTS(N)	11	11	128	429	3.35	3	41.7	59.7	546
1940 NEW YORK GIANTS(N)	11	9	132	474	3.59	1	44.0	84.9	603
1941 NEW YORK GIANTS(N)	11	11	100	332	3.32	4	33.8	68.1	423
1942 NEW YORK GIANTS(N)	11	8	51	116	2.27	3	13.3	19.6	148
1943 NEW YORK GIANTS(N)	10	10	37	69	1.86	0	6.9	10.3	97
TOTAL 8 YEARS	*88*	*80*	*919*	*3142*	*3.42*	*17*	*37.6*	*69.1*	*3920*

FLOYD LITTLE	LG	G	ATT	YDS	AVG	TD	AYD/G	AYD/L	Y/14G
1967 DENVER BRONCOS(A)	14	13	130	381	2.93	1	27.9	30.4	381
1968 DENVER BRONCOS(A)	14	11	158	584	3.70	3	43.9	55.7	584
1969 DENVER BRONCOS(A)	14	9	146	729	4.99	6	56.4	84.6	729
1970 DENVER BRONCOS(N)	14	14	209	901	4.31	3	66.5	79.2	901
1971 DENVER BRONCOS(N)	14	14	284	1133	3.99	6	85.2	100.0	1133
1972 DENVER BRONCOS(N)	14	14	216	859	3.98	9	67.8	72.4	859
1973 DENVER BRONCOS(N)	14	14	256	979	3.82	12	78.5	51.8	979
1974 DENVER BRONCOS(N)	14	14	117	312	2.67	1	23.0	21.5	312
1975 DENVER BRONCOS(N)	14	14	125	445	3.56	2	33.2	23.5	445
TOTAL 9 YEARS	*126*	*117*	*1641*	*6323*	*3.85*	*43*	*53.6*	*63.6*	*6323*

OLLIE MATSON	LG	G	ATT	YDS	AVG	TD	AYD/G	AYD/L	Y/14G
1952 CHICAGO CARDINALS(N)	12	11	96	344	3.58	3	31.2	37.6	401
1954 CHICAGO CARDINALS(N)	12	12	101	506	5.01	4	45.5	48.4	590
1955 CHICAGO CARDINALS(N)	12	12	109	475	4.36	1	40.4	46.1	554
1956 CHICAGO CARDINALS(N)	12	12	192	924	4.81	5	81.2	78.2	1078
1957 CHICAGO CARDINALS(N)	12	12	134	577	4.31	6	53.1	61.7	673
1958 CHICAGO CARDINALS(N)	12	12	129	505	3.91	5	46.3	32.7	589
1959 LOS ANGELES RAMS(N)	12	12	161	863	5.36	6	76.9	62.8	1007
1960 LOS ANGELES RAMS(N)	12	12	61	170	2.79	1	15.0	13.4	198
1961 LOS ANGELES RAMS(N)	14	14	24	181	7.54	2	14.4	13.5	181

OLLIE MATSON

	LG	G	ATT	YDS	AVG	TD	AYD/G	AYD/L	Y/14G
1962 LOS ANGELES RAMS(N)	14	13	3	0	0.00	0	0.0	0.0	0
1963 DETROIT LIONS(N)	14	8	13	20	1.54	0	1.4	1.0	20
1964 PHILADELPHIA EAGLES(N)	14	12	96	404	4.21	4	31.7	29.3	404
1965 PHILADELPHIA EAGLES(N)	14	14	22	103	4.68	2	8.8	7.2	103
1966 PHILADELPHIA EAGLES(N)	14	14	29	101	3.48	1	7.9	8.5	101
TOTAL 14 YEARS	180	170	1170	5173	4.42	40	31.0	47.4	5900

HUGH McELHENNY

	LG	G	ATT	YDS	AVG	TD	AYD/G	AYD/L	Y/14G
1952 SAN FRANCISCO 49ERS(N)	12	12	98	684	6.98	6	62.0	74.8	798
1953 SAN FRANCISCO 49ERS(N)	12	12	112	503	4.49	3	44.4	47.7	587
1954 SAN FRANCISCO 49ERS(N)	12	6	64	515	8.05	6	47.9	50.9	601
1955 SAN FRANCISCO 49ERS(N)	12	12	90	327	3.63	4	30.6	34.9	382
1956 SAN FRANCISCO 49ERS(N)	12	12	185	916	4.95	8	83.0	79.9	1069
1957 SAN FRANCISCO 49ERS(N)	12	12	102	478	4.69	1	40.7	47.3	558
1958 SAN FRANCISCO 49ERS(N)	12	12	113	451	3.99	6	42.6	30.1	526
1959 SAN FRANCISCO 49ERS(N)	12	10	18	67	3.72	1	6.4	5.2	78
1960 SAN FRANCISCO 49ERS(N)	12	9	95	347	3.65	0	28.9	25.8	405
1961 MINNESOTA VIKINGS(N)	14	13	120	570	4.75	3	42.9	40.3	570
1962 MINNESOTA VIKINGS(N)	14	11	50	200	4.00	0	14.3	12.0	200
1963 NEW YORK GIANTS(N)	14	14	55	175	3.18	0	12.5	8.8	175
1964 DETROIT LIONS(N)	14	8	22	48	2.18	0	3.4	3.2	48
TOTAL 13 YEARS	164	143	1124	5281	4.70	38	34.5	45.0	5996

WILBERT MONTGOMERY

	LG	G	ATT	YDS	AVG	TD	AYD/G	AYD/L	Y/14G
1977 PHILADELPHIA EAGLES(N)	14	14	45	183	4.07	2	14.5	10.2	183
1978 PHILADELPHIA EAGLES(N)	16	14	259	1220	4.71	9	81.9	82.9	1068
1979 PHILADELPHIA EAGLES(N)	16	16	338	1512	4.47	9	100.1	84.9	1323
1980 PHILADELPHIA EAGLES(N)	16	12	193	778	4.03	8	53.6	41.6	681
1981 PHILADELPHIA EAGLES(N)	16	15	286	1402	4.90	8	92.6	82.2	1227
1982 PHILADELPHIA EAGLES(N)	9	8	114	515	4.52	7	65.0	69.1	801
1983 PHILADELPHIA EAGLES(N)	16	5	29	139	4.79	0	8.7	7.0	122
1984 PHILADELPHIA EAGLES(N)	16	16	201	789	3.93	2	50.6	36.0	690
1985 DETROIT LIONS(N)	16	7	75	251	3.35	0	15.7	13.4	220
TOTAL 9 YEARS	135	107	1540	6789	4.41	45	53.6	63.9	6314

LENNY MOORE

	LG	G	ATT	YDS	AVG	TD	AYD/G	AYD/L	Y/14G
1956 BALTIMORE COLTS(N)	12	12	86	649	7.55	8	60.8	58.5	757
1957 BALTIMORE COLTS(N)	12	12	98	488	4.98	3	43.2	50.2	569
1958 BALTIMORE COLTS(N)	12	12	82	598	7.29	7	55.7	39.4	698
1959 BALTIMORE COLTS(N)	12	12	92	422	4.59	2	36.8	30.1	492
1960 BALTIMORE COLTS(N)	12	12	91	374	4.11	4	34.5	30.7	436
1961 BALTIMORE COLTS(N)	14	13	92	648	7.04	7	51.3	48.3	648
1962 BALTIMORE COLTS(N)	14	10	106	470	4.43	2	35.0	29.4	470
1963 BALTIMORE COLTS(N)	14	7	27	136	5.04	2	11.1	7.9	136
1964 BALTIMORE COLTS(N)	14	14	157	584	3.72	16	53.1	49.1	584
1965 BALTIMORE COLTS(N)	14	12	133	464	3.49	5	36.7	30.0	464
1966 BALTIMORE COLTS(N)	14	13	63	209	3.32	3	17.1	18.2	209
1967 BALTIMORE COLTS(N)	14	14	42	132	3.14	4	12.3	13.1	132
TOTAL 12 YEARS	158	143	1069	5174	4.84	63	36.7	37.3	5596

MARION MOTLEY

	LG	G	ATT	YDS	AVG	TD	AYD/G	AYD/L	Y/14G
1946 CLEVELAND BROWNS(A)	14	13	73	601	8.23	5	46.5	84.7	601
1947 CLEVELAND BROWNS(A)	14	14	146	889	6.09	8	69.2	60.1	889
1948 CLEVELAND BROWNS(A)	14	14	157	964	6.14	5	72.4	100.0	964
1949 CLEVELAND BROWNS(A)	12	12	113	570	5.04	8	54.2	75.3	665
1950 CLEVELAND BROWNS(N)	12	12	140	810	5.79	3	70.0	100.0	945
1951 CLEVELAND BROWNS(N)	12	11	61	273	4.48	1	23.6	27.2	319
1952 CLEVELAND BROWNS(N)	12	12	104	444	4.27	1	37.8	45.7	518
1953 CLEVELAND BROWNS(N)	12	12	32	161	5.03	0	13.4	14.4	188
1955 PITTSBURGH STEELERS(N)	12	7	2	8	4.00	0	0.7	0.8	9
TOTAL 9 YEARS	*114*	*107*	*828*	*4720*	*5.70*	*31*	*44.1*	*72.5*	*5098*

BRONKO NAGURSKI

	LG	G	ATT	YDS	AVG	TD	AYD/G	AYD/L	Y/14G
1930 CHICAGO BEARS(N)	14	13	111	550	4.95	5	42.9	100.0	550
1931 CHICAGO BEARS(N)	13	10	88	446	5.07	2	35.8	84.7	480
1932 CHICAGO BEARS(N)	14	14	111	496	4.47	4	38.3	88.4	496
1933 CHICAGO BEARS(N)	13	13	128	533	4.16	1	41.8	63.2	574
1934 CHICAGO BEARS(N)	13	13	123	586	4.76	7	50.5	60.5	631
1935 CHICAGO BEARS(N)	12	5	37	137	3.70	1	12.3	28.8	160
1936 CHICAGO BEARS(N)	12	11	122	529	4.34	3	46.6	63.0	617
1937 CHICAGO BEARS(N)	11	10	73	343	4.70	1	32.1	38.2	437
1943 CHICAGO BEARS(N)	10	9	16	84	5.25	1	9.4	14.0	118
TOTAL 9 YEARS	*112*	*98*	*809*	*3704*	*4.58*	*25*	*35.3*	*68.8*	*4063*

WALTER PAYTON

	LG	G	ATT	YDS	AVG	TD	AYD/G	AYD/L	Y/14G
1975 CHICAGO BEARS(N)	14	13	196	679	3.46	7	53.5	37.9	679
1976 CHICAGO BEARS(N)	14	14	311	1390	4.47	13	108.6	96.0	1390
1977 CHICAGO BEARS(N)	14	14	339	1852	5.46	14	142.3	100.0	1852
1978 CHICAGO BEARS(N)	16	16	333	1395	4.19	11	94.1	95.3	1221
1979 CHICAGO BEARS(N)	16	16	369	1610	4.36	14	109.4	92.7	1409
1980 CHICAGO BEARS(N)	16	16	317	1460	4.61	6	95.0	73.6	1278
1981 CHICAGO BEARS(N)	16	16	339	1222	3.60	6	80.1	71.1	1069
1982 CHICAGO BEARS(N)	9	9	148	596	4.03	1	67.3	71.6	927
1983 CHICAGO BEARS(N)	16	16	314	1421	4.53	6	92.6	74.5	1243
1984 CHICAGO BEARS(N)	16	16	381	1684	4.42	11	112.1	79.9	1474
1985 CHICAGO BEARS(N)	16	16	324	1551	4.79	9	102.6	87.8	1357
1986 CHICAGO BEARS(N)	16	16	321	1333	4.15	8	88.3	73.2	1166
1987 CHICAGO BEARS(N)	15	12	146	533	3.65	4	38.2	38.6	497
TOTAL 13 YEARS	*194*	*190*	*3838*	*16726*	*4.36*	*110*	*91.9*	*79.9*	*15562*

JOE PERRY

	LG	G	ATT	YDS	AVG	TD	AYD/G	AYD/L	Y/14G
1948 SAN FRANCISCO 49ERS(A)	14	14	77	562	7.30	10	47.3	65.3	562
1949 SAN FRANCISCO 49ERS(A)	12	12	115	783	6.81	8	71.9	100.0	914
1950 SAN FRANCISCO 49ERS(N)	12	12	124	647	5.22	5	58.1	83.0	755
1951 SAN FRANCISCO 49ERS(N)	12	11	136	677	4.98	3	58.9	67.9	790
1952 SAN FRANCISCO 49ERS(N)	12	12	158	725	4.59	8	67.1	81.0	846
1953 SAN FRANCISCO 49ERS(N)	12	12	192	1018	5.30	10	93.2	100.0	1188
1954 SAN FRANCISCO 49ERS(N)	12	12	173	1049	6.06	8	94.1	100.0	1224
1955 SAN FRANCISCO 49ERS(N)	12	11	156	701	4.49	2	60.1	68.6	818
1956 SAN FRANCISCO 49ERS(N)	12	12	115	520	4.52	3	45.8	44.1	607
1957 SAN FRANCISCO 49ERS(N)	12	8	97	454	4.68	3	40.3	46.9	530
1958 SAN FRANCISCO 49ERS(N)	12	12	125	758	6.06	4	66.5	47.0	884

JOE PERRY

	LG	G	ATT	YDS	AVG	TD	AYD/G	AYD/L	Y/14G
1959 SAN FRANCISCO 49ERS(N)	12	10	139	602	4.33	3	52.7	43.0	702
1960 SAN FRANCISCO 49ERS(N)	12	8	36	95	2.64	1	8.8	7.8	111
1961 BALTIMORE COLTS(N)	14	13	168	675	4.02	3	50.4	47.4	675
1962 BALTIMORE COLTS(N)	14	11	94	359	3.82	0	25.6	21.6	359
1963 SAN FRANCISCO 49ERS(N)	14	9	24	98	4.08	0	7.0	4.9	98
TOTAL 16 YEARS	200	179	1929	9723	5.04	71	52.2	66.3	11061

JOHN RIGGINS

	LG	G	ATT	YDS	AVG	TD	AYD/G	AYD/L	Y/14G
1971 NEW YORK JETS(N)	14	14	180	769	4.27	1	55.6	65.3	769
1972 NEW YORK JETS(N)	14	12	207	944	4.56	7	72.4	77.3	944
1973 NEW YORK JETS(N)	14	11	134	482	3.60	4	37.3	24.6	482
1974 NEW YORK JETS(N)	14	10	169	680	4.02	5	52.1	48.8	680
1975 NEW YORK JETS(N)	14	14	238	1005	4.22	8	77.5	54.9	1005
1976 WASHINGTON REDSKINS(N)	14	14	162	572	3.53	3	43.0	38.0	572
1977 WASHINGTON REDSKINS(N)	14	5	68	203	2.99	0	14.5	10.2	203
1978 WASHINGTON REDSKINS(N)	16	15	248	1014	4.09	5	66.5	67.3	887
1979 WASHINGTON REDSKINS(N)	16	16	260	1153	4.43	9	77.7	65.9	1009
1981 WASHINGTON REDSKINS(N)	16	15	195	714	3.66	13	52.8	46.8	625
1982 WASHINGTON REDSKINS(N)	9	8	177	553	3.12	3	64.8	68.9	860
1983 WASHINGTON REDSKINS(N)	16	15	375	1347	3.59	24	99.2	79.8	1179
1984 WASHINGTON REDSKINS(N)	16	14	327	1239	3.79	14	86.2	61.4	1084
1985 WASHINGTON REDSKINS(N)	16	12	176	677	3.85	8	47.3	40.5	592
TOTAL 14 YEARS	203	175	2916	11352	3.89	104	61.0	58.8	10891

GEORGE ROGERS

	LG	G	ATT	YDS	AVG	TD	AYD/G	AYD/L	Y/14G
1981 NEW ORLEANS SAINTS(N)	16	16	378	1674	4.43	13	112.8	100.0	1465
1982 NEW ORLEANS SAINTS(N)	9	6	122	535	4.39	3	62.8	66.8	832
1983 NEW ORLEANS SAINTS(N)	16	13	256	1144	4.47	5	74.6	60.1	1001
1984 NEW ORLEANS SAINTS(N)	16	16	239	914	3.82	2	58.4	41.6	800
1985 WASHINGTON REDSKINS(N)	16	15	231	1093	4.73	7	72.7	62.2	956
1986 WASHINGTON REDSKINS(N)	16	15	303	1203	3.97	18	86.4	71.6	1053
1987 WASHINGTON REDSKINS(N)	15	11	163	613	3.76	6	44.9	45.4	572
TOTAL 7 YEARS	104	92	1692	7176	4.24	54	74.2	67.8	6679

GALE SAYERS

	LG	G	ATT	YDS	AVG	TD	AYD/G	AYD/L	Y/14G
1965 CHICAGO BEARS(N)	14	14	166	867	5.22	14	71.9	58.8	867
1966 CHICAGO BEARS(N)	14	14	229	1231	5.38	8	93.6	100.0	1231
1967 CHICAGO BEARS(N)	14	13	186	880	4.73	7	67.9	72.2	880
1968 CHICAGO BEARS(N)	14	9	138	856	6.20	2	62.6	62.6	856
1969 CHICAGO BEARS(N)	14	14	236	1032	4.37	8	79.4	100.0	1032
1970 CHICAGO BEARS(N)	14	2	23	52	2.26	0	3.7	4.4	52
1971 CHICAGO BEARS(N)	14	2	13	38	2.92	0	2.7	3.2	38
TOTAL 7 YEARS	98	68	991	4956	5.00	39	54.6	79.2	4956

O. J. SIMPSON

	LG	G	ATT	YDS	AVG	TD	AYD/G	AYD/L	Y/14G
1969 BUFFALO BILLS(A)	14	13	181	697	3.85	2	51.2	76.8	697
1970 BUFFALO BILLS(N)	14	8	120	488	4.07	5	38.4	45.8	488
1971 BUFFALO BILLS(N)	14	14	183	742	4.05	5	56.6	66.4	742
1972 BUFFALO BILLS(N)	14	14	292	1251	4.28	6	93.6	100.0	1251
1973 BUFFALO BILLS(N)	14	14	332	2003	6.03	12	151.6	100.0	2003

	LG	G	ATT	YDS	AVG	TD	AYD/G	AYD/L	Y/14G
1974 BUFFALO BILLS(N)	14	14	270	1125	4.17	3	82.5	77.2	1125
1975 BUFFALO BILLS(N)	14	14	329	1817	5.52	16	141.2	100.0	1817
1976 BUFFALO BILLS(N)	14	14	290	1503	5.18	8	113.1	100.0	1503
1977 BUFFALO BILLS(N)	14	7	126	557	4.42	0	39.8	28.0	557
1978 SAN FRANCISCO 49ERS(N)	16	10	161	593	3.68	1	37.7	38.2	519
1979 SAN FRANCISCO 49ERS(N)	16	13	120	460	3.83	3	30.6	26.0	403
TOTAL 11 YEARS	*158*	*135*	*2404*	*11236*	*4.67*	*61*	*75.0*	*78.8*	*11104*

JIM TAYLOR

	LG	G	ATT	YDS	AVG	TD	AYD/G	AYD/L	Y/14G
1958 GREEN BAY PACKERS(N)	12	12	52	247	4.75	1	21.4	15.1	288
1959 GREEN BAY PACKERS(N)	12	12	120	452	3.77	6	42.7	34.9	527
1960 GREEN BAY PACKERS(N)	12	12	230	1101	4.79	11	100.9	89.9	1285
1961 GREEN BAY PACKERS(N)	14	14	243	1307	5.38	15	104.1	97.9	1307
1962 GREEN BAY PACKERS(N)	14	14	272	1474	5.42	19	118.9	100.0	1474
1963 GREEN BAY PACKERS(N)	14	14	248	1018	4.10	9	79.1	55.9	1018
1964 GREEN BAY PACKERS(N)	14	13	235	1169	4.97	12	92.1	85.0	1169
1965 GREEN BAY PACKERS(N)	14	13	207	734	3.55	4	55.3	45.2	734
1966 GREEN BAY PACKERS(N)	14	14	204	705	3.46	4	53.2	56.8	705
1967 NEW ORLEANS SAINTS(N)	14	14	130	390	3.00	2	29.3	31.2	390
TOTAL 10 YEARS	*134*	*132*	*1941*	*8597*	*4.43*	*83*	*70.4*	*69.8*	*8897*

STEVE VAN BUREN

	LG	G	ATT	YDS	AVG	TD	AYD/G	AYD/L	Y/14G
1944 PHILADELPHIA EAGLES(N)	10	9	80	444	5.55	5	49.4	59.7	622
1945 PHILADELPHIA EAGLES(N)	10	10	143	832	5.82	15	98.2	100.0	1165
1946 PHILADELPHIA EAGLES(N)	11	9	116	529	4.56	5	52.6	91.3	673
1947 PHILADELPHIA EAGLES(N)	12	12	217	1008	4.65	13	94.8	100.0	1176
1948 PHILADELPHIA EAGLES(N)	12	11	201	945	4.70	10	87.1	100.0	1103
1949 PHILADELPHIA EAGLES(N)	12	12	263	1146	4.36	11	104.7	100.0	1337
1950 PHILADELPHIA EAGLES(N)	12	10	188	629	3.35	4	55.8	79.6	734
1951 PHILADELPHIA EAGLES(N)	12	10	112	327	2.92	6	32.3	37.2	382
TOTAL 8 YEARS	*91*	*83*	*1320*	*5860*	*4.44*	*69*	*72.0*	*88.6*	*7191*

PASSING

KEN ANDERSON

	LG	G	ATT	COM	YDS	AVG	TD	INT	Y-RATE	L-RATE	Y/14G
1971 CINCINNATI BENGALS(N)	14	11	131	72	777	5.93	5	4	4.94	56.3	777
1972 CINCINNATI BENGALS(N)	14	13	301	171	1918	6.37	7	7	5.56	72.2	1918
1973 CINCINNATI BENGALS(N)	14	14	329	179	2428	7.38	18	12	6.29	88.4	2428
1974 CINCINNATI BENGALS(N)	14	13	328	213	2667	8.13	18	10	7.31	100.0	2667
1975 CINCINNATI BENGALS(N)	14	13	377	228	3169	8.41	21	11	7.65	100.0	3169
1976 CINCINNATI BENGALS(N)	14	14	338	179	2367	7.00	19	14	5.70	66.5	2367
1977 CINCINNATI BENGALS(N)	14	14	323	166	2145	6.64	11	11	5.45	81.0	2145
1978 CINCINNATI BENGALS(N)	16	12	319	173	2219	6.96	10	22	4.17	63.2	1942
1979 CINCINNATI BENGALS(N)	16	15	339	189	2340	6.90	16	10	6.05	83.0	2048
1980 CINCINNATI BENGALS(N)	16	13	275	166	1778	6.47	6	13	4.56	63.0	1556
1981 CINCINNATI BENGALS(N)	16	16	479	300	3754	7.84	29	10	7.50	100.0	3285
1982 CINCINNATI BENGALS(N)	9	9	309	218	2495	8.07	12	9	7.15	92.3	3881
1983 CINCINNATI BENGALS(N)	16	13	297	198	2333	7.86	12	13	6.29	82.3	2041
1984 CINCINNATI BENGALS(N)	16	11	275	175	2107	7.66	10	12	6.06	71.2	1844
1985 CINCINNATI BENGALS(N)	16	3	32	16	170	5.31	2	0	5.94	76.7	149
1986 CINCINNATI BENGALS(N)	16	8	23	11	171	7.43	1	2	3.96	52.8	150
TOTAL 16 YEARS	*235*	*192*	*4475*	*2654*	*32838*	*7.34*	*197*	*160*	*6.17*	*82.0*	*32365*

SAMMY BAUGH

	LG	G	ATT	COM	YDS	AVG	TD	INT	Y-RATE	L-RATE	Y/14G
1937 WASHINGTON REDSKINS(N)	11	11	171	81	1127	6.59	8	14	3.37	63.9	1434
1938 WASHINGTON REDSKINS(N)	11	10	128	63	853	6.66	6	11	3.27	71.3	1086
1939 WASHINGTON REDSKINS(N)	11	8	96	53	518	5.40	6	9	1.80	32.0	659
1940 WASHINGTON REDSKINS(N)	11	11	177	111	1367	7.72	12	10	5.86	100.0	1740
1941 WASHINGTON REDSKINS(N)	11	11	193	106	1236	6.40	10	19	2.49	29.6	1573
1942 WASHINGTON REDSKINS(N)	11	11	225	132	1524	6.77	16	11	5.28	86.8	1940
1943 WASHINGTON REDSKINS(N)	10	10	239	133	1754	7.34	23	19	4.72	49.4	2456
1944 WASHINGTON REDSKINS(N)	10	8	146	82	849	5.82	4	8	3.62	61.6	1189
1945 WASHINGTON REDSKINS(N)	10	8	182	128	1669	9.17	11	4	8.79	100.0	2337
1946 WASHINGTON REDSKINS(N)	11	11	161	87	1163	7.22	8	17	2.97	53.3	1480
1947 WASHINGTON REDSKINS(N)	12	12	354	210	2938	8.30	25	15	7.10	100.0	3428
1948 WASHINGTON REDSKINS(N)	12	12	315	185	2599	8.25	22	23	5.66	79.4	3032
1949 WASHINGTON REDSKINS(N)	12	12	255	145	1903	7.46	18	14	5.70	87.7	2220
1950 WASHINGTON REDSKINS(N)	12	11	166	90	1130	6.81	10	11	4.43	64.1	1318
1951 WASHINGTON REDSKINS(N)	12	12	154	67	1104	7.17	7	17	2.66	37.5	1288
1952 WASHINGTON REDSKINS(N)	12	7	33	20	152	4.61	2	1	3.85	58.2	177
TOTAL 16 YEARS	*179*	*165*	*2995*	*1693*	*21886*	*7.31*	*188*	*203*	*4.89*	*71.7*	*27356*

TERRY BRADSHAW

	LG	G	ATT	COM	YDS	AVG	TD	INT	Y-RATE	L-RATE	Y/14G
1970 PITTSBURGH STEELERS(N)	14	13	218	83	1410	6.47	6	24	1.79	22.4	1410
1971 PITTSBURGH STEELERS(N)	14	14	373	203	2259	6.06	13	22	3.75	42.7	2259
1972 PITTSBURGH STEELERS(N)	14	14	308	147	1887	6.13	12	12	4.76	61.9	1887
1973 PITTSBURGH STEELERS(N)	14	10	180	89	1183	6.57	10	15	3.38	47.5	1183
1974 PITTSBURGH STEELERS(N)	14	8	148	67	785	5.30	7	8	3.34	45.8	785
1975 PITTSBURGH STEELERS(N)	14	14	286	165	2055	7.19	18	9	6.40	83.6	2055
1976 PITTSBURGH STEELERS(N)	14	10	192	92	1177	6.13	10	9	4.54	53.0	1177
1977 PITTSBURGH STEELERS(N)	14	14	314	162	2523	8.04	17	19	5.85	87.0	2523
1978 PITTSBURGH STEELERS(N)	16	16	368	207	2915	7.92	28	20	6.24	94.6	2551
1979 PITTSBURGH STEELERS(N)	16	16	472	259	3724	7.89	26	25	6.06	83.1	3259
1980 PITTSBURGH STEELERS(N)	16	15	424	218	3339	7.88	24	22	6.11	84.5	2922
1981 PITTSBURGH STEELERS(N)	16	14	370	201	2887	7.80	22	14	6.69	89.3	2526
1982 PITTSBURGH STEELERS(N)	9	9	240	127	1768	7.37	17	11	6.01	77.6	2750
1983 PITTSBURGH STEELERS(N)	16	1	8	5	77	9.63	2	0	12.13	158.7	67
TOTAL 14 YEARS	*201*	*168*	*3901*	*2025*	*27989*	*7.17*	*212*	*210*	*5.30*	*71.6*	*27353*

JOHN BRODIE

	LG	G	ATT	COM	YDS	AVG	TD	INT	Y-RATE	L-RATE	Y/14G
1957 SAN FRANCISCO 49ERS(N)	12	5	21	11	160	7.62	2	3	2.14	24.6	187
1958 SAN FRANCISCO 49ERS(N)	12	12	172	103	1224	7.12	6	13	4.06	56.6	1428
1959 SAN FRANCISCO 49ERS(N)	12	12	64	30	354	5.53	2	7	0.92	10.7	413
1960 SAN FRANCISCO 49ERS(N)	12	11	207	103	1111	5.37	6	9	3.70	40.5	1296
1961 SAN FRANCISCO 49ERS(N)	14	14	283	155	2588	9.14	14	12	7.73	100.0	2588
1962 SAN FRANCISCO 49ERS(N)	14	14	304	175	2272	7.47	18	16	5.70	75.5	2272
1963 SAN FRANCISCO 49ERS(N)	14	3	61	30	367	6.02	3	4	3.56	45.4	367
1964 SAN FRANCISCO 49ERS(N)	14	14	392	193	2498	6.37	14	16	4.89	54.4	2498
1965 SAN FRANCISCO 49ERS(N)	14	13	391	242	3112	7.96	30	16	6.88	87.5	3112
1966 SAN FRANCISCO 49ERS(N)	14	14	427	232	2810	6.58	16	22	4.64	51.5	2810
1967 SAN FRANCISCO 49ERS(N)	14	14	349	168	2013	5.77	11	16	4.02	60.1	2013
1968 SAN FRANCISCO 49ERS(N)	14	14	404	234	3020	7.48	22	21	5.68	69.0	3020

	LG	G	ATT	COM	YDS	AVG	TD	INT	Y-RATE	L-RATE	Y/14G
1969 SAN FRANCISCO 49ERS(N)	14	12	347	194	2405	6.93	16	15	5.45	76.4	2405
1970 SAN FRANCISCO 49ERS(N)	14	14	378	223	2941	7.78	24	10	7.22	90.4	2941
1971 SAN FRANCISCO 49ERS(N)	14	14	387	208	2642	6.83	18	24	4.50	51.3	2642
1972 SAN FRANCISCO 49ERS(N)	14	6	110	70	905	8.23	9	8	5.77	75.0	905
1973 SAN FRANCISCO 49ERS(N)	14	14	194	98	1126	5.80	3	12	3.18	44.7	1126
TOTAL 17 YEARS	230	200	4491	2469	31548	7.02	214	224	5.26	66.2	32023

LEN DAWSON

	LG	G	ATT	COM	YDS	AVG	TD	INT	Y-RATE	L-RATE	Y/14G
1957 PITTSBURGH STEELERS(N)	12	3	4	2	25	6.25	0	0	6.25	71.7	29
1958 PITTSBURGH STEELERS(N)	12	4	6	1	11	1.83	0	2	−13.17	−183.4	13
1959 PITTSBURGH STEELERS(N)	12	12	7	3	60	8.57	1	0	10.00	116.4	70
1960 CLEVELAND BROWNS(N)	12	2	13	8	23	1.77	0	0	1.77	19.4	27
1961 CLEVELAND BROWNS(N)	14	6	15	7	85	5.67	1	3	−2.67	−34.5	85
1962 DALLAS TEXANS(A)	14	14	310	189	2759	8.90	29	17	7.37	100.0	2759
1963 KANSAS CITY CHIEFS(A)	14	14	352	190	2389	6.79	26	19	5.10	74.9	2389
1964 KANSAS CITY CHIEFS(A)	14	14	354	199	2879	8.13	30	18	6.69	100.0	2879
1965 KANSAS CITY CHIEFS(A)	14	14	305	163	2262	7.42	21	14	6.04	100.0	2262
1966 KANSAS CITY CHIEFS(A)	14	14	284	159	2527	8.90	26	10	8.23	100.0	2527
1967 KANSAS CITY CHIEFS(A)	14	14	357	206	2651	7.43	24	17	5.96	96.4	2651
1968 KANSAS CITY CHIEFS(A)	14	14	224	131	2109	9.42	17	9	8.37	100.0	2109
1969 KANSAS CITY CHIEFS(A)	14	8	166	98	1323	7.97	9	13	4.99	65.1	1323
1970 KANSAS CITY CHIEFS(N)	14	13	262	141	1876	7.16	13	14	5.25	65.7	1876
1971 KANSAS CITY CHIEFS(N)	14	14	301	167	2504	8.32	15	13	6.87	78.3	2504
1972 KANSAS CITY CHIEFS(N)	14	14	305	175	1835	6.02	13	12	4.67	60.7	1835
1973 KANSAS CITY CHIEFS(N)	14	9	101	66	725	7.18	2	5	5.15	72.4	725
1974 KANSAS CITY CHIEFS(N)	14	14	235	138	1573	6.69	7	13	4.50	61.6	1573
1975 KANSAS CITY CHIEFS(N)	14	12	140	93	1095	7.82	5	4	6.89	90.1	1095
TOTAL 19 YEARS	258	209	3741	2136	28711	7.67	239	183	6.11	83.6	28731

JOHN ELWAY

	LG	G	ATT	COM	YDS	AVG	TD	INT	Y-RATE	L-RATE	Y/14G
1983 DENVER BRONCOS(N)	16	11	259	123	1663	6.42	7	14	4.26	55.7	1455
1984 DENVER BRONCOS(N)	16	15	380	214	2598	6.84	18	15	5.53	65.0	2273
1985 DENVER BRONCOS(N)	16	16	605	327	3891	6.43	22	23	5.08	65.7	3405
1986 DENVER BRONCOS(N)	16	16	504	280	3485	6.91	19	13	6.13	81.7	3049
1987 DENVER BRONCOS(N)	15	12	410	224	3198	7.80	19	12	6.95	94.9	2985
TOTAL 5 YEARS	79	70	2158	1168	14835	6.87	85	77	5.66	73.7	13167

DAN FOUTS

	LG	G	ATT	COM	YDS	AVG	TD	INT	Y-RATE	L-RATE	Y/14G
1973 SAN DIEGO CHARGERS(N)	14	10	194	87	1126	5.80	6	13	3.10	43.6	1126
1974 SAN DIEGO CHARGERS(N)	14	11	237	115	1732	7.31	8	13	5.18	70.8	1732
1975 SAN DIEGO CHARGERS(N)	14	10	195	106	1396	7.16	2	10	4.95	64.8	1396
1976 SAN DIEGO CHARGERS(N)	14	14	359	208	2535	7.06	14	15	5.57	65.0	2535
1977 SAN DIEGO CHARGERS(N)	14	4	109	69	869	7.97	4	6	5.86	87.1	869
1978 SAN DIEGO CHARGERS(N)	16	15	381	224	2999	7.87	24	20	6.14	93.2	2624
1979 SAN DIEGO CHARGERS(N)	16	16	530	332	4082	7.70	24	24	6.12	83.9	3572
1980 SAN DIEGO CHARGERS(N)	16	16	589	348	4715	8.01	30	24	6.68	92.4	4126
1981 SAN DIEGO CHARGERS(N)	16	16	609	360	4802	7.89	33	17	7.17	95.6	4202
1982 SAN DIEGO CHARGERS(N)	9	9	330	204	2883	8.74	17	11	7.75	100.0	4485
1983 SAN DIEGO CHARGERS(N)	16	10	340	215	2975	8.75	20	15	7.35	96.2	2603
1984 SAN DIEGO CHARGERS(N)	16	13	507	317	3740	7.38	19	17	6.24	73.4	3273
1985 SAN DIEGO CHARGERS(N)	16	14	430	254	3638	8.46	27	20	7.00	90.4	3183

DAN FOUTS

	LG	G	ATT	COM	YDS	AVG	TD	INT	Y-RATE	L-RATE	Y/14G
1986 SAN DIEGO CHARGERS(N)	16	12	430	252	3031	7.05	16	22	5.12	68.2	2652
1987 SAN DIEGO CHARGERS(N)	15	11	364	206	2517	6.91	10	15	5.34	72.9	2349
TOTAL 15 YEARS	*222*	*181*	*5604*	*3297*	*43040*	*7.68*	*254*	*242*	*6.19*	*82.3*	*40726*

OTTO GRAHAM

	LG	G	ATT	COM	YDS	AVG	TD	INT	Y-RATE	L-RATE	Y/14G
1946 CLEVELAND BROWNS(A)	14	14	174	95	1834	10.54	17	5	10.22	100.0	1834
1947 CLEVELAND BROWNS(A)	14	14	269	163	2753	10.23	25	11	9.32	100.0	2753
1948 CLEVELAND BROWNS(A)	14	14	333	173	2713	8.15	25	15	6.87	87.2	2713
1949 CLEVELAND BROWNS(A)	12	12	285	161	2785	9.77	19	10	8.86	100.0	3249
1950 CLEVELAND BROWNS(N)	12	12	253	137	1943	7.68	14	20	4.68	67.7	2267
1951 CLEVELAND BROWNS(N)	12	12	265	147	2205	8.32	17	16	6.25	88.2	2573
1952 CLEVELAND BROWNS(N)	12	12	364	181	2816	7.74	20	24	5.32	80.5	3285
1953 CLEVELAND BROWNS(N)	12	12	258	167	2722	10.55	11	9	9.41	100.0	3176
1954 CLEVELAND BROWNS(N)	12	12	240	142	2092	8.72	11	17	5.99	85.4	2441
1955 CLEVELAND BROWNS(N)	12	12	185	98	1721	9.30	15	8	8.17	100.0	2008
TOTAL 10 YEARS	*126*	*126*	*2626*	*1464*	*23584*	*8.98*	*174*	*135*	*7.33*	*90.0*	*26298*

BOB GRIESE

	LG	G	ATT	COM	YDS	AVG	TD	INT	Y-RATE	L-RATE	Y/14G
1967 MIAMI DOLPHINS(A)	14	12	331	166	2005	6.06	15	18	4.06	65.8	2005
1968 MIAMI DOLPHINS(A)	14	13	355	186	2473	6.97	21	16	5.53	66.1	2473
1969 MIAMI DOLPHINS(A)	14	9	252	121	1695	6.73	10	16	4.27	55.7	1695
1970 MIAMI DOLPHINS(N)	14	14	245	142	2019	8.24	12	17	5.61	70.2	2019
1971 MIAMI DOLPHINS(N)	14	14	263	145	2089	7.94	19	9	7.13	81.2	2089
1972 MIAMI DOLPHINS(N)	14	6	97	53	638	6.58	4	4	5.13	66.7	638
1973 MIAMI DOLPHINS(N)	14	13	218	116	1422	6.52	17	8	5.65	79.5	1422
1974 MIAMI DOLPHINS(N)	14	13	253	152	1968	7.78	16	15	5.74	78.6	1968
1975 MIAMI DOLPHINS(N)	14	10	191	118	1693	8.86	14	13	6.53	85.4	1693
1976 MIAMI DOLPHINS(N)	14	13	272	162	2097	7.71	11	12	6.13	71.5	2097
1977 MIAMI DOLPHINS(N)	14	14	307	180	2252	7.34	22	13	6.15	91.3	2252
1978 MIAMI DOLPHINS(N)	16	11	235	148	1791	7.62	11	11	5.98	90.8	1567
1979 MIAMI DOLPHINS(N)	16	14	310	176	2160	6.97	14	16	5.10	69.9	1890
1980 MIAMI DOLPHINS(N)	16	5	100	61	790	7.90	6	4	6.70	92.7	691
TOTAL 14 YEARS	*202*	*161*	*3429*	*1926*	*25092*	*7.32*	*192*	*172*	*5.62*	*75.1*	*24499*

ARNIE HERBER

	LG	G	ATT	COM	YDS	AVG	TD	INT	Y-RATE	L-RATE	Y/14G
1930 GREEN BAY PACKERS(N)	14	10	31	9	183	5.90	3	3	2.52	37.4	183
1931 GREEN BAY PACKERS(N)	14	3	11	5	45	4.09	0	0	4.09	74.1	45
1932 GREEN BAY PACKERS(N)	14	14	101	37	639	6.33	9	9	3.21	70.7	639
1933 GREEN BAY PACKERS(N)	13	11	126	56	656	5.21	4	12	1.24	21.3	706
1934 GREEN BAY PACKERS(N)	13	12	115	42	799	6.95	8	12	2.95	99.9	860
1935 GREEN BAY PACKERS(N)	12	11	106	40	729	6.88	8	6	5.08	100.1	851
1936 GREEN BAY PACKERS(N)	12	12	173	77	1239	7.16	11	13	4.42	100.1	1446
1937 GREEN BAY PACKERS(N)	11	9	104	47	676	6.50	7	10	2.85	53.9	860
1938 GREEN BAY PACKERS(N)	11	9	55	22	336	6.11	4	4	3.56	77.8	428
1939 GREEN BAY PACKERS(N)	11	10	139	57	1107	7.96	8	9	5.63	99.9	1409
1940 GREEN BAY PACKERS(N)	11	10	89	38	560	6.29	5	7	3.31	56.6	713
1944 NEW YORK GIANTS(N)	10	9	86	36	651	7.57	6	8	4.08	69.4	911
1945 NEW YORK GIANTS(N)	10	10	80	35	641	8.01	9	8	4.64	52.8	897
TOTAL 13 YEARS	*156*	*130*	*1216*	*501*	*8261*	*6.79*	*82*	*101*	*3.73*	*74.2*	*9948*

RON JAWORSKI

	LG	G	ATT	COM	YDS	AVG	TD	INT	Y-RATE	L-RATE	Y/14G
1974 LOS ANGELES RAMS(N)	14	5	24	10	144	6.00	0	1	4.13	56.4	144
1975 LOS ANGELES RAMS(N)	14	14	48	24	302	6.29	0	2	4.42	57.7	302
1976 LOS ANGELES RAMS(N)	14	5	52	20	273	5.25	1	5	1.12	13.0	273
1977 PHILADELPHIA EAGLES(N)	14	14	346	166	2183	6.31	18	21	4.10	60.9	2183
1978 PHILADELPHIA EAGLES(N)	16	16	398	206	2487	6.25	16	16	4.84	73.5	2176
1979 PHILADELPHIA EAGLES(N)	16	16	374	190	2669	7.14	18	12	6.17	84.7	2335
1980 PHILADELPHIA EAGLES(N)	16	16	451	257	3529	7.82	27	12	7.23	99.9	3088
1981 PHILADELPHIA EAGLES(N)	16	16	461	250	3095	6.71	23	20	5.26	70.1	2708
1982 PHILADELPHIA EAGLES(N)	9	9	286	167	2076	7.26	12	12	5.79	74.7	3229
1983 PHILADELPHIA EAGLES(N)	16	16	446	235	3315	7.43	20	18	6.07	79.4	2901
1984 PHILADELPHIA EAGLES(N)	16	13	427	234	2754	6.45	16	14	5.35	62.9	2410
1985 PHILADELPHIA EAGLES(N)	16	16	484	255	3450	7.13	17	20	5.62	72.6	3019
1986 PHILADELPHIA EAGLES(N)	16	10	245	128	1405	5.73	8	6	4.96	66.1	1229
TOTAL 13 YEARS	*193*	*166*	*4042*	*2142*	*27682*	*6.85*	*176*	*159*	*5.51*	*74.0*	*25997*

BERT JONES

	LG	G	ATT	COM	YDS	AVG	TD	INT	Y-RATE	L-RATE	Y/14G
1973 BALTIMORE COLTS(N)	14	8	108	43	539	4.99	4	12	0.36	5.1	539
1974 BALTIMORE COLTS(N)	14	11	270	143	1610	5.96	8	12	4.26	58.3	1610
1975 BALTIMORE COLTS(N)	14	14	344	203	2483	7.22	18	8	6.69	87.5	2483
1976 BALTIMORE COLTS(N)	14	14	343	207	3104	9.05	24	9	8.57	100.0	3104
1977 BALTIMORE COLTS(N)	14	14	393	224	2686	6.83	17	11	6.01	89.3	2686
1978 BALTIMORE COLTS(N)	16	3	42	27	370	8.81	4	1	8.69	131.9	324
1979 BALTIMORE COLTS(N)	16	4	92	43	643	6.99	3	3	5.85	80.2	563
1980 BALTIMORE COLTS(N)	16	15	446	248	3134	7.03	23	21	5.42	75.0	2742
1981 BALTIMORE COLTS(N)	16	15	426	244	3094	7.26	21	20	5.64	75.2	2707
1982 LOS ANGELES RAMS(N)	9	4	87	48	527	6.06	2	4	4.22	54.4	820
TOTAL 10 YEARS	*143*	*102*	*2551*	*1430*	*18190*	*7.13*	*124*	*101*	*5.83*	*78.0*	*17578*

DAVE KRIEG

	LG	G	ATT	COM	YDS	AVG	TD	INT	Y-RATE	L-RATE	Y/14G
1980 SEATTLE SEAHAWKS(N)	16	1	2	0	0	0.00	0	0	0.00	0.0	0
1981 SEATTLE SEAHAWKS(N)	16	7	112	64	843	7.53	7	5	6.14	81.9	738
1982 SEATTLE SEAHAWKS(N)	9	3	78	49	501	6.42	2	2	5.53	71.3	779
1983 SEATTLE SEAHAWKS(N)	16	9	243	147	2139	8.80	18	11	7.51	98.2	1872
1984 SEATTLE SEAHAWKS(N)	16	16	480	276	3671	7.65	32	24	6.06	71.3	3212
1985 SEATTLE SEAHAWKS(N)	16	16	532	285	3602	6.77	27	20	5.59	72.2	3152
1986 SEATTLE SEAHAWKS(N)	16	15	375	225	2921	7.79	21	11	7.03	93.7	2556
1987 SEATTLE SEAHAWKS(N)	15	12	294	178	2131	7.25	23	15	5.73	78.3	1989
TOTAL 8 YEARS	*120*	*79*	*2116*	*1224*	*15808*	*7.47*	*130*	*88*	*6.21*	*80.1*	*14297*

SONNY JURGENSEN

	LG	G	ATT	COM	YDS	AVG	TD	INT	Y-RATE	L-RATE	Y/14G
1957 PHILADELPHIA EAGLES(N)	12	10	70	33	470	6.71	5	8	2.29	26.2	548
1958 PHILADELPHIA EAGLES(N)	12	12	22	12	259	11.77	0	1	9.73	135.5	302
1959 PHILADELPHIA EAGLES(N)	12	12	5	3	27	5.40	1	0	7.40	86.1	32
1960 PHILADELPHIA EAGLES(N)	12	12	44	24	486	11.05	5	1	11.16	122.2	567
1961 PHILADELPHIA EAGLES(N)	14	14	416	235	3723	8.95	32	24	7.12	92.1	3723
1962 PHILADELPHIA EAGLES(N)	14	14	366	196	3261	8.91	22	26	6.31	83.6	3261
1963 PHILADELPHIA EAGLES(N)	14	9	184	99	1413	7.68	11	13	5.10	65.1	1413
1964 WASHINGTON REDSKINS(N)	14	14	385	207	2934	7.62	24	13	6.72	74.7	2934
1965 WASHINGTON REDSKINS(N)	14	13	356	190	2367	6.65	15	16	5.05	64.1	2367
1966 WASHINGTON REDSKINS(N)	14	14	436	254	3209	7.36	28	19	6.04	67.1	3209
1967 WASHINGTON REDSKINS(N)	14	14	508	288	3747	7.38	31	16	6.57	98.2	3747
1968 WASHINGTON REDSKINS(N)	14	12	292	167	1980	6.78	17	11	5.67	68.9	1980

SONNY JURGENSEN

YEAR	LG	G	ATT	COM	YDS	AVG	TD	INT	Y-RATE	L-RATE	Y/14G
1969 WASHINGTON REDSKINS(N)	14	14	442	274	3102	7.02	22	15	5.99	84.0	3102
1970 WASHINGTON REDSKINS(N)	14	14	337	202	2354	6.99	23	10	6.33	79.3	2354
1971 WASHINGTON REDSKINS(N)	14	5	28	16	170	6.07	0	2	2.86	32.5	170
1972 WASHINGTON REDSKINS(N)	14	7	59	39	633	10.73	2	4	8.02	104.1	633
1973 WASHINGTON REDSKINS(N)	14	14	145	87	904	6.23	6	5	5.10	71.7	904
1974 WASHINGTON REDSKINS(N)	14	14	167	107	1185	7.10	11	5	6.41	87.6	1185
TOTAL 18 YEARS	244	218	4262	2433	32224	7.56	255	189	6.16	79.4	32431

BOBBY LAYNE

YEAR	LG	G	ATT	COM	YDS	AVG	TD	INT	Y-RATE	L-RATE	Y/14G
1948 CHICAGO BEARS(N)	12	11	52	16	232	4.46	3	2	3.31	46.4	271
1949 NEW YORK BULLDOGS(N)	12	12	299	155	1796	6.01	9	18	3.60	55.4	2095
1950 DETROIT LIONS(N)	12	12	336	152	2323	6.91	16	18	4.98	72.1	2710
1951 DETROIT LIONS(N)	12	12	332	152	2403	7.24	26	23	4.90	69.3	2804
1952 DETROIT LIONS(N)	12	12	287	139	1999	6.97	19	20	4.49	67.9	2332
1953 DETROIT LIONS(N)	12	12	273	125	2088	7.65	16	21	4.77	50.7	2436
1954 DETROIT LIONS(N)	12	12	246	135	1818	7.39	14	12	5.76	82.2	2121
1955 DETROIT LIONS(N)	12	12	270	143	1830	6.78	11	17	4.35	53.3	2135
1956 DETROIT LIONS(N)	12	12	244	129	1909	7.82	9	17	5.06	68.7	2227
1957 DETROIT LIONS(N)	12	11	179	87	1169	6.53	6	12	3.85	44.1	1364
1958 DETROIT LIONS(N) PITTSBURGH STEELERS(N)	12	12	294	145	2510	8.54	14	12	7.18	100.0	2928
1959 PITTSBURGH STEELERS(N)	12	12	297	142	1986	6.69	20	21	4.18	48.6	2317
1960 PITTSBURGH STEELERS(N)	12	12	209	103	1814	8.68	13	17	5.64	61.8	2116
1961 PITTSBURGH STEELERS(N)	14	8	149	75	1205	8.09	11	16	3.99	51.7	1205
1962 PITTSBURGH STEELERS(N)	14	13	233	116	1686	7.24	9	17	4.34	57.5	1686
TOTAL 15 YEARS	184	175	3700	1814	26768	7.23	196	243	4.81	64.0	30748

NEIL LOMAX

YEAR	LG	G	ATT	COM	YDS	AVG	TD	INT	Y-RATE	L-RATE	Y/14G
1981 ST. LOUIS CARDINALS(N)	16	14	236	119	1575	6.67	4	10	4.94	65.8	1378
1982 ST. LOUIS CARDINALS(N)	9	9	205	109	1367	6.67	5	6	5.60	72.2	2126
1983 ST. LOUIS CARDINALS(N)	16	13	354	209	2636	7.45	24	11	6.73	88.0	2307
1984 ST. LOUIS CARDINALS(N)	16	16	560	345	4614	8.24	28	16	7.45	87.6	4037
1985 ST. LOUIS CARDINALS(N)	16	16	471	265	3214	6.82	18	12	6.06	78.3	2812
1986 ST. LOUIS CARDINALS(N)	16	14	421	240	2583	6.14	13	12	5.16	68.8	2260
1987 ST. LOUIS CARDINALS(N)	15	12	463	275	3387	7.32	24	12	6.67	91.1	3161
TOTAL 7 YEARS	104	94	2710	1562	19376	7.15	116	79	6.27	80.7	18082

SID LUCKMAN

YEAR	LG	G	ATT	COM	YDS	AVG	TD	INT	Y-RATE	L-RATE	Y/14G
1939 CHICAGO BEARS(N)	11	11	51	23	636	12.47	5	4	9.92	176.2	809
1940 CHICAGO BEARS(N)	11	11	105	48	941	8.96	4	9	5.49	93.6	1198
1941 CHICAGO BEARS(N)	11	11	119	68	1181	9.92	9	6	8.41	100.0	1503
1942 CHICAGO BEARS(N)	11	11	105	57	1023	9.74	10	13	5.12	84.1	1302
1943 CHICAGO BEARS(N)	10	10	202	110	2194	10.86	28	12	9.57	100.0	3072
1944 CHICAGO BEARS(N)	10	7	143	71	1018	7.12	11	11	4.43	75.3	1425
1945 CHICAGO BEARS(N)	10	10	217	117	1725	7.95	14	10	6.52	74.2	2415
1946 CHICAGO BEARS(N)	11	11	229	110	1826	7.97	17	16	5.57	100.0	2324
1947 CHICAGO BEARS(N)	12	12	323	176	2712	8.40	24	31	4.82	67.9	3164
1948 CHICAGO BEARS(N)	12	12	163	89	1047	6.42	13	14	3.36	47.1	1222
1949 CHICAGO BEARS(N)	12	11	50	22	200	4.00	1	3	1.50	23.1	233
1950 CHICAGO BEARS(N)	12	11	37	13	180	4.86	1	2	2.70	39.1	210
TOTAL 12 YEARS	133	128	1744	904	14683	8.42	137	131	5.82	81.3	18877

DAN MARINO

	LG	G	ATT	COM	YDS	AVG	TD	INT	Y-RATE	L-RATE	Y/14G
1983 MIAMI DOLPHINS(N)	16	11	296	173	2210	7.47	20	6	7.23	94.6	1934
1984 MIAMI DOLPHINS(N)	16	16	564	362	5084	9.01	48	17	8.51	100.0	4449
1985 MIAMI DOLPHINS(N)	16	16	567	336	4137	7.30	30	21	6.16	79.6	3620
1986 MIAMI DOLPHINS(N)	16	16	623	378	4746	7.62	44	23	6.66	88.8	4153
1987 MIAMI DOLPHINS(N)	15	12	444	263	3245	7.31	26	13	6.58	89.8	3029
TOTAL 5 YEARS	*79*	*71*	*2494*	*1512*	*19422*	*7.79*	*168*	*80*	*7.02*	*90.1*	*17184*

DON MEREDITH

	LG	G	ATT	COM	YDS	AVG	TD	INT	Y-RATE	L-RATE	Y/14G
1960 DALLAS COWBOYS(N)	12	6	68	29	281	4.13	2	5	1.12	12.2	328
1961 DALLAS COWBOYS(N)	14	8	182	94	1161	6.38	9	11	4.15	53.7	1161
1962 DALLAS COWBOYS(N)	14	13	212	105	1679	7.92	15	8	6.93	91.8	1679
1963 DALLAS COWBOYS(N)	14	14	310	167	2381	7.68	17	18	5.62	71.7	2381
1964 DALLAS COWBOYS(N)	14	12	323	158	2143	6.63	9	16	4.68	52.0	2143
1965 DALLAS COWBOYS(N)	14	14	305	141	2415	7.92	22	13	6.72	85.4	2415
1966 DALLAS COWBOYS(N)	14	13	344	177	2805	8.15	24	12	7.28	80.8	2805
1967 DALLAS COWBOYS(N)	14	11	255	128	1834	7.19	16	16	5.00	74.7	1834
1968 DALLAS COWBOYS(N)	14	13	309	171	2500	8.09	21	12	7.02	85.3	2500
TOTAL 9 YEARS	*124*	*104*	*2308*	*1170*	*17199*	*7.45*	*135*	*111*	*5.87*	*73.0*	*17246*

JOE MONTANA

	LG	G	ATT	COM	YDS	AVG	TD	INT	Y-RATE	L-RATE	Y/14G
1979 SAN FRANCISCO 49ERS(N)	16	16	23	13	96	4.17	1	0	4.61	63.2	84
1980 SAN FRANCISCO 49ERS(N)	16	15	273	176	1795	6.58	15	9	5.64	78.0	1571
1981 SAN FRANCISCO 49ERS(N)	16	16	488	311	3565	7.31	19	12	6.59	87.8	3119
1982 SAN FRANCISCO 49ERS(N)	9	9	346	213	2613	7.55	17	11	6.61	85.3	4065
1983 SAN FRANCISCO 49ERS(N)	16	16	515	332	3910	7.59	26	12	7.05	92.3	3421
1984 SAN FRANCISCO 49ERS(N)	16	16	432	279	3630	8.40	28	10	8.01	94.1	3176
1985 SAN FRANCISCO 49ERS(N)	16	15	494	303	3653	7.39	27	13	6.76	87.3	3196
1986 SAN FRANCISCO 49ERS(N)	16	8	307	191	2236	7.28	8	9	6.22	83.0	1957
1987 SAN FRANCISCO 49ERS(N)	15	13	398	266	3054	7.67	31	13	6.98	95.4	2850
TOTAL 9 YEARS	*136*	*124*	*3276*	*2084*	*24552*	*7.49*	*172*	*89*	*6.80*	*88.5*	*23439*

JOE NAMATH

	LG	G	ATT	COM	YDS	AVG	TD	INT	Y-RATE	L-RATE	Y/14G
1965 NEW YORK JETS(A)	14	14	340	164	2220	6.53	18	15	5.07	84.0	2220
1966 NEW YORK JETS(A)	14	14	471	232	3379	7.17	19	27	5.00	60.7	3379
1967 NEW YORK JETS(A)	14	14	491	258	4007	8.16	26	28	6.12	99.1	4007
1968 NEW YORK JETS(A)	14	14	380	187	3147	8.28	15	17	6.66	79.6	3147
1969 NEW YORK JETS(A)	14	14	361	185	2734	7.57	19	17	5.98	78.1	2734
1970 NEW YORK JETS(N)	14	5	179	90	1259	7.03	5	12	4.30	53.8	1259
1971 NEW YORK JETS(N)	14	4	59	28	537	9.10	5	6	5.37	61.2	537
1972 NEW YORK JETS(N)	14	13	324	162	2816	8.69	19	21	6.36	82.6	2816
1973 NEW YORK JETS(N)	14	6	133	68	966	7.26	5	6	5.61	78.9	966
1974 NEW YORK JETS(N)	14	14	361	191	2616	7.25	20	22	5.06	69.2	2616
1975 NEW YORK JETS(N)	14	14	326	157	2286	7.01	15	28	3.61	47.2	2286
1976 NEW YORK JETS(N)	14	11	230	114	1090	4.74	4	16	1.78	20.8	1090
1977 LOS ANGELES RAMS(N)	14	6	107	50	606	5.66	3	5	3.84	57.1	606
TOTAL 13 YEARS	*182*	*143*	*3762*	*1886*	*27663*	*7.35*	*173*	*220*	*5.18*	*70.7*	*27663*

BRIAN SIPE

	LG	G	ATT	COM	YDS	AVG	TD	INT	Y-RATE	L-RATE	Y/14G
1974 CLEVELAND BROWNS(N)	14	10	108	59	603	5.58	1	7	2.76	37.7	603
1975 CLEVELAND BROWNS(N)	14	7	88	45	427	4.85	1	3	3.43	44.9	427
1976 CLEVELAND BROWNS(N)	14	14	312	178	2113	6.77	17	14	5.30	61.8	2113

BRIAN SIPE

	LG	G	ATT	COM	YDS	AVG	TD	INT	Y-RATE	L-RATE	Y/14G
1977 CLEVELAND BROWNS(N)	14	9	195	112	1233	6.32	9	14	3.55	52.8	1233
1978 CLEVELAND BROWNS(N)	16	16	399	222	2906	7.28	21	15	6.12	92.8	2543
1979 CLEVELAND BROWNS(N)	16	16	535	286	3793	7.09	28	26	5.43	74.4	3319
1980 CLEVELAND BROWNS(N)	16	16	554	337	4132	7.46	30	14	6.86	94.9	3616
1981 CLEVELAND BROWNS(N)	16	16	567	313	3876	6.84	17	25	5.15	68.7	3392
1982 CLEVELAND BROWNS(N)	9	6	185	101	1064	5.75	4	8	4.02	51.9	1655
1983 CLEVELAND BROWNS(N)	16	16	496	291	3566	7.19	26	23	5.63	73.7	3120
TOTAL 10 YEARS	145	126	3439	1944	23713	6.90	154	149	5.39	73.3	22020

KEN STABLER

	LG	G	ATT	COM	YDS	AVG	TD	INT	Y-RATE	L-RATE	Y/14G
1970 OAKLAND RAIDERS(N)	14	3	7	2	52	7.43	0	1	1.00	12.5	52
1971 OAKLAND RAIDERS(N)	14	14	48	24	268	5.58	1	4	2.04	23.3	268
1972 OAKLAND RAIDERS(N)	14	14	74	44	524	7.08	4	3	5.80	75.3	524
1973 OAKLAND RAIDERS(N)	14	14	260	163	1997	7.68	14	10	6.49	91.3	1997
1974 OAKLAND RAIDERS(N)	14	14	310	178	2469	7.96	26	12	7.06	96.6	2469
1975 OAKLAND RAIDERS(N)	14	14	293	171	2296	7.84	16	24	4.70	61.4	2296
1976 OAKLAND RAIDERS(N)	14	12	291	194	2737	9.41	27	17	7.70	89.9	2737
1977 OAKLAND RAIDERS(N)	14	13	294	169	2176	7.40	20	20	5.02	74.6	2176
1978 OAKLAND RAIDERS(N)	16	16	406	237	2944	7.25	16	30	4.32	65.6	2576
1979 OAKLAND RAIDERS(N)	16	16	498	304	3615	7.26	26	22	5.79	79.5	3163
1980 HOUSTON OILERS(N)	16	16	457	293	3202	7.01	13	28	4.53	62.7	2802
1981 HOUSTON OILERS(N)	16	13	285	165	1988	6.98	14	18	4.62	61.7	1740
1982 NEW ORLEANS SAINTS(N)	9	8	189	117	1343	7.11	6	10	5.04	65.1	2089
1983 NEW ORLEANS SAINTS(N)	16	14	311	176	1988	6.39	9	18	4.08	53.4	1740
1984 NEW ORLEANS SAINTS(N)	16	3	70	33	339	4.84	2	5	1.91	22.5	297
TOTAL 15 YEARS	217	184	3793	2270	27938	7.37	194	222	5.24	71.0	26925

BART STARR

	LG	G	ATT	COM	YDS	AVG	TD	INT	Y-RATE	L-RATE	Y/14G
1956 GREEN BAY PACKERS(N)	12	9	44	24	325	7.39	2	3	4.77	64.8	379
1957 GREEN BAY PACKERS(N)	12	12	215	117	1489	6.93	8	10	5.20	59.7	1737
1958 GREEN BAY PACKERS(N)	12	12	157	78	875	5.57	3	12	2.32	32.4	1021
1959 GREEN BAY PACKERS(N)	12	12	134	70	972	7.25	6	7	5.35	62.3	1134
1960 GREEN BAY PACKERS(N)	12	12	172	98	1358	7.90	4	8	6.03	66.1	1584
1961 GREEN BAY PACKERS(N)	14	14	295	172	2418	8.20	16	16	6.30	81.5	2418
1962 GREEN BAY PACKERS(N)	14	14	285	178	2438	8.55	12	9	7.55	100.1	2438
1963 GREEN BAY PACKERS(N)	14	13	244	132	1855	7.60	15	10	6.37	81.4	1855
1964 GREEN BAY PACKERS(N)	14	14	272	163	2144	7.88	15	4	7.77	86.4	2144
1965 GREEN BAY PACKERS(N)	14	14	251	140	2055	8.19	16	9	7.21	91.6	2055
1966 GREEN BAY PACKERS(N)	14	14	251	156	2257	8.99	14	3	9.01	100.0	2257
1967 GREEN BAY PACKERS(N)	14	14	210	115	1823	8.68	9	17	5.47	81.7	1823
1968 GREEN BAY PACKERS(N)	14	13	171	109	1617	9.46	15	8	8.23	100.0	1617
1969 GREEN BAY PACKERS(N)	14	11	148	92	1161	7.84	9	6	6.63	93.0	1161
1970 GREEN BAY PACKERS(N)	14	14	255	140	1645	6.45	8	13	4.47	56.0	1645
1971 GREEN BAY PACKERS(N)	14	4	45	24	286	6.36	0	3	3.36	38.2	286
TOTAL 16 YEARS	214	196	3149	1808	24718	7.85	152	138	6.36	78.9	25555

ROGER STAUBACH

	LG	G	ATT	COM	YDS	AVG	TD	INT	Y-RATE	L-RATE	Y/14G
1969 DALLAS COWBOYS(N)	14	6	47	23	421	8.96	1	2	7.26	101.8	421
1970 DALLAS COWBOYS(N)	14	8	82	44	542	6.61	2	8	2.46	30.8	542
1971 DALLAS COWBOYS(N)	14	13	211	126	1882	8.92	15	4	8.78	100.0	1882
1972 DALLAS COWBOYS(N)	14	4	20	9	98	4.90	0	2	0.40	5.2	98
1973 DALLAS COWBOYS(N)	14	14	286	179	2428	8.49	23	15	6.93	97.5	2428
1974 DALLAS COWBOYS(N)	14	14	360	190	2552	7.09	11	15	5.52	75.5	2552

1975 DALLAS COWBOYS(N)	14	13	348	198	2666	7.66	17	16	6.08	79.5	2666
1976 DALLAS COWBOYS(N)	14	14	369	208	2715	7.36	14	11	6.40	74.6	2715
1977 DALLAS COWBOYS(N)	14	14	361	210	2620	7.26	18	9	6.63	98.6	2620
1978 DALLAS COWBOYS(N)	16	15	413	231	3190	7.72	25	16	6.59	99.9	2791
1979 DALLAS COWBOYS(N)	16	16	461	267	3586	7.78	27	11	7.29	100.0	3138
TOTAL 11 YEARS	158	131	2958	1685	22700	7.67	153	109	6.53	88.5	21853

FRAN TARKENTON	LG	G	ATT	COM	YDS	AVG	TD	INT	Y-RATE	L-RATE	Y/14G
1961 MINNESOTA VIKINGS(N)	14	14	280	157	1997	7.13	18	17	5.04	65.2	1997
1962 MINNESOTA VIKINGS(N)	14	14	329	163	2595	7.89	22	25	5.14	68.0	2595
1963 MINNESOTA VIKINGS(N)	14	14	297	170	2311	7.78	15	15	6.01	76.8	2311
1964 MINNESOTA VIKINGS(N)	14	14	306	171	2506	8.19	22	11	7.29	81.0	2506
1965 MINNESOTA VIKINGS(N)	14	14	329	171	2609	7.93	19	11	7.00	89.0	2609
1966 MINNESOTA VIKINGS(N)	14	14	358	192	2561	7.15	17	16	5.62	62.3	2561
1967 NEW YORK GIANTS(N)	14	14	377	204	3088	8.19	29	19	6.69	100.0	3088
1968 NEW YORK GIANTS(N)	14	14	337	182	2555	7.58	21	12	6.60	80.2	2555
1969 NEW YORK GIANTS(N)	14	14	409	220	2918	7.13	23	8	6.82	95.6	2918
1970 NEW YORK GIANTS(N)	14	14	389	219	2777	7.14	19	12	6.24	78.1	2777
1971 NEW YORK GIANTS(N)	14	13	386	226	2567	6.65	11	21	4.49	51.1	2567
1972 MINNESOTA VIKINGS(N)	14	14	378	215	2651	7.01	18	13	5.94	77.2	2651
1973 MINNESOTA VIKINGS(N)	14	14	274	169	2113	7.71	15	7	7.11	100.0	2113
1974 MINNESOTA VIKINGS(N)	14	13	351	199	2598	7.40	17	12	6.35	86.8	2598
1975 MINNESOTA VIKINGS(N)	14	14	425	273	2994	7.04	25	13	6.26	81.8	2994
1976 MINNESOTA VIKINGS(N)	14	13	412	255	2961	7.19	17	8	6.73	78.5	2961
1977 MINNESOTA VIKINGS(N)	14	9	258	155	1734	6.72	9	14	4.63	68.8	1734
1978 MINNESOTA VIKINGS(N)	16	16	572	345	3468	6.06	25	32	3.98	60.4	3035
TOTAL 18 YEARS	254	246	6467	3686	47003	7.27	342	266	5.95	77.4	46570

JOE THEISMANN	LG	G	ATT	COM	YDS	AVG	TD	INT	Y-RATE	L-RATE	Y/14G
1974 WASHINGTON REDSKINS(N)	14	9	11	9	145	13.18	1	0	14.09	192.8	145
1975 WASHINGTON REDSKINS(N)	14	14	22	10	96	4.36	1	3	−1.32	−17.2	96
1976 WASHINGTON REDSKINS(N)	14	14	163	79	1036	6.36	8	10	4.09	47.7	1036
1977 WASHINGTON REDSKINS(N)	14	14	182	84	1097	6.03	7	9	4.19	62.2	1097
1978 WASHINGTON REDSKINS(N)	16	16	390	187	2593	6.65	13	18	4.91	74.4	2269
1979 WASHINGTON REDSKINS(N)	16	16	395	233	2797	7.08	20	13	6.11	83.8	2447
1980 WASHINGTON REDSKINS(N)	16	16	454	262	2962	6.52	17	16	5.31	73.5	2592
1981 WASHINGTON REDSKINS(N)	16	16	496	293	3568	7.19	19	20	5.76	76.8	3122
1982 WASHINGTON REDSKINS(N)	9	9	252	161	2033	8.07	13	9	6.98	90.0	3162
1983 WASHINGTON REDSKINS(N)	16	16	459	276	3714	8.09	29	11	7.64	100.1	3250
1984 WASHINGTON REDSKINS(N)	16	16	477	283	3391	7.11	24	13	6.39	75.0	2967
1985 WASHINGTON REDSKINS(N)	16	11	301	167	1774	5.89	8	16	3.77	48.7	1552
TOTAL 12 YEARS	177	167	3602	2044	25206	7.00	160	138	5.72	75.9	23736

Y. A. TITTLE	LG	G	ATT	COM	YDS	AVG	TD	INT	Y-RATE	L-RATE	Y/14G
1948 BALTIMORE COLTS(A)	14	14	289	161	2522	8.73	16	9	7.88	100.0	2522
1949 BALTIMORE COLTS(A)	12	11	289	148	2209	7.64	14	18	5.33	60.1	2577
1950 BALTIMORE COLTS(N)	12	12	315	161	1884	5.98	8	19	3.52	50.9	2198
1951 SAN FRANCISCO 49ERS(N)	12	12	114	63	808	7.09	8	9	4.24	59.8	943
1952 SAN FRANCISCO 49ERS(N)	12	12	208	106	1407	6.76	11	12	4.70	71.1	1642
1953 SAN FRANCISCO 49ERS(N)	12	10	259	149	2121	8.19	20	16	6.18	65.7	2475
1954 SAN FRANCISCO 49ERS(N)	12	12	295	170	2205	7.47	9	9	6.41	91.4	2573
1955 SAN FRANCISCO 49ERS(N)	12	12	287	147	2185	7.61	17	28	3.82	46.7	2549

Y. A. TITTLE

	LG	G	ATT	COM	YDS	AVG	TD	INT	Y-RATE	L-RATE	Y/14G
1956 SAN FRANCISCO 49ERS(N)	12	10	218	124	1641	7.53	7	12	5.37	73.0	1915
1957 SAN FRANCISCO 49ERS(N)	12	12	279	176	2157	7.73	13	15	5.78	66.3	2517
1958 SAN FRANCISCO 49ERS(N)	12	11	208	120	1467	7.05	9	15	4.24	59.1	1712
1959 SAN FRANCISCO 49ERS(N)	12	10	199	102	1331	6.69	10	15	3.80	44.2	1553
1960 SAN FRANCISCO 49ERS(N)	12	9	127	69	694	5.46	4	3	4.72	51.7	810
1961 NEW YORK GIANTS(N)	14	13	285	163	2272	7.97	17	12	6.67	86.3	2272
1962 NEW YORK GIANTS(N)	14	14	375	200	3224	8.60	33	20	7.08	93.7	3224
1963 NEW YORK GIANTS(N)	14	13	367	221	3145	8.57	36	14	7.83	100.0	3145
1964 NEW YORK GIANTS(N)	14	14	281	147	1798	6.40	10	22	3.23	35.9	1798
TOTAL 17 YEARS	214	201	4395	2427	33070	7.52	242	248	5.54	70.5	36422

JOHNNY UNITAS

	LG	G	ATT	COM	YDS	AVG	TD	INT	Y-RATE	L-RATE	Y/14G
1956 BALTIMORE COLTS(N)	12	12	198	110	1498	7.57	9	10	5.75	78.1	1748
1957 BALTIMORE COLTS(N)	12	12	301	172	2550	8.47	24	17	6.73	77.2	2975
1958 BALTIMORE COLTS(N)	12	10	263	136	2007	7.63	19	7	7.16	99.7	2342
1959 BALTIMORE COLTS(N)	12	12	367	193	2899	7.90	32	14	7.05	82.1	3382
1960 BALTIMORE COLTS(N)	12	12	378	190	3099	8.20	25	24	6.00	65.7	3616
1961 BALTIMORE COLTS(N)	14	14	420	229	2990	7.12	16	24	4.93	63.8	2990
1962 BALTIMORE COLTS(N)	14	14	389	222	2967	7.63	23	23	5.56	73.6	2967
1963 BALTIMORE COLTS(N)	14	14	410	237	3481	8.49	20	12	7.66	97.8	3481
1964 BALTIMORE COLTS(N)	14	14	305	158	2824	9.26	19	6	9.00	100.0	2824
1965 BALTIMORE COLTS(N)	14	11	282	164	2530	8.97	23	12	7.87	100.0	2530
1966 BALTIMORE COLTS(N)	14	14	348	195	2748	7.90	22	24	5.43	60.2	2748
1967 BALTIMORE COLTS(N)	14	14	436	255	3428	7.86	20	16	6.67	99.7	3428
1968 BALTIMORE COLTS(N)	14	5	32	11	139	4.34	2	4	−0.66	−8.0	139
1969 BALTIMORE COLTS(N)	14	13	327	178	2342	7.16	12	20	4.78	67.0	2342
1970 BALTIMORE COLTS(N)	14	14	321	166	2213	6.89	14	18	4.81	60.2	2213
1971 BALTIMORE COLTS(N)	14	13	176	92	942	5.35	3	9	3.22	36.7	942
1972 BALTIMORE COLTS(N)	14	8	157	88	1111	7.08	4	6	5.61	72.9	1111
1973 SAN DIEGO CHARGERS(N)	14	5	76	34	471	6.20	3	7	2.45	34.4	471
TOTAL 18 YEARS	242	211	5186	2830	40239	7.76	290	253	6.12	77.1	42248

NORM VAN BROCKLIN

	LG	G	ATT	COM	YDS	AVG	TD	INT	Y-RATE	L-RATE	Y/14G
1949 LOS ANGELES RAMS(N)	12	8	58	32	601	10.36	6	2	9.84	151.5	701
1950 LOS ANGELES RAMS(N)	12	12	233	127	2061	8.85	18	14	6.91	100.1	2405
1951 LOS ANGELES RAMS(N)	12	12	194	100	1725	8.89	13	11	7.01	99.0	2013
1952 LOS ANGELES RAMS(N)	12	12	205	113	1736	8.47	14	17	5.42	82.0	2025
1953 LOS ANGELES RAMS(N)	12	12	286	156	2393	8.37	19	14	6.83	72.6	2792
1954 LOS ANGELES RAMS(N)	12	12	260	139	2637	10.14	13	21	7.01	100.0	3077
1955 LOS ANGELES RAMS(N)	12	12	272	144	1890	6.95	8	15	4.76	58.3	2205
1956 LOS ANGELES RAMS(N)	12	12	124	68	966	7.79	7	12	4.00	54.3	1127
1957 LOS ANGELES RAMS(N)	12	12	265	132	2105	7.94	20	21	5.13	58.9	2456
1958 PHILADELPHIA EAGLES(N)	12	12	374	198	2409	6.44	15	20	4.44	61.8	2811
1959 PHILADELPHIA EAGLES(N)	12	12	340	191	2617	7.70	16	14	6.31	73.5	3053
1960 PHILADELPHIA EAGLES(N)	12	12	284	153	2471	8.70	24	17	6.85	75.1	2883
TOTAL 12 YEARS	144	140	2895	1553	23611	8.16	173	178	5.99	76.8	27546

DANNY WHITE

	LG	G	ATT	COM	YDS	AVG	TD	INT	Y-RATE	L-RATE	Y/14G
1976 DALLAS COWBOYS(N)	14	14	20	13	213	10.65	2	2	7.15	83.4	213
1977 DALLAS COWBOYS(N)	14	14	10	4	35	3.50	0	1	−1.00	−14.9	35

1978 DALLAS COWBOYS(N)	16	16	34	20	215	6.32	0	1	5.00	75.9	188
1979 DALLAS COWBOYS(N)	16	16	39	19	267	6.85	1	2	4.79	65.8	234
1980 DALLAS COWBOYS(N)	16	16	436	260	3287	7.54	28	25	5.60	77.5	2876
1981 DALLAS COWBOYS(N)	16	16	391	223	3098	7.92	22	13	6.99	93.2	2711
1982 DALLAS COWBOYS(N)	9	9	247	156	2079	8.42	16	12	6.88	88.8	3234
1983 DALLAS COWBOYS(N)	16	16	533	334	3980	7.47	29	23	6.07	79.4	3483
1984 DALLAS COWBOYS(N)	16	14	233	126	1580	6.78	11	11	5.13	60.3	1383
1985 DALLAS COWBOYS(N)	16	14	450	267	3157	7.02	21	17	5.78	74.7	2762
1986 DALLAS COWBOYS(N)	16	7	153	95	1157	7.56	12	5	6.88	91.7	1012
1987 DALLAS COWBOYS(N)	15	11	362	215	2617	7.23	12	17	5.45	74.4	2443
TOTAL 12 YEARS	*180*	*163*	*2908*	*1732*	*21685*	*7.46*	*154*	*129*	*5.99*	*79.0*	*20573*

RECEIVING

DANNY ABRAMOWICZ	*LG*	*G*	*NO*	*YDS*	*AVG*	*TD*	*AYD/G*	*AYD/L*	*Y/14G*
1967 NEW ORLEANS SAINTS(N)	14	14	50	721	14.42	6	55.8	57.2	50
1968 NEW ORLEANS SAINTS(N)	14	14	54	890	16.48	7	68.6	80.9	54
1969 NEW ORLEANS SAINTS(N)	14	14	73	1015	13.90	7	77.5	90.0	73
1970 NEW ORLEANS SAINTS(N)	14	14	55	906	16.47	5	68.3	78.4	55
1971 NEW ORLEANS SAINTS(N)	14	14	37	657	17.76	5	50.5	59.9	37
1972 NEW ORLEANS SAINTS(N)	14	13	38	668	17.58	7	52.7	66.8	38
1973 NEW ORLEANS SAINTS(N)									
SAN FRANCISCO 49ERS(N)	14	14	37	460	12.43	1	33.6	39.0	37
1974 SAN FRANCISCO 49ERS(N)	14	14	25	369	14.76	1	27.1	31.0	25
TOTAL 8 YEARS	*112*	*111*	*369*	*5686*	*15.41*	*39*	*54.3*	*68.0*	*369*

LANCE ALWORTH	*LG*	*G*	*NO*	*YDS*	*AVG*	*TD*	*AYD/G*	*AYD/L*	*Y/14G*
1962 SAN DIEGO CHARGERS(A)	14	8	10	226	22.60	3	18.3	21.2	10
1963 SAN DIEGO CHARGERS(A)	14	14	61	1205	19.75	11	93.9	89.8	61
1964 SAN DIEGO CHARGERS(A)	14	14	61	1235	20.25	13	97.5	83.9	61
1965 SAN DIEGO CHARGERS(A)	14	14	69	1602	23.22	14	124.4	100.0	69
1966 SAN DIEGO CHARGERS(A)	14	14	73	1383	18.95	13	108.1	100.0	73
1967 SAN DIEGO CHARGERS(A)	14	11	52	1010	19.42	9	78.6	71.7	52
1968 SAN DIEGO CHARGERS(A)	14	14	68	1312	19.29	10	100.9	100.0	68
1969 SAN DIEGO CHARGERS(A)	14	14	64	1003	15.67	4	74.5	74.5	64
1970 SAN DIEGO CHARGERS(N)	14	14	35	608	17.37	4	46.3	53.1	35
1971 DALLAS COWBOYS(N)	14	12	34	487	14.32	2	36.2	43.0	34
1972 DALLAS COWBOYS(N)	14	14	15	195	13.00	2	15.4	19.5	15
TOTAL 11 YEARS	*154*	*143*	*542*	*10266*	*18.94*	*85*	*72.2*	*81.0*	*542*

JIM BENTON	*LG*	*G*	*NO*	*YDS*	*AVG*	*TD*	*AYD/G*	*AYD/L*	*Y/14G*
1938 CLEVELAND RAMS(N)	11	10	21	418	19.90	5	42.5	73.4	27
1939 CLEVELAND RAMS(N)	11	11	27	388	14.37	7	41.6	50.6	34
1940 CLEVELAND RAMS(N)	11	9	22	351	15.95	3	34.6	51.0	28
1942 CLEVELAND RAMS(N)	11	8	23	345	15.00	1	32.3	25.7	29
1943 CHICAGO BEARS(N)	10	9	13	235	18.08	3	26.5	29.9	18
1944 CLEVELAND RAMS(N)	10	10	39	505	12.95	6	56.5	59.1	55
1945 CLEVELAND RAMS(N)	10	9	45	1067	23.71	8	114.7	100.0	63
1946 LOS ANGELES RAMS(N)	11	11	63	981	15.57	6	94.6	100.0	80
1947 LOS ANGELES RAMS(N)	12	11	35	511	14.60	6	47.6	56.3	41
TOTAL 9 YEARS	*97*	*88*	*288*	*4801*	*16.67*	*45*	*54.1*	*69.7*	*375*

RAYMOND BERRY

	LG	G	NO	YDS	AVG	TD	AYD/G	AYD/L	Y/14G
1955 BALTIMORE COLTS(N)	12	12	13	205	15.77	0	17.1	21.9	15
1956 BALTIMORE COLTS(N)	12	12	37	601	16.24	2	51.8	47.5	43
1957 BALTIMORE COLTS(N)	12	12	47	800	17.02	6	71.7	100.0	55
1958 BALTIMORE COLTS(N)	12	12	56	794	14.18	9	73.7	75.1	65
1959 BALTIMORE COLTS(N)	12	12	66	959	14.53	14	91.6	100.0	77
1960 BALTIMORE COLTS(N)	12	12	74	1298	17.54	10	116.5	100.0	86
1961 BALTIMORE COLTS(N)	14	12	75	873	11.64	0	62.4	68.5	75
1962 BALTIMORE COLTS(N)	14	14	51	687	13.47	3	51.2	48.0	51
1963 BALTIMORE COLTS(N)	14	9	44	703	15.98	3	52.4	48.7	44
1964 BALTIMORE COLTS(N)	14	12	43	663	15.42	6	51.6	55.6	43
1965 BALTIMORE COLTS(N)	14	14	58	739	12.74	7	57.8	55.3	58
1966 BALTIMORE COLTS(N)	14	14	56	786	14.04	7	61.1	62.8	56
1967 BALTIMORE COLTS(N)	14	7	11	167	15.18	1	12.6	13.0	11
TOTAL 13 YEARS	170	154	631	9275	14.70	68	58.6	69.6	680

FRED BILETNIKOFF

	LG	G	NO	YDS	AVG	TD	AYD/G	AYD/L	Y/14G
1965 OAKLAND RAIDERS(A)	14	14	24	331	13.79	0	23.6	19.0	24
1966 OAKLAND RAIDERS(A)	14	10	17	272	16.00	3	21.6	20.0	17
1967 OAKLAND RAIDERS(A)	14	14	40	876	21.90	5	66.1	60.4	40
1968 OAKLAND RAIDERS(A)	14	14	61	1037	17.00	6	78.4	77.7	61
1969 OAKLAND RAIDERS(A)	14	14	54	837	15.50	12	68.4	68.4	54
1970 OAKLAND RAIDERS(N)	14	14	45	768	17.07	7	59.9	68.7	45
1971 OAKLAND RAIDERS(N)	14	14	61	929	15.23	9	72.8	86.4	61
1972 OAKLAND RAIDERS(N)	14	14	58	802	13.83	7	62.3	78.9	58
1973 OAKLAND RAIDERS(N)	14	14	48	660	13.75	4	50.0	58.0	48
1974 OAKLAND RAIDERS(N)	14	14	42	593	14.12	7	47.4	54.3	42
1975 OAKLAND RAIDERS(N)	14	11	43	587	13.65	2	43.4	53.1	43
1976 OAKLAND RAIDERS(N)	14	13	43	551	12.81	7	44.4	50.4	43
1977 OAKLAND RAIDERS(N)	14	14	33	446	13.52	5	35.4	55.4	33
1978 OAKLAND RAIDERS(N)	16	16	20	285	14.25	2	19.1	24.4	18
TOTAL 14 YEARS	198	190	589	8974	15.24	76	49.2	61.8	587

CLIFF BRANCH

	LG	G	NO	YDS	AVG	TD	AYD/G	AYD/L	Y/14G
1972 OAKLAND RAIDERS(N)	14	14	3	41	13.67	0	2.9	3.7	3
1973 OAKLAND RAIDERS(N)	14	13	19	290	15.26	3	22.9	26.5	19
1974 OAKLAND RAIDERS(N)	14	13	60	1092	18.20	13	87.3	100.0	60
1975 OAKLAND RAIDERS(N)	14	14	51	893	17.51	9	70.2	86.0	51
1976 OAKLAND RAIDERS(N)	14	14	46	1111	24.15	12	87.9	100.0	46
1977 OAKLAND RAIDERS(N)	14	13	33	540	16.36	6	42.9	67.0	33
1978 OAKLAND RAIDERS(N)	16	16	49	709	14.47	1	44.9	57.6	43
1979 OAKLAND RAIDERS(N)	16	14	59	844	14.31	6	56.5	68.1	52
1980 OAKLAND RAIDERS(N)	16	16	44	858	19.50	7	58.0	63.1	39
1981 OAKLAND RAIDERS(N)	16	16	41	635	15.49	1	40.3	43.3	36
1982 LOS ANGELES RAIDERS(N)	9	9	30	575	19.17	4	68.3	54.8	47
1983 LOS ANGELES RAIDERS(N)	16	12	39	696	17.85	5	46.6	48.5	34
1984 LOS ANGELES RAIDERS(N)	16	14	27	401	14.85	0	25.1	23.9	24
1985 LOS ANGELES RAIDERS(N)	16	4	0	0	0.00	0	0.0	0.0	0
TOTAL 14 YEARS	205	182	501	8685	17.34	67	45.6	66.4	485

KEN BURROUGH	LG	G	NO	YDS	AVG	TD	AYD/G	AYD/L	Y/14G
1970 NEW ORLEANS SAINTS(N)	14	12	13	196	15.08	2	15.4	17.7	13
1971 HOUSTON OILERS(N)	14	13	25	370	14.80	1	27.1	32.2	25
1972 HOUSTON OILERS(N)	14	14	26	521	20.04	4	40.1	50.8	26
1973 HOUSTON OILERS(N)	14	14	43	577	13.42	2	42.6	49.5	43
1974 HOUSTON OILERS(N)	14	11	36	492	13.67	2	36.6	41.9	36
1975 HOUSTON OILERS(N)	14	14	53	1063	20.06	8	81.6	100.0	53
1976 HOUSTON OILERS(N)	14	14	51	932	18.27	7	71.6	81.4	51
1977 HOUSTON OILERS(N)	14	14	43	816	18.98	8	64.0	100.0	43
1978 HOUSTON OILERS(N)	16	16	47	624	13.28	2	40.3	51.6	41
1979 HOUSTON OILERS(N)	16	16	40	752	18.80	6	50.8	61.2	35
1980 HOUSTON OILERS(N)	16	2	4	91	22.75	0	5.7	6.2	4
1981 HOUSTON OILERS(N)	16	16	40	668	16.70	7	46.1	49.6	35
TOTAL 12 YEARS	*176*	*156*	*421*	*7102*	*16.87*	*49*	*43.1*	*63.2*	*405*

HAROLD CARMICHAEL	LG	G	NO	YDS	AVG	TD	AYD/G	AYD/L	Y/14G
1971 PHILADELPHIA EAGLES(N)	14	9	20	288	14.40	0	20.6	24.4	20
1972 PHILADELPHIA EAGLES(N)	14	13	20	276	13.80	2	21.1	26.8	20
1973 PHILADELPHIA EAGLES(N)	14	14	67	1116	16.66	9	86.1	100.0	67
1974 PHILADELPHIA EAGLES(N)	14	14	56	649	11.59	8	52.1	59.7	56
1975 PHILADELPHIA EAGLES(N)	14	14	49	639	13.04	7	50.6	62.0	49
1976 PHILADELPHIA EAGLES(N)	14	14	42	503	11.98	5	39.5	44.9	42
1977 PHILADELPHIA EAGLES(N)	14	14	46	665	14.46	7	52.5	82.0	46
1978 PHILADELPHIA EAGLES(N)	16	16	55	1072	19.49	8	72.0	92.2	48
1979 PHILADELPHIA EAGLES(N)	16	16	52	872	16.77	11	61.4	74.0	46
1980 PHILADELPHIA EAGLES(N)	16	16	48	815	16.98	9	56.6	61.6	42
1981 PHILADELPHIA EAGLES(N)	16	16	61	1028	16.85	6	68.0	73.1	53
1982 PHILADELPHIA EAGLES(N)	9	9	35	540	15.43	4	64.4	51.7	54
1983 PHILADELPHIA EAGLES(N)	16	15	38	515	13.55	3	34.1	35.4	33
1984 DALLAS COWBOYS(N)	16	2	1	7	7.00	0	0.4	0.4	1
TOTAL 14 YEARS	*203*	*182*	*590*	*8985*	*15.23*	*79*	*48.2*	*66.5*	*578*

WES CHANDLER	LG	G	NO	YDS	AVG	TD	AYD/G	AYD/L	Y/14G
1978 NEW ORLEANS SAINTS(N)	16	16	35	472	13.49	2	30.8	39.4	31
1979 NEW ORLEANS SAINTS(N)	16	16	65	1069	16.45	6	70.6	85.1	57
1980 NEW ORLEANS SAINTS(N)	16	16	65	975	15.00	6	64.7	70.4	57
1981 NEW ORLEANS SAINTS(N) SAN DIEGO CHARGERS(N)	16	16	69	1142	16.55	6	75.1	80.8	60
1982 SAN DIEGO CHARGERS(N)	9	8	49	1032	21.06	9	124.7	100.0	76
1983 SAN DIEGO CHARGERS(N)	16	16	58	845	14.57	5	55.9	58.2	51
1984 SAN DIEGO CHARGERS(N)	16	15	52	708	13.62	6	48.0	45.9	46
1985 SAN DIEGO CHARGERS(N)	16	15	67	1199	17.90	10	81.2	95.7	59
1986 SAN DIEGO CHARGERS(N)	16	16	56	874	15.61	4	57.1	53.1	49
1987 SAN DIEGO CHARGERS(N)	15	10	39	617	15.82	2	42.5	49.1	36
TOTAL 10 YEARS	*152*	*144*	*555*	*8933*	*16.10*	*56*	*62.5*	*70.3*	*521*

DWIGHT CLARK	LG	G	NO	YDS	AVG	TD	AYD/G	AYD/L	Y/14G
1979 SAN FRANCISCO 49ERS(N)	16	16	18	232	12.89	0	14.5	17.5	16
1980 SAN FRANCISCO 49ERS(N)	16	16	82	991	12.09	8	66.9	72.9	72
1981 SAN FRANCISCO 49ERS(N)	16	16	85	1105	13.00	4	71.6	76.9	74
1982 SAN FRANCISCO 49ERS(N)	9	9	60	913	15.22	5	107.0	85.8	93

DWIGHT CLARK

	LG	G	NO	YDS	AVG	TD	AYD/G	AYD/L	Y/14G
1983 SAN FRANCISCO 49ERS(N)	16	16	70	840	12.00	8	57.5	59.8	61
1984 SAN FRANCISCO 49ERS(N)	16	16	52	880	16.92	6	58.8	56.1	46
1985 SAN FRANCISCO 49ERS(N)	16	16	54	705	13.06	10	50.3	59.3	47
1986 SAN FRANCISCO 49ERS(N)	16	16	61	794	13.02	2	50.9	47.3	53
1987 SAN FRANCISCO 49ERS(N)	15	8	24	290	12.08	5	22.7	26.2	22
TOTAL 9 YEARS	*136*	*129*	*506*	*6750*	*13.34*	*48*	*53.2*	*62.8*	*485*

TOM FEARS

	LG	G	NO	YDS	AVG	TD	AYD/G	AYD/L	Y/14G
1948 LOS ANGELES RAMS(N)	12	12	51	698	13.69	4	61.5	68.1	60
1949 LOS ANGELES RAMS(N)	12	12	77	1013	13.16	9	91.9	100.0	90
1950 LOS ANGELES RAMS(N)	12	12	84	1116	13.29	7	98.8	100.0	98
1951 LOS ANGELES RAMS(N)	12	7	32	528	16.50	3	46.5	33.5	37
1952 LOS ANGELES RAMS(N)	12	12	48	600	12.50	6	55.0	48.5	56
1953 LOS ANGELES RAMS(N)	12	8	23	278	12.09	4	26.5	27.7	27
1954 LOS ANGELES RAMS(N)	12	10	36	546	15.17	3	48.0	45.3	42
1955 LOS ANGELES RAMS(N)	12	12	44	569	12.93	2	49.1	63.1	51
1956 LOS ANGELES RAMS(N)	12	2	5	49	9.80	0	4.1	3.7	6
TOTAL 9 YEARS	*108*	*87*	*400*	*5397*	*13.49*	*38*	*53.5*	*70.1*	*467*

GARY GARRISON

	LG	G	NO	YDS	AVG	TD	AYD/G	AYD/L	Y/14G
1966 SAN DIEGO CHARGERS(A)	14	14	46	642	13.96	4	48.7	45.1	46
1967 SAN DIEGO CHARGERS(A)	14	14	44	772	17.55	2	56.6	51.6	44
1968 SAN DIEGO CHARGERS(A)	14	14	52	1103	21.21	10	85.9	85.2	52
1969 SAN DIEGO CHARGERS(A)	14	10	40	804	20.10	7	62.4	62.4	40
1970 SAN DIEGO CHARGERS(N)	14	14	44	1006	22.86	12	80.4	92.3	44
1971 SAN DIEGO CHARGERS(N)	14	14	42	889	21.17	6	67.8	80.4	42
1972 SAN DIEGO CHARGERS(N)	14	14	52	744	14.31	7	58.1	73.7	52
1973 SAN DIEGO CHARGERS(N)	14	7	14	292	20.86	2	22.3	25.9	14
1974 SAN DIEGO CHARGERS(N)	14	14	41	785	19.15	5	59.6	68.3	41
1975 SAN DIEGO CHARGERS(N)	14	14	27	438	16.22	2	32.7	40.1	27
1976 SAN DIEGO CHARGERS(N)	14	2	2	58	29.00	1	4.9	5.5	2
1977 HOUSTON OILERS(N)	14	2	1	5	5.00	0	0.4	0.6	1
TOTAL 12 YEARS	*168*	*133*	*405*	*7538*	*18.61*	*58*	*48.3*	*66.2*	*405*

JOHN GILLIAM

	LG	G	NO	YDS	AVG	TD	AYD/G	AYD/L	Y/14G
1967 NEW ORLEANS SAINTS(N)	14	13	22	264	12.00	1	19.6	20.1	22
1968 NEW ORLEANS SAINTS(N)	14	14	24	284	11.83	0	20.3	23.9	24
1969 ST. LOUIS CARDINALS(N)	14	14	52	997	19.17	9	77.6	90.1	52
1970 ST. LOUIS CARDINALS(N)	14	14	45	952	21.16	5	71.6	82.1	45
1971 ST. LOUIS CARDINALS(N)	14	14	42	837	19.93	3	61.9	73.5	42
1972 MINNESOTA VIKINGS(N)	14	14	47	1035	22.02	7	78.9	100.0	47
1973 MINNESOTA VIKINGS(N)	14	14	42	907	21.60	8	70.5	81.8	42
1974 MINNESOTA VIKINGS(N)	14	14	26	578	22.23	5	44.9	51.4	26
1975 MINNESOTA VIKINGS(N)	14	14	50	777	15.54	7	60.5	74.1	50
1976 MINNESOTA VIKINGS(N)	14	14	21	292	13.90	2	22.3	25.3	21
1977 MINNESOTA VIKINGS(N) NEW ORLEANS SAINTS(N)	14	12	11	133	12.09	1	10.2	16.0	11
TOTAL 11 YEARS	*154*	*151*	*382*	*7056*	*18.47*	*48*	*48.9*	*69.0*	*382*

BOB HAYES	LG	G	NO	YDS	AVG	TD	AYD/G	AYD/L	Y/14G
1965 DALLAS COWBOYS(N)	14	13	46	1003	21.80	12	80.2	76.7	46
1966 DALLAS COWBOYS(N)	14	14	64	1232	19.25	13	97.3	100.0	64
1967 DALLAS COWBOYS(N)	14	13	49	998	20.37	10	78.4	80.4	49
1968 DALLAS COWBOYS(N)	14	14	53	909	17.15	10	72.1	85.0	53
1969 DALLAS COWBOYS(N)	14	10	40	746	18.65	4	56.1	65.2	40
1970 DALLAS COWBOYS(N)	14	13	34	889	26.15	10	70.6	81.1	34
1971 DALLAS COWBOYS(N)	14	14	35	840	24.00	8	65.7	78.0	35
1972 DALLAS COWBOYS(N)	14	12	15	200	13.33	0	14.3	18.1	15
1973 DALLAS COWBOYS(N)	14	13	22	360	16.36	3	27.9	32.3	22
1974 DALLAS COWBOYS(N)	14	12	7	118	16.86	1	9.1	10.5	7
1975 SAN FRANCISCO 49ERS(N)	14	5	6	119	19.83	0	8.5	10.4	6
TOTAL 11 YEARS	*154*	*133*	*371*	*7414*	*19.98*	*71*	*52.8*	*74.4*	*371*

CHARLEY HENNIGAN	LG	G	NO	YDS	AVG	TD	AYD/G	AYD/L	Y/14G
1960 HOUSTON OILERS(A)	14	14	44	722	16.41	6	55.9	49.1	44
1961 HOUSTON OILERS(A)	14	14	82	1746	21.29	12	133.3	100.0	82
1962 HOUSTON OILERS(A)	14	14	54	867	16.06	8	67.6	78.3	54
1963 HOUSTON OILERS(A)	14	14	61	1051	17.23	10	82.2	78.6	61
1964 HOUSTON OILERS(A)	14	14	101	1546	15.31	8	116.1	100.0	101
1965 HOUSTON OILERS(A)	14	14	41	578	14.10	4	44.1	35.5	41
1966 HOUSTON OILERS(A)	14	14	27	313	11.59	3	24.5	22.7	27
TOTAL 7 YEARS	*98*	*98*	*410*	*6823*	*16.64*	*51*	*74.8*	*76.9*	*410*

HARLON HILL	LG	G	NO	YDS	AVG	TD	AYD/G	AYD/L	Y/14G
1954 CHICAGO BEARS(N)	12	12	45	1124	24.98	12	103.7	97.8	53
1955 CHICAGO BEARS(N)	12	12	42	789	18.79	9	73.3	94.1	49
1956 CHICAGO BEARS(N)	12	12	47	1128	24.00	11	103.2	94.6	55
1957 CHICAGO BEARS(N)	12	8	21	483	23.00	2	41.9	58.5	25
1958 CHICAGO BEARS(N)	12	8	27	365	13.52	3	32.9	33.6	32
1959 CHICAGO BEARS(N)	12	11	36	578	16.06	3	50.7	55.3	42
1960 CHICAGO BEARS(N)	12	12	5	98	19.60	0	8.2	7.0	6
1961 CHICAGO BEARS(N)	14	14	3	51	17.00	0	3.6	4.0	3
1962 PITTSBURGH STEELERS(N)	14	7	7	101	14.43	0	7.2	6.8	7
TOTAL 9 YEARS	*112*	*96*	*233*	*4717*	*20.24*	*40*	*45.7*	*73.1*	*270*

TONY HILL	LG	G	NO	YDS	AVG	TD	AYD/G	AYD/L	Y/14G
1977 DALLAS COWBOYS(N)	14	14	2	21	10.50	0	1.5	2.3	2
1978 DALLAS COWBOYS(N)	16	16	46	823	17.89	6	55.2	70.7	40
1979 DALLAS COWBOYS(N)	16	16	60	1062	17.70	10	72.6	87.6	53
1980 DALLAS COWBOYS(N)	16	16	60	1055	17.58	8	70.9	77.2	53
1981 DALLAS COWBOYS(N)	16	16	46	953	20.72	4	62.1	66.7	40
1982 DALLAS COWBOYS(N)	9	9	35	526	15.03	1	59.6	47.8	54
1983 DALLAS COWBOYS(N)	16	12	49	801	16.35	7	54.4	56.6	43
1984 DALLAS COWBOYS(N)	16	11	58	864	14.90	5	57.1	54.6	51
1985 DALLAS COWBOYS(N)	16	15	74	1113	15.04	7	73.9	87.2	65
1986 DALLAS COWBOYS(N)	16	16	49	770	15.71	3	50.0	46.5	43
TOTAL 10 YEARS	*151*	*141*	*479*	*7988*	*16.68*	*51*	*56.3*	*68.0*	*443*

ELROY HIRSCH	LG	G	NO	YDS	AVG	TD	AYD/G	AYD/L	Y/14G
1946 CHICAGO ROCKETS(A)	14	14	27	347	12.85	3	26.9	40.8	27
1947 CHICAGO ROCKETS(A)	14	5	10	282	28.20	3	22.3	25.9	10

ELROY HIRSCH

	LG	G	NO	YDS	AVG	TD	AYD/G	AYD/L	Y/14G
1948 CHICAGO ROCKETS(A)	14	5	7	101	14.43	1	7.9	10.8	7
1949 LOS ANGELES RAMS(N)	12	12	22	326	14.82	4	30.5	33.2	26
1950 LOS ANGELES RAMS(N)	12	12	42	687	16.36	7	63.1	63.8	49
1951 LOS ANGELES RAMS(N)	12	12	66	1495	22.65	17	138.8	100.0	77
1952 LOS ANGELES RAMS(N)	12	10	25	590	23.60	4	52.5	46.3	29
1953 LOS ANGELES RAMS(N)	12	12	61	941	15.43	4	81.8	85.4	71
1954 LOS ANGELES RAMS(N)	12	12	35	720	20.57	3	62.5	59.0	41
1955 LOS ANGELES RAMS(N)	12	9	25	460	18.40	2	40.0	51.4	29
1956 LOS ANGELES RAMS(N)	12	12	35	603	17.23	6	55.3	50.7	41
1957 LOS ANGELES RAMS(N)	12	12	32	477	14.91	6	44.8	62.4	37
TOTAL 12 YEARS	150	127	387	7029	18.16	60	50.9	64.4	444

BILLY HOWTON

	LG	G	NO	YDS	AVG	TD	AYD/G	AYD/L	Y/14G
1952 GREEN BAY PACKERS(N)	12	12	53	1231	23.23	13	113.4	100.0	62
1953 GREEN BAY PACKERS(N)	12	8	25	463	18.52	4	41.9	43.8	29
1954 GREEN BAY PACKERS(N)	12	12	52	768	14.77	2	65.7	61.9	61
1955 GREEN BAY PACKERS(N)	12	12	44	697	15.84	5	62.3	80.0	51
1956 GREEN BAY PACKERS(N)	12	12	55	1188	21.60	12	109.0	100.0	64
1957 GREEN BAY PACKERS(N)	12	12	38	727	19.13	5	64.8	90.3	44
1958 GREEN BAY PACKERS(N)	12	12	36	507	14.08	2	43.9	44.8	42
1959 CLEVELAND BROWNS(N)	12	12	39	510	13.08	1	43.3	47.3	46
1960 DALLAS COWBOYS(N)	12	11	23	363	15.78	4	33.6	28.8	27
1961 DALLAS COWBOYS(N)	14	14	56	785	14.02	4	58.9	64.8	56
1962 DALLAS COWBOYS(N)	14	14	49	706	14.41	6	54.7	51.3	49
1963 DALLAS COWBOYS(N)	14	11	33	514	15.58	3	38.9	36.1	33
TOTAL 12 YEARS	150	142	503	8459	16.82	61	60.5	66.6	564

DON HUTSON

	LG	G	NO	YDS	AVG	TD	AYD/G	AYD/L	Y/14G
1935 GREEN BAY PACKERS(N)	12	10	18	420	23.33	6	40.0	100.0	21
1936 GREEN BAY PACKERS(N)	12	12	34	536	15.76	8	51.3	100.0	40
1937 GREEN BAY PACKERS(N)	11	11	41	552	13.46	7	56.5	85.8	52
1938 GREEN BAY PACKERS(N)	11	10	32	548	17.13	9	58.0	100.0	41
1939 GREEN BAY PACKERS(N)	11	11	34	846	24.88	6	82.4	100.0	43
1940 GREEN BAY PACKERS(N)	11	11	45	664	14.76	7	66.7	98.3	57
1941 GREEN BAY PACKERS(N)	11	11	58	738	12.72	10	76.2	100.0	74
1942 GREEN BAY PACKERS(N)	11	11	74	1211	16.36	17	125.5	100.0	94
1943 GREEN BAY PACKERS(N)	10	10	47	776	16.51	11	88.6	100.0	66
1944 GREEN BAY PACKERS(N)	10	10	58	866	14.93	9	95.6	100.0	81
1945 GREEN BAY PACKERS(N)	10	10	47	834	17.74	9	92.4	80.6	66
TOTAL 11 YEARS	120	117	488	7991	16.38	99	74.8	96.8	635

HAROLD JACKSON

	LG	G	NO	YDS	AVG	TD	AYD/G	AYD/L	Y/14G
1968 LOS ANGELES RAMS(N)	14	2	0	0	0.00	0	0.0	0.0	0
1969 PHILADELPHIA EAGLES(N)	14	14	65	1116	17.17	9	86.1	100.0	65
1970 PHILADELPHIA EAGLES(N)	14	14	41	613	14.95	5	47.4	54.3	41
1971 PHILADELPHIA EAGLES(N)	14	14	47	716	15.23	3	53.3	63.2	47
1972 PHILADELPHIA EAGLES(N)	14	14	62	1048	16.90	4	77.7	98.5	62
1973 LOS ANGELES RAMS(N)	14	14	40	874	21.85	13	71.7	83.3	40
1974 LOS ANGELES RAMS(N)	14	14	30	514	17.13	5	40.3	46.2	30
1975 LOS ANGELES RAMS(N)	14	14	43	786	18.28	7	61.1	74.9	43

	LG	G	NO	YDS	AVG	TD	AYD/G	AYD/L	Y/14G
1976 LOS ANGELES RAMS(N)	14	14	39	751	19.26	5	57.2	65.1	39
1977 LOS ANGELES RAMS(N)	14	14	48	666	13.88	6	51.9	81.0	48
1978 NEW ENGLAND PATRIOTS(N)	16	16	37	743	20.08	6	50.2	64.3	32
1979 NEW ENGLAND PATRIOTS(N)	16	16	45	1013	22.51	7	67.7	81.6	39
1980 NEW ENGLAND PATRIOTS(N)	16	16	35	737	21.06	5	49.2	53.5	31
1981 NEW ENGLAND PATRIOTS(N)	16	16	39	669	17.15	0	41.8	45.0	34
1983 SEATTLE SEAHAWKS(N)	16	15	8	126	15.75	1	8.5	8.8	7
TOTAL 15 YEARS	*220*	*207*	*579*	*10372*	*17.91*	*76*	*50.6*	*72.4*	*559*

ROY JEFFERSON	LG	G	NO	YDS	AVG	TD	AYD/G	AYD/L	Y/14G
1965 PITTSBURGH STEELERS(N)	14	10	13	287	22.08	1	21.2	20.3	13
1966 PITTSBURGH STEELERS(N)	14	14	32	772	24.13	4	58.0	59.6	32
1967 PITTSBURGH STEELERS(N)	14	13	29	459	15.83	4	35.6	36.6	29
1968 PITTSBURGH STEELERS(N)	14	14	58	1074	18.52	11	84.6	99.7	58
1969 PITTSBURGH STEELERS(N)	14	14	67	1079	16.10	9	83.5	96.9	67
1970 BALTIMORE COLTS(N)	14	14	44	749	17.02	7	58.5	67.1	44
1971 WASHINGTON REDSKINS(N)	14	14	47	701	14.91	4	52.9	62.8	47
1972 WASHINGTON REDSKINS(N)	14	14	35	550	15.71	3	41.4	52.5	35
1973 WASHINGTON REDSKINS(N)	14	14	41	595	14.51	1	43.2	50.2	41
1974 WASHINGTON REDSKINS(N)	14	14	43	654	15.21	4	49.6	56.8	43
1975 WASHINGTON REDSKINS(N)	14	13	15	255	17.00	2	19.6	24.1	15
1976 WASHINGTON REDSKINS(N)	14	14	27	364	13.48	2	27.4	31.2	27
TOTAL 12 YEARS	*168*	*162*	*451*	*7539*	*16.72*	*52*	*48.0*	*64.2*	*451*

CHARLIE JOINER	LG	G	NO	YDS	AVG	TD	AYD/G	AYD/L	Y/14G
1969 HOUSTON OILERS(A)	14	7	7	77	11.00	0	5.5	5.5	7
1970 HOUSTON OILERS(N)	14	9	28	416	14.86	3	31.9	36.6	28
1971 HOUSTON OILERS(N)	14	14	31	681	21.97	7	53.6	63.6	31
1972 HOUSTON OILERS(N) CINCINNATI BENGALS(N)	14	12	24	439	18.29	2	32.8	41.5	24
1973 CINCINNATI BENGALS(N)	14	5	13	214	16.46	0	15.3	17.7	13
1974 CINCINNATI BENGALS(N)	14	14	24	390	16.25	1	28.6	32.7	24
1975 CINCINNATI BENGALS(N)	14	14	37	726	19.62	5	55.4	67.9	37
1976 SAN DIEGO CHARGERS(N)	14	14	50	1056	21.12	7	80.4	91.5	50
1977 SAN DIEGO CHARGERS(N)	14	14	35	542	15.49	6	43.0	67.2	35
1978 SAN DIEGO CHARGERS(N)	16	16	33	607	18.39	1	38.6	49.4	29
1979 SAN DIEGO CHARGERS(N)	16	16	72	1008	14.00	4	65.5	79.0	63
1980 SAN DIEGO CHARGERS(N)	16	16	71	1132	15.94	4	73.3	79.7	62
1981 SAN DIEGO CHARGERS(N)	16	16	70	1188	16.97	7	78.6	84.5	61
1982 SAN DIEGO CHARGERS(N)	9	9	36	545	15.14	0	60.6	48.6	56
1983 SAN DIEGO CHARGERS(N)	16	16	65	960	14.77	3	61.9	64.3	57
1984 SAN DIEGO CHARGERS(N)	16	16	61	793	13.00	6	53.3	50.9	53
1985 SAN DIEGO CHARGERS(N)	16	16	59	932	15.80	7	62.6	73.8	52
1986 SAN DIEGO CHARGERS(N)	16	15	34	440	12.94	2	28.8	26.7	30
TOTAL 18 YEARS	*263*	*239*	*750*	*12146*	*16.19*	*65*	*48.7*	*63.6*	*712*

STEVE LARGENT	LG	G	NO	YDS	AVG	TD	AYD/G	AYD/L	Y/14G
1976 SEATTLE SEAHAWKS(N)	14	14	54	705	13.06	4	53.2	60.5	54
1977 SEATTLE SEAHAWKS(N)	14	14	33	643	19.48	10	53.1	82.9	33
1978 SEATTLE SEAHAWKS(N)	16	16	71	1168	16.45	8	78.0	99.9	62
1979 SEATTLE SEAHAWKS(N)	16	15	66	1237	18.74	9	82.9	100.0	58

STEVE LARGENT

	LG	G	NO	YDS	AVG	TD	AYD/G	AYD/L	Y/14G
1980 SEATTLE SEAHAWKS(N)	16	16	66	1064	16.12	6	70.3	76.5	58
1981 SEATTLE SEAHAWKS(N)	16	16	75	1224	16.32	9	82.1	88.3	66
1982 SEATTLE SEAHAWKS(N)	9	8	34	493	14.50	3	58.1	46.6	53
1983 SEATTLE SEAHAWKS(N)	16	15	72	1074	14.92	11	74.0	76.9	63
1984 SEATTLE SEAHAWKS(N)	16	16	74	1164	15.73	12	80.3	76.7	65
1985 SEATTLE SEAHAWKS(N)	16	16	79	1287	16.29	6	84.2	99.3	69
1986 SEATTLE SEAHAWKS(N)	16	16	70	1070	15.29	9	72.5	67.4	61
1987 SEATTLE SEAHAWKS(N)	15	13	58	912	15.72	8	66.1	76.4	54
TOTAL 12 YEARS	180	175	752	12041	16.01	95	72.2	81.3	695

DANTE LAVELLI

	LG	G	NO	YDS	AVG	TD	AYD/G	AYD/L	Y/14G
1946 CLEVELAND BROWNS(A)	14	14	40	843	21.08	8	65.9	100.0	40
1947 CLEVELAND BROWNS(A)	14	13	49	799	16.31	9	63.5	73.7	49
1948 CLEVELAND BROWNS(A)	14	8	25	463	18.52	5	36.6	49.8	25
1949 CLEVELAND BROWNS(A)	12	10	28	475	16.96	7	45.4	49.6	33
1950 CLEVELAND BROWNS(N)	12	12	37	565	15.27	5	51.3	51.9	43
1951 CLEVELAND BROWNS(N)	12	12	43	586	13.63	6	53.8	38.8	50
1952 CLEVELAND BROWNS(N)	12	8	21	336	16.00	4	31.3	27.6	25
1953 CLEVELAND BROWNS(N)	12	12	45	783	17.40	6	70.3	73.4	53
1954 CLEVELAND BROWNS(N)	12	12	47	802	17.06	7	72.7	68.6	55
1955 CLEVELAND BROWNS(N)	12	12	31	492	15.87	4	44.3	57.0	36
1956 CLEVELAND BROWNS(N)	12	11	20	344	17.20	1	29.5	27.1	23
TOTAL 11 YEARS	138	124	386	6488	16.81	62	51.5	60.2	431

JAMES LOFTON

	LG	G	NO	YDS	AVG	TD	AYD/G	AYD/L	Y/14G
1978 GREEN BAY PACKERS(N)	16	16	46	818	17.78	6	54.9	70.3	40
1979 GREEN BAY PACKERS(N)	16	15	54	968	17.93	4	63.0	76.0	47
1980 GREEN BAY PACKERS(N)	16	16	71	1226	17.27	4	79.1	86.1	62
1981 GREEN BAY PACKERS(N)	16	16	71	1294	18.23	8	85.9	92.3	62
1982 GREEN BAY PACKERS(N)	9	9	35	696	19.89	4	81.8	65.6	54
1983 GREEN BAY PACKERS(N)	16	16	58	1300	22.41	8	86.3	89.7	51
1984 GREEN BAY PACKERS(N)	16	16	62	1361	21.95	7	89.4	85.4	54
1985 GREEN BAY PACKERS(N)	16	16	69	1153	16.71	4	74.6	87.9	60
1986 GREEN BAY PACKERS(N)	16	15	64	840	13.13	4	55.0	51.2	56
1987 LOS ANGELES RAIDERS(N)	15	12	41	880	21.46	5	62.0	71.6	38
TOTAL 10 YEARS	152	147	571	10536	18.45	54	72.9	78.9	526

DON MAYNARD

	LG	G	NO	YDS	AVG	TD	AYD/G	AYD/L	Y/14G
1958 NEW YORK GIANTS(N)	12	12	5	84	16.80	0	7.0	7.1	6
1960 NEW YORK TITANS(A)	14	14	72	1265	17.57	6	94.6	83.2	72
1961 NEW YORK TITANS(A)	14	14	43	629	14.63	8	50.6	38.0	43
1962 NEW YORK TITANS(A)	14	14	56	1041	18.59	8	80.1	92.6	56
1963 NEW YORK JETS(A)	14	12	38	780	20.53	9	62.1	59.4	38
1964 NEW YORK JETS(A)	14	14	46	847	18.41	8	66.2	57.0	46
1965 NEW YORK JETS(A)	14	14	68	1218	17.91	14	97.0	78.0	68
1966 NEW YORK JETS(A)	14	14	48	840	17.50	5	63.6	58.8	48
1967 NEW YORK JETS(A)	14	14	71	1434	20.20	10	109.6	100.0	71
1968 NEW YORK JETS(A)	14	13	57	1297	22.75	10	99.8	98.9	57
1969 NEW YORK JETS(A)	14	10	47	938	19.96	6	71.3	71.3	47
1970 NEW YORK JETS(N)	14	10	31	525	16.94	0	37.5	43.0	31

	LG	G	NO	YDS	AVG	TD	AYD/G	AYD/L	Y/14G
1971 NEW YORK JETS(N)	14	14	21	408	19.43	2	30.6	36.3	21
1972 NEW YORK JETS(N)	14	14	29	510	17.59	2	37.9	48.0	29
1973 NEW YORK JETS(N)	14	2	1	18	18.00	0	1.3	1.5	1
TOTAL 15 YEARS	*208*	*185*	*633*	*11834*	*18.70*	*88*	*61.1*	*71.8*	*634*

TOMMY McDONALD	LG	G	NO	YDS	AVG	TD	AYD/G	AYD/L	Y/14G
1957 PHILADELPHIA EAGLES(N)	12	12	9	228	25.33	3	21.5	30.0	11
1958 PHILADELPHIA EAGLES(N)	12	10	29	603	20.79	9	57.8	58.9	34
1959 PHILADELPHIA EAGLES(N)	12	12	47	846	18.00	10	78.8	86.1	55
1960 PHILADELPHIA EAGLES(N)	12	12	39	801	20.54	13	77.6	66.6	46
1961 PHILADELPHIA EAGLES(N)	14	14	64	1144	17.88	13	91.0	100.0	64
1962 PHILADELPHIA EAGLES(N)	14	14	58	1146	19.76	10	89.0	83.4	58
1963 PHILADELPHIA EAGLES(N)	14	14	41	731	17.83	8	57.9	53.9	41
1964 DALLAS COWBOYS(N)	14	14	46	612	13.30	2	45.1	48.6	46
1965 LOS ANGELES RAMS(N)	14	14	67	1036	15.46	9	80.4	76.9	67
1966 LOS ANGELES RAMS(N)	14	13	55	714	12.98	2	52.4	53.9	55
1967 ATLANTA FALCONS(N)	14	14	33	436	13.21	4	34.0	34.9	33
1968 CLEVELAND BROWNS(N)	14	9	7	113	16.14	1	8.8	10.4	7
TOTAL 12 YEARS	*160*	*152*	*495*	*8410*	*16.99*	*84*	*57.8*	*68.0*	*516*

BOBBY MITCHELL	LG	G	NO	YDS	AVG	TD	AYD/G	AYD/L	Y/14G
1958 CLEVELAND BROWNS(N)	12	12	16	131	8.19	3	13.4	13.7	19
1959 CLEVELAND BROWNS(N)	12	12	35	351	10.03	4	32.6	35.6	41
1960 CLEVELAND BROWNS(N)	12	12	45	612	13.60	6	56.0	48.1	53
1961 CLEVELAND BROWNS(N)	14	14	32	368	11.50	3	28.4	31.2	32
1962 WASHINGTON REDSKINS(N)	14	14	72	1384	19.22	11	106.7	100.0	72
1963 WASHINGTON REDSKINS(N)	14	14	69	1436	20.81	7	107.6	100.0	69
1964 WASHINGTON REDSKINS(N)	14	14	60	904	15.07	10	71.7	77.2	60
1965 WASHINGTON REDSKINS(N)	14	14	60	867	14.45	6	66.2	63.3	60
1966 WASHINGTON REDSKINS(N)	14	14	58	905	15.60	9	71.1	73.1	58
1967 WASHINGTON REDSKINS(N)	14	14	60	866	14.43	6	66.1	67.8	60
1968 WASHINGTON REDSKINS(N)	14	14	14	130	9.29	0	9.3	11.0	14
TOTAL 11 YEARS	*148*	*148*	*521*	*7954*	*15.27*	*65*	*58.1*	*68.4*	*537*

STANLEY MORGAN	LG	G	NO	YDS	AVG	TD	AYD/G	AYD/L	Y/14G
1977 NEW ENGLAND PATRIOTS(N)	14	14	21	443	21.10	3	33.8	52.8	21
1978 NEW ENGLAND PATRIOTS(N)	16	16	34	820	24.12	5	54.4	69.7	30
1979 NEW ENGLAND PATRIOTS(N)	16	16	44	1002	22.77	12	70.1	84.6	39
1980 NEW ENGLAND PATRIOTS(N)	16	16	45	991	22.02	6	65.7	71.5	39
1981 NEW ENGLAND PATRIOTS(N)	16	13	44	1029	23.39	6	68.1	73.2	39
1982 NEW ENGLAND PATRIOTS(N)	9	9	28	584	20.86	3	68.2	54.7	44
1983 NEW ENGLAND PATRIOTS(N)	16	16	58	863	14.88	2	55.2	57.4	51
1984 NEW ENGLAND PATRIOTS(N)	16	13	38	709	18.66	5	47.4	45.3	33
1985 NEW ENGLAND PATRIOTS(N)	16	15	39	760	19.49	5	50.6	59.7	34
1986 NEW ENGLAND PATRIOTS(N)	16	16	84	1491	17.75	10	99.4	92.5	74
1987 NEW ENGLAND PATRIOTS(N)	15	9	40	672	16.80	3	46.8	54.1	37
TOTAL 11 YEARS	*166*	*153*	*475*	*9364*	*19.71*	*60*	*60.0*	*68.4*	*440*

OZZIE NEWSOME	LG	G	NO	YDS	AVG	TD	AYD/G	AYD/L	Y/14G
1978 CLEVELAND BROWNS(N)	16	16	38	589	15.50	2	38.1	48.8	33
1979 CLEVELAND BROWNS(N)	16	16	55	781	14.20	9	54.4	65.6	48

OZZIE NEWSOME

	LG	G	NO	YDS	AVG	TD	AYD/G	AYD/L	Y/14G
1980 CLEVELAND BROWNS(N)	16	16	51	594	11.65	3	39.0	42.4	45
1981 CLEVELAND BROWNS(N)	16	16	69	1002	14.52	6	66.4	71.4	60
1982 CLEVELAND BROWNS(N)	9	8	49	633	12.92	3	73.7	59.1	76
1983 CLEVELAND BROWNS(N)	16	16	89	970	10.90	6	64.4	66.9	78
1984 CLEVELAND BROWNS(N)	16	16	89	1001	11.25	5	65.7	62.7	78
1985 CLEVELAND BROWNS(N)	16	16	62	711	11.47	5	47.6	56.1	54
1986 CLEVELAND BROWNS(N)	16	16	39	417	10.69	3	27.9	26.0	34
1987 CLEVELAND BROWNS(N)	15	12	34	375	11.03	0	25.0	28.9	32
TOTAL 10 YEARS	152	148	575	7073	12.30	42	49.3	56.5	538

DREW PEARSON

	LG	G	NO	YDS	AVG	TD	AYD/G	AYD/L	Y/14G
1973 DALLAS COWBOYS(N)	14	14	22	388	17.64	2	29.1	33.8	22
1974 DALLAS COWBOYS(N)	14	14	62	1087	17.53	2	79.1	90.6	62
1975 DALLAS COWBOYS(N)	14	14	46	822	17.87	8	64.4	78.9	46
1976 DALLAS COWBOYS(N)	14	14	58	806	13.90	6	61.9	70.3	58
1977 DALLAS COWBOYS(N)	14	14	48	870	18.13	2	63.6	99.3	48
1978 DALLAS COWBOYS(N)	16	16	44	714	16.23	3	46.5	59.6	39
1979 DALLAS COWBOYS(N)	16	15	55	1026	18.65	8	69.1	83.3	48
1980 DALLAS COWBOYS(N)	16	16	43	568	13.21	6	39.3	42.7	38
1981 DALLAS COWBOYS(N)	16	16	38	614	16.16	3	40.3	43.3	33
1982 DALLAS COWBOYS(N)	9	9	26	382	14.69	3	45.8	36.7	40
1983 DALLAS COWBOYS(N)	16	14	47	545	11.60	5	37.2	38.7	41
TOTAL 11 YEARS	159	156	489	7822	16.00	48	52.2	66.0	475

PETE PIHOS

	LG	G	NO	YDS	AVG	TD	AYD/G	AYD/L	Y/14G
1947 PHILADELPHIA EAGLES(N)	12	12	23	382	16.61	7	37.7	44.6	27
1948 PHILADELPHIA EAGLES(N)	12	12	46	766	16.65	11	73.0	80.9	54
1949 PHILADELPHIA EAGLES(N)	12	11	34	484	14.24	4	43.7	47.5	40
1950 PHILADELPHIA EAGLES(N)	12	12	38	447	11.76	6	42.3	42.7	44
1951 PHILADELPHIA EAGLES(N)	12	12	35	536	15.31	5	48.8	35.2	41
1952 PHILADELPHIA EAGLES(N)	12	12	12	219	18.25	1	19.1	16.8	14
1953 PHILADELPHIA EAGLES(N)	12	12	63	1049	16.65	10	95.8	100.0	74
1954 PHILADELPHIA EAGLES(N)	12	12	60	872	14.53	10	81.0	76.4	70
1955 PHILADELPHIA EAGLES(N)	12	12	62	864	13.94	7	77.8	100.0	72
TOTAL 9 YEARS	108	107	373	5619	15.06	61	57.7	71.1	435

ART POWELL

	LG	G	NO	YDS	AVG	TD	AYD/G	AYD/L	Y/14G
1959 PHILADELPHIA EAGLES(N)	12	12	0	0	0.00	0	0.0	0.0	0
1960 NEW YORK TITANS(A)	14	14	69	1167	16.91	14	93.4	82.0	69
1961 NEW YORK TITANS(A)	14	14	71	881	12.41	5	66.5	49.9	71
1962 NEW YORK TITANS(A)	14	14	64	1130	17.66	8	86.4	100.0	64
1963 OAKLAND RAIDERS(A)	14	14	73	1304	17.86	16	104.6	100.0	73
1964 OAKLAND RAIDERS(A)	14	14	76	1361	17.91	11	105.1	90.5	76
1965 OAKLAND RAIDERS(A)	14	14	52	800	15.38	12	65.7	52.8	52
1966 OAKLAND RAIDERS(A)	14	14	53	1026	19.36	11	81.1	75.1	53
1967 BUFFALO BILLS(N)	14	6	20	346	17.30	4	27.6	28.3	20
1968 MINNESOTA VIKINGS(N)	14	1	1	31	31.00	0	2.2	2.6	1
TOTAL 10 YEARS	138	117	479	8046	16.80	81	64.2	77.4	479

SONNY RANDLE

	LG	G	NO	YDS	AVG	TD	AYD/G	AYD/L	Y/14G
1959 CHICAGO CARDINALS(N)	12	8	15	202	13.47	1	17.7	19.3	18
1960 ST. LOUIS CARDINALS(N)	12	12	62	893	14.40	15	86.9	74.6	72

	LG	G	NO	YDS	AVG	TD	AYD/G	AYD/L	Y/14G
1961 ST. LOUIS CARDINALS(N)	14	14	44	591	13.43	9	48.6	53.5	44
1962 ST. LOUIS CARDINALS(N)	14	14	63	1158	18.38	7	87.7	82.2	63
1963 ST. LOUIS CARDINALS(N)	14	14	51	1014	19.88	12	81.0	75.3	51
1964 ST. LOUIS CARDINALS(N)	14	7	25	517	20.68	5	40.5	43.6	25
1965 ST. LOUIS CARDINALS(N)	14	14	51	845	16.57	9	66.8	63.9	51
1966 ST. LOUIS CARDINALS(N)	14	14	17	218	12.82	2	17.0	17.5	17
1967 SAN FRANCISCO 49ERS(N)	14	14	33	502	15.21	4	38.7	39.7	33
1968 SAN FRANCISCO 49ERS(N)									
DALLAS COWBOYS(N)	14	9	4	56	14.00	1	4.7	5.6	4
TOTAL 10 YEARS	*136*	*120*	*365*	*5996*	*16.43*	*65*	*48.9*	*61.0*	*378*

AHMAD RASHAD

	LG	G	NO	YDS	AVG	TD	AYD/G	AYD/L	Y/14G
1972 ST. LOUIS CARDINALS(N)	14	14	29	500	17.24	3	37.9	48.0	29
1973 ST. LOUIS CARDINALS(N)	14	13	30	409	13.63	3	31.4	36.4	30
1974 BUFFALO BILLS(N)	14	14	36	433	12.03	4	33.8	38.7	36
1976 MINNESOTA VIKINGS(N)	14	13	53	671	12.66	3	50.1	56.9	53
1977 MINNESOTA VIKINGS(N)	14	14	51	681	13.35	2	50.1	78.2	51
1978 MINNESOTA VIKINGS(N)	16	16	66	769	11.65	8	53.1	68.0	58
1979 MINNESOTA VIKINGS(N)	16	16	80	1156	14.45	9	77.9	93.9	70
1980 MINNESOTA VIKINGS(N)	16	16	69	1095	15.87	5	71.6	77.9	60
1981 MINNESOTA VIKINGS(N)	16	16	58	884	15.24	7	59.6	64.1	51
1982 MINNESOTA VIKINGS(N)	9	7	23	233	10.13	0	25.9	20.8	36
TOTAL 10 YEARS	*143*	*139*	*495*	*6831*	*13.80*	*44*	*50.8*	*65.6*	*474*

PETE RETZLAFF

	LG	G	NO	YDS	AVG	TD	AYD/G	AYD/L	Y/14G
1956 PHILADELPHIA EAGLES(N)	12	10	12	159	13.25	0	13.3	12.2	14
1957 PHILADELPHIA EAGLES(N)	12	12	10	120	12.00	0	10.0	14.0	12
1958 PHILADELPHIA EAGLES(N)	12	12	56	766	13.68	2	65.5	66.8	65
1959 PHILADELPHIA EAGLES(N)	12	10	34	595	17.50	1	50.4	55.1	40
1960 PHILADELPHIA EAGLES(N)	12	12	46	826	17.96	5	73.0	62.7	54
1961 PHILADELPHIA EAGLES(N)	14	14	50	769	15.38	8	60.6	66.6	50
1962 PHILADELPHIA EAGLES(N)	14	8	30	584	19.47	3	43.9	41.1	30
1963 PHILADELPHIA EAGLES(N)	14	14	57	895	15.70	4	66.8	62.1	57
1964 PHILADELPHIA EAGLES(N)	14	12	51	855	16.76	8	66.8	71.9	51
1965 PHILADELPHIA EAGLES(N)	14	14	66	1190	18.03	10	92.1	88.1	66
1966 PHILADELPHIA EAGLES(N)	14	14	40	653	16.33	6	50.9	52.3	40
TOTAL 11 YEARS	*144*	*132*	*452*	*7412*	*16.40*	*47*	*54.7*	*63.0*	*478*

MAC SPEEDIE

	LG	G	NO	YDS	AVG	TD	AYD/G	AYD/L	Y/14G
1946 CLEVELAND BROWNS(A)	14	14	24	564	23.50	7	45.3	68.7	24
1947 CLEVELAND BROWNS(A)	14	14	67	1146	17.10	6	86.1	100.0	67
1948 CLEVELAND BROWNS(A)	14	12	58	816	14.07	4	61.1	83.1	58
1949 CLEVELAND BROWNS(A)	12	12	62	1028	16.58	7	91.5	100.0	72
1950 CLEVELAND BROWNS(N)	12	12	42	548	13.05	1	46.5	47.0	49
1951 CLEVELAND BROWNS(N)	12	10	34	589	17.32	3	51.6	37.2	40
1952 CLEVELAND BROWNS(N)	12	12	62	911	14.69	5	80.1	70.6	72
TOTAL 7 YEARS	*90*	*86*	*349*	*5602*	*16.05*	*33*	*65.9*	*77.3*	*382*

JOHN STALLWORTH

	LG	G	NO	YDS	AVG	TD	AYD/G	AYD/L	Y/14G
1974 PITTSBURGH STEELERS(N)	14	13	16	269	16.81	1	19.9	22.8	16
1975 PITTSBURGH STEELERS(N)	14	11	20	423	21.15	4	33.1	40.5	20

JOHN STALLWORTH	LG	G	NO	YDS	AVG	TD	AYD/G	AYD/L	Y/14G
1976 PITTSBURGH STEELERS(N)	14	8	9	111	12.33	2	9.4	10.6	9
1977 PITTSBURGH STEELERS(N)	14	14	44	784	17.82	7	61.0	95.3	44
1978 PITTSBURGH STEELERS(N)	16	16	41	798	19.46	9	55.5	71.1	36
1979 PITTSBURGH STEELERS(N)	16	16	70	1183	16.90	8	78.9	95.2	61
1980 PITTSBURGH STEELERS(N)	16	3	9	197	21.89	1	12.9	14.1	8
1981 PITTSBURGH STEELERS(N)	16	16	63	1098	17.43	5	71.8	77.2	55
1982 PITTSBURGH STEELERS(N)	9	9	27	441	16.33	7	56.8	45.5	42
1983 PITTSBURGH STEELERS(N)	16	4	8	100	12.50	0	6.3	6.5	7
1984 PITTSBURGH STEELERS(N)	16	16	80	1395	17.44	11	94.1	89.9	70
1985 PITTSBURGH STEELERS(N)	16	16	75	937	12.49	5	61.7	72.7	66
1986 PITTSBURGH STEELERS(N)	16	11	34	466	13.71	1	29.8	27.7	30
1987 PITTSBURGH STEELERS(N)	15	11	41	521	12.71	2	36.1	41.7	38
TOTAL 14 YEARS	208	164	537	8723	16.24	63	45.0	68.2	502

LYNN SWANN	LG	G	NO	YDS	AVG	TD	AYD/G	AYD/L	Y/14G
1974 PITTSBURGH STEELERS(N)	14	12	11	208	18.91	2	16.3	18.7	11
1975 PITTSBURGH STEELERS(N)	14	14	49	781	15.94	11	63.6	78.0	49
1976 PITTSBURGH STEELERS(N)	14	12	28	516	18.43	3	39.0	44.4	28
1977 PITTSBURGH STEELERS(N)	14	14	50	789	15.78	7	61.4	95.9	50
1978 PITTSBURGH STEELERS(N)	16	16	61	880	14.43	11	61.9	79.3	53
1979 PITTSBURGH STEELERS(N)	16	13	41	808	19.71	5	53.6	64.7	36
1980 PITTSBURGH STEELERS(N)	16	13	44	710	16.14	7	48.8	53.1	39
1981 PITTSBURGH STEELERS(N)	16	13	34	505	14.85	5	34.7	37.3	30
1982 PITTSBURGH STEELERS(N)	9	9	18	265	14.72	0	29.4	23.6	28
TOTAL 9 YEARS	129	116	336	5462	16.26	51	46.3	64.2	324

CHARLEY TAYLOR	LG	G	NO	YDS	AVG	TD	AYD/G	AYD/L	Y/14G
1964 WASHINGTON REDSKINS(N)	14	14	53	814	15.36	5	61.7	66.5	53
1965 WASHINGTON REDSKINS(N)	14	13	40	577	14.43	3	43.4	41.5	40
1966 WASHINGTON REDSKINS(N)	14	14	72	1119	15.54	12	88.5	91.0	72
1967 WASHINGTON REDSKINS(N)	14	12	70	990	14.14	9	77.1	79.1	70
1968 WASHINGTON REDSKINS(N)	14	14	48	650	13.54	5	50.0	59.0	48
1969 WASHINGTON REDSKINS(N)	14	14	71	883	12.44	8	68.8	79.9	71
1970 WASHINGTON REDSKINS(N)	14	10	42	593	14.12	8	48.1	55.2	42
1971 WASHINGTON REDSKINS(N)	14	6	24	370	15.42	4	29.3	34.7	24
1972 WASHINGTON REDSKINS(N)	14	14	49	673	13.73	7	53.1	67.2	49
1973 WASHINGTON REDSKINS(N)	14	14	59	801	13.58	7	62.2	72.2	59
1974 WASHINGTON REDSKINS(N)	14	14	54	738	13.67	5	56.3	64.5	54
1975 WASHINGTON REDSKINS(N)	14	14	53	744	14.04	6	57.4	70.3	53
1977 WASHINGTON REDSKINS(N)	14	12	14	158	11.29	0	11.3	17.6	14
TOTAL 13 YEARS	182	165	649	9110	14.04	79	54.4	67.7	649

LIONEL TAYLOR	LG	G	NO	YDS	AVG	TD	AYD/G	AYD/L	Y/14G
1959 CHICAGO BEARS(N)	12	8	0	0	0.00	0	0.0	0.0	0
1960 DENVER BRONCOS(A)	14	12	92	1235	13.42	12	96.8	85.1	92
1961 DENVER BRONCOS(A)	14	14	100	1176	11.76	4	86.9	65.2	100
1962 DENVER BRONCOS(A)	14	14	77	908	11.79	4	67.7	78.3	77
1963 DENVER BRONCOS(A)	14	14	78	1101	14.12	10	85.8	82.0	78
1964 DENVER BRONCOS(A)	14	14	76	873	11.49	7	67.4	58.0	76
1965 DENVER BRONCOS(A)	14	14	85	1131	13.31	6	85.1	68.4	85

1966 DENVER BRONCOS(A)	14	14	35	448	12.80	1	32.7	30.3	35
1967 HOUSTON OILERS(A)	14	8	18	233	12.94	1	17.4	15.8	18
1968 HOUSTON OILERS(A)	14	9	6	90	15.00	0	6.4	6.4	6
TOTAL 10 YEARS	*138*	*121*	*567*	*7195*	*12.69*	*45*	*55.4*	*67.7*	*567*

OTIS TAYLOR	*LG*	*G*	*NO*	*YDS*	*AVG*	*TD*	*AYD/G*	*AYD/L*	*Y/14G*
1965 KANSAS CITY CHIEFS(A)	14	14	26	446	17.15	5	35.4	28.5	26
1966 KANSAS CITY CHIEFS(A)	14	14	58	1297	22.36	8	98.4	91.0	58
1967 KANSAS CITY CHIEFS(A)	14	14	59	958	16.24	11	76.3	69.6	59
1968 KANSAS CITY CHIEFS(A)	14	11	20	420	21.00	4	32.9	32.6	20
1969 KANSAS CITY CHIEFS(A)	14	14	41	696	16.98	7	54.7	54.7	41
1970 KANSAS CITY CHIEFS(N)	14	13	34	618	18.18	3	46.3	53.1	34
1971 KANSAS CITY CHIEFS(N)	14	14	57	1110	19.47	7	84.3	100.0	57
1972 KANSAS CITY CHIEFS(N)	14	14	57	821	14.40	6	62.9	79.7	57
1973 KANSAS CITY CHIEFS(N)	14	14	34	565	16.62	4	43.2	50.2	34
1974 KANSAS CITY CHIEFS(N)	14	10	24	375	15.63	2	28.2	32.3	24
TOTAL 10 YEARS	*140*	*132*	*410*	*7306*	*17.82*	*57*	*56.3*	*67.2*	*410*

WESLEY WALKER	*LG*	*G*	*NO*	*YDS*	*AVG*	*TD*	*AYD/G*	*AYD/L*	*Y/14G*
1977 NEW YORK JETS(N)	14	14	35	740	21.14	3	55.0	85.9	35
1978 NEW YORK JETS(N)	16	16	48	1169	24.35	8	78.1	100.0	42
1979 NEW YORK JETS(N)	16	9	23	569	24.74	5	38.7	46.6	20
1980 NEW YORK JETS(N)	16	11	18	376	20.89	1	24.1	26.3	16
1981 NEW YORK JETS(N)	16	13	47	770	16.38	9	53.8	57.8	41
1982 NEW YORK JETS(N)	9	9	39	620	15.90	6	75.6	60.6	61
1983 NEW YORK JETS(N)	16	16	61	868	14.23	7	58.6	60.9	53
1984 NEW YORK JETS(N)	16	12	41	623	15.20	7	43.3	41.4	36
1985 NEW YORK JETS(N)	16	12	34	725	21.32	5	48.4	57.1	30
1986 NEW YORK JETS(N)	16	16	49	1016	20.73	12	71.0	66.0	43
1987 NEW YORK JETS(N)	15	3	9	190	21.11	1	13.3	15.4	8
TOTAL 11 YEARS	*166*	*131*	*404*	*7666*	*18.98*	*64*	*50.0*	*62.3*	*385*

BILLY WILSON	*LG*	*G*	*NO*	*YDS*	*AVG*	*TD*	*AYD/G*	*AYD/L*	*Y/14G*
1951 SAN FRANCISCO 49ERS(N)	12	9	18	268	14.89	3	24.8	17.9	21
1952 SAN FRANCISCO 49ERS(N)	12	9	23	304	13.22	3	27.8	24.5	27
1953 SAN FRANCISCO 49ERS(N)	12	12	51	840	16.47	10	78.3	81.8	60
1954 SAN FRANCISCO 49ERS(N)	12	12	60	830	13.83	5	73.3	69.2	70
1955 SAN FRANCISCO 49ERS(N)	12	12	53	831	15.68	7	75.1	96.5	62
1956 SAN FRANCISCO 49ERS(N)	12	12	60	889	14.82	5	78.3	71.8	70
1957 SAN FRANCISCO 49ERS(N)	12	11	52	757	14.56	6	68.1	95.0	61
1958 SAN FRANCISCO 49ERS(N)	12	9	43	592	13.77	5	53.5	54.5	50
1959 SAN FRANCISCO 49ERS(N)	12	10	44	540	12.27	4	48.3	52.8	51
1960 SAN FRANCISCO 49ERS(N)	12	4	3	51	17.00	1	5.1	4.4	4
TOTAL 10 YEARS	*120*	*100*	*407*	*5902*	*14.50*	*49*	*53.3*	*69.4*	*475*